ARIS AND PHILLIPS CLA

CW01511612

AESCHYLUS

Agamemnon

Edited with a Translation, Introduction and Commentary by

Edith Hall

LIVERPOOL UNIVERSITY PRESS

First published 2024
Liverpool University Press
4 Cambridge Street
Liverpool, L69 7ZU

This paperback edition published 2025

British Library Cataloguing-in-Publication Data
A British Library CIP Record is available.

ISBN 978-1-80085-628-8 (hardback)
ISBN 978-1-83624-429-5 (paperback)
eISBN 978-1-80085-508-3

Cover image: Fragments of a Lucanian vase (c. 400 BCE) in the Herbert Cahn Collection, Basel. Drawing reproduced courtesy of Becky Brewis.

Typeset by Carnegie Book Production, Lancaster
Printed and bound by CPI Group (UK) Ltd, Croydon CR0 4YY

CONTENTS

*This one is for my all my graduate students, past and present,
from whom I've learned more than they have ever learned from me*

ILLUSTRATIONS

ACKNOWLEDGEMENTS

Several scholars have helped me enormously in the preparation of this edition, especially Christopher Collard, Alan Sommerstein and Ahuvia Kahane, although any and all errors are entirely my responsibility. Becky Brewis drew Figures 6 and 7 (the latter is also the cover image) and has kindly given permission for them to be reproduced here. Rachel Chamberlain and the team at Carnegie Book Production did sterling work on a complicated book. Georgia Poynder, Richard Poynder, and Durham University graduate Lucia-Allegra Perricone generously compiled the meticulous index. I would like to thank Adrian Phillips for suggesting I tackle *Agamemnon* in the first place, and especially Clare Litt at Liverpool University Press for consistent encouragement, especially at moments of recent crisis for me in terms of both professional employment and health. I have been lucky enough to teach this incomparable play to superb graduate students at Leiden University, thanks to Ineke Sluiter, and at Durham, as well as to undergraduates at Swarthmore and Royal Holloway University of London. I have learned a great deal from supervising Dr Caroline Latham's KCL doctoral dissertation on stage translations of the *Oresteia*, and especially from Dr Helen Eastman's outstanding production of *Agamemnon* in the original language at the University of Cambridge in 2010, with an excellent musical score by Alex Silverman that evoked Aeschylus' authentic rhythms. The translation published here formed the basis of the surtitles used in that production. I have been talking about Aeschylus for more than 30 years with Professor Fiona Macintosh and the poet Tony Harrison. My understanding of the play was greatly enhanced by a research project I conducted at the Archive of Performances of Greek and Roman Drama at Oxford University, alongside Pantelis Michelakis and Oliver Taplin, as well as Fiona, from 2002 to 2005. My husband Richard Poynder has been a constant and indispensable support.

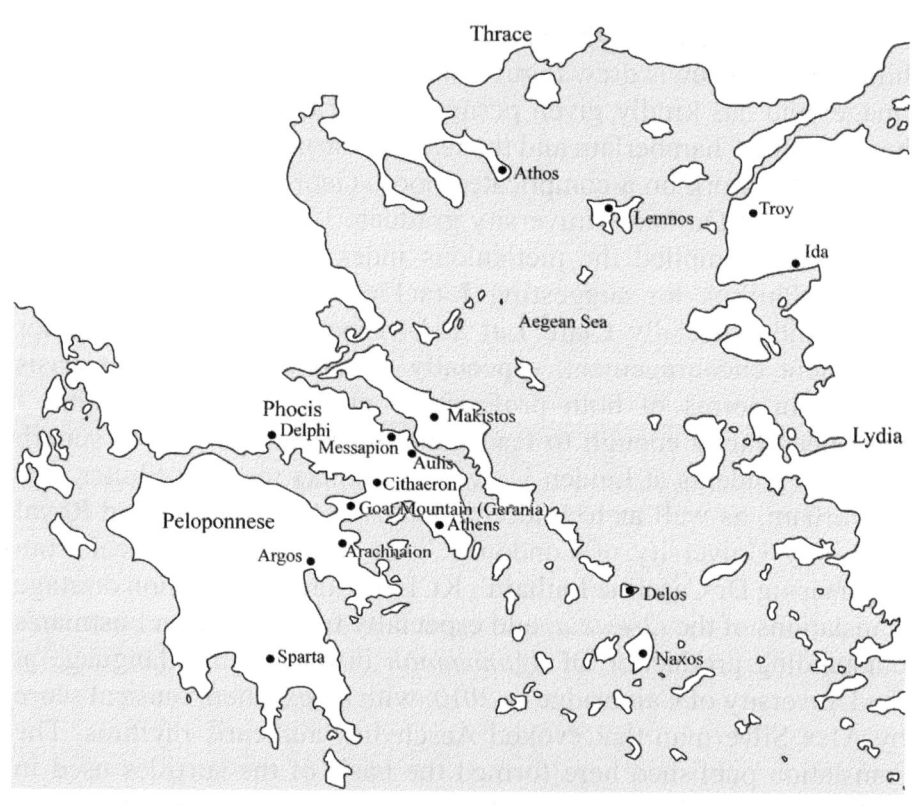

Greece and the Aegean Sea: Topography of places
mentioned in *Agamemnon*

INTRODUCTION

1. A PLAY ABOUT PAIN

A rooftop lookout; an account of a disastrous multiple shipwreck; a domineering queen who speaks in riddles; a king on a magnificent vehicle with a mysterious veiled woman; the spreading and trampling of priceless textiles; a scene of vatic possession ending in a clairvoyant prophetess's walk to certain death; offstage screaming; the queen in blood-drenched clothes boasting over corpses; her confrontation with a citizen chorus who fail to banish her; and their showdown with her lover, nearly exploding into civil war—these thrilling scenes in *Agamemnon* reveal Aeschylus as the titanic father of theatre. The tragedy has a foundational status shared by few other artworks in the world repertoire, besides being the first and greatest play in the only extant ancient Greek tragic trilogy.

Agamemnon is the earliest surviving revenge tragedy,[1] the first sustained examination of the psychology of murder, the first tragedy with a female protagonist, the first set outside a household and the inspiration behind countless ancient and modern paintings, sculptures, poems, poetic practices, novels and works for enactment on stages and screens (Figure 1). It was chosen as the first ever play to be performed in the oldest modern festival of ancient drama, inaugurated by the Italian National Institute of Ancient Drama (INDA) in the ancient Greek theatre of Syracuse in 1914.[2] Aeschylus' *Agamemnon* carries 'an almost unbearable weight of historical and cosmic meaning'.[3] It could not be more appropriate that he was supposed to have said, when he felt he had been unfairly defeated in a drama competition, that his tragedies were devoted to Time (Athen. *Deipn.* 8.347e).

---

1 Kerrigan (1996).
2 Michelakis (2005) 9–10, 17.
3 Otis (1981) 20.

Figure 1. Agamemnon about to tread on the tapestries. Anonymous drawing of a production of Sergey Ivanovich Taneyev's opera *Oresteya*, performed in 1917–18 at the Theatre of the Council of Workers' Deputies in Moscow. Author's personal collection.

Agamemnon is also a study of suffering. The opening sentence, 'I implore the gods to set me free from these ordeals', is delivered by an actor playing a working man. He is perched atop the palace of the Atreidai at Argos, one autumn dawn in the late Bronze Age. But the audience to whom he spoke at the play's première were in another place and time—the theatre of Dionysus in the god's sanctuary on the south-west slope of the Athenians' acropolis in the spring of 458 BCE, during the democratic era, when their empire was growing apace.

Unlike *Eumenides*, *Agamemnon* makes little reference to the future, at least beyond the imminent murders of Clytemnestra and Aegisthus that will be enacted in the following play. But its entire intellectual and moral thrust was designed to address its original audience's contemporary concerns. Greek tragedy was, amongst other things, an interpretation of heroic myth from the perspective of the Athenian democratic citizen. When we read or enact it, we are operating on triple time levels: our own, that of Aeschylus' Greek audience two and half millennia before us, and the Mycenaean past, as Aeschylus' contemporaries in turn believed it had been experienced, at least another six centuries before them.

The opening sentence crystallises the emotional dynamic of the *Oresteia*: humans suffer as they await some resolution, by divine ordinance, of a terrifying period of history. There have been multiple bereavements. A striking feature of *Agamemnon* is the death wishes. The Herald says that, now he has returned home, he would be content to die (539), and the chorus respond that their life has been made so difficult under the city's current administration that death would be preferable (550). Clytemnestra claims that she has tried often to hang herself (875–6), and one of the chorus-men says, while Agamemnon is being murdered, that it would be far better to die than live under a tyranny (1364–5). Afterwards, the chorus long to meet a swift and painless death in the form of 'everlasting sleep' (1448–50). Aegisthus twice declares his willingness to die (1610–11, 1652).

The Watchman's word for ordeals is the plural of the noun *ponos*, 'pain', or 'labour', one of a semantic complex of terms for miserable sensations and emotions, besides the ubiquitous *kaka*, 'bad things' or 'evils'; this, along with its singular, its adverbial form and appearance in compounds, occurs no fewer than 42 times. There are more than 30 words beginning with the prefix *dus-*, 'hard' or 'difficult'. There are more than 80 instances of the privative initial alpha, creating an aural wall of negativity. There are over 100 instances of words referring to pain, suffering, grief, despair, anxiety, emotional burdens and shuddering, including *algos, achos, pathos, duai, pēmonē, pēma, odunē* and *mogeros*. The other terms that dominate the emotional register are hatred, terror, envy and—perhaps paradoxically—hope: one of the chorus' refrains, borrowed from the seer Calchas and paraphrased by major characters, is 'Sing the song of sorrow, but may good prevail' (121, 139, 160). It is not that the chorus are advocating 'pessimism of the intellect, optimism of the will'. Their sentiment means 'lament what you have suffered in the past as much as you need, but believe that the future may be better'. This is a perfect therapeutic mantra in the face of suicidal despair. Oscar Wilde, who had been affected by a performance of *Agamemnon* in Greek in 1880, chose this resonant Greek line as the epitaph to his famous poem 'Tristitiae'.[4]

Everyone in *Agamemnon* suffers and has suffered, but the anguish of two victims is underscored by their youth and innocence and the terrible beauty of the poetry in which the preludes to their distressing deaths are depicted. The preparations for the knifing of Iphigenia over the altar of Artemis ten years previously are described by the chorus in vivid detail, foregrounding her terror; Cassandra foresees her own execution. The prominence given to the gruesome killings of guiltless females in the society portrayed in Aeschylus' Argos is crucial to the play's ethical as well as emotional impact. It marks a crucial shift from the portrayal of the Trojan War in the *Iliad*, where the sacrifice of Iphigenia has been erased even from the memories of Aulis which occasionally surface. It is quite unlike the tone of Greek epic when Aeschylus' Herald characterises men who die in war being 'led out for sacrifice' (641).

2. POLITICAL AND HISTORICAL CONTEXT

Aeschylus, son of Euphorion, was born in about 525 BCE, two decades before the revolution that led to the instalment of the Athenian democracy in 507. He came from Eleusis, a settlement in the far west of Attica renowned for its cult of Demeter and its Mysteries. His family was wealthy and upper class. There may be no truth in the tradition that when he was a child he had been visited in a dream by Dionysus, who found him asleep in his father's vineyard and ordered him to compose tragedy (Paus. 1.21.2). But Aeschylus was certainly prolific (he produced more than 90 plays) and successful, and took the genre to new levels of artistic brilliance and prestige. We are fortunate to be able to date all seven surviving plays attributed to him except *Prometheus Bound*, which he may not have written.[5] He first competed at Athens in his mid-20s in 499 BCE, and won his first victory in 484. Afterwards, he

---

4　Wilde (2010) 757. Hall (2023) and (2024) 174. On terms for anxiety in Aeschylus, see Schnyder (1995).
5　See further Hall (2010b) 230.

won first prize at least 12 further times, including with his last Athenian production, the *Oresteia*, in 458, a couple of years before his death.

When Aeschylus was growing into manhood he witnessed epoch-defining events—the tyrannical rule of Pisistratus' two sons, the assassination of one of them (Hipparchus), the expulsion of the other (Hippias) and the jockeying for position between rival aristocratic factions that had culminated in Cleisthenes' assumption of leadership and his democratic reforms of 507 BCE. The fledgling democracy faced a momentous challenge with the Persian invasion of 490 BCE, and Aeschylus was in his physical prime—about 35—when Darius finally invaded mainland Greece, bringing the deposed Hippias with him. The poet himself almost certainly fought at the battle of Marathon; his brother died because of a wound inflicted there (Herodotus 6.114). When Xerxes led the second invasion in 480, Aeschylus was witness to the crumbling of the Greek defence in Boeotia, the terrifying march of Xerxes on Athens, the evacuation of the civic centre, its subsequent sacking and the eventual Greek victories at Salamis, Plataea and Mycale. Aeschylus had then lived amongst the ruins of his ravaged—but free—city.

That democratic city was also growing its own domestic empire. The Athenians' identity, as democrats who had secured freedom with their hands on their oars at Salamis, was intertwined with their aspiration to be leaders of other Greeks.[6] Defeating the Persians allowed them to increase their own power across the Aegean. Ostensibly in 'defence' of Greece, the Athenians built up the alliance of city-states which evolved into a mighty sea-based empire. Any pretence that the 'alliance' was not an empire could no longer be sustained after the islanders of Naxos seceded in 468. Athens crushed them and Naxos lost her independence. The theme of violent imperialism is a factor in *Agamemnon* (see 338–42), but it is displaced onto Argive prehistory.[7]

Athenian imperial expansion was led by Cimon, the son of Miltiades, hero of Marathon. But Cimon fell from grace after an unsuccessful attempt in 462 BCE to help the Spartans when their helots revolted. He was ostracised; any sense of Athenian loyalty to

---

6   Meiggs (1943).
7   Salanitro (1966); Stella (1994) 73–4.

Sparta vanished altogether. It was now imperative that the Athenians secure a new alliance with the other great central Peloponnesian city-state of Argos. Argos had suffered at Spartan hands, and was also afflicted by internal civil conflicts, almost certainly resulting in a democratic constitution consolidated by 460 BCE;[8] this would have made it even more attractive to the Athenians as a potential ally. The treaty was concluded in 462, and a resounding aetiology for it is provided in Orestes' last speech in *Eumenides*, after his acquittal in the brand-new murder court in magnanimous Athens. He swears an oath of eternal friendship between the Argives and the Athenians and promises to safeguard it even posthumously from his tomb (762–74).

But there was another topical factor. The Watchman, the Herald, Clytemnestra and the chorus of *Agamemnon* all complain that their sleep is disturbed by anxious thoughts; Clytemnestra uses a striking phrase of the Greek soldiers at Troy, at last able to 'sleep like happy men the whole night through with no need for a guard' after Troy has finally fallen (336–7). In 458 BCE Athens was recovering from devastating civic violence, some of which had taken place furtively behind closed doors in a primal class struggle ultimately caused by the extension of rights to the lowest class of citizens, the thetes, by Cleisthenes' reforms. Thetes were still excluded from access to the substantial powers exercised by the ancient Council of the Areopagus. The aristocratic Areopagites met on the 'Rock of Ares' from which they took their name. But a radical democrat and former general named Ephialtes had campaigned to divide this august body's powers between the three core institutions of the city which *were* open to all male citizens: the Assembly, the Council which advised it, and the lawcourts. These measures produced bloodshed in the streets and an oligarchic plot to destabilise the democracy. Ephialtes was assassinated in 461 BCE; the identity of the murderer was never discovered (Antiphon 5.68). Aeschylus' audience members in 458 BCE may indeed have recently experienced difficulty sleeping without fear in their beds.

Ephialtes' ally Pericles now came to the forefront of politics and the powers of the Areopagus were duly restricted to jurisdiction in some

---

8   Robinson (2011) 10–18.

homicide cases. Orestes' trial for murdering his mother is presented in *Eumenides*, the third tragedy of the *Oresteia*, performed just three years after Ephialtes' murder, as the institution's foundational first trial. His death and those of others lent resonance to Athena's ban on factional violence (*Eum.* 858–63).

Aeschylus won a famous victory with this tetralogy, for which the official funder (*chorēgos*) was Xenocles of Aphidna, an age-old town in north-eastern Attica; sadly, the final play, the satyr drama *Proteus*, has not been preserved. It took a light-hearted look at a journey home from Troy by another member of the same family. It dramatised Menelaus' meeting in Egypt with the sea-divinity Proteus, recounted in *Odyssey* book 4. Aeschylus was aware of the version of Helen's story, told by the archaic lyric poet Stesichorus, in which she stayed with Proteus during the Trojan War, and perhaps this featured in the satyr play.[9]

But the Ephialtic revolution affects how we interpret the trilogy politically. Does the *Oresteia* criticise the reforms of the Areopagus by celebrating its status as a sacred institution, with unique authority, founded according to Zeus' will by his daughter Athena? Or does it take the democrats' side by celebrating the Areopagus primarily as a court of law that adjudicated in homicide trials? Scholars have tended to pick sides according to whether their own politics—and therefore, predictably, their characterisation of Aeschylus' politics—are conservative or more progressive. But there is a third answer to the question, and it becomes attractive if we consider the nature of Aeschylus' audience. He wanted to win the drama competition and succeeded in doing so. The judges in the competition chose the tragedian whose works they rated most highly, but they were unlikely to vote against what had emerged as the popular choice as indicated by audience reaction. Aeschylus has clothed his primeval Areopagus in mythical and poetic dress so consciously ambiguous that it can sustain multiple interpretations. He seems to have achieved the difficult task of portraying Athenian constitutional history in a way that pleased people of diverse political persuasions equally.[10]

---

9   Sommerstein (2010) 77–80.

10   Hall (2010b) 225–6.

The poetry of the *Oresteia* is infused with archaic-sounding proverbial wisdom. The moral sayings 'the doer will suffer' and 'blood for blood' resound through its choruses. Perhaps the most significant is the phrase 'learning [comes] through suffering' (176–83). The trilogy portrays how a whole society changed in response to the things people suffered, a change echoed in the shift from a house to public space. It is only in the final tragedy, *Eumenides*, that the scene changes first to the Delphic oracle of Apollo, and then to an institutional arena in the centre of Athens.

These settings link the old story of the Peloponnesian Atreidai and their family curse not only to the most important centre of prophecy in the Greek world but also to the city-state laying claim to imperial leadership of much of that world. This allows the trilogy to suggest what had been the real historical development of the archaic Greek city-state from the constitutional monarchy apparently portrayed in *Agamemnon*, through to the tyranny maintained by Clytemnestra and Aegisthus, following their violent coup, in *Choephori*, and thence to the Athenian proto-democracy in *Eumenides*. This last tragedy, uniquely, portrays a city that can govern itself without either tyrant or king and where lawcourts in which the jurors are regular Athenian citizens will be a central organ in the maintenance not only of democracy but of civic order. The foundations for this celebration of trial by jury are laid in *Agamemnon* with a dense network of legal language and imagery (see below, p. 65).

But the inauguration of the historical Athenian democracy had also raised the question of the place of women in such a society. Under monarchy and tyranny, and even in the fifth century BCE in most non-Athenian Greek city-states, women were more visible and powerful in public, civic life, and their freedoms less curtailed. *Agamemnon* offers bald accounts of the suffering of powerless young women in ancient Aulis and Argos, depicts Clytemnestra's intelligence as equal to that of any man and allows her to express her frustrations with a patriarchal political system that had not implemented any legal mechanism to prosecute Agamemnon for killing their daughter. This portrait reveals unease with Clytemnestra's political position. The issue of the correct place of women in public life will not be resolved until the end of *Eumenides*, where Athenian women, excluded from juries and sovereign bodies, are granted roles in the sphere of religion.

3. THE ARGIVE CONSTITUTION IN *AGAMEMNON*

The Watchman seems to have fond memories of his King, and to look forward to his return, since the household is not, in his view, being run correctly (18–19). But he is warily silent on other topics and his optimism about the future seems compromised. The power of the monarch (or his regent, who, the chorus state emphatically at 257–8, is Clytemnestra) is great: the chorus tell the Herald that they have feared someone in Argos while the army has been away (548–50). But the royal power is not unlimited; as Aristotle says, the difference between a tyranny and a monarchy is that in the latter the single ruler's supremacy is subject to a degree of regulation (*Rhet.* 1.1366a). The chorus, who more than once speak as if they are representatives of the whole citizen body, believe that they have the authority to speak publicly about their collective memories of national events (104). They feel entitled to interrogate Clytemnestra about the authenticity of her news (271–80). They regard it as their responsibility to thank the gods for the victory (317–19, 352–4). They act as the spokesmen for those who have been bereaved by the war not just in Argos but in all Greece (427–48). In the context of the war fatalities, they tell us that they are aware (457–8) that it 'is a grave matter when citizens speak resentfully' and that there is such a thing as 'a curse ratified by the people'. Later, they seem in touch with public opinion when they tell Cassandra that 'the whole city resounds' with talk of the fate of Thyestes' children (1106).

When Agamemnon arrives, we can assess how this imagined political system was expected to operate when its King was present. The chorus is surprisingly frank in their opening address to Agamemnon (783–809, Figure 2), stating that they disapproved of his 'sacrifices to stir up bravado' at the mustering of the fleet (although, as Clytemnestra points out later at 1412–17, they had done nothing to punish him). They seem directive in their advice that he 'will in time discover by enquiry' how each Argive has behaved in his absence (808–9). Agamemnon is hardly fulsome in his address to the chorus; he ignores their reference

Figure 2. The chorus greet Agamemnon. An anonymous late nineteenth-century engraving. Author's personal collection.

to the sacrifice of Iphigenia. Yet he acknowledges that he is mindful of their (other) sentiments (829–31); he announces that 'we shall set up an assembly to debate and deliberate' about the gods and the city-state (844–6); the word for an assembly (*panēguris*) is not connected with the one the Athenians used for their democratic assembly (*ekklēsia*), but the term 'deliberate' is etymologically connected with the Athenians' label for their Council (*boulē*).

Clytemnestra is intent on addressing the Argive elders herself (855–76), even though she has been invited to do so by neither them nor Agamemnon. She apostrophises them here as 'citizens' and 'respected body of Argive elders', using the neuter noun *presbos*, but not clarifying whether this citizen body has any official or constitutional status. When she repeats this label, after the death of Agamemnon, it is with a derisive, sarcastic edge, underlining that, whatever the chorus' claims to respectful treatment based on their seniority, she does not care whether they like what she has done or resent it (1393). But it is in her explanation of Orestes' absence to Agamemnon that the language of comparative constitutions is first introduced. Clytemnestra claims that Strophius, the Phocian ally who has taken in Orestes, had warned her about 'twin disasters'— the danger facing Agamemnon at Troy 'and the possibility that the populace might talk itself into anarchy and overthrow the council' (822–4). Here again, the 'people' (*dēmos*) is conceived as potentially dangerous; moreover, it might overthrow the council (and on this occasion the standard noun, *boulē*, is used) by talking itself into *anarchia* or a system with no leader at all (see 881–4*).

The precise status of the chorus' identity as a community is never elucidated.[11] They do not seem to be precisely equivalent to the 'council' that Clytemnestra fears might be overthrown, nor to the assembly (*panēguris*) which Agamemnon proposes to work with, nor to the chorus of elders in *Persians* who introduce themselves as a body called 'The Faithful', formally selected to oversee Xerxes' domain in his absence by virtue of their seniority (*presbeia, Pers.* 4). Yet the elders respond to Agamemnon's death cries by deciding to pool 'deliberations (*bouleumata*) about a safe strategy' (*Ag.* 1346–7); they then stage what can certainly be understood as a miniature democratic debate, 12 different opinions being expressed, each in a couplet, probably delivered by each citizen chorus-man in turn. Nothing in *Agamemnon* has produced such divergent critical responses, and they have largely been determined by the authors' own political views. An Edwardian don might write that the contrast drawn 'between the decisiveness of the heroic personages and the imbecility of the council reveals a glimpse of the anti-democratic tendencies of the poet',[12] while Dodds interpreted it as a model

---

11   See the excellent remarks of Winnington-Ingram (1954) 23–4 and especially n.4.

12   Sidgwick (1905) xii n.1. This line of argument can be traced to Müller (1835), but that treatise could not take into account the Aristotelian *Athenian Constitution*, which had not yet been discovered.

democratic *agōn*.[13] Podlecki compromises: Aeschylus, a moderate democrat, would have been disturbed by the more radical recent reforms.[14]

Readers must decide for themselves, although the impact of this fascinating sequence partly depends on how a director chooses to stage it. The chorus certainly identify the pressing issues: that the situation is urgent enough to require help from fellow townspeople, that speed is of the essence if the perpetrators are to be apprehended in the act and that the murder of the hereditary monarch implies that someone is attempting to establish a tyranny; yet, if Agamemnon is already dead, then there's not much that can be done to restore him. But the most important priority in all democratic deliberation is soon specified: the verification of information and establishment of certainty.[15] At this point verification is spectacularly provided with the gloating 'confession' of Clytemnestra, blood-drenched, over her victims' corpses.

The final section of the play clarifies the nature of the new political situation. The citizen community represented by the chorus feel they have the formal right to curse and expel Clytemnestra and to condemn Aegisthus to death (1409–11, 1615–16). But they fail. Nor is it ever elucidated whether they did have such rights when Agamemnon authorised the sacrifice of Iphigenia, and chose not to implement them, or whether under their constitution no sanctions were available to the citizens for the prosecution of the legitimate hereditary monarch himself; his crime was committed, moreover, at Aulis, perhaps outside their geopolitical area of jurisdiction.

But the regime run by Clytemnestra and Aegisthus is a tyranny won by a violent coup executed by individuals other than the hereditary successor (who would be Orestes). It is a regime in which Aegisthus, at any rate, feels the citizen chorus have no right to express dissent and

---

13   See Dodds (1960), especially 20, where references to the *dēmos* in Agamemnon are emphasised. Dodds' main point is that political concerns are an integral part of the drama throughout the trilogy; Winnington-Ingram (1954) shows how the debate is quite consistent with the characterisation of the chorus elsewhere in the play.

14   Podlecki (1999) 80–100.

15   Hall (2009) 70–9.

may lose their liberty if he so chooses. The chorus, meanwhile, insist that the Argive temperament is not suited to grovelling before evil men (1665). The altercation is about to erupt into physical violence—class-based stasis outside the Argive palace—when Clytemnestra appears and succeeds in establishing a nervous temporary armistice: it may, however, be significant that, while she feels the need to address the chorus emolliently as 'respected old men' (1657), she no longer calls them *presbos* or 'senior body'.

Clytemnestra's intervention fended off an immediate threat from the Argive *dēmos* to the couple's absolute power. The situation in *Choephori* is a stalemate: the new tyranny is universally resented. By choosing to make the chorus of *Choephori* women who are enslaved, Aeschylus keeps the spotlight off the experience of the Argive citizenry under this regime until the final scene, but he also implies that there are no functioning civic bodies for debate or consultation. When Orestes appears over their corpses, he asks onlookers to view the 'twofold tyranny' that had destroyed his household (973–4). He asks 'all Argives' to bear witness in time to the way he has acted (1039–40), as if the community represented by the male chorus of *Agamemnon* were bodily present (1039–40); the chorus say that he has 'liberated' the entire Argive city-state (1046) by assassinating the tyrants. The city, it is implied, will be without a leader until the return of Orestes, now in flight from the Erinyes. But, as we learn in *Eumenides*, he will inaugurate an eternal alliance between them and the now king-free citizens of Athens.

4. PLOT, TEMPORALITY AND STRUCTURE

The Argives, along with the warriors of other Greek city-states, have been away at Troy for ten years, after Agamemnon sacrificed his daughter Iphigenia to Artemis to enable his fleet to sail. His wife Clytemnestra has been ruling in his place. She tells the chorus that a beacon relay has indicated that the Greeks have been victorious. The chorus remain sceptical until a Herald arrives to say that, although a storm destroyed most of the fleet, Agamemnon's arrival is imminent. When the King appears, ostentatiously, on a vehicle, with his Trojan captive Cassandra beside him, Clytemnestra persuades him to walk over purple cloths into the palace. Cassandra erupts into song and speech, delivering prophecies, seeing ghosts and describing preparations for murder going on inside the palace before entering it. The chorus hear Agamemnon's death cries; Clytemnestra appears, rejoicing, over the corpses of both Agamemnon and Cassandra. In a long confrontation, the chorus try to banish her, but she withstands them. Suddenly Aegisthus, Agamemnon's cousin and now Clytemnestra's lover, enters with his bodyguard and tries to impose his authority as ruler on the chorus. They refuse to accept it. It is only when Clytemnestra emerges for the last time that an uneasy truce is called.

At 1673 lines, *Agamemnon* is the longest surviving Greek tragedy except for three late plays: Euripides' *Helen* and *Phoenician Women* and Sophocles' *Oedipus at Colonus*. The dominant atmosphere is tense anticipation. Nearly all the first half is spent waiting for the arrival of Agamemnon home from Troy; he first appears at or shortly after line 782. But there are nearly 600 lines to go before his death cries are heard; only the last 300 deal with the relationship between the new tyrants of Argos and their mutinous subjects. The plot stages a homecoming (*nostos*) that ends in disaster, reversing the successful *nostos* recounted in the *Odyssey*;[16] the catastrophic homecoming was subsequently adopted as a structure in many plays, since it 'provides a model for how tragedy can explore so many of its favourite questions, revolving around the house, the family, the return, and the possibilities that this brings with it of integration or disintegration; and of course the deeply problematic issues of revenge'.[17] The 'homecoming plays' illuminate the social context of Athens and its 'home front'.[18] The new empire required much longer military deployments overseas. *Agamemnon* was especially relevant to the families of Athenian soldiers and sailors. It addresses the problems experienced both by wives waiting at home and their returning menfolk.

---

16   Hall (1997).
17   Easterling (2005) 31.
18   Weiberg (2022).

Of all the extant Greek tragedies, *Agamemnon* is most obsessed with the past, the antecedent acts and events which have made the present crisis, at the precise moment of Agamemnon's homecoming, inevitable. All the long choral songs until Agamemnon's death deal with the past. They paint graphic pictures of the impatient Greek army and fleet and the sacrifice of Iphigenia, before going further back in time to Helen's elopement and arrival in Troy. The Watchman recalls his sufferings over the last year and the happier days before Agamemnon left. The Herald recalls the physical suffering of the Greek soldiers at Troy and the storm which destroyed so many of those who had survived combat. Clytemnestra complains about her misery during the long years when Agamemnon was away and later argues with the chorus about Agamemnon's escape from punishment for the sacrifice of Iphigenia. Aegisthus' consciousness is dominated by the Thyestean feast that took place decades ago when he was still an infant. The Watchman and the Herald voice the desire to forget; Clytemnestra and Aegisthus are both motivated by long-remembered grievances. But the chorus' recollections, fears and presentiments 'serve to bridge past, present, and future, opening up, as it were, the field of present action' long before the arrival of Cassandra.[19] It is with Cassandra that past, present and future crimes are fused—Atreus, Agamemnon and Orestes: 'the three generations stand before our eyes as one'.[20] She also faces her memories, both good and bad, of life in Troy, with no motive other than to voice her pain.[21]

There are various ways in which the structure of the play has been analysed. Durand, for example, spotlights the concept of conflicted relationships, and how they are described in the tragedy, regardless of whether the parties are represented on stage. In his account, the play serially reflects on the conflicts between Greeks and Trojans, Greeks and Artemis, Zeus and Ouranos, Zeus and Paris, Cassandra and Apollo, Clytemnestra and Agamemnon, Thyestes and Atreus, and Aegisthus and the Argives, while pointing to Orestes' imminent

---

19   Brault (2009) 201.
20   de Romilly (1968) 80.
21   Wians (2009) 193.

showdown with the tyrants.[22] Sailor and Stroup, on the other hand, see the first half of the play as revolving around 'three crimes of the House of Atreus': the sacrifice of Iphigenia, the wasting of lives at Ilion and the treading of the textiles.[23] It is also notable that the death of Agamemnon is evoked three times from three different perspectives: Cassandra's predictions, Agamemnon's screams and Clytemnestra's vaunting reenactment over his corpse. But such thematic divisions are better suited to narrative poetry than to theatrical.

From the perspective of the performers, and who needs to be on stage in what mask, a revealing approach is to look at exits and entrances in the manner pioneered by Oliver Taplin.[24] Nobody makes more than one entrance except Clytemnestra, who makes no fewer than six, and probably seven (see 83–4*). The play can be seen as falling into 15 episodes, and these are used as sub-headings in the commentary.[25] The chorus are present, and always highly engaged, from their entrance song beginning at line 40. They have seven substantial musical sequences: their entrance song (*parodos*), three lyric choral odes (*stasima*), a separate run of anapaests between nos. 2 and 3 when they get into formation for welcoming Agamemnon, and two long semi-lyric interchanges (*amoibaia*) with Cassandra and then Clytemnestra.[26]

No episode features more than two individual characters verbally interacting (although see the note on 1651, which might require a third actor immediately before Clytemnestra's final entrance). But the triangle of Clytemnestra/Agamemnon/Cassandra requires three speaking

22   Durand (2005) 79–95.
23   Sailor and Stroup (1999).
24   Taplin (1977).
25   This breakdown is similar but not identical to that in Föllinger (2009) 117–18; it differs in its actorly focus on who is presenting and performing.
26   The history of the labelling of such sequences is fraught (Zimmermann (1985) 150–2). Aristotle called a 'lament' shared between chorus and an actor a *kommos* (*Poet.* 1452b), but neither of the semi-lyric exchanges in *Agamemnon* is, strictly speaking, a lament. The term *epirrhema* originally designates a particular metrical unit in comedy and I have avoided it; it was made popular by Kranz (1919) 318–19; see Peretti (1939); for its use in ancient and modern scholarship see Taplin (1977) 86 n.2. For a more recent discussion see Popp (1971).

actors, unless two successive actors wear Cassandra's mask, one while she is present silently and the other (who would on this allocation of roles previously have played Agamemnon) for her divination scene. This would require some swift opportunity for the speaking Cassandra actor to replace the mute one on stage (it is conceivably possible that Cassandra disappeared briefly while descending from the vehicle at 1069–71). But, given that three actors are required for *Choephori* 900–2 and *Eumenides* 607–777, such speculation is unnecessary.

It is likely that, in addition to the Clytemnestra-protagonist, one actor played the male individuals, who do not sing—the Watchman, Herald, Agamemnon and Aegisthus—and the other the young singing Cassandra: ancient actors often specialised in male or female roles, and some were skilled at messenger-type orations, such as those delivered by the Herald, or lyric solo arias.[27] The same actor taking the roles of Agamemnon and Aegisthus could exploit his voice to suggest the family resemblance of these first cousins; Epictetus said that the only part of an actor's own physical presence which was not disguised or erased was his voice (*Discourses* 1.29.6). For actors and chorus-men, the 15 episodes break down as follows:

i 1–39 The Watchman
ii 40–256 Chorus (*parodos*: Calchas, Hymn to Zeus, sacrifice of Iphigenia)
iii 257–354 Chorus and Clytemnestra: beacon relay speech
iv 355–487 Chorus alone (*stasimon* 1: Helen, Menelaus, war dead)
v 488–586 Chorus and the Herald (announcement of victory at Troy)
vi 587–612 Chorus, the Herald and Clytemnestra
vii 613–80 Chorus and the Herald (Herald on the storm and shipwrecks)
viii 681–781 Chorus alone (*stasimon* 2: Helen, Paris, lion cub analogy, family crimes)
ix 782–974 Chorus (anapaests), Agamemnon, Clytemnestra (silent Cassandra)

---

27 Hall (2002); Green (2002).

x 975–1068 Chorus (*stasimon* 3: terror), silent Cassandra, Clytemnestra

xi 1069–330 Chorus and Cassandra, no longer silent: *amoibaion*

xii 1331–71 Chorus alone (and briefly Agamemnon from offstage)

xiii 1372–1576 Chorus and Clytemnestra in confrontation: *amoibaion*

xiv 1577–1653 Chorus and Aegisthus

xv 1654–73 Chorus, Clytemnestra and Aegisthus

5. CHARACTERS

5.i The Watchman

Aeschylus' earlier surviving tragedies are opened by choruses of state counsellors (*Persians*) or aristocratic Egyptian sisters (*Suppliants*), or by a king (*Seven against Thebes*). The importance attached in the *Oresteia* to the repercussions that crises in the topmost social class inflict on more humble people is signalled at its opening by Aeschylus' choice of a working person, the night Watchman, as first speaker. He used to be patronised by supercilious Victorian scholars such as Frederick Paley, who invited his reader to 'observe the mixture of sententiousness and forcible homeliness in the speech of this servant',[28] who is a 'rustic wit'; Brooks Otis said his language was 'characteristic' of his 'lower-class personality'.[29] But the Watchman fared better in the twentieth century, by 1976 being described as 'an utterly captivating figure';[30] Seamus Heaney's response to *Agamemnon*, in his poem cycle 'Mycenae Lookout', uses the voice of the Watchman to comment on the misery caused by the Trojan War and the arrogance of the Argive ruling class.[31] The Watchman also draws spectators in, symbiotically, as fellow viewers; he is looking for information about the progress of the Trojan War: thus 'the script and even physical staging of *Agamemnon* puts us in the

---

28 Paley (1845) 5 and comment on line 21.
29 Otis (1981) 18.
30 Vaughn (1976) 353.
31 Heaney (1996) 34–46.

position of Watchmen, yet Watchmen with a liminal or uncertain status'.[32]

The Watchman evinces the primal emotions of terror and hope which dominate the play and trilogy; he introduces several of the most significant themes—light versus darkness, sleep and wakefulness, androgyny, animals, speech and silence, music and dance—but the form taken by his speech is equally programmatic in that it is inchoate and wandering. His meandering train of thought is reflected in an asyntactical style. His second word is *men*, a particle that usually marks a clause or sentence to be followed by an antithetical one marked by the partner particle *de*, but the *de* never comes. It 'cannot appear because it is not logically called for in the Watchman's train of thought'.[33] This train of thought is not ordered by, for example, logical deduction, antitheses or linear chronology, but by 'morphogenetic' (see below) evolution from one image to another— light, fire, the fall of Troy, the manly woman, fear which makes sleep impossible. It is marked by abrupt transitions, appositional construction, a distorted ring composition and asyndeton; this sets up the idiom of wandering thoughts and difficulty in understanding what transpires, central to the opaque epistemology of the play.

5.ii The Chorus

One passage in *Agamemnon* implies that there are 12 chorus-men (1348–471), each of whom delivers a short passage of speech; it is possible, however, that there were 15.[34] Aeschylus could have chosen a chorus of slaves, or Argive women, or youths too young to have been conscripted. But, at 67 years of age, he opted for a chorus of elderly citizens. This decision perhaps allowed the greatest freedom in expressing the civic memory of the Argive city-state. They explore the trauma of a community living in fear of a cruel regime, the need for secrecy about expression of true opinion and the brutalising effect

---

32   Nicholson (2018) 105.
33   Vaughn (1976) 336.
34   I have assumed, with most modern scholars, that the number of elders in *Agamemnon* was twelve, as the dialogue at 1348–71 indicates. See Sansone (2016) 233–7, and, in general on ancient Greek tragic chorus size, Kaimio (1970).

of mass bereavement. They fluctuate between expressing themselves as 'citizen advisers, inspired sages, and submissive and ineffectual dependents of the august royal family'.[35] In their insistence on drawing distinctions between what they can and cannot control in their shared destiny, they offer a role model for all communities struggling with collective pain.[36]

They do much of the psychological work, responding to the miserable actions of their overlords. They are adept at describing their emotions. They have also learned over the many years of miserable waiting that they must sometimes 'park' their feelings and try to exist in the present moment (251–4). The extensive vocabulary and imagery they deploy to express their psychic state is dominated by anxiety. When exploring their inner thoughts with only the audience to listen, or talking to the Herald and Cassandra, they are impressively candid about their desperation. They think about the experience of the younger Argives slaughtered in brutal hoplite warfare at Troy (65–8). We are told that grief afflicts every household that sent out a man to war who returned as ashes in an urn (428–34). They were never able to lament their dead kinsmen in person and honour them with the burial rites so important to every ancient Greek extended family.

But their act of imagining the fates of their loved ones is preceded and supplemented by their communal acts of deliberate recollection, as they search for explanations for their present misery in events which took place years ago. They embark on this work of memory straightaway as they enter in their parodos (40–6): it is ten years since the Atreidai's taskforce set sail. They retell the omen of the eagles and the hares which took place outside the palace, and report Calchas' divination speech. They must have accompanied the taskforce to Aulis, for they describe harrowingly the misery of the ordinary soldiers when the fleet was marooned by adverse winds there—starvation, disease and rotting ships (192–8). They remember that Calchas had suggested to the Atreidai, stranded at

35   Griffith (1995) 81. The oscillations in the chorus' emotions and their centrality to the ethics of *Agememnon* are well brought out in Gantz (1983).
36   This was appreciated by Vellacott (1984) 97–106; see also Hall (2023).

Aulis, what is euphemistically called the 'remedy' that had made them weep. Although the chorus did not see Iphigenia's death throes, they describe in the most distressing stanzas the preparations for the sacrifice (230–41). The effect is that of a psychiatric patient on the couch who needs to offload some great burden of remembered trauma before he can operate in the real world.

Aeschylus makes us conscious of their old age and infirmity. They were not allowed to join the military expedition ten years ago; to an Athenian, this means that they are all now a minimum of 70 years old. They lean on staffs (79–82). Yet, like Nestor in the *Iliad* (4.318–21), they are proud of the authority that their seniority lends to their words (105–6). The most touching moments in the play occur at moments of transgenerational understanding between these elderly Greeks and the young foreigner Cassandra, despite her crazy behaviour. They express admiration for her courage as well as pity (1069, 1166, 1296–8).

One of their most remarkable speech-acts is their greeting to Agamemnon. They open with a denunciation of hypocrisy—of people who pretend to feel sorry for the unfortunate, and those who fake pleasure in other people's success (793–8). This introduces their astonishingly brave public condemnation of Agamemnon's sacrifice of Iphigenia (798–803). Nevertheless, they say, as spokesmen of the city, that they are fostering no hard feelings and extend their goodwill. They can compromise, apparently, and are still hopeful that better days have already come. But this chorus of non-aristocratic citizens have not lost their moral compass, and in the closing episode they rediscover a spirit of resistance and a physical courage which are inspiring in the extreme. Despite their misery, which is felt in both the mind and the body, there is resistance and hope to be found in the great choral odes of this drama.

5.iii Clytemnestra

The role of Clytemnestra is demanding. It requires an actor to convey qualities associated with both men and women. That there is something androgynous about her is suggested by the Watchman's first reference as a 'woman who thinks like a man in her expectant heart' (10–11).

A central issue in the entire trilogy is the nature of 'proper' feminine conduct. *Agamemnon* comes up with no satisfactory answer.

One 'unfeminine' feature of Clytemnestra is that she has no apparent interest in weaving, despite being in control of a vast quantity of textiles. An obviously 'masculine' characteristic is that she wants political power. This is stressed by the term *kratos*, which means 'power' or 'right to command'. The first verb used of her is *kratei*, 'commands' or 'decrees' (11). Later the chorus address her formally: 'I have come, Clytemnestra, to honour your sovereignty (*kratos*)'; they explain that 'it is right to pay respect to the leader's wife when he is absent from his throne' (258–60). But the chorus' need to rationalise why they respect her power suggests that they are not entirely comfortable with the situation.

She wields her power imperiously. She dominates the doorway into the palace and controls the exits and entrances of others.[37] The audience hears her delivering commands to the chorus, to the Herald, to Agamemnon, to her serving women, to Cassandra and to Aegisthus—that is, to every character she encounters. Almost all her injunctions are obeyed; only Cassandra refuses to submit. The foreign princess appears not to understand Clytemnestra's order to climb down from the carriage and enter the house, although acknowledging later that she understands Greek well (1035–59, 1254). But Cassandra's flouting of Clytemnestra's authority is exceptional; after killing her husband, the Queen consolidates her hold on political power. Her own words close the play, with the idea of her *kratos* prominent. She says to Aegisthus, 'We—I and you—shall put things in good order and be in command of this house' (1673).

There is much discussion, focused on Clytemnestra, of what kinds of behaviour are identifiably 'masculine' or 'feminine' (it may have been Clytemnestra who uttered the sentence 'It is not right to revile a woman', the sole fragment (fr. 91) of Aeschylus' lost *Iphigenia*). Agamemnon accuses her, in a political context, of being 'unfeminine'; when she tells him to take no notice of his subjects, he replies that it is not the conduct *of a woman* to desire conflict with the people (940). Yet,

---

37   Blasina (2003) 60–1.

sometimes, when Clytemnestra's behaviour is described as 'masculine' it seems to be a sign of approval. She prays that the Greeks avoid committing sacrilege at Troy, concluding that her speech has been that 'of a woman' (348), for women often deliver advice on religious matters in Greek literature without compromising their feminine virtue. But the chorus here respond that she has spoken 'with good sense, like a sensible man' (351). Expressing ideas that are deemed to be 'like a man's' is not *necessarily* a bad thing for a woman to do.

In Greek antiquity, revenge was gendered feminine, as it has dominantly been gendered since; the portrait of Clytemnestra and her relationship with the Erinyes in the *Oresteia* was foundational to this conceptualisation.[38] The outraged chorus banish her from Argos. But Clytemnestra, a lone woman confronted by 12 angry men, is not intimidated. She says she is prepared to use physical violence to fight for the command of Argos on equal terms with its men. Yet she is no feminist. She is quite unlike Euripides' Medea, who complains about the unfairness of women's position in society. Clytemnestra does not apparently care about women in general. Her concern is less to change society's rules than to play and win by exactly those rules with the freedom of a man. She is aware that she exists in a society which has sexual stereotypes and different protocols for women and men. But her reaction is not to say that these stereotypes are inequitable.

The chorus suspect that Clytemnestra has been too quick to trust unreliable signs. They reflect that it is just like a woman to give thanks before good news is confirmed. Moreover, it is her womanish instructions to sacrifice that have been too persuasive, for rumours, when uttered by a woman, die down quickly (479–87). They question her reliability and concern for truth. They use against her the standard stereotype which saw all women as foolish and gullible, yet plausible pedlars of falsehood and gossip. Clytemnestra does not voice objections to the existence of these stereotypes. But she *is* insulted at being accused of behaving in accordance with them. Once the victory at Troy has been formally declared, she rebukes the chorus not for their sexist beliefs but for implying that she had behaved as a woman

---

38   Hall (2018b).

Figure 3. 'Clytemnestra and the Elders', by Adolfo de Carolis, reproduced
from *Tragedie di Eschilo*, translated by Ettore Romagnoli, vol. 2.
Bologna: Zanichelli (1921).
Author's personal collection.

would. After announcing Agamemnon's death, she comes close to
denying that she is a woman at all. The chorus have baulked at her
boasts; she reprimands them for testing her out as if she were 'an
inane woman' (1401). Is her primary objection to being considered
inane or to being considered a woman? She implies that in killing her
husband she has transcended her 'inane' sex.

Clytemnestra's physical presence is so powerful that the chorus
do not try to stop her committing murder or to arrest her afterwards
(Figure 3). She also intervenes, displaying a cool head in a crisis, when
the chorus and Aegisthus' entourage are about to fight in the final scene.
She tells Aegisthus to desist and instructs the elders to return home. She
speaks unapologetically but diplomatically, saying that she would be
pleased if all the suffering were over: 'We have been sorely kicked by
god's heavy hoof. That is what a woman says, if anyone thinks it worth
taking note' (1660–1). Her last initiative thus consists of her effective
intervention in violence between men. Such an action might be seen by
Aeschylus' audience as conventionally 'female'; but within a few lines

she is concluding the play with that power-hungry announcement to Aegisthus that they are now jointly in command (1673).

Some critics have argued that after the murders she appears in her own way as 'possessed' as Cassandra, 'almost insane with triumph', taken over by an 'unnatural force' which dies down by the time she returns to the stage to join Aegisthus.[39] Dodds claimed that when she insists that she is inseparable from the alastor or spirit of vengeance that is repaying Atreus for his crimes (1497–1504) Clytemnestra realises with dismay that she has merely been the puppet of the vengeance spirit and that this breaks her psychologically.[40] She is certainly aware of playing her role in the transgenerational pattern of violence, and in *Choephori* is made anxious by an ominous dream. But her anger against Agamemnon is an infinitely more important motive, and the supposed signs within *Agamemnon* of her losing control over herself or of events at Argos are based on little evidence.

She maintains control partly by the force of her language and the skilful deployment in her rhetoric of keywords such as woman/wife, man/husband, father, mother, offspring and dog.[41] She makes unsettling allusions to the wider world beyond the sphere of the household and to disturbing myths about the violent hero Heracles (870, 1040). She knows about elaborate hunting nets (1375–6), the gathering of sea-purple from the deepest oceans (958–60) and even metallurgy (612). Her speech describing the beacon relay is remarkable for its picturesque details of geography and topography: the men she has stationed to watch for the sign that Troy has been taken stand at intervals all the way from the vanquished city to the island of Lemnos and Mount Athos in northern Greece, down the mainland and across the Peloponnese to Argos. She is familiar with the customs of barbarian royal courts. When she asks Agamemnon to avoid putting his foot on the naked earth, she refers to the taboo

---

39   Murray (1920) xii–xiii.
40   Dodds (1960) 30. For a discussion of different interpretations of these lines see Neuburg (1991).
41   265, 316, 600, 602–604, 606, 607, 612, 896; see Chesi (2014) 10–44.

which prevented kings of Persia from touching the ground with their feet. When she prostrates herself before her husband, she is imitating the salaam of a Persian menial before his Great King (918–22). She even knows ancient Egyptian poetry. Her bizarre speech in praise of Agamemnon, where she calls him the watchdog of the stables, forestay of the ship, the pillar of the roof, only child to a father, land appearing to sailors bereft of hope, the fairest day after a storm and spring-water to a thirsty traveller (896–901), paraphrases an Egyptian hymn to a monarch of the Middle Kingdom.[42]

Yet Clytemnestra's language also underlines her identity as a woman and a mother.[43] Some aspects of her forcefulness stem from conventionally 'female' forms of exercising power. First, she furthers her goals by using her access, as a woman, to the women of the city and to religious ritual. The chorus describe the way she has lit all Argos up with the flames of burning sacrifices (85–96). She and her women, as she proudly recalls, stood in different places throughout the city, shrieking the women's conventional victory cry (594–8). Second, she can use sex appeal. She tells the chorus that she has no fear 'as long as Aegisthus kindles the fire on my hearth' (1435). This ambiguous phrase indicates that Aegisthus is effeminate, an indoor man; but it also has erotic overtones.

Third, Clytemnestra's guile is not untypical of women in Greek literature. The chorus are more shocked by her committing the murder than her use of cunning to do so. It is suggested that even regicide could have been performed according to more conventional expectations of male and female behaviour. The chorus ask Aegisthus why he did not kill Agamemnon himself (1643–5). They imply that it was contrary to the natural law of the sexes if Aegisthus plotted Agamemnon's death while Clytemnestra physically carried it out. Yet Aegisthus insists that 'the entrapment was obviously a woman's task' (1636), and Clytemnestra's genius for deception has been demonstrated earlier. The play thus portrays Clytemnestra as capable equally of 'feminine' guile and 'masculine' force.

---

42   See Hall (1989) 206.
43   McClure (1999) 7.

Fourth, Clytemnestra is herself a dazzling actress, word-perfect in the 'role' of a noble wife. She asks the Herald, 'what pleasure is greater in a woman's eyes than to open the gates for her husband returning from campaign?' (602–3). She follows this with her biggest lie in the play, denying that she knows anything of adultery and insisting that she has faithfully guarded Agamemnon's household. The Herald seems to be impressed, for he comments that when 'such a boast is full of truth it does a high-minded wife no shame to utter it' (613–14).

While she may change costume or accessories for some of her six or seven entrances, to underline her attempts to control appearances, the inner workings of Clytemnestra's mind are closed to the audience. When we have seen her mendacity in action, it is difficult to know when—indeed if—she speaks with honesty during her 'Iphigenia defence'. Aeschylus has cast doubt on her virtues as a mother by drawing attention to the way she sent her boy-child Orestes away (877–85). But even this cannot annul the force of her references to Agamemnon's sacrifice of Iphigenia, the darling daughter he thought no more of killing than if she had been an animal, the baby Clytemnestra remembers giving birth to in agony, the child whose right to Justice was ignored (1414–18, 1432). Clytemnestra can argue with the passionate conviction of a bereaved mother. This dimension of her power emerges when the chorus repeat Calchas' prophecy long ago at Aulis, predicting 'a terrible, resilient, treacherous housekeeper, a remembering wrath that avenges a child' (153–5).

The *Oresteia* concludes that fathers are more important than mothers, that men are more important than women, and that women's only public role is in religion. Clytemnestra may well, therefore, have been designed to demonstrate what happens in a nightmarish city where women with manlike thoughts stake a claim to sovereignty, thus 'proving' the necessity of the Athenian social system in which men excluded women from power. Her very frightfulness may have been felt to justify patriarchy.[44] But by *imagining* a woman who can add to her female cunning and maternal rage the ability to think like a man, by *inventing* a woman of huge intelligence who can play the

---

44   Zeitlin (1984), especially 160.

male games of politics and violence, Aeschylus created a phenomenal challenge to sexism, ancient or modern. By destroying the husband to whom she should be subordinate, she inverts the normative gender hierarchy and raises questions that are not satisfactorily answered even in *Eumenides* when the traditional order is re-established.[45]

5.iv The Herald

The Herald has often been regarded as a cheery soul, even if he becomes infected by the chorus' gloom,[46] and his scene said to function as a relatively optimistic interlude before Agamemnon's ominous arrival. But this is to misinterpret the tone, which was well described by Hugh Lloyd-Jones: 'The description of the war's horrors is further amplified in the speeches of the Herald, all the more effectively because of his pathetic determination to look on the more cheerful aspects of the situation.'[47] Responses to the Herald have sometimes been marked by the same class-based derision as the Watchman has prompted. Some have found him a typical low-ranking soldier: 'he is not very intelligent, he is garrulous, and like a soldier back from the trenches in the first world war he is determined to talk about his own sufferings'; he speaks 'an ungrammatical flood of reminiscence and reflection'.[48] But this is to overlook both the respect accorded to tragic actors who took on the challenge of messengers' emotive narratives (a character in a comedy by Eubulus said that the tragic actor Nikostratos was famous for his performance in messenger roles (fr. 134)),[49] and the relatively high status of heralds in Greek epic and tragedy; at least one ancient scholar believed this herald was the important individual known as Talthybius, Agamemnon's personal herald in the *Iliad* (1.320; see below, p. 57[50]); Agamemnon, so careful

---

45   Irigaray (2018).
46   Conacher (1987) 25: the chorus 'gradually infect the cheerful Herald with their own mood of gloom'.
47   Lloyd-Jones (1970) 10.
48   Postgate (1969) 47, 9; see also Fraenkel (1950) vol. 2, 293.
49   Green (2002) 100–2, 107–11.
50   See Wartelle (1971) 158.

about his self-promotion as victor, would have been unlikely to entrust the news of his imminent arrival to an incompetent speaker. Much of the Herald's first speech sounds like a prepared oration of which the contents had been approved by high command (507–37); so does the last part of his second, which even contains text that would serve as an victory epigram to be carved on a stone and erected in temples (573–82). The third speech, the description of the storm (636–80), contains strained syntax perhaps intended to express his state of shock, yet it is still mostly in 'the elevated style customary in messenger speeches'.[51]

A herald's task is to deliver exciting narrative and put past action before the mind's eye, just like an epic rhapsode. The term *kērux* is cognate with a Sanskrit word *karu* meaning 'bard', and may once have denoted a pre-Homeric professional ancestor who performed the function of both announcing and memorialising news.[52] The first half of the second speech is different in tone. The Herald describes, in realistic and painful detail, the acute physical discomforts which the regular Greek militiamen endured both on board and in the camps. It is a remarkable 'worm's-eye view' of warfare usually glorified in grandiose terms. Leahy has shown how it would have spoken to Aeschylus' audience, who had been involved in continuous campaigning since the Persian Wars. The stress the Herald lays on the hardships that winter brought to the encampment

> suggests conditions such as may have been endured at the siege of Eion, which seems to have lasted through the winter of 476/75 B.C., and perhaps at Sestos-only a few miles from Troy itself—where the Athenians stayed on into the winter to invest the city after the other Greeks had sailed home.[53]

But, rhetorically speaking, the Herald's emphasis on self-sacrifice can be seen as designed to make the return to the language of official victory announcement at 575, by way of contrast, all the more impressive.

---

51 Leahy (1974) 2; see also von Wilamowitz-Moellendorff (1914) 170–1.

52 Barrett (2002) 57.

53 Leahy (1974) 5–6.

5.v Agamemnon

Aeschylus inherited a characterisation of Agamemnon from the *Iliad*, which presents him as a mean-minded, arrogant and self-important monarch, wholly insensitive to the needs of his comrades and brutal to women—even the daughter of a priest—whom he treats as sex objects and exchange commodities. He has casually insulted Apollo, demands absolute obedience as the most high-status king on the Greek side, is susceptible to flattery, vacillates and relies heavily on his quick-thinking lieutenant, Odysseus, just to hold the army together. Aeschylus does little to alter this picture and offers a compelling portrait of the type of man he is. Commentators have often bent over backwards to present the Aeschylean Agamemnon to their readers as a palatable personality. Fraenkel argued, on the tenuous evidence of the Watchman's speech, that in *Agamemnon* he is shown to have been regarded as a kind master, respected and deeply loved by his people. But even if we accept this, he has come back from Troy deeply unloveable.[54] Although Agamemnon's death is shocking, he makes a poor impression. I am not in much disagreement with F.L. Lucas, who found him 'forcible-feeble; stiff yet weak; not great, but the shadow of greatness'.[55] He is brusque to the chorus and perfunctory in his thanks to the gods, ignores Clytemnestra and boasts about his violent achievements. And, throughout the play, his stature as an agent from the perspectives of religion, politics and ethics is scrutinised minutely.

There are aspects of his conduct that impugn his status from all three perspectives, leading to intense disagreement amongst scholars as to

---

54   Fraenkel (1950) vol. 2, 26. Comparing Agamemnon with the Herald, Fraenkel became fulsome (vol. 2, 294): Agamemnon is 'a model of perfect restraint' and 'a great gentleman'; his 'reflections on the ways of men the fruit of mature wisdom'. Elsner (2017) 43 explains Fraenkel's interpretation as resulting from his trauma as a Jewish refugee from Nazism: 'Fraenkel's famous misreading of Agamemnon's character in the play is effectively the product of a refugee's extraordinarily complex mix of projections about—and interpretations of—his own place in a new society, foreign to so many of his reflexes, and an imagined return to his old society turned not only alien but murderous in his absence.'
55   Lucas (1954) 61.

the extent and nature of Agamemnon's guilt. He leads an army which has committed sacrilege in its desecration of Trojan shrines (338–42, 527–8). Politically speaking, the chorus imply that the protracted war Agamemnon initiated and has led has caused acute resentment. Third, he insults his wife by bringing his concubine to share her house. Although in Athens men were allowed multiple sexual partners while female adultery was punished, there is an immanent rule discernible in tragedy by which the installation of a concubine in the marital home is censured. Every man who attempts it in tragedy suffers death shortly thereafter: the other two are Heracles in Sophocles' *Women of Trachis* and Neoptolemus in Euripides' *Andromache*, where Orestes remarks that it is a bad thing for a man to have two women he shares one bed with (909). The ideology underlying this story pattern is a refraction through a mythical prism of the same culturally endorsed notion which leads the orator Apollodorus to praise Lysias because he refrained from bringing home his girlfriends out of respect for his wife and mother ([Dem.] 59.22).[56]

But Clytemnestra's over-riding reason for killing Agamemnon is that he killed their daughter, in violation of the most basic ancient taboo on kin-killing, and has never yet been punished for it. How much guilt does this version of the myth imply he had incurred at Aulis? The controversy revolves around four inter-related issues. Why is Artemis angry in the first place and what did the omen of the eagles witnessed by the chorus truly signify? Was a military attack on Troy the will of Zeus? What exactly did Calchas say at Aulis? And did Agamemnon have any choice when he authorised the sacrifice of Iphigenia? The reason for the prolonged scholarly debate is simple; just as the *Oresteia*'s position on the Ephialtic reforms is left ambiguous by allegorical language, so *Agamemnon*'s presentation of these four issues is ambivalent and incomplete. Spectators and scholars must judge for themselves.

First, why is Artemis angry? The chorus recall the omen they had witnessed outside the palace in Argos a decade ago; two eagles had devoured a pregnant hare, foetuses and all. Calchas, the seer,

---

56   Hall (2010b) 153–4.

had identified the eagles as symbolising Agamemnon and Menelaus (123–5), and interpreted their supremacy as predicting a future victory over Troy and the taking of its livestock (126–8). But Calchas warns that the omen does not signify unmarred good fortune. Artemis is angry with the eagles because she protects animals and their unborn offspring (130–45). Calchas already has an inkling that Artemis may retaliate by imposing adverse winds that will prevent the Greek fleet from launching, and by 'precipitating another sacrifice' which is inedible (i.e., not of an animal) and which has some connection with child-avenging (146–58). He asks Apollo to intervene to ward off such an action by his sister.

There is no suggestion that either Agamemnon or Menelaus has offended Artemis beforehand, as in some versions of the myth. In the cyclic epic *Cypria*, Agamemnon went hunting when the taskforce had assembled at Aulis. He killed a deer and boasted that he had surpassed Artemis. It was in consequence of this boast that Artemis had become angry (*Cypria* Arg. par. 8). In a variant story, his offence was that he shot a goat sacred to the goddess or failed to fulfil a promise that he would sacrifice his best sheep to her, since he throttled the golden lamb that had appeared in his flock and kept it in a chest (ps.-Apollod. *Bibl.* E 2.10). But no such offence is even mentioned in *Agamemnon*. Artemis is said by Calchas to be angry with these eagles. She uses her influence in the natural world to put Agamemnon into a position where he could abandon the war project, or not. She does not compel him: it is the 'kind of man Agamemnon is' that determines the outcome.[57] The chorus seem to believe Calchas, but the audience does not need to agree wholeheartedly with them. Scholars have proposed that the devoured offspring of the hare could represent multiple beings besides the Trojans' livestock: Iphigenia, Trojan dead, Cassandra, or Thyestes' children, who will become prominent later in the play;[58] Aeschylus' Greek, however, could simultaneously encompass all these referents, and more. Via his baffled chorus, he is inviting us on a cognitive journey, but, even

---

57   Peradotto (1969a) 250.
58   For a conspectus of scholarly views, see Conacher (1987) 76–83.

by the end of *Agamemnon*, little has become clear except the principle that cycles of violence are self-perpetuating.

The second question asks whether Zeus Xeinios (protector both of people vulnerable in alien jurisdictions and of their hosts) has commanded that the Greeks punish the Trojans for taking Helen, a claim made by Menelaus in the *Iliad* vaunting over Peisander's corpse (13.622–8), but never confirmed in that epic by Zeus himself. Most commentators have assumed that it is the case in *Agamemnon*, but this requires that we believe the chorus to be the unmediated mouthpiece for Aeschylus' own views; instead, he may be portraying them as anxiously uncertain about the true nature of Zeus and as clinging rather desperately to their traditional conviction that the victory over Troy was an instance of 'divine wrath' inflicting 'reprisals, in due course, for the outrage done to the laws of hospitality and to Zeus, protector of the hearth' (501–3). Other texts as well as some passages of *Agamemnon* show us that the inevitability of the Trojan War and the assumption that Zeus Xeinios insisted on it were not unquestioned. The idea that a war should be fought merely for the sake of a woman, and someone else's woman at that, had been challenged repeatedly in the *Iliad*. In *Agamemnon*, the chorus' emphasis on the horrific scale of the war fatalities also undermines the notion that the war was necessary or even desirable.

The third debate centres on what Calchas said at Aulis. The chorus' wording is enigmatic: 'the seer intoned another remedy' to the overlords, the first remedy he attempted having been a request to Apollo to intervene and dissuade his sister. This 'other' remedy is 'worse' than the terrible weather and Calchas 'implicates Artemis'; it makes the Atreidai weep (199–205). Agamemnon *understands* it as meaning that he must kill his virgin female child by the altar, even though this expedient is 'worse' than the current predicament. But Aeschylus leaves it unclear whether Calchas had been so explicit.

Moreover, there always remains the possibility that experts in augury might make a false diagnosis; even the chorus of *Agamemnon* think that no good may come of them (1132–5). In the *Iliad*, Priam says to Hecuba that he might not have credited a seer who divines from sacrifices, or a priest, if they had instructed him to go to the

Achaeans' camp, since the instructions given by such men can be deemed false and not followed; he believes the mandate to go and ransom Hector's corpse solely because it been delivered to him directly by Iris, a divinity he had actually seen and heard (24.220–4).

The appearance of birds may not even have prophetic significance. When an eagle drops a writhing snake in the middle of the Trojans, the authorial voice tells us that the Trojans shuddered when they saw it, 'a portent of aegis-bearing Zeus' (*Iliad* 12.208–9). But the statement that the snake was a portent is syntactically so positioned as to leave it ambiguous whether this is the opinion of the authorial voice or the focalised view of the shuddering Trojans. Polydamas, who is neither a seer nor a priest, pleads with Hector to retreat. He believes that the omen means that the Trojans will end up retreating in disarray, with many fatalities. He reinforces this view with the claim that this would be the interpretation of a prophet 'who had clear knowledge of omens in his mind and whom the people believe' (12.228–9). But Hector has been told, by Iris, the will of Zeus: he must remain on the battlefield until Agamemnon leaves it (11.199–209, 11.284–91). He is disinclined to believe Polydamas' interpretation of the incident of the eagle and the snake. It could just be, after all, a coincidence. He tells Polydamas that he would rather trust in the message he has personally received from Zeus than in what he thinks is a random zoological event. He continues (12.237–40):

> But you tell us to obey long-winged birds
> that I neither pay attention to nor concern myself with,
> whether they move on the right towards the dawn and sun,
> or on the left towards the murky darkness.
> Let us obey the advice of great Zeus,
> who is king of all mortals and immortals.

Aeschylus' Agamemnon has received neither a personal visitation nor a message from any god.

The majority of commentators feel that Zeus Xenios *has* commanded the Trojan War because they want to represent Agamemnon's experience at Aulis as 'the ultimate tragic situation, faced with a choice which must bring disaster whichever path he chooses'.[59] They see him as caught between two absolute and conflicting religious imperatives—to pursue the war to punish the Trojans' violation of *xenia* and to avoid kin-killing at all costs. But Agamemnon himself does not even cite the violation of *xenia* here. The pressure he states is his reluctance 'to become a deserter of my fleet, failing my allies' (213–14). This is a purely secular and political pressure; it may or may not be meant to remind the audience of the tradition (not mentioned in the play but featuring in the *Cypria*) that the suitors of Helen had sworn an oath to recover her if ever she should be taken from the one amongst them lucky enough to become her husband (see also Apollod. *Bibl.* 3.10.9).

Aeschylean ambiguity reaches its apex with the image the chorus use to represent the moment that Agamemnon made up his mind: he 'put on the yoke-strap of necessity' (219). The image crystallises the tragedy's challenge to the distinction between compelled and freely chosen action (he put it on himself, the verb being in the active voice, but what he put on was a curb symbolising metaphysical compulsion, *Ananke*). Most commentators have seen Agamemnon as a helpless puppet under the sway of supranatural forces; Lesky saw freedom of human will and metaphysical compulsion in this play as a unity that cannot be divided.[60] But this passage can be read in more than one way. Bernard Williams argues that to interpret Agamemnon's agency thus 'simply misrepresents the text';[61] if Agamemnon is obliged to sacrifice Iphigenia, it is Agamemnon who makes it obligatory. Martha Nussbaum responded to Williams that Agamemnon's choice is bound by rational necessity.[62] If Nussbaum is correct, Aeschylus is

> showing that Agamemnon is shouldering the painful burden that he must in light of his character—at least if he is to remain a recognizably rational agent. This, in turn, means that not only does Aeschylus see

---

59   Edwards (1978) 24; see also Denniston and Page (1957) xxiv.
60   Lesky (1966); this is a reading of great subtlety that deserves close attention, even though I disagree with his conclusion.
61   Williams (1993) 133.
62   Nussbaum (2001) 34.

the decision to sacrifice Iphigenia as rationally required, but that we should as well.[63]

Robert Parker points out, correctly in my view, that Agamemnon's reported characterisation of the longing 'for a sacrifice to stop the wind and for a maiden's blood' as *'themis'*, or 'right from a religious perspective', is a self-justifying assertion at once refuted by the chorus, who baldly denounce his decision as sacrilegious (215–21).[64] The compulsion, moreover, could refer not to the ineluctability of the decision but to the inevitability of the *consequences* of his decision, especially since the chorus go on to decry it as impious, unholy, the *cause* of woe—its purpose not to vindicate Zeus Xeinios but 'to avenge a woman' (218–26). The chorus later state, unambiguously, that they disapprove of the poor judgement Agamemnon exercised at Aulis (801–3). The question of Agamemnon's culpability or innocence is therefore not only left wide open, but the weight of the chorus' memories inclines towards inculpating him. This is certainly the way Euripides interpreted the same myth in his reworking of this great chorus as the action of *Iphigenia in Aulis*; in that searing tragedy, there is scant emphasis on the oracle delivered by Calchas (it is only summarised, and in *oratio obliqua*, at 89–91), no further omen, no angry bird, no inspection of entrails. There is no guidance from any priestly figure, no divination of the will of heaven. There is no new communication from the gods during the entire play.[65] Agamemnon even criticises all seers as frauds, while failing to contest Calchas' faintly recalled pronouncement. Euripides' presentation of the myth, informed by this Aeschylean choral ode, implies that the suffering Iphigenia must undergo is not only avoidable, but that it remains so until the 11th hour.[66]

The crass complacency with which Agamemnon describes his victory jars on the ears of an audience 'who have heard what the campaign has cost in terms of human suffering'.[67] In scholarship, a

---

63   Coates (2023) 122.
64   Parker (2009) 131–2.
65   See Foley (1985) 66, 96–100.
66   Hall (2005b).
67   Leahy (1974) 21.

major focus has been on the question of why Agamemnon so suddenly gives in to Clytemnestra in consenting to walk on the cloths, when he has explicitly rejected the request previously (944–57). There is no justification in the argument that Aeschylus had no interest in characterisation and that he only decides to comply because it was dramatically necessary: character is not completely subordinated to plot in Greek tragedy, even though until recently this was fashionable to assert.[68] Nor is the idea persuasive that the audience are to sense the influence of Zeus at work.[69] In practice, much depends on how the actors use intonation and gesture; the text works well if Clytemnestra is presented as defeating her less strong-willed spouse by psychological attrition. But some have claimed that he agreed out of a gentlemanly impulse not to worst a woman in public;[70] others (more plausibly given his insensitivity in other matters) that he either secretly or subconsciously wanted to accept the invitation all along,[71] or that he hopes Clytemnestra will 'repay him by graciously admitting his war-prize concubine into the palace'.[72]

Agamemnon's taste for exhibiting his worldly possessions is made concrete in the figure of his war spoil Cassandra (see Figure 4). It is only hubristic humans shortly to die who enter on vehicles in Greek tragedy; non-pedestrian entry signified theatrically that mortal characters were getting above themselves. But riding on a vehicle, however magnificent, was not in itself a crime. Nor was a sexual relationship with a war captive, even for a married man. Clytemnestra sees the relationship with Cassandra, and the way Agamemnon has humiliated her by the public display of his infidelity, as providing additional justifications for murdering him (1438–47).

His self-important agreement to tread the tapestries betrays an arrogance that comes close to sacrilege. Putting fabric instead of shoe

---

68 Dawe (1963) 50. A crucial intervention here was the utterly sensible and sensitive discussion of Easterling (1973).
69 Lloyd-Jones (1970) 67.
70 Fraenkel (1950) vol. 2, 441.
71 E.g., Denniston and Page (1957) 151.
72 Meridor (1987) 39.

Figure 4. Agamemnon's entrance. A staging in Paris in 1886, engraving in
La République illustrée for 28 January. Author's personal collection.

leather between his feet and the earth has metaphysical ramifications.
The gods, even Agamemnon realises, do not like to see humans
honoured in such ways (918–25). Clytemnestra activates a more
political meaning. She throws herself to the ground and performs a
salaam before her husband, in a manner that the Greeks despised when
they saw it practised by the courtiers of the Persian King. She reminds
him that Priam, an Asiatic king, would, in Agamemnon's position,
happily have walked on textiles. And, despite his professed misgivings,
Agamemnon walks like a god, or a tyrant. Clytemnestra's strategy has
been designed to demonstrate something important about Agamemnon
to the Argives. By forcing him to play the role of a man who fancied
himself equivalent to a barbarian autocrat, she is attempting to add
political legitimacy to his death—to present it as a political assassination. In Athens, a citizen could be acquitted of murder if he could

prove that his victim had been intending to overthrow the democracy. Perhaps Clytemnestra is trying to rouse popular support for a deed really motivated by her personal feud with her husband.

Persuading Agamemnon to behave like a barbarian monarch will have chimed with contemporary ideas.[73] After the Persian Wars, many members of Athenian aristocratic families were suspected of harbouring tyrannical aspirations, and therefore accused of colluding with Persia and plotting to overthrow the democracy. Ostraka from this period graphically illustrate the fusion of the concepts 'pro-tyrant' and 'pro-Persian'; Callias son of Cratias, a leading candidate for ostracism in this period, is nicknamed 'the Mede', and on one ostrakon is actually caricatured in Persian clothes.[74] Pausanias and Themistocles, heroes of the war against Persia, paradoxically provide the prototypes of Aeschylus' Agamemnon, seduced by 'barbarian' luxury and power.[75] After his famous generalship at Plataea, Pausanias the Spartan allegedly began to become arrogant and tyrannical, and gave way to the temptation of colluding with Persia (Thuc. 1.94–5). When his overtures from the Hellespont to the Persian King met with an encouraging response (Thuc. 1.130),

> he thought even more of himself and was unable to live any more in the usual way, but used to depart from Byzantium dressed in Median clothing, accompanied by Median and Egyptian bodyguards, and held Persian-style banquets … . He made himself inaccessible and treated everyone so highhandedly that no one was able to go near him.

Themistocles learned the language and customs of the Persian court and retired to enjoy its hospitality (Thuc. 1. 138). Aeschylus may not be referring to any historical individual, but to the abstract principle, of which these men's careers were concrete illustrations, indicated in Euripides' *Orestes* by the verb *barbaroō* (485), 'adopt barbarian ways'.

73　See Dover (1977). For discussions of the reasons why Agamemnon yields, see Simpson (1971) and Meridor (1987).

74　Daux (1968) 732; Thomsen (1972) 97–8; Hall (1989) 59, 203.

75　On Pausanias and Persia see e.g. Blamire (1970).

5.vi Cassandra

Cassandra is silent on stage for longer than she is vocal. Aeschylean characters' initial silences were discussed throughout antiquity.[76] Plutarch preserves an anecdote in which he and the tragedian Ion of Chios saw a boxer receive a bad blow at the Isthmian games; the crowd roared. Aeschylus nudged Ion and said, 'See what training does for you! The one knocked down keeps quiet, and only the spectators cry out' (*On Progress in Virtue* 79d). Cassandra's silent presence adds mystery to her trauma as victim of very recent enslavement and near-shipwreck (and probably rape) and to her complex combination of the archetypal figures of seer, virgin bride and sacrificial victim.[77] Functionally, she is 'part lyric instrument, part dramatic personality'.[78] But she is also a heroic personage with psychological stature. As the sole character to resist Clytemnestra's authority, Cassandra maintains an independence from the action and 'comes closest of all the characters in the *Oresteia* to a Homeric hero'.[79]

Her stage identity, articulated in the priestly accoutrements that she eventually discards, is, however, that of seer. The minute Clytemnestra has entered the palace, Cassandra bursts into a terrible song to Apollo. In her prophetic frenzy she describes, only minutes before Agamemnon's death cries are heard, Clytemnestra's preparations for his murder. Her ravings also encompass laments for the fall of Troy, a prediction that Agamemnon will be avenged and a repudiation of Apollo, who has inflicted such suffering on her. In the end she asserts what little autonomy she can by entering the palace, of her own free will, to certain death. But the impact of her unforgettable scene, which left a profound impression on the literature of subsequent antiquity,[80] and has recently been treated to an outstanding analysis by Emily

---

76   Taplin (1972). For other perspectives on silences in *Agamemnon* see Nooter (2017) 81–2 and Montiglio (2000) 212: they are 'are choked voices, loaded with anguish and foreboding'.
77   Doyle (2008) 5.
78   Conacher (1987) 40.
79   Macleod (1982) 231–2.
80   Easterling (2005); Mazzoldi (2001); Brault (2009).

Figure 5. Phoebe Baines as Cassandra with the Chorus in Helen
Eastman's production at Cambridge in 2010. Photo reproduced courtesy
of the Cambridge University Greek Play Committee.

Pillinger,[81] has much to do with its relationship to the experience of the
theatrical spectator. Like every audience member, Cassandra is aware
of things far beyond the palace façade, in the past and the future; like
them, she knows that in the immediate present something horrific is
happening inside. But she is as helpless in the face of Agamemnon's
suffering as any spectator, and, like them, is a mortal, subject to death
herself (Figure 5). Her sad last lines, which equate human life with a
painted image that can be wiped away at any time by a wet sponge, are
a crystallisation of all tragic metaphysics (1327–30).

Some of her language is in the riddling and allegorical style
associated with oracles: Agamemnon is a bull and Clytemnestra a
cow (1125–60).[82] Some of her utterances could well be compared with

---

81   Pillinger (2019) 28–73.
82   On the special oracular qualities of Cassandra's imagery and diction, see Pucci

Heraclitus' comment on Pythian predictions: 'The lord whose oracle is in Delphi neither declares nor conceals, but gives a sign' (22 Heraclitus B 93). The chorus obliquely compare the difficulty of understanding her with the incomprehensibility of the Pythian oracles (1255). But this can be over-stated. She herself can see, and expresses with terrible clarity, the problem undermining the Argive royal family. She points to the spectres of the little children served up at the Thyestean feast, diminutive ghosts who died in and haunt the house forming the scenic background to the tragedy. 'Do you see those young creatures', she demands of the chorus, 'beside the house, like figures in dreams? They are the children slaughtered by their own kindred; their hands are full of the meat of their own flesh; they are clear to me, holding their vitals and entrails, which their father tasted' (1217–22).

How is the Cassandra scene related to the oracular performances of the Pythia, the priestess of Apollo at the Delphic oracle, of whom we meet a prehistoric example at the opening of *Eumenides*? Cassandra is inspired by Apollo; her predictions about Orestes' return and the matricide are in accordance with what we learn about the Delphic oracle and Apollo's edicts in the subsequent tragedies. Plutarch's description of a Pythia in his own day, who believed that the ritual preparations had indicated it was not an appropriate time for her to prophesy, but nevertheless became possessed, sounds not dissimilar to Cassandra (*Cessation of Oracles* 51): 'it was at once plain from the harshness of her voice that she was not responding properly; she was like a labouring ship and was filled with a mighty and baleful spirit'. The poor woman, hysterical and with a frightful shriek, attempted suicide and died a few days later. An obstacle in seeing Cassandra as a proto-Pythia, however, is the form and metre of her utterances. In Herodotus and most other sources, the oracles that issued from Delphi take the form of the dactylic hexameter, whereas Cassandra uses the wild, emotive dochmiac, and the plainer iambic trimeter that in Greek drama represents speech in prose. Here, the work of Lisa Maurizio suggests a solution. She has argued that during a divinatory ritual the priestesses delivered oracles

---

(1996) 167–88. There are some indirectly illuminating riddles preserved in later Greek poetry analysed in Luz (2013).

in states of spirit possession in a variety of types and forms, metrical and otherwise.[83] There is debate about the precise process by which the oracles 'quoted' in, for example, Herodotus, were (re)formulated for public consumption and record.[84]

Cassandra may therefore partly be understood as a mythical forebear or aetiological precursor of the true Pythian priestess of *Eumenides*. She breaks her silence by bursting into song in the agitated dochmiac metre, 'that strange checked, cross-weaving rhythm', which never appears before Greek tragedy (and only once after it,[85] in a context with a relationship to tragic performance).[86] It consists of the equivalent of eight short notes, in which some pairs (2 and 3, 4 and 5, 7 and 8) could be and usually were replaced by a single long (e.g. v – – v – or v vv – v –). It was not well understood even by metrical specialists in later antiquity.[87] Cassandra's dochmiac singing is likened by the chorus (also using dochmiacs) to the song of the nightingale (1140–9). The comparison was presumably reinforced by the lost melody, and certainly by the 'twittering' effect produced by the high proportion of short syllables in the resolved dochmiacs of this interchange; the chorus' description of Cassandra's melody as a 'tuneless tune' (*nomon anomon*) itself scans as five short syllables consecutively.

Cassandra, however, shifts the focus from the bird's voice to her winged body, reminding us that the singing actor playing her is engaged in an emphatically physical activity. Her singing contains numerous exclamations, where there may well have been freedom for her to extemporise moans and cries in ways that extended beyond the strict metre: one of the musical papyri suggests that accomplished singing actors had considerable room for creative input when performing the lyrics sung by a mantic character such as Cassandra. It is a fragment

---

83 Maurizio (1995) and (1997). See also Fontenrose (1978) 196–227.

84 The different views are listed in Bowden (2005) 51 n.15; see also Flower (2008).

85 Else (1977) 79. See also Seidler (1811).

86 West (1992) 142–5.

87 Fries (2016). For a statistical study of all the different types of dochmiac used by all the tragedians, including in *Agamemnon*, see Conomis (1964).

of a scene from a post-classical tragedy on the fall of Troy in which Cassandra deliriously describes Hector's last battle against Achilles, but the papyrus includes the word 'song' on seven occasions before verses probably delivered by her. These seem to be musical directions to the actor playing Cassandra to improvise sung preludes to the words he had to memorise.[88]

5.vii Aegisthus

The sudden appearance of Aegisthus after Clytemnestra's uneasy accommodation with the chorus (1577) confirms that he was involved in the slaughter but does not clarify how. The functions of his scene are to vindicate Cassandra's sense that the house is haunted by the murdered children of Thyestes, explain Aegisthus' enmity against Agamemnon and spell out the new political situation in Argos. But it also allows Aeschylus, with a few deft strokes, to paint a character-portrait of an unlovely tyrant.

He arrives with a bodyguard, the sign of someone who knows or fears he is unpopular and/or likes to make an exhibition of his wealth and status, like Pausanias the Spartan (see above). The possession of a bodyguard could be used to prove that an individual was aiming at installing a tyranny (Aristot. *Rhet.* 1.1357b). Aegisthus does not mention Clytemnestra, but claims to have 'taken on' Agamemnon himself, to make amends for the Thyestean feast (1608–11). The chorus, who understand him as meaning that he had personally killed their King, respond that he will be cursed and banished (1612–16); he now makes such shocking, arrogant and violent threats against them, based on their lower social status and their infirmity (1621–3), that the audience would be wholly in sympathy with the revulsion they feel towards him. They portray him as a man who shirks military duty and lives under the protection of a woman; we believe them. He now claims that she was responsible for the trickery involved in the murder, implying that he did the actual deed; we do not believe him.

They insist that Orestes may still be alive, and may come to kill Aegisthus and restore moral order (1646–8). Aegisthus, enraged,

---

88   Unassigned Greek tragic fr. 649 = POxy. 2746, first edited by Coles (1968).

calls his bodyguard to attention (1650). The chorus, nothing daunted, exhort each other to resist. They are not going to run away at this decisive moment (1651). When Aegisthus says he is ready to fight to the death, the chorus say they embrace the opportunity to kill him (1653). Clytemnestra intervenes, and diplomatically tries to persuade the old men to go home, but Aegisthus reveals his petty egocentrism in three brilliantly written lines, complaining peevishly to his more pragmatic partner that he should not have to tolerate being insulted (1662–4). The play ends with this impasse. The chorus have refused to submit, but Clytemnestra has prevented actual violence—civil war— erupting for the time being, despite her rebarbative lover's best efforts.

Yet the Aegisthus scene is often best remembered for the oration which precedes this exciting showdown (1577–1611). He explains that his father and Agamemnon's had engaged in a similar dynastic struggle one generation previously. Atreus had killed, dismembered and served up the elder two of Thyestes' three sons to him at a banquet. Aegisthus escaped ending up in a saucepan with his brothers, an escape he seems to explain by saying that he had at the time been just a tiny baby (1606). Even though something has happened to shorten or distort the transmitted Greek text of Aegisthus' description of the atrocity, and even though it does not approach the nauseating extension and detail of the equivalent passage in Seneca's *Thyestes* (749–88), it certainly conveys the physical reality of the occasion when, just inside the walls the audience can see, the tiny bodies were literally 'butchered', devoured and regurgitated.

6. RELIGION

6.i Gods

Agamemnon conveys the full complexity of ancient Greek religion as well as the bafflement that humans feel when attempting to comprehend what is being done by the superhuman agents and forces working behind the empirically discernible surface of the world. In the third play of the *Oresteia*, the curtain between humans and superhuman will finally be drawn back, to reveal the ghost of the dead Clytemnestra, the ravening chthonic Erinyes and the Olympian gods

Apollo, Hermes and Athena. But, for the time being, in *Agamemnon*, divining the metaphysical reasons for human suffering must rely entirely on guesswork, traditional theological explanations and seers' interpretations of omens.

When the Herald arrives at the palace, he salutes all the supernatural entities he feels are appropriate (508–21), and they offer a helpful cross section of the pantheon. The Earth and the Sunlight are cosmic elements worshipped across the Greek world; Zeus is supreme god for all the Greeks, but also has a special place in Argive local cult, as do the specific heroes of the city who the Herald says sent the taskforce on its way. It is striking that, in *Agamemnon*, Athena, Goddess of Victory, is not thanked for her sterling support of the Greeks at Troy; Zeus' wife Hera is also completely overlooked, which is remarkable since she was the most important Olympian at Argos, outside which there was an archaic sanctuary of the goddess and famous festivals in her honour; her favourite places were Argos, Sparta and Mycenae, the very three Peloponnesian cities associated with the Atreidai (*Il.* 4. 51). Perhaps the trilogy's gynaecophobic thrust is to blame for this goddess's loss of independent divine agency and status; Hera is once named in *Eumenides*, but in the mouth of Clytemnestra's divine adversary, Apollo, and merely as Zeus' wife: Apollo tells the chorus that their defence of Clytemnestra overlooks the wedding vows made between Hera and Zeus and all married couples (213–14).

Gods had special spheres of competence as well as discrete regions where they were most highly honoured; the Herald acknowledges Apollo's capacity to inflict plague as he had done at Troy, and asks him to heal now instead. He also invokes the god of his own profession, Hermes (514–15). Hermes does not feature elsewhere in *Agamemnon*, but is to be called on at crucial moments in *Choephori*; in its opening line Orestes invokes him, as the god who conducts souls of the dead to the nether world, to assist Orestes in communicating with his father; later, the chorus invoke him as god of trickery to help Orestes deceive his mother (1–2, 726–7). Hermes accompanies Orestes and Apollo as a silent escort in *Eumenides* (88–94).

The war-god Ares, who received a cult in few classical cities except Thebes, is associated by the chorus and the Herald with the belligerence of the Greek leadership and the conduct of their army at Troy; in the third strophe of the chorus' great ode after Clytemnestra's description of the beacon relay, Ares' venal temperament as the god who exchanges human corpses like gold currency seems to oust Zeus' justice as the chief motivation for the Greek invasion of the Troad.[89] But, later, Ares comes to symbolise domestic killing as well (48, 74–6, 108–15, 374–6, 472, 642, 645, 1509–12).

Artemis plays a pivotal role in the entire trilogy when the chorus recollect that it was to her as goddess of wild animals that Iphigenia was sacrificed, but she is never mentioned subsequently to those stanzas in the entire *Oresteia*; this only adds to the mysterious nature of her involvement. Athena, who will play the decisive role in *Eumenides*, is never mentioned in *Agamemnon*. Hephaestus, as fire-god, is central to the imagery of Clytemnestra's speech about the beacon relay (281–316) but otherwise does not feature.

Apollo rivals Zeus for prominence in *Agamemnon*, from the moment when the chorus wonder which immortal hears vulture parents bereft of their young, and nominate as candidates Apollo, Pan and Zeus, in that order (55–7). Calchas begged Apollo under his cult title Paian, 'Healer', to intercede with his sister Artemis and 'heal' the problem of the offence she had taken (142). A statue of Pythian Apollo, standing outside the palace alongside those of Zeus and Hermes, is addressed by the Herald (509–11). Cassandra later recoils from this statue, and physically feels the unseen presence of Apollo. She senses him scrutinising and stripping her. He dominates the entire 200 lines from her first, terrifying apostrophe (1073), 'O Apollo O Apollo', to her statement that he has brought her to her fatal predicament (1276). Apollo's influence is also to be profound on Orestes' psyche in *Choephori*, and this god finally becomes a physical presence in *Eumenides* (from line 64, where he visits his own oracle at Delphi) as Orestes' protector and advocate. During Cassandra's scene, Apollo's cult titles Loxias, Aguieus and Lycian are all used (1074, 1081–2, 1257). Amidst the bafflement about the gods' involvement in *Agamemnon*, Apollo's intimate relationship

---

89 Conacher (1987) 22. On Ares' role in the rest of the *Oresteia* as well, see Higgins (1978).

with Cassandra and his instrumentality in her acquisition of unerring prophetic powers provide a rare point of certainty.[90]

The plethora of deaths discussed produces several grim references to Hades, god of the Underworld. The Herald talks of deaths of his comrades at sea as 'a marine Hades' (667). Cassandra describes the net in which Clytemnestra traps Agamemnon as the 'net of Hades' (1115), calls Clytemnestra 'mother of Hades' (1235–6) and addresses the palace doors as those of Hades (1291). Clytemnestra disturbingly boasts to Agamemnon's citizens over his corpse that she has sacrificed him to 'infernal Hades' (1386–7).

But the presiding divinity of Agamemnon is Zeus, from whom the Atreidai received their kingly prerogative (43–4). The chorus want to believe that Zeus, in his capacity as Xeinios, 'who ensures correct treatment of hosts and guests, sent the sons of Atreus against Alexander, for the sake of a woman mated with many men' (60–3). They repeat this view more emphatically after the Herald's report of the victory (701–3). The Herald, at least publicly, agrees with this line of argument, adjuring the chorus to greet Agamemnon warmly, as 'befits the one who has demolished Troy to its foundations with the mattock of Zeus the Avenger' (523–5), and claims the victory has been won 'by favour of Zeus' (581–2). But Agamemnon himself does not attribute the victory to Zeus, preferring to emphasise Argive valour (810, 823–9). Clytemnestra, meanwhile, believes that Zeus is on her side, cryptically asking him as god of fulfilment, in front of Cassandra and the chorus, to consummate her prayers (973–4). She makes a sinister reference to Zeus as weather-god (970–2, see also the chorus' different point at 1014–15*) and one to a domestic aspect of Zeus as the god who protected a household's possessions (1036–7*).

Zeus, however, also punishes those who accumulate wealth unjustly or in excess, sing the chorus, in a context where they have been thinking about the Atreidai (469–70); Clytemnestra's cavalier attitude to consumption of valuables strikes a jarring note in the light of this stanza. The chorus know that death is final because Zeus

---

90   On the four passages dealing with Apollo in *Agamemnon*, which increase in elaboration, see Roberts (1984) 63–6.

punished Asclepius for bringing a man back to life (1022–4). Outraged and bewildered by the murder, they still try to comfort themselves with the notion there must be a divine cosmic order behind all this, ordained by Zeus (1485–8), and that he will ensure that Clytemnestra will one day receive her just deserts (1563–4).

They chorus want to maintain a belief in traditional theodicy, and above all in the providential Justice of Zeus, which will one day, they remain for the most part convinced, punish wrongdoers and restore moral order. They believe that the punishment of the Trojans for breaking Zeus' law of *xenia* is proof that the gods *do* concern themselves with mortals, like the Trojans, who commit sacrilege (367–72). They even say that the killing of Agamemnon must be 'the work of Zeus, cause of all, implementer of all', and ask 'what mortal dealings are conducted without Zeus?' (1485–7), although they immediately modify the apparent certainty of this by another question asking whether any element of what has happened is not 'divinely' executed, rather than executed by Zeus (1488).

Discussion of Zeus in *Agamemnon* has always centred on the enigmatic and beautiful 'Hymn to Zeus' (161–83), which interrupts the extended entrance song of the chorus at the point where they have remembered Calchas' ambivalent interpretation of the omen of the eagles; it thus precedes their account of the brutal sacrifice of Iphigenia. It creates the impression that they are attempting to reassure themselves that Zeus is indeed in charge of events, and that there is a purpose behind them, before they relive Iphigenia's trauma and their own. In strange wording they address Zeus as 'whoever he may be', underlining their own metaphysical uncertainty. But they *are* certain that, if they are to relieve their own anxiety, they must sing in praise of Zeus as 'the one who put mortals on the path of understanding, who ordained the law that learning comes from suffering' (174–8). Even the unwilling learn this wisdom, and divine favour comes only with great severity (179–83).

As the chorus insist to themselves that suffering does have a constructive purpose, in that mortals learn from it, and that this law is ordained by Zeus, they point out that there is no other entity that can be compared with him. This is an ancient idea: in the *Iliad*,

Zeus himself is never compared with anything or anyone else, the supreme Greek deity inheriting from those of Ancient Near Eastern Literature a legacy of incomparability.[91] The chorus allude briefly to (although avoid naming) the supreme gods who went before Zeus, his grandfather Ouranos and father Kronos, who vanquished Ouranos before being vanquished himself by Zeus (169–73). The old citizens, however, seem uneasy with the details of this myth of succession achieved through intrafamilial violence.[92]

This hymn was used by some scholars in the nineteenth century to define Aeschylus as a proto-Christian poet and his view of Zeus as somehow adumbrating a monotheistic worldview. Others did not accept that he was in any sense a monotheist, but nevertheless maintained that the religious sensibility surrounding the awe in which Zeus is held, especially in the *Oresteia*, reveals that Aeschylus' theological views represented an 'advance' on archaic conceptions. Gilbert Murray saw the advance as lying precisely in the chorus' statement that Zeus has introduced a new imperative, that what is produced by suffering is wisdom, or understanding (177).[93] This was trenchantly repudiated by Lloyd-Jones in *The Justice of Zeus*, first published in 1971, but elaborating an argument that he had first put forward in 1956; he claimed that everything said about Zeus in Aeschylus had previously been articulated by Hesiod or Homer.

Fontenrose argued that Zeus operates as head of a team of Olympians, much as he does in the *Iliad*, and that he supports Agamemnon and Orestes throughout the trilogy in opposition to Clytemnestra and her chthonic allies.[94] But this requires us to insist, despite the subtle nuances, ambivalences and contradictions within Aeschylus' dialogic text,[95] that Zeus Xeinios rather than Ares the

---

91　Ready (2012).
92　How uneasy depends on a textual crux well discussed by Pope (1974), although I have not adopted his suggestion.
93　Murray (1940) 101.
94　Fontenrose (1971).
95　Overlooked by e.g. Smith (1980), who tries and fails to pin down a unitary meaning on the 'Hymn to Zeus'.

corpse-exchanger required the sacrifice of Iphigenia and the assault on Troy. It also requires that we close our ears to the questions that the play asks, in particular how we should evaluate the justice dispensed by a top god who fails to avenge the slaughter of two blameless teenage girls.

6.ii Ritual Performed and Evoked

Ritual mediates and lends pattern to suffering, which is the subject-matter of tragedy. Time, too, is experienced in similar ways in ritual and in drama. 'The events of the *Agamemnon* when performed exist in the same temporal relation to their audience as the singing of the paean or the dithyramb', and 'in the same way each is infinitely repeatable'.[96] Aeschylus' great ritual scenes contribute much to his bewitching of experience. Rituals of several kinds are enacted or recollected and also evoked in the imagery of the play; elements of sung ritual genres are fused with other material in complex choral odes. The Watchman says that the news brought by the beacon will inspire choral dances in Argos (23–4). He suggests that Clytemnestra initiate triumphal shouts in the city (27–8), which she later says she did (588, 594–6). The chorus advocate pealing forth praise songs for Zeus (174) and recall how Iphigenia used to sing at her father's symposia in her pure, virginal voice (245). The Herald and Agamemnon formally invoke the city's gods on their return (503–20, 810–12).

Clytemnestra has organised sacrifices on the city's altars to all its gods (87–95) and the performance of the victory cry (594–7). The chorus remember the sacrifice of Iphigenia (148–51, 184–247). Cassandra, the chorus and Clytemnestra frame the deaths of Cassandra and Agamemnon as animal sacrifices (1277–8, 1298, 1385–8, 1502–5). Clytemnestra swears an oath to the chorus that she has justice on her side (1431–7), while Aegisthus reconstructs in memory his father calling down his terrifying formal curse on Atreus' family line (1600–2).

The chorus contrast the marriage hymn they imagine being performed when Helen arrived in Troy with the dirges for the dead

---

96   Easterling (1993) 20, 9.

now to be heard there (705–16). In their terror they say that internally they are singing the lament of the Erinyes (989–1002). Cassandra's addresses to Apollo, they feel, are not appropriate hymns to the gods, for they sound more like ritual laments (1078–9). Cassandra sees and hears a chorus of Erinyes singing a cacophonous hymn (1085–91)—a chorus prefiguring the one which will become physically discernible and audible to the audience in *Eumenides*. Agamemnon's lack of a public funeral and a formal eulogy is regretted by the chorus and applauded by Clytemnestra (1548–55).

The motif of the wedding that leads to catastrophe is omnipresent. The chorus imagine the wedding song performed in Troy for Paris and Helen, but also the dirges which have now replaced the happy music (700–16). Cassandra is aware that the wrecked marriage of Atreus to Aerope is still casting a fateful shadow (1192–3). There are also the disrupted marriages of Helen's sister Clytemnestra and Helen to the brothers Agamemnon and Menelaus, and the quasi-marriage of Cassandra. Her presence, albeit first silent and then overpoweringly vocal, offers 'a sustained evocation of the negative elements in the situation of a bride';[97] she is removed from the house of her father and mother, taken in a vehicle to her 'husband' Agamemnon's residence and greeted by her rival, a woman householder who would normally become her mother-in-law. But she is also, in an equally distorted way, the bride of Apollo.[98]

6.iii The Erinyes and the Family Curse

For the ancient Greeks of Aeschylus' time, the legacy of past deeds was conceptualised more concretely, more extremely, and more physically than it is in our modern notions of internal guilt which torments the malefactor. Murderers (and there was no crime more serious than murder within the family) were tormented not so much by their own consciences as by the Erinyes, or vengeance-spirits, of the murdered victim. The Erinyes could only be appeased by the blood of the murderer, or vicariously by the blood of his or her children. When

---

97   Seaford (1987) 128. See also Rehm (1994) 43–58 and McNeil (2005).
98   Mitchell-Boyask (2006) 270–85; Doyle (2008) 58–62.

this blood was spilt on the ground, they drank it voraciously from their subterranean home beneath it.[99] In drinking human blood, and in their association with hunting, bloodhounds and tearing flesh, all of which will be stressed when they physically appear in *Eumenides*, the Erinyes have their own cannibalistic qualities.

The centrality of the Erinyes to the *Oresteia* is, however, set up by several important passages in *Agamemnon*, where the opposition between the Erinyes and the Olympians that emerges in *Eumenides* is by no means clear: in some passages the Erinyes are portrayed as being included in the dispensation of Zeus.[100] The chorus imagine eagles wheeling, mourning and seeking vengeance for the loss of their young as an Erinys that brings punishment (55–9); although the context implies a comparison with the vengeful Atreidai, the simile also reminds the audience of Clytemnestra, awaiting revenge for her daughter Iphigenia. Later, they reflect that the Erinyes do eventually bring murderers to account (461–6). Helen's effect on Troy (and consequently on the Argives) was that of an Erinys who brings tears (748–9). And Cassandra describes another group of terrifying Erinyes haunting the palace, reminiscent of the cannibalised children, but associated, rather, with the crime of adultery which had resulted in the Thyestean feast, for Thyestes seduced his brother's wife, Aerope (1186–93).

The Erinyes bring with them the story of their own strange genesis, as members of the primordial family in Greek myth described in Hesiod's *Theogony* and briefly alluded to in the 'Hymn to Zeus' in *Agamemnon*. This was one of the Greeks' oldest narratives and part of their core identity and cultural curriculum. The Erinyes are some of the youngest in the long line of siblings produced in the first sexual mating, between Gaia and the son she has produced alone, Ouranos. They are thus primeval, but also low-status among this primordial generation; they are framed, forever, as the junior sisters of mighty beings. But several of the core themes and images in Hesiod's account of the original, conflicted, family in the universe reverberate within

---

99   The Erinyes' role in revenge is discussed at length in Hall (2018).
100   Solmsen (1949) 186–7.

Aeschylus' account of the later, conflicted royal family at Argos in the Peloponnese.

In the *Theogony*, the Erinyes are said to have originated materially in the blood falling on Gaia, and socially within a phenomenally dysfunctional family *already* encompassing patriarchal privilege, incest, inter-generational violence, conflict between sexual partners and co-parents, mother–child collusion, castration and child abuse. To summarise Hesiod's account of the background to the arrival of retributive justice—the fundamental theme of *Agamemnon*—in the universe (132–92): Gaia lay with Ouranos and gave birth to several children, including 'Kronos of the crooked counsel', who 'hated his vigorous father'. Then she gave birth to a series of monstrous sons including the Cyclopes, and they were all 'hated by their own father from the first'. He stuffed them back inside their mother, so she persuaded Kronos to castrate him. When Kronos threw his father's genitals on the ground, Gaia received the 'bloody droplets' and gave birth to the Erinyes. From the white foam that issued from bits of the genitals thrown into the sea, there was born Aphrodite.

In this primal scene of crime and counter-crime, the first felon is the patriarch. Ouranos represses all except one of his younger group of children and their mother. The oldest of this group, although not himself oppressed by his father, castrates him. It is at this pivotal moment that the Erinyes are born, between the second and third acts of violence in what is to become an infinite cycle. They mark the instant when the process, rather than finding a solution in the form of a doublet, a punishment to fit a crime (which is what Clytemnestra at the end of *Agamemnon* fervently wishes the day's murders comprise: see 1558–60), forever loses all possibility of being limited and indeed becomes triple and escalates. It is also the moment when reciprocal violence is no longer a matter of straightforward tit for tat. Kronos' intervention, and the genesis of the unlimited, plural Erinyes, underline the potential for revenge to be redirected and for collateral damage.

Moreover, just after the birth of the Erinyes, the upshot of the castration of Ouranos is the first, primordial curse. The wounded patriarch declares that on Kronos and the hidden-away sons, there will later come vengeance (*tisis*) for their evil deed. This, as the

Greeks knew, would expand in significance beyond the family to become the first great *political* struggle for power in the universe, when Zeus overcomes Kronos and the Olympians wrest supremacy from the Titans and Giants; in *Agamemnon*, where a similar curse operates, the revenge wreaked by Clytemnestra, with an unknowable amount of assistance from Aegisthus, is not only an act of personal and domestic revenge but part of a life-and-death struggle for absolute sovereign power, which she turns into a tyranny, in Argos.

The symbolic importance of this threefold movement establishing an irreversible process of crime and counter-crime, which is marked in Hesiod by the birth of the Erinyes and the first curse, is dazzlingly dramatised in the *Oresteia*.[101] The Hesiodic situation resembles that in *Agamemnon*. Here, too, there is a family curse, although the details of its genesis and first effects amidst earlier generations are not clearly spelled out. There are frustratingly uninformative references to Pelops (1600) and to an ancestor somehow embroiled in the saga of the family curse, Pleisthenes (1569, 1602).[102] In *Agamemnon*, however, just as there were different reasons why Ouranos and Kronos were hated, the reasons for the killing of Agamemnon are plural and confused, and the audiences is reminded of shocking collateral damage in the deaths of the innocent Iphigenia and Cassandra. Just as the birth of Aphrodite in Hesiod introduces a sexual edge to the revenge instinct embodied in her sisters, the Erinyes, extra-marital sexual desire further taints the vengeful relationships in *Agamemnon*. There is another similarity between the dysfunctional families of Hesiod and Aeschylus, and that is the centrality of the theme of the curse.

A range of images and vocabulary is applied to the curse on the house of Atreus in *Agamemnon*.[103] The chorus recall Calchas' prophetic description of the Clytemnestra-shaped Wrath (*Mēnis*) which would be the legacy of the sacrifice to Artemis (a sacrifice that would cause the wife to stop respecting the husband): she is a

---

101 On the importance of the number three in Aeschylus' presentation of revenge cycles, see Clay (1969).

102 For the little we know about him see Dalzell (1970).

103 On the family curse in the *Oresteia* see above all Gagné (2013) 394–416.

treacherous 'housekeeper' (153–5). It is the outsider, Cassandra, who sings of the insatiable civil war (*stasis*) that afflicts the Argive royal clan (1117).[104] There is a notion that some fiend or malevolent spirit (*daimōn*) has occupied the household and ravens for blood like an Erinys. The chorus accuses the '*daimōn* who has befallen on the house and the two descendants of Tantalus' (i.e. Agamemnon and Aegisthus) of operating through Clytemnestra (1469). Clytemnestra responds that they are correct to name 'the thrice-gorged *daimōn* of this race'; it is through him that bloodlust replicates itself (1475–80). She sexualises the fiend's bloodthirstiness by calling it an *erōs*. But she hopes—in vain—that in killing Agamemnon she has stopped the cycle of reciprocal violence and wants to make a compact with the familial *daimōn* (1568–70). She later prays that the suffering the family has endured already will prove sufficient, visualising the fiend as a horse or bull which has kicked them (1660).

The Athenian audience in 458 BCE were accustomed to the idea of a family curse, arising from a sacrilegious killing, which afflicted prominent citizens at the top of the political ladder. Two of the most distinguished statesmen in the half-century history of the democracy, Pericles and his great-uncle Cleisthenes, both belonged to the Alcmaeonid family, which had fallen under a curse in the seventh century BCE. Their ancestor Megacles had authorised the killing of the followers of Cylon of Athens during an attempted coup, even though Cylon had taken refuge as a suppliant in Athena's temple (Hdt. 5.71; Thuc. 1.126). Although the Alcmaeonids had been rehabilitated, the curse was still a live issue in Athenian memory and public rhetoric, and believed to be passed down across generations. As Solon had put it (fr. 13.29–32), 'But one man pays the penalty at once, another later, and if they themselves escape the penalty and the pursuing destiny of the gods does not overtake them, it assuredly comes at another time; the innocent pay the penalty, either their children or a later progeny.'

In Hesiod, the Erinyes' position within the first ever dysfunctional, strife-ridden family is precise. They are generated immediately before

---

104   Garvie (2010) 70.

the curse—the threat of the *counter*-counter-crime—is delivered. This critical moment establishes a law of cosmic penology which is played out in every Greek mythical cycle. The law is re-enacted in *Agamemnon*, where Clytemnestra, who describes herself as a semi-supernatural embodiment of vengeance, kills her husband in a counter-crime for the sacrifice of Iphigenia just before Orestes must return to murder his mother and Aegisthus in the third swing of the pendulum, the counter-counter-crime.

The curse is also linked, in some obscure way, to the wealth that the family has accumulated, and which Clytemnestra displays immoderately by lining the palace entrance with priceless cloth. The chorus warn that it is easier to practise virtue in the grimy houses of the poor; virtue is incompatible with 'gold-encrusted mansions' (773–80). They believe that wealthy people are more likely to desecrate the altar of Justice, but that wealth cannot protect them from destruction, eventually, by the gods and their agents, the Erinyes. The gods, they desperately want to believe, are not heedless of people with blood on their hands (380–3).

7. SENSORY THEATRE

Here is a translation of most of the ancient summarising introductory note prefixed to papyrus copies of Agamemnon, its 'hypothesis':

> When Agamemnon departed to Ilium, he promised Clytemnestra that if he took Ilium he would signal to her that the same day via beacon-fires. So Clytemnestra installed a watchman for a wage to look out for the beacon-fire. And when he saw it he reported it, but she sends for the crowd of elders, so as to tell them about the beacon-fires. As a result the chorus assembles. When they hear the news they sing the victory-song. Not much later Talthybius appears and describes what happened on the voyage. Agamemnon comes on a wagon. Another wagon follows him, in which are the war spoils and Cassandra. He on the one hand approaches the house with Clytemnestra, while Cassandra on the other hand, before entering the palace, prophesies both her own and Agamemnon's death and the matricide of Orestes, and leaps inside as one about to die, having cast

of her priestly ribbons. This part of the drama creates *ekplēxis*, since it elicits both terrified amazement and pity in sufficient measure, for Aeschylus portrays the killing of Agamemnon in a distinctive way on stage. He passes over Cassandra's death, but displays her corpse. He makes Aegisthus and Clytemnestra each justify the killing on a single ground: for her, it is the killing of Iphigenia; but for him, it is what happened to his father Thyestes at Atreus' hands.

Cassandra's scene was apparently much admired for its power to elicit *ekplēxis* (terrified amazement) and pity in full measure, and one detail the writer specifies is when she discards her priestly garlands. The quality of *ekplēxis* is particularly associated with the visual impact of tragic theatre, for example in a scholion on Sophocles' *Ajax* 346, where the hero is displayed amongst the cattle he has slaughtered. The scholiast concluded that the theatrical machine, the *ekkuklēma*, must have been used here 'to bring the spectator to *ekplēxis*', because things 'are more pathetic when they are actually seen'.

Other sources corroborate that the ancients admired Aeschylus, as do directors today, for his command of the visual resources of theatre. *Agamemnon* gradually restricts its vision. It opens on a vertical axis, inaugurated by the stargazing Watchman on the roof, the flames of sacrifices that shoot to the heavens, the soaring vultures in similes and eagles in omens, the numerous references to flying birds (49–52, 136, 276, 394, 426, 563–9, 1147) and the fires of the beacon relays on mountain tops. But it moves to the horizontal in Agamemnon's scene as he walks to his death. Scholars now understand better how to read an ancient theatre script differently from a text designed for delivery by, for example, an epic rhapsode, a soloist singing at a symposium with a lyre, or an epinician chorus, precisely because the visual dimension of performed drama was integral to the meanings created by the words. Aeschylus is sensitive to how fundamentally significant communication via the eyes is to the theatrical experience, presumably further heightened by the ways that paint, aperture, facial position and focal direction were emphasised by the convention of the mask.

From the moment when the Watchman talks about closing his eyelids in sleep (15), chorus and characters also draw explicit attention to the role that eyes play in the emotional communication between them. Iphigenia, recall the chorus, struck each one of the men officiating at her sacrifice with piteous shafts from her eyes (240–2). Menelaus, deprived of eye contact with Helen, has lost all libido (418). Zeus smites right in the eyes those men who have received praise beyond their deserts (469–70) and Agamemnon prays that he may not be struck from the eyes of any envious god (947). The Herald asks the statues in front of the palace to greet the King with shining eyes (520), and the chorus' eyes fill with tears at the sight of the Herald (541). The chorus imagine erotic glances exchanged at Troy (741) and say Justice leaves the houses of the wicked rich with her eyes averted (777–8). Agamemnon believes that a good judge of character can't be taken in by the look in the eyes of a false flatterer (796), even though he completely misjudges Clytemnestra's flattery himself. Clytemnestra speaks of the damage done to her eyes by nocturnal weeping fits (889); the chorus stress the importance of their own eye-witnessing of the return of Agamemnon from Troy (988–9). Cassandra speaks of her prophecy as no more glancing out from beneath veils like a bride (1178–9) and hopes her eyes will close painlessly in death (1294). Aegisthus asks why the chorus, although being able to see, do not comprehend what is going on (1623).

References to taste and smell heighten the physical experience of the audience; these are linked with the background of the Thyestean feast and help prepare for the literally bloodthirsty Erinyes of *Eumenides*. There is a cluster of disturbing images of bodily ingestion, especially of blood and human flesh. The chorus inaugurate this imagery by singing that grief is 'devouring' their peace of mind (103), just before they recall the repulsive omen of the eagles eating the foetuses of a pregnant hare (119). Clytemnestra imagines the Argive soldiers rampaging round Troy, grabbing whatever breakfast they can (331). The chorus' allegorical lion cub suffers hunger pangs that make it wheedle its master for food (725–6). Agamemnon compares the Greek army to a raving lion who slurped the blood of Trojan royalty (827–8). Both Clytemnestra and Cassandra, although to markedly different effect, speak of fresh water that relieves thirst (901, 1157).

Cassandra, says Clytemnestra, must now eat the coarse bread of slavery (1041), although before the captive has time to eat anything, Clytemnestra, her own appetite for bloodshed finally satisfied, revels in the extra gourmet delicacy that Cassandra's death has added to her own carnal pleasure (1445–6) and describes Agamemnon as drinking to the dregs the very wine-bowl of miseries he had himself prepared for the household (1398–9).

Clytemnestra defines the altar flames the Argive women are tending as scented with fragrant incense (596–7), but most references to smell are sinister.[105] Cassandra, like the Erinyes in the subsequent plays, is compared with a hound on the scent (*Ag.* 1093–94, 1184–85, *Cho.* 924, *Eum.* 244–47) and smells the blood being shed inside the house when Agamemnon is murdered. The chorus try to reassure her that it is the regular smell of animal sacrifices at the hearth; she has reeled back and insists, however, that it smells like the putrid air coming from a tomb (1308–12).

Actors' physicality informs theatre scripts in ways that make them fundamentally different from, for example, epic poetry.[106] The abundance of references to hands is one example, suggestive of gesture accompanying both speech and song: the Watchman imagines clasping Agamemnon's hand in his (34–5), the chorus recalls Agamemnon's hands stained with his own daughter's blood (210), and the lion-cub that turns its face towards its master's hand (725), visions of Helen slip through Menelaus' hands (425), in unrighteous homes hands are fouled (777), Clytemnestra tells the chorus to use their hands in ordering Cassandra to obey (1061), Cassandra sees Clytemnestra stretching out her hands prior to assaulting Agamemnon (1110–11), and the hands of the children of Thyestes full of their own meat (1220). The chorus want to catch the killers with blood on their hands (1357), Clytemnestra praises the work of her own right hand in killing Agamemnon (1405), the chorus also speak of her murderous hand (1496, 1520), Clytemnestra imagines Iphigenia and Agamemnon's hands in embrace in the

---

105   On the olfactory dimensions of the *Oresteia*, see further Lather (2018).
106   See especially Griffith (1998).

Underworld (1559), Aegisthus speaks of the crime committed by Atreus' hand (1582) and the way Atreus had mutilated the hands of Thyestes' butchered sons (1594).

Feet, kicking and trampling are even more significant than hands, the theme being made powerfully visual when Agamemnon demands that a slave remove his footwear before he walks over the purple tapestries (944–57); Cassandra may also trample on the insignia of her prophetic office when she has thrown them to the ground at 1266–7. These physical actions have been anticipated by the chorus' images of immoral men who trample sacred matters underfoot (372) or kick the altar of justice into obscurity (383–4), and Clytemnestra's proverbial statement that it is human nature to kick a man when he is down (884–5). The image is picked up later by Cassandra's reference to Thyestes 'trampling' on the sanctity of his brother's marriage bed (1193), Clytemnestra's image of hope, for her, not treading in the house of fear (1434), Aegisthus' report that Thyestes sealed his curse on Atreus by kicking the dining table (1601), and warning to the chorus not to 'kick against the pricks' (1624); these pictures reach their climax with Clytemnestra's final reference to the malevolent spirit that has kicked the household with its heavy hoof (1660).[107]

Chorus-men and actors are acutely conscious of their own breathing patterns and need to be in perfect control of their air supply; as the chorus sing at 105–6, a divine power of song still breathes on them. The vocabulary and imagery of in- and exhalation is peculiarly prominent in *Agamemnon*, emphasising the subjective experience of inhabiting a mammalian body in moments of panic, aggression, desire and death. The chorus sing of men who breathe in a more warlike way than is appropriate (375–6) and recall that the Atreidai 'breathed in unison with the strokes of fortune' at 187. Agamemnon breathed as if the wind had changed when he made the decision to sacrifice Iphigenia (219). The Herald wonders whether any of the crews of the other Greek ships still live and breathe (671), Cassandra speaks of a wave of prophetic inspiration blowing over her like a fresh wind (1180–1), says that Apollo approached her like a wrestler, 'breathing

---

107   Levine (2015) 255–63.

desire' (1206), and calls Clytemnestra a mother of Hades breathing violence (1235–6). Even the house is an organism which breathes bloody slaughter (1309). Agamemnon lies in the net, having breathed out his life (1493, 1517; see also 1389).

The somatic emphasis extends to Aeschylus' depiction of workings of the mind and the emotions, for both of which he uses distinctively violent language; both cerebral activity and psychological turmoil are experienced in a series of organs whose functions are hard to define and differentiate:[108] the heart (*kear*, 11, or *kardia*, 169, 977, 1028, 1121, 1402), breast or chest (*sternon* or *sterna*, 76), midriff, mind or seat of the passions (*phrēn, phrenes*, 103, 219, 275, 492, 502, 805, 895, 983, 996, 1034, 1064, 1084, 1143, cf. 1140, 1308, 1427, 1491, 1549, 1622), thoughts or consciousness (*phrontis*, 165, 1530), liver (*hēpar*, 432), diaphragm, understanding (*prapides*, 802), soul, heart, seat of emotion (*thumos*, 993), innards (*splanchna*, 995), and brain or mind (a compound with *nous*, 1172).[109] Ancient actors will have conceived their own emotions as intimately related to all these parts of their physiology and this will have affected the way they used the bodies as vehicles for expressing emotional disturbance.

8. VERBAL IMAGERY AND VISUALISED SPECTACLE

8.i Darkness and Light

The network of metaphors and images in *Agamemnon* is breathtakingly bold and complex, 'a resonant poetic labyrinth' which has been much discussed.[110] Just as characters are conceived theatrically in terms of concrete objects, whether they are seen or not (e.g. Agamemnon is imagined and seen in vessels—ship, vehicle, bath, tomb),[111] so an image conjured in the poetry often becomes visually concrete later; the chorus describe the hunting-net which Night threw over Troy

---

108   But see the scrupulous analysis of Thalmann (1986).
109   Aeschylus' use of these terms is discussed in detail in Sullivan (1997), and the instances in *Agamemnon* tabulated at 156–60.
110   Garner (1990) 29. See especially Petrounias (1976) 129–61.
111   Blasina (2003) 143–4.

(357–61); this adumbrates the physical net in which Agamemnon was trapped by his wife, revealed to the audience at 1371; multiple military metaphors are instantiated in the armed bodyguard who march into view with Aegisthus at 1577.[112]

It is difficult to discuss most examples of this technique without an appreciation of how they are expanded in the following two tragedies. References to statues and visual illustrations prefigure Electra's weaving that shows beasts in *Choephori* (232–3) and Athena's statue in *Eumenides* (235–6, 409). The numerous references to pouring, streaming liquids and sticky substances in *Agamemnon* become physically palpable in the libations poured by the chorus in *Choephori* and the mucus oozing from the eyes of the Erinyes in *Eumenides*. There are allusions in *Agamemnon* to the ghostly children haunting the house, visualisations of Iphigenia, Agamemnon and Cassandra in the Underworld (1555–8, 1160–1) and many references to phantoms, dreams, sleep, hunting and dogs;[113] these prefigure the tableau in *Eumenides* when the sleeping Erinyes dream that the ghost of Clytemnestra awakens them and they embark on their pursuit of Orestes, baying like hunting hounds on the scent of prey.

The entire trilogy moves from the pre-dawn darkness of the Watchman's scene and the light we hear flashes from fire to fire in the beacon relay, to the visible torches with which Athena and the citizen women of Athens escort the Erinyes to their new Athenian home at the conclusion of the trilogy (*Eum.* 1022, 1029, 1041–2).[114] This has a metatheatrical dimension. 'That the Watchmen can hear as well as see the fires' message also transmits an invitation to recognize how theatrical spectatorship involves a poetic coordination and even altered deployment of the senses, enabling remote images and fictional stories to become visible, three-dimensional, alive, and moving'.[115] There

---

112   Golden (1958) 75–106.
113   3*, 179–80*, 274*, 357*, 414–15*. There is much to be learned on ancient Greek views of those who have died violently and are now restless chthonic presences from Johnston (1999).
114   Peradotto (1964); Irwin (1974) 111–200.
115   Nicholson (2018) 109.

are mystery-cultic overtones to this, since firelight and torchlight are associated with some religious cults, especially those of the Eleusinian Mysteries and Dionysus, the god overseeing the entire performance of the *Oresteia*.[116] Equally, the preponderance of darkness, murk and the colour black in the poetry of *Agamemnon* becomes starkly visible in the black Erinyes (*Eum.* 52).[117] In *Agamemnon*, too, not only the Erinyes (462–3), but other destructive and dangerous forces are dark or black: divine grudges (132–4), *Atē* ('Ruin', 769) and Ares (1511). The character of an unjust man is 'black right through' (390–5); reprehensible children are 'black blights' on their household (769–70); the murder weapon has a handle of black horn (1127); a murder victim's blood is black (1019–20, as is Agamemnon's (1390). The chorus describe depressed and metaphysically confused minds as 'dark' (546, 1030–2). And, as so often in Greek tragedy, dying is presented as a passage from daylight to darkness, by the chorus (1121–3; see also 1646) and by Cassandra as she calls on Helios to witness (1323) her passing.[118]

But the opposition of light and darkness is neither simple nor binary, since the light can be equally threatening. Clytemnestra, plotting revenge, is responsible for the firelight rising to heaven all over the city (92–3), the reason for which the chorus assume will become clear at daybreak (254). She uses a proverb about the arrival of dawn and the arrival of daylight (264, 279) and monopolises the image of torchlight through her beacon relay speech (281–315). Aegisthus greets the light of the day that he believes has brought justice but has in fact brought terrible bloodshed and perpetuated the family curse (1577). The chorus sing that the man seduced by Persuasion into injustice sustains an injury that cannot be hidden: it 'stands out like a light' (387–9). The Herald is glad to arrive in the bright light of day (504) and equates the imminent return of Agamemnon to the appearance of light in darkness (521–2), but neither chorus nor audience feels anything but

---

116   Furley (1981); Parasinou (2003); Patera (2010); Paleothodoros (2010).

117   Aguirre (2010). On light and darkness in the *Oresteia* see also Petrounias (1976) 244–54.

118   Hall (2010b) 93–4.

apprehension at his news. And when he reports the shipwreck, it is only when 'the bright sun's light arose' that survivors could see that the sea was 'abloom with corpses' (658–9).

8.ii Legal Language

An example of the eventual concretisation of a preoccupation of the poetry is the appearance of the jurors and the votes they cast in urns at the climax of *Eumenides* (744–54). Winnington-Ingram rightly called the whole *Oresteia* a 'vast exploration of justice',[119] because the conflicts discussed in the earlier plays are frequently cast in legalistic language.[120] The chorus frame the Trojan War in legal terms in their opening anapaests, where Menelaus is presented as the plaintiff opposing Priam (41); Agamemnon says that the gods themselves unanimously cast their ballots 'in the bloody urn in favour of the murderous destruction of Ilium' (814–16).[121] Clytemnestra and Cassandra use the language of swearing oaths in legal contexts (1432–3, 1569–70). The theme continues in *Choephori*, where 'Justice' cries out for bloodshed (*Choeph.* 311–13) and Orestes claims that his actions have not been without Justice (1027).[122] The urns in which the jurors of *Eumenides* cast their ballots (742) have been foreshadowed by several different kind of urn and other hollow container: in *Agamemnon*, it is the urns containing the ashes of the war dead and the metal bath tub in which Agamemnon's corpse is displayed (1539–40); in *Choephori*, it is the vases carried by the women of the chorus as they arrive at Agamemnon's tomb (99).

8.iii Mammalian Reproduction

The tragedy uses the imagery of human genesis and reproduction, 'paedogonic' imagery, to expand its cosmic and ethical scope. Mammalian gestation is central to the chorus' sung account of the omen which precipitated the sacrifice of Iphigenia: two eagles had

---

119   Winnington-Ingram (1983) 75.
120   Daube (1939); the same goes for all Aeschylus' plays (Robertson (1939)).
121   Cohen (1986).
122   See Meinel (2015) 113–15c.

appeared near the palace, and had devoured a pregnant hare, including her unborn brood (114–20). Even the alternation of day and night is conceptualised in terms of childbirth (264–50, 279). An illuminating animal image occurs in the chorus' actual description of the sacrifice of Iphigenia. The play implies that Agamemnon has inherited his infanticidal tendencies from his father Atreus, who blurred that vital distinction between animals and beasts by forcing his brother into anthropophagy. Agamemnon blurs this distinction by offering a human sacrifice instead of an animal one, producing the master motif of the perverted sacrifice identified in a brilliant article by Froma Zeitlin.[123] Greek literature universally presents human sacrifice as an abomination, practised only by Carthaginians and other barbarians on the margins of the civilised world. Yet Agamemnon chose to have his daughter Iphigenia sacrificed 'like a kid' (231–38); she has a bit in her mouth to gag her, like a young animal, and is substituted for the fawn or other wild beast which would have been the customary offering to Artemis.

The omen of the eagles also makes concrete the overarching theme of the child-destroying family curse, a curse which affects children born to the household even before their birth. Agamemnon was once the innocent little child of Atreus; the stage building representing Atreus' physical house, a psychoanalytical critic might suggest, becomes itself an enormous, toxic, lethal womb. It disgorges the bloodied corpse of Agamemnon, killed like a defensive baby in amniotic fluid of his homecoming bath; he is dragged alongside Cassandra, stillborn or aborted in a sinister parody of a multiple birth, through the vulva-like doors of the palace into the harsh daylight of Argos. In the polysemic world of Aeschylean poetry it is not too outrageous to see the killing of Agamemnon and Cassandra, enclosed within the stage doors, as prefigured by the omen where the eagles killed the unborn children of the hare, still embryos in the mother's womb.

The terminology of begetting, conception and engendering formulates the ethical ideas at the heart of the play's conception of

---

123 Zeitlin (1965) with her postscript (1966). Many have followed in her pioneering footsteps: see e.g. Kanellakis (2020).

human action. When the chorus await the return of their King and try to sort out their thoughts about the Argive crisis, they assert that it is 'the evil deed which thereafter begets more evil deeds' of the same pedigree (758–60). They chorus believe that it is not prosperity itself which causes the destruction of a household (a traditional and widespread view), but a single iniquitous deed. The evil deed begets more evil deeds (758–60). The criminal act spawns more criminal acts. The chorus' metaphorical family of parent crimes and child crimes then almost imperceptibly mutates into the physical reality of a human family: the doer of the evil deed begets further doers of evil deeds. With another slide between concrete and metaphorical families the doer then becomes the deed again: an act of hubris in the past, the chorus continue, 'begets' an act of hubris in the present; the 'children' of hubris curse the household, but are in fact replicas of their hubristic parents (763–66).

There can be no clearer statement that the miseries of a household are the direct result of former crimes in the past. Modern readers often interpret the curse psychoanalytically as a metaphor for the way that abusive behaviour is repeated down generations through imitation of each child's treatment at the hands of traumatised parents, or, more subtly, as a pathological compulsion to repeat traumatic events from several generations ago which 'imprint themselves upon the psyche and demand an action, unconsciously, in the present'.[124]

8.iv More Fauna

Aeschylus' decision to frame ethical choice as reproductive biological imperative suggests that the 'system' of reciprocal killing is embedded deep within nature. The implication is that humans can only escape the bloody 'natural order' with the dawning of a new enlightened age of reason, in which they can demarcate themselves off from animals and create a higher system of law administered by communities (like democratic Athens) which transcend biological ties. Here the imagery of reproduction becomes inseparable from the proliferation of animal imagery (which has been more carefully

---

124   Coles (2011) 6–7.

studied by scholars in the past than the repertoire of reproductive terms).[125]

The humans at the infantile stage of social development depicted in *Agamemnon* find it almost impossible to conceptualise the universe they inhabit without resorting to analogies with the law of the jungle, or at the very least to the law of the farmyard and of the hunt. The Watchman who delivers the prologue already describes himself as a 'hound', who must place the 'ox' of silence on his tongue (3; 36). The Argives were like a ravening lion who drank the blood of Troy (824–28). Clytemnestra complains that buzzing mosquitoes awoke her from her dreams (891–94); but she herself strikes one speaker or another as a hound, a snake, a lioness (1258–59), a croaking raven (1473), and twice as a spider in whose web Agamemnon dies (1115; 1492). Mere nature seems inadequate to furnish beasts adequate to compare her with: she is likened to two supernatural monsters, the amphisbaena (1233, the serpent born from the blood shed by the decapitated Medusa), and the human-devouring Scylla (1233–6). At the end of the play the chorus insultingly refer to her and Aegisthus as a hen and a cock (1671), but Cassandra has previously called Aegisthus a 'cowardly lion' (1223–5). Agamemnon is equated with a bull, a hound and a lion (1125–26). Cassandra is variously likened to a swallow (1050), a newly captured wild animal (1063), a hound (1093), a nightingale (1141–42), a sacrificial ox (1298) and a swan (1445–46), who saves its last song for the moment of its death.

All these images suggest that in the primitive mythical world of Argos, before the invention of civic justice in the evolving Athenian democracy, humans were social and psychological infants who still behaved like bloodthirsty animals. The images also imply that they could only think about one another in the images of the bestiary, like insults thrown around a playground, or the animal figures in children's fables and nursery rhymes.[126] It is perhaps in Helen that the connection between the reproductive imagery and the imagery of the jungle is

---

125   See e.g. Heath (1999) with further refences; Heath (2005) 217–33; Kanellakis (2020).

126   Well brought out in West (1979).

most brilliantly welded. Helen, who arrived in Troy as the beautiful bride of Paris, yet who acted like an Erinys and caused the annihilation of the city, is associated with the potent idea of a lion cub fostered in a household. At first the cub is an adorable, gentle companion, allowed to play with children and nursed in the arms like a newborn baby; as it grows up, however, it turns fierce and violent, causing carnage and destruction, as did both Helen and Paris (717–36).[127] Aegisthus, Clytemnestra and Agamemnon are also connected through imagery with lions. It is tempting to speculate that Aeschylus was perfectly aware that lions were not only an important symbol of power encoded in the art and architecture of the Bronze-Age palaces of kings such as Agamemnon, but – like his tragic humans – are one of the very few mammalian creatures capable of eating their own children.[128]

8.v The House

The very first sentence draws attention to the palace roof (3). The scenery also showed statues of gods including Zeus, Apollo and Hermes (509–11) and palace doors, which Cassandra addresses as the gates of Hades (1291). The house often seems to be thought of as sentient; the Watchman implies that it is a voiceless witness to what goes on inside it (34–9), a notion repeated by Cassandra (1090–2). The Herald addresses the edifice directly (518); Clytemnestra arrogantly says that her house 'doesn't know how to be poor' (962). The audience is made powerfully aware of four important objects within: the marriage bed (27*), the banqueting table (243–5*), the family hearth (427–8*) and Agamemnon's bath, which is triumphantly revealed by Clytemnestra at 1372. Other passages suggest further activities behind the scenes, especially the unguents for sacrifice that Clytemnestra prepares 'deep inside the palace' (96*). But the house also has a metaphysical status as the material representative of the family line through time, haunted by ghosts and attacked by malign supernatural spirits. It is no surprise that Aeschylus chooses an architectural metaphor to describe Orestes'

---

127   See further Knox (1952) and Nappa (1994).
128   See Younger (1978) and Hall (2019) 272–7 on the lion-similes in relation to filicide in Euripides' *Medea*.

longed-for return: Cassandra predicts that he will put the copingstone on the edifice of his family's devastation (1283).

9. SOUNDSCAPE, VOICES, VOCALITY

The play is an overwhelming aural performance in itself, an example of the *Gesamtkunstwerk* that was provided in the Theatre of Dionysus by the combination of visual enactment with melodic and rhythmic dance, song, monologue, dialogue, sung responsion and metrical effects.[129] The audience are also treated to intense aural experiences in Agamemnon's death cries and Cassandra's mantic utterances, described by the chorus as 'a tune with cacophonous shrieks and piercing refrains?' (1152–3), and Clytemnestra's victory cry (see 1236–8, 1427). There is a range of exclamatory noises (*iou, iō, iē, pheu, ōmoi* and *ototoi*, especially in the mouths of the chorus and Cassandra[130]) and vocabulary describing vocalisations (*klangē, laskein, kōkuein, stenein, baüzein* and *oimōzein*), especially those expressing grief. Certain stylistic features such as polyptoton have dramatic acoustic properties (see below). But the poetry of the play evokes a secondary soundscape of quoted voices, individual and collective, animal noises and the cries and songs of birds, as well as references to musical performances and choral dancing.

Sarah Nooter has shown that *Agamemnon* is 'unique in its reliance on choral quoting and the depiction of offstage voices, which draw the attention of audiences to the force of vocalized absence and, at the same time, to the displacement of vocal presence'.[131] Rumour and expressions of resentment swirl in this city-state, or are expected to (487–8, 863, 938, 1106). The women of Argos are spoken of as if they form an offstage secondary chorus, joining in the shout of triumph

---

129   See the Metrical Appendix and the rhythmically sensitive discussions of Scott (1984) 22–78, Edwards (2002) 62–98 and Bierl (2016).

130   411*, 503*, 1072*, 1141–3*, 1214*, 1343*. Aristotle describes 'meaningless' sounds, which he associates with animals, as *agrammoi logoi* at *de Interpretatione* 16a 28 and *History of Animals* 1.488a 33.

131   Nooter (2017) 124; see also Bierl (2016).

led by the palace (28). We hear of war-cries bellowed by the Atreidai (48–9). The chorus describe the prophetic voice in which Calchas intoned his prophecies (156, 202), remember Iphigenia calling on her father in terror (228–9), cite voices in praise of the war dead and the criticism snarled at the Atreidai by the bereaved (452–6); they tell the Herald that they have often sighed out loud during the war (547). Clytemnestra imagines the mingled cries at Troy—the laments of the bereaved Trojans and the victory cries of the Greeks (321–9). The Herald is anxious about making this victory day ill-omened by reporting the bad news about the storm (636), a process he calls intoning a victory-song of the Erinyes (645). He speculates on what the others who were struck by the storm are saying now, if they are still alive (670–1). Agamemnon says that the envious man groans when he witnesses the successes of others (838). Cassandra can hear ghostly babies howling inside the palace (1096) and predicts that henceforward she will chant prophecies in the Underworld (1160). Aegisthus evokes his father's scream and curse on the descants of Pelops (1599–603).

The terrifying song of the Erinyes, which will not be heard by the audience until *Eumenides*, can already be heard within the mind of the chorus (900–1) and by Cassandra (1117–20, 1186–91). Wilson and Taplin argue that the language about music and especially choruses in *Agamemnon* and the rest of the *Oresteia*, what Weiss calls Aeschylus' 'metamusicality', 'is also exploited in complex and subtle ways to reflect upon the social and political order; and that disruptions or distortions in the social order find their counterpart in the musical order'. Moreover, this also supplies generically self-referential commentary on the place of the theatre in the polis, an aetiology of tragedy itself.[132]

10. STYLE AND LANGUAGE

It is an underestimation to say that Aeschylus' style and sound are distinctive. The ancients were intensely aware of this, as Aristophanes' affectionate caricature of Aeschylus' works in *Frogs* richly testifies.[133]

---

132 Weiss (2023); Wilson and Taplin (1993) 169.
133 See Scharffenberger (2007).

Sophocles is even supposed to have said that, if Aeschylus did succeed at poetry, it was serendipitously, without any knowledge of how to do so (Athen. *Deipn.* 1.22a). Aeschylean style as well as stage effects were associated by ancient critics with what they called *onkos*, 'bigness' or grandeur'.[134] A particular feature is strings of adjectives beginning with the privative alpha, which produce strong assonance for emphasis as well as providing singers with the opportunity for wide open mouths that allow them to maximise a ringing tone and volume (768–71). Aristophanes associated this with Aeschylus, as Euripides' characterisation of his 'unbridled undisciplined unguarded mouth, un-circumlocutory, pompous-bundle-spoken' demonstrates (*Frogs* 837–9). F.L. Lucas believed the best description of Aeschylus occurs in his own poetry, in a line from *Suppliants*, where the despairing chorus use compounded adjectives to wish they could escape to some 'sheer and goat-untrodden, far-withdrawn and lonely-hearted, eagle-haunted, beetling crag' (794–6). Tony Harrison's translation for the National Theatre's *Oresteia* in 1981 looked to old English and Norse poetry to find equivalent compounded 'kennings' that would suggest this remarkable feature of Aeschylean diction.[135]

All this makes for rewarding but fiendishly difficult reading: 'To read the *Oresteia* is to be sentenced to hard labour in the prison house of language' declared Mark Golden;[136] nor does it make for easy translation. Aeschylus often omits conjunctions and particles (asyndeton), or whole words and phrases (ellipse), writes in anacolouthon (changing syntactical structure in the middle of a sentence)[137] or inserts abrupt parentheses, consolidating the disjointed ambiguity that was precisely explored in Peter Stein's pioneering 1980 production of the *Oresteia* at the Berlin Schaubühne.[138]

---

134   Easterling (2005) 28–9; Podlecki (2006). Stylistic *onkos* is defined at Aristot. *Rhet.* 3.1407b26 and *Poet.* 1459b28.
135   Hall (2021b) 59–77; Taplin (2005).
136   Golden (1994) 378.
137   Berti (1930) 268–73.
138   See Case (1980).

By far the best study of Aeschylus' style remains a monograph by William Bedell Stanford, professor of Greek at Trinity College Dublin, published in 1942;[139] my discussion here and many remarks in the commentary owe more to it than I can express. The year before, he had published a dazzling study of the poet Gerard Manley Hopkins, professor of Greek at University College Dublin, showing that Hopkins' extraordinary synaesthetic style and obscurity owed much of their strangeness to Aeschylus,[140] and I believe Stanford's views on the Greek tragedian were much shaped by thinking about Hopkins' creative reactions. Hopkins wrote to fellow Aeschylus admirer Robert Bridges that Aeschylus 'is always forgetting he said a thing before. Indeed he never did, but tried to say it two or three times—something rich and profound but not by him distinctly apprehended; so he goes at it again and again like a canary trying to learn the *Bluebells of Scotland*'.[141]

Hopkins, however, usually took the kind of style he shared with Aeschylus far more seriously, as 'barbarous in beauty' and possessing 'a kind of raw nakedness and unmitigated violence'.[142] Aeschylus' repetitions have received appreciation subsequently, especially his chains of constantly evolving images and manipulation of key terms and their cognates; a favourite term for this has been 'agglutination, in which thought is continually in dynamism, meaning in suspension'.[143] Agglutination is itself a metaphorical term derived from medicine, where it denotes the amassing of red blood cells or bacteria, suspended in liquid, into clumps. But this label seems to me to misrepresent how Aeschylean semantic and imagistic clustering and recapitulation are constantly evolving, through shifts in emphasis, or supplementation, or a new association or interaction with another field of metaphor. A better analogy seems to me to be morphogenesis.

Morphogenesis is the dynamic biological process that causes an organic cell, tissue or organism such as an embryo or tumour to

---

139 Stanford (1942); there are also good insights in Earp (1948) and Finley (1955).
140 Stanford (1941).
141 Letter of January 1888, quoted in Stanford (1941) 360.
142 Stanford (1941) 366–7.
143 Matheson (1966) 101.

develop in new and different ways and into new shapes. Aeschylus' use of earlier poetry (in the lyrics above all, and drawn from Homer and Hesiod above all[144]) is equally morphogenetic, in that he rarely offers a simple quotation, but adapts, expands or inflects the wording as his own aesthetic organism evolves. The same can be said of his proclamatory verse in longer speeches and in the Cassandra scene. This often resembles what has been called the 'orational style' in the fragments of Heraclitus, which 'includes alliteration, internal "sound links", assonance, consonance, parallelism, chiasmus, word plays, onomatopoeia'.[145] These aural devices developed to serve mnemonic needs, but suit poetry because they are aurally arresting.[146]

Other salient features include enjambement (235–8*), neologisms, often repeated,[147] rare words, rhetorical questions (hypophora, 212–13, 1487–8, 490–1), interlaced polyptoton (338–40), *figura etymologica*, exclamations, triple anaphora (1553), oxymoron (1272), scathing litotes (249, 649) and elaborate periphrasis (970–2). Proverbial and sententious language is prominent everywhere in Aeschylus, but particularly so in *Agamemnon* (see 36–7*, 121, 264–5*), where the ethical confusion makes all the characters and the chorus unusually concerned to identify any jointly held moral or religious certainties and beliefs that are part of the common stock; they thus acquire a new intensity.[148] Sometimes our attention is explicitly drawn to the gnomic nature of what characters are saying (264–5*; see also 750–4).

Aeschylean stichomythia sometimes gets overlooked in favour of his great orations and lyrical episodes, but it rewards equally detailed study. It is more combative, 'bolder and more experimental' in *Agamemnon* than in other Aeschylean plays.[149] And analysis of

---

144 Sideras (1971); Østerud (1976).
145 Maurizio (2013), discussing Robb (1983).
146 Robb (1983) documents the occurrence of these devices in some of Heraclitus' sayings.
147 The neologisms of *Agamemnon* have been treated to an expert discussion by Citti (1994) 39–85, which rewards detailed study.
148 See de Romilly (1970).
149 Myres (1950) 23; Schein (1979).

particles in the stichomythic exchange between Clytemnestra and Agamemnon, for example, has revealed his hesitation and serious misgivings about the action he is being persuaded to perform: particles show that Clytemnestra seizes the initiative and keeps her husband's responses firmly under control, because she has come to the stichomythia with a plan.[150]

11. SOURCES AND ANTECEDENTS

If Aeschylus really said that his tragedies were slices of fish taken from the banquets of Homer (Athenaeus 8.347d), then 'he probably meant by "Homer" not just the *Iliad* and the *Odyssey*, but the whole of what later came to be called the Epic Cycle and perhaps, even more broadly, the entire corpus of archaic narrative epic'.[151] The epics narrating the run-up to the Trojan War (the *Cypria*) and the return of Agamemnon (part of the *Nostoi*) have not survived. The *Cypria* 'took in everything from Zeus' first design for the war to the point where the *Iliad* begins',[152] including material dealt with in the choral odes of *Agamemnon*—the departure of Helen and the gathering of the Achaeans at Aulis; the *Nostoi* included Menelaus' unsuccessful attempt to return and Agamemnon's fateful homecoming.[153] But the loss of the texts impedes understanding of the extent to which Aeschylus made innovations in the story. He certainly did not agree with the epic precursors on every significant detail. Artemis, for example, in the earlier mythical tradition had been angry with Agamemnon for specific reasons involving his sacrilege.[154]

In the *Odyssey*, Aegisthus is the sole murderer mentioned in connection with Agamemnon by Zeus (1.29–43). Nestor's version of the death of Agamemnon (3.263–75, 3.305–10) makes Aegisthus the chief plotter; Clytemnestra at first resisted his scheme. But Aegisthus

---

150   van Emde Boas (2017).
151   Sommerstein (1996) 337.
152   West (2015) 99.
153   Danek (2015) 377–8.
154   They are reviewed by De Paoli (2018). See 1584–6*.

seduced her, removing and killing the minstrel whom Agamemnon had left to guard her. He ruled Mycenae for seven years until Orestes killed him and Clytemnestra. Menelaus recalls what Proteus had told him (4.514–47). When Agamemnon returned to Argos, Aegisthus was in power. He invited Agamemnon to a feast and killed him; all the followers of both cousins died too. There is no mention of Clytemnestra. But the account given by the shade of Agamemnon in the Underworld paints a much darker picture of Clytemnestra's involvement (11.409–34; see also 24.95–6, 24.199–202). Aegisthus killed him and his comrades, with Clytemnestra's help, after inviting him to a feast. Clytemnestra killed Cassandra beside him. She then disrespected his corpse by neglecting to close his eyes and mouth.[155] Hesiod may have alluded to the murder (in a supplement to the text of fr. 19.30) and spoke of Clytemnestra's sexual relationship with Aegisthus (fr. 247.5–6). The surviving fragments of Stesichorus' *Oresteia* show that it dealt with the trickery involved in the sacrifice of Iphigenia (frr. 181a.25–7), a detail which suggests that the lyric poet was more interested in Clytemnestra's psychological justification for killing Agamemnon than he has usually been given credit for.[156] The visual record offers no evidence for Clytemnestra acting alone before *Agamemnon*, although an eighth-century terracotta pinax from Gortyn *possibly* shows Clytemnestra and Aegisthus attacking a seated Agamemnon; two shield bands from Olympia and Aegina also depict a woman attacking a man.[157]

In *Pythian* 11.26–40, Pindar says that Clytemnestra sent Cassandra and Agamemnon to the Underworld with her bronze blade, and asks whether her motive was vengeance for Iphigenia or her sexual relationship with Aegisthus. Unfortunately, we do not know whether this epinician ode was composed before or after *Agamemnon*. But, in

---

155   The treatments of this story in the *Odyssey* are admirably discussed by Föllinger (2003) 60–1.

156   Finglass (2018b) 34–5.

157   Heraklion 11512, but see Fittschen (1969) 189 with n.891. The Argive shield bands are reproduced in Prag (1985) A3 plate 2a and A4 plate 2b–c. For further discussion see Brize (1980) 15–19 and especially Föllinger (2003) 64–5.

a sense, it does not matter. In the absence of so much archaic poetry, especially the *Cypria* and Stesichorus' *Oresteia*, we can do little more than guess that Aeschylus took his theatrical opportunity to elaborate on Clytemnestra's dominance, and may have been the first poet to make her kill her husband single-handedly. A theatrical poet, moreover, has a huge range of effects at his disposal, especially scenery, costume, props, masks, stage action, entrances and exits, posture and gesture, dance, contrasting voices and metrical gearshifts. We do not need to know how much of the storyline Aeschylus shared with other poets in order to appreciate these.[158]

12. THE AFTERLIFE AND INFLUENCE OF *AGAMEMNON* IN ANTIQUITY

The poetry of *Agamemnon*, however incomprehensible some may have found it, soon became embedded in the Athenian consciousness, especially in the minds of the playwrights that came after him. The *Oresteia* may well have been revived in the early 420s, inspiring and informing Euripides' 'Orestean' tragedies *Iphigenia in Tauris*, *Electra* and *Orestes*.[159] Easterling has shown how some of the *Oresteia*'s language seems to have turned almost into catch phrases:[160] the thirsty dust (495, cf. Soph. *Ant.* 246–7, 429); Helen as sacker of cities (690, cf. Eur. *IA* 1476, 1511); the mattock of Zeus (526, cf. Soph. fr. 727, from the lost play *Chryses*, parodied by Aristophanes at *Birds* 1240); 'a bitter end of marriage rites' (745, cf. Eur. *Med.* 1388). Coo has argued for the influence of *Agamemnon* on both Sophocles' *Women of Trachis* and his famous lost tragedy *Tereus*.[161] But when Euripides consciously writes plays which remake Aeschylean material, especially *Iphigenia in Aulis* in the case of *Agamemnon*, Easterling demonstrates how the linguistic texture of the new tragedy reformulates famous

158 On the literary sources see also Garvie (1986) ix–xxvi; Gantz (1993) 664–85; Bowie (2015) 113–20.
159 Schol. Ar. *Ach* 10; see Meinel (2015) 140–4.
160 Easterling (2005) 30–1.
161 Coo (2013) 357–61.

phrases to 'point up crucially ironic difference'.[162] A fine example is how Euripides redevelops what the chorus of Agamemnon call the King's 'yoke-strap of necessity' (218) as the more idiomatic 'bonds of necessity' (*IA* 43), in the mouth of the King himself. The *Oresteia* was certainly appreciated by Aristophanes, who parodically not only quotes *Choephori* in *Frogs* but reworks several of the trilogy's motifs in *Wasps*.[163]

  Yet the influence of Aeschylus' *Agamemnon* exerted itself in the form of reaction when it came to the unpleasant arrogance of Agamemnon and the unforgettable portrait of Clytemnestra.[164] Agamemnon's own scene lies behind the anecdote about the Cynic philosopher Diogenes which describes him trampling on Plato's carpets when Plato was enjoying, too much for Diogenes' taste, the extravagant hospitality of the court of Dionysius I, tyrant of Syracuse (Diogenes Laertius 6.2.26). An Etrurian sculptor in the second century CE decorated an alabaster urn with a scene in which Clytemnestra takes the principal role in the murder of Agamemnon (Figure 6), but this is the sole certain ancient visual illustration of the murder of Agamemnon post-dating the *Oresteia* which makes Clytemnestra the primary agent in her husband's slaughter.[165] Literary versions which make her both mastermind and executor of the crime are also rare, one exception being Philostratus' even later *Cassandra*, an ekphrasis of a painting written in about 300 CE (*Imagines* 2.10). Yet the Aeschylean Clytemnestra's impact was swift: when the legal speech-writer Antiphon composed the case for the prosecution in the mid-fifth-century trial of a woman accused of murdering her husband, he invoked a parallel with Clytemnestra (Antiphon 1.17). More than a millennium later, Procopius makes his power-crazed Byzantine empress Theodora allude to Clytemnestra's

---

162 Easterling (2005) 30.

163 Wyles (2020b).

164 On Agamemnon in tragedies by all three tragedians, see Merker (2011).

165 The urn is now in the Florence Archaeological Museum (Knoepfler (1993) fig. 75 = LIMC 'Agamemnon' no. 96). Two Erinyes flank Clytemnestra while she attacks Agamemnon. He is seated and his upper body has a piece of fabric thrown over it. Aegisthus, most unusually, is not depicted.

Figure 6. Etruscan alabaster urn in Beni Archeologici della Toscana, Florence (second century CE). Drawing reproduced courtesy of Becky Brewis.

sinister speech 'There is the sea … ' at a moment of political crisis (*History of the Wars* 1.24.33–7).

Most of the evidence for Clytemnestra's reception in antiquity suggests, however, that she was soon widely replaced by a less domineering character, of a type perhaps implied by the more sympathetic woman in Sophocles' *Electra* or Euripides' *Electra* and *Iphigenia in Aulis*. This different conception of Clytemnestra may have been invented by Aeschylus himself (in his lost *Iphigenia*) or by Ion of Chios a generation later. Between Ion's first competition (in 452 or 449) and his death (before 421), he wrote a tragic *Agamemnon*. It was sufficiently famous for Didymus to write a commentary upon it in Alexandria in the first century BCE (Athen. *Deipn.* 11.468d).

Like Sophocles in his *Electra*, Ion may well have decided against Aeschylus' spousal slaughter in the bathroom, returning to those Homeric accounts of Agamemnon's death in which Aegisthus played the leading role, at a banquet.[166]

The picture of the murder offered by the surviving *hypothesis* to *Agamemnon* (see above) does not exactly square with the version in the Aeschylean text. The hypothesis claims that 'Aeschylus has Agamemnon murdered in a distinctive way on stage' 15–16). The earlier part of this summary has contained at least one piece of information which Taplin has plausibly argued probably derives from Hellenistic performance practices—two vehicles rather than one.[167] The theatre contemporary with the hypothesis writer may have played up the display of Agamemnon's booty, as performances of Accius' Roman tragedy on the theme certainly did by the mid-first century BCE (see below).

The 'distinctive way' suggests the confining textile or robe which appears in so many versions of the murder of Agamemnon. It is a possibility that the spectacular taste of the Hellenistic theatre could have produced (mimed?) enactments of this exciting scene? The author of the hypothesis might be responding to contemporary theatrical taste which enjoyed the representation of sensational violence more than fifth-century audiences had enjoyed them.[168] But it is more likely that he had no experience of Aeschylus' play in performance. He

---

166   See von Blumenthal (1939). Ion's death by 421 is fixed by a reference in Aristophanes' *Peace* (832–5), which was certainly produced that year. Hyginus (117) and Servius Auctus on Virgil, *Aen.* 11.268–9 preserve yet another version where Agamemnon was killed while offering a sacrifice. The *Agamemnon* of Ion (or of Aeschylus, or even another unidentifiable tragedian) may have been produced at the Lenaea in 419, of which no further evidence survives than the three first letters of the name (tr. fr. adesp. 1). On the other hand, the play could have been an *Agaue*.

167   Taplin (1977) 304–5.

168   The possibility that some ancient audiences actually saw Agamemnon being killed was at least envisaged by Verrall, whose response to the hypothesis was to remark circumspectly that 'our knowledge of ancient scenery is not such as to warrant any positive assertion on details of this kind' (Verrall (1889) lvi–vii), and

could have seen two vehicles in another play on the same theme—Ion's *Agamemnon* included a reference to horse-related luxury (*hippikon chlidos*, fr. 3)—but have made the mistake concerning the murder in *Agamemnon* through misunderstanding fifth-century theatre conventions, as Taplin suspected.[169] In this case the hypothesis writer's confusion might result from a difficulty, born of *ignorance* of the play in performance, in understanding that Cassandra can actually see through walls—that her commentary on the death of Agamemnon is clairvoyant rather than empirically observed.

Seeing the hypothesis's strange account of the murder as resulting from an inexperience of the play in performance might illuminate the near-absence from the ancient Greek world of certainly identified depictions, which post-date the *Oresteia*, of the murder of Agamemnon.[170] This absence becomes conspicuous by comparison with the numerous vase-paintings depicting scenes from both the *Choephori* and the *Eumenides*—illustrations of the tomb of Agamemnon, the recognition of Electra and Orestes, the deaths of Clytemnestra and Aegisthus, and Orestes with Erinyes.[171] Amongst the few possible representations (besides the alabaster urn, Figure 6) all are doubtful and in none does Clytemnestra act alone.

There is the Dokimasia painter's brilliant calyx-crater in Boston, which Vermeule argues is a response to the *Oresteia* (although most scholars date it to 470–460 BC).[172] On this vase Aegisthus is

---

who did not deserve the opprobrium heaped on his head by subsequent scholars as a result.

169   Taplin (1977) 304.

170   In the Louvre there is one imperial sculpture from Volterra (a 2nd-century CE alabaster urn), on which Aegisthus and Clytemnestra simultaneously attack Agamemnon, who is seated and draped in fabric, while a mysterious young man enters at the side. This may be related to Pacuvius' lost tragedy *Dulorestes* (on which see below).

171   See Prag (1985); Knoepfler (1993); Trendall and Webster (1971) 40–9. For the depiction of Orestes about to slay Clytemnestra, who is showing her breast to him, on a red-figured neck-amphora from Paestum, see Trendall (1987) 183–4, no. 418 and plate 129a.

172   Boston 63.1246, Prag (1985) plates 3–4; Vermeule (1966).

Figure 7. Fragments of a Lucanian vase (c. 400 BCE) in the Herbert Cahn Collection, Basel. Drawing reproduced courtesy of Becky Brewis.

unambivalently portrayed as the killer; Clytemnestra, although running in to help with an axe, is 'no more than an enthusiastic if not very useful supporter'.[173] If this represents the *Oresteia*, then the painter (like many dramatists subsequently) modified the Aeschylean version to make Clytemnestra less important. There are two other possible candidates. One is a fragmentary Lucanian crater of about 400 BCE (see Figure 7 and the cover to this book), on which the faces, especially the eyes and the wrinkles, suggest theatrical masks. Here a woman, not in the first flush of youth, appears to be holding in her left hand the greaves of the mature, bearded, seated man; her

173   Prag (1985) 4.

right hand seems to be on his head. The left hand of a third party is visibly pressing the seated man's head down, probably in preparation for striking a blow with his(?) other hand. If this image represents Clytemnestra and Agamemnon, then she is not attacking her husband single-handedly as she claims in Aeschylus' *Agamemnon*.[174] The other possible candidate is a Campanian krater in Leningrad on which a woman uses a weapon that looks like a golf club to attack a man; although he is a warrior, he is unbearded and wears a Phrygian cap, which seems unlikely for Agamemnon.[175]

Could the dearth of illustrations of Aeschylus' *Agamemnon* relate to the absence of evidence for any revival of this play, either on its own or as part of the trilogy? Can we discount the possibility that the other two plays were often performed without *Agamemnon*? Could it be relevant that in *Frogs*, when asked to recite the prologue of what is termed the *Oresteia*, Aeschylus offers the opening lines not of *Agamemnon* but of *Choephori* (1124, 1128)?[176] Playwrights subsequent to Aeschylus graphically tamed the Clytemnestra of the *Agamemnon*, and not just because this play was so good that it 'seems to have been regarded as an unapproachable model'.[177] These playwrights had other, more ideological reasons, and they found two suggestive details already lurking in *Choephori*. One was a tender, sexualised side to Clytemnestra, who can openly and sincerely call Aegisthus 'beloved' (895), and whose motives are now explicitly presented as including *erōs* (597).[178] The other was the tempting possibility that Agamemnon was killed by Aegisthus.

---

174   Fig. 37 in Knoepfler (1993) 55; the fragment is not included in LIMC. For a full discussion see Cambitoglou et al. (1997) 14–17.

175   K28 in Kossatz-Deissmann (1978).

176   This is not to deny that there are allusions to the text of *Agamemnon* in *Frogs*, above all at 1284–92, which is built around some lines of the opening chorus (*Ag.* 108–11).

177   Pearson (1917) vol. 1, 219, in the context of his excellent discussion of Sophocles' fragmentary *Iphigenia*.

178   There may, of course, be a sexual double entendre at *Ag.* 1654. But see the sensitive comment of Garvie (1986) 291, on *Choeph.* 893, where Clytemnestra, with obvious sincerity, apostrophises the dead Aegisthus as *philtat' Aigisthou bia*:

Aegisthus, when depicted as Agamemnon's murderer, invariably uses a sword. Clytemnestra, on the other hand, was predominantly associated with the 'manslaying axe' which she so memorably demands in *Choephori* when realising her mortal danger (889): although one hydria approximately contemporary with the *Oresteia* may conceivably show her with a sword over the prostrate body of Cassandra (Prague, Charles University, 60.31), she certainly wields an axe, for example, in the rare illustration of her murder of Cassandra on a cup by the Marlay Painter.[179] *Pelekus* ('Axe') was the nickname acquired by a tragic actor called Demetrios (perhaps as early as the fifth or fourth century BCE) on account of a role connected with 'the death of Agamemnon'.[180] *Choephori* thus dominated the tradition, rather than *Agamemnon*, where the weapon is twice envisaged as a sword.[181] In *Choephori* Orestes calls the murder weapon *Aegisthus'* sword (1011). *Choephori*, acted without *Agamemnon*, implies that Clytemnestra was neither the sole nor the primary agent in the murder of her husband. If we only had *Choephori* we would think that Aegisthus killed Agamemnon with a sword, assisted by the axe-armed Clytemnestra.

It is likely that by the fourth century, at least, the first play was often dropped from performances of *Choephori* and *Eumenides*, whether separately or together.[182] In the Roman world there are few signs of an *Agamemnon* with an Amazonian Clytemnestra of the Aeschylean type, although it would be good to know more about Pacuvius' *Dulorestes*, which apparently involved Orestes taking the role of a slave in the household of Aegisthus and Clytemnestra.[183] The 12 surviving lines of Livius Andronicus' *Aegisthus* (late third

---

'The pathos of Clytemnestra's words contrasts strikingly with Orestes' tone ... . Unimpressive we know him [Aegisthus] to be, he was still loved by Clytaemnestra. It is a side of her that hardly emerged in *Ag.*'

179　ARV 1280.64 = Ferrara T 264, 435–430 BCE; reproduced in Easterling (2005) 35 as fig. 1.2; see also p. 422.

180　Hesychius δ 837 = Stephanis (1988) no. 610.

181　See 1260–3*.

182　Hall (2005a) 57–61.

183　This tragedy seems to have included elaborate rhetoric: see Erasmo (2004) 34–5.

century BCE) include references to the division of the Trojan booty and to dolphins accompanying the voyage (2–6);[184] in one fragment (7) the speaker forbids his listeners to discuss an unspecified subject within an unidentified woman's hearing, which looks likely to be Agamemnon talking about Cassandra. The most interesting fragment from our perspective is that which implies that the murder was performed at a banquet rather than in a bath: 'He seats himself upon the royal chair / And Clytemnestra is next to him; the third / Their daughters occupy' (9–10). One other fragment features an individual claiming *maiestas*, and the right to absolute obedience, while giving the order that a female is to be led away: 'You must endure the duty of obedience / To what my majesty demands. Lead you / This woman from the temple' (14). The speaker here, on the analogy of Seneca's *Agamemnon* 997, is likely to be Aegisthus. The evidence, such as it is, therefore points forward to the Clytemnestra of Seneca rather than backwards to the Clytemnestra of Aeschylus.

The most important Roman Republican play on this theme was by Lucius Accius (acclaimed in Seneca's day as the greatest of all Roman tragedians), who wrote his influential *Clytemnestra* in the second half of the second century BCE. *Clytemnestra* was sufficiently popular to be revived in the following century, at the gala staged to celebrate the opening of Pompey's theatre in 55 BCE; Cicero complained of the spectacle 'of hundreds of mules' (*Fam.* 7.1.2), which suggests that the acting text of Accius' version demanded or at least permitted Agamemnon's entrance to be accompanied by a spectacular military procession. It is likely that Accius' Clytemnestra was no Argive termagant but a more 'feminine' figure, subsidiary to her lover. The fragments suggest that prominence was given to her fraught relationship with her love rival Cassandra, who believed it to be her last day alive (fr. 243–6).[185] The fragments are unhelpful on

---

184   These and all subsequent references to Livius Andronicus and Accius are cited (with very slight alterations to the English translations) from Warmington (1935–40).

185   It is possible that the play is to be identified with Accius' *Aegisthus*, which included a speech in which a character spoke about the 'might of government', *vis*

the identity of the principal architect of the murder of Agamemnon. Yet they do positively imply that Clytemnestra's sexual jealousy of Cassandra and Aegisthus' imposition of tyrannical rule were dimensions of Accius' interpretation of the story, while there is no evidence for a politicised Clytemnestra, a Clytemnestra acting alone, or the daughter-avenging motive. The secondary status to which Clytemnestra is relegated in the fully surviving Latin versions by Ovid and by Seneca was probably already a standard feature of republican Roman theatre.

Sadly we know little about the tragedy *Clytemnestra* by the Ephesian poet Polemaios, performed at a festival at Magnesia on the Maeander in the first half of the first century BCE, because it would have provided a bridge between the Greek and the Roman worlds at a time when revivals of the old Roman plays were popular.[186] By the last days of the Roman Republic, Agamemnon was a familiar mythical figure. Champlin has argued that this was a result of widespread familiarity with stage plays. Agamemnon's presence in the Roman imagination made it easy for Pompeius Magnus to foster what in his opponent's hands turned out to be an unfortunate comparison between himself and Agamemnon; his notorious gala revival of Accius' *Clytemnestra* was part of this propaganda. Augustus, on the other hand, promoted a comparison between himself and Orestes: they were both young leaders who had avenged the murder of their father. Each had also put down his father's insurgent wives, ensconced in love-nests with new swains: to Augustus' public, Cleopatra had thus become Clytemnestra.[187] This equation may have made it more dangerous for poets to trifle with the Atreidai.

---

imperi, breaking men's fierce spirits (frr. 8–9), a remark that women are more easily hardened (*callent*) than men (frr. 10–11), and a reference to a man, presumably Orestes, whose 'hand is fouled and spattered by his mother's blood' (fr. 12). Accius also wrote an *Agamemnon's Children* (*Agamemnonidae*).

186   A Magnesian inscription records the victory of an actor called Artemidorus, son of Artemidorus and grandson of Dioscorides, in the Romaia at Magnesia on the Maeander, some time in the first half of the first century BCE; the play he performed was Polemaios' *Clytemnestra* (Stephanis (1988) 416 = tr. fr. 155.1).

187   See Champlin (2003), especially 308–10, 297–300.

Polemaios' Ephesian *Clytemnestra* may, however, have been more interested in sexual love than in Roman dynastic politics. It may have been known by Ovid, whose version in the *Ars Amatoria* (2.387–408) presents us with the most eviscerated ancient Clytemnestra. Ovid's narrator is urging that people in love—for example, Clytemnestra—can become vindictive if they discover they have been betrayed. And, along with Ovid's sexy heroine, the most influential Clytemnestra until 130 years ago was Seneca's neurotic adulteress.

Ovid's humorous rewriting of Clytemnestra certainly informed Seneca's more serious presentation of her character, as Tarrant demonstrates in his Senecan commentary.[188] Unlike Ovid, the Roman tragedian does not absolutely exclude Iphigenia from the argument. But his Clytemnestra remains, in comparison with Aeschylus' heroine, an apolitical character, a feature exaggerated by the replacement of the male chorus of Argive citizens with females uninterested in the constitutional ramifications of the domestic crisis they are witnessing. The opening lines delivered by Seneca's Clytemnestra set the agenda for her character delineation: she regrets, in a manner remote from Aeschylus' amoral heroine, the disappearance of good character, justice, propriety, *pietas*, fidelity and decency (112–13). The state of mind of Seneca's queen is marked by anguish and psychological fragmentation. She is also self-confessedly amorous; her dominant motives, it is stressed, are sexual passion for Aegisthus and sexual jealousy of Cassandra. Finally, she is psychologically frail; she is shown struggling with the immorality even of *complicity* in the killing of her husband.

Under emotional pressure from Aegisthus, according to Cassandra's account of the crime, she is involved in the murder of her husband. Clytemnestra persuades Agamemnon to don the confining garment at his own victory banquet (897–900). Aegisthus strikes the first blow, but it fails to penetrate deep enough to cause death.[189]

---

188   Tarrant (1976), subject index s.v. 'Ovid'.
189   At this point the text draws on both the Homeric conception of the murder as orchestrated at a banquet by Aegisthus and the Aeschylean notion of Aegisthus' inadequacy as a male: here and here alone Cassandra calls him *semivir* (890). The evisceration of Clytemnestra in this play has even led some translators to assume

Thereupon Clytemnestra strikes with her axe, partially decapitating Agamemnon, and, together, 'the son of Thyestes and the sister of Helen' complete their bloody task (897–907). Thus, in Seneca's reading, the leading agent in both the original plan for the murder, and its execution, is Aegisthus. It is Aegisthus, moreover, who is unquestionably in political charge at the end of the play, when Clytemnestra asks for his help in controlling both Electra and Cassandra, and it is he who commands the palace guard and the Argive dungeons.[190] Yet Clytemnestra is by no means without a capacity for cruelty and violence, the relationship between the two lovers being to a certain extent co-dependent. The text seems locked in a struggle between different versions of Clytemnestra (Seneca knew both Aeschylus and Ovid, as well as intervening plays[191]).

The perennial controversy about Senecan performance has tended to operate in misleading isolation from what we know about the *variety* of genres of ancient entertainment connected with tragedy, in all of which there survive traces of the 'return of Agamemnon' theme. For example, certain features in the Senecan messenger's elaborate description of the storm may even have entered the narrative tradition because of their treatment in a mechanical puppet-show, a five-act *Nauplius*, described in Hero of Alexandria's technical treatise *On Automata*.[192] Besides declamation and puppet-shows, moreover, tragic material could take the form of a sung recital by a masked performer (*tragoedus, tragicus cantor*), a practice which is attested as late as the fifth century CE, or of a ballet to choral accompaniment (ancient

---

that the term *semivir* refers disparagingly to Clytemnestra, and her inability to strike deep enough to kill a man. See e.g. Harris (1904), 303 (interestingly, a female translator).

190   Several critics have tried to find strong reminders of the Iphigenia-motivation in the later parts of the play, for example in the imagery describing Agamemnon's death (e.g. Shelton (1983) 176), but their need to find Iphigenia where she is not speaks louder than the alleged textual echoes themselves.

191   See further Brook (2019); Rodrigues (2020).

192   Heron, *Peri Automatopoiētikēs* ch. 22.3–6, par. 264 in the Teubner edition of Wilhelm Schmidt (1899); the material may have been taken from Philo of Byzantium (see Tarrant (1976) 21).

pantomime), or of a mixture of these elements.[193] Philostratus tells of an itinerant professional singer, whose repertoire of 'tragic arias' included Nero's own *Oresteia* (*Vit. Ap.* 4.39), and that in the time of Herodes Atticus 'the affairs of the Pelopids' were still standard topics dealt with in Pythian competitions in tragic singing (*Vit. Soph.* 2.7). St Augustine speaks of a special class of actor whose speaking voice supplemented specialist danced or sung performances, citing the example of an actor who speaks Agamemnon's words 'in theatrical tales' (*On the Sermon on the Mount* 2.2.5). Pantomimes became the major route by which citizens of the Roman empire had access to Greek tragedy. We know from Seneca himself, Apuleius, and Claudian that the murder (*sphagē*) of Agamemnon was a theme of the tragic dance; both Clytemnestra and Cassandra are named as figures in this medium.[194]

13. RECEPTION FROM THE RENAISSANCE TO THE TWENTY-FIRST CENTURY

The Senecan text survived when the puppet shows, tragic arias and pantomime libretti had been lost (the church fathers, who were opposed to performed theatre, seem still to have had at least some knowledge of Senecan tragedy[195]). Since the fifteenth century, the Latin tragedy has exerted an incalculable subterranean influence. Its poetry and sententiae are a presence in the European imagination from the first appearance of Andreas Bellfortis' *editio princeps* of Seneca's tragedies in Ferrara in 1484, through playwrights including May, Shakespeare, Kyd and Webster, to Hofmannsthal's *Electra*. Almost throughout that entire period the Senecan version also fundamentally affected the shape taken by Clytemnestra in plays about the death of Agamemnon. The Clytemnestras of Ovid's *Ars Amatoria* and Seneca's *Agamemnon* were implicated far more heavily than Aeschylus' vengeful queen

---

193   Hall (2002); Hall and Wyles (2008).
194   See Sen. *ad Lucil.* 80.7, Apul. *apol.* 78, Claudian *in Eutrop.* 2.405; Wüst (1949) 847–50; Kokolakis (1959).
195   See Weismann (1972) 38.

in Agamemnon plays in and after the Renaissance until the late Victorian era. The *subterranean* influence of the Aeschylean tragedy must not be disregarded.[196] But the texts which underlay the English, German, French and Italian dramas and operas on the theme before the nineteenth century, in addition to those by Ovid and Seneca, were medieval mythological compendia drawing on the Christian poem *Orestis Tragoedia* by Blossius Aemilius Dracontius, which was probably composed in Carthage in the late fifth century CE. The prime motive of Dracontius' lascivious Clytemnestra is sexual feeling towards Aegisthus;[197] this Latin epyllion was significant in the creation of the Christian ethical perspective on the amorous medieval Clytemnestra, who usually manufactures the robe and persuades Agamemnon to put it on, while Aegisthus strikes the blows.

The texts ultimately drawing on Ovid, Seneca and/or Dracontius would certainly include Hans Sachs' Shrovetide morality play *Clitemnestra* (1554), the deeply Senecan *Clytemnestre* (1589) of Pierre Matthieu and the *Agamemnon* of Sieur Arnauld of Provence (1642). Claude Boyer's *Agamemnon*, first performed at the Théâtre Guénégaud in Paris on 12 March 1680, is a more original tragedy concerning Orestes' doomed love for Cassandra, but Clytemnestra remains her Senecan self, nervously conducting an adulterous affair with the evil (although oddly absent) Egiste, and nursing her resentments about Briseis as well as Cassandra; these command more attention than the death of Iphigenia.[198] The sexually driven Clytemnestra who had emerged in antiquity, in reaction against Aeschylus' matriarchal androgyne, became the *canonical* Clytemnestra of the sixteenth to early nineteenth centuries, the early modern and neoclassical Clytemnestra.

---

196   See Tarrant (1976) 180, 196, 228, commentary on Seneca, *Agamemnon* lines 56, 115 and 299 respectively; Ewbank (2005).

197   See especially lines 126–8 and 227–70 in the Budé edition of Bouquet and Wolff (1995), and Bouquet's Introduction to it, especially 30–1. Dracontius was interested in the dominant women of tragedy; his secular poetry also included a *Medea*. The *Orestis Tragoedia* includes the delightful detail that Electra takes the rescued Orestes off to enrol him at university in Athens (284–90).

198   See Boyer (1680) 12.

For centuries the politicised, Amazonian Clytemnestra's advocacy—indeed symbolic incarnation—of the maternally transmitted kinship bond became irrelevant; along with the neurotic adulteress of the Senecan *Agamemnon* tradition, it was the victimised wife and mother in Euripides' *Iphigenia in Aulis* who provided the dominant source material for composers of libretti about the Atreidai.[199]

Seneca's queen, morally weaker than her men and secondary to the power struggle between them, found new resonances in the politicised but essentially moral theatre of the neoclassical period, which revelled in assassinations, dynastic struggles, battles over succession, *coups d'etats* and revolutions. Often coloured by the Clytemnestra of Sophocles' *Electra*, she was also attractive to the creators of political allegory, a dominant force in the shaping of ancient tragedy for performance before the nineteenth century. The ideological taboos and imperatives of this era meant that Aeschylus' Clytemnestra could not have been tolerated on the public stage. Neoclassical plays on the story which did draw on the Aeschylean version as well as the Latin successors include James Thomson's *Agamemnon* (first performed at Drury Lane in 1738),[200] which was translated into German at least three times in the mid-eighteenth century, and admired by no less a critic than Gotthold Lessing.[201] It almost certainly lies behind Wilhelm von Humboldt's interest in translating the Aeschylean version into metrical German, and it was von Humboldt's translation that was used by Wagner.[202]

Thomson's Whig *Agamemnon* play also influenced Alfieri, whose twin verse tragedies *Agamennone* and *Oreste* became popular in Britain after they appeared in English translation in 1815.[203] Thomson's version was also translated into French and performed in Paris in 1780;[204] this revival probably lies behind Citizen Louis Jean

---

199   See Phillippo (2005) and Reynolds (2005).
200   See Hall and Macintosh (2005) 104–15; Vedelago (2020).
201   Lessing, 'Vorrede' to Thomson (1756) 3–14.
202   von Humboldt (1816); see further Ewans (2005).
203   Di Martino (2019).
204   See Thomson (1780) and Wartelle (1978) 24.

SCENE FROM THE "AGAMEMNON," BY ÆCHYLUS.

Figure 8. Clytemnestra's last entrance, in the production of *Agamemnon* at
Balliol College, Oxford, in June 1880. Engraving in *The Graphic* no. 552
(26 June 1880). Author's personal collection.

Nepomucene Lemercier's attraction to the political potential of the
story. Lemercier's important adaptation, performed at the Théâtre
de la République, late April (Floreal) 1797, assumes a contemporary
political charge as Cassandra predicts that the fall of the tyrant
assassins of Agamemnon is itself imminent (V.xi).[205]

It was not until the late nineteenth century that Aeschylus' own
tragedy was to be staged. The play was important in the revival of
interest in staging Greek plays, traceable to Lewis Campbell's circle
in south-eastern Scotland in the 1870s,[206] followed by a production
in the original Greek at Balliol College, Oxford, in 1880 (Figure 8).
A clearer vision of Aeschylus' achievement in the creation of his

---

205 On parodies and comic versions of Agamemnon tragedies in France, Italy
and England, some of which involved racy cross-dressing, see Hall (2005a) 73–4
n.62.
206 Hall and Macintosh (2005) 451–3.

Clytemnestra is thus made possible by reminding ourselves that in her Aeschylean form this heroine has been intolerable on the stage or in the public imagination until the last decades of the nineteenth century, exactly the chronological point at which women's rights as both political agents and as parents finally began to be discussed with gravity. Yet the erotic, Senecan Clytemnestra lingered on in some quarters: there is no more sensual husband-slayer than Christine Mannon in Eugene O'Neill's 1931 *Mourning Becomes Electra*. The Mannons' New England Doric mansion has seen neither infanticide nor power struggle: Christine prefers Adam Brant to her husband Ezra because he is better in bed.

The authentic Aeschylean Clytemnestra began to speak in a voice once again immediate and relevant only when she could address a late nineteenth-century audience, even if their increasingly sympathetic response to her arguments was different from the revulsion it is probable was felt by Aeschylus' contemporaries. It was as late as the twentieth century, shortly after women received the vote in the USA, that Henry Lister, author of a revisionist American *Clytemnestra* in 1923, could remotely expect to be taken seriously when he wrote: 'The modern enfranchisement of women has ... placed the sexes on an equal basis. In making Clytemnestra the heroine instead of the villain of the play the author asks the world, newly awakened to the rights of women, whether Clytemnestra was guilty or not guilty.'[207] From the middle of the twentieth century social theorists already recognised that nothing less than the violent subversion of rule by men is at stake in Aeschylus' Argos; Winnington-Ingram, decades before modern feminism, identified the corrosive effect of Clytemnestra's jealousy of Agamemnon's status *as a man*. Simone de Beauvoir regarded the *Oresteia* as representing the triumph of patriarchy, and Kate Millett said that the door it slammed on women was not to be re-opened until Ibsen's Nora walked out of her doll's house in 1879.[208]

---

207   Lister (1923) 'Preface', p. 8.
208   de Beauvoir (1972) 111 n.9; Millett (1971) 115; further references in Goldhill (1986) 53–4. For more recent feminist and critical theory see Njoya (2020).

More recently, Zeitlin's pioneering structuralist analysis showed the importance to the configuration of Clytemnestra of the Amazonian archetype and its fundamental threat to patriarchy. In an adaptation of Greek tragedy by a woman, at that time a rarity, Dacia Maraini's *I sogni di Clitennestra* (1981) was first performed in English as *Dreams of Clytemnestra* in 1989. There now exist several detailed and illuminating scholarly studies of the uniqueness of the Aeschylean Clytemnestra, written in the light of the late twentieth-century feminist revolution.[209] Ted Hughes' sinuous translation of the *Oresteia* was directed by a woman, Katie Mitchell, at the National Theatre in 1999, and made interesting use of the visible pregnancy of Anastasia Hille, who played Clytemnestra; I felt this viscerally as I was pregnant with one of my daughters when I saw it. The figure of the dead Iphigenia also haunted the stage throughout.[210] In Marina Carr's affecting *Ariel* (2002), performed at the Abbey Theatre, Dublin, the relationships between the Clytemnestra-figure (Frances Fermoy) and all four of her children, dead and alive, are the psychological centre of the action.[211]

Agamemnon has addressed racial injustice, too. When on 4 April 1968 Robert F. Kennedy was obliged to inform an Indianapolis crowd, containing a large proportion of African Americans, of the death in Memphis of Martin Luther King, he quoted Edith Hamilton's translation of *Agamemnon* 179–83: 'He who learns must suffer. In our sleep, pain which cannot forget falls drop by drop upon the heart until, in our own despair, against our will, comes wisdom through the awful grace of God.'[212] During the last decade of the Cold War, titans of international theatre saw how the *Oresteia* addressed not only women's rights, but democracy, imperialism, ethnicity and economic inequality, as well as providing rich potential for avant-garde theatrical and aesthetic experimentation. A series of era-defining productions by Peter Hall and Tony Harrison, Peter Stein, Karolos Koun, Ariane

---

209   Zeitlin (1984). See especially Foley (2001) 202–34; McClure (1999) 72–99.
210   On Hughes' and also Tony Harrison's translations see especially Latham (2016).
211   See Carr (2002) especially 74–5; Hall (2005b).
212   Hamilton (1957/1964) 34; see Hallett (2016) 221–3; Casazza (2003).

Mnouchkine and Silviu Purcarete in the 1980s and 1990s educated the theatregoing public in Greek tragedy as never before.[213]

Yaël Farber's *Molora* adapted *Agamemnon* and *Choephori* to the specific historical South African moment of transition to democracy and the hearings of the Truth and Reconciliation Commission after the end of apartheid.[214] Milo Rau's *Orestes in Mosul* used the *Oresteia* to address crises in Iraq and Muslim oppression of homosexuality.[215] The therapeutic potential of Aeschylus' epic enactment of the intergenerational effects of trauma has been increasingly acknowledged by psychoanalysts and psychotherapists,[216] in part because the *Oresteia* and in particular a certain passage in *Agamemnon* (832–8) were central to psychoanalyst Melanie Klein's theories relating to envy, the splitting of the Mother and the persecutory superego.[217] Colm Tóibín's searing *The House of Names* (2017) is the most distinguished retelling of the *Oresteia* in recent fiction, following a gentle, gay Orestes' painful emergence from the agony of his family and nation's past, tinged with Irish colouring, into a new, more hopeful, embrace of fatherhood.[218]

14. TEXTS AND COMMENTARIES

It is amazing that we can enjoy *Agamemnon* at all. Aeschylus was less read in antiquity than Sophocles or Euripides, and it was only a series of fortunate accidents that led to the precious manuscript, dating to about 1000 CE and containing much of the seven plays we can now read complete, arriving in Italy in about 1423. It is the Codex Laurentianus, called 'M', short for 'Mediceus' because it belonged to the Medici family. Unfortunately, it is missing most of *Agamemnon* (lines 311–1066 and 1160–673), forcing editors to use later manuscripts from the thirteenth to the fifteenth centuries, whose readings are less

---

213   Macintosh et al. (2005); Llewellyn-Jones (2021); Marshall (2023).
214   Röttger (2019).
215   Devoldere (2019). On other important productions, see Baudou (2017).
216   Hall (2024).
217   Klein (1963).
218   See Hall (2022b).

reliable: papyri containing verses from *Agamemnon* are exiguous and horribly mutilated.[219] The gap in this manuscript is one reason for the relative paucity of ancient scholarly annotations (scholia) on this play, although the Byzantine scholar Demetrius Triclinius preserved, in addition to his own intelligent suggestions, some ancient scholia;[220] there must, however, have been study of the play in antiquity because there are many citations in lexicographers, especially Hesychius.[221]

The gap in M also caused the fusion in the first printed editions of what little was available of *Agamemnon* with *Choephori*—the Aldine in 1518, and those by Turnebus (1552) and Robortello (also 1552).[222] The problem was solved by Vettori, whose 1557 edition separated *Agamemnon* from *Choephori* and could draw on another manuscript containing the whole of *Agamemnon*.[223] Other editions which adopted Vettori's breakthrough findings soon followed;[224] by 1663 the English poet Thomas Stanley produced a thoughtful edition that provided, for the first time, a translation and commentary suited to a non-specialist audience, which explained historical and philosophical matters as well as literary ones.[225]

The text as printed here is a result of many centuries of philological labour, from Triclinius and Thomas Magister in the thirteenth century onwards. There have been breakthroughs in our understanding of the manuscript tradition quite recently, especially Roger Dawe's demonstration that the texts of Aeschylus were transmitted 'horizontally'

---

219   Wartelle (1971) 310–15.

220   The *Agamemnon* scholia on M and those in Triclinius' recension are included in Smith (1976).

221   Easterling (2005) 26 and nn.5–7; Wartelle (1971), index s.v. Hesychius.

222   Ewbank (2005) 39–40.

223   Rosenmeyer (1982) 1–28 offers a masterclass in explaining how the texts of Aeschylus arrived in our modern printed editions via ancient papyri collected in libraries including Alexandria, school selections, Byzantine scriptoria, early printing presses, academic study and serial editing by professional philologists. On the survival to the Renaissance and the first printed edition see Mund-Dopchie (1984), especially 124–49 on Vettori.

224   See Gruys (1981).

225   See the detailed appreciation of Stanley's achievement in Arnold (1984).

by scribes who were already making choices between readings in different manuscripts rather than just copying out a single one, and Martin West's Teubner edition, which was the first based on knowledge of all the known manuscripts dated to before the fifteenth century.[226] The names of certain scholars recur insistently in the apparatus criticus, reflecting the combination of hard work, erudition and intellectual brilliance that they put into the task of editing: Turnebus, Auratus, Scaliger, Casaubon, Hermann, Dindorf, Blomfield, Wilamowitz, Campbell, Porson, Blomfield, Hartung, Wellauer, Paley, Canter, Pauw, Stanley, Schütz, Hartung, Pearson, Klausen, Enger, Dobree, Margoliouth, Martin West. Editing the Greek text sometimes feels like going on an intense reading holiday with a transhistorical group of (male) scholars vying for the prize of their name appearing most frequently in the critical apparatus.

There are half a dozen manuscripts which include plays of the *Oresteia*. Their collation and recension are matters of huge complexity, but four of them are of by far the most importance.[227] These are the symbols used in the apparatus criticus.

M Mediceus: the important tenth- or early eleventh-century Laurentian manuscript 32.9 in Florence, which is the unique source for *Choephori* but for *Agamemnon* offers only lines 1–310 and 1067–159.

V Venetus: the thirteenth-century manuscript in the Biblioteca Nazionale Marciana in Venice, which has been renumbered as cod. gr. 468 instead of 653, contains the full trilogy and an additional version of lines 1–348.

Tr Triclinius: early fourteenth-century manuscript in the Biblioteca Nazionale in Naples, cod. II F 31.

F The fourteenth-century Laurentian manuscript 31.8 in Florence, written by a man named Constantius, which contains all of *Agamemnon*.

---

226   West (1990); Dawe (1964); for a full account, see Garvie (2016) 26.
227   See Turyn (1943) especially 100–16. Dawe (1964), although crucial in changing attitudes to the way scribes operated, is devoted to the collation of the manuscripts of *Prometheus*, *Septem* and *Persians* rather than the *Oresteia*.

Full familiarity with the history of the manuscripts and their editing is of course not required to undertake a production in performance or close study of the tragedy as a poetic playscript and document of the Athenian cultural imagination.

There are some passages where serious emendation is essential if any correct syntax or meaning is to be established (e.g. 556–7, 713–15), and a few where one or more lines have dropped out of the manuscript tradition (e.g. after 7, 287, 1005–7*). Yet, despite the plethora of enormously long scholarly publications exhaustively and exhaustingly discussing every tiny detail of manuscript variants and every conjectural emendation that has ever been proposed,[228] mercifully there are hardly any occasions where a textual problem really matters to the meaning or dramatic effect. Aesthetically speaking, however, the corruption of a few passages of high-flown poetry (e.g. 412–13, 984–7*) is acutely disappointing.

Commentators on *Agamemnon* over the last 150 years include some of the most controversial and colourful characters in the history of classical scholarship. A.W. Verrall's 1889 edition 'immediately made history';[229] it was notable for unconventional claims, including the proposal that Aegisthus had conspired in 'faking' the beacon relay by lighting the last fire to alert Clytemnestra to the imminent arrival of Agamemnon so that she could begin to execute their plot for a coup.[230] Ulrich von Wilamowitz-Moellendorff was a titanic figure whose 'late Romantic', Wagnerian outlook fundamentally affected his comments on Aeschylus.[231] Gilbert Murray's OCT text (1937, which needed to be replaced by Denys Page's new OCT in 1972 after Dawe's intervention), verse translation of *Agamemnon* (1920) and monograph *Aeschylus* (1939) were partly so influential because he was a famous and respected figure for reasons other than holding the Oxford Regius Chair of Greek, as one of the brains behind the League of Nations, the first incarnation of the United Nations. This led him to help

---

228 E.g., Thiel (1993).
229 Postgate (1969) 8.
230 This spawned a host of publications in response, e.g. Hoernle (1921).
231 Citti (2006) 69–72.

Jewish academics facing persecution in Germany, including Eduard Fraenkel, the author of the colossal three-volume *Agamemnon* edition that has dominated scholarship on the play ever since. Jaś Elsner has persuasively argued that its 'themes of catastrophe—so potently close to the thematics of the long war, exile, and murder in the 1930s and 1940s ... proved a perfect cipher for Fraenkel's own working out of his responses to much more contemporary issues'; his consequent mental energy produced the commentary that has correctly been called 'perhaps the most erudite that any Greek play has ever had' by another distinguished commentator on Aeschylus.[232] It was published in 1950 and had been developed in the course of Fraenkel's celebrated weekly seminars at Oxford University, attended in 1940 by the novelist Iris Murdoch. She later recalled 'that terrifying class of Fraenkel's— it was the most frightening part of my university education';[233] she wrote a poem entitled 'The Agamemnon Class, 1939', which equated terror of failing to identify the tense of an ancient Greek verb with her generation's growing apprehension of the scale of the war: 'Between line eighty three and line a thousand / It seemed to us our innocence / Was lost, our youth laid waste, / In that pellucid unforgiving air'.[234] Denys Page, the Regius Professor at Cambridge who was held in awe because he had worked on Ultra intelligence material at the Government Code & Cypher School based at Bletchley Park during World War II, revised John Denniston's unpublished commentary. Although Page's outspoken support of the Greek dictatorship of 1967–74 was widely resented by many students, the jointly authored 1957 edition is the one which most English-speaking undergraduates, including myself, have used ever since, at least until Simon's Goldhill's student guide to the *Oresteia* was published in 1992. David Raeburn and Oliver Thomas' accessible textbook came out in 2012, visually supplemented by the ebook *Agamemnon: A Performance History*,

---

232   Elsner (2017) 36; Rose (1952) 130. For a striking isolated reference to recent Nazi history in Fraenkel's edition, which otherwise almost completely avoids such contemporary allusions, see the note in my commentary on lines 716–19*.
233   Conradi (2001) 615n.
234   Murdoch (1977); see Umachandran (2019).

which was released free online by the Archive of Performances of Greek & Roman Drama in 2020.[235]

The translation and other publications of *Agamemnon* by Hugh Lloyd-Jones, whose own terrifying Oxford seminars on Sophoclean textual criticism I attended in the 1980s as the sole woman amongst 12 men, have also informed my thinking. The contribution made to my appreciation of the acoustic and poetic aspects of the play by the commentary of Pierre Judet de la Combe (2001), who had advised Ariane Mnouchkine on her landmark production *Les Atrides* (1990–3), is all-pervasive. The many other works I have found invaluable include everything ever written on the *Oresteia* by Froma Zeitlin, Helene Foley and Pat Easterling, Simon Goldhill's monograph (1984), Desmond Conacher's literary commentary (1987), Alan Sommerstein's annotated Loeb translation (2009) and Enrico Medda's substantial Italian edition (2017). Alex Garvie's commentary on *Choephori* (1986) and Sommerstein's on *Eumenides* (1989a) have been indispensable as well.

15. CONCLUSION

The cultural impact of *Agamemnon* can be felt across multifarious media, even when it is not explicitly named as an influence, for example in some of the greatest works of nineteenth-century fiction. Victorian authors were fascinated by both its ethics and metaphysics. George Eliot wrote a chilling rephrasing of lines 658–66 in *Romola*: 'Our deeds are like children that are born to us; they live and act apart from our will: nay, children may be strangled, but deeds never; they have an indestructible life both in and out of our consciousness.'[236] In Thomas Hardy's *Jude the Obscure* (1895), when Jude and Sue discover their three children dead, Jude quotes the chorus of *Agamemnon* (67–8) almost exactly: 'Nothing can be done,' he replied. 'Things are as they are, and will be brought to their destined issue.'[237] Clytemnestra, along

---

235   https://www.apgrd.ox.ac.uk/ebooks-agamemnon; I contributed an audio discussion to this resource. See also Taplin and Billings (2018) and p. 103 n.250.
236   Eliot (1887) 174. See Easterling (1991).
237   Hardy (2002) 358.

with Elizabeth Martha Browne, a servant of lowly background, was a model for the heroine of *Tess of the d'Urbervilles* (1891). Tess is hanged at the end of her novel for stabbing her abusive seducer Alec d'Urberville to death in their bed; Browne was the last woman to be publicly hanged in the county of Dorset in 1856, after killing her drunken husband with an axe. At the age of 16, Hardy, along with hundreds of other local people, went to witness the execution of the 'Dorset Clytemnestra', and never forgot it.[238]

Agamemnon's philosophical heft comes from its combination of ethical/political and metaphysical stature with the third branch of Greek philosophy emergent in Aeschylus' day—epistemology, which asks how we know things and whether we can ever be certain. The play is a sustained enquiry into the nature and limitations of human knowledge. It has been argued that Aeschylus was himself pessimistic about the potential of human enquiry to lead to episte-mological certainty, unlike the pioneers of Greek natural science and philosophy—especially Xenophanes, Heraclitus, Anaxagoras, Pythagoras and Empedocles, whose ideas have sometimes (contro-versially) been said to have influenced his thought or at least to have informed it in less direct ways.[239] Even the illustration of the situation by comparison with other myths, in the time-honoured manner of the lyric poets, repeatedly fails as the exempla turn out to prove negatives. Clytemnestra says that false rumour suggested that Agamemnon had as many wounds as Geryon after Heracles' assault (869–72). She reminds Cassandra that even Heracles had submitted to slavery, but Cassandra does not submit (1040–1). Cassandra denies that she can be compared with Procne, who was turned into a bird and not murdered (1142–9; see fig. 7). The chorus reflect that no doctor with magical powers can resurrect a dead man, as Asclepius once did (1019–24). Aegisthus *contrasts* the chorus' angry utterances with the song of Orpheus (1627–33).

---

238   Purdy and Millgate (1988) vol. 7, 5.
239   See Gladigow (1962); Goldhill (1984) 7 n.17, 82 n.133, 121 n.32; Kirk et al. (1983) 354–5; Seaford (2012) 240–57, 293–303; Scapin (2020).

Asseverations of truth proliferate,[240] but everyone at some point is not believed, lies, evades or distorts the truth except for Cassandra, and even she once deceived a god; a lie, we are told, can be divine (478).[241] Silence can be as telling as speech; as Harriott writes of the pervasive animal imagery, 'the animal's inability to speak, its reliance on wordless action, is only one element, but on some occasions it is the most important element'.[242] Signals, dreams, omens and their interpretation, clairvoyant visions, inherited proverbial wisdom and eye-witness reports are all manifested and their reliability subjected to critique. Comprehension of what is happening, and why, is systematically compromised. The chorus sing of the possibility of learning, but, like them, audiences or readers struggle, often without success, to understand.[243] There is some absurdity, even a 'wind of grim comedy',[244] blowing through the chorus' failure to follow some of the things said by both Clytemnestra and Cassandra, sometimes relieving, more often intensifying, the grandeur of the tragic atmosphere.

It is that mournful grandeur which has more than anything else defined the image of Aeschylus in the cultural tradition in and ever since his own times. In the English-speaking world he became a byword for rugged elevation, just in time for the Romantic poets and artists (Figure 9), as soon as his complete plays were first translated into English by Robert Potter in 1777.

William Hazlitt described 'the high-wrought trumpet-tongued eloquence of Æschylus'.[245] Samuel Taylor Coleridge struck a typical note in identifying Aeschylus' 'sublime simplicity' and the 'terrible, malignant, and persecuting' picture he offered of religion.[246] Philip Bailey recommended his philosophically minded audience, 'Read

---

240   Gemin (2020).
241   Golden (1994) 379; Park (2023) 35–42.
242   Harriot (1982) 13; there are excellent remarks on the speechlessness of babies and children in *Agamemnon* in Golden (1994) 378–83.
243   Goldhill (1984) 28.
244   Bennett (1929) 140.
245   Hazlitt (1825) 68.
246   Coleridge (1851) 10.

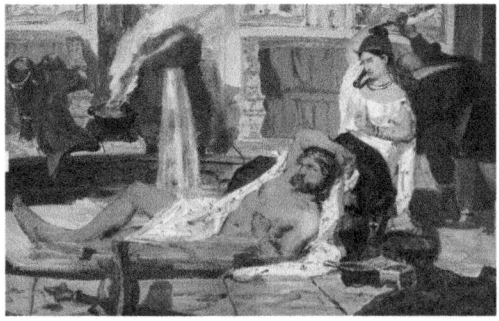

Figure 9. Print of a drawing by David Scott depicting the murder of Agamemnon, c. 1837. Author's personal collection.

mighty Æschylus, whose harmonies, / Polysyllabic, would, in days like these, / Crush critics' jaws, or else their theories'.[247] Mortimer Collins summed up Aeschylus' achievement as 'gloom sublime'.[248] When Lawrence Durrell visited Argos, he observed,

> In this land one encounters always
> Agamemnon, Agamemnon; the voice
> Of water falling on hair in caves,
> The stonebreaker's hammer on walls.[249]

But neither Aeschylus' intellectual clout nor his atmospheric grandeur should prevent us from appreciating just how emotionally powerful his writing can be. The deaths of Iphigenia and Cassandra contain more effective pathos than almost anything in world literature. As Jonathan Swift put it, when using verse to explain why this tragedian was his favourite of all time:

> But above all I prefer Æschylus,
> Whose moving Touches, when they please, kill us.[250]

---

247 Bailey (1858) 1–2.
248 Collins (1871) 30.
249 Durrell (1985) 105–6.
250 Swift (1937) 987–8, 'A Letter to the Reverend Dr. SH---N'. See also Taplin and Billings (2018) and Addendum p. 525.

Agamemnon

ΑΓΑΜΕΜΝΩΝ

ΤΑ ΤΟΥ ΔΡΑΜΑΤΟΣ ΠΡΟΣΩΠΑ
ΦΥΛΑΞ
ΧΟΡΟΣ ΓΕΡΟΝΤΩΝ ΑΡΓΕΙΩΝ
ΚΛΥΤΑΙΜΗΣΤΡΑ
ΚΗΡΥΞ
ΑΓΑΜΕΜΝΩΝ
ΚΑΣΣΑΝΔΡΑ
ΑΙΓΙΣΘΟΣ

Φύλαξ
θεοὺς μὲν αἰτῶ τῶνδ᾽ ἀπαλλαγὴν πόνων
φρουρᾶς ἐτείας μῆκος, ἣν κοιμώμενος
στέγαις Ἀτρειδῶν ἄγκαθεν, κυνὸς δίκην,
ἄστρων κάτοιδα νυκτέρων ὁμήγυριν,
καὶ τοὺς φέροντας χεῖμα καὶ θέρος βροτοῖς
λαμπροὺς δυνάστας, ἐμπρέποντας αἰθέρι
ἀστέρας, ὅταν φθίνωσιν, ἀντολάς τε τῶν.
καὶ νῦν φυλάσσω λαμπάδος τὸ σύμβολον,
αὐγὴν πυρὸς φέρουσαν ἐκ Τροίας φάτιν
ἁλώσιμόν τε βάξιν· ὧδε γὰρ κρατεῖ   10
γυναικὸς ἀνδρόβουλον ἐλπίζον κέαρ.
εὖτ᾽ ἂν δὲ νυκτίπλαγκτον ἔνδροσόν τ᾽ ἔχω
εὐνὴν ὀνείροις οὐκ ἐπισκοπουμένην
ἐμήν· φόβος γὰρ ἀνθ᾽ ὕπνου παραστατεῖ,
τὸ μὴ βεβαίως βλέφαρα συμβαλεῖν ὕπνῳ·
ὅταν δ᾽ ἀείδειν ἢ μινύρεσθαι δοκῶ,
ὕπνου τόδ᾽ ἀντίμολπον ἐντέμνων ἄκος,
κλαίω τότ᾽ οἴκου τοῦδε συμφορὰν στένων
οὐχ ὡς τὰ πρόσθ᾽ ἄριστα διαπονουμένου.
νῦν δ᾽ εὐτυχὴς γένοιτ᾽ ἀπαλλαγὴ πόνων   20
εὐαγγέλου φανέντος ὀρφναίου πυρός.

2 ἣν Tr F: δ᾽ ἦν M V.

AGAMEMNON

CHARACTERS IN THE DRAMA
Watchman
Chorus of old Argive men
Clytemnestra
Herald
Agamemnon
Cassandra
Aegisthus

Watchman [*alone on the palace roof, speaking*]
I implore the gods to set me free from these ordeals,
the protracted year-long lookout that I keep at night,
like a dog, propped up on my elbow on the roof of the Atreidai.
I know all about the stars which congregate at night,
—both those that bring winter weather to mortals, and those that
   bring summer,
brilliant, lordly stars, standing out from the heavens—
when they set and when they rise.
And I'm still looking out for the torch-signal,
the gleam of fire bringing word from Troy,
and word of its capture. For so decrees   10
the woman who thinks like a man in her expectant heart.
Whenever I bed down here at night, uneasy and dew-sodden,
I never have any dreams. Terror, not sleep, is my companion,
and stops me closing my eyelids securely in slumber.
When I feel like singing or humming a tune,
using music as a cure for sleepiness,
I cry aloud, groaning for this household's predicament:
it's not being managed properly as it used to be.
I hope that I may now receive a happy discharge from my duties,   20
that the fire which brings good news will flash through the darkness....

ὦ χαῖρε λαμπτὴρ νυκτός, ἡμερήσιον
φάος πιφαύσκων καὶ χορῶν κατάστασιν
πολλῶν ἐν Ἄργει, τῆσδε συμφορᾶς χάριν.
ἰοὺ ἰού.
Ἀγαμέμνονος γυναικὶ σημαίνω τορῶς
εὐνῆς ἐπαντείλασαν ὡς τάχος δόμοις
ὀλολυγμὸν εὐφημοῦντα τῇδε λαμπάδι
ἐπορθιάζειν, εἴπερ Ἰλίου πόλις
ἑάλωκεν, ὡς ὁ φρυκτὸς ἀγγέλλων πρέπει·   30
αὐτός τ᾽ ἔγωγε φροίμιον χορεύσομαι.
τὰ δεσποτῶν γὰρ εὖ πεσόντα θήσομαι
τρὶς ἓξ βαλούσης τῆσδέ μοι φρυκτωρίας.
γένοιτο δ᾽ οὖν μολόντος εὐφιλῆ χέρα
ἄνακτος οἴκων τῇδε βαστάσαι χερί.
τὰ δ᾽ ἄλλα σιγῶ· βοῦς ἐπὶ γλώσσῃ μέγας
βέβηκεν· οἶκος δ᾽ αὐτός, εἰ φθογγὴν λάβοι,
σαφέστατ᾽ ἂν λέξειεν· ὡς ἑκὼν ἐγὼ
μαθοῦσιν αὐδῶ κοὐ μαθοῦσι λήθομαι.

Χορός
δέκατον μὲν ἔτος τόδ᾽ ἐπεὶ Πριάμου   40
μέγας ἀντίδικος,
Μενέλαος ἄναξ ἠδ᾽ Ἀγαμέμνων,
διθρόνου Διόθεν καὶ δισκήπτρου
τιμῆς ὀχυρὸν ζεῦγος Ἀτρειδᾶν
στόλον Ἀργείων χιλιοναύτην,
τῆσδ᾽ ἀπὸ χώρας
ἦραν, στρατιῶτιν ἀρωγήν,
μέγαν ἐκ θυμοῦ κλάζοντες Ἄρη
τρόπον αἰγυπιῶν, οἵτ᾽ ἐκπατίοις
ἄλγεσι παίδων ὕπατοι λεχέων   50
στροφοδινοῦνται
πτερύγων ἐρετμοῖσιν ἐρεσσόμενοι,
δεμνιοτήρη
πόνον ὀρταλίχων ὀλέσαντες·

26 σημαίνω Μ: σημανῶ cett.   30 ἀγγέλλων Tr: ἀγγέλων Μ V F.   40 Πριάμου V Tr F:
Πριάμῳ Μ.

O watch fire—welcome!—lighting up the night like day,
inspiring abundant choral dances in Argos to celebrate this event!
Hallo there! Hallo!
I'm signalling clearly to Agamemnon's wife
to rise from bed at speed
and raise the shout of triumph in the palace
in response to this torchlight, if the city of Troy
has really been taken, as the fire-signal emphatically announces!   30
And I'll dance the prelude myself.
For I'll count my masters' luck at the dice as my own,
since this beacon has thrown me a triple six of the dice.
And so may the King come home, and may I
clasp his hand in welcome with this hand of mine.
About the other things I'm saying nothing; a big bull
has trodden on my tongue. Yet the house itself, if it could give voice,
could tell the truth most unerringly. I prefer to speak to
those who know, and when it comes to those who don't, lose my memory.
[*Exit the Watchman. Enter the chorus from the direction of the city*]

Chorus [*they intone as they move*]
This is the tenth year now since Priam's   40
great adversary,
King Menelaus and Agamemnon,
the strong pair, the sons of Atreus,
honourably yoked by Zeus to a double throne and sceptre,
raised a thousand-strong Argive fleet of ships,
a martial force from this land to help their mission.
They bellowed the war-cry loudly in their fury,
like vultures grieving for their young
in remote places, and wheeling   50
high above their nests,
rowing the air on their oarlike wings,
bereft of the labour of minding their young.

ὕπατος δ᾽ ἀίων ἤ τις Ἀπόλλων
ἢ Πὰν ἢ Ζεὺς οἰωνόθροον
γόον ὀξυβόαν τῶνδε μετοίκων
ὑστερόποινον
πέμπει παραβᾶσιν Ἐρινύν.
οὕτω δ᾽ Ἀτρέως παῖδας ὁ κρείσσων   60
ἐπ᾽ Ἀλεξάνδρῳ πέμπει ξένιος
Ζεὺς πολυάνορος ἀμφὶ γυναικὸς
πολλὰ παλαίσματα καὶ γυιοβαρῆ
γόνατος κονίαισιν ἐρειδομένου
διακναιομένης τ᾽ ἐν προτελείοις
κάμακος θήσων Δαναοῖσιν
Τρωσί θ᾽ ὁμοίως. ἔστι δ᾽ ὅπῃ νῦν
ἔστι· τελεῖται δ᾽ ἐς τὸ πεπρωμένον·
οὔθ᾽ ὑποκαίων οὔθ᾽ ὑπολείβων
οὔτε δακρύων ἀπύρων ἱερῶν   70
ὀργὰς ἀτενεῖς παραθέλξει.
ἡμεῖς δ᾽ ἀτίται σαρκὶ παλαιᾷ
τῆς τότ᾽ ἀρωγῆς ὑπολειφθέντες
μίμνομεν ἰσχὺν
ἰσόπαιδα νέμοντες ἐπὶ σκήπτροις.
ὅ τε γὰρ νεαρὸς μυελὸς στέρνων
ἐντὸς ἀνᾴσσων
ἰσόπρεσβυς, Ἄρης δ᾽ οὐκ ἔνι χώρᾳ,
τό θ᾽ ὑπέργηρων φυλλάδος ἤδη
κατακαρφομένης, τρίποδας μὲν ὁδοὺς   80
στείχει, παιδὸς δ᾽ οὐδὲν ἀρείων
ὄναρ ἡμερόφαντον ἀλαίνει.
σὺ δέ, Τυνδάρεω
θύγατερ, βασίλεια Κλυταιμήστρα,
τί χρέος; τί νέον; τί δ᾽ ἐπαισθομένη,
τίνος ἀγγελίας
πειθοῖ περίπεμπτα θυοσκεῖς;
πάντων δὲ θεῶν τῶν ἀστυνόμων,
ὑπάτων, χθονίων,

69 ὑποκαίων Casaubon: ὑποκλαίων codd.   77 ἀνᾴσσων Hermann: ἀνάσσων codd.
79 τό θ᾽ ὑπέργηρων Tr: τίθιπεργήρωσ M: τόθιπεργήρωσ V F.   87 πειθοῖ M: πυθοῖ F:
πευθοῖ Scaliger.   θυοσκεῖς Turnebus: θυοσκινεῖσ codd.

But one of those on high—perhaps Apollo,
or Pan or Zeus—hears the shrill screaming
lament of the birds, residents of the sky,
and sends overdue
punishment against the offenders in revenge.
This is how almighty Zeus,   60
who ensures correct treatment of hosts and guests,
sent the sons of Atreus against Alexander,
for the sake of a woman mated with many men;
his purpose was to inflict, on Greeks and Trojans alike,
countless clashes that exhaust the limbs,
knees pressed down into the dust
and the spear-shaft shattered as the ceremony of battle commences.
It is how it now is. It's being fulfilled in line with destiny.
By offering neither burnt sacrifice, nor libation,
nor tears shall a man assuage   70
the implacable wrath caused by unhallowed rites.
But we, disregarded by reason of our elderly flesh,
excluded then from the mission,
are waiting, leaning on our staffs,
no stronger than children.
For fresh excitement springs up
in the chest, but it's like an old man;
it doesn't make a soldier;
in the same way, advanced old age,
its leaves already withering away, wends its way   80
with three feet, and wanders around, no stronger than a child,
like a dream that appears in the daytime.
But you, Tyndareus' daughter,
Queen Clytemnestra, what's the matter?
What's the news? What indication
or persuasive report have you received
that makes you send orders round to perform sacrifices?
For all the gods we cultivate in our city
—the supreme ones, the gods of the Underworld,

τῶν τ᾽ οὐρανίων τῶν τ᾽ ἀγοραίων,   90
βωμοὶ δώροισι φλέγονται·
ἄλλη δ᾽ ἄλλοθεν οὐρανομήκης
λαμπὰς ἀνίσχει,
φαρμασσομένη χρίματος ἁγνοῦ
μαλακαῖς ἀδόλοισι παρηγορίαις,
πελάνῳ μυχόθεν βασιλείῳ.
τούτων λέξασ᾽ ὅ τι καὶ δυνατὸν
καὶ θέμις, αἴνει παιών τε γενοῦ
τῆσδε μερίμνης,
ἦ νῦν τοτὲ μὲν κακόφρων τελέθει,   100
τοτὲ δ᾽ ἐκ θυσιῶν ἀγανὴ φαίνουσ᾽
ἐλπὶς ἀμύνει φροντίδ᾽ ἄπληστον
καὶ θυμοβόρον φρενὶ λύπην

κύριός εἰμι θροεῖν ὅδιον κράτος αἴσιον ἀνδρῶν   *strophe 1*
ἐκτελέων· ἔτι γὰρ θεόθεν καταπνείει
πειθώ, μολπᾶν
ἀλκάν, ξύμφυτος αἰών·
ὅπως Ἀχαιῶν δίθρονον κράτος, Ἑλλάδος ἥβας
ξύμφρονα ταγάν,   110
πέμπει ξὺν δορὶ καὶ χερὶ πράκτορι
θούριος ὄρνις Τευκρίδ᾽ ἐπ᾽ αἶαν,
οἰωνῶν βασιλεὺς βασιλεῦσι νεῶν ὁ κελαινός, ὅ τ᾽ ἐξόπιν ἀργᾶς,
φανέντες ἴκταρ μελάθρων χερὸς ἐκ δοριπάλτου
παμπρέπτοις ἐν ἕδραισιν,
βοσκόμενοι λαγίναν, ἐρικύμονα φέρματα γένναν,
βλαβέντα λοισθίων δρόμων.   120
αἴλινον αἴλινον εἰπέ, τὸ δ᾽ εὖ νικάτω.

98   αἴνει Wieseler: αἰνεῖν M V: εἰπεῖν F.   101   φαίνουσ᾽ Tr F: φαίνεισ M: φανθεῖσ᾽ Pauw.
103   καὶ Blaydes: τῆν codd.   106   πειθὼ μολπὰν codd., in M correctum ex μολπᾶν.
110   ξύμφρονα ταγάν recc.: ξύμφρονα τᾶν γᾶν M.   111   καὶ χερὶ Ar. *Ran.* 1289: δίκας
codd.   114   ἀργᾶς Blomfield: ἀργίασ codd.   119   ἐρικύμονα recc.: ἐρικύματα M.
φέρματα Hartung: φέρματι codd.

the gods of the heavens, and of the marketplace—   90
their altars are ablaze with offerings.
Everywhere flames are rising
all the way to heaven,
bewitched by the soft, simple encouragement
of pure balm, a salve
from deep inside the palace.
You should tell us whatever is
possible and right about these things,
and mend my troubled mind,
which one minute feels apprehension,   100
and the next hope, glowing gently from the sacrifices,
which shields me from the avid anxiety
and the sorrow destroying my peace of mind.

Chorus *[sing and dance]*
I have the authority to speak out loud of the leaders'
   omen of victory,   *strophe 1*
received on the journey. For in my old age, persuasion,
the power of songs, is still breathed on me from the gods.
I sing how the Achaean commanders,
with their double throne, the unified leadership
of the young men of Hellas—   110
how a furious bird-omen sent them in arms and with an avenging hand
against the Teucrian land,
the birds' king to the kings of ships
—two of them, one black, one with a white tail—
appeared close to the palace on the right,
in a very conspicuous place,
eating baby hares, creatures still in the womb,
deprived of a last escape.   120
Sing the song of sorrow, but may good prevail.

κεδνὸς δὲ στρατόμαντις ἰδὼν δύο λήμασι δισσοὺς   *antistrophe 1*
Ἀτρεΐδας μαχίμους ἐδάη
πομπούς τ᾽ ἀρχάς· οὕτω δ᾽ εἶπε τεράζων·
'χρόνῳ μὲν ἀγρεῖ Πριάμου πόλιν ἅδε κέλευθος,
  πάντα δὲ πύργων
κτήνη πρόσθε τὰ δημιοπληθέα
  Μοῖρ᾽ ἀλαπάξει πρὸς τὸ βίαιον·   130
οἷον μή τις ἄγα θεόθεν κνεφά-
  σῃ προτυπὲν στόμιον μέγα Τροίας
στρατωθέν. οἴκτῳ γὰρ ἐπί-
φθονος Ἄρτεμις ἁγνὰ
πτανοῖσιν κυσὶ πατρὸς
αὐτότοκον πρὸ λόχου μογερὰν πτάκα θυομένοισιν,
στυγεῖ δὲ δεῖπνον αἰετῶν.'
αἴλινον αἴλινον εἰπέ, τὸ δ᾽ εὖ νικάτω.

'τόσον περ εὔφρων ἁ καλὰ   *mesode* 140
δρόσοισι λεπτοῖς μαλερῶν λεόντων
πάντων τ᾽ ἀγρονόμων φιλομάστοις
θηρῶν ὀβρικάλοισι τερπνά,
τούτων αἴτει ξύμβολα κρᾶναι,
δεξιὰ μέν, κατάμομφα δὲ φάσματα †στρουθῶν†.
ἰήιον δὲ καλέω Παιᾶνα,
μή τινας ἀντιπνόους Δαναοῖς χρονί-
  ας ἐχενῇδας ἀπλοίας   150
τεύξῃ, σπευδομένα θυσίαν ἑτέραν ἄνομόν τιν᾽, ἄδαιτον,
νεικέων τέκτονα σύμφυτον, οὐ δει-
  σήνορα. μίμνει γὰρ φοβερὰ παλίνορτος
οἰκονόμος δολία, μνάμων μῆνις τεκνόποινος.'
τοιάδε Κάλχας ξὺν μεγάλοις ἀγαθοῖς ἀπέκλαγξεν
μόρσιμ᾽ ἀπ᾽ ὀρνίθων ὁδίων οἴκοις βασιλείοις·

---

129 πρόσθε τὰ Tr F: προσθετὰ M.   131 ἄγα Hermann: ἄτα codd.   134 οἴκτῳ Auratus,
Scaliger: οἴκῳ codd.   140 ἁ καλὰ F: καλὰ M V.   141 δρόσοισι λεπτοῖς Wellauer:
δρόσοισιν ἀέλπτοισ M: δρόσοισιν ἀέπτοις F.   λεόντων Pearson, cf. Et. Mag. 377.40:
ὄντων M.   145 στρουθῶν M V: τῶν στρουθῶν F: κρίνω Page.

The trusted army seer, noting that the   *antistrophe 1*
two warlike Atreidai were of two tempers,
identified the hare-devourers with the leaders of the army,
and spoke, interpreting the portents thus:
'In time this expedition shall take Priam's city,
and, before its ramparts, Fate shall violently ravage
its abundant publicly owned livestock in its entirety.
Only let no godsent grudge
darken the great marshalled curb of Troy,   130
forged beforehand. For, out of pity,
pure Artemis is angry
with the winged hounds of her father
for sacrificing a distressed, cowering creature,
along with her unborn brood.
She loathes the eagles' feast'.
Sing the song of sorrow, but may good prevail.

'The Beautiful One is so well-disposed   *mesode* 140
to raging lions' tiny cubs,
and so delights in the suckling young
of all creatures that roam the countryside,
that she demands the fulfilment of the meaning of these joint signs—
they are auspicious; but the apparition was marred.
And I call on Paean with the cry *iē*
to prevent her from frustrating the Danaans' voyage
by imposing adverse winds of long duration
and precipitating another sacrifice—a lawless one,
which cannot be eaten, craftsman of family conflict   150
and disrespect of woman towards man. For there awaits
a terrible, resilient, treacherous housekeeper, a remembering wrath that
    avenges a child'.
Such fateful things, along with many blessings, did Calchas shout out to
    the royal palace,
inferring them from the bird-omens as the journey began.

τοῖς δ᾽ ὁμόφωνον
αἴλινον αἴλινον εἰπέ, τὸ δ᾽ εὖ νικάτω.

Ζεύς, ὅστις ποτ᾽ ἐστίν, εἰ τόδ᾽ αὐ-   *strophe 2*   160
   τῷ φίλον κεκλημένῳ,
τοῦτό νιν προσεννέπω.
οὐκ ἔχω προσεικάσαι
   πάντ᾽ ἐπισταθμώμενος
πλὴν Διός, εἰ τὸ μάταν ἀπὸ φροντίδος ἄχθος
χρὴ βαλεῖν ἐτητύμως.

οὐδ᾽ ὅστις πάροιθεν ἦν μέγας,   *antistrophe 2*
   παμμάχῳ θράσει βρύων,
οὐδὲ λέξεται πρὶν ὤν·   170
ὃς δ᾽ ἔπειτ᾽ ἔφυ, τριακ-
   τῆρος οἴχεται τυχών.
Ζῆνα δέ τις προφρόνως ἐπινίκια κλάζων
τεύξεται φρενῶν τὸ πᾶν·

τὸν φρονεῖν βροτοὺς ὁδώ-   *strophe 3*
   σαντα, τὸν πάθει μάθος
θέντα κυρίως ἔχειν.
στάζει δ᾽ ἔν θ᾽ ὕπνῳ πρὸ καρδίας
μνησιπήμων πόνος· καὶ παρ᾽ ἄ-   180
   κοντας ἦλθε σωφρονεῖν.
δαιμόνων δέ που χάρις βίαιος
   σέλμα σεμνὸν ἡμένων.

καὶ τόθ᾽ ἡγεμὼν ὁ πρέσ-   *antistrophe 3*
   βυς νεῶν Ἀχαιικῶν,
μάντιν οὔτινα ψέγων,
ἐμπαίοις τύχαισι συμπνέων,
εὖτ᾽ ἀπλοίᾳ κεναγγεῖ βαρύ-
   νοντ᾽ Ἀχαιικὸς λεώς,

---

165   τὸ μάταν Pauw: τόδε μάταν M V F.   170   οὐδὲ λέξεται H.L. Ahrens: οὐδὲν λέξαι M V
F: οὐδέν τι λέξαι Tr.   182   βίαιος Turnebus: βιαίως codd.

And in tune with this,
sing the song of sorrow, but may good prevail. 160

Zeus, whoever he may be—if this designation *strophe 2*
meets his approval,
that is how I address him.
I have no point of comparison,
as I weigh everything up,
except for Zeus, if I must truly cast
this fruitless burden from my anxious thoughts.

The one who once was great, *antistrophe 2*
swelling with overconfidence in every battle— 170
his past existence shall not be discussed.
And the one who came next
met his victor and is gone.
But whoever earnestly peals forth a victory praise-song for Zeus,
he'll acquire good sense about everything—

praising him as the one who put mortals on the path of
    understanding, *strophe 3*
who ordained the law
that learning comes from suffering.
Anguish from remembered pain
drips over the heart in sleep; 180
and wisdom comes even to the unwilling.
It seems to me that the favour of the gods,
sitting augustly on the deck of the ship, comes with severity.

And then the older commander *antistrophe 3*
of the Achaean ships,
without censuring the seer,
breathed in unison with the strokes of fortune,
when the Achaean taskforce
were oppressed, unable to sail, their supplies running out,

Χαλκίδος πέραν ἔχων παλιρρόχ-   190
θοις ἐν Αὐλίδος τόποις·

πνοαὶ δ᾽ ἀπὸ Στρυμόνος μολοῦσαι   *strophe 4*
κακόσχολοι νήστιδες δύσορμοι,
βροτῶν ἄλαι,
ναῶν τε καὶ πεισμάτων ἀφειδεῖς,
παλιμμήκη χρόνον τιθεῖσαι
τρίβῳ κατέξαινον ἄνθος Ἀργεί-
ων· ἐπεὶ δὲ καὶ πικροῦ
χείματος ἄλλο μῆχαρ   200
βριθύτερον πρόμοισιν
μάντις ἔκλαγξεν προφέρων
Ἄρτεμιν, ὥστε χθόνα βάκ-
τροις ἐπικρούσαντας Ἀτρεί-
δας δάκρυ μὴ κατασχεῖν·

ἄναξ δ᾽ ὁ πρέσβυς τότ᾽ εἶπε φωνῶν·   *antistrophe 4*
‘βαρεῖα μὲν κὴρ τὸ μὴ πιθέσθαι,
βαρεῖα δ᾽, εἰ
τέκνον δαΐξω, δόμων ἄγαλμα,
μιαίνων παρθενοσφάγοισιν
ῥείθροις πατρῴους χέρας πέλας βω-   210
μοῦ· τί τῶνδ᾽ ἄνευ κακῶν,
πῶς λιπόναυς γένωμαι
ξυμμαχίας ἁμαρτών;
παυσανέμου γὰρ θυσίας
παρθενίου θ᾽ αἵματος ὀρ-
γᾷ περιόργως ἐπιθυ-
μεῖν θέμις. εὖ γὰρ εἴη.’

ἐπεὶ δ᾽ ἀνάγκας ἔδυ λέπαδνον   *strophe 5*
φρενὸς πνέων δυσσεβῆ τροπαίαν
ἄναγνον ἀνίερον, τόθεν   220

190–1 παλιρρόχθοις H.L. Ahrens: παλιρρόθοις codd. 194 τε add. Porson. 206 τότ᾽ Stanley: τόδ᾽ codd. 207 πιθέσθαι Turnebus: πείθεσθαι codd. 210 ῥείθροις Tr: ῥεέθροισ M. 211 πέλας βωμοῦ Blomfield: βωμοῦ πέλας codd. 212 πῶς λιπόναυς Tr: τί· πῶς λ(ε)ιπόναυς τε M V F.

opposite Chalcis, in the Aulis region 190
where the reverse tides rush.

Winds that came from the Strymon *strophe 4*
caused unwanted leisure, hunger, detention at anchor,
and men to wander, sparing neither
ships nor cables.
Doubling the length of the delay,
they crushed the flower of Argos
by attrition.
Then the seer intoned
another remedy to the chieftains, 200
graver even
than the bitter winter weather,
implicating Artemis, so that the Atreidai,
beating the ground with their staffs,
could not hold back tears.

The senior king then spoke, saying, *antistrophe 4*
'A dire calamity it is to disobey,
but dire it is if I must smite my child,
the ornament of the household,
defiling a father's hands 210
with streams of a maiden's blood
before the altar. Which alternative is not dire?
How am I to become a deserter of my fleet,
failing my allies?
It's legitimate in anger
to long angrily for a sacrifice
to stop the wind and for a maiden's blood.
May all be well.'

But when he put on the yoke-strap of necessity, *strophe 5*
as if blowing a sacrilegious wind of change—unholy, unhallowed—
from his mind—from then on he made a decision 220

τὸ παντότολμον φρονεῖν μετέγνω.
βροτοὺς θρασύνει γὰρ αἰσχρόμητις
τάλαινα παρακοπὰ πρωτοπήμων.
ἔτλα δ᾽ οὖν θυτὴρ γενέ-
σθαι θυγατρός, γυναικοποί-
νων πολέμων ἀρωγὰν
καὶ προτέλεια ναῶν.

λιτὰς δὲ καὶ κληδόνας πατρῴους   *antistrophe 5*
παρ᾽ οὐδὲν αἰῶ τε παρθένειον
ἔθεντο φιλόμαχοι βραβῆς.   230
φράσεν δ᾽ ἀόζοις πατὴρ μετ᾽ εὐχὰν
δίκαν χιμαίρας ὕπερθε βωμοῦ
πέπλοισι περιπετῆ παντὶ θυμῷ
προνωπῆ λαβεῖν ἀέρ-
δην, στόματός τε καλλιπρῴ-
ρου φυλακᾷ κατασχεῖν
φθόγγον ἀραῖον οἴκοις,

βίᾳ χαλινῶν τ᾽ ἀναύδῳ μένει.   *strophe 6*
κρόκου βαφὰς δ᾽ ἐς πέδον χέουσα
ἔβαλλ᾽ ἕκαστον θυτήρ-   240
ων ἀπ᾽ ὄμματος βέλει φιλοίκτῳ,
πρέπουσά θ᾽ ὡς ἐν γραφαῖς, προσεννέπειν
θέλουσ᾽, ἐπεὶ πολλάκις
πατρὸς κατ᾽ ἀνδρῶνας εὐτραπέζους
ἔμελψεν, ἁγνᾷ δ᾽ ἀταύρωτος αὐδᾷ πατρὸς
φίλου τριτόσπονδον εὔποτμον παιᾶνα φίλως ἐτίμα—

τὰ δ᾽ ἔνθεν οὔτ᾽ εἶδον οὔτ᾽ ἐννέπω·   *antistrophe 6*
τέχναι δὲ Κάλχαντος οὐκ ἄκραντοι.
Δίκα δὲ τοῖς μὲν παθοῦ-   250
σιν μαθεῖν ἐπιρρέπει· τὸ μέλλον δ᾽,
ἐπεὶ γένοιτ᾽, ἂν κλύοις· πρὸ χαιρέτω·

223 βροτοὺς Spanheim: βροτοῖσ M.   229 αἰῶ τε K. O. Müller: αἰῶνα codd.   236 φυλακᾷ
Blomfield: φυλακὰν codd.   245 ἁγνᾷ...αὐδᾷ recc.: ἁγνὰ...αὐδὰ M.   247 παιᾶνα Hartung:
αἰῶνα codd.   251 δ᾽ add. Elmsley.   252 πρὸ χαιρέτω H.L. Ahrens: προχαιρέτω codd.

to dare to think the unthinkable.
For making wretched, delusional, disgraceful plans,
the first cause of woe, emboldens men.
And so he brought himself to become
the sacrificer of his daughter,
putting her into the service of a war fought to avenge a woman
as the sacrifice to precede the voyage.

But the warlike leaders disregarded   *antistrophe 5*
her entreaties and her cries of 'father'
and her virgin life. After a prayer   230
her father told the ministrants
to seize her confidently and hold her falling forwards,
high over the altar, like a young she-goat,
her yellow-dyed robes falling around her,
and with a gag to stop her lovely mouth
from uttering a curse against the household

with the violence and silencing force of the bit.   *strophe 6*
Shedding to the ground her yellow-dyed robes,
she kept on striking each one of the sacrificers
with a shaft from her piteous eye,
standing out as if in a picture,   240
yearning to speak, since many times
she had sung for the men
at her father's welcoming banquet-table,
and with her pure, virginal voice
used lovingly to pay homage to her beloved father's
chant for blessing at the third libation.

What happened next I did not see and am not telling.   *antistrophe 6*
What Calchas' arts predicted was not unfulfilled.
Justice inclines her scales
so that people who've suffered learn from it.   250
But you'll hear about the future when it comes. Until then, let it be.

ἴσον δὲ τῷ προστένειν.
τορὸν γὰρ ἥξει σύνορθρον αὐγαῖς.
πέλοιτο δ' οὖν τἀπὶ τούτοισιν εὖ πρᾶξις, ὡς
θέλει τόδ' ἄγχιστον Ἀπίας γαί-
ας μονόφρουρον ἕρκος.

ἥκω σεβίζων σόν, Κλυταιμήστρα, κράτος·
δίκη γάρ ἐστι φωτὸς ἀρχηγοῦ τίειν
γυναῖκ' ἐρημωθέντος ἄρσενος θρόνου.   260
σὺ δ' εἴ τι κεδνὸν εἴτε μὴ πεπυσμένη
εὐαγγέλοισιν ἐλπίσιν θυηπολεῖς,
κλύοιμ' ἂν εὔφρων· οὐδὲ σιγώσῃ φθόνος.

Κλυταιμήστρα
εὐάγγελος μέν, ὥσπερ ἡ παροιμία,
ἕως γένοιτο μητρὸς εὐφρόνης πάρα.
πεύσῃ δὲ χάρμα μεῖζον ἐλπίδος κλυεῖν·
Πριάμου γὰρ ᾑρήκασιν Ἀργεῖοι πόλιν.
Χορός
πῶς φής; πέφευγε τοὔπος ἐξ ἀπιστίας.
Κλυταιμήστρα
Τροίαν Ἀχαιῶν οὖσαν· ἦ τορῶς λέγω;
Χορός
χαρά μ' ὑφέρπει δάκρυον ἐκκαλουμένη.   270
Κλυταιμήστρα
εὖ γὰρ φρονοῦντος ὄμμα σοῦ κατηγορεῖ.
Χορός
τί γὰρ τὸ πιστόν; ἔστι τῶνδέ σοι τέκμαρ;
Κλυταιμήστρα
ἔστιν· τί δ' οὐχί; μὴ δολώσαντος θεοῦ.
Χορός
πότερα δ' ὀνείρων φάσματ' εὐπειθῆ σέβεις;
Κλυταιμήστρα
οὐ δόξαν ἂν λάβοιμι βριζούσης φρενός.

---

254 σύνορθρον Wellauer: σύνορθον M: σύναρθρον F Trl Fa.   αὐγαῖς Hermann: αὐταῖς
codd.   255 εὖ πρᾶξις Lobeck: εὔπραξις codd.   261 εἴ τι Auratus: εἴτε codd.   272 τί
γὰρ τὸ πιστόν; Prien: τί γάρ; τὸ πιστὸν M.

Worrying about it is equivalent to weeping prematurely.
It shall become clear as it dawns with the first daylight.
And so may what's to follow this turn out well,
which is the desire
of this lone guardian and defender of the Apian land,
closest to the King.

[Enter Clytemnestra from the palace. The chorus now converse with her]

Clytemnestra, I come to honour your sovereignty.
For it's right to pay respect to the leader's wife
when he's absent from his throne.   260
As for you, I'd like to know whether you've heard good news,
or are organising sacrifices because you've heard nothing
and hope for good news. But I hold no grudge if you say nothing.

Clytemnestra
There's a proverb—let dawn be born full of good tidings from her mother,
    night-time.
You're about to hear something more joyful than you hoped for:
The Argives have taken Priam's city!

Chorus
What are you saying? It's difficult to grasp since it seems unbelievable.

Clytemnestra
Troy is under Achaean control. Is that clear enough?

Chorus
I'm beginning to feel elated and am close to tears.

Clytemnestra
Yes, your face indicates your goodwill.   270

Chorus
So what's the proof? Do you have corroboration?

Clytemnestra
Certainly I do, unless some god has tricked me.

Chorus
Is it the phantom-figures of dreams that have convinced you?

Clytemnestra
I wouldn't accept the fantasy of a mind that was asleep.

Χορός
ἀλλ᾽ ἦ σ᾽ ἐπίανέν τις ἄπτερος φάτις;
Κλυταιμήστρα
παιδὸς νέας ὣς κάρτ᾽ ἐμωμήσω φρένας.
Χορός
ποίου χρόνου δὲ καὶ πεπόρθηται πόλις;
Κλυταιμήστρα
τῆς νῦν τεκούσης φῶς τόδ᾽ εὐφρόνης λέγω.
Χορός
καὶ τίς τόδ᾽ ἐξίκοιτ᾽ ἂν ἀγγέλων τάχος ;   280
Κλυταιμήστρα
Ἥφαιστος Ἴδης λαμπρὸν ἐκπέμπων σέλας.
φρυκτὸς δὲ φρυκτὸν δεῦρ᾽ ἀπ᾽ ἀγγάρου πυρὸς
ἔπεμπεν· Ἴδη μὲν πρὸς Ἑρμαῖον λέπας
Λήμνου· μέγαν δὲ πανὸν ἐκ νήσου τρίτον
Ἀθῷον αἶπος Ζηνὸς ἐξεδέξατο,
ὑπερτελής τε, πόντον ὥστε νωτίσαι,
ἰσχὺς πορευτοῦ λαμπάδος πρὸς ἡδονὴν
                    *
πεύκη τὸ χρυσοφεγγές, ὥς τις ἥλιος,
σέλας παραγγείλασα Μακίστου σκοπαῖς·
ὁ δ᾽ οὔτι μέλλων οὐδ᾽ ἀφρασμόνως ὕπνῳ   290
νικώμενος παρῆκεν ἀγγέλου μέρος·
ἑκὰς δὲ φρυκτοῦ φῶς ἐπ᾽ Εὐρίπου ῥοὰς
Μεσσαπίου φύλαξι σημαίνει μολόν.
οἱ δ᾽ ἀντέλαμψαν καὶ παρήγγειλαν πρόσω
γραίας ἐρείκης θωμὸν ἅψαντες πυρί.
σθένουσα λαμπὰς δ᾽ οὐδέπω μαυρουμένη,
ὑπερθοροῦσα πεδίον Ἀσωποῦ, δίκην
φαιδρᾶς σελήνης, πρὸς Κιθαιρῶνος λέπας
ἤγειρεν ἄλλην ἐκδοχὴν πομποῦ πυρός.
φάος δὲ τηλέπομπον οὐκ ἠναίνετο   300
φρουρὰ πλέον καίουσα τῶν εἰρημένων·
λίμνην δ᾽ ὑπὲρ Γοργῶπιν ἔσκηψεν φάος·
ὄρος τ᾽ ἐπ᾽ Αἰγίπλαγκτον ἐξικνούμενον

282 ἀγγάρου ex Etym. Magn. Canter: ἀγγέλου codd.   284   πανὸν ex Athen. 15.700e
Casaubon: φανὸν codd.   Post 287 lacunam statuit Paley.   289 σκοπαῖς Turnebus:
σκοπάς codd.   297 πεδίον Ἀσωποῦ recc.: παιδίον ὠποῦ M.

Chorus
Has some premature rumour fed your hopes then?
Clytemnestra
You really do despise my intelligence as if I were a little girl.
Chorus
So at what time has the sacking of the city taken place?
Clytemnestra
As I say, it was during last night, the one that gave birth to today.
Chorus
And what kind of messenger could arrive so quickly?   280
Clytemnestra
Hephaestus, sending his dazzling blaze out from Ida.
From one beacon-flame to another the message was sent
towards us by courier of fire: Ida to the Hermaean crag
of Lemnos; from that island, the peak of Zeus' Athos
received the great torch third,
and, soaring high over the surface of the sea,
the power of the torchlight travelled gleefully.
[*line(s) missing*]
The pinewood torch, gleaming as golden as some kind of sun,
passed the flame's message to the lookout points of Makistos.
The mountain, without delay and without giving in   290
witlessly to sleep, carried out his task as messenger.
The beacon's light came from far across the flowing Euripus
and gave the signal to the watchmen on Messapion.
They, kindling a heap of withered bush heather,
lit it up in answer and passed the message on.
The torchlight, now getting stronger and not losing any clarity,
leapt across the plain of Asopus, like
a beaming moon, to craggy Cithaeron
and started up another stage in the relay of fire.
The lookout team there did not spurn the light, sent from far away,   300
but made a bigger blaze than they had been told to do.
The light shot across Lake Gorgopis,
arrived at Goat Mountain,

ὤτρυνε θεσμὸν μὴ χρονίζεσθαι πυρός.
πέμπουσι δ᾽ ἀνδαίοντες ἀφθόνῳ μένει
φλογὸς μέγαν πώγωνα, καὶ Σαρωνικοῦ
πορθμοῦ κάτοπτον πρῶν᾽ ὑπερβάλλειν πρόσω
φλέγουσαν· ἔστ᾽ ἔσκηψεν εὖτ᾽ ἀφίκετο
Ἀραχναῖον αἶπος, ἀστυγείτονας σκοπάς·
κἄπειτ᾽ Ἀτρειδῶν ἐς τόδε σκήπτει στέγος   310
φάος τόδ᾽ οὐκ ἄπαππον Ἰδαίου πυρός.
τοιοίδε τοί μοι λαμπαδηφόρων νόμοι,
ἄλλος παρ᾽ ἄλλου διαδοχαῖς πληρούμενοι·
νικᾷ δ᾽ ὁ πρῶτος καὶ τελευταῖος δραμών.
τέκμαρ τοιοῦτον σύμβολόν τέ σοι λέγω
ἀνδρὸς παραγγείλαντος ἐκ Τροίας ἐμοί.

Χορός
θεοῖς μὲν αὖθις, ὦ γύναι, προσεύξομαι.
λόγους δ᾽ ἀκοῦσαι τούσδε κἀποθαυμάσαι
διηνεκῶς θέλοιμ᾽ ἄν, ὡς λέγοις, πάλιν.

Κλυταιμήστρα
Τροίαν Ἀχαιοὶ τῇδ᾽ ἔχουσ᾽ ἐν ἡμέρᾳ.   320
οἶμαι βοὴν ἄμεικτον ἐν πόλει πρέπειν.
ὄξος τ᾽ ἄλειφά τ᾽ ἐγχέας ταὐτῷ κύτει
διχοστατοῦντ᾽ ἄν, οὐ φίλω, προσεννέποις.
καὶ τῶν ἁλόντων καὶ κρατησάντων δίχα
φθογγὰς ἀκούειν ἔστι, συμφορᾶς διπλῆς.
οἱ μὲν γὰρ, ἀμφὶ σώμασιν πεπτωκότες
ἀνδρῶν κασιγνήτων τε καὶ φυταλμίων
παῖδες γερόντων, οὐκέτ᾽ ἐξ ἐλευθέρου
δέρης ἀποιμώζουσι φιλτάτων μόρον·
τοὺς δ᾽ αὖτε νυκτίπλαγκτος ἐκ μάχης πόνος   330
νήστεις πρὸς ἀρίστοισιν ὧν ἔχει πόλις
τάσσει, πρὸς οὐδὲν ἐν μέρει τεκμήριον,
ἀλλ᾽ ὡς ἕκαστος ἔσπασεν τύχης πάλον.
ἐν δ᾽ αἰχμαλώτοις Τρωϊκοῖς οἰκήμασιν

---

304   χρονίζεσθαι Casaubon: χαρίζεσθαι codd.   307   κάτοπτον Canter: κάτοπτρον codd.
308   ἔστ᾽...εὖτ᾽ Hermann: εἴτ᾽... εἴτ᾽ codd.   312–1007   e Med. cod. exciderunt.
312   τοιοίδε τοί μοι Schütz: τοιοίδ᾽ ἔτοιμοι codd.   319   λέγοις Tr: λέγεις V.   322   ἐγχέας
Canter: ἐκχέας codd.   323   φίλω Portus: φίλως codd.   331   νήστεις Tr: νῆστις F.
334   δ᾽ add. Pauw.

and urged the rite of fire to make no delay.
Igniting a vast beard of flame with unlimited forcefulness,
these watchmen drove it forward so that its blaze
even reached past the cape that faces
the Saronic gulf, until it shot down on arrival
to the lookout-point near our city, on steep Arachnaion;
and then it shot onto the very roof here of the Atreidai,   310
this light which is directly descended from the fire of Ida.
These were the torch-bearers; according to my instructions,
which were carried out in turn, each took over from the other.
The winner is the one who ran both first and last legs of the relay.
That's the sort of evidence and corroboration I give you,
the message from Troy my husband has sent to me.

Chorus

Woman, I'll offer prayers to the gods shortly.
But I'd like to hear this account again and marvel at it,
so please tell it again straight through to the end.

Clytemnestra

Today the Achaeans hold Troy.   320
Within the city I believe that there are loud conflicting voices.
If you pour vinegar and oil into the same container
they stay separate—hostile to one another, you could say.
So you can hear quite different cries from the
conquered and the conquerors, since they have different fates.
For the defeated have collapsed on the corpses
of their husbands and brothers, and children
on the bodies of their elderly fathers,
grieving loudly, captives now, over their loved ones' fate.
But for the victors, on the other hand, a busy night's work after the battle   330
has worked up a huge appetite for whatever breakfast
they can find in the city, not according to rank,
but according to whatever straw each man just happened to draw.
And they've already taken up quarters in captured Trojan houses,

ναίουσιν ἤδη, τῶν ὑπαιθρίων πάγων
δρόσων τ᾽ ἀπαλλαγέντες, ὡς δ᾽ εὐδαίμονες
ἀφύλακτον εὐδήσουσι πᾶσαν εὐφρόνην.
εἰ δ᾽ εὐσεβοῦσι τοὺς πολισσούχους θεοὺς
τοὺς τῆς ἁλούσης γῆς θεῶν θ᾽ ἱδρύματα,
οὔ τᾶν ἑλόντες αὖθις ἀνθαλοῖεν ἄν.   340
ἔρως δὲ μή τις πρότερον ἐμπίπτῃ στρατῷ
πορθεῖν ἃ μὴ χρή, κέρδεσιν νικωμένους.
δεῖ γὰρ πρὸς οἴκους νοστίμου σωτηρίας
κάμψαι διαύλου θάτερον κῶλον πάλιν·
θεοῖς δ᾽ ἀναμπλάκητος εἰ μόλοι στρατός,
ἐγρηγορὸς τὸ πῆμα τῶν ὀλωλότων
γένοιτ᾽ ἄν, εἰ πρόσπαια μὴ τύχοι κακά.
τοιαῦτά τοι γυναικὸς ἐξ ἐμοῦ κλύεις·
τὸ δ᾽ εὖ κρατοίη μὴ διχορρόπως ἰδεῖν.
πολλῶν γὰρ ἐσθλῶν τήνδ᾽ ὄνησιν εἱλόμην.   350

Χορός
γύναι, κατ᾽ ἄνδρα σώφρον᾽ εὐφρόνως λέγεις.
ἐγὼ δ᾽ ἀκούσας πιστά σου τεκμήρια
θεοὺς προσειπεῖν εὖ παρασκευάζομαι.
χάρις γὰρ οὐκ ἄτιμος εἴργασται πόνων.

ὦ Ζεῦ βασιλεῦ καὶ Νὺξ φιλία
μεγάλων κόσμων κτεάτειρα,
ἥτ᾽ ἐπὶ Τροίας πύργοις ἔβαλες
στεγανὸν δίκτυον, ὡς μήτε μέγαν
μήτ᾽ οὖν νεαρῶν τιν᾽ ὑπερτελέσαι
μέγα δουλείας   360
γάγγαμον, ἄτης παναλώτου.
Δία τοι ξένιον μέγαν αἰδοῦμαι
τὸν τάδε πράξαντ᾽ ἐπ᾽ Ἀλεξάνδρῳ
τείνοντα πάλαι τόξον, ὅπως ἂν
μήτε πρὸ καιροῦ μήθ᾽ ὑπὲρ ἄστρων
βέλος ἠλίθιον σκήψειεν.

---

336 δ᾽ εὐδαίμονες Stanley: δυσδαίμονες codd.   340 οὔ τᾶν ἑλόντες Hermann: οὐκ ἀνελ-
V: οὐκ ἄν γ᾽ ἑλ- F.   346 ἐγρηγορὸς Porson: ἐγρήγορον codd.   350 τήνδ᾽ Hermann: τὴν
codd.

released from the frost and dewfall
they suffered outdoors, and will sleep like happy men
the whole night through, with no need for a guard.
If they properly respect the gods who dwell in the vanquished
country's citadel, and its gods' shrines,
the captors will not themselves be vanquished in their turn.   340
I hope that no desire now impels the army,
overcome by greed for gain, to loot things they shouldn't.
To get home safely they have to pass the turning-post
and run the length of the whole racetrack back again.
Even if our forces returned without forsaking the gods at all,
the misery of the dead might be awakened,
regardless of any fresh calamities that might befall.
That is what I have to say to you—a woman's words.
But may what is good prevail, unambiguously and visibly.
This benefit is the one I favour over multiple blessings.   350
Chorus
Woman, you speak with good sense, like a sensible man.
For my part, having heard your reliable evidence,
I'm getting ready to address proper prayers to the gods.
A valuable reward for our troubles has been achieved.

[*Exit Clytemnestra into the palace. The chorus starts intoning*]

O Zeus my King—and kindly Night,
provider of great glory,
you who threw an impermeable mesh
over the ramparts of Troy, so that
neither adult nor any of the young ones
could escape the great net of slavery,   360
all-embracing ruin.
Zeus, great guardian of strangers, I venerate
for this achievement, bending his bow
against Alexander at length, to ensure that he shot his arrow
neither prematurely
nor in vain beyond the stars.

[*Singing and dancing*]

Διὸς πλαγὰν ἔχουσιν εἰπεῖν,   *strophe 1*
πάρεστιν τοῦτό γ᾽ ἐξιχνεῦσαι.
ἔπραξαν ὡς ἔκρανεν. οὐκ ἔφα τις
θεοὺς βροτῶν ἀξιοῦσθαι μέλειν   370
ὅσοις ἀθίκτων χάρις
πατοῖθ᾽· ὁ δ᾽ οὐκ εὐσεβής.
πέφανται δ᾽ ἐκτίνου-
    σα τόλμα τῶν Ἄρη
πνεόντων μεῖζον ἢ δικαίως,
φλεόντων δωμάτων ὑπέρφευ
ὑπὲρ τὸ βέλτιστον. ἔστω δ᾽ ἀπή-
    μαντον, ὥστ᾽ ἀπαρκεῖν
εὖ πραπίδων λαχόντα.   380
    οὐ γὰρ ἔστιν ἔπαλξις
    πλούτου πρὸς κόρον ἀνδρὶ
    λακτίσαντι μέγαν Δίκας
       βωμὸν εἰς ἀφάνειαν.

βιᾶται δ᾽ ἁ τάλαινα Πειθώ,   *antistrophe 1*
προβούλου παῖς ἄφερτος Ἄτας.
ἄκος δὲ πᾶν μάταιον. οὐκ ἐκρύφθη,
πρέπει δέ, φῶς αἰνολαμπές, σίνος·
κακοῦ δὲ χαλκοῦ τρόπον   390
τρίβῳ τε καὶ προσβολαῖς
μελαμπαγὴς πέλει
    δικαιωθείς, ἐπεὶ
διώκει παῖς ποτανὸν ὄρνιν,
πόλει πρόστριμμα θεὶς ἄφερτον.
λιτᾶν δ᾽ ἀκούει μὲν οὔτις θεῶν,
    τὸν δ᾽ ἐπίστροφον τῶν
φῶτ᾽ ἄδικον καθαιρεῖ.
    οἷος καὶ Πάρις ἐλθὼν

---

368 πάρεστιν Hartung: πάρεστι codd. τοῦτο γ᾽ Tr: τοῦτ᾽ F. 369 ἔπραξαν Hermann: ὡς ἔπραξεν codd. 374–5 ἐκτίνουσα τόλμα τῶν Ἄρη Hartung: ἐγγόνους ἀτολμήτων codd. 383 μέγαν Canter: μεγάλα codd. 386 προβούλου παῖς Hartung: προβουλόπαις codd. 391 τε Tr: om. F. προσβολαῖς Pearson: προβολαῖς codd. 394 ποτανὸν Schütz: πτανὸν codd. 395 θεὶς ἄφερτον Wilamowitz: ἄφερτον θεὶς F: ἄφερτον ἐνθεὶς Tr. 397 τῶν Klausen: τῶνδε F.

It's what they call 'the stroke of Zeus'.   *strophe 1*
It's possible to track this down.
They fared as he ordained. Someone said
that the gods don't think it's worth concerning themselves with mortals   370
by whom the favour of things which must not be touched
is trampled underfoot. That man has no piety.
The penalty has been shown to be paid
by the daring of those who breathe war
in excess of what's right,
their homes teeming far beyond
what's best. Let one's livelihood
bring no harm, but be sufficient for
the person of good sense.
For wealth provides no protection   380
to the man who has insatiably
kicked the great altar of Justice
into obscurity.

Wretched Persuasion, intolerable daughter   *antistrophe 1*
of premeditated Ruin, forces him on.
Every remedy is futile. The wound can't be hidden
but stands out like a light of frightful gleam.
Just like base metal
rubbed by the touchstone,
when tested he is proved   390
to be black right through—he's like
a child chasing a bird on the wing—
having marked his city with an intolerable taint.
The gods, rather than listening to his prayers,
destroy the unjust man
involved in such things.
That was what Paris was like,

ἐς δόμον τὸν Ἀτρειδᾶν　　　　　　　　　400
ἤσχυνε ξενίαν τράπε-
ζαν κλοπαῖσι γυναικός.

λιποῦσα δ᾽ ἀστοῖσιν ἀσπίστορας　　　*strophe 2*
κλόνους λοχίσμους τε καὶ
　　ναυβάτας ὁπλισμούς,
ἄγουσά τ᾽ ἀντίφερνον Ἰλίῳ φθορὰν
βέβακε ῥίμφα διὰ
　　πυλᾶν ἄτλητα τλᾶσα· πολλὰ δ᾽ ἔστενον
τόδ᾽ ἐννέποντες δόμων προφῆται·
᾽ἰὼ ἰὼ δῶμα δῶμα καὶ πρόμοι,　　　　410
ἰὼ λέχος καὶ στίβοι φιλάνορες.
πάρεστι †σιγὰς ἄτιμος ἀλοίδορος
　　ἄδιστος ἀφεμένων† ἰδεῖν.
πόθῳ δ᾽ ὑπερποντίας
φάσμα δόξει δόμων ἀνάσσειν.
　　εὐμόρφων δὲ κολοσσῶν
　　ἔχθεται χάρις ἀνδρί·
　　ὀμμάτων δ᾽ ἐν ἀχηνίαις
　　　ἔρρει πᾶσ᾽ Ἀφροδίτα.᾽

᾽ὀνειρόφαντοι δὲ πενθήμονες　　　*antistrophe 2* 420
πάρεισι δόξαι φέρου-
　　σαι χάριν ματαίαν.
μάταν γάρ, εὖτ᾽ ἂν ἐσθλά τις δοκῶν ὁρᾷ,
παραλλάξασα διὰ
　　χερῶν βέβακεν ὄψις, οὐ μεθύστερον
πτεροῖς ὀπαδοῦσ᾽ ὕπνου κελεύθοις.᾽
τὰ μὲν κατ᾽ οἴκους ἐφ᾽ ἑστίας ἄχη
τάδ᾽ ἐστί, καὶ τῶνδ᾽ ὑπερβατώτερα.
τὸ πᾶν δ᾽ ἀφ᾽ Ἕλλανος αἴας συνορμένοισι πέν-
θει᾽ ἀτλησικάρδιος　　　　　　　　　430

404　λοχισμούς Heyse: λογχίμους F.　　408　πολλὰ δ᾽ ἔστενον Tr: πολὺ δ᾽ ἀνέστενον F.
410　ἰὼ ἰὼ δῶμα δῶμα Tr: ἰὼ δῶμα F.　　412　σιγὰσ ἄτιμοσ ἀλοίδοροσ codd.: σιγὰς ἄτιμυος
ἀλοιδόρους Hermann.　　413　ἄδιστος codd.: ἄλγιστ᾽ Enger.　ἀφεμένων codd.: ἀφημένων
Dindorf.　　423　ὁρᾷ Scholefield: ὁρᾶν codd.　426　ὀπαδοῦσ᾽ Dobree: ὀπαδοῖς codd.
429　Ἕλλανος Bamberger: Ἑλλάδος codd.　συνορμένοισι Schwerdt: συνορμένοις codd.

when he arrived at the home of the Atreidai,   400
and shamed hospitality's table
by stealing a wife.

Leaving behind, for her own people,   *strophe 2*
the tumult of shield-bearing soldiers,
the formation of companies and the arming of ships' crews,
and bringing destruction to Troy in place of a dowry,
she stepped lightly through the gate,
daring what should not be dared.
The palace seers began groaning copiously, saying,
'Alas, alas for the house, the house and its overlords,   410
alas for the marriage-bed and the traces of her lovemaking.
You can see how in his acute grief he sits apart,
silent, dishonoured, but unreproachful.
In his yearning for her across the sea
a wraith shall seem to rule the household.
The grace of beautiful statues
is hateful to the husband.
In the absence of eye contact
all sexual desire has departed.

Mournful apparitions are present in his dreams   *antistrophe 2* 420
bringing futile joy.
For it's futile when someone imagines he sees something good,
but the apparition, slipping through his arms,
is gone momentarily,
following on wings the paths of sleep'.
Such are the sorrows of hearth and home,
but there are sorrows which surpass even these.
For everyone who set out from Greece,
unbearable heartbreak

δόμοις ἑκάστου πρέπει.
πολλὰ γοῦν θιγγάνει πρὸς ἧπαρ·
  οὓς μὲν γάρ τις ἔπεμψεν
  οἶδεν, ἀντὶ δὲ φωτῶν
  τεύχη καὶ σποδὸς εἰς ἑκά-
    στου δόμους ἀφικνεῖται.

ὁ χρυσαμοιβὸς δ' Ἄρης σωμάτων	*strophe 3*
καὶ ταλαντοῦχος ἐν μάχῃ δορὸς	
πυρωθὲν ἐξ Ἰλίου	440
φίλοισι πέμπει βαρὺ	

ψῆγμα δυσδάκρυτον ἀν-
  τήνορος σποδοῦ γεμί-
  ζων λέβητας εὐθέτους.
στένουσι δ' εὖ λέγοντες ἄνδρα τὸν μὲν ὡς μάχης ἴδρις,
τὸν δ' ἐν φοναῖς καλῶς πεσόντ'—
  ἀλλοτρίας διαὶ γυναι-
  κός· τὰ δὲ σῖγά τις βαΰ-
  ζει, φθονερὸν δ' ὑπ' ἄλγος ἕρ-   450
  πει προδίκοις Ἀτρείδαις.
οἱ δ' αὐτοῦ περὶ τεῖχος
θήκας Ἰλιάδος γᾶς
εὔμορφοι κατέχουσιν· ἐχ-
  θρὰ δ' ἔχοντας ἔκρυψεν.

βαρεῖα δ' ἀστῶν φάτις ξὺν κότῳ·	*antistrophe 3*
δημοκράντου δ' ἀρᾶς τίνει χρέος.	
μένει δ' ἀκοῦσαί τί μοι	
μέριμνα νυκτηρεφές.	460

τῶν πολυκτόνων γὰρ οὐκ
  ἄσκοποι θεοί. κελαι-
  ναὶ δ' Ἐρινύες χρόνῳ
τυχηρὸν ὄντ' ἄνευ δίκας

---

431 δόμοις Porson: δόμων F.   433 τις add. Porson.   444 εὐθέτους Auratus: εὐθέτου codd.   448 διαὶ Hermann: διὰ codd.: γε διὰ Tr.   458 δημοκράντου Porson: δημοκράτου codd.   459 μοι Karsten: μου F.

universally dominates their homes.
Many things touch the heart.   430
For everyone knows
whom they sent out, but instead of men
urns and ashes return
to the homes of each one.

Ares, who exchanges bodies like gold currency,   *strophe 3*
and who holds the scales in spear-battles,
sends from Ilium to loved ones
weighty residue from the fires,
bringing bitter tears—
easily stowed urns crammed with ash instead of men.   440
They groan, praising
one man for his skill in battle,
another for falling nobly amidst the slaughter
for the sake of another man's wife—
so someone snarls under their breath,   450
and resentful anguish creeps against their advocates, the Atreidai.
But those beautiful men occupy graves
there, around the walls of Ilium.
The enemy earth has concealed its occupiers.

It's a grave matter when citizens speak resentfully.   *antistrophe 3*
It pays the debt of a curse ratified by the people.
In my anxiety I anticipate hearing something
still benighted in gloom.   460
For gods aren't heedless of people
with blood on their hands. In time
the black Erinyes, by attrition and reversal,

παλιντυχεῖ τριβᾷ βίου
τιθεῖσ᾽ ἀμαυρόν, ἐν δ᾽ ἀί-
στοις τελέθοντος οὔτις ἀλ-
κά· τὸ δ᾽ ὑπερκόπως κλύειν
εὖ βαρύ· βάλλεται γὰρ ὄσ-
σοις Διόθεν κάρανα.   470
κρίνω δ᾽ ἄφθονον ὄλβον·
μήτ᾽ εἴην πτολιπόρθης
μήτ᾽ οὖν αὐτὸς ἁλοὺς ὑπ᾽ ἄλλων βίον κατίδοιμι.

πυρὸς δ᾽ ὑπ᾽ εὐαγγέλου   *epode*
πόλιν διήκει θοὰ
βάξις· εἰ δ᾽ ἐτήτυμος,
τίς οἶδεν, ἤ τι θεῖόν ἐστί πῃ ψύθος.
τίς ὧδε παιδνὸς ἢ φρενῶν κεκομμένος,
φλογὸς παραγγέλμασιν   480
νέοις πυρωθέντα καρδίαν ἔπειτ᾽
    ἀλλαγᾷ λόγου καμεῖν;
ἐν γυναικὸς αἰχμᾷ πρέπει
πρὸ τοῦ φανέντος χάριν ξυναινέσαι.
πιθανὸς ἄγαν ὁ θῆλυς ὅρος ἐπινέμεται
ταχύπορος· ἀλλὰ ταχύμορον
γυναικογήρυτον ὄλλυται κλέος.

τάχ᾽ εἰσόμεσθα λαμπάδων φαεσφόρων
φρυκτωρίας τε καὶ πυρὸς παραλλαγάς,   490
εἴτ᾽ οὖν ἀληθεῖς εἴτ᾽ ὀνειράτων δίκην
τερπνὸν τόδ᾽ ἐλθὸν φῶς ἐφήλωσεν φρένας.
κήρυκ᾽ ἀπ᾽ ἀκτῆς τόνδ᾽ ὁρῶ κατάσκιον
κλάδοις ἐλαίας· μαρτυρεῖ δέ μοι κάσις
πηλοῦ ξύνουρος διψία κόνις τάδε,
ὡς οὔτ᾽ ἄναυδος οὔτε σοι δαίων φλόγα
ὕλης ὀρείας σημανεῖ καπνῷ πυρός,

---

465   παλιντυχεῖ Scaliger: παλιντυχῇ codd.   468   ὑπερκόπως Grotius: ὑπερκότως codd.
477   ἐτήτυμος Auratus: ἐτητύμος codd.   478   τι...πῃ H.L. Ahrens: τοι...μὴ codd.
483   γυναικὸς Scaliger: ἐν γυναικὸς F.   490   φρυκτωρίας Wilamowitz: φρυκτωριῶν F.

cast into obscurity
the man who prospers through injustice.
When a man is among the unseen
there's no help for him.
To be spoken about with excessive praise
is perilous. The exalted
are smitten in their eyes by Zeus. 470
I favour the felicity that attracts no envy.
May I neither be a sacker of cities,
nor be captured myself and witness
my life under others' control.

Announced by a beacon bearing good news, *epode*
a swift report has gone across the city.
But who knows whether it's true,
or some deceit practised by the gods?
Who is so childlike or mindless,
when his heart has been inflamed by news 480
reported by a beacon-fire,
then to struggle when the story changes?
A woman's fighting temperament
obviously gives assent to what it wants to hear before things are clarified.
A woman's mind is too gullible, its boundaries too quickly infringed.
But rumour uttered by a woman
quickly meets its end.

[*speaking*]
We'll know soon know whether the glowing lights,
the beacon signals and fire relay, 490
are true, or whether, like dreams, the pleasure
bestowed by the light's arrival deceived our minds.

[*Enter the Herald from the direction of the harbour*]

I see there a herald garlanded with olive-twigs
coming from the shore. He's encrusted
with dusty dried mud, evidence
that he's not about to use the mute language of fire or smoke signals
by kindling a flame from mountain wood.

ἀλλ᾽ ἦ τὸ χαίρειν μᾶλλον ἐκβάξει λέγων—
τὸν ἀντίον δὲ τοῖσδ᾽ ἀποστέργω λόγον·
εὖ γὰρ πρὸς εὖ φανεῖσι προσθήκη πέλοι.—   500
ὅστις τάδ᾽ ἄλλως τῇδ᾽ ἐπεύχεται πόλει,
αὐτὸς φρενῶν καρποῖτο τὴν ἁμαρτίαν.

Κῆρυξ
ἰὼ πατρῷον οὖδας Ἀργείας χθονός,
δεκάτου σε φέγγει τῷδ᾽ ἀφικόμην ἔτους,
πολλῶν ῥαγεισῶν ἐλπίδων μιᾶς τυχών.
οὐ γάρ ποτ᾽ ηὔχουν τῇδ᾽ ἐν Ἀργείᾳ χθονὶ
θανὼν μεθέξειν φιλτάτου τάφου μέρος.
νῦν χαῖρε μὲν χθών, χαῖρε δ᾽ ἡλίου φάος,
ὕπατός τε χώρας Ζεύς, ὁ Πύθιός τ᾽ ἄναξ,
τόξοις ἰάπτων μηκέτ᾽ εἰς ἡμᾶς βέλη·   510
ἅλις παρὰ Σκάμανδρον ἦσθ᾽ ἀνάρσιος·
νῦν δ᾽ αὖτε σωτὴρ ἴσθι καὶ παιώνιος,
ἄναξ Ἄπολλον. τούς τ᾽ ἀγωνίους θεοὺς
πάντας προσαυδῶ, τόν τ᾽ ἐμὸν τιμάορον
Ἑρμῆν, φίλον κήρυκα, κηρύκων σέβας,
ἥρως τε τοὺς πέμψαντας, εὐμενεῖς πάλιν
στρατὸν δέχεσθαι τὸν λελειμμένον δορός.
ἰὼ μέλαθρα βασιλέων, φίλαι στέγαι,
σεμνοί τε θᾶκοι, δαίμονές τ᾽ ἀντήλιοι,
εἴ που πάλαι, φαιδροῖσι τοισίδ᾽ ὄμμασι   520
δέξασθε κόσμῳ βασιλέα πολλῷ χρόνῳ.
ἥκει γὰρ ὑμῖν φῶς ἐν εὐφρόνῃ φέρων
καὶ τοῖσδ᾽ ἅπασι κοινὸν Ἀγαμέμνων ἄναξ.
ἀλλ᾽ εὖ νιν ἀσπάσασθε, καὶ γὰρ οὖν πρέπει
Τροίαν κατασκάψαντα τοῦ δικηφόρου
Διὸς μακέλλῃ, τῇ κατείργασται πέδον.
βωμοὶ δ᾽ ἄιστοι καὶ θεῶν ἱδρύματα,
καὶ σπέρμα πάσης ἐξαπόλλυται χθονός.
τοιόνδε Τροίᾳ περιβαλὼν ζευκτήριον
ἄναξ Ἀτρείδης πρέσβυς εὐδαίμων ἀνὴρ   530
ἥκει, τίεσθαι δ᾽ ἀξιώτατος βροτῶν

---

504 δεκάτου Jacob: δεκάτῳ F.   511 ἦσθ᾽ Askew: ἦλθες Tr.   512 καὶ παιώνιος Dobree:
καὶ παγώνιος F: κἀπαγώνιος Tr.   520 εἴ που Auratus: ἦπου codd.   522 ὑμῖν Tr: ἡμῖν F.

He'll speak out in words that will either make us exult even more, or—
but I'm not keen on news of the opposite kind.
May more good news be added to what we already know.   500
Whoever prays otherwise for this city,
may he harvest the fruit of his own mind's misjudgement.

Herald

Greetings, earth of my Argive fatherland;
on this bright day I've reached you ten years on.
Though many of my hopes have been shattered, one has been fulfilled.
I never expressed confidence that I would die here on Argive ground
and receive the funeral I yearn for. So now, I greet the earth, I greet
   the sunlight,
and our country's supreme god, Zeus, and the Pythian lord—
may you shoot no more arrows against us!
You were troublesome enough beside the Scamander!   510
So now be our saviour and healer,
Lord Apollo. And I greet all the gods of the assembly,
and my own protector Hermes, much-loved herald, by heralds revered;
and the heroes who sent us on our mission, asking them to give
a friendly reception to the forces who've survived combat.
I salute you, palace of my kings, well-loved buildings,
and consecrated seats and gods in the sun,
if ever you welcomed the King long ago with a shine in these eyes of yours,
then do so now, after all this time, in a proper manner.   520
For he has returned, bringing in the darkness
a light you share with all these people here—Agamemnon the King.
So greet him warmly, for it surely befits
the one who has demolished Troy to its foundations
with the mattock of Zeus the Avenger,
The land has been completely tamed with it.
The altars and shrines of the gods have been obliterated,
and the population of the whole country wiped out.
Such is the yoke he has cast upon the neck of Troy;
the King, Atreus' elder son, returns a man blessed by fortune,   530
of men alive today the most worthy

τῶν νῦν· Πάρις γὰρ οὔτε συντελὴς πόλις
ἐξεύχεται τὸ δρᾶμα τοῦ πάθους πλέον.
ὀφλὼν γὰρ ἁρπαγῆς τε καὶ κλοπῆς δίκην
τοῦ ῥυσίου θ᾽ ἥμαρτε καὶ πανώλεθρον
αὐτόχθονον πατρῷον ἔθρισεν δόμον.
διπλᾶ δ᾽ ἔτεισαν Πριαμίδαι θἀμάρτια.

Χορός
κῆρυξ Ἀχαιῶν χαῖρε τῶν ἀπὸ στρατοῦ.

Κῆρυξ
χαίρω γε· τεθνάναι δ᾽ οὐκέτ᾽ ἀντερῶ θεοῖς.

Χορός
ἔρως πατρῴας τῆσδε γῆς σ᾽ ἐγύμνασεν;   540

Κῆρυξ
ὥστ᾽ ἐνδακρύειν γ᾽ ὄμμασιν χαρᾶς ὕπο.

Χορός
τερπνῆς ἄρ᾽ ἦστε τῆσδ᾽ ἐπήβολοι νόσου.

Κῆρυξ
πῶς δή; διδαχθεὶς τοῦδε δεσπόσω λόγου.

Χορός
τῶν ἀντερώντων ἱμέρῳ πεπληγμένοι.

Κῆρυξ
ποθεῖν ποθοῦντα τήνδε γῆν στρατὸν λέγεις;

Χορός
ὡς πόλλ᾽ ἀμαυρᾶς ἐκ φρενός μ᾽ ἀναστένειν.

Κῆρυξ
πόθεν τὸ δύσφρον τοῦτ᾽ ἐπῆν στύγος φρενῶν;

Χορός
πάλαι τὸ σιγᾶν φάρμακον βλάβης ἔχω.

Κῆρυξ
καὶ πῶς; ἀπόντων κοιράνων ἔτρεις τινάς;

Χορός
ὡς νῦν, τὸ σὸν δή, καὶ θανεῖν πολλὴ χάρις.   550

Κῆρυξ
εὖ γὰρ πέπρακται. ταῦτα δ᾽ ἐν πολλῷ χρόνῳ

---

539 γε add. Enger (τεθνᾶναι codd.). οὐκέτ᾽ Tr: οὐκ F. 541 ἐκδακρύειν Tr. 542 ἦστε H. L. Ahrens: ἴστε F: ἦτε Tr. 544 πεπληγμένοι Tyrwhitt: πεπληγμένος codd. 546 μ᾽ add. Scaliger. 547 φρενῶν Hermann: στρατῷ codd.: λεῷ Heimsoeth. 550 ὡς Auratus: ὧν codd.

to be honoured. For neither Paris nor his affiliate city
can boast that his feat exceeded the scale of their suffering.
Convicted of abduction and theft as well,
he forfeited the property he had stolen
and mowed down his ancestral home and its very land in utter ruin.
Priam's sons have paid a double penalty for their crimes.

Chorus
Greetings, Herald from the Achaean army!

Herald
Greetings indeed. I'm happy to die now if the gods so will it.

Chorus
Did craving for your fatherland here oppress you? 540

Herald
Yes, so that my eyes are filled with of tears of joy.

Chorus
The affliction affecting you brings gratification.

Herald
How so? If you explain I'll master the meaning of what you say.

Chorus
The people you longed for loved you in return.

Herald
You mean that our country missed the army as much as the other way round?

Chorus
We felt so dejected that we often sighed out loud.

Herald
What caused this hateful misery?

Chorus
I've long since maintained that silence is the best policy.

Herald
And why so? Were you afraid of anyone while the rulers were away?

Chorus
So much so that—as you said—even death would now be a pleasure. 550

Herald
Yes. There's been a good outcome. But when it comes to the long view

τὰ μέν τις ἂν λέξειεν εὐπετῶς ἔχειν,
τὰ δ᾽ αὖτε κἀπίμομφα. τίς δὲ πλὴν θεῶν
ἅπαντ᾽ ἀπήμων τὸν δι᾽ αἰῶνος χρόνον;
μόχθους γὰρ εἰ λέγοιμι καὶ δυσαυλίας,
σπαρνὰς παρήξεις καὶ κακοστρώτους, τί δ᾽ οὐ
στένοντες, †οὐ λαχόντες† ἤματος μέρος;
τὰ δ᾽ αὖτε χέρσῳ καὶ προσῆν πλέον στύγος·
εὐναὶ γὰρ ἦσαν δηΐων πρὸς τείχεσιν·
ἐξ οὐρανοῦ δὲ κἀπὸ γῆς λειμώνιαι   560
δρόσοι κατεψάκαζον, ἔμπεδον σίνος
ἐσθημάτων, τιθέντες ἔνθηρον τρίχα.
χειμῶνα δ᾽ εἰ λέγοι τις οἰωνοκτόνον,
οἷον παρεῖχ᾽ ἄφερτον Ἰδαία χιών,
ἢ θάλπος, εὖτε πόντος ἐν μεσημβριναῖς
κοίταις ἀκύμων νηνέμοις εὕδοι πεσών·
τί ταῦτα πενθεῖν δεῖ; παροίχεται πόνος·
παροίχεται δέ, τοῖσι μὲν τεθνηκόσιν
τὸ μήποτ᾽ αὖθις μηδ᾽ ἀναστῆναι μέλειν.
τί τοὺς ἀναλωθέντας ἐν ψήφῳ λέγειν,   570
τὸν ζῶντα δ᾽ ἀλγεῖν χρὴ τύχης παλιγκότου;
καὶ πολλὰ χαίρειν συμφοραῖς καταξιῶ.
ἡμῖν δὲ τοῖς λοιποῖσιν Ἀργείων στρατοῦ
νικᾷ τὸ κέρδος, πῆμα δ᾽ οὐκ ἀντιρρέπει·
ὡς κομπάσαι τῷδ᾽ εἰκὸς ἡλίου φάει
ὑπὲρ θαλάσσης καὶ χθονὸς ποτωμένοις·
‘Τροίαν ἑλόντες δή ποτ᾽ Ἀργείων στόλος
θεοῖς λάφυρα ταῦτα τοῖς καθ᾽ Ἑλλάδα
δόμοις ἐπασσάλευσαν ἀρχαῖον γάνος.’
τοιαῦτα χρὴ κλύοντας εὐλογεῖν πόλιν   580
καὶ τοὺς στρατηγούς· καὶ χάρις τιμήσεται
Διὸς τόδ᾽ ἐκπράξασα. πάντ᾽ ἔχεις λόγον.
Χορός
νικώμενος λόγοισιν οὐκ ἀναίνομαι·
ἀεὶ γὰρ ἡβᾷ τοῖς γέρουσιν εὖ μαθεῖν.

552 ἂν Auratus: εὖ codd.   556 κακοστρώτους Tr: κακοτρώτους F.   557 οὐ λαχόντες
corrupta: οὐ κλαίοντες Jacob: ἀσχάλλοντες Margoliouth.   560 δὲ Porson: γὰρ codd.

one could say that some things have fallen out well
while others are regrettable. But who, except the gods,
can avoid suffering for their entire lifetime?
For if I were to detail the hardships—our grim berths,
the terrible bedding in narrow gangways—everything
was lamentable, every hour of the day.
Things were even more vile on dry land too.
Our sleeping quarters were at the enemy's walls.
Drops of rain from the sky and field dew   560
kept dribbling on us, a constant threat
to our clothing and making our hair look wild.
And if one were to describe the wintry weather that killed the birds
when the snows of Ida rendered it intolerable,
or the heat, when the winds failed and the sea fell asleep,
waveless on his noonday couch—
but what's the point in grieving over this? Our suffering is past.
It's past, while the dead need never worry about coming to life again.
Why enumerate the lives expended?   570
Why should a living person feel aggrieved about bad luck?
The situation demands a celebration of these misfortunes.
In our case, as survivors of the Argive force,
the benefits have prevailed; the losses do not weigh as heavy in the scales.
So it's seemly for us, as we fly over sea and land,
to make this boast on this bright day:
'An Argive taskforce once took Troy,
and nailed up these spoils for the gods in temples across Greece
as a dazzling ornament from the olden days'.
Everyone who hears such things must acclaim the city   580
and the generals. And the favour of Zeus, which
accomplished this, shall be venerated. You've heard the whole story.

Chorus

Your words have won the day, I don't deny it.
In old people, the ability to learn always stays young.

δόμοις δὲ ταῦτα καὶ Κλυταιμήστρᾳ μέλειν
εἰκὸς μάλιστα, σὺν δὲ πλουτίζειν ἐμέ.

Κλυταιμήστρα
ἀνωλόλυξα μὲν πάλαι χαρᾶς ὕπο,
ὅτ᾽ ἦλθ᾽ ὁ πρῶτος νύχιος ἄγγελος πυρός,
φράζων ἅλωσιν Ἰλίου τ᾽ ἀνάστασιν.
καί τίς μ᾽ ἐνίπτων εἶπε, 'φρυκτωρῶν δία   590
πεισθεῖσα Τροίαν νῦν πεπορθῆσθαι δοκεῖς;
ἦ κάρτα πρὸς γυναικὸς αἴρεσθαι κέαρ.'
λόγοις τοιούτοις πλαγκτὸς οὖσ᾽ ἐφαινόμην.
ὅμως δ᾽ ἔθυον, καὶ γυναικείῳ νόμῳ
ὀλολυγμὸν ἄλλος ἄλλοθεν κατὰ πτόλιν
ἔλασκον εὐφημοῦντες ἐν θεῶν ἕδραις
θυηφάγον κοιμῶντες εὐώδη φλόγα.
καὶ νῦν τὰ μάσσω μὲν τί δεῖ σέ μοι λέγειν;
ἄνακτος αὐτοῦ πάντα πεύσομαι λόγον.
ὅπως δ᾽ ἄριστα τὸν ἐμὸν αἰδοῖον πόσιν   600
σπεύσω πάλιν μολόντα δέξασθαι·—τί γὰρ
γυναικὶ τούτου φέγγος ἥδιον δρακεῖν,
ἀπὸ στρατείας ἀνδρὶ σώσαντος θεοῦ
πύλας ἀνοῖξαι;—ταῦτ᾽ ἀπάγγειλον πόσει·
ἥκειν θ᾽ ὅπως τάχιστ᾽ ἐράσμιον πόλει·
γυναῖκα πιστὴν δ᾽ ἐν δόμοις εὕροι μολὼν
οἵαν περ οὖν ἔλειπε, δωμάτων κύνα
ἐσθλὴν ἐκείνῳ, πολεμίαν τοῖς δύσφροσιν,
καὶ τἄλλ᾽ ὁμοίαν πάντα, σημαντήριον
οὐδὲν διαφθείρασαν ἐν μήκει χρόνου.   610
οὐδ᾽ οἶδα τέρψιν οὐδ᾽ ἐπίψογον φάτιν
ἄλλου πρὸς ἀνδρὸς μᾶλλον ἢ χαλκοῦ βαφάς.

Κῆρυξ
τοιόσδ᾽ ὁ κόμπος τῆς ἀληθείας γέμων
οὐκ αἰσχρὸς ὡς γυναικὶ γενναίᾳ λακεῖν.

Χορός
αὕτη μὲν οὕτως εἶπε μανθάνοντί σοι
τοροῖσιν ἑρμηνεῦσιν εὐπρεπῶς λόγον.

587   ἀνωλόλυξα μὲν Stephanus: ἀνωλολύξαμεν F.   598   σέ μοι Wiesler: σ᾽ ἐμοὶ codd.
605   θ᾽ add. Blaydes.

These matters are likely to be of particular concern to the palace
and Clytemnestra, besides being advantageous to me.
[*Enter Clytemnestra from the palace*]
Clytemnestra
I raised a joyful shout much earlier,
when the first messenger arrived at night in the form of fire,
reporting the capture and desolation of Troy.
Someone said to me in reproach, 'Are you swayed   590
by beacon fires to believe that Troy has been sacked?
It really is just like a woman to get excited'.
By words such as these I was being made out to be deluded.
Nevertheless I continued to make offerings, and the women,
as is their custom, raised the loud shout everywhere across the town,
applauding the gods in their shrines,
calming the fragrant flame with sacrificial offerings.
So why should you report any more to me now?
I'll hear the full account from the King himself.
I'll hurry to welcome my revered husband   600
in the best way possible as he comes back.
For what pleasure is greater in a woman's eyes
than to open the gates for her husband returning from campaign,
when god has saved his life? Deliver this message to my husband:
he should come as soon as possible, for his city yearns for him.
When he comes he'll find his faithful wife at home,
just exactly as he left her, a loyal dog guarding
his household, hostile to those who bear him ill-will,
the same in every detail, having broken
no seal this long-extended time.   610
For I know no more about gratification with any other man
or a scandalous reputation than I do about dipping bronze.
[*Clytemnestra exits into the house*]
Herald
When such a boast is full of truth
it does a high-minded wife no shame to utter it.
Chorus
She delivered a speech like that to indoctrinate you,
although to astute interpreters it's a façade.

σὺ δ᾽ εἰπέ, κῆρυξ, Μενέλεων δὲ πεύθομαι.
εἰ νόστιμός τε καὶ σεσωσμένος πάλιν
ἥκει σὺν ὑμῖν, τῆσδε γῆς φίλον κράτος.

Κῆρυξ
οὐκ ἔσθ᾽ ὅπως λέξαιμι τὰ ψευδῆ καλὰ   620
ἐς τὸν πολὺν φίλοισι καρποῦσθαι χρόνον.

Χορός
πῶς δῆτ᾽ ἂν εἰπὼν κεδνὰ τἀληθῆ τύχοις;
σχισθέντα δ᾽ οὐκ εὔκρυπτα γίγνεται τάδε.

Κῆρυξ
ἀνὴρ ἄφαντος ἐξ Ἀχαιικοῦ στρατοῦ,
αὐτός τε καὶ τὸ πλοῖον. οὐ ψευδῆ λέγω.

Χορός
πότερον ἀναχθεὶς ἐμφανῶς ἐξ Ἰλίου,
ἢ χεῖμα, κοινὸν ἄχθος, ἥρπασε στρατοῦ;

Κῆρυξ
ἔκυρσας ὥστε τοξότης ἄκρος σκοποῦ·
μακρὸν δὲ πῆμα συντόμως ἐφημίσω.

Χορός
πότερα γὰρ αὐτοῦ ζῶντος ἢ τεθνηκότος   630
φάτις πρὸς ἄλλων ναυτίλων ἐκλῄζετο;

Κῆρυξ
οὐκ οἶδεν οὐδεὶς ὥστ᾽ ἀπαγγεῖλαι τορῶς,
πλὴν τοῦ τρέφοντος Ἡλίου χθονὸς φύσιν.

Χορός
πῶς γὰρ λέγεις χειμῶνα ναυτικῷ στρατῷ
ἐλθεῖν τελευτῆσαί τε δαιμόνων κότῳ;

Κῆρυξ
εὔφημον ἦμαρ οὐ πρέπει κακαγγέλῳ
γλώσσῃ μιαίνειν· χωρὶς ἡ τιμὴ θεῶν.
ὅταν δ᾽ ἀπευκτὰ πήματ᾽ ἄγγελος πόλει
στυγνῷ προσώπῳ πτωσίμου στρατοῦ φέρῃ,
πόλει μὲν ἕλκος ἓν τὸ δήμιον τυχεῖν,   640
πολλοὺς δὲ πολλῶν ἐξαγισθέντας δόμων
ἄνδρας διπλῇ μάστιγι, τὴν Ἄρης φιλεῖ,

618 τε Hermann: γε codd.   622 τύχοις Porson: τύχης F Tr.   624 ἀνὴρ Hermann· ἀνὴρ codd.   639 στυγνῷ F: σμοιῷ M. Schmidt, cf. Hesychius σ1270.

But tell us, Herald, I want to know whether Menelaus,
our country's dear sovereign, is returning alive,
and has arrived with you.

Herald

I can't tell friends agreeable lies   620
that they could enjoy for any length of time.

Chorus

If only you could tell us news both true and pleasing!
It's difficult to conceal it when the two are at variance.

Herald

The man disappeared from the Achaean taskforce,
himself and his ship. I tell no lie.

Chorus

Was he seen putting out to sea from Ilium,
or did a storm, a blight on everybody, snatch him away from the fleet?

Herald

You've hit the target like a consummate archer.
You've described protracted agony concisely.

Chorus

Was he alive or dead according to the rumour   630
circulating amongst the other seamen?

Herald

Nobody knows so as to provide clear information
except the Sun, who nurtures the natural world.

Chorus

So how do you say that the storm came upon the fleet
through the rancour of the gods, and how it ended?

Herald

It's not right to pollute an auspicious day by voicing bad news.
They should be kept apart for the sake of honouring the gods.
When a grim-faced messenger brings to a city
dreaded sorrows with news of an army's fall,
on the one hand a single communal wound inflicted on the state,   640
but, on the other hand, many men led out for sacrifice from many homes,
by the twofold whip which Ares loves—

δίλογχον ἄτην, φοινίαν ξυνωρίδα·
τοιῶνδε μέντοι πημάτων σεσαγμένον
πρέπει λέγειν παιᾶνα τόνδ᾽ Ἐρινύων.
σωτηρίων δὲ πραγμάτων εὐάγγελον
ἥκοντα πρὸς χαίρουσαν εὐεστοῖ πόλιν,
πῶς κεδνὰ τοῖς κακοῖσι συμμείξω, λέγων
χειμῶν᾽ Ἀχαιοῖς οὐκ ἀμήνιτον θεῶν;
ξυνώμοσαν γάρ, ὄντες ἔχθιστοι τὸ πρίν,   650
πῦρ καὶ θάλασσα, καὶ τὰ πίστ᾽ ἐδειξάτην
φθείροντε τὸν δύστηνον Ἀργείων στρατόν.
ἐν νυκτὶ δυσκύμαντα δ᾽ ὠρώρει κακά.
ναῦς γὰρ πρὸς ἀλλήλαισι Θρήκιαι πνοαὶ
ἤρεικον· αἱ δὲ κεροτυπούμεναι βίᾳ
χειμῶνι τυφῶ σὺν ζάλῃ τ᾽ ὀμβροκτύπῳ
ᾤχοντ᾽ ἄφαντοι ποιμένος κακοῦ στρόβῳ.
ἐπεὶ δ᾽ ἀνῆλθε λαμπρὸν ἡλίου φάος,
ὁρῶμεν ἀνθοῦν πέλαγος Αἰγαῖον νεκροῖς
ἀνδρῶν Ἀχαιῶν ναυτικοῖς τ᾽ ἐρειπίοις.   660
ἡμᾶς γε μὲν δὴ ναῦν τ᾽ ἀκήρατον σκάφος
ἤτοι τις ἐξέκλεψεν ἢ ᾽ξῃτήσατο
θεός τις, οὐκ ἄνθρωπος, οἴακος θιγών.
Τύχη δὲ σωτὴρ ναῦν θέλουσ᾽ ἐφέζετο,
ὡς μήτ᾽ ἐν ὅρμῳ κύματος ζάλην ἔχειν
μήτ᾽ ἐξοκεῖλαι πρὸς κραταίλεως χθόνα.
ἔπειτα δ᾽ Ἅιδην πόντιον πεφευγότες,
λευκὸν κατ᾽ ἦμαρ, οὐ πεποιθότες τύχῃ,
ἐβουκολοῦμεν φροντίσιν νέον πάθος,
στρατοῦ καμόντος καὶ κακῶς σποδουμένου.   670
καὶ νῦν ἐκείνων τ᾽ εἴ τίς ἐστιν ἐμπνέων,
λέγουσιν ἡμᾶς ὡς ὀλωλότας, τί μήν;
ἡμεῖς τ᾽ ἐκείνους ταὔτ᾽ ἔχειν δοξάζομεν.
γένοιτο δ᾽ ὡς ἄριστα. Μενέλεως γὰρ οὖν
πρῶτόν τε καὶ μάλιστα προσδόκα μολεῖν.
εἰ δ᾽ οὖν τις ἀκτὶς ἡλίου νιν ἱστορεῖ

---

644 σεσαγμένον Schütz: σεσαγμένων codd.   649 Ἀχαιοῖς...θεῶν Dobree: Ἀχαιῶν...θεοῖς codd.   655 κεροτυπούμεναι Wasse: κερωτυπούμεναι codd.   660 ναυτικοῖς τ᾽ ἐρειπίοις Auratus: ναυτικῶν τ᾽ ἐριπίων codd.   671 τ᾽ add. Hartung.   672 τί μήν Linwood: τί μή codd.   673 ταὔτ᾽ Stanley: ταῦτ᾽ codd.

double-edged destruction, a gory double blow—
it's when indeed he's laden with sorrows of this kind
that he should intone this victory-song of the Erinyes.
But for a man coming with good news of deliverance
to a city rejoicing in its happiness—
how shall I combine good with bad as I report
the storm, not unconnected with divine wrath, that afflicted the Achaeans?
For fire and sea, former bitterest of enemies,   650
swore an alliance and offered as pledge
the joint destruction of the miserable Achaean fleet.
The difficulties had arisen with rough waves during the night.
Winds from Thrace kept making the ships crash into each other.
They were gouged forcefully by the horns
of the wintry typhoon and the gusts of pelting rain;
they disappeared, whirled out of sight by a malign herdsman.
But when the bright sun's light arose
we saw the Aegean Sea abloom with corpses
of Achaean men amidst the wreckage of the ships.   660
But we ourselves and our ship, its hull ungouged—
some being, a god rather than a human, rescued us
by stealthy action or verbal appeal, and laid a hand on our helm.
And Fortune, of her own accord, took her seat as Saviour on board,
so we did not take in storm-waves at anchor
and did not run aground on rocky shores.
Then, having escaped a watery death,
in the pale daylight, scarcely believing what had befallen,
we paid close attention to this fresh disaster,
our fleet debilitated and badly battered.   670
And now, if any of those men are alive,
they are saying that we are dead. Why wouldn't they?
We imagine the same to be the case with them.
May things work out for the best. First and most importantly
anticipate that Menelaus will arrive.
So if any ray of the sun discovers him

καὶ ζῶντα καὶ βλέποντα, μηχαναῖς Διός,
οὔπω θέλοντος ἐξαναλῶσαι γένος,
ἐλπίς τις αὐτὸν πρὸς δόμους ἥξειν πάλιν.
τοσαῦτ᾽ ἀκούσας ἴσθι τἀληθῆ κλύων.   680

Χορός
τίς ποτ᾽ ὠνόμαζεν ὧδ᾽   *strophe 1*
    ἐς τὸ πᾶν ἐτητύμως—
μή τις ὄντιν᾽ οὐχ ὁρῶμεν προνοί-
    αισι τοῦ πεπρωμένου
γλῶσσαν ἐν τύχᾳ νέμων;—
τὰν δορίγαμβρον ἀμφινει-
    κῆ θ᾽ Ἑλέναν; ἐπεὶ πρεπόντως
ἑλέναυς, ἕλανδρος, ἑλέ-
    πτολις, ἐκ τῶν ἁβροτίμων   690
προκαλυμμάτων ἔπλευσε
ζεφύρου γίγαντος αὔρᾳ,
πολύανδροί τε φεράσπιδες κυναγοὶ
    κατ᾽ ἴχνος πλατᾶν ἄφαντον
κελσάντων Σιμόεντος ἀ-
    κτὰς ἐπ᾽ ἀεξιφύλλους
δι᾽ Ἔριν αἱματόεσσαν.

Ἰλίῳ δὲ κῆδος ὀρ-   *antistrophe 1*
    θώνυμον τελεσσίφρων   700
μῆνις ἤλασεν, τραπέζας ἀτί-
    μωσιν ὑστέρῳ χρόνῳ
καὶ ξυνεστίου Διὸς
πρασσομένα τὸ νυμφότι-
    μον μέλος ἐκφάτως τίοντας,
†ὑμέναιον ὃς† τότ᾽ ἐπέρ-
    ρεπεν γαμβροῖσιν ἀείδειν·
μεταμανθάνουσα δ᾽ ὕμνον

689 ἑλέναυς Blomfield: ἑλένας F.   695 πλατᾶν Heath: πλάταν codd.
697 ἐπ᾽ ἀεξιφύλλους Casaubon: ἐπ᾽ ἀξιφύλλους Tr: εἰς ἀεξιφύλλους F.   701 ἤλασεν
Porson: ἤλασε codd.   702 ἀτίμωσιν Canter: ἀτίμως ἵν᾽ FF: ἀτίμως Tr.

alive and well—by the machinations of Zeus,
if he does not yet want to wipe the race out—
there's a hope that he'll come home again.
Having listened this far, be sure you've heard the truth.   680
[*Exit the Herald to the harbour*]

Chorus [*singing and dancing*]
Who was it who once decided   *strophe 1*
on giving such a completely suitable name to Helen,
the bride of the spear, the cause of the conflict?
Was it some invisible being,
who had foresight of what was destined to happen,
whose tongue hit on the truth?
For true to her name,
she meant Hell for ships, Hell for men,
Hell for a city, when she   690
sailed out and away
from her luxurious, expensive
draperies, wafted by the breath of the strong west wind;
a vast force of shielded huntsmen
followed in the oars' traces as they vanished,
when they beached her ship on the leafy banks
of the river Simois—
sent by Strife to create carnage.

For divine wrath, working its will,   *antistrophe 1*
inflicted on Ilium
a marriage whose name meant misery.   700
Divine wrath took reprisals, in due course,
for the outrage done to the laws of hospitality
and to Zeus, protector of the hearth,
punishing those who baldly sang
the song in honour of the bride,
the marriage hymn,
which fell that day
on the groom's family to sing.
But Priam's ancient city   710

Πριάμου πόλις γεραιὰ 710
πολύθρηνον μέγα που στένει κικλήσκου-
σα Πάριν τὸν αἰνόλεκτρον,
παμπορθῆ †πολύθρηνον αἰ-
ῶν' ἀμφὶ πολίταν†
μέλεον αἷμ' ἀνατλᾶσα.

ἔθρεψεν δὲ λέοντος ἶ-   *strophe 2*
   νιν δόμοις ἀγάλακτον οὕ-
   τως ἀνὴρ φιλόμαστον,
ἐν βιότου προτελείοις 720
ἄμερον, εὐφιλόπαιδα
καὶ γεραροῖς ἐπίχαρτον.
πολέα δ' ἔσκ' ἐν ἀγκάλαις
νεοτρόφου τέκνου δίκαν,
φαιδρωπὸς ποτὶ χεῖρα σαί-
   νων τε γαστρὸς ἀνάγκαις.

χρονισθεὶς δ' ἀπέδειξεν ἦ-   *antistrophe 2*
   θος τὸ πρὸς τοκέων· χάριν
γὰρ τροφεῦσιν ἀμείβων
μηλοφόνοισι σὺν ἄταις 730
δαῖτ' ἀκέλευστος ἔτευξεν·
αἵματι δ' οἶκος ἐφύρθη,
ἄμαχον ἄλγος οἰκέταις
μέγα σίνος πολυκτόνον.
ἐκ θεοῦ δ' ἱερεύς τις ἄ-
   'τας δόμοις προσεθρέφθη.

πάραυτα δ' ἐλθεῖν ἐς Ἰλίου πόλιν   *strophe 3*
λέγοιμ' ἂν φρόνημα μὲν
   νηνέμου γαλάνας,

714–15 παμπορθῆ Seidler: παμπρόσθη codd. αἰῶν' ἀμφὶ codd.: αἰῶνα διαὶ Emper
717–18 λέοντος ἶνιν Conington: λέοντα σίνιν codd. 723 ἔσκ' Casaubon: ἔσχ'
codd. 727 ἦθος Conington: ἔθος codd. 729 γὰρ τροφεῦσιν Tr: τροφᾶς γὰρ F.
730 μηλοφόνοισι σὺν Fix: μηλοφόνοισιν F. 736 προσεθρέφθη Porson (προσετρέφθη
Heath): προσετράφη codd.

has learned to sing a different tune,
and I expect is howling noisy dirges,
calling Paris the bridegroom from Hell.
For Troy has endured total annihilation,
her whole life now one big lamentation
for the blood so miserably shed by her citizens.

A man thus reared *strophe 2*
a lion cub in his home,
forcibly weaned while still craving breast milk.
Tame in his early life, 720
he was good with children
and a joy to the elderly.
Often he was held in the arms
like a newborn child,
with his beaming face turned towards his master's hand,
cajoling him into satisfying his hunger pangs.

But in time he grew up and evinced *antistrophe 2*
his true disposition, inherited from his parents,
returning the favour to his foster-parents;
he prepared a feast of slaughtered sheep, 730
wiping out the flock.
The house was befouled with blood,
its inhabitants suffered insurmountable grief
at the damage, the extent of the butchery.
By divine will he was reared to be
a priest of ruin to the household.

At first, I would say, there came to Ilium *strophe 3*
a disposition
of unruffled calm,

ἀκασκαῖον δ᾽ ἄγαλμα πλούτου,   740
μαλθακὸν ὀμμάτων βέλος,
δηξίθυμον ἔρωτος ἄνθος.
παρακλίνασ᾽ ἐπέκρανεν
      δὲ γάμου πικρὰς τελευτάς,
δύσεδρος καὶ δυσόμιλος
συμένα Πριαμίδαισιν,
πομπᾷ Διὸς ξενίου,
νυμφόκλαυτος Ἐρινύς.

παλαίφατος δ᾽ ἐν βροτοῖς γέρων λόγος   *antistrophe 3* 750
τέτυκται, μέγαν τελε-
      σθέντα φωτὸς ὄλβον
τεκνοῦσθαι μηδ᾽ ἄπαιδα θνῄσκειν,
ἐκ δ᾽ ἀγαθᾶς τύχας γένει
βλαστάνειν ἀκόρεστον οἰζύν.
δίχα δ᾽ ἄλλων μονόφρων εἰ-
      μί· τὸ δυσσεβὲς γὰρ ἔργον
μετὰ μὲν πλείονα τίκτει,
σφετέρᾳ δ᾽ εἰκότα γέννᾳ.   760
οἴκων γὰρ εὐθυδίκων
καλλίπαις πότμος αἰεί.

φιλεῖ δὲ τίκτειν Ὕβρις   *strophe 4*
      μὲν παλαιὰ νεά-
      ζουσαν ἐν κακοῖς βροτῶν
ὕβριν τότ᾽ ἢ τόθ᾽, ὅτε τὸ κύ-
      ριον μόλῃ φάος τόκου,
δαίμονά τε τὰν ἄμαχον ἀπόλε-
      μον, ἀνίερον Θράσος, μελαί-
      νας μελάθροισιν Ἄτας,   770
εἰδομέναν τοκεῦσιν.

---

740 δ᾽ add. Porson.   758 δυσσεβὲς γὰρ Pauw: γὰρ δυσσεβὲς codd.   766 ὅτε Klausen:
ὅταν codd.   767 φάος τόκου H.L. Ahrens: νεαρὰ φάους κότον codd.   768 τὰν Hermann:
τὸν codd.

a pleasing ornament of wealth, 740
soft glances passed between eyes,
sexual attraction so sharp it hurts.
But then she changed tack
and brought her marriage to a bitter end,
a curse on the people she lived with and talked to,
driven against the children of Priam
with Zeus god of guests escorting her,
a spirit of revenge whose marriage brought woe.

An ancient saying was created by mankind *antistrophe 3* 750
long ago: when a man's success
grows to adulthood
it produces offspring and doesn't die childless,
and from good fortune
grows the family's insatiable despair.
But I have a mind of my own and disagree.
It's the ungodly deed
that engenders more ungodliness,
bearing a family likeness. 760
For in upright households
children always turn out well.

Amongst wicked people, *strophe 4*
old Outrage tends eventually
to produce a new outrage,
when the appointed day of birth arrives.
With it come the spirit of Recklessness—
uncontrollable, unmanageable, unholy—
a black blight on the household, 770
a blight which takes after its parents.

Δίκα δὲ λάμπει μὲν ἐν   *antistrophe 4*
  δυσκάπνοις δώμασιν,
  τὸν δ' ἐναίσιμον τίει {βίον}.
τὰ χρυσόπαστα δ' ἔδεθλα σὺν
  πίνῳ χερῶν παλιντρόποις
ὄμμασι λιποῦσ', ὅσια προσέμολε, δύναμιν οὐ σέβουσα πλούτου παράσημον αἴνῳ·   780
πᾶν δ' ἐπὶ τέρμα νωμᾷ.

ἄγε δή, βασιλεῦ, Τροίας πτολίπορθ',
Ἀτρέως γένεθλον,
πῶς σε προσείπω; πῶς σε σεβίζω
μήθ' ὑπεράρας μήθ' ὑποκάμψας
καιρὸν χάριτος;
πολλοὶ δὲ βροτῶν τὸ δοκεῖν εἶναι
προτίουσι δίκην παραβάντες.
τῷ δυσπραγοῦντι τ' ἐπιστενάχειν   790
πᾶς τις ἕτοιμος· δῆγμα δὲ λύπης
οὐδὲν ἐφ' ἧπαρ προσικνεῖται·
καὶ ξυγχαίρουσιν ὁμοιοπρεπεῖς
ἀγέλαστα πρόσωπα βιαζόμενοι.
ὅστις δ' ἀγαθὸς προβατογνώμων,
οὐκ ἔστι λαθεῖν ὄμματα φωτός,
τὰ δοκοῦντ' εὔφρονος ἐκ διανοίας
ὑδαρεῖ σαίνειν φιλότητι.
σὺ δέ μοι τότε μὲν στέλλων στρατιὰν
Ἑλένης ἕνεκ', οὐ γάρ σ' ἐπικεύσω,   800
κάρτ' ἀπομούσως ἦσθα γεγραμμένος,
οὐδ' εὖ πραπίδων οἴακα νέμων
θράσος ἐκ θυσιῶν
ἀνδράσι θνήσκουσι κομίζων.

---

775 βίον seclusit H.L. Ahrens.   776 ἔδεθλα Auratus: ἐσθλὰ codd.   778 προσέμολε
Hermann: προσέβα τοῦ codd.   783 πτολίπορθ' Blomfield: πολίπορθ' codd.   790 τ'
Hermann: δ' codd.   800 σ' add. Musgrave.   803 θράσος ἐκ θυσιῶν H.L. Ahrens: θάρσος
ἑκούσιον codd.

But Uprightness shines brightly *antistrophe 4*
in smoky, shabby homes
and honours the right-thinking man.
With averted eyes she leaves
gold-encrusted mansions,
where hands have been fouled,
and moves to innocent homes.
She does not respect
the power that comes with wealth falsely praised, 780
and she steers everything to its conclusion.

[*During the following intoned choral passage, Agamemnon enters from
the direction of the harbour, on a carriage with Cassandra; Clytemnestra
enters from the palace with women slaves carrying elaborately decorated
purple textiles*]

Chorus [*intoning*]
Greetings, my King, Troy's destroyer,
offspring of Atreus.
How shall I salute you? How shall I honour you
without either exceeding or falling short
of the appropriate degree of politeness?
Many people think that appearances are paramount,
and overstep what's right.
And when someone's unsuccessful, everyone's prepared
to respond with a sigh. But no real pang of misery 790
penetrates to their core.
They join in the joy of others, feigning similar expressions,
and force themselves to smile.
But a good judge of livestock
can't be taken in by the look in the eyes of a man
who fakes an attitude of goodwill
although his fawning esteem is a sham.
Then, when you were marshalling the army
for Helen's sake—for I won't hide it from you—
you were portrayed most inartistically in my eyes, 800
as exercising poor judgement
in using sacrifices to stir up bravado
in dying men.

νῦν δ᾽ οὐκ ἀπ᾽ ἄκρας φρενὸς οὐδ᾽ ἀφίλως
εὔφρων πόνον εὖ τελέσασιν <ἐγώ>.
γνώσῃ δὲ χρόνῳ διαπευθόμενος
τόν τε δικαίως καὶ τὸν ἀκαίρως
πόλιν οἰκουροῦντα πολιτῶν.

Ἀγαμέμνων
πρῶτον μὲν Ἄργος καὶ θεοὺς ἐγχωρίους   810
δίκη προσειπεῖν, τοὺς ἐμοὶ μεταιτίους
νόστου δικαίων θ᾽ ὧν ἐπραξάμην πόλιν
Πριάμου· δίκας γὰρ οὐκ ἀπὸ γλώσσης θεοὶ
κλύοντες ἀνδροθνῆτας Ἰλίου φθορὰς
ἐς αἱματηρὸν τεῦχος οὐ διχορρόπως
ψήφους ἔθεντο· τῷ δ᾽ ἐναντίῳ κύτει
ἐλπὶς προσῄει χειρὸς οὐ πληρουμένῳ.
καπνῷ δ᾽ ἁλοῦσα νῦν ἔτ᾽ εὔσημος πόλις.
ἄτης θύελλαι ζῶσι· συνθνῄσκουσα δὲ
σποδὸς προπέμπει πίονας πλούτου πνοάς.   820
τούτων θεοῖσι χρὴ πολύμνηστον χάριν
τίνειν, ἐπείπερ καὶ πάγας ὑπερκότους
ἐφραξάμεσθα καὶ γυναικὸς οὕνεκα
πόλιν διημάθυνεν Ἀργεῖον δάκος,
ἵππου νεοσσός, ἀσπιδηφόρος λεώς,
πήδημ᾽ ὀρούσας ἀμφὶ Πλειάδων δύσιν·
ὑπερθορὼν δὲ πύργον ὠμηστὴς λέων
ἄδην ἔλειξεν αἵματος τυραννικοῦ.
θεοῖς μὲν ἐξέτεινα φροίμιον τόδε·
τὰ δ᾽ ἐς τὸ σὸν φρόνημα, μέμνημαι κλύων,   830
καὶ φημὶ ταὐτὰ καὶ συνήγορόν μ᾽ ἔχεις.
παύροις γὰρ ἀνδρῶν ἐστι συγγενὲς τόδε,
φίλον τὸν εὐτυχοῦντ᾽ ἄνευ φθόνου σέβειν.
δύσφρων γὰρ ἰὸς καρδίαν προσήμενος
ἄχθος διπλοίζει τῷ πεπαμένῳ νόσον,
τοῖς τ᾽ αὐτὸς αὐτοῦ πήμασιν βαρύνεται
καὶ τὸν θυραῖον ὄλβον εἰσορῶν στένει.

---

806   πόνον Bourdelot: πόνος codd.   823   ἐφραξάμεσθα Francken: ἐπραξάμεσθα codd.
825   ἀσπιδηφόρος Blomfield: ἀσπιδήστροφος F: ἀσπιδόστροφος Tr.   831   ταὐτὰ Auratus:
ταῦτα codd.   835   πεπαμένῳ Porson: πεπαμμένῳ F.

But now, with all my heart and with no hard feelings
I extend goodwill to those who have successfully completed their labours.
You will in time discover by enquiry
which citizens have acted uprightly in guarding the state,
and which unsuitably.

Agamemnon [*speaks*]
First, it's right that I greet Argos and the local gods   810
who share the credit for my safe return
and for the penalty I exacted from Priam's city.
For the gods did not hear any cases made,
but unanimously cast their ballots in the bloody urn
in favour of the murderous destruction of Ilium.
The only thing that went near the other urn was hope.
Even now the city's fall is still obvious from the smoke.
The winds of destruction are still blowing,
and the dying embers discharge the greasy vapours of erstwhile wealth.   820
For this we owe the gods a permanent debt of gratitude,
since we put up a fence of fury round the city,
and for a woman's sake it has been pulverised by the beast of Argos,
the horse's offspring, the shield-bearing army
that leapt and charged at the waning of the Pleiades.
Vaulting high over the ramparts, the ravenous lion
slurped his fill of royal blood.
This has been my extended preliminary address to the gods.
But in regard to your sentiments, which I heard and am mindful of,   830
I say the same thing and advocate your view.
For hardly anyone is by nature capable
of valuing, without envy, a friend's success.
The venom of malice, settling on the heart,
doubles the burden borne by the man with this malady.
He's weighed down by his own pain,
but also groans when he witnesses others' success.

εἰδὼς λέγοιμ' ἄν, εὖ γὰρ ἐξεπίσταμαι
ὁμιλίας κάτοπτρον, εἴδωλον σκιᾶς
δοκοῦντας εἶναι κάρτα πρευμενεῖς ἐμοί.   840
μόνος δ' Ὀδυσσεύς, ὅσπερ οὐχ ἑκὼν ἔπλει,
ζευχθεὶς ἕτοιμος ἦν ἐμοὶ σειραφόρος·
εἴτ' οὖν θανόντος εἴτε καὶ ζῶντος πέρι
λέγω. τὰ δ' ἄλλα πρὸς πόλιν τε καὶ θεοὺς
κοινοὺς ἀγῶνας θέντες ἐν πανηγύρει
βουλευσόμεσθα. καὶ τὸ μὲν καλῶς ἔχον
ὅπως χρονίζον εὖ μενεῖ βουλευτέον·
ὅτῳ δὲ καὶ δεῖ φαρμάκων παιωνίων,
ἤτοι κέαντες ἢ τεμόντες εὐφρόνως
πειρασόμεσθα πῆμ' ἀποστρέψαι νόσου.   850
νῦν δ' ἐς μέλαθρα καὶ δόμους ἐφεστίους
ἐλθὼν θεοῖσι πρῶτα δεξιώσομαι,
οἵπερ πρόσω πέμψαντες ἤγαγον πάλιν.
νίκη δ' ἐπείπερ ἕσπετ', ἐμπέδως μένοι.

Κλυταιμήστρα
ἄνδρες πολῖται, πρέσβος Ἀργείων τόδε,
οὐκ αἰσχυνοῦμαι τοὺς φιλάνορας τρόπους
λέξαι πρὸς ὑμᾶς· ἐν χρόνῳ δ' ἀποφθίνει
τὸ τάρβος ἀνθρώποισιν. οὐκ ἄλλων πάρα
μαθοῦσ', ἐμαυτῆς δύσφορον λέξω βίον
τοσόνδ' ὅσον περ οὗτος ἦν ὑπ' Ἰλίῳ.   860
τὸ μὲν γυναῖκα πρῶτον ἄρσενος δίχα
ἧσθαι δόμοις ἔρημον ἔκπαγλον κακόν,
πολλὰς κλύουσαν κληδόνας παλιγκότους·
καὶ τὸν μὲν ἥκειν, τὸν δ' ἐπεσφέρειν κακοῦ
κάκιον ἄλλο πῆμα, λάσκοντας δόμοις.
καὶ τραυμάτων μὲν εἰ τόσων ἐτύγχανεν
ἀνὴρ ὅδ', ὡς πρὸς οἶκον ὠχετεύετο
φάτις, τέτρηται δικτύου πλείω λέγειν.
εἰ δ' ἦν τεθνηκώς, ὡς ἐπλήθυον λόγοι,

---

850 πῆμ' ἀποστρέψαι νόσου Porson: πήματος τρέψαι νόσον codd.   863 κληδόνας
Auratus: ἡδονὰς codd.   868 τέτρηται H.L.Ahrens: τέτρωται codd.   869 ἐπλήθυον
Porson: ἐπλήθυνον codd.

I speak with knowledge (for I understand the mirror of social interaction),
that the loyalty professed by some towards me is a shadowy illusion.   840
Only Odysseus, the one man who didn't want to sail to Troy,
once he was harnessed to my cause, readily worked in partnership.
This statement applies regardless of whether he's alive or dead.
As for other matters, in regard to the state and our collective gods,
we shall set up an assembly to debate
and deliberate. Where things are going well
we need to consider how to maintain them permanently.
But where there's also need of healing medicine,
whether by cauterisation or surgery, we shall try
graciously to avert the pain associated with the disease.   850
Now I'll advance into the palace and to the household hearth
to salute the gods first of all,
who once sent me forth, and have brought me back again.
May my attendant Victory remain constant!

Clytemnestra

Citizens, you respected elders of Argos,
I'm not ashamed to address you on the subject
of my love for my man. People get over
their timidity eventually. From my own experience and no one else's
I can describe my own intolerable life
during the entire time that he was beneath the walls of Ilium.   860
For a start, it's a terrible hardship for a woman
to sit at home alone, deprived of her husband,
receiving incessant malign rumours,
and for one messenger after another to arrive reporting
a calamity worse than the one before, shrieking it out to the whole household.
When it comes to injuries, if my husband here had received the number
suggested by the rumours that kept being conveyed to the house,
you'd say that there were more holes in him than in a net.
And if he'd died as frequently as reports were indicating,

τρισώματός τᾶν Γηρυὼν ὁ δεύτερος 870
πολλὴν ἄνωθεν, τὴν κάτω γὰρ οὐ λέγω,
χθονὸς τρίμοιρον χλαῖναν ἐξηύχει λαβεῖν,
ἅπαξ ἑκάστῳ κατθανὼν μορφώματι.
τοιῶνδ' ἕκατι κληδόνων παλιγκότων
πολλὰς ἄνωθεν ἀρτάνας ἐμῆς δέρης
ἔλυσαν ἄλλοι πρὸς βίαν λελημμένης.
ἐκ τῶνδέ τοι παῖς ἐνθάδ' οὐ παραστατεῖ,
ἐμῶν τε καὶ σῶν κύριος πιστωμάτων,
ὡς χρῆν, Ὀρέστης· μηδὲ θαυμάσῃς τόδε.
τρέφει γὰρ αὐτὸν εὐμενὴς δορύξενος 880
Στρόφιος ὁ Φωκεύς, ἀμφίλεκτα πήματα
ἐμοὶ προφωνῶν, τόν θ' ὑπ' Ἰλίῳ σέθεν
κίνδυνον, εἴ τε δημόθρους ἀναρχία
βουλὴν καταρρίψειεν, ὥστε σύγγονον
βροτοῖσι τὸν πεσόντα λακτίσαι πλέον.
τοιάδε μέντοι σκῆψις οὐ δόλον φέρει.
ἔμοιγε μὲν δὴ κλαυμάτων ἐπίσσυτοι
πηγαὶ κατεσβήκασιν, οὐδ' ἔνι σταγών.
ἐν ὀψικοίτοις δ' ὄμμασιν βλάβας ἔχω
τὰς ἀμφί σοι κλαίουσα λαμπτηρουχίας 890
ἀτημελήτους αἰέν. ἐν δ' ὀνείρασιν
λεπταῖς ὑπαὶ κώνωπος ἐξηγειρόμην
ῥιπαῖσι θωύσσοντος, ἀμφί σοι πάθη
ὁρῶσα πλείω τοῦ ξυνεύδοντος χρόνου.
νῦν ταῦτα πάντα τλᾶσ' ἀπενθήτῳ φρενὶ
λέγοιμ' ἂν ἄνδρα τόνδε τῶν σταθμῶν κύνα,
σωτῆρα ναὸς πρότονον, ὑψηλῆς στέγης
στῦλον ποδήρη, μονογενὲς τέκνον πατρί,
γαῖαν φανεῖσαν ναυτίλοις παρ' ἐλπίδα,
κάλλιστον ἦμαρ εἰσιδεῖν ἐκ χείματος, 900
ὁδοιπόρῳ διψῶντι πηγαῖον ῥέος·
τερπνὸν δὲ τἀναγκαῖον ἐκφυγεῖν ἅπαν.
τοιοῖσδέ τοί νιν ἀξιῶ προσφθέγμασιν.

---

870 τᾶν Wellauer: τ' ἂν codd.   871 del. Schütz.   872 λαβεῖν Paley: λαβών codd.
878 πιστωμάτων Spanheim: πιστευμάτων codd.   898 στῦλον Tr: στόλον F.   899 γαῖαν
Blomfield: καὶ γῆν F.   903 τοί νιν Schütz: τοίνυν F.

like a second Geryon with three bodies   870
he'd boast that he had three times been covered with earth
(a large amount needed for his upper half, though I can't tell about the lower),
having died once in each of his three forms.
On account of such malign rumours as these
other people often cut me down from nooses
which I'd forced around my neck.
These are the reasons why our child, trustee
of our mutual pledges, does not stand beside me
as he ought—Orestes. Don't be surprised at this.
Our ally Stropheus the Phocian, who's well disposed to us,   880
is raising him, after forewarning me
about twin disasters—the danger you were in at Ilium,
and the possibility that the populace might talk itself into anarchy
and overthrow the council;
it's human nature to kick a man when he's down.
This explanation involves no deceit.
As for myself, my streaming tears have dried up.
Not one drop remains.
But my eyes are sore from staying up all night,
weeping at the watchfires laid for you   890
but neglected always. I was repeatedly woken by the low hum
of a buzzing mosquito from dreams in which I witnessed
you suffer more than was possible during the time I was asleep.
Now, however, after coping with all this, with my mind freed from sorrow,
I'd salute my husband here as the dog that watches the cattle pens,
the forestay on which the ship's safety depends, the pillar
supporting the high roof from a firm foundation,
an only child to a father, land appearing to seamen when hope is lost,
a lovely day dawning after a storm,   900
spurting spring-water to a thirsty traveller.
It's always pleasurable to relieve a pressing need.
I really consider him worthy of salutations of this kind.

φθόνος δ᾽ ἀπέστω· πολλὰ γὰρ τὰ πρὶν κακὰ
ἠνειχόμεσθα. νῦν δέ μοι, φίλον κάρα,
ἔκβαιν᾽ ἀπήνης τῆσδε, μὴ χαμαὶ τιθεὶς
τὸν σὸν πόδ᾽, ὦναξ, Ἰλίου πορθήτορα.
δμῳαί, τί μέλλεθ᾽, αἷς ἐπέσταλται τέλος
πέδον κελεύθου στορνύναι πετάσμασιν;
εὐθὺς γενέσθω πορφυρόστρωτος πόρος   910
ἐς δῶμ᾽ ἄελπτον ὡς ἂν ἡγῆται δίκη.
τὰ δ᾽ ἄλλα φροντὶς οὐχ ὕπνῳ νικωμένη
θήσει δικαίως σὺν θεοῖς εἱμαρμένα.

Ἀγαμέμνων
Λήδας γένεθλον, δωμάτων ἐμῶν φύλαξ,
ἀπουσίᾳ μὲν εἶπας εἰκότως ἐμῇ·
μακρὰν γὰρ ἐξέτεινας· ἀλλ᾽ ἐναισίμως
αἰνεῖν, παρ᾽ ἄλλων χρὴ τόδ᾽ ἔρχεσθαι γέρας·
καὶ τἄλλα μὴ γυναικὸς ἐν τρόποις ἐμὲ
ἄβρυνε, μηδὲ βαρβάρου φωτὸς δίκην
χαμαιπετὲς βόαμα προσχάνῃς ἐμοί,   920
μηδ᾽ εἵμασι στρώσασ᾽ ἐπίφθονον πόρον
τίθει· θεούς τοι τοῖσδε τιμαλφεῖν χρεών·
ἐν ποικίλοις δὲ θνητὸν ὄντα κάλλεσιν
βαίνειν ἐμοὶ μὲν οὐδαμῶς ἄνευ φόβου.
λέγω κατ᾽ ἄνδρα, μὴ θεόν, σέβειν ἐμέ.
χωρὶς ποδοψήστρων τε καὶ τῶν ποικίλων
κληδὼν αὐτεῖ· καὶ τὸ μὴ κακῶς φρονεῖν
θεοῦ μέγιστον δῶρον. ὀλβίσαι δὲ χρὴ
βίον τελευτήσαντ᾽ ἐν εὐεστοῖ φίλῃ.
εἰ πάντα δ᾽ ὣς πράσσοιμ᾽ ἄν, εὐθαρσὴς ἐγώ.   930
Κλυταιμήστρα
καὶ μὴν τόδ᾽ εἰπὲ μὴ παρὰ γνώμην ἐμοί.
Ἀγαμέμνων
γνώμην μὲν ἴσθι μὴ διαφθεροῦντ᾽ ἐμέ.
Κλυταιμήστρα
ηὔξω θεοῖς δείσας ἂν ὧδ᾽ ἔρξειν τάδε;

909 στορνύναι Elmsley: στρωννύναι F.   933 ἔρξειν Headlam: ἔρδειν F.

But let envy absent itself: we were previously enduring
many hardships. So now, dear one, please get down from
the carriage, but don't touch the earth,
my King, with the foot that's conquered Ilium.
What are you waiting for, slave women—you, to whom
the office has been assigned of covering his path with material?
Hurry up! Let his path be swathed in purple,   910
so that Justice may conduct him into a home he did not expect to see.
I'll organise everything else with vigilant mindfulness,
and in the right way in accordance with the gods and what is ordained.
[*The slave women spread the textiles and Agamemnon dismounts from the
vehicle*]

Agamemnon

Child of Leda, guardian of my household,
your speech has well complemented the length of my absence,
since it was very long! But it's by other people
than you that the appropriate tributes should be paid.
As for the rest, stop cosseting me like a woman,
and don't, like some barbarian man,
prostrate yourself on the ground, gaping at me as you clamour,   920
and don't bring down envy in my path by swathing
it in fabrics! It's the gods who should be honoured in this way.
I don't believe a mortal can tread on beautiful tapestries
without feeling afraid. Respect me as a man, not a god, I tell you.
Rumours run rife even without foot rugs
and patterned fabrics. Good sense is
the best gift the gods can give.
Only the man who dies content can be called happy.
If I always act in accordance with these principles, I am confident in
    this respect.   930

Clytemnestra

But next, tell me your true opinion on this question.

Agamemnon

You can be sure that I won't compromise my true opinion.

Clytemnestra

If you were afraid, would you make a vow to the gods to do this?

Ἀγαμέμνων
εἴπερ τις εἰδώς γ᾽ εὖ τόδ᾽ ἐξεῖπεν τέλος.
Κλυταιμήστρα
τί δ᾽ ἂν δοκεῖ σοι Πρίαμος, εἰ τάδ᾽ ἤνυσεν;
Ἀγαμέμνων
ἐν ποικίλοις ἂν κάρτα μοι βῆναι δοκεῖ.
Κλυταιμήστρα
μή νυν τὸν ἀνθρώπειον αἰδεσθῇς ψόγον.
Ἀγαμέμνων
φήμη γε μέντοι δημόθρους μέγα σθένει.
Κλυταιμήστρα
ὁ δ᾽ ἀφθόνητός γ᾽ οὐκ ἐπίζηλος πέλει.
Ἀγαμέμνων
οὔτοι γυναικός ἐστιν ἱμείρειν μάχης.   940
Κλυταιμήστρα
τοῖς δ᾽ ὀλβίοις γε καὶ τὸ νικᾶσθαι πρέπει.
Ἀγαμέμνων
ἦ καὶ σὺ νίκην τήνδε δήριος τίεις;
Κλυταιμήστρα
πιθοῦ· κρατεῖς μέντοι παρείς γ᾽ ἑκὼν ἐμοί.
Ἀγαμέμνων
ἀλλ᾽ εἰ δοκεῖ σοι ταῦθ᾽, ὑπαί τις ἀρβύλας
λύοι τάχος, πρόδουλον ἔμβασιν ποδός.
καὶ τοῖσδέ μ᾽ ἐμβαίνονθ᾽ ἀλουργέσιν θεῶν
μή τις πρόσωθεν ὄμματος βάλοι φθόνος.
πολλὴ γὰρ αἰδὼς δωματοφθορεῖν ποσὶν
φθείροντα πλοῦτον ἀργυρωνήτους θ᾽ ὑφάς.
τούτων μὲν οὕτω· τὴν ξένην δὲ πρευμενῶς   950
τήνδ᾽ ἐσκόμιζε· τὸν κρατοῦντα μαλθακῶς
θεὸς πρόσωθεν εὐμενῶς προσδέρκεται.
ἑκὼν γὰρ οὐδεὶς δουλίῳ χρῆται ζυγῷ.
αὕτη δὲ πολλῶν χρημάτων ἐξαίρετον
ἄνθος, στρατοῦ δώρημ᾽, ἐμοὶ ξυνέσπετο.

---

934 ἐξεῖπεν Auratus: ἐξεῖπον F. 935 δοκεῖ Stanley· δοκῇ F. 943 κρατεῖς ... παρείς
Weil: κράτος ... πάρες F. 948 δωματοφθορεῖν Schütz: σωματοφθορεῖν F. 954 αὕτη
Auratus: αὐτὴ F.

Agamemnon
Yes, if someone with expertise declared I should perform it as a duty.
Clytemnestra
And don't you think that Priam would have done it, if he had succeeded
    as you have?
Agamemnon
Yes, I think he would certainly walk on tapestries.
Clytemnestra
Then disregard the censure of ordinary mortals.
Agamemnon
And yet the voice of the people is an important force.
Clytemnestra
The man who isn't envied doesn't have anything worth vying for.
Agamemnon
It isn't womanly to be keen on fighting.   940
Clytemnestra
True, but it in successful people even conceding victory can be appropriate.
Agamemnon
Do you really value this victory in combat?
Clytemnestra
Do it! You're still in charge if you give in to me of your own free will.
Agamemnon
Well, if that's how you see it, let someone quickly
undo my shoes, which serve my footsteps like slaves.
And while I walk upon these purple products of the sea,
may no envy strike me from the eye of a god far away.
For there's much at issue in wasting household resources
and harming wealth and expensive textiles with one's feet.
So much for this. Give this foreign woman a gracious welcome.   950
A god looks approvingly from afar on a gentle overlord,
since nobody assumes the yoke of slavery of their own free will.
She's an outstanding ornament worth a great deal of money,
a gift from the army, and she joined my train.

ἐπεὶ δ᾽ ἀκούειν σοῦ κατέστραμμαι τάδε,
εἶμ᾽ ἐς δόμων μέλαθρα πορφύρας πατῶν.

Κλυταιμήστρα
ἔστιν θάλασσα, τίς δέ νιν κατασβέσει;
τρέφουσα πολλῆς πορφύρας ἰσάργυρον
κηκῖδα παγκαίνιστον, εἱμάτων βαφάς.   960
οἶκος δ᾽ ὑπάρχει τῶνδε σὺν θεοῖς ἅλις
ἔχειν· πένεσθαι δ᾽ οὐκ ἐπίσταται δόμος.
πολλῶν πατησμὸν δ᾽ εἱμάτων ἂν ηὐξάμην,
δόμοισι προυνεχθέντος ἐν χρηστηρίοις,
ψυχῆς κόμιστρα τῆσδε μηχανωμένη.   965
ῥίζης γὰρ οὔσης φυλλὰς ἵκετ᾽ ἐς δόμους,
σκιὰν ὑπερτείνασα σειρίου κυνός.
καὶ σοῦ μολόντος δωματῖτιν ἑστίαν,
θάλπος μὲν ἐν χειμῶνι σημαίνεις μολόν·
ὅταν δὲ τεύχῃ Ζεὺς ἀπ᾽ ὄμφακος πικρᾶς   970
οἶνον, τότ᾽ ἤδη ψῦχος ἐν δόμοις πέλει,
ἀνδρὸς τελείου δῶμ᾽ ἐπιστρωφωμένου.
Ζεῦ, Ζεῦ τέλειε, τὰς ἐμὰς εὐχὰς τέλει·
μέλοι δέ τοι σοὶ τῶν περ ἂν μέλλῃς τελεῖν.

Χορός
τίπτε μοι τόδ᾽ ἐμπέδως   *strophe 1*
δεῖμα προστατήριον
καρδίας τερασκόπου ποτᾶται,
μαντιπολεῖ δ᾽ ἀκέλευστος ἄμισθος ἀοιδά,
οὐδ᾽ ἀποπτύσαι δίκαν   980
δυσκρίτων ὀνειράτων
θάρσος εὐπειθὲς ἵ-
    ζει φρενὸς φίλον θρόνον;
χρόνος δ᾽ ἐπεὶ πρυμνησίων ξυνεμβολαῖς

959 ἰσάργυρον Salmasius: εἰς ἄργυρον F.   961 ἅλις Karsten: ἄναξ F.   963 δ᾽
εἱμάτων Canter: δειμάτων F.   965 μηχανωμένη Scaliger: μηχανωμένης F.   969 μολόν
Voss: μολών F.   970 Ζεὺς Scaliger: Ζεύς τ᾽ F.   972 ἐπιστρωφωμένου Victorius:
ἐπιστροφωμένου Tr: ἐπιστρεφωμένου F.   982 εὐπειθὲς Jacob: εὐπιθὲς F.   982–3 ἵζει
Scaliger: ἵξει Tr F.   984 ξυνεμβολαῖς Schneider: ξυνεμβόλοις codd.

But since I've been compelled to listen to you about this,
I'll step on purple fabrics as I go into my palace home.
[*He walks over the textiles and enters the palace*]
Clytemnestra
There is the sea, and who shall drain it dry?
It produces the liquor of abundant purple-fish for dying clothes,
never fading and worth its weight in silver.   960
The household is such that it possesses, thanks to gods,
a sufficiency of these things. Our house doesn't know how to be poor.
I'd have made a vow to have many textiles trampled on
if the house had been allocated this task by oracles
and I was working out how pay a ransom for this person's life.
While the root remains, leaves still grow into the house,
spreading their shade against the searing Dog Star.
With your arrival at the domestic hearth,
you signal that warmth has come in wintertime.
And when Zeus produces wine from the bitter,   970
unripe grape, then coolness permeates the house,
if the man who is its consummate head is in residence.
Zeus, Zeus the fulfiller, consummate my prayers!
It's for you to fulfil what you intend to do.
[*Clytemnestra enters the palace, followed by her slave women*]

Chorus [*sing and dance*]
Why does this terror   *strophe 1*
hover relentlessly
in front of my soothsaying soul?
Why does my song, unbidden and unwaged, make prophecies?
Why doesn't a reassuring sense of courage   980
occupy the throne of my mind
and discard the terror
like an incomprehensible dream?
Time has grown old

†ψαμμίας ἀκάτα† παρή-
    βησεν, εὖθ᾽ ὑπ᾽ Ἴλιον
ὦρτο ναυβάτας στρατός.

πεύθομαι δ᾽ ἀπ᾽ ὀμμάτων   *antistrophe 1*
νόστον, αὐτόμαρτυς ὤν·
τὸν δ᾽ ἄνευ λύρας ὅμως ὑμνῳδεῖ   990
θρῆνον Ἐρινύος αὐτοδίδακτος ἔσωθεν
θυμός, οὐ τὸ πᾶν ἔχων
ἐλπίδος φίλον θράσος.
σπλάγχνα δ᾽ οὔτοι ματᾴ-
    ζει πρὸς ἐνδίκοις φρεσὶν
τελεσφόροις δίναις κυκλούμενον κέαρ.
εὔχομαι δ᾽ ἐξ ἐμᾶς
    ἐλπίδος ψύθη πεσεῖν
ἐς τὸ μὴ τελεσφόρον.   1000

μάλα γέ τοι τὸ μεγάλας ὑγιείας   *strophe 2*
ἀκόρεστον τέρμα· νόσος γάρ
γείτων ὁμότοιχος ἐρείδει.
καὶ πότμος εὐθυπορῶν
*
ἀνδρὸς ἔπαισεν ἄφαντον ἕρμα.
καὶ πρὸ μέν τι χρημάτων
κτησίων ὄκνος βαλὼν
σφενδόνας ἀπ᾽ εὐμέτρου,   1010
οὐκ ἔδυ πρόπας δόμος
πημονᾶς γέμων ἄγαν,
οὐδ᾽ ἐπόντισε σκάφος.
πολλά τοι δόσις ἐκ Διὸς ἀμφιλα-
    φής τε καὶ ἐξ ἀλόκων ἐπετειᾶν
νῆστιν ὤλεσεν νόσον.

985 ψαμμίας ἀκάτα παρήβησεν F: ψάμμος (Wecklein): ἄμπτα Wilamowitz. 990 ὅμως
Auratus: ὅπως F. 991 Ἐρινύος Porson: ἐρινvὸσ F. 999 ψύθη Stephanus: ψύδη F.
1001 τὸ μεγάλας Paley: τᾶς πολλᾶς codd. 1005 Excidunt post vel ante 1005 eiusdem
metri versus. 1012 πημονᾶς Victorius: πημονὰς codd.

since the mooring-cables were cast from the sterns
so the sand flew
when the army set sail for Ilium.

I know they've returned   *antistrophe 1*
from the evidence which I've seen with my own eyes.
But my heart sings inside me nevertheless   990
the lyreless lament of the Erinyes
which it has taught itself, for it can't fully feel
the welcome confidence that hope brings.
Not without reason do my innards speak to me,
my heart racing as it beats, in waves of fulfilment,
along with my sense of what's right.
I pray that my expectations
will turn out false,
and will be unfulfilled.   1000

Really excellent health knows   *strophe 2*
no bounds. But its neighbour, disease, shares
a common wall with it and leans on it hard.
And a man's destiny, although travelling in a straight direction,
[*line missing*]
strikes an invisible reef.
But if trepidation has previously jettisoned
a part of the wealth of possessions,
by judicious use of the ship's crane,   1010
the household is saved from sinking entire,
overloaded with misery,
and doesn't submerge its hull.
The ample, abundant gift from Zeus
and annual ploughing of furrows
oust the disease of famine.

τὸ δ᾽ ἐπὶ γᾶν πεσὸν ἅπαξ θανάσιμον   *antistrophe 2*
πρόπαρ ἀνδρὸς μέλαν αἷμα τίς ἂν   1020
πάλιν ἀγκαλέσαιτ᾽ ἐπαείδων;
οὐδὲ τὸν ὀρθοδαῆ
τῶν φθιμένων ἀνάγειν
Ζεὺς †αὖτ᾽ ἔπαυσ᾽† ἐπ᾽ ἀβλαβείᾳ.
εἰ δὲ μὴ τεταγμένα
μοῖρα μοῖραν ἐκ θεῶν
εἶργε μὴ πλέον φέρειν,
προφθάσασα καρδία
γλῶσσαν ἂν τάδ᾽ ἐξέχει.
νῦν δ᾽ ὑπὸ σκότῳ βρέμει   1030
θυμαλγής τε καὶ οὐδὲν ἐπελπομέ-
     να ποτὲ καίριον ἐκτολυπεύσειν
ζωπυρουμένας φρενός.

Κλυταιμήστρα
εἴσω κομίζου καὶ σύ, Κασάνδραν λέγω,
ἐπεί σ᾽ ἔθηκε Ζεὺς ἀμηνίτως δόμοις
κοινωνὸν εἶναι χερνίβων, πολλῶν μέτα
δούλων σταθεῖσαν κτησίου βωμοῦ πέλας·
ἔκβαιν᾽ ἀπήνης τῆσδε, μηδ᾽ ὑπερφρόνει.
καὶ παῖδα γάρ τοί φασιν Ἀλκμήνης ποτὲ   1040
πραθέντα τλῆναι δουλίας μάζης τυχεῖν.
εἰ δ᾽ οὖν ἀνάγκη τῆσδ᾽ ἐπιρρέποι τύχης,
ἀρχαιοπλούτων δεσποτῶν πολλὴ χάρις.
οἳ δ᾽ οὔποτ᾽ ἐλπίσαντες ἤμησαν καλῶς,
ὠμοί τε δούλοις πάντα καὶ παρὰ στάθμην.
ἔχεις παρ᾽ ἡμῶν οἷά περ νομίζεται.
Χορός
σοί τοι λέγουσα παύεται σαφῆ λόγον.
ἐντός δ᾽ ἁλοῦσα μορσίμων ἀγρευμάτων
πείθοι᾽ ἄν, εἰ πείθοι᾽· ἀπειθοίης δ᾽ ἴσως.

1019 πεσὸν Auratus: πεσόνθ᾽ codd.   1024 ἀπέπαυσεν Hartung: ἂν ἔπαυσεν Martin:
κατένευσεν West. αὖτ᾽ ἔπαυσ᾽ codd.   1401 δουλίας μάζης τυχεῖν Enger: δουλείας μάζης
βία F.   1048 ἁλοῦσα Haupt: ἂν οὖσα codd.

But once a murdered man's dark blood   *antistrophe 2*
has fallen before him to the ground,   1020
who can call him back to life by incantations?
Not even he who properly knew
how to bring men back from the dead
was allowed by Zeus to do so without being harmed.
But if one fate ordained by the gods
didn't prevent another fate
from gaining the upper hand,
my heart could take precedence over my tongue
and become open to view.
But as it is, my heart drones in darkness,   1030
distressed and without hope
that it will ever unravel anything
in due season when my soul catches light.

[*Enter Clytemnestra from the palace*]
Clytemnestra [*speaks*]
Get yourself indoors too—Cassandra, I mean,
since Zeus has benevolently made you
a joint partaker in the holy water of this house, standing amidst
numerous slaves at the altar of the god who guards possessions.
Get down from this carriage, and don't be overly proud.
For they say that once even Alcmena's son   1040
endured being sold and eating the coarse bread of slavery.
So if this fate bears down of necessity,
it's something to be grateful for if the masters inherit ancient wealth.
But those who have reaped a fine harvest when they never expected to
are savage to slaves in every respect, even beyond the general rule.
You're having from us the treatment that's customary.
Chorus [*to Cassandra*]
It's you to whom she's finished speaking, and her meaning is clear.
Since you're caught in destiny's hunting nets,
you may obey, if you're compliant; but perhaps you'll disobey.

Κλυταιμήστρα
ἀλλ᾽ εἴπερ ἐστι μὴ χελιδόνος δίκην   1050
ἀγνῶτα φωνὴν βάρβαρον κεκτημένη,
ἔσω φρενῶν λέγουσα πείθω νιν λόγῳ.

Χορός
ἕπου. τὰ λῷστα τῶν παρεστώτων λέγει.
πείθου λιποῦσα τόνδ᾽ ἁμαξήρη θρόνον.

Κλυταιμήστρα
οὔτοι θυραίαν τῇδ᾽ ἐμοὶ σχολὴ πάρα
τρίβειν· τὰ μὲν γὰρ ἑστίας μεσομφάλου
ἕστηκεν ἤδη μῆλα πρὸς σφαγὰς πάρος,
ὡς οὔποτ᾽ ἐλπίσασι τήνδ᾽ ἕξειν χάριν.
σὺ δ᾽ εἴ τι δράσεις τῶνδε, μὴ σχολὴν τίθει.
εἰ δ᾽ ἀξυνήμων οὖσα μὴ δέχῃ λόγον,   1060
σὺ δ᾽ ἀντὶ φωνῆς φράζε καρβάνῳ χερί.

Χορός
ἑρμηνέως ἔοικεν ἡ ξένη τοροῦ
δεῖσθαι· τρόπος δὲ θηρὸς ὡς νεαιρέτου.

Κλυταιμήστρα
ἦ μαίνεταί γε καὶ κακῶν κλύει φρενῶν,
ἥτις λιποῦσα μὲν πόλιν νεαίρετον
ἥκει, χαλινὸν δ᾽ οὐκ ἐπίσταται φέρειν,
πρὶν αἱματηρὸν ἐξαφρίζεσθαι μένος.
οὐ μὴν πλέω ῥίψασ᾽ ἀτιμασθήσομαι.

Χορός
ἐγὼ δ᾽, ἐποικτίρω γάρ, οὐ θυμώσομαι.
ἴθ᾽, ὦ τάλαινα, τόνδ᾽ ἐρημώσασ᾽ ὄχον,   1070
εἴκουσ᾽ ἀνάγκῃ τῇδε καίνισον ζυγόν.

Κασάνδρα
ὀτοτοτοῖ πόποι δᾶ.   *strophe 1*
ὦπολλον ὦπολλον.

1055 τῇδ᾽ Musgrave: τήνδ᾽ F.   1057 πάρος Musgrave: πύρος F.   1071 εἴκουσ᾽
Robortello: ἑκοῦσ᾽ codd.

Clytemnestra [*to the chorus*]
Well, unless she speaks   1050
some unknown barbarian language, like a swallow,
I'm inducing her with words she understands.
Chorus [*to Cassandra*]
Follow her. Under the circumstances, what she says is best.
Obey her and leave your seat in the carriage.
Clytemnestra
I don't have leisure-time to waste outside here:
the animals have already long taken their place
near the central hearth for sacrifice—
gratification such as we never hoped to experience.
[*to Cassandra*] You there—don't dawdle if you're to take any part in this.
If you don't understand and don't grasp my meaning—   1060
[*to the chorus*] and you there, tell her with a barbarous hand instead of speech.
Chorus
It seems that the foreign woman needs a lucid interpreter;
she's acting like a wild creature that's just been seized.
Clytemnestra
No, she's crazed and listening to her blighted mind,
because she's come after leaving her city that's just been seized,
and doesn't know how to tolerate the bit,
until she has discharged her temper in bloody spume.
No, I'll not throw more words away on being disrespected.
[*Exit Clytemnestra into the palace*]
Chorus
I, however, since I pity her, won't be angry.
Come, wretched woman, and leave this carriage.   1070
Give in to necessity and try on this new yoke.

Cassandra [*sings*]   *strophe 1*
Otototoi popoi da!
O Apollo O Apollo.

Χορός
τί ταῦτ᾽ ἀνωτότυξας ἀμφὶ Λοξίου;
οὐ γὰρ τοιοῦτος ὥστε θρηνητοῦ τυχεῖν.

Κασσσάνδρα
ὀτοτοτοῖ πόποι δᾶ.   *antistrophe 1*
ὦπολλον ὦπολλον.

Χορός
ἡ δ᾽ αὖτε δυσφημοῦσα τὸν θεὸν καλεῖ
οὐδὲν προσήκοντ᾽ ἐν γόοις παραστατεῖν.

Κασσάνδρα
Ἄπολλον Ἄπολλον   *strophe 2* 1080
ἀγυιᾶτ᾽, ἀπόλλων ἐμός.
ἀπώλεσας γὰρ οὐ μόλις τὸ δεύτερον.

Χορός
χρήσειν ἔοικεν ἀμφὶ τῶν αὐτῆς κακῶν.
μένει τὸ θεῖον δουλίᾳ περ ἐν φρενί.

Κασσάνδρα
Ἄπολλον Ἄπολλον   *antistrophe 2* 1085
ἀγυιᾶτ᾽, ἀπόλλων ἐμός.
ἆ ποῖ ποτ᾽ ἤγαγές με; πρὸς ποίαν στέγην;

Χορός
πρὸς τὴν Ἀτρειδῶν· εἰ σὺ μὴ τόδ᾽ ἐννοεῖς,
ἐγὼ λέγω σοι· καὶ τάδ᾽ οὐκ ἐρεῖς ψύθη.

Κασσάνδρα
μισόθεον μὲν οὖν, πολλὰ συνίστορα   *strophe 3* 1090
αὐτοφόνα κακὰ †κάρτάναι†
ἀνδρος σφαγεῖον καὶ πεδορραντήριον.

1084   περ ἐν Schütz: παρ᾽ ἐν M: παρὲν F: παρὸν Tr.   1091   καρατόμα Kayser: καὶ
ἀρτάνας Lachmann: κάρτάναι M: κάρτάνας Tr.   1092   σφαγεῖον Turnebus: σφάγιον codd.

Chorus [*speak*]
Why did you start wailing *ototoi* in connection with Loxias?
It's not appropriate for him to be associated with mourning.

Cassandra [*sings*]   *antistrophe 1*
Otototoi popoi da!
O Apollo O Apollo.

Chorus [*speak*]
Once again she's addressing with ill-omened words
the god whose presence doesn't belong in laments.

Cassandra [*sings*]   *strophe 2* 1080
Apollo Apollo,
god of the streets, my destroyer.
For you've destroyed me utterly a second time.

Chorus [*speak*]
She seems about to prophesy about her own troubles.
The divine spark survives in a mind even though it's enslaved.

Cassandra [*sings*]
Apollo Apollo,   *antistrophe 2*
god of the streets, my destroyer.
Aah, wherever have you brought me? To what kind of house?

Chorus [*speak*]
To that of the Atreidai; I'm telling you this
in case you don't realise; you'll not deny it's true.

Cassandra [*sings*]
No, it's a house that hates the gods, witness to   *strophe 3* 1090
copious foul kin-murders, beheadings—
a human abattoir, floors spattered with blood.

Χορός
ἔοικεν εὖρις ἡ ξένη κυνὸς δίκην
εἶναι, ματεύει δ᾽ ὧν ἀνευρήσει φόνον.

Κασσάνδρα
μαρτυρίοισι γὰρ τοῖσδ᾽ ἐπιπείθομαι·   *antistrophe 3*
κλαιόμενα τάδε βρέφη σφαγάς,
ὀπτάς τε σάρκας πρὸς πατρὸς βεβρωμένας.

Χορός
καὶ μὴν κλέος σοῦ μαντικὸν πεπυσμένοι
ἦμεν· προφήτας δ᾽ οὔτινας μαστεύομεν.

Κασσάνδρα
ἰὼ πόποι, τί ποτε μήδεται;   *strophe 4* 1100
τί τόδε νέον ἄχος; μέγα
μέγ᾽ ἐν δόμοισι τοῖσδε μήδεται κακὸν
ἄφερτον φίλοισιν, δυσίατον; ἀλκὰ δ᾽
ἑκὰς ἀποστατεῖ.

Χορός
τούτων ἄιδρίς εἰμι τῶν μαντευμάτων.
ἐκεῖνα δ᾽ ἔγνων· πᾶσα γὰρ πόλις βοᾷ.

Κασσάνδρα
ἰὼ τάλαινα, τόδε γὰρ τελεῖς,   *antistrophe 4*
τὸν ὁμοδέμνιον πόσιν
λουτροῖσι φαιδρύνασα—πῶς φράσω τέλος;
τάχος γὰρ τόδ᾽ ἔσται· προτείνει δὲ χεὶρ ἐκ   1110
χερὸς ὀρέγματα.

Χορός
οὔπω ξυνῆκα· νῦν γὰρ ἐξ αἰνιγμάτων
ἐπαργέμοισι θεσφάτοις ἀμηχανῶ.

1094   ἀνευρήσει Porson: ἂν εὑρήσῃ M: ἐφευρήσει F.   1095   μαρτυρίοισι Pauw:
μαρτυρίοις codd.   τοῖσδ᾽ ἐπιπείθομαι Abresch: τοῖσδε πεπείθομαι codd.   1098   καὶ μὴν
Paley: ἤμην M.   1111   ὀρέγματα Hermann: ὀρεγόμενα M: ὀρεγμένα cett.

Chorus [*speak*]
The foreigner seems keen-scented, like a dog,
and is on a trail where she'll detect murder.

Cassandra [*sings*]
Yes, for these are my proofs: *antistrophe 3*
these babies howling at their own slaughter,
their flesh roasted and devoured by their father.

Chorus [*speak*]
Yes, we've been informed of your famous mantic power,
but we're not looking for any prophets.

Cassandra [*sings*]
Iō popoi! Whatever's the plan?   *strophe 4* 1100
What's this new anguish?
Massive, massive trouble planned within this house,
intolerable to loved ones, incurable.
And help is far away.

Chorus [*speak*]
I have no idea about these divinations.
But I understood the others; the whole city resounds with them.

Cassandra [*sings*]
Iō wretched woman, is this what you're doing,   *antistrophe 4*
bathing your husband, who shares your bed,
to make him glisten? How shall I speak of the conclusion?
It will be done soon; she's stretching out first this hand   1110
and then the other.

Chorus [*speak*]
I still don't understand, for I'm baffled now,
by obscure prophecies emanating from riddles.

Κασσάνδρα
ἒ ἒ, παπαῖ παπαῖ, τί τόδε φαίνεται;   *strophe 5*
ἦ δίκτυόν τί γ᾽ Ἅιδου;
ἀλλ᾽ ἄρκυς ἡ ξύνευνος, ἡ ξυναιτία
φόνου. στάσις δ᾽ ἀκόρετος γένει
κατολολυξάτω θύματος λευσίμου.

Χορός
ποίαν Ἐρινὺν τήνδε δώμασιν κέλῃ
ἐπορθιάζειν; οὔ με φαιδρύνει λόγος.   1120
ἐπὶ δὲ καρδίαν ἔδραμε κροκοβαφὴς
σταγών, ἅτε καιρία πτώσιμος
ξυνανύτει βίου δύντος αὐγαῖς·
ταχεῖα δ᾽ ἄτα πέλει.

Κασσάνδρα
ἆ ἆ, ἰδοὺ ἰδού· ἄπεχε τῆς βοὸς   *antistrophe 5*
τὸν ταῦρον· ἐν πέπλοισι
μελαγκέρῳ λαβοῦσα μηχανήματι
τύπτει· πίτνει δ᾽ ἐν ἐνύδρῳ τεύχει.
δολοφόνου λέβητος τύχαν σοι λέγω.

Χορός
οὐ κομπάσαιμ᾽ ἂν θεσφάτων γνώμων ἄκρος   1130
εἶναι, κακῷ δέ τῳ προσεικάζω τάδε.
ἀπὸ δὲ θεσφάτων τίς ἀγαθὰ φάτις
βροτοῖς τέλλεται; κακῶν γὰρ διαὶ
πολυεπεῖς τέχναι θεσπιῳδὸν
φόβον φέρουσιν μαθεῖν.

Κασσάνδρα
ἰὼ ἰὼ ταλαίνας κακόποτμοι τύχαι·   *strophe 6*
τὸ γὰρ ἐμὸν θροῶ πάθος ἐπεγχύδαν.
ποῖ δή με δεῦρο τὴν τάλαιναν ἤγαγες;
οὐδέν ποτ᾽ εἰ μὴ ξυνθανουμένην. τί γάρ;

1115 Ἅιδου Schütz: ἀΐδου codd.   1117 ἀκόρετος Bothe: ἀκόρεστος codd.   1122 καιρία Dindorf: καὶ δορία M.   1128 ἐν add. Schütz.   1133 τέλλεται Emperius: στέλλεται codd. διαὶ Hermann: διὰ M.   1137 ἐπεγχύδαν Headlam: ἐπεγχέασα codd.

Cassandra [*sings*]

E, e, papai papai, what's this that appears?   *strophe 5*
Is it some hunting-net of Hades?
It's a snare that sleeps with him, the accomplice
in murder. Let the faction that never gets enough of this family
raise the triumphal cry over a condemned victim.

Chorus [*speak*]

What is this Erinys in the house that you're ordering
to raise a cry? Your words don't cheer me.   1120

[*sing*] Yellow-stained drops course
over my heart, falling at the critical moment,
and waning with the last rays of life's light:
destruction comes speedily.

Cassandra [*sings*]

Ah! Ah! Look, look! keep the bull   *antistrophe 5*
away from the cow! She's holding him
in cloths and stabs him with a device
that has a handle of black horn. He collapses in the vessel of water.
It's a fate in a treacherous, murderous bath I'm speaking of.

Chorus [*speak*]

I don't claim to be good at judging oracles,   1130
but I think these mean something bad.

[*sing*] What good pronouncement ever comes
to mortals from oracles? Through predicting bad things,
their skill and wordiness make men learn
how to be frightened of prophecy.

Cassandra [*sings*]   *strophe 6*

Iō iō, the misery of my ill-fated destiny.
I lament my suffering, pouring it in on top.
Why did you bring me here in my misery?
For no reason except to die, and not alone. For what else?

Χορός

φρενομανής τις εἶ θεοφόρητος, ἀμ-   1140
φὶ δ᾽ αὐτᾶς θροεῖς
νόμον ἄνομον, οἷά τις ξουθὰ
ἀκόρετος βοᾶς, φεῦ, ταλαίναις φρεσίν
Ἴτυν Ἴτυν στένουσ᾽ ἀμφιθαλῆ κακοῖς
ἀηδὼν μόρον.

Κασσάνδρα

ἰὼ ἰὼ λιγείας βίος ἀηδόνος·   *antistrophe 6*
περέβαλον γάρ οἱ πτεροφόρον δέμας
θεοὶ γλυκύν τ᾽ αἰῶνα κλαυμάτων ἄτερ·
ἐμοὶ δὲ μίμνει σχισμὸς ἀμφήκει δορί.

Χορός

πόθεν ἐπισσύτους θεοφόρους τ᾽ ἔχεις   1150
ματαίους δύας,
τὰ δ᾽ ἐπίφοβα δυσφάτῳ κλαγγᾷ
μελοτυπεῖς ὁμοῦ τ᾽ ὀρθίοις ἐν νόμοις;
πόθεν ὅρους ἔχεις θεσπεσίας ὁδοῦ
κακορρήμονας;

Κασσάνδρα

ἰὼ γάμοι γάμοι Πάριδος ὀλέθριοι φίλων.   *strophe 7*
ἰὼ Σκαμάνδρου πάτριον ποτόν.
τότε μὲν ἀμφὶ σὰς ἀϊόνας τάλαιν᾽
ἠνυτόμαν τροφαῖς·
νῦν δ᾽ ἀμφὶ Κωκυτόν τε κἀχερουσίους   1160
ὄχθους ἔοικα θεσπιῳδήσειν τάχα.

Χορός

τί τόδε τορὸν ἄγαν ἔπος ἐφημίσω;
νεόγνος ἂν ἀΐων μάθοι.
πέπληγμαι δ᾽ ὑπαὶ δάκει φοινίῳ

1143   ἀκόρετος Aldina: ἀκόρεστος codd.   1145   μόρον Page: βίον codd.   1146   βίος
ἀηδόνος Page: ἀηδόνος μόρον codd.   1147   περέβαλον Wieseler: περεβάλοντο M.
1148   αἰῶνα Μγρ: ἀγῶνα codd.   1163   ἂν ἀΐων Karsten: ἀνθρώπων F Tr.   1164   ὑπαὶ Tr:
ὑπὸ codd. F.   δάκει Hermann: δήγματι codd.

Chorus [*sing*]
Your mind is crazed and you're possessed by a god,   1140
voicing an unmelodic melody
about your own plight, like the chirruping nightingale,
insatiably crying out—alas—as she groans 'Itys, Itys'
in her misery-loving heart,
for a death so abundant in sorrows.

Cassandra [*sings*]   *antistrophe 6*
Iō iō, for the life of the clear-voiced nightingale!
For the gods wrapped her up in a winged body
and gave her a sweet life free from tears.
But what awaits me is being split open by a double-edged shaft.

Chorus [*sing*]
Where do these agonising onslaughts of divine possession   1150
come from to no purpose?
And why do you set these horrors to a tune
with cacophonous shrieks and piercing refrains?
How can you know what the limits are
to your ominous prophetic course?

Cassandra [*sings*]
Iō the marriage, the marriage of Paris, lethal to those close to him. *strophe 7*
Iō the waters of the Scamander, drunk by my ancestors.
I used then to be raised and nurtured
on your shores, miserable as I am,
but now it seems that I'll soon chant my prophecies   1160
beside the Cocytus and on the banks of the Acheron.

Chorus [*sing*]
What is this that you've uttered, words whose meaning is all too clear?
A newborn if he heard them could understand.
I'm assaulted by murderous pain,

δυσαλγεῖ τύχᾳ μινυρὰ θρεομένας,
θραύματ᾽ ἐμοὶ κλύειν.

Κασσάνδρα
ἰὼ πόνοι πόνοι πόλεος ὀλομένας τὸ πᾶν.   *antistrophe 7*
ἰὼ πρόπυργοι θυσίαι πατρὸς
πολυκανεῖς βοτῶν ποιονόμων· ἄκος δ᾽
        οὐδὲν ἐπήρκεσαν   1170
τὸ μὴ πόλιν μὲν ὥσπερ οὖν ἔχει παθεῖν.
ἐγὼ δὲ θερμόνους τάχ᾽ ἐν πέδῳ βαλῶ.

Χορός
ἑπόμενα προτέροισι τάδ᾽ ἐφημίσω.
καί τίς σε κακοφρονῶν τίθη-
        σι δαίμων ὑπερβαρὴς ἐμπίτνων
μελίζειν πάθη γοερὰ θανατοφόρα.
τέρμα δ᾽ ἀμηχανῶ.

Κασσάνδρα
καὶ μὴν ὁ χρησμὸς οὐκέτ᾽ ἐκ καλυμμάτων
ἔσται δεδορκὼς νεογάμου νύμφης δίκην·
λαμπρὸς δ᾽ ἔοικεν ἡλίου πρὸς ἀντολὰς   1180
πνέων ἐσᾴξειν, ὥστε κύματος δίκην
κλύζειν πρὸς αὐγὰς τοῦδε πήματος πολὺ
μεῖζον· φρενώσω δ᾽ οὐκέτ᾽ ἐξ αἰνιγμάτων.
καὶ μαρτυρεῖτε συνδρόμως ἴχνος κακῶν
ῥινηλατούσῃ τῶν πάλαι πεπραγμένων.
τὴν γὰρ στέγην τήνδ᾽ οὔποτ᾽ ἐκλείπει χορὸς
ξύμφθογγος οὐκ εὔφωνος· οὐ γὰρ εὖ λέγει.
καὶ μὴν πεπωκώς γ᾽, ὡς θρασύνεσθαι πλέον,
βρότειον αἷμα κῶμος ἐν δόμοις μένει,
δύσπεμπτος ἔξω, συγγόνων Ἐρινύων.   1190
ὑμνοῦσι δ᾽ ὕμνον δώμασιν προσήμεναι
πρώταρχον ἄτην· ἐν μέρει δ᾽ ἀπέπτυσαν

1165 δυσαλγεῖ Auratus: δυσαγγεῖ codd.   1167 ὀλομένας Casaubon: ὀλωμένας F:
ὀλουμένας Tr.   1174 κακοφρονῶν Schütz: κακοφρονεῖν F.   1181 ἐσᾴξειν Bothe: ἐσ ἥξειν
codd.   1182 κλύζειν Auratus: κλύειν codd.   1192 πρώταρχον Tr: πρώταρχος F.

while you, because of your agonising fate, whimper horribly and shriek,
heart-breaking for me to hear.

Cassandra [*sings*]

Iō the ordeals, the ordeals of my city, completely destroyed! *antistrophe 7*
Iō the frequent sacrifices of grazing animals
slaughtered by my father to save its walls;
but they effected no cure that prevented   1170
the city from suffering as she does.
And I, my mind inflamed, shall soon collapse to the ground.

Chorus [*sing*]

This statement confirms your previous words.
And some malevolent weighty spirit
descends on you and makes you sing
about distress, suffering and death.
I've no idea where it will end.

Cassandra [*speaks*]

And indeed my prophecy will no longer glance out
from behind her veils like a newly-wed bride.
It will spring up on me like a fresh wind blowing   1180
against the rising sun, to surge against its rays
like a wave, far greater than this calamity.
I'll not explain through riddles any more.
And be my witnesses, following me close
as I track the odour of crimes committed long ago.
For a chorus singing in cacophonous unison
is never absent; what it says is not good.
A troupe of revelling kinfolk of the Erinyes
have guzzled human blood, so as to assert themselves the more,
and wait in the house, impossible to drive out.   1190
Sitting within the house, they chant their chant
about the original felony, each in turn spurning

εὐνὰς ἀδελφοῦ τῷ πατοῦντι δυσμενεῖς.
ἥμαρτον, ἢ κυρῶ τι τοξότης τις ὥς;
ἢ ψευδόμαντίς εἰμι θυροκόπος φλέδων;
ἐκμαρτύρησον προυμόσας τό μ' εἰδέναι
λόγῳ παλαιὰς τῶνδ' ἁμαρτίας δόμων.

Χορός
καὶ πῶς ἂν ὅρκος, πῆγμα γενναίως παγέν,
παιώνιος γένοιτο; θαυμάζω δέ σε,
πόντου πέραν τραφεῖσαν ἀλλόθρουν πόλιν   1200
κυρεῖν λέγουσαν, ὥσπερ εἰ παρεστάτεις.

Κασσάνδρα
μάντις μ' Ἀπόλλων τῷδ' ἐπέστησεν τέλει.

Χορός
μῶν καὶ θεός περ ἱμέρῳ πεπληγμένος;

Κασσάνδρα
προτοῦ μὲν αἰδὼς ἦν ἐμοὶ λέγειν τάδε.

Χορός
ἁβρύνεται γὰρ πᾶς τις εὖ πράσσων πλέον.

Κασσάνδρα
ἀλλ' ἦν παλαιστὴς κάρτ' ἐμοὶ πνέων χάριν.

Χορός
ἦ καὶ τέκνων εἰς ἔργον ἦλθετην νόμῳ;

Κασσάνδρα
ξυναινέσασα Λοξίαν ἐψευσάμην.

Χορός
ἤδη τέχναισιν ἐνθέοις ᾑρημένη;

Κασσάνδρα
ἤδη πολίταις πάντ' ἐθέσπιζον πάθη.   1210

Χορός
πῶς δῆτ' ἄνατος ἦσθα Λοξίου κότῳ;

Κασσάνδρα
ἔπειθον οὐδέν' οὐδέν, ὡς τάδ' ἤμπλακον.

Χορός
ἡμῖν γε μὲν δὴ πιστὰ θεσπίζειν δοκεῖς.

1194 κυρῶ Korais: τηρῶ F.   1198 πῆγμα Auratus: πῆμα codd.   1199 σε Auratus: σου
codd.   1203 in codd. post 1204: correxit Hermann.   1207 ἦλθετην Elmsley: ἦλθετον F.
1211 ἄνατος Canter: ' ἄνακτος codd.   1212 οὐδέν' οὐδέν Canter: οὐδὲν οὐδὲν codd.

the brother's marriage bed and loathing its abuser.
Have I missed the target or made a hit like an archer?
Or am I a false prophet, knocking at your door to talk nonsense?
Bear witness on oath that I know the misdeeds
of this household, spoken of since long ago.

Chorus [*speaks*]
And how could an oath, even a pledge honourably given,
provide a cure? But I'm amazed that even though
you were raised overseas, you speak the truth,   1200
as if you'd been present, about a house that speaks another tongue.

Cassandra
The seer Apollo imposed this function on me.

Chorus
Was he lovestruck even though he's a god?

Cassandra
Before now I was ashamed to speak of this.

Chorus
Delicacy is more of an option when someone's enjoying good fortune.

Cassandra
But he wrestled with me, heavily breathing desire.

Chorus
Did you two join in the rite that might produce children?

Cassandra
I gave my consent but deceived Loxias.

Chorus
Were you already possessed of the god-inspired art?

Cassandra
I was already foretelling what the citizens would suffer.   1210

Chorus
How did no damage come to you from Loxias' anger?

Cassandra
Because of that error, I became unable to convince anyone of anything.

Chorus
Yet to us you seem indeed to divine the truth.

Κασσάνδρα
ἰοὺ ἰού, ὢ ὢ κακά.
ὑπ᾽ αὖ με δεινὸς ὀρθομαντείας πόνος
στροβεῖ ταράσσων φροιμίοις δυσφροιμίοις.
ὁρᾶτε τούσδε τοὺς δόμοις ἐφημένους
νέους, ὀνείρων προσφερεῖς μορφώμασιν;
παῖδες θανόντες ὡσπερεὶ πρὸς τῶν φίλων,
χεῖρας κρεῶν πλήθοντες οἰκείας βορᾶς,   1220
σὺν ἐντέροις τε σπλάγχν᾽, ἐποίκτιστον γέμος,
πρέπουσ᾽ ἔχοντες, ὧν πατὴρ ἐγεύσατο.
ἐκ τῶνδε ποινὰς φημὶ βουλεύειν τινὰ
λέοντ᾽ ἄναλκιν ἐν λέχει στρωφώμενον
οἰκουρόν, οἴμοι, τῷ μολόντι δεσπότῃ
ἐμῷ· φέρειν γὰρ χρὴ τὸ δούλιον ζυγόν·
νεῶν δ᾽ ἄπαρχος Ἰλίου τ᾽ ἀναστάτης
οὐκ οἶδεν οἷα γλῶσσα μισητῆς κυνὸς
λείξασα κἀκτείνασα φαιδρὸν οὖς, δίκην
Ἄτης λαθραίου τεύξεται κακῇ τύχῃ.   1230
τοιάδε τόλμα· θῆλυς ἄρσενος φονεὺς
ἔστιν. τί νιν καλοῦσα δυσφιλὲς δάκος
τύχοιμ᾽ ἄν; ἀμφίσβαιναν, ἢ Σκύλλαν τινὰ
οἰκοῦσαν ἐν πέτραισι, ναυτίλων βλάβην,
θύουσαν Ἅιδου μητέρ᾽ ἄσπονδόν τ᾽ Ἄρη
φίλοις πνέουσαν; ὡς δ᾽ ἐπωλολύξατο
ἡ παντότολμος, ὥσπερ ἐν μάχης τροπῇ,
δοκεῖ δὲ χαίρειν νοστίμῳ σωτηρίᾳ.
καὶ τῶνδ᾽ ὅμοιον εἴ τι μὴ πείθω· τί γάρ;
τὸ μέλλον ἥξει. καὶ σύ μ᾽ ἐν τάχει παρὼν   1240
ἄγαν γ᾽ ἀληθόμαντιν οἰκτίρας ἐρεῖς.
Χορός
τὴν μὲν Θυέστου δαῖτα παιδείων κρεῶν
ξυνῆκα καὶ πέφρικα, καὶ φόβος μ᾽ ἔχει
κλύοντ᾽ ἀληθῶς οὐδὲν ἐξῃκασμένα.
τὰ δ᾽ ἄλλ᾽ ἀκούσας ἐκ δρόμου πεσὼν τρέχω.

1216 δυσφροιμίοις add. Hermann: ἐφημένους (e proximo versu) codd. eiciendum.
1227 δ᾽ add. Voss.   1229 λείξασα Tyrwhitt, κἀκτείνασα Canter, φαιδρὸν οὖς H.L. Ahrens:
λέξασα καὶ κτείνασα φαιδρόνους codd.   1235 Ἄρη Porson: ἀρὰν codd.   1240 μ᾽ ἐν
Auratus: μὴν codd.   1242 παιδείων Schütz: παιδίων codd.

Cassandra

Iou iou, ah, ah, misery!
Once again the awful pain of true divination
makes me reel, agitating me with its unwanted onset.
Do you see those young ones who've taken their seat
in the house, looking like figures in dreams?
Like children killed by their kinfolk,
they stand out conspicuously, their hands brimming
with the meat of their own flesh, along with   1220
the entrails and innards—most pitiful cargo—which their father tasted.
I can tell from them that a strengthless housekeeping lion
turns over in bed and plots, alas, against my master
(for I must bear the yoke of slavery) as he returns.
The admiral of the fleet and the destroyer of Ilium
is unaware what evil fate she will furnish him with,
having licked him with the tongue of a hateful hound
and cocked her gleaming ear towards him, like clandestine Ruin.
Such is her daring: she's a female murderer of a male.   1230
What kind of unlovely monster should I
call her? An amphisbaena, or a Scylla
living on rocks to cause harm to sailors,
a seething mother of Hades, who breathes war without respite
on family members? How she raised the triumph shout,
this all-daring woman, as in the battle rout,
feigning delight at his safe return!
It's all the same whether I convince anyone of any of this. So what?
The future will come. And you, soon you'll be present,   1240
pitying me, and call me a prophet who speaks all too truly.

Chorus

Thyestes' feasting on his children's flesh I understood
and I shuddered and terror seizes me
as I hear the truth, rather than any semblance of it.
But I completely lose track about the other things I heard.

Κασσάνδρα
Ἀγαμέμνονός σέ φημ᾽ ἐπόψεσθαι μόρον.
Χορός
εὔφημον, ὦ τάλαινα, κοίμησον στόμα.
Κασσάνδρα
ἀλλ᾽ οὔτι παιὼν τῷδ᾽ ἐπιστατεῖ λόγῳ.
Χορός
οὔκ, εἴπερ ἔσται γ᾽· ἀλλὰ μὴ γένοιτό πως.
Κασσάνδρα
σὺ μὲν κατεύχῃ, τοῖς δ᾽ ἀποκτείνειν μέλει.   1250
Χορός
τίνος πρὸς ἀνδρὸς τοῦτ᾽ ἄχος πορσύνεται;
Κασσάνδρα
ἦ κάρτα τἄρα παρεκόπης χρησμῶν ἐμῶν
Χορός
τοῦ γὰρ τελοῦντος οὐ ξυνῆκα μηχανήν.
Κασσάνδρα
καὶ μὴν ἄγαν γ᾽ Ἕλλην᾽ ἐπίσταμαι φάτιν.
Χορός
καὶ γὰρ τὰ πυθόκραντα· δυσμαθῆ δ᾽ ὅμως.
Κασσάνδρα
παπαῖ, οἷον τὸ πῦρ· ἐπέρχεται δέ μοι.
ὀτοτοῖ, Λύκει᾽ Ἄπολλον, οἲ ἐγὼ ἐγώ.
αὕτη δίπους λέαινα συγκοιμωμένη
λύκῳ, λέοντος εὐγενοῦς ἀπουσίᾳ,
κτενεῖ με τὴν τάλαιναν· ὡς δὲ φάρμακον   1260
τεύχουσα κἀμοῦ μισθὸν ἐνθήσειν κότῳ
ἐπεύχεται, θήγουσα φωτὶ φάσγανον
ἐμῆς ἀγωγῆς ἀντιτείσασθαι φόνον.
τί δῆτ᾽ ἐμαυτῆς καταγέλωτ᾽ ἔχω τάδε,
καὶ σκῆπτρα καὶ μαντεῖα περὶ δέρῃ στέφη;
σὲ μὲν πρὸ μοίρας τῆς ἐμῆς διαφθερῶ.
ἴτ᾽ ἐς φθόρον· πεσόντα γ᾽ ὧδ᾽ ἀμείψομαι.

1249   εἴπερ ἔσται Schütz: εἰ πάρεσται codd.   1252   κάρτα τἄρα παρεκόπης Hartung: κάρτ᾽ ἄρ᾽ ἄν παρεσκόπης codd.   1255   δυσμαθῆ Tr: δυσπαθῆ cett.   1258   δίπους Victorius: δίπλους codd.   1261   ἐνθήσειν Tr: ἐνθήσει cett.   1263   ἀντιτείσεσθαι (-τίσ-) Blomfield: ἀντιτίσασθαι F.   1267   πεσόντα γ᾽ (Jacob): πεσόντα θ᾽ ὧδ Verrall: πεσόντ᾽ ἀγαθῶ δ᾽ codd.

Cassandra
I say you'll look on Agamemnon dead.
Chorus
Don't speak inauspicious words.
Cassandra
But there is no healing god in charge of this prediction.
Chorus
No indeed, if it is to be. But may it somehow not happen!
Cassandra
You do your praying: their concern is killing.   1250
Chorus
And which man is organising this woeful deed?
Cassandra
You're surely deluded about the meaning of my prophecies.
Chorus
That's because I don't understand the strategy of the man doing it.
Cassandra
And yet I know the Greek language all too well.
Chorus
So do the Pythian oracles, but they're still hard to comprehend.
Cassandra
Papai! The fire; it's coming on me!
Ototoi, Lycian Apollo, *oi* me, me.
This two-footed lioness mating with the wolf
when the noble lion's away
will put me to death in my misery. As if concocting a drug,   1260
she boasts she'll blend a fee for me too in with her rage,
sharpening her sword against the man,
murdering him in reprisal for bringing me here.
So why do I keep these things that make me ridiculous,
my staff and prophetic garlands round my neck?
You I shall destroy before my own death.
Go to destruction! By throwing you down I repay you.

ἄλλην τιν᾽ ἄτης ἀντ᾽ ἐμοῦ πλουτίζετε.
ἰδοὺ δ᾽ Ἀπόλλων αὐτὸς ἐκδύων ἐμὲ
χρηστηρίαν ἐσθῆτ᾽, ἐποπτεύσας δέ με   1270
κἂν τοῖσδε κόσμοις καταγελωμένην μέγα
φίλων ὑπ᾽ ἐχθρῶν οὐ διχορρόπως, μάτην—
καλουμένη δὲ φοιτὰς ὡς ἀγύρτρια
πτωχὸς τάλαινα λιμοθνὴς ἠνεσχόμην—
καὶ νῦν ὁ μάντις μάντιν ἐκπράξας ἐμὲ
ἀπήγαγ᾽ ἐς τοιάσδε θανασίμους τύχας.
βωμοῦ πατρῴου δ᾽ ἀντ᾽ ἐπίξηνον μένει,
θερμῷ κοπείσης φοινίῳ προσφάγματι.
οὐ μὴν ἄτιμοί γ᾽ ἐκ θεῶν τεθνήξομεν.
ἥξει γὰρ ἡμῶν ἄλλος αὖ τιμάορος,   1280
μητροκτόνον φίτυμα, ποινάτωρ πατρός·
φυγὰς δ᾽ ἀλήτης τῆσδε γῆς ἀπόξενος
κάτεισιν, ἄτας τάσδε θριγκώσων φίλοις·
ὀμώμοται γὰρ ὅρκος ἐκ θεῶν μέγας,
ἄξειν νιν ὑπτίασμα κειμένου πατρός.
τί δῆτ᾽ ἐγὼ κάτοικτος ὧδ᾽ ἀναστένω;
ἐπεὶ τὸ πρῶτον εἶδον Ἰλίου πόλιν
πράξασαν ὡς ἔπραξεν, οἳ δ᾽ εἷλον πόλιν
οὕτως ἀπαλλάσσουσιν ἐν θεῶν κρίσει,
ἰοῦσα πράξω· τλήσομαι τὸ κατθανεῖν.   1290
Ἅιδου πύλας δὲ τάσδ᾽ ἐγὼ προσεννέπω·
ἐπεύχομαι δὲ καιρίας πληγῆς τυχεῖν,
ὡς ἀσφάδαστος, αἱμάτων εὐθνησίμων
ἀπορρυέντων, ὄμμα συμβάλω τόδε.
Χορός
ὦ πολλὰ μὲν τάλαινα, πολλὰ δ᾽ αὖ σοφὴ
γύναι, μακρὰν ἔτεινας. εἰ δ᾽ ἐτητύμως
μόρον τὸν αὑτῆς οἶσθα, πῶς θηλάτου
βοὸς δίκην πρὸς βωμὸν εὐτόλμως πατεῖς;

1268 ἄτης Stanley: ἄτην codd.   1271 μέγα Hermann: μετὰ F.   1284–post 1290 codd:
huc transtulit Hermann.   1285 ἄξειν F: ἄξει Tr.   1286 κάτοικτος Scaliger: κάτοικος
codd.   1288 εἷλον Musgrave: εἶχον codd.   1291 τάσδ᾽ ἐγὼ Auratus: τὰς λέγω codd.
1295 δ᾽ αὖ Tr: δὲ F.

Enrich some other woman by ruining her.
Look, Apollo himself is stripping me
of my prophetic outfit, having watched closely   1270
as I was hugely derided, even in this finery,
by friends turned enemies, all alike, in vain—
I put up with being called a wandering vagabond,
a wretched beggar woman starving to death,
and now the prophet has undone me, the prophetess,
and led me to such a fatal predicament as this.
Instead of my father's altar, a chopping-block awaits me,
where I'll be struck down in a hot and gory sacrifice.
But we shall not die unavenged by the gods.
Another shall come to avenge us in turn,   1280
a mother-killing offspring to get redress for his father.
An exile, a wanderer, alienated from this land,
he's returning to put the copingstone on his family's devastation.
For a great oath has been sworn by the gods
that his dead father's prostrate corpse will bring him back.
So why do I lament so pitifully?
Because I saw, first, that the city of Ilium
had undergone what she underwent, and those
who took her, by judgement of the gods, ending up like this—
I'm going to meet my fate. I'll submit to dying.   1290
I address these doors as those of Hades.
But I pray that I'll receive a fatal blow,
so that these eyes of mine close without a struggle,
my blood flowing away in an easeful death.
Chorus
You've been talking at length, O woman, about many sad things
and many wise ones. If you truly know
you are to die, how is it that you're walking
with such courage towards the altar, like an ox driven by a god?

Κασσάνδρα
οὐκ ἔστ᾽ ἄλυξις, οὔ, ξένοι, χρόνον πλέω.
Χορός
ὁ δ᾽ ὕστατός γε τοῦ χρόνου πρεσβεύεται.   1300
Κασσάνδρα
ἥκει τόδ᾽ ἦμαρ· σμικρὰ κερδανῶ φυγῇ.
Χορός
ἀλλ᾽ ἴσθι τλήμων οὖσ᾽ ἀπ᾽ εὐτόλμου φρενός.
Κασσάνδρα
οὐδεὶς ἀκούει ταῦτα τῶν εὐδαιμόνων.
Χορός
ἀλλ᾽ εὐκλεῶς τοι κατθανεῖν χάρις βροτῷ.
Κασσάνδρα
ἰὼ πάτερ σοῦ σῶν τε γενναίων τέκνων.
Χορός
τί δ᾽ ἐστὶ χρῆμα; τίς σ᾽ ἀποστρέφει φόβος;
Κασσάνδρα
φεῦ φεῦ.
Χορός
τί τοῦτ᾽ ἔφευξας; εἴ τι μὴ φρενῶν στύγος.
Κασσάνδρα
φόνον δόμοι πνέουσιν αἱματοσταγῆ,
Χορός
καί πῶς; τόδ᾽ ὄζει θυμάτων ἐφεστίων.   1310
Κασσάνδρα
ὅμοιος ἀτμὸς ὥσπερ ἐκ τάφου πρέπει,
Χορός
οὐ Σύριον ἀγλάισμα δώμασιν λέγεις.
Κασσάνδρα
ἀλλ᾽ εἶμι κἀν δόμοισι κωκύσουσ᾽ ἐμὴν
Ἀγαμέμνονός τε μοῖραν. ἀρκείτω βίος.
ἰὼ ξένοι,
οὔτοι δυσοίζω θάμνον ὡς ὄρνις φόβῳ
ἄλλως· θανούσῃ μαρτυρεῖτέ μοι τόδε,
ὅταν γυνὴ γυναικὸς ἀντ᾽ ἐμοῦ θάνῃ,

1299 χρόνον Hermann: χρόνῳ codd.   1303–4 transponit Heath.   1305 σῶν Auratus:
τῶν codd.   1309 φόνον Tr: φόβον F.   1317 ἄλλως Hermann: ἀλλ᾽ ὡς codd.

Cassandra

There's no longer time for escape.

Chorus

Yet the one who's last has time on his side.   1300

Cassandra

This day has come. I'll profit little from running away.

Chorus

But be sure that you bear misery courageously.

Cassandra

No happy people are talked about like that.

Chorus

But surely for a mortal to die commendably is good.

Cassandra

Iō for you, father, and your noble children!

Chorus

What's going on? What terror turns you away?

Cassandra

Alas, alas!

Chorus

Why are you saying 'alas'? Unless there's something hateful in your mind.

Cassandra

The house reeks of murder and dripping blood.

Chorus

How so? That's the smell from the victims sacrificed at the hearth.   1310

Cassandra

The vapour's like what comes out of a tomb.

Chorus

You don't mean Syrian incense enhancing the halls.

Cassandra

So I'll enter the house, to bewail my fate
and Agamemnon's. Let that be enough of life.
Iō, strangers,
I'm not afraid for no reason, as a bird fears a bush.
Once I'm dead, bear witness to this for me,
when a woman shall die in return for me, also a woman,

ἀνήρ τε δυσδάμαρτος ἀντ' ἀνδρὸς πέσῃ.
ἐπιξενοῦμαι ταῦτα δ' ὡς θανουμένη.   1320
Χορός
ὦ τλῆμον, οἰκτίρω σε θεσφάτου μόρου.
Κασσάνδρα
ἅπαξ ἔτ' εἰπεῖν ῥῆσιν ἢ θρῆνον θέλω
ἐμὸν τὸν αὐτῆς. ἡλίῳ δ' ἐπεύχομαι
πρὸς ὕστατον φῶς <δεσπότου> τιμαόροις
ἐχθροὺς φόνευσιν τὴν ἐμὴν τίνειν ὁμοῦ,
δούλης θανούσης, εὐμαροῦς χειρώματος.
ἰὼ βρότεια πράγματ'· εὐτυχοῦντα μὲν
σκιᾷ τις ἂν πρέψειεν· εἰ δὲ δυστυχῇ,
βολαῖς ὑγρώσσων σπόγγος ὤλεσεν γραφήν.
καὶ ταῦτ' ἐκείνων μᾶλλον οἰκτίρω πολύ.   1330

Χορός
τὸ μὲν εὖ πράσσειν ἀκόρεστον ἔφυ
πᾶσι βροτοῖσιν· δακτυλοδείκτων δ'
οὔτις ἀπειπὼν εἴργει μελάθρων,
μηκέτ' ἐσέλθῃς, τάδε φωνῶν.
καὶ τῷδε πόλιν μὲν ἑλεῖν ἔδοσαν
μάκαρες Πριάμου·
θεοτίμητος δ' οἴκαδ' ἱκάνει.
νῦν δ' εἰ προτέρων αἷμ' ἀποτείσῃ
καὶ τοῖσι θανοῦσι θανὼν ἄλλων
ποινὰς θανάτων ἐπικράνῃ,   1340
τίς ἂν ἐξεύξαιτο βροτῶν ἀσινεῖ
δαίμονι φῦναι τάδ' ἀκούων;

Ἀγαμέμνων
ὤμοι, πέπληγμαι καιρίαν πληγὴν ἔσω.

1323   ἡλίου Jacob: ἡλίῳ F.   1324   δεσπότου: M. Schmidt: τοῖς ἐμοῖς (ex 1325) codd.
1325   ἐχθροὺς Pearson, φόνευσιν Bothe, τὴν ἐμὴν Heller: ἐχθροῖς φονεῦσι τοῖς ἐμοῖς F.
1328   σκιᾷ Wiesler: σκιά codd. ἂν πρέψειεν Boissonade: ἂν τρέψειεν Porson: ἀντρέψειεν
codd.   1332   βροτοῖσιν Pauw: βροτοῖς codd.   1334   μηκέτ' ἐσέλθῃς Hermann: μηκέτι
δ' εἰσέλθῃς F.   1338   ἀποτείσῃ Sidgwick: ἀποτίσει codd.   1340   ἐπικράνῃ Sidgwick:
ἐπικράνει codd.   1341   ἐξεύξαιτο Schneidewin: εὔξαιτο F.

and a man shall fall in return for a man with an evil wife.
As your guest, about to die, I claim this favour. 1320
Chorus
O poor woman, I pity you for the death you foretell.
Cassandra
There's one more speech—or lament, my own lament—
I want to utter. I pray to the sun, to my last daylight,
that my enemies may pay to my master's avengers
a penalty for my murder, too,
for putting to death a slave, an easy achievement.
Iō for the human condition! When successful,
one could liken it to a sketch; but when it's unfortunate,
a wet sponge wipes the picture out with its strokes.
And this fate I pity far more than the other one. 1330
[*Cassandra exits into the palace*]

Chorus [*intones*]
It's human nature not to get enough
of prosperity: nobody denies it entry
to notable palaces,
saying these words, 'No further entry'.
The blessed ones even bestowed on him
the capture of Priam's town;
he returns home honoured by gods.
But if he's now to pay the penalty
for earlier bloodshed,
and by dying on behalf of the dead
bring to fulfilment punishment for other deaths, 1340
what human being, if he heard this, could boast
that he was born with a destiny free from harm?

Agamemnon [*shouts from inside the palace*]
Ōmoi, I've been struck a fatal blow indoors!

Χορός
σῖγα· τίς πληγὴν ἀυτεῖ καιρίως οὐτασμένος;

Ἀγαμέμνων
ὤμοι μάλ' αὖθις, δευτέραν πεπληγμένος.

Χορός
τοὔργον εἰργάσθαι δοκεῖ μοι βασιλέως οἰμώγμασιν.
ἀλλὰ κοινωσώμεθ' ἤν πως ἀσφαλῆ βουλεύματα.

—ἐγὼ μὲν ὑμῖν τὴν ἐμὴν γνώμην λέγω,
πρὸς δῶμα δεῦρ' ἀστοῖσι κηρύσσειν βοήν.—
—ἐμοὶ δ' ὅπως τάχιστά γ' ἐμπεσεῖν δοκεῖ   1350
καὶ πρᾶγμ' ἐλέγχειν σὺν νεορρύτῳ ξίφει.—
—κἀγὼ τοιούτου γνώματος κοινωνὸς ὢν
ψηφίζομαί τι δρᾶν· τὸ μὴ μέλλειν δ' ἀκμή.—
—ὁρᾶν πάρεστι· φροιμιάζονται γὰρ ὡς
τυραννίδος σημεῖα πράσσοντες πόλει.—
—χρονίζομεν γάρ. οἱ δὲ τῆς μελλοῦς κλέος
πέδον πατοῦντες οὐ καθεύδουσιν χερί.—
—οὐκ οἶδα βουλῆς ἧστινος τυχὼν λέγω.
τοῦ δρῶντός ἐστι καὶ τὸ βουλεῦσαι πέρι.—
—κἀγὼ τοιοῦτός εἰμ', ἐπεὶ δυσμηχανῶ   1360
λόγοισι τὸν θανόντ' ἀνιστάναι πάλιν.—
—ἦ καὶ βίον τείνοντες ὧδ' ὑπείξομεν
δόμων καταισχυντῆρσι τοῖσδ' ἡγουμένοις;—
—ἀλλ' οὐκ ἀνεκτόν, ἀλλὰ κατθανεῖν κρατεῖ·
πεπαιτέρα γὰρ μοῖρα τῆς τυραννίδος.—
—ἦ γὰρ τεκμηρίοισιν ἐξ οἰμωγμάτων
μαντευσόμεσθα τἀνδρὸς ὡς ὀλωλότος;—
—σάφ' εἰδότας χρὴ τῶνδε θυμοῦσθαι πέρι·
τὸ γὰρ τοπάζειν τοῦ σάφ' εἰδέναι δίχα.—
—ταύτην ἐπαινεῖν πάντοθεν πληθύνομαι,   1370
τρανῶς Ἀτρείδην εἰδέναι κυροῦνθ' ὅπως.

1347 ἤν Weil: ἄν codd.   1356 τῆς μελλοῦς Trypho: τῆς μελλούσης F: μελλούσης Tr.
1362 τείνοντες Auratus: κτείνοντες codd.   1368 θυμοῦσθαι E.A.I. Ahrens: μυθοῦσθαι codd.

Chorus [*speaking rapidly*]
Be silent: who's shouting that he's fatally wounded?

Agamemnon
Ōmoi once again, I've been struck a second time.

Chorus [*speaking rapidly*]
To judge from the King's groans, it seems to me that the deed is done.
But let's pool advice on any way of finding safety.
[*speaking in regular metre of dialogue, each chorus-man delivering two lines*]
—I'm telling you what I think—that we should summon
the townspeople here to the palace to help.
—But I think we should apprehend them as fast as possible   1350
and lay charges while the sword still drips fresh blood.
—I share this view too and vote to do something.
Hesitation is useless at a critical time.
—It's plain to see: their prefatory actions
signal that they are imposing a tyranny on the city.
—Yes, we're wasting time. But they're trampling
the very name of hesitation on the ground and their hands aren't idle.
—I don't know what plan could occur to me to suggest.
The person carrying out a deed needs to do the planning too.
—I agree with this too, since I know no means   1360
to bring a dead man back to life by talking.
—So we should prolong our lives just to surrender
to the rule of people who disgrace the house?
—No, that's intolerable. It's better to die—
for that's a less bitter fate than tyranny.
—Shall we divine from the evidence just of groans
that the man's dead?
—Our anger about this must be based on certain knowledge.
Guesswork is not the same as knowing for certain.
—With the support of the majority on all sides I approve this policy—
to acquire clear information about the condition of Atreus' son.   1370

Κλυταιμήστρα
πολλῶν πάροιθεν καιρίως εἰρημένων
τἀναντί' εἰπεῖν οὐκ ἐπαισχυνθήσομαι.
πῶς γάρ τις ἐχθροῖς ἐχθρὰ πορσύνων, φίλοις
δοκοῦσιν εἶναι, πημονῆς ἀρκύστατ' ἂν
φράξειεν, ὕψος κρεῖσσον ἐκπηδήματος;
ἐμοὶ δ' ἀγὼν ὅδ' οὐκ ἀφρόντιστος πάλαι
νείκης παλαιᾶς ἦλθε, σὺν χρόνῳ γε μήν·
ἕστηκα δ' ἔνθ' ἔπαισ' ἐπ' ἐξειργασμένοις.
οὕτω δ' ἔπραξα, καὶ τάδ' οὐκ ἀρνήσομαι·   1380
ὡς μήτε φεύγειν μήτ' ἀμύνεσθαι μόρον,
ἄπειρον ἀμφίβληστρον, ὥσπερ ἰχθύων,
περιστιχίζω, πλοῦτον εἵματος κακόν.
παίω δέ νιν δίς· κἀν δυοῖν οἰμωγμάτοιν
μεθῆκεν αὐτοῦ κῶλα· καὶ πεπτωκότι
τρίτην ἐπενδίδωμι, τοῦ κατὰ χθονὸς
Ἅιδου νεκρῶν σωτῆρος εὐκταίαν χάριν.
οὕτω τὸν αὐτοῦ θυμὸν ὁρμαίνει πεσών·
κἀκφυσιῶν ὀξεῖαν αἵματος σφαγὴν
βάλλει μ' ἐρεμνῇ ψακάδι φοινίας δρόσου,   1390
χαίρουσαν οὐδὲν ἧσσον ἢ διοσδότῳ
γάνει σπορητὸς κάλυκος ἐν λοχεύμασιν.
ὡς ὧδ' ἐχόντων, πρέσβος Ἀργείων τόδε,
χαίροιτ' ἄν, εἰ χαίροιτ', ἐγὼ δ' ἐπεύχομαι.
εἰ δ' ἦν πρεπόντων ὥστ' ἐπισπένδειν νεκρῷ,
τῷδ' ἂν δικαίως ἦν, ὑπερδίκως μὲν οὖν.
τοσῶνδε κρατῆρ' ἐν δόμοις κακῶν ὅδε
πλήσας ἀραίων αὐτὸς ἐκπίνει μολών.

Χορός
θαυμάζομέν σου γλῶσσαν, ὡς θρασύστομος,
ἥτις τοιόνδ' ἐπ' ἀνδρὶ κομπάζεις λόγον.   1400

Κλυταιμήστρα
πειρᾶσθέ μου γυναικὸς ὡς ἀφράσμονος·
ἐγὼ δ' ἀτρέστῳ καρδίᾳ πρὸς εἰδότας

1375 πημονῆς Auratus: πημονὴν codd. ἀρκύστατ' ἂν Elmsley: ἀρκύστατον
codd.   1378 νείκης Heath: νίκης codd.   1383 περιστιχίζω Tr: περιστοιχίζων
F.   1384 οἰμωγμάτοιν Elmsley: οἰμώγμασιν F.   1387 Διὸς Enger: Ἅιδου F.
1391–2 διοσδότῳ γάνει Porson: Διὸς νότῳ γᾶν εἰ codd.   1396 τῷδ' Tyrwhitt: ταδ' codd.

Clytemnestra [*appearing from the house over the corpses to speak*]
Many things were said earlier to suit the occasion
and I'll not be ashamed to say the opposite.
For how can anyone wanting to hurt his enemies,
who seem to be friends, fence the prey in with hunting-nets
too high for it to jump out over them?
This struggle arose from an old dispute, and was of old
given no little thought by me; given time, it has indeed taken place.
I stand where I struck; the deed has been done.
This is what I did, and I'll not deny it.   1380
To prevent him escaping or avoiding his fate,
I threw all round him an impenetrable net,
as if for fish, a costly, evil textile.
I struck him twice. And with the second groan
his limbs went limp on the spot. I dealt his fallen body
yet a third blow, as a prayer of gratitude
to infernal Hades, saviour of corpses.
Thus he lay and gasped out his life;
and as he breathed out sharp jets of blood
he struck me with dingy drizzles of gory dew,   1390
which I delighted in no less than the sown earth is refreshed
by Zeus' gift of rain when the flower-buds are born.
Since this is the situation, you revered citizens of Argos,
be joyful, if you feel joy; I exult in it.
If it were proper to make libations over a corpse,
it would be done with justice over him—with more than justice.
He filled the mixing-bowl with so many cursed tribulations,
and on return has drunk the very last drop.

Chorus
I'm astonished by your tongue, your insolent mouth—
a woman who delivers such a boasting speech over your husband!   1400

Clytemnestra
You're testing me out as if I were an inane woman:
but my heart doesn't tremble as I address people who are aware—

λέγω· σὺ δ᾽ αἰνεῖν εἴτε με ψέγειν θέλεις
ὅμοιον. οὗτός ἐστιν Ἀγαμέμνων, ἐμὸς
πόσις, νεκρὸς δέ, τῆσδε δεξιᾶς χερὸς
ἔργον, δικαίας τέκτονος. τάδ᾽ ὧδ᾽ ἔχει.

Χορός

τί κακόν, ὦ γύναι,   *strophe 1*
χθονοτρεφὲς ἐδανὸν ἢ ποτὸν
πασαμένα ῥυτᾶς ἐξ ἁλὸς ὀρόμενον
τόδ᾽ ἐπέθου θύος, δημοθρόους τ᾽ ἀράς;
ἀπέδικες ἀπέταμες· ἀπόπολις δ᾽ ἔσῃ   1410
μῖσος ὄβριμον ἀστοῖς.

Κλυταιμήστρα

νῦν μὲν δικάζεις ἐκ πόλεως φυγὴν ἐμοὶ
καὶ μῖσος ἀστῶν δημόθρους τ᾽ ἔχειν ἀράς,
οὐδὲν τότ᾽ ἀνδρὶ τῷδ᾽ ἐναντίον φέρων·
ὃς οὐ προτιμῶν, ὡσπερεὶ βοτοῦ μόρον,
μήλων φλεόντων εὐπόκοις νομεύμασιν,
ἔθυσεν αὐτοῦ παῖδα, φιλτάτην ἐμοὶ
ὠδῖν᾽, ἐπῳδὸν Θρῃκίων ἀημάτων.
οὐ τοῦτον ἐκ γῆς τῆσδε χρῆν σ᾽ ἀνδρηλατεῖν,
μιασμάτων ἄποιν᾽; ἐπήκοος δ᾽ ἐμῶν   1420
ἔργων δικαστὴς τραχὺς εἶ. λέγω δέ σοι
τοιαῦτ᾽ ἀπειλεῖν, ὡς παρεσκευασμένης
ἐκ τῶν ὁμοίων χειρὶ νικήσαντ᾽ ἐμοῦ
ἄρχειν· ἐὰν δὲ τοὔμπαλιν κραίνῃ θεός,
γνώσῃ διδαχθεὶς ὀψὲ γοῦν τὸ σωφρονεῖν.

Χορός

μεγαλόμητις εἶ,   *antistrophe 1*
περίφρονα δ᾽ ἔλακες. ὥσπερ οὖν
φονολιβεῖ τύχᾳ φρὴν ἐπιμαίνεται,
λίπος ἐπ᾽ ὀμμάτων αἵματος εὖ πρέπει·

1408 ῥυτᾶς Stanley: ῥυσᾶς codd.   1410 ἀπόπολις Casaubon: ἄπολις codd.   1414 τότ᾽
Voss: τόδ᾽ codd.   1418 ἀημάτων Canter: τε λημμάτων codd.   1419 χρῆν Porson: χρή
codd.

it's all the same whether you want to praise
or blame me—that this is Agamemnon, my husband,
but a corpse—the work of this right hand of mine,
a rightful craftsman. That is how the matter stands.

Chorus [*sing*]
What foul thing have you fed upon, O woman,   *strophe 1*
eaten or drunk, nourished by the earth
or rising from the churning sea, so as to take on
this sacrifice and the pronouncement of the people's curse?
You cast him out, you cut him off, and an outcast you shall be yourself,   1410
mightily hated by the citizens.

Clytemnestra [*speaks*]
So now you sentence *me* to banishment from the city,
and to incur the hatred of its citizens and the pronouncement of the
    public curse,
having then brought no charge against this man here.
A man who paid no heed to the sacrifice of his own child
as if she were a pasture animal, even though
sheep abounded in his fleecy flocks.
The most beloved product of my labour pains
was used to cast a spell on Thracian winds.
Shouldn't you have banished this man from this land
in requital for his polluting acts? But when you hear   1420
about *my* deeds you are a harsh judge. I tell you,
you threaten me thus on the understanding that
I'm prepared, if you defeat me by force on equal terms,
for you to rule over me. But if god ordains the opposite,
you'll surely know, though taught late in the day, how to control yourselves.

Chorus [*sing*]
You think a great deal of yourself,   *antistrophe 1*
and have bellowed overbearingly. Just as
your mind is crazed by this instance of bloodletting,
congealed blood is clear to see on your face.

ἀτίετον ἔτι σὲ χρὴ στερομέναν φίλων
τύμμα τύμματι τεῖσαι.   1430

Κλυταιμήστρα
καὶ τήνδ᾽ ἀκούεις ὁρκίων ἐμῶν θέμιν·
μὰ τὴν τέλειον τῆς ἐμῆς παιδὸς Δίκην,
Ἄτην Ἐρινύν θ᾽, αἷσι τόνδ᾽ ἔσφαξ᾽ ἐγώ,
οὔ μοι φόβου μέλαθρον ἐλπὶς ἐμπατεῖ,
ἕως ἂν αἴθῃ πῦρ ἐφ᾽ ἑστίας ἐμῆς
Αἴγισθος, ὡς τὸ πρόσθεν εὖ φρονῶν ἐμοί.
οὗτος γὰρ ἡμῖν ἀσπὶς οὐ σμικρὰ θράσους.
κεῖται γυναικὸς τῆσδε λυμαντήριος,
Χρυσηίδων μείλιγμα τῶν ὑπ᾽ Ἰλίῳ·
ἥ τ᾽ αἰχμάλωτος ἥδε καὶ τερασκόπος   1440
καὶ κοινόλεκτρος τοῦδε, θεσφατηλόγος
πιστὴ ξύνευνος, ναυτίλων δὲ σελμάτων
ἰστοτριβής. ἄτιμα δ᾽ οὐκ ἐπραξάτην.
ὁ μὲν γὰρ οὕτως, ἡ δέ τοι κύκνου δίκην
τὸν ὕστατον μέλψασα θανάσιμον γόον
κεῖται, φιλήτωρ τοῦδ᾽, ἐμοὶ δ᾽ ἐπήγαγεν
εὐνῆς παροψώνημα τῆς ἐμῆς χλιδῆς.

Χορός
φεῦ, τίς ἂν ἐν τάχει, μὴ περιώδυνος,   *strophe 2*
    μηδὲ δεμνιοτήρης,
μόλοι τὸν αἰεὶ φέρουσ᾽ ἐν ἡμῖν   1450
Μοῖρ᾽ ἀτέλευτον ὕπνον, δαμέντος
φύλακος εὐμενεστάτου καὶ
πολέα τλάντος γυναικὸς διαί·
πρὸς γυναικὸς δ᾽ ἀπέφθισεν βίον.

ἰὼ ἰὼ παράνους Ἑλέναν   *ephymnion*
μία τὰς πολλάς, τὰς πάνυ πολλὰς
ψυχὰς ὀλέσασ᾽ ὑπὸ Τροίᾳ.

1430   τύμμα τύμματι Casaubon: τύμμα τύμμα codd.   1435   ἐμῆς Porson: ἐμὰς codd.
1443   ἰσοτριβής Pauw: ἰστοτριβής codd.   1450   ἂν Emperius: ἐν F.   1452   εὐμενεστάτου
Franz: εὐμενεστάτου καὶ F.   1453   πολέα Haupt: πολλὰ F.   1455   ἰὼ ἰὼ Blomfield: ἰὼ
codd.   παράνους Hermann: παρανόμους codd.

Dishonoured and deprived of friends,
for each strike you must still be struck in requital. 1430

Clytemnestra [*speaks*]
Hear now the just ordinance of my oath.
By Justice fulfilled for my daughter,
by Ruin and the Erinys, to whom I sacrificed this man,
hope does not tread for me in the house of fear,
as long as Aegisthus kindles the fire on my hearth,
staying loyal to me as formerly.
For he is no small shield of confidence to me.
Here lies the man who inflicted outrages on me, his wife,
but was the fondling of every Chryseis at Troy.
So does his war captive and diviner 1440
and bed partner, his trusted soothsaying paramour,
who was pounded by the sailors' masts beside their benches.
The fate of them both was not unworthy.
She, like a swan, has sung her last death-dirge,
and lies here, his lover, but to my bed
she's brought a dainty extra morsel to relish.

Chorus [*sing*]
Alas! I wish that some fate—neither agonising   *strophe 2*
nor protracted—would come to me,
bringing eternal, everlasting sleep, 1450
since my most gracious protector
has been slain, having endured
much on account of a woman;
at a woman's hand he lost his life.

Iō iō demented Helen,   *ephymnion*
one woman who destroyed so many—
so very many—lives beneath Ilium,

νῦν τελέαν πολύμναστον ἐπηνθίσω
δι' αἷμ' ἄνιπτον. ἦ τις ἦν τότ' ἐν δόμοις   1460
ἔρις ἐρίδματος ἀνδρὸς οἰζύς.

Κλυταιμήστρα
μηδὲν θανάτου μοῖραν ἐπεύχου
τοῖσδε βαρυνθείς·
μηδ' εἰς Ἑλένην κότον ἐκτρέψῃς,
ὡς ἀνδρολέτειρ', ὡς μία πολλῶν
ἀνδρῶν ψυχὰς Δαναῶν ὀλέσασ'
ἀξύστατον ἄλγος ἔπραξεν.

Χορός
δαῖμον, ὃς ἐμπίτνεις δώμασι καὶ διφυί-   *antistrophe 2*
    οισι Τανταλίδαισιν,
κράτος τ' ἰσόψυχον ἐκ γυναικῶν   1470
καρδιόδηκτον ἐμοὶ κρατύνεις.
ἐπὶ δὲ σώματος δίκαν [μοι]
κόρακος ἐχθροῦ σταθεῖσ' ἐκνόμως
ὕμνον ὑμνεῖν ἐπεύχεται < ∪ –>.

Κλυταιμήστρα
νῦν δ' ὤρθωσας στόματος γνώμην,
τὸν τριπάχυντον
δαίμονα γέννης τῆσδε κικλήσκων.
ἐκ τοῦ γὰρ ἔρως αἱματολοιχὸς
νείρᾳ τρέφεται, πρὶν καταλῆξαι
τὸ παλαιὸν ἄχος, νέος ἰχώρ.   1480

Χορός
ἦ μέγαν οἰκονόμον   *strophe 3*
δαίμονα καὶ βαρύμηνιν αἰνεῖς,

1458   τελέαν Wilamowitz: δὲ τελείαν F.   1460   ἦ τις Schütz: ἥτις codd.   1468   ἐμπίτνεις
Canter: ἐμπίπτεις codd.   1469   διφυίοισι Hermann: διφυεῖσι codd.   1470   τ' add.
Hermann.   1471   καρδιόδηκτον Abresch: καρδία δηκτὸν codd.   1472   δίκαν Dindorf: ·
δίκαν μοι F.   1473   σταθεῖσ' Stanley: σταθεὶς codd.   1474   lacunam statuit Pauw (cf. 1454).
1476   τριπάχυντον Bamberger: τριπάχυιον codd.   1479   νείρᾳ Wellauer: νείρει codd.
1481   οἰκονόμον Schneider: οἴκοις τοῖσδε codd.

now you have festooned yourself with your final, unforgettable flowers,
through blood that cannot be washed away. The strife   1460
which has brought the man misery was truly inbuilt into the house of old.

Clytemnestra [*intones*]
Don't pray for death as your fate,
weighed down by these thoughts.
And don't divert your rage against Helen,
calling her the man-killer who, by individually
destroying many Danaan souls,
inflicted infinite pain.

Chorus [*sing*]
Malign spirit, you swoop down onto the house   *antistrophe 2*
and onto the two Tantalids,
and you exert rule through women   1470
whose heart-breaking regime reflects their temperament.
Perched over his body,
like a hateful crow, she discordantly
sings her vaunting song.

Clytemnestra [*intones*]
Now you've put your stated opinion right,
giving name to the thrice-fattened
malign spirit of this family.
For lust for lapping blood
is nourished by him in the belly,
and before the old pain abates,   1480
new blood is discharged.

Chorus [*sing*]
Truly you tell of a spirit that keeps house   *strophe 3*
and is heavy with wrath.

φεῦ φεῦ, κακὸν αἶνον ἀτη-
ρᾶς τύχας ἀκορέστου·
ἰὼ ἰὼ, διαὶ Διὸς
παναιτίου πανεργέτα·
τί γὰρ βροτοῖς ἄνευ Διὸς τελεῖται;
τί τῶνδ᾽ οὐ θεόκραντόν ἐστιν;

ἰὼ ἰὼ βασιλεῦ βασιλεῦ,   *ephymnion*
πῶς σε δακρύσω;   1490
φρενὸς ἐκ φιλίας τί ποτ᾽ εἴπω;
κεῖσαι δ᾽ ἀράχνης ἐν ὑφάσματι τῷδ᾽
ἀσεβεῖ θανάτῳ βίον ἐκπνέων.
ὤμοι μοι κοίταν τάνδ᾽ ἀνελεύθερον
δολίῳ μόρῳ δαμεὶς <δάμαρτος>
ἐκ χερὸς ἀμφιτόμῳ βελέμνῳ.

Κλυταιμήστρα
αὐχεῖς εἶναι τόδε τοὔργον ἐμόν;
μηδ᾽ ἐπιλεχθῇς
Ἀγαμεμνονίαν εἶναί μ᾽ ἄλοχον.
φανταζόμενος δὲ γυναικὶ νεκροῦ   1500
τοῦδ᾽ ὁ παλαιὸς δριμὺς ἀλάστωρ
Ἀτρέως χαλεποῦ θοινατῆρος
τόνδ᾽ ἀπέτεισεν,
τέλεον νεαροῖς ἐπιθύσας.

Χορός
ὡς μὲν ἀναίτιος εἶ   *antistrophe 3*
τοῦδε φόνου τίς ὁ μαρτυρήσων;
πῶς πῶς; πατρόθεν δὲ συλλή-
πτωρ γένοιτ᾽ ἂν ἀλάστωρ.
βιάζεται δ᾽ ὁμοσπόροις
ἐπιρροαῖσιν αἱμάτων   1510
μέλας Ἄρης, ὅποι δίκαν προβαίνων
πάχνᾳ κουροβόρῳ παρέξει.

1495 δάμαρτος add. Enger, idem 1519.   1511 δίκαν Scholefield: δὲ καὶ codd.   προβαίνων
Canter: προσβαίνων codd.

Alas, alas, an evil tale of ruinous
fate, never satisfied!
Iō iē, it's the work of Zeus,
cause of all, implementer of all.
For what mortal dealings are conducted without Zeus?
What part of what has happened here is not divinely executed?

Iō iō, my King, my King,   *ephymnion*
how shall I weep for you?   1490
Whatever can I say from the heart of a friend?
You're lying in this spider's web
having breathed your last in an impious death;
ōmoi moi, you lie on this dishonourable bed,
slain in a treacherous killing by your wife's hand,
with a double-edged weapon.

Clytemnestra [*intones*]
Are you proclaiming that the deed was mine?
Do not suppose I am Agamemnon's woman.
Taking on the appearance of this cadaver's wife,   1500
the ancient, bitter spirit of retaliation
against Atreus and his foul feast
has offered this man as payment,
an adult sacrifice to supplement that of young ones.

Chorus [*sing*]
You, not to blame   *antistrophe 3*
for this murder?! Who will testify to that?
How? How? But the spirit of retaliation
might be an accomplice
coming from a father's side.
Black Ares comes on with force
amidst streams of kindred blood,   1510
advancing to the place where he'll grant redress
for the congealed blood of children devoured.

ἰὼ ἰὼ βασιλεῦ βασιλεῦ,   *ephymnion*
πῶς σε δακρύσω;
φρενὸς ἐκ φιλίας τί ποτ᾽ εἴπω;
κεῖσαι δ᾽ ἀράχνης ἐν ὑφάσματι τῷδ᾽
ἀσεβεῖ θανάτῳ βίον ἐκπνέων.
ὤμοι μοι κοίταν τάνδ᾽ ἀνελεύθερον
δολίῳ μόρῳ δαμεὶς <δάμαρτος>
ἐκ χερὸς ἀμφιτόμῳ βελέμνῳ.   1520

Κλυταιμήστρα
οὔτ᾽ ἀνελεύθερον οἶμαι θάνατον
τῷδε γενέσθαι.
οὐδὲ γὰρ οὗτος δολίαν ἄτην
οἴκοισιν ἔθηκ᾽;
ἀλλ᾽ ἐμὸν ἐκ τοῦδ᾽ ἔρνος ἀερθέν.
τὴν πολυκλαύτην Ἰφιγενείαν,
ἄξια δράσας ἄξια πάσχων
μηδὲν ἐν Ἅιδου μεγαλαυχείτω,
ξιφοδηλήτῳ,
θανάτῳ τείσας ἅπερ ἦρξεν.

Χορός
ἀμηχανῶ φροντίδος στερηθεὶς   *strophe 4* 1530
εὐπάλαμον μέριμναν
ὅπα τράπωμαι, πίτνοντος οἴκου.
δέδοικα δ᾽ ὄμβρου κτύπον δομοσφαλῆ
τὸν αἱματηρόν· ψακὰς δὲ λήγει.
Δίκην δ᾽ ἐπ᾽ ἄλλο πρᾶγμα θηγάνει βλάβης
πρὸς ἄλλαις θηγάναισι Μοῖρα.
ἰὼ γᾶ γᾶ, εἴθ᾽ ἔμ᾽ ἐδέξω,
πρὶν τόνδ᾽ ἐπιδεῖν ἀργυροτοίχου
δροίτης κατέχοντα χάμευναν.   1540
τίς ὁ θάψων νιν; τίς ὁ θρηνήσων;
ἢ σὺ τόδ᾽ ἔρξαι τλήσῃ, κτείνασ᾽

1519   δάμαρτος add Enger, idem 1495.   1526   πολυκλαύτην Ἰφιγενείαν Porson:
πολύκλαυτόν τ᾽ Ἰφιγένειαν F.   1527   ἄξια ante δράσας Hermann: ἀνάξια codd.
1531   εὐπάλαμον Hermann: εὐπάλαμνον codd.   1535   θηγάνει Hermann: θήγει F.

Iō iō, my King, my King,   *ephymnion*
How shall I weep for you?
Whatever can I say from the heart of a friend?
You are lying in this spider's web
having breathed your last in an impious death;
ōmoi moi, you lie on this dishonourable bed,
slain in a treacherous killing by your wife's hand,
with a double-edged weapon.   1520

Clytemnestra [*intones*]
I don't think he died
an unworthy death,
for didn't he too impose ruin on
the household by treachery?
He snatched away my offspring by him,
the much-bewailed Iphigenia.
His fitting agony befits what he did.
So let him make no big boasts in Hades,
having paid the penalty of execution by the sword
for what he started.   1530

Chorus [*sing*]
I'm deprived of any mental resource   *strophe 4*
to deal with this, and have no idea
where to turn with the household collapsing.
I fear the loud rattle of a home-wrecking
deluge of blood: it isn't just drizzling any more.
Fate is sharpening Justice's blade
for another damaging deed on other sharpening blocks.
Iō earth, earth, I wish you'd taken me
before I witnessed this man occupying
a silver-sided bathtub.   1540
Who's going to bury him? Who'll lament him?
Are you going to bring yourself to do this, to bewail

ἄνδρα τὸν αὐτῆς ἀποκωκῦσαι
ψυχῇ τ᾽ ἄχαριν χάριν ἀντ᾽ ἔργων
μεγάλων ἀδίκως ἐπικρᾶναι;
τίς δ᾽ ἐπιτύμβιον αἶνον ἐπ᾽ ἀνδρὶ θείῳ
σὺν δακρύοις ἰάπτων
ἀληθείᾳ φρενῶν πονήσει;   1550

Κλυταιμήστρα
οὐ σὲ προσήκει τὸ μέλημ᾽ ἀλέγειν
τοῦτο· πρὸς ἡμῶν
κάππεσε, κάτθανε, καὶ καταθάψομεν,
οὐχ ὑπὸ κλαυθμῶν τῶν ἐξ οἴκων,
ἀλλ᾽ Ἰφιγένειά νιν ἀσπασίως
θυγάτηρ, ὡς χρή,
πατέρ᾽ ἀντιάσασα πρὸς ὠκύπορον
πόρθμευμ᾽ ἀχέων
περὶ χεῖρε βαλοῦσα φιλήσει.

Χορός
ὄνειδος ἥκει τόδ᾽ ἀντ᾽ ὀνείδους.   *antistrophe 4* 1560
δύσμαχα δ᾽ ἔστι κρῖναι.
φέρει φέροντ᾽, ἐκτίνει δ᾽ ὁ καίνων.
μίμνει δὲ μίμνοντος ἐν θρόνῳ Διὸς
παθεῖν τὸν ἔρξαντα· θέσμιον γάρ.
τίς ἂν γονὰν ἀραῖον ἐκβάλοι δόμων;
κεκόλληται γένος πρὸς ἄτᾳ.

Κλυταιμήστρα
ἐς τόνδ᾽ ἐνέβης ξὺν ἀληθείᾳ
χρησμόν. ἐγὼ δ᾽ οὖν
ἐθέλω δαίμονι τῷ Πλεισθενιδῶν
ὅρκους θεμένη τάδε μὲν στέργειν,   1570
δύστλητά περ ὄνθ᾽· ὃ δὲ λοιπόν, ἰόντ᾽

1545 ψυχῇ τ᾽ E.A.J. Ahrens: ψυχὴν codd.   1547 ἐπιτύμβιον αἶνον Voss: ἐπιτύμβιος αἶνος
codd.   1551 μέλημ᾽ ἀλέγειν Karsten: μέλημα λέγειν codd.   1555 Ἰφιγένειά νιν Auratus:
Ἰφιγένεια ἵν᾽ codd.   1559 χεῖρε Porson: χεῖρα codd.   1563 θρόνῳ Schütz· χρόνῳ
codd.   1565 ἀραῖον Hermann: ῥᾷον codd.   1566 πρὸς ἄτᾳ Blomfield: προσάψαι codd.
1567 ἐνέβης Canter: ἐνέβη codd.

your own husband after killing him,
and complete this unjustly with a favour that is no favour to his soul,
in return for momentous deeds?
Who, while tearfully delivering
a eulogy over the grave of the godlike man,
shall feel sincere mental pain? 1550

Clytemnestra [*intones*]
It's not for you to concern yourself
with this responsibility. At our hands
down he fell, down he was struck, and down there we shall bury him.
There'll be no weeping by those outside the household.
But his daughter Iphigenia
shall encounter her father with an embrace,
as she ought, beside the fast-flowing
ford of miseries,
throw her harms around him and kiss him.

Chorus [*sing*]
This blaming arises in return for blame. *antistrophe 4* 1560
The battle outcome is hard to judge.
The defeater is defeated; the killer pays the penalty.
While Zeus remains on his throne, it remains true
that the doer suffers, for that is the rule.
Who could cast the family curse out from the house?
The family line is welded to destruction.

Clytemnestra [*intones*]
You've hit with truth
on this oracular statement. So for my part
I'm willing to make a sworn agreement
with the malign spirit of the Pleisthenids
to acquiesce in what has happened, 1570
although it's hard to bear. For the future,

ἐκ τῶνδε δόμων ἄλλην γενεὰν
τρίβειν θανάτοις αὐθένταισι.
κτεάνων τε μέρος
βαιὸν ἐχούσῃ πᾶν ἀπόχρη μοι
μανίας μελάθρων
ἀλληλοφόνους ἀφελούσῃ.

Αἴγισθος
ὦ φέγγος εὖφρον ἡμέρας δικηφόρου.
φαίην ἂν ἤδη νῦν βροτῶν τιμαόρους
θεοὺς ἄνωθεν γῆς ἐποπτεύειν ἄχη,
ἰδὼν ὑφαντοῖς ἐν πέπλοις Ἐρινύων   1580
τὸν ἄνδρα τόνδε κείμενον φίλως ἐμοί,
χερὸς πατρῴας ἐκτίνοντα μηχανάς.
Ἀτρεὺς γὰρ ἄρχων τῆσδε γῆς, τούτου πατήρ,
πατέρα Θυέστην τὸν ἐμόν, ὡς τορῶς φράσαι,
αὐτοῦ δ᾽ ἀδελφόν, ἀμφίλεκτος ὢν κράτει,
ἠνδρηλάτησεν ἐκ πόλεώς τε καὶ δόμων.
καὶ προστρόπαιος ἑστίας μολὼν πάλιν
τλήμων Θυέστης μοῖραν ηὗρετ᾽ ἀσφαλῆ,
τὸ μὴ θανὼν πατρῷον αἱμάξαι πέδον,
αὐτός· ξένια δὲ τοῦδε δύσθεος πατὴρ   1590
Ἀτρεύς, προθύμως μᾶλλον ἢ φίλως, πατρὶ
τὠμῷ, κρεουργὸν ἦμαρ εὐθύμως ἄγειν
δοκῶν, παρέσχε δαῖτα παιδείων κρεῶν.
τὰ μὲν ποδήρη καὶ χερῶν ἄκρους κτένας
ἔθρυπτ᾽, ἄνωθεν ...
*
   ... ἀνδρακὰς καθήμενος.
ἄσημα δ᾽ αὐτῶν αὐτίκ᾽ ἀγνοίᾳ λαβὼν
ἔσθει βορὰν ἄσωτον, ὡς ὁρᾷς, γένει.
κἄπειτ᾽ ἐπιγνοὺς ἔργον οὐ καταίσιον
ᾤμωξεν, ἀμπίπτει δ᾽ ἀπὸ σφαγὴν ἐρῶν,
μόρον δ᾽ ἄφερτον Πελοπίδαις ἐπεύχεται,   1600

1574–6 μοι δ᾽ ἀλληλοφόνους μανίας μελάθρων codd: δ᾽ eiecit Canter, ordinem mutavit
Erfurdt. 1585 αὐτοῦ δ᾽ Elmsley: αὐτοῦ τ᾽ codd. 1595 lacunam indicaverunt Hense et
Wilamowitz. 1599 ἀμπίπτει δ᾽ Canter: ἄν, πίπτει codd. σφαγὴν Auratus: σφαγῆς codd.

let him be willing, for his part, to leave this house and
wear down another family with intrafamilial deaths.
For me, the possession of a small share of wealth
is wholly sufficient,
if I can rid the palace
of the madness of reciprocal murders.

[*Exit Clytemnestra into the house; enter Aegisthus with bodyguards*]

Aegisthus [*speaks*]
O kindly light of the day that has brought justice!
Now at last I can say that the gods who wreak revenge
for mortals do oversee from on high the miseries on earth.
I welcome the sight of this man lying here   1580
in clothes woven by the Erinyes,
fully expiating the schemes carried out at his father's hand.
For his father Atreus, when ruling this land,
when his sovereignty was disputed,
banished my father Thyestes—his brother,
to make it clear—from the city and the house.
When poor Thyestes returned again,
a suppliant at the hearth, he met a safe fate personally,
since he did not die and spill his blood on the ancestral earth.
This man here's godless father Atreus   1590
offered my father hospitality with more zeal than love,
pretending to mark the day generously by serving meat,
but the feast consisted of his children's flesh.
He broke off the toes, and the fingers from the hands,
and from the upper part…

[*line(s) missing*]
                    …sitting on his own.
Straightaway taking, in ignorance, parts he did not recognise,
he ate food which, as you see, couldn't salvage the family line.
And when he realised his ill-omened deed
he screamed, and fell backwards from the slaughtered flesh, spewing it out.
He invoked an intolerable doom on the Pelopids,   1600

λάκτισμα δείπνου ξυνδίκως τιθεὶς ἀρᾷ,
οὕτως ὀλέσθαι πᾶν τὸ Πλεισθένους γένος.
ἐκ τῶνδέ σοι πεσόντα τόνδ᾽ ἰδεῖν πάρα.
κἀγὼ δίκαιος τοῦδε τοῦ φόνου ῥαφεύς.
τρίτον γὰρ ὄντα μ᾽ ἐπὶ δυσαθλίῳ πατρὶ
συνεξελαύνει τυτθὸν ὄντ᾽ ἐν σπαργάνοις·
τραφέντα δ᾽ αὖθις ἡ δίκη κατήγαγεν.
καὶ τοῦδε τἀνδρὸς ἡψάμην θυραῖος ὤν,
πᾶσαν συνάψας μηχανὴν δυσβουλίας.
οὕτω καλὸν δὴ καὶ τὸ κατθανεῖν ἐμοί,   1610
ἰδόντα τοῦτον τῆς δίκης ἐν ἕρκεσιν.

Χορός
Αἴγισθ᾽, ὑβρίζειν ἐν κακοῖσιν οὐ σέβω.
σὺ δ᾽ ἄνδρα τόνδε φὴς ἑκὼν κατακτανεῖν,
μόνος δ᾽ ἔποικτον τόνδε βουλεῦσαι φόνον·
οὔ φημ᾽ ἀλύξειν ἐν δίκῃ τὸ σὸν κάρα
δημορριφεῖς, σάφ᾽ ἴσθι, λευσίμους ἀράς.

Αἴγισθος
σὺ ταῦτα φωνεῖς νερτέρᾳ προσήμενος
κώπῃ, κρατούντων τῶν ἐπὶ ζυγῷ δορός;
γνώσῃ γέρων ὢν ὡς διδάσκεσθαι βαρὺ
τῷ τηλικούτῳ, σωφρονεῖν εἰρημένον.   1620
δεσμὸς δὲ καὶ τὸ γῆρας αἵ τε νήστιδες
δύαι διδάσκειν ἐξοχώταται φρενῶν
ἰατρομάντεις. οὐχ ὁρᾷς ὁρῶν τάδε;
πρὸς κέντρα μὴ λάκτιζε, μὴ παίσας μογῇς.

Χορός
γύναι, σὺ τοὺς ἥκοντας ἐκ μάχης μένων
οἰκουρὸς εὐνὴν ἀνδρὸς αἰσχύνας ἅμα
ἀνδρὶ στρατηγῷ τόνδ᾽ ἐβούλευσας μόρον;

Αἴγισθος
καὶ ταῦτα τἄπη κλαυμάτων ἀρχηγενῆ.
Ὀρφεῖ δὲ γλῶσσαν τὴν ἐναντίαν ἔχεις.
ὁ μὲν γὰρ ἦγε πάντ᾽ ἀπὸ φθογγῆς χαρᾷ,   1630

1602 ὀλέσθαι Porson: ὀλέσθη codd.   1604 δυσαθλίῳ Schömann: δέκ᾽ ἀθλίῳ codd.
1613 τόνδε φὴς Pauw: τόνδ᾽ ἔφης codd.   1624 παίσας (ex schol. Pind. *Pyth.* 2) Hermann:
πίσας vel πήσας codd.   1625 μένων Wieseler: νέον codd.   1626 αἰσχύνας Wieseler:
αἰσχύνουσ᾽ codd.

with a kick to the table testifying to the righteousness of the curse:
'Thus shall the entire family line of Pleisthenes perish'.
These are the reasons why you see this man fallen here.
And I'm the designer of this murder, and rightly so.
For me, the third son, he drove out, together with my
utterly miserable father, when I was a baby in swaddling clothes.
But Justice has brought me back again in adulthood.
Outsider though I was, I took this man on,
pondering every kind of unpleasant scheme.
So now even death would be fine to me, 1610
since I see him in the nets of Justice.

Chorus [*speak*]
Aegisthus, I do not respect insulting behaviour during hard times.
You say that you wilfully killed this man,
and planned this pitiful murder on your own.
I say that you—you personally, be assured—will
in justice not evade public curses and death by stoning.

Aegisthus
You say this although sitting at the lower oar,
when those with power over the ship sit on the top deck?
You're old: you'll find out how oppressive it is to be taught
at your age, when the lesson is self-control. 1620
In terms of schooling the elderly,
fetters and hunger pangs are the most outstanding physicians
of the mind. Do you have eyes and not see this?
Don't kick against the pricks, in case you suffer as you strike.

Chorus
You woman! Lingering until men returned from war,
keeping house, and having shamed a husband's bed,
did you at the same time plot this fate for a military commander?

Aegisthus
These words too shall give you reason to weep.
Your voice is the opposite of Orpheus's.
For he led every being to him with his delightful voice, 1630

σὺ δ᾽ ἐξορίνας νηπίοις ὑλάγμασιν
ἄξῃ· κρατηθεὶς δ᾽ ἡμερώτερος φανῇ.

Χορός
ὡς δὴ σύ μοι τύραννος Ἀργείων ἔσῃ,
ὃς οὐκ, ἐπειδὴ τῷδ᾽ ἐβούλευσας μόρον,
δρᾶσαι τόδ᾽ ἔργον οὐκ ἔτλης αὐτοκτόνως.

Αἴγισθος
τὸ γὰρ δολῶσαι πρὸς γυναικὸς ἦν σαφῶς·
ἐγὼ δ᾽ ὕποπτος ἐχθρὸς ἦ παλαιγενής.
ἐκ τῶν δὲ τοῦδε χρημάτων πειράσομαι
ἄρχειν πολιτῶν· τὸν δὲ μὴ πειθάνορα
ζεύξω βαρείαις οὔτι μοι σειραφόρον   1640
κριθῶντα πῶλον· ἀλλ᾽ ὁ δυσφιλὴς σκότῳ
λιμὸς ξύνοικος μαλθακόν σφ᾽ ἐπόψεται.

Χορός
τί δὴ τὸν ἄνδρα τόνδ᾽ ἀπὸ ψυχῆς κακῆς
οὐκ αὐτὸς ἠνάριζες, ἀλλά νιν γυνὴ
χώρας μίασμα καὶ θεῶν ἐγχωρίων
ἔκτειν᾽; Ὀρέστης ἆρά που βλέπει φάος,
ὅπως κατελθὼν δεῦρο πρευμενεῖ τύχῃ
ἀμφοῖν γένηται τοῖνδε παγκρατὴς φονεύς;

Αἴγισθος
ἀλλ᾽ ἐπεὶ δοκεῖς τάδ᾽ ἔρδειν καὶ λέγειν, γνώσῃ τάχα
Χορός
*
Αἴγισθος
εἶα δή, φίλοι λοχῖται, τοὔργον οὐχ ἑκὰς τόδε.   1650
Χορός
εἶα δή, ξίφος πρόκωπον πᾶς τις εὐτρεπιζέτω.
Αἴγισθος
ἀλλὰ κἀγὼ μὴν πρόκωπος οὐκ ἀναίνομαι θανεῖν.
Χορός
δεχομένοις λέγεις θανεῖν σε· τὴν τύχην δ᾽ αἱρούμεθα.

1631 νηπίοις Auratus: ἠπίοις codd.   1638 τῶν δὲ Auratus: τῶνδε codd.   1640 μοι
Pauw: μὴ codd.   1641 σκότῳ Scaliger: κότῳ codd.   1644 νιν Stanley: σὺν codd.   Post
1649 versum excidisse indicat Hermann.   1650 Aigistho dat Stanley: choro codd.
1653 αἱρούμεθα Auratus: ἐρούμεθα codd.

but you've provoked me with your childish yelps
and shall be led away. Once you've been overpowered you'll seem calmer.
Chorus
So am I really to think you're going to be the Argives' tyrant,
when although you plotted this man's fate,
you didn't have the courage to carry out the killing yourself?
Aegisthus
The entrapment was obviously a woman's task.
I was under suspicion as an enemy of his from long ago.
I'll endeavour to rule the citizens
using this man's money. On anyone insubordinate
I'll impose a heavy yoke; he'll not be my   1640
well-fed trace-horse. Hateful starvation, combined
with darkness, shall see him softened up.
Chorus
Why then, in the vileness of your heart,
Didn't you slay this man yourself—but his wife
killed him, a pollution to this land
and this land's gods? Maybe Orestes is alive
so that he can return here, and, with fortune in his favour
become killer of them both, victorious in the contest.

Aegisthus [*the metre used by all changes to the rapid trochaic tetrameter
until the end of the play*]
Since you've a mind to do and say such things, you'll soon learn.
Chorus
[*line spoken by the chorus missing*]
Aegisthus
Come on, my loyal guards, your work is not far to seek.   1650
Chorus
Come on indeed; let everyone draw their sword and get ready.
Aegisthus
But I too have drawn my sword and don't spurn death.
Chorus
You talk of your death to accepting ears. We embrace the opportunity.

Κλυταιμήστρα
μηδαμῶς, ὦ φίλτατ᾽ ἀνδρῶν, ἄλλα δράσωμεν κακά.
ἀλλὰ καὶ τάδ᾽ ἐξαμῆσαι πολλά, δύστηνον θέρος.
πημονῆς δ᾽ ἅλις γ᾽ ὑπάρχει· μηδὲν αἱματώμεθα.
στείχετ᾽ αἰδοῖοι γέροντες πρὸς δόμους πεπρωμένους [τούσδε]
πρὶν παθεῖν ἔρξαντες· ἀρκεῖν χρῆν τάδ᾽ ὡς ἐπράξαμεν.
εἰ δέ τοι μόχθων γένοιτο τῶνδ᾽ ἅλις, δεχοίμεθ᾽ ἄν,
δαίμονος χηλῇ βαρείᾳ δυστυχῶς πεπληγμένοι.   1660
ὧδ᾽ ἔχει λόγος γυναικός, εἴ τις ἀξιοῖ μαθεῖν.

Αἴγισθος
ἀλλὰ τούσδ᾽ ἐμοὶ ματαίαν γλῶσσαν ὧδ᾽ ἀπανθίσαι
κἀκβαλεῖν ἔπη τοιαῦτα δαίμονος πειρωμένους,
σώφρονος γνώμης θ᾽ ἁμαρτεῖν τὸν κρατοῦντά <θ᾽ ὑβρίσαι.>

Χορός
οὐκ ἂν Ἀργείων τόδ᾽ εἴη, φῶτα προσσαίνειν κακόν.

Αἴγισθος
ἀλλ᾽ ἐγώ σ᾽ ἐν ὑστέραισιν ἡμέραις μέτειμ᾽ ἔτι.

Χορός
οὔκ, ἐὰν δαίμων Ὀρέστην δεῦρ᾽ ἀπευθύνῃ μολεῖν.

Αἴγισθος
οἶδ᾽ ἐγὼ φεύγοντας ἄνδρας ἐλπίδας σιτουμένους.

Χορός
πρᾶσσε, πιαίνου, μιαίνων τὴν δίκην, ἐπεὶ πάρα.

Αἴγισθος
ἴσθι μοι δώσων ἄποινα τῆσδε μωρίας χάριν.   1670

Χορός
κόμπασον θαρσῶν, ἀλέκτωρ ὥστε θηλείας πέλας.

Κλυταιμήστρα
μὴ προτιμήσῃς ματαίων τῶνδ᾽ ὑλαγμάτων· ἐγὼ
καὶ σὺ θήσομεν κρατοῦντε τῶνδε δωμάτων καλῶς.

1654   δράσωμεν Victorius: δράσομεν codd.   1655   θέρος Schütz: ὁ ἔρως codd.
1656   ὑπάρχει Scaliger: ὕπαρχε codd.   αἱματώμεθα Jacob: ἡματώμεθα codd.
1657   στείχετ᾽ αἰδοῖοι Ahrens: στείχετε δ᾽ οἱ codd. τούσδε seclusit Auratus.
1658   ἔρξαντες· ἀρκεῖν Hermann: ἔρξαντες καιρὸν codd.   1659   δεχοίμεθ᾽ Martin: γ᾽
ἐχοίμεθ᾽ codd.   1662   τούσδ᾽ ἐμοὶ Voss: τούσδε μοι codd.   1663   δαίμονος Casaubon:
δαίμονας codd.   1664   ἁμαρτεῖν τὸν Casaubon: ἁμαρτῆτον codd.   θ᾽ ὑβρίσαι add.
Blomfield.   1671   ὥστε Scaliger: ὥσπερ codd.   1672–3   ἐγὼ et καλῶς addiderunt Canter et
Auratus e schol.

Clytemnestra [*entering from the palace*]
O dearest of men, let's do not one more bad thing.
Even these are a substantial and miserable harvest to reap.
There's enough calamity. Let's shed no more blood.
Go to your appointed homes, respected elders, before you suffer
for your actions: what we did here must suffice.
Surely, if these troubles were to prove sufficient, I would be content.
We've been sorely kicked by god's heavy hoof.   1660
That's what a woman says, if anyone thinks it worth taking note.
Aegisthus
But it's intolerable that these men should pluck flowers of rash speech
    against me
tossing out such language, jeopardising their destiny,
and to make such a mistake in judgement, insulting their overlord.
Chorus
It wouldn't be the way of the Argives to grovel before an evil man.
Aegisthus
But I remain in your midst in the days to come.
Chorus
Not if god directs Orestes' return here.
Aegisthus
I have personal knowledge of how exiles feed on hope.
Chorus
Carry on, get fat as you pollute justice, since you can.
Aegisthus
Be sure that you'll pay me penalties for this stupidity.   1670
Chorus
Boast away to build up your confidence, like a cock beside his hen.
Clytemnestra
Pay no heed to these men's idle yelps. We—I and you
—shall put things in good order and be joint rulers of this house.

[*The chorus presumably depart in the direction of the town. Clytemnestra
and Aegisthus enter the palace together, perhaps leaving the bodyguard to
remain, menacingly, outside*]

COMMENTARY

Where a numeral specifying line numbers is followed by an asterisk, it means that there is additional discussion in the commentary on the lines in question. Line numbers, with or without asterisks, where no other source is indicated, always refer to the Greek text of *Agamemnon*. For the editions and abbreviations used see the separate Bibliography.

i]   1–39   THE WATCHMAN

Summary

The play opens with the speech of a Watchman, visible on the roof of the palace building; the scenery also reveals the palace doors and some statues of gods (509–11*). The two side passages leading into the theatre between the stage and the dancing area represent routes to the city centre and the harbour respectively. The Watchman is at first lying down, probably propping his head up with one hand (3). The audience is kept guessing his precise whereabouts until line 24, since Agamemnon's palace had been situated by many previous poets in Lacedaemon: see Beer (2020). He begins the speech as a prayer asking for release from his labours, but his mind quickly wanders to other topics. When (21–2) he catches sight of the beacon signal emanating from the north, on the Arachnaion mountain (309), indicating that Troy has been taken, he leaps up; he even embarks on a private solo dance at 31, so excited is he at the new development. The opening speech is a model of the playwright's craft. It tells the audience where the play is set (Agamemnon's palace at Argos), but offers a cosmic overview by locating the action beneath a night sky that arches eastward to Troy. It indicates the precise point in mythical time (many years after the Greek army left for Troy), the precise time of day (it is still dark) and who is in charge (the wife of Agamemnon, who 'thinks like a man'). The Watchman introduces animal imagery that is to weave in and out of the fabric of both play and trilogy, and recurring antitheses such as light versus darkness, speech and silence, memory and forgetting, sleep and wakefulness. His speech sets the emotional agenda by conveying his personal attitude to the situation, which seems to be sad and resentful, and certainly critical of the current management of the household. His explicit concluding statement—that there are things going on which he is not prepared to talk about—sets up the tension of a world dominated by secrecy and lies.

1   implore the gods: The very first words of the play establish its interest in humans' frustration with the gods' apparent indifference to their suffering. The Watchman uses the (untranslated) particle *men*, which would normally be followed by a contrasting idea marked by the particle *de*, but his train of thought alters before an antithesis can be formulated. **to set me free:** Lit. 'for release'. The feminine noun *apallagē* and the verb from the same stem are suited to a play which portrays people attempting to escape from desperate plights. The Herald uses the cognate verb to describe the Argive soldiers' delivery from frost and dew now they have taken Troy (336); Cassandra uses the cognate verb in a much darker reference to the way things ended up for Agamemnon (1288). **from these ordeals:** The noun *ponos* can indicate a range of unpleasant experiences, from work or toil to the fruits of labour (see below, 54*), to physical or psychological agony (179–80*) and what Troy suffered at the hands of the Greeks (1167). The same phrase, 'to set me free from these labours', is repeated in the last sentence of this first, despondent part of the Watchman's speech (20*). Bowie (1993) 24 hears an allusion to the Eleusinian Mysteries, at the culmination of which a brilliant light blazed, signalling that the initiates would enter a blissful afterlife when they died.

2   the protracted year-long lookout: Lit., '[over the] length of a year-long lookout' (*mēkos* is in the type of accusative implying that the verb covers the entire period of an extension of time (cf. Xen. *Anab.* 1.2.6)). This detail has probably been appropriated from *Odyssey* 4.524–8, where Menelaus reports Proteus as saying that Aegisthus had set a lookout man to watch out for Agamemnon's return a year before he arrived. **that I keep at night:** The middle tense of the verb from which the present participle *koimoumenos* derives means 'sleep', but is also used of animals lying down at night (*Od.* 14.411) and (as here) of guards keeping watch outdoors at night (Xen. *Cyr.* 1.2.4).

3   like a dog: On prepositional *dikan* see 231–5*. In *Choephori* (447) Electra will use the identical phrase of the way she was kept kennelled in her room when Agamemnon was killed. In comparing himself with a dog, the Watchman introduces the first of many comparisons with fauna (see Introduction, pp. 67–9) and the first of serial references to dogs in the play (see Lilja (1976) 54–7) and in the trilogy (Saayman (2014)). Clytemnestra, Agamemnon and Cassandra are all explicitly compared with dogs and

Aegisthus implicitly compares the chorus' cries with dog yelps: see 607–8*, 895–6*, 965–7*, 1093–4*, 1228–30*, 1631–2* and 1672–3*. The comparison here is double-edged; it suggests a complaint about being kept outside the comfort of the house, deprived of sleep at the natural time, but also the trust that is placed in the Watchman to carry out his duty faithfully. Any watchdog waiting for his master to return from the Trojan War is reminiscent of the sad story in the *Odyssey* of Argos, Odysseus' loyal dog, kept in discomfort outside the palace doors. He recognises the disguised Odysseus before any human except Telemachus does, and dies forthwith (17.291–327). But dogs were also strongly associated with female divinities such as Artemis and Hecate, which may suggest to the audience that the Watchman's orders come from Clytemnestra before he actually says so later in his speech. **propped up on my elbow:** This circumlocution is necessary to translate the adverb *ankathen*. A scholion here suggests that it is a contracted form of *anakathen*, and equivalent to *anōthen*, meaning 'from on high' or 'on high', which is possible. But *ankathen* is used in relation to Orestes' arms embracing the statue of Athena early in *Eumenides* (80), perhaps in a deliberate echo of this passage. **on the roof:** The physical house, along with its roof, to which the Watchman calls the spectator's attention, is to play an unprecedented role in this tragedy (see Introduction, pp. 69–70). **of the Atreidai:** This can mean either the two brothers who are sons of Atreus, Agamemnon and Menelaus, consistently presented as a nearly equal pair in ancient Greek literature (see 407–10*, 842*), or the collective descendants of Atreus down the generations.

4   stars which congregate at night: Lit., 'the assembly of nocturnal stars'. The feminine noun *homēguris* is used in Homer of an assembly of the gods (*Il.* 20.142) and in Pindar specifically of the assembly convened by Zeus (*Isthm.* 7.46), so this term lends the Watchman's words a note of reverence and awe. On the evocation of the universe through the play's use of the vertical axis see Introduction, p. 58. On stars see 6–7*, 365, 826*, 965–7*.

5   winter weather ... summer: The Watchman deploys the standard pairing of nouns for these two seasons (Hom. *Od.* 7.118). Experience of extremes of weather is also a theme in songs of the chorus (at Aulis, 198–204), the speeches of the Herald (the storm at sea, 654–6) and Clytemnestra (ceremonial language praising Agamemnon, 968–9, 970–2), the imagery used by Cassandra (1180–1*) and the chorus' terror of a storm of rain beating on the house (1533–4*). Although astronomical knowledge was well developed by the fifth century, both by seafarers for use in navigation and in the cosmological speculations of the presocratic thinkers (see Gregory (2016)), the reference to constellations and star movements as indicators of seasonal changes in the weather will have put the audience in mind above all of Hesiod's *Works and Days*.

6–7 brilliant, lordly stars: Lit., 'brilliant lords, the stars standing out from heaven'. The masculine noun *dunastēs* in reference to a star is a bold image, since it is usually used of a divine potentate such as Zeus (Soph. *Ant.* 608) or a mortal one (Hdt. 2.32), and it thus introduces the concept of powerful and high-status rulers, central to the play, by oblique visual means. **standing out from the heavens:** The verb *emprepein* from which the participle *emprepontas*, 'standing out' is formed, like its near-equivalent *prepein*, 'be conspicuous', 'stand out', often refers to an entity which is perceived as distinct from its background or other similar entities by one of the senses, usually vision. See further 29–30*, 242–3*. See also on astronomical movements in connection with the Atreidai at 1584–6*.

8 And I'm still looking out: Lit., 'Even now I'm looking out'. **torch-signal:** Lit., 'sign of the torch'; *phulassein* plus accusative can mean, as here, 'lie in wait for something'. Using fire signals to communicate military messages across distances is already attested in a simile in the *Iliad*; the flames which Athena makes gleam from Achilles' head when he goes to encourage the beleaguered Achaeans resembles the glare of beacon-fires ignited by men on a besieged island signalling that they need assistance (18.211–13). See also Theognis 549–50, 'The voiceless messenger rouses tearful war, Cyrnus, when it shows from the far-beaming lookout place'. Beacon-relays were one of the inventions attributed to the clever Greek at Troy, Palamedes; curiously, two of the others also feature, if obliquely, in this speech: astronomy (see Soph. *Nauplios* fr. 432.8–11, schol. Eur. *Or.* 432, Alcidamas *Od.* 22) and the game of dice (see below, 32*). At least some were listed by the titular hero in Aeschylus' *Palamedes*, for which unfortunately we have no date of first production (fr. 181a, 182 and 182a). Historically, Aeschylus and his audience had been witnesses to the Persians' use of beacon-relays at the time of Xerxes' invasion: see below, 280*. **the gleam:** This is in the accusative since it is in apposition to *sumbolon*. **word:** The feminine noun *phatis* can refer to several kinds of significant speech, and its multivalence is explored in this play, where it assumes different meanings, including 'rumour' (278, 456, 864–5), a 'divine voice' speaking through oracles (1132) and a particular human language (1254).

10–11 For so decrees … expectant heart: Lit., 'For so the woman's manly-deliberating expectant heart commands'. The messenger tells us that it is a woman from whom he takes his orders. The verb *kratein* is potent, usually meaning to hold the *kratos* or sovereign or executive power, and words with this stem will become increasingly important in this play about the contestation of political power, especially in the mouths of Aegisthus and Clytemnestra (see 17*, 258, 324–5*, 17*, 1617–19*, 1631–2*, 1672–3*). The woman who gives the Watchman orders is no ordinary one, for she deliberates like a man (compare the *androphrōn gunē*, 'manly thinking woman' of Sophocles fr. 943): it is interesting to find Damascius, a late Neoplatonist, use Aeschylus' term as a compliment in his description of Damiane, the wife of the philosopher Asclepiodotus, who he says was 'extremely modest', 'highminded and male-deliberating (*androboulon*) in her housekeeping' as well as 'restrained and inviolable as cohabitee' (*Life of Isidore* fr. 130.2). It was proverbial that women could not deliberate; 'a woman just does not deliberate with an eye to expedience' (*Monostichoi* 106, see also 355), and 'a man who takes a woman's advice when he fears downfall actually deliberates his downfall into being' (the New Comedy poet Philemon's fr. 177 in the edition of Kock (1884) 528). The developed capacity to deliberate (*bouleuesthai*) as a fully autonomous moral agent is denied to women in Aristotle's *Politics* 1.1260a (see Hall (2009) 86–9 and (2016a) 39). The crucial issues of Clytemnestra's mental acuity and the degree to which it challenges gender stereotypes are thus established at the outset of the play. The *boul-* stem is used at crucial junctures later, of both formal civic deliberations and secret murder plots (881–4*, 844–6, 1123–6, 1346–7*). **expectant:** Hope (*elpis*), hopelessness, and fearful anticipation are to become key emotions in the choral songs as well as the speeches of the characters (see 12–14* and 20–1*).

12–14   Whenever I bed down here at night, uneasy and dew-sodden, I never have any dreams: Lit., 'Whenever I have my night-wandering-causing dewy bed it is not visited by dreams.' The Watchman never dreams because he can never get any sleep. The unusual compound adjective *nuktiplanktos* recurs at 330 and also characterises fear in *Libation-Bearers* (524, 751). On dreams see 274* and on wandering see 77–9*. The Herald later complains about the dew which made sleeping uncomfortable at Troy (333–4*, see also 141), but, for Clytemnestra, dew is positive: see 1390*. The Herald, another working man, also complains about the inadequate bedding he was forced to endure on the Troy campaign (556–7*), but it is the adulterous beds of the ruling class that are most prominent (see 27*). **Terror:** This is the most prevalent emotion in the play and discussed in detail by Avezzù (2018); see also, on suspense, Benarowski (2015): the chorus have been living in a state of fear (549–50), say terror hovers in front of their soul (976), feel dread when Cassandra alludes to the Thyestean feast (1243) and anticipate a deluge of blood that will wreck the house (1533); Agamemnon says no-one can walk on tapestries without feeling afraid (924), while Cassandra turns away from the palace in terror (1306) and insists that what she fears is real (1316–17). Only Aegisthus and Clytemnestra seem immune to trepidation, Clytemnestra declaring that hope does not tread for her in the house of fear while Aegisthus is there for her (1434–5).

15   eyelids: In Homer, sleep is poured on or removed from eyelids (e.g. *Od.* 20.54, *Il.* 10.187). But eyes, eyelids and the gaze are of central concern to the tragedy (see 240* and Introduction, pp. 58–9). **securely:** The Watchman implies that he does occasionally doze off, but that his terrified state of mind causes him to wake up repeatedly.

16   When I feel like singing or humming a tune: Lit., 'when I think/ intend to sing or hum'. This is the first of serial references to music-making in the play: see Introduction, p. 71. There was a proverb current in the fifth century BCE, 'singing on watch', *phrouras aidōn* (Ar. *Clouds* 720). *minuresthai* is used of the nightingale at Soph. *OC* 671, and the first elderly woman in Aristophanes' *Ecclesiazusae* describes herself leaning out of her window to attract a male passerby and 'humming [*minuromenē*] some song to myself' (880).

17   using music as a cure for sleepiness: Lit., 'shredding in [herbs for] a cure sung against sleep', or 'cutting into a root to drain sap for a cure against sleep'. The Watchman uses a metaphor suggesting both magical and medicinal means for staying awake—singing or humming is like preparing a herbal stimulant and warbling an incantation against drowsiness at the same time. On the theme of sleep see 179–80*. Further medical imagery denotes households afflicted by violence, minds afflicted by psychic suffering and political corruption that needs to be rooted out. The chorus want their anxiety to be 'healed' (99) and later tell the Herald that his weeping is an affliction that pleases them (542), although silence is the best medicinal antidote to harm (548). Agamemnon, rather chillingly, says that in correcting faults in the Argive political system he will act like a doctor, where necessary using cauterisation or surgery (849–50*); the chorus, however, while comparing moral soundness with physical health, say that health is like a building which shares a party wall with disease and is thus dialectically inextricable from it (1001–4). They ruminate that no incantations can bring back a man from the dead (1021). Cassandra sees the house of Atreus as suffering from an incurable health problem (1103), while Priam's sacrifices at Troy effected no cure for that city's ailment, either (1169–70). The chorus do not see how swearing an oath to Cassandra that they will remember her predictions can have any healing effect on the situation (1199), while she insists that, since no healing god is present, it does not matter what she says (1248). Aegisthus, like Agamemnon, prefers to configure himself as dishing out medicine as a form of discipline, telling the mutinous chorus that hunger and bondage are excellent 'physicians of the mind' at 1623. Parallels in Hippocratic texts with each of these terms are suggested by Dumortier (1935a). On Aeschylus' medical imagery, see also Fowler (1967) 40–7.

18   I cry aloud, groaning: The semantic range in this play for vocal and audible expressions of sorrow is extensive (Introduction, p. 70). Both *klaiein* and *stenein* denote standard Homeric responses by men to grief (*Il.* 8.364, *Od.* 21.247). The actor playing the Watchman may well have interpolated a groan outside the formal metrical structure before or after delivering this line.

19   managed properly: The passive participle means, literally, 'thoroughly laboured at', another instance of a word incorporating the continuing theme of *ponos*, toil/pain (1*). The woman who thinks like a man is apparently not managing her husband's household conscientiously in his absence as the audience know, from the *Odyssey*, Penelope is concurrently supervising Odysseus' palace in Ithaca.

20–1   I hope that I may now receive a happy discharge from my duties, that the fire which brings good news will flash through the darkness: Lit., 'May fortunate release from labours now happen, the fire that-brings-good-news appearing in-the-darkness'. The Watchman in his closing wish repeats the same phrase for being set free from labours, *ponoi*, as he used in the opening line; on hope see also 10–11*. As an ancient scholiast observed, there is presumably a short pause here before the Watchman first senses the light through the night sky.

22–4   O watch fire: In Homer, the masculine noun *lamptēr* seems to mean the grate in which a pinewood torch or fire would be set, but the addition of 'of night' makes it clear that it is a watch fire designed to be seen through darkness (cf. Soph. *Ajax* 286, Eur. *IA* 34, Xen. *Symp.* 5.2). **welcome:** The imperative of *chairein*, 'to rejoice', is the standard form of greeting another person in ancient Greek literature, here addressed to an inanimate object, just as the Herald will later use the same word to greet his native land and the sun (508). Dio Cassius 69.18 claims that it was more appropriate for greetings made early in the day. **lighting up the night like day:** Lit., 'showing forth light [like that] of day'. Clytemnestra's account of the beacon relay indicates that the fire seen here by the Watchman was lit on Mount Arachnaion, which Pausanias said lay between Argos and Epidauros (2.25.10). See 309*. On light and darkness see Introduction, pp. 63–5. **inspiring abundant choral dances in Argos to celebrate this event:** Lit., '[showing forth] numerous choral dances in Argos for the sake of this event!' The participle 'inspiring', or something like it, needs to be inserted to make sense in English; in the Greek, *piphauskōn*, 'showing forth', governs the light and the formation (*katastasin*) of the choruses. A *choros* entails simultaneous dancing and singing, here celebratory; this is the standard reaction of communities in Greek tragedy to joyful news (cf. Eur. *Alc.* 1154–5). The notion of choruses becomes a leitmotiv of the play and entire trilogy (see Introduction, p. 71). But although this fire supposedly brings joyful news, the Watchman's uneasy conclusion to the speech undermines the celebratory image. As Gantz (1977) 28 argues, 'fire repeatedly serves to symbolize the destructive aspects of vengeance'.

25   Hallo there! Hallo! The exclamation *iou iou*, a loud shout, can express joy, despair or surprise (see 1214*), but the Watchman's explanation here shows that it can also be used to get someone else's attention.

26   I'm signalling clearly: The Watchman explains the *purpose* of his shouting in the previous line. The play's intense concern with different forms of verbal and non-verbal communication, inaugurated by the receipt of the beacon signal by the Watchman, is thus further developed. The adverb *torōs* implies a shrill or piercing quality as well as clarity. The stem *tor-* is favoured by Aeschylus in discussing communication, knowledge and its sources in *Agamemnon*: see 632 (of a messenger's tidings), 1062 (of an interpreter), 254 (of what will happen in the future) and 1584 (of imparting information). **Agamemnon's wife:** Clytemnestra is called many things in this play, few of them complimentary, beginning with ambiguous 'the woman who thinks like a man' (see 10–11*). Here the Watchman, who is apparently loyal to Agamemnon, reminds the audience that she is only in control of the household because she is married to its true master.

27   to rise from bed: The audience is asked to picture Clytemnestra in her bedchamber, which, given their familiarity with the *Odyssey*, will have raised the question in their minds of the whereabouts of Aegisthus. The bed Clytemnestra once shared with Agamemnon is on several other minds (1123–6*, 1108–9, 1447, 1498–9*, 1626), but Clytemnestra points out that Cassandra and Agamemnon are now bed partners (1440–3). The chorus are grimly aware that the only bed Agamemnon now sleeps in is his death bed (1494). Menelaus' bed, which Helen abandoned, is also mentioned (412*) and her new bed in Troy probably evoked at 690–2*.

28   raise the shout of triumph: An *ololugmos* is a ritual cry, or ululation, high-pitched, and lent its trilling quality by repeatedly clicking the tongue to the soft palate while howling. For this and other words using the same core onomatopoeic *olol-* stem in this play see 587 and 1118*. Some scholars have seen the *ololugmos* as the aural symbol that points towards the eventual resolution of the tragic conflict in the trilogy (Goheen (1955) 124–25). It is attested in ancient Egyptian texts as well as Greek literature; Herodotus thinks that the Greeks adopted the practice from Libya (1.189.3), 'for the women of that country ululate very well'. It is still practised all over Africa and the Middle East. In ancient Greek literature it is usually performed by women invoking a god (Hom. *Il.* 6.301), in response to good news (Eur. *Or.* 1137) or at the instant when blood is drawn from an animal when it is sacrificed (see the professional woman wailer at sacrifices designated an *ololuktria* at SIG 982.25 and Pulleyn (1997) 178–80). In epic and tragedy, it can be a vindictive response to the slaughter of a hated individual (Hom. *Od.* 22.408, Aesch. *Choeph.* 387), although here the participle *euphēmounta* specifically defines it as triumphant. The Watchman envisages Clytemnestra as the leader who instigates (*eporthiazein*) a triumphant chorus of palace women welcoming Agamemnon home.

29–30   if ... really been taken: The *-per* in *eiper*, translated here by 'really', heightens the hint of doubt introduced by the conditional; this sets the stage for the chorus' later scepticism about whether the message of the beacon-relay is entirely to be trusted (274–80). But any doubt is contrasted by the Watchman with the clarity of the fire-signal. **emphatically announces:** Lit., 'is conspicuous announcing'. On *prepei* see above, 6–7*; the fire-signal stands out visibly from the sky as the shining stars do.

31   dance the prelude: The noun *phroimion* is a contracted form of *proomion*, 'prelude'. Choral dances were often preceded by short overtures played on musical instruments; at the opening of Pindar *Pyth.* 1.4, the poet says that his lyre gives instructions to the singers with its 'chorus-leading preludes' (*proomia*). It would be dramatically effective for the Watchman to make a few dance steps or gestures at this point. This striking image draws metatheatrical attention to the function of the Watchman's speech as prelude to the entire play and tetralogy: see Introduction, pp. 18–19.

32   For I'll count ... as my own: Lit., 'For I will count my masters' lucky [dice] fallings as my own.' In English we tend to say 'throw' of the dice rather than 'fall'. The metaphor which equates strokes of fate with throws of the dice, often those thrown by gods (although here it is by the beacon-signal) was common: see Soph. fr. 895 ('the dice of Zeus always fall well'),

Eur. *Suppl.* 330, Ar. *Thesm.* 414. Socrates thought that the game of dice had been invented by the Egyptian god Theuth (Plato, *Phaedr.* 274c–d), and the Lydians claimed it was their invention (Hdt. 1.94), but early examples from Mesopotamia have survived (see, e.g., British Museum no. 1880,1112.2092). Knucklebones with four numbered sides (*astralagoi*) were also used in games of chance in distant antiquity; in the *Iliad* we hear that Patroclus as a child had killed Amphidamas' son when he became angry over a game of knucklebones (23.88). The Greeks usually credited the invention of six-sided cubic dice to the Greek hero Palamedes, who was said to have invented board games, such as draughts (*pessoi*), suitable for relieving the boredom of the Greeks at Troy (Gorgias, *Palamedes* 30). For his invention of six-sided dice with their faces specifically numbered one to six (*kuboi*) see Sophocles' *Nauplios* fr. 429 and *Palamedes* fr. 479.4, schol. Eur. *Or.* 432 and Pausanias 2.20.3. Achilles and Ajax are depicted playing a game involving both a board and dice on Exekias' beautiful black-figured amphora in the Vatican (Cat. 16757). The words inscribed near their mouths suggest that Achilles has thrown a four and Ajax a three respectively. Aeschylus' approximate coeval Polygnotus painted Palamedes himself playing draughts with Thersites and Salaminian Ajax, all three of them enemies of Odysseus, in his *Nekyia* on the walls of the Lesche of the Cnidians at Delphi (Paus. 10.31.1–2). On the social role and significance of games in ancient Greek literature see Kurke (1999). **masters':** Aeschylus' characters and chorus use a range of terms to designate the status of Agamemnon and his close family (see 34–9*, 83–4*). Here the Watchman's use of the plural suggests that he is thinking of the entire household. Words with the *despot-* stem have a range of meanings from 'head of the household' (see Aesch. *Eum.* 60) to master of slaves (Plato, *Parm.* 133d); the newly enslaved Cassandra uses it of Agamemnon at 1224 and it almost certainly means that the Watchman would have been understood to be a slave by Aeschylus' audience here (see the discussion of Griffith (1995) 79 with n.64). But in political contexts *despotēs* means something closer to the English 'despot', an absolute ruler (Aesch. *Eum.* 527, 696; Eur. *Her.* 28, Hdt. 3.89, Thuc. 6.77).

33   beacon: The feminine noun *phruktōria* more literally means the act of making signals by fire-beacons (see also below 490, Soph. fr. 432.6, from his *Nauplius*, Eur. *Rhes.* 55, Ar. *Birds* 1161). **triple six:** The game of dice was divided into groups of three throws or a throw of three dice simultaneously. The best score was three sixes: see Plato, *Laws* 12.968e. On gaming with dice see also 998–1000*. There is a sixth-century Athenian clay model of a dicing game board in the National Museum in Copenhagen, illustrated in

Ussing (1884) plate 1. The number three is to prove fundamental to the entire play and trilogy as it was not only to Greek religion, theology, taxonomy and other aspects of Greek life but also to ancient Indian, Egyptian, Babylonian, Phrygian and Scythian cultures too (Lease (1919) 63–4). An Aristotelian treatise observed that 'the triad is the number of the complete whole, inasmuch as it contains a beginning, a middle, and an end. Nature herself has provided us with this number for use in the holy service of the gods' (*de Caelo* 1.1). An anonymous late antique treatise entitled *Theology of Arithmetic*, which draws on Pythagorean numerological ideas, goes further: 'The triad, the first odd number, is called perfect by some, because it is the first number to signify the totality–the beginning, middle, and end. When people exalt extraordinary events, they derive words from the triad and talk of "thrice blessed", "thrice fortunate". Prayers and libations are performed three times. Triangles both reflect and are the first substantiation of being plane; and there are three kinds of triangle–equilateral, isosceles, and scalene' (Waterfield (1988) 51; see Zhmud (2016) 321). The number three was integral to the drama competitions, where three tragedians and three comic poets competed; choral lyric's ancient structure seems to have been based on the ancient tripartite structure of strophe, antistrophe and epode (Usener (1903) 1–2). The same applied to athletics competitions; three sprinters compete at Patroclus' funeral games (*Iliad* 23.741–51); Zeus is the third supreme deity after Ouranos and Kronos and in *Agamemnon* his victory is compared with a wrestler who wins the best of three bouts (171–2*). Hesiod's *Theogony* contains no fewer than 15 triads of divinities (Usener (1903) 4; see also Mehrlein (1959)). Magical spells routinely invoke triads of divinities or supernatural spirits, or invoke individual ones as triform; the most spectacular example is a prayer to Selene designed to reinforce any spell, which calls on her as 'triple-sounding, triple-headed, triple-voiced … triple-pointed, triple-faced, triple-necked, and goddess of the triple ways', with fire 'in triple baskets'; she frequents 'the triple way' (*PGM* 4.2820–5 in Betz (1986) 91). Clytemnestra makes a bizarre comparison between rumours of the death of Agamemnon at Troy and the mythical triple-bodied Geryon (870). In prayers and oaths, naming three gods was standard practice, reflected in *Agamemnon* in the chorus' speculation that one of the gods was listening, 'perhaps Apollo, or Pan or Zeus' (55–7). The chorus sing that old age wanders on three feet, perhaps in a reference to the riddle of the Sphinx (77–9). Iphigenia used to sing the ritual chant for her father at his symposia when the third libation was poured, to Zeus Saviour (245–7*); a crucial refrain is repeated by the chorus three times (158–9). Cassandra experiences three waves of delirium (1256*).

The threefold polyptoton of words with the *than-* stem at 1339–40 reinforces acoustically the iterative pattern of reciprocal murder. Clytemnestra strikes Agamemnon three blows (1384–7*; see also 1553*). The curse the chorus pronounce on her is rhetorically tripartite (1411*). Clytemnestra dedicates her 'sacrifice' to three significant female deities, Justice, Ruin and Erinys (1432–3*). The malign spirit that has wrecked the household is 'thrice-fattened' (1476–7*). Aegisthus reminds us that he was the third son of Thyestes (1605). Three-part utterances are rhetorically and poetically forceful: Clytemnestra uses the same verb—*skēptein*—three times between 300 and 310, adding rhetorical emphasis to the final climactic stages of the message's journey. At 406 the chorus uses three semi-rhyming feminine participles alluding to Helen's nefarious actions. At 454–5 the three words beginning with *ech-* or *ek-* produce a powerful assonantal effect, bolstering the sense of despair at the war fatalities. At 530, the assonance of three words beginning with alpha heightens the ceremonial ring of the address to Agamemnon. At 689–91* the chorus use three compounds punning grimly on Helen's name in the first syllable of each to emphasise the destruction she wrought on ships, men and a city, but at 738–42* they stress the joy with which she was received in Troy using three phrases in apposition, of which the subjects are neuter nouns. Agamemnon uses triple negative imperatives at the crucial moment in his altercation with Clytemnestra (618–22*).

34–9   And so may the King ... mine: lit. 'And so may [the opportunity] happen that, the King having come home, [I am able] to raise his welcome hand in this hand'. Here Agamemnon is called an *anax*, a standard word for a ruler or king in tragedy (Eur. *Phoen.* 17, *Or.* 349). In Homer it means 'king', 'man of high rank' or 'lord', and is especially associated with Agamemnon, the '*anax* of men' (*Il.* 1.442). The chorus (206, 530) and Clytemnestra (599) also call him *anax*; the chorus also use it of Menelaus (42). **I'm saying nothing:** Lit., 'I am silent'. Silence and the suppression of open expression of opinion or emotion, and economy with information and the truth, are here established as central concerns of the play: Iphigenia is later said to have been gagged to suppress her voice (235–8*, 240*, 242–3*); the abandoned Menelaus sat apart in lonely silence (412–13*); the chorus sing of the silent protests of angry townspeople (445–51*) and say that they learned long ago that the best policy is silence (548). **big bull ... tongue:** The Watchman's blunt proverbial image, found in both Theognis (815) and several other fifth-century texts (see Fraenkel (1950) vol. 2, 17), is framed within the first of the play's many gnomic sayings: see Introduction, p. 74. But it also heralds several references to bulls in the contexts of sex or lethal force (see

245–7*, 654–6*, 1125–6*, 1127*, 1295–8*). Aristophanes was laughing at Aeschylus' bull imagery when he made Aeacus in *Frogs* say that when he heard that he was to compete with Euripides word by word, 'he certainly stooped down and glowered like a bull' (804). Euripides accuses him there of making his characters 'speak a dozen bull-words with eyebrows and crests' (924–5). **the house itself ... most unerringly:** The material reality of the palace buildings is brought to the audience's attention, here in the first of several articulations of the idea that house walls themselves are speechless witnesses to what goes in inside them (see Introduction, pp. 69–70). On the noun *phthongos*, 'voice', see 324–5*. The adjective *saphēs*, here adverbially used in the superlative plural, can mean not just 'clear' but 'truthful' or 'accurate' as well, especially of prophetic and oracular speech (Soph. *OT* 390, 1011, *OC* 623). **I prefer ... memory:** Lit., 'I willingly speak to those who have learned and decide to forget with those who have not learned'. The Watchman is talking to himself and addressing an imaginary audience; characters and choruses in tragedy never address the external audience, with the possible exception of Electra in Eur. *Or.* 128. For this meaning of *lēthomai* see Hom. *Il.* 9.537. On memory and forgetting see 154–5, 179–80, 231–5, 821–4, 1105, 1316, 1459 and Introduction, p. 15.

ii] 40–257 THE CHORUS (AND SILENT CLYTEMNESTRA?)

Summary

As the Watchman disappears, probably down into the palace, the sun is assumed to rise, and the chorus of elderly Argive men enter the orchestra, leaning on sticks, from the direction of their imagined city centre. In due course they explain that they have come to the palace to ask Queen Clytemnestra why she has ordered the women of the city to embark on rituals of celebration. But the main purpose of this exceptionally long choral episode—which occupies nearly an eighth of this exceptionally long play— is to establish the dire emotional state in which the Argive community is languishing and to enquire into the historical and theological reasons for this predicament in the hope that there is some divine purpose behind everything which will lead to a just and happier conclusion. Structurally, the sequence consists of a long run of anapaests as the chorus file in (40–103), to take up their places for the long lyric parodos; this consists of six pairs of metrically corresponding stanzas, of which only the first is followed by a metrically unique stanza or 'mesode'. But the slight shifts in subject matter are not precisely coterminous with shifts in lyric metre or stanza end.

40–103 Anapaests

The anapaests recall the departure of the Argive taskforce ten years ago, articulating the 'official', public justification for it, that Zeus had sent the sons of Atreus against Troy to punish them for violating his taboo on abusing the law of reciprocal respect between guests and hosts in taking Helen. The chorus express their hope that everything will work out for the best, while referring grimly to the implacable divine wrath that attends on unspecified 'unhallowed rites'. They explain that they were already too old to have joined the army when it departed and regret their age and infirmity. Clytemnestra probably briefly appears in silence (83–4*), for the chorus then ask her why the women are performing sacrifices across the city and express their need for emotional reassurance that all is well (for the use of these and other anapaests in *Agamemnon*, see Moore (2024), 29–31).

40 Priam's: The figure of the Trojan King, who the audience will know has very recently been killed, assumes great importance later in the play both as a point of comparison with the Argive King Agamemnon and as the father of Paris and of Cassandra (126–7, 537, 935, 1306, 1335–6).

41 adversary: The Greek *antidikos* means specifically an adversary at law, properly a prosecutor, but it is also applied to the defendant (Aeschines 2.165, Antiphon 1.2, Lys. 7.13). The metaphor lends a quasi-legal authority to the Atreidai's declaration of war on Priam and Troy. The themes both of legal processes, culminating in Orestes' trial in *Eumenides*, and justice (*dikē*) more generally, are thus introduced at the impact-making moment of the chorus' first sentence; legal terms meaning 'advocate', 'testimony', 'prosecutor', 'corroboration' and various types of charge and punishment recur densely throughout *Agamemnon*. See Introduction, p. 65 and 250–1*, 272*, 390–5*, 445–51*, 493–5*, 535–6*, 813–17*, 830–1*, 821–3*, 1231–3, 1377–8*, 1412–13*, 1506*, 1601 and 1613*.

43–4 the strong pair … sceptre: Lit., 'the pair of Atreidai, strong [because] of the double-throned and double-sceptred prerogative [they receive] from Zeus'—the first time the supreme Olympian is named in the tragedy. The pair of brothers are one of the significant doublets in the play, which also include the two vultures the chorus will shortly compare them with (49–50), the omen of the two eagles (108–15), the sisters Clytemnestra and Helen, the brothers Atreus and Thyestes and the two butchered sons of Thyestes (1605–6). Kingly power and its symbol, the sceptre, was bestowed upon mortals by Zeus (so Agamemnon at Hom. *Il.* 2.102–7), who was often depicted with a sceptre as well as a thunderbolt and/or eagle himself. See, e.g., the neck-amphora dated 480–470 BCE, attributed to the Berlin Painter, in the British Museum (cat. no. 1867,0508.1114). The *Orphic Hymn to Zeus* addresses him as (amongst other things) 'Son of Kronos, sceptre-holding, descending from above, sturdy-hearted' (15.6–7 in Athanassakis (1977)). Zeus dominates the theology of the play: see Introduction, pp. 48–51. The presentation of the central Peloponnesian mythical royal house of Atreus as based on a double monarchy was related both to the myth of the Dioscuri as divine twins, who received an important Spartan cult, and to the historically attested dual kingship at Sparta, the two kings being drawn from the Agid and the Eurypontid clans. This was much discussed by ancient historians and constitutional writers (Miller (1998)); the lyric poets (not to mention the Spartans themselves) tended to place both brothers at Sparta, while the Greek tragedians explained the geopolitics of the myth in different ways to suit their purposes, sometimes locating Menelaus' palace at Sparta rather than Argos and/or Agamemnon's at Mycenae (see Hall (2018c)).

45–7 raised … mission: Lit., 'raised a thousand-shipped armament of Argives, a martial aid'. The 'thousand ships' is a poetic approximation: the catalogue of ships on the Greek side in the *Iliad* lists 1186 ships, which Thucydides (1.10.4) rounds up to 1200. The indicative of the verb *aeirein* often applies to getting an army on the march or a fleet of ships under sail. On ships and ship imagery see 108–15*.

48 They bellowed … fury: Lit., 'shouting great Ares in their fury'. The verb *klazein* means 'scream loudly'; it is often used of birds (Hom. *Il.* 17.756), dogs (Hom. *Od.* 14.30) or Zeus letting forth the sound of thunder (Pind. *Pyth.* 4.23) as well as warriors shouting (Hom. *Il.* 2.222). **war-cry:** The proper name of the war-god could stand metonymically for 'war', 'death' or 'slaughter' (Hom. *Il.* 2.381, Soph. *OC* 1046, Aesch. *PV* 861), and by extension a 'warlike spirit' (as below 78*, Eur. *Phoen.* 134, Soph. *El.* 1242, Ar. *Plut.* 328). But the participle that governs it here means making a sound, so 'Ares' must stand for the actual war-cry for which Menelaus at least was famous, as his Homeric epithet 'good at the war-cry' indicates (e.g. *Il.* 2.408). The passage introduces Ares, who will later symbolise the aggressive and brutal objectives of the expedition against Troy (374–6*), challenging the chorus' proposal that the Greeks were commanded by Zeus to punish the Trojans for their contravention of the laws of *xenia*. **fury:** The masculine noun *thumos* has a wide range of meanings ('soul', 'mind', 'temper') including, as here, anger or the seat of anger (see, e.g., Eur. *Med.* 1079, Hom. *Il.* 17.254); in Thuc. 2.11 it is opposed to *logismos*, 'rationality'.

49–50 vultures: These noisy birds are in archaic poetry a favourite subject in similes about fighting men; they are memorably described in the Hesiodic

Shield of Heracles (405–6), functioning as a comparand for the combatants Cycnus and Heracles, as 'curving-taloned hooked-beak vultures, screaming loudly over a high cliff'. **grieving for their young in remote places:** Lit., 'which in remote griefs for their children'. A scholiast here explains the adjective *ekpatios* as meaning 'lonely'. Aeschylus draws on the famous vulture simile which occurs when Telemachus finally recognises his father in the *Odyssey* (16.216–19), and they wailed aloud more vehemently than 'sea-eagles, or vultures with crooked talons, whose young the country-folk have taken from their nest before they were fledged'. But he may also be reworking a version of the fable of the fox and the eagle related by Archilochus (frr. 172–8); they were friends until the eagle seized the fox's cubs to feed its young: see Garner (1990) 29–30, 32. These vulture chicks are the first newborn creatures to be mentioned in the play, prefiguring the theme of suffering babies recalled in Cassandra's reference to Itys, a child killed and cooked by his mother (1144–5*) and several references to Thyestes' children. These reach a climax in the evocations of the Thyestean feast by Cassandra (1096–7, 1217–22), the chorus (1106) and Aegisthus (1590–1602), and especially in Aegisthus' statement that he was still a baby in swaddling clothes at the time (1606*). This in turn foreshadows the nurse Cilissa's speech about caring for the infant Orestes in *Choephori* (746–61). The chorus' lion-cub allegory also stresses that it was at first an adorable newborn like a human baby (723–4,* 763–7*).

51–4 and wheeling … young: Lit., 'they wheel high above their beds, rowing with oars of wings, having lost the bed-watching labour of their young'. On winged beings see 390–5. **high above:** On the play's portrait of the vertical axis of the universe, introduced by the Watchman's observation of the stars, see 4*, 51–4*, 92–3*, 364–5 and Introduction, p. 58. On the adjective *hupatos* see below, 55–7*, 88–91*. **nests:** The primary meaning of the neuter noun *lechos* is 'bed', especially 'marriage-bed' (see 411*), but in English 'nest' is the required translation here (cf. Soph. *Ant.* 425). **rowing the air on their oarlike wings:** The Greeks often compared the movement and appearance of an oared ship with a bird in flight and *vice versa*: see, e.g., Eur. *Hipp.* 752. A large proportion of Aeschylus' audience consisted of highly trained and experienced oarsmen, and metaphors from rowing abound in classical Athenian literature and *Agamemnon* (see 108–15* and Hall (2022a)). In *Persians* 1046 the chorus perform movements which involve 'rowing' with their arms: see Hall (1996) 176. **labour of minding:** On the recurrent term *ponos* see 1*. The adjective *demniotērēs*, 'bed-watching', is a remarkable compound, which means something even more sinister at 1449*.

55–7 But one of those on high—perhaps Apollo, or Pan or Zeus—hears the shrill screaming lament of the birds, residents of the sky: Lit., 'But one of those on high, Apollo or Pan or Zeus, perceiving the bird-uttered sharp-shouted lament of these metics.' The chorus assume that when predators kill another creature's young in the natural world, they are punished by one of the gods who hears their cries of lament. The chorus do not include Artemis, who would be the obvious divine defender of the hunted young of wild fauna (142*). The uncertainty about which god would be responsible is typical of the play's portrait of human theological bewilderment (see Introduction, pp. 45–8). **on high:** The adjective *hupatos*, 'topmost', is often used as a title of Zeus alone; see 88–91* and 509. Here it also cements the relationship between the vultures (described as *hupatoi* at 51–4*) and the gods. **Apollo:** The chorus propose him as a possibility because he punishes and destroys wicked and overbearing men with his unerring bows and arrows (Hom. *Il.* 24.604, *Od.* 11.318). It was believed by some ancient authorities, but denied by Socrates in Plato's *Cratylus* (404c5–8, 404d8–e2, 405e1–4), that his name was etymologically connected with the verb *apollusthai*, 'destroy'. See 1081*. **Pan:** He is a candidate because he lives in the wild and especially on mountain ridges (Hom. *Hymn to Pan* 14.4–11); his home is Arcadia, with its three mountain ranges in the central Peloponnese (his worship at Athens had been introduced only at the time of the battle of Marathon—see Paus. 8.26.2). He was also the god of flocks, both wild and tame, and responsible for their increase. **Zeus:** Zeus' panhellenic portfolio included the punishment of those who break fundamental taboos by committing crimes such as murder, betraying a host or guest, and breaking oaths: see 60–2*. **hears the shrill screaming lament:** Lit., 'hearing the bird-uttered sharply shouted lament'. Aeschylus' poetic soundscape, inaugurated by the Watchman's reference to his attempts to keep himself awake by singing or humming (16*), is here expanded to accommodate the screams of vultures in flight. The masculine noun *goos* is a standard term for wailed lamentation by both women and men in archaic and classical Greek poetry: cf. Hom. *Od.* 4.103, 758; Pind. *Pyth.* 3.103; Aesch. *Pers.* 949; Soph. *Aj.* 529 and 629 (of the nightingale). Birds, wings and flying feature regularly in the play's imaginary: see Introduction, p. 58. **residents of the sky:** Lit., 'metics of these [gods]'. See Cerri (2012) and, on the theme of *metoikia* across the *Oresteia*, Dougherty (2017). In Athens, a metic was a resident non-Athenian with specific but limited rights (Thuc. 2.13, Ar. *Ach.* 508). It is disputed whether the *met-* originally referred to one who has *changed* residence or *shares it with* full citizens.

The word becomes significant at the end of *Eumenides* when the chorus of Erinyes accept the status of Athenian metics (869, 1011). The image of gods and vultures sharing the same aerial space, within a simile illustrating what is fundamentally a theological speculation, typifies Aeschylus' evocation of the scale of the cosmic order which is so difficult for his humans to understand in this play.

58–9 sends overdue punishment against the offenders in revenge: Lit., 'sends a late-punishing Erinys against the offenders'. In *Choephori*, Orestes says that Zeus sends a late-punishing retribution/destruction for wicked deeds (382–3); see also 155*. Fraenkel (1950) vol. 2, 38 is correct that these 'weighty new compounds emphasize one of the central ideas of the *Oresteia*'; *parabasin* is the aorist masculine plural participle of *parabainein*, 'go beyond' or 'trangress', in the dative case. The idea that the gods might punish one bird or animal for predating on another, as if fauna are subject to the same rules as human beings, is startling: the chorus' thoughts have slipped from the creatures in the simile to the comparands—the Atreidai— before the simile is syntactically over. **revenge:** This is placed last in this long sentence in the translation to suggest the force of the Greek *Erinun* at both sentence- and line-end. The Erinyes, supernatural female embodiments and agents of reprisal, were conceived by Earth from the bloody droplets which fell from Ouranos' groin when Kronos castrated him (Hes. *Theog.* 183–5; see Hall (2018a)), although in *Eumenides* they pray to Night as their mother who gave birth to them 'as retribution for the blind and sighted' (321–3). Their principal function is to punish violations of the 'unwritten laws' of the Greeks (on which see Hall (2010b) 159–61) proscribing offences against kin, recipients of oaths, suppliants and vulnerable strangers. Although it is not common for men as opposed to women to be said to possess or to be like an *Erinys*, Hecuba dreams that Paris will be an *Erinys* at Pindar fragment 52i(A).19–21 (*Paean* 8a). See Finglass (2005). This Erinys inaugurates the central function that the Erinyes are to play in the entire *Oresteia*— they are seen by Orestes at the end of *Choephori* and form the chorus of *Eumenides*. But the idea of a parent awaiting long-delayed revenge must also remind the audience of Clytemnestra, awaiting vengeance for the loss of her daughter Iphigenia (154–5*). Later, the chorus reflect that the black Erinyes bring down the unrighteous man 'and reverse his fortunes by wearing him down' (461–6). Helen herself is seen as a bride whose effect on Troy (and consequently on the Argives) was that of an Erinys who brings tears (748–9). Cassandra describes the revelling kindred Erinyes haunting the house (1186–93).

60–2   who ensures correct treatment of hosts and guests: This lengthy periphrasis is necessary to translate the full force of Zeus' epithet *xenios*, which is closely related to his function as protector of suppliants. Weak translations that refer to 'hospitality' fail to convey the life-and-death importance in the ancient world of an ethical/religious system which assumed a dreadful punishment awaited those who threatened the safety either of people travelling in alien territory and lodging with strangers or of the strangers they encountered abroad. This is explained (in vain) by Odysseus to Polyphemus in Hom. *Od.* 266–71, despite Odysseus' own breaching of the code of *xenia* by entering the Cyclops' cave uninvited: 'but we, thus visiting you, have come as suppliants to your knees, hoping that you will give us some token of guest-friendship or give us some other gift as is due to strangers. So come on, most powerful one, respect the gods. We are your suppliants, and Zeus is the avenger of suppliants and strangers—Zeus, the strangers' god—who always looks after strangers, who need protection.' The chorus in *Agamemnon* assume that Alexander will be punished by the Atreidai, as instruments of the justice of Zeus, because he breached *xenia* when he took his host Menelaus's wife away with him after visiting. **sent:** Lit., 'sends'. The present tense, which reinforces by repetition the comparison between the vultures and the Atreidai, may be an example of a vivid present in exciting narration. But since the chorus do not yet know that Troy has been taken, in their eyes Zeus is still continuing to send revenge to Troy. **Alexander:** The chorus (although inclined, like most ancient Greek authors, to blame Helen rather than Greek militarism for the Trojan War (Hall (2010b) 177–8)), in their first mention of the supposed culprit are unambivalent that the individual on whom vengeance must be taken is the Trojan prince with whom she left Sparta. Both Homer and the tragedians use both names for him, Paris and Alexander: although attempts have been made to argue that the Greeks use 'Alexander' and the Trojans 'Paris' unless they are talking to Greeks (de Jong (1987)) or *vice versa* (Stinton (1965) 36 n.2), neither distinction stands up to investigation; although the motif of the two names, one given him by Hecuba and one by the shepherd who adopted him, was exploited by Euripides in his *Alexander* according to its hypothesis (T iii = POxy 3650.14; see further 720*) and *Trojan Women* (919–22, 941–2), tragedies performed together in 415 BCE, it is not known who bestowed which name (Lloyd (1989)). Aeschylus uses 'Paris' five times (*Ag.* 399, 532, 713, 1156) and in a fragment (*POxy.* 2253 a 6 = fr. 451k.6) and 'Alexandros' twice (*Ag.* 61, 363, exclusively in anapaests). **For the sake of a woman:** Blaming all the death and destruction caused by the Trojan War on Helen is a commonplace in ancient Greek literature from Homer onwards: see, e.g., Odysseus' complaint at *Od.* 11.438, 'many of us died for the sake of Helen'. In this play alone see versions of this cliché at 445–51*, 799–801*, 821–4* and 1448–54. **mated with many men:** The chorus do not use the name 'Helen', as they are to do with such effect at 687–9, but the reference to her is unmistakable. The adjective *poluanōr* elsewhere has neutral and even positive overtones (of the much-frequented seat of Apollo at Delphi, Eur. *IT* 1281, or a populous city, Ar. *Birds* 1313), but when applied to a woman in a patriarchal society it is virtually equivalent to 'promiscuous'. In the *Oresteia* Helen is only ever sexually associated with Menelaus and Alexander, although there was an early ancient tradition that after Alexander's death she was in a relationship with his brother, the Trojan Deiphobus (*Little Iliad* arg. 2, perhaps Hom. *Od.* 4.274–6, 8.517–520; Verg. *Aen.* 6.511–512); other ancient sources claim that she had been raped when still a child by Theseus (Apollodorus, *Bibl. Ep.* 1.3, Diodorus 4.63.1–3, and Plutarch, *Life of Theseus* 31–34).

63–7 his purpose was to inflict, on Greeks and Trojans alike, countless clashes that exhaust the limbs, knees pressed down into the dust and the spear-shaft shattered as the ceremony of battle commences: Lit., 'intending to inflict, on Danaans and Trojans alike, many limb-weighing-down wrestling-bouts, the knee being planted in the dust and the spear-shaft scraped in the ceremonies that precede [battle]'. On wrestling imagery see 171–2*. This is a negative, rare and precious expression of the subjective experience of the brutality of hoplite warfare from the perspective of the soldier (Hanson (1991) 72). It is also perhaps reminiscent of Eumaeus' wish in the *Odyssey* that Helen's family would perish, because she 'loosed the knees' of many men (14.68–71). The reference to countless clashes affecting both Greeks and Trojans may have brought to mind the tradition that Zeus had a plan to destroy the Achaeans (*Il.* 1.5 with schol. D ad loc.) as part of a scheme to depopulate the world, after Earth had complained of being over-burdened. See 678* and Hall (2025) chapter I section 1. Heavy weights and weighing imagery interweave throughout the play, adding to the oppressive and fateful atmosphere. Intellectual deliberation is imagined by the chorus as weighing things up (161–3*); Ares is conceived as balancing the scales of warriors' fate in battle, like a merchant weighing gold (438*); simultaneous good and bad outcomes are conceptualised as being weighed against one another in the balance (349, 574; see also 1272 and 1042) and an obligation falls on the Trojans like a scale pan sinking down (704–8). Suffering weighed the Greeks down at Aulis (184–91); calamity is heavy

(206), the ashes of the war dead are now 'weighty residue from the fires' (440–4); envy weighs people down (836), Clytemnestra says the chorus are weighed down with miserable thoughts (1463), and the *daimōn* afflicting the house is heavy with wrath (1482); Aegisthus threatens weighty punishments (1619–20) and imposing a heavy yoke (1640–2). **ceremony ... commences:** The neuter plural noun *proteleia* usually refers to a sacrifice performed before a solemn ritual, especially an initiation or wedding (Eur. *IA* 720, Plat. *Laws* 6.774e): these men are sacrificed to enable Menelaus' marriage to Helen to be renewed. Although LSJ suggests that it means, more generally, 'beginnings' here, the image of a sacrifice is not inappropriate to the first blood that is shed in a war, and it inaugurates the constant theme of the play and trilogy of the corrupted sacrifice so brilliantly analysed by Zeitlin (1965); see also Rehm (1994) 43; Seaford (2012) 190–1 and 227*, 720*.

67–8 It is how it now is. It's being fulfilled in line with destiny: The gnomic language and the sense of helpless inertia in the face of evolving events are both typical of this chorus' idiom of self-expression. On the important concept of things being brought to their proper end (*telos*) or fulfilment see 751*. **destiny:** Here, *peprōmenon* is the singular perfect passive neuter participle of *porein*, 'furnish', used substantively with a definite article. For this metaphysical sense see 684*, Eur. *Ion* 1388 and *Rhes.* 634.

69–71 By offering neither burnt sacrifice, nor libation, nor tears shall a man assuage the implacable wrath caused by unhallowed rites: Lit., 'Neither applying fire nor pouring out nor weeping shall [anyone] assuage the unbending angers [caused by] unburnt offerings.' The adjective *apuros* does not usually have a negative connotation, but in the context it is clear that chorus are alluding to sacrificial rites or offerings (*hiera* can mean either) that were improperly conducted, leading to implacable anger. The chorus' cryptic form of expression leaves it entirely open whether the reference is to an angry human, perhaps Clytemnestra or Aegisthus, or to the gods, or both. **assuage:** The *thelg-* stem in this verb implies an element of magical enchantment and possibly trickery: see Hom. *Od.* 12.40 (of the Sirens), 14.387 (coupled with lying), Pind. *Nem.* 4.3.

72 disregarded: The adjective *atitai*, 'without honour', is related to the verb *tiein*, 'revere', on which see below, 531*. **flesh:** This is a graphic and elemental way of talking about their ageing physical capacities. The feminine noun *sarx*, often in the plural, is often to be found in association with corpses being devoured by dogs, wolves and birds of prey (Hom. *Il.* 8.380, *Od.* 19.450, Aesch. *Sept.* 1040), with the flesh of those dying from poison falling off their bones (Eur. *Med.* 1200) or chunks of cooked sacrificial meat ('three chunks' of a bull are specified along with its tongue on an inscription from Amorgos (Vermaseren (1982) no. 650 fr. B.7); see below, 1097*). Since Athenian men were still liable for military service until the age of 60 ([Aristot.] *Ath. Pol.* 53.4), and the chorus are talking about being excluded from the campaign ten years ago, they would have been imagined to be septuagenarians. They regret their old age, and express its frustrations in exquisite poetic language (77–9*), while proudly claiming that their ability to bear sung witness to the past has not diminished (104*) and acknowledging that one is never too old to learn something new (584*). Their physical appearance adds pathos to Clytemnestra's description of the miserable situation of other old men at Troy, on the opposite side of the Aegean Sea (326–8), as well as the elderly who adored the allegorical lion-cub (721–2*), and the chorus' brave response to Aegisthus' cruel taunts about their advancing years (1619–20*). The theme of old age probably prompts the chorus' own description of a traditional saying as 'elderly' (750–4*). **excluded:** For this sense of *hupoleipein* in the passive with a genitive see Hdt. 1.165.

74–5 are waiting: The verb *mimnein*, denoting holding out, waiting or awaiting something, often in a military context of an expected attack (*Il.* 5.94, 13.713), is closely connected with death at Clytemnestra's hands in *Agamemnon*. It is used of the child-avenging wrath that Calchas said will wait in the house (154–5); Cassandra says that being split by a weapon awaits her (1149). The play's uniquely tense atmosphere is also partly dependent on its evocation of the length of time between actions and the retributive responses they trigger in both mortals and gods (1149*, 1563*). **leaning on our staffs, no stronger than children:** Lit., 'supporting our childlike strength on our staffs'. There is an echo of this at *Eum.* 34–8, when the priestess of Apollo crawls on hands and feet out of the inner sanctum of his temple at Delphi in shock after glimpsing the Erinyes, 'because an old woman, overcome with fear, is nothing, or rather she is like a child'. The chorusmen's appearance can be helpfully visualised by looking at the vase-painting depicting a group of agitated men, several of them elderly, leaning on walking sticks, on the exterior of the red-figure kylix by the Tithonus painter in Boston, Museum of Fine Arts, 95.28. Although the idea of helpless and defenceless young offspring has already been launched by the chorus' simile of the vultures wheeling over empty nests (51–4*), the chorus' sad reflection on their physical vulnerability introduces serial negative comparisons with the powers of children. These are used by the chorus to derogate not only their own physical strength (see also 77–9*), but people with ill-judged optimism (390–5*) and Clytemnestra's alleged credulity (479*). She resents being taken no more seriously than if she were a little girl (277*). Aegisthus accuses the chorus of yelping childishly (1631–2*). But such figurative language also highlights the helplessness of victimised children, a central theme of the play.

76   fresh excitement: Lit., 'youthful bone-marrow'; on *nearos* see 359*. The masculine noun *muelos* can refer either to marrow spurting from the spine of a mortally injured warrior (Hom. *Il.* 20.482) or to marrow as nutritious food (Hom. *Il.* 22.501). It is not often used metaphorically (although see Eur. *Hipp.* 255) and might be interpreted here more literally—the marrow is still being renewed in their bones but it is the degenerate marrow of old men. Either way, the physical nature of the language is strikingly bald and in line with the tragedy's uncompromising carnality (72*). **doesn't make a soldier:** Lit., 'Ares [is] not in place', a difficult phrase which has been interpreted variously, although the general sense is not in doubt: see Medda (2012). For the metaphorical use of the war-god's name as meaning 'warlike spirit' see 48* and, on Ares in the rest of the play, 374–6*.

77–9   advanced old age: The noun is formed by using the neuter singular form, with definite article, of the rare adjective *hupergērōs*, 'exceedingly old' (cf. Lucian, *Dial. Mort.* 27.9). In Gissen Papyrus I.59, col. 4 line 14, it seems to have a technical sense exempting someone in a list of candidates for civic liturgies. Aeschylus daringly imagines advanced old age as an organism itself, first as a plant whose leaves are withering, second as a walking-stick-using childlike human figure, and third as an immaterial figure in a vision: on phantoms see 414–15*. **its leaves already withering away:** The *kata-* prefix intensifies the root verb *karphein* (transitive 'wither'), often used of human skin becoming wrinkled (*Od.* 13.398, Hes. *Works* 575); there is, unusually, in Aeschylus, an explicit echo here of Archilochus fr. 188.1–2. **wends its way with three feet:** Lit., 'walks its three-footed paths'; *tripous* can refer to a three-legged object such as a table (as a noun in Xen. *Anab.* 7.3.21), but is used proverbially of a man whose age means he leans on a staff (Hes. *Works* 533, cf. Eur. *Tro.* 275); on the number three see 33* and on old age 72*. **and wanders around, no stronger than a child:** The play features the language of wandering in both body and mind as part of its picture of a confused group of people who are not sure what direction destiny is taking them in: see also 12–14*, 593, 192–5, 330–3*, 593, 1282. Aeschylus' audience may already have known a version of the Sphinx's riddle solved by Oedipus and put as a question in *Anth. Pal.* 14.64; this says that it is as a crawling child on four legs that the human being is weakest, which may have prompted the chorus' train of thought here, making them repeat the comparison of themselves with feeble children (74–5*).

80   like a dream that appears in daytime: The neuter noun *onar* usually meant a dream experienced while asleep *as opposed* to a vision, phantasm or apparition seen when awake (Hom. *Od.* 19.547, 20.90; Plato, *Politicus* 278e). Aeschylus is stressing just how faint and shadowy the chorus feel their presence is. Cassandra later likens to figures in dreams the ghosts of the children of Thyestes whom she (although no-one else) can see (1218*).

83–4   But you, Tyndareus' daughter: The chorus might conceivably address a character not visible to the audience, but the most obvious interpretation of this passage is that the actor playing Clytemnestra has appeared on stage and conducts some ritual business at an altar (for a survey of discussions see Pool (1983)). Her silence in response to the chorus' series of direct questions of increasing length would heighten the suspense. Not far short of 200 lines will pass before she does eventually speak. She may leave the stage at about 103* or even possibly continue with her ritual activities while the chorus perform the parodos. The chorus do not yet know that news has arrived from Troy, although before the old men arrived on stage, the audience learned from the Watchman that he had signalled the information to Clytemnestra. Addressing Clytemnestra as the daughter of Tyndareus will probably have brought Helen, the other famous women raised as a daughter by Tyndareus, to mind: see 914. **Queen Clytemnestra:** Finally, the woman who has already inspired a sinister periphrasis (10–11*) is named. The feminine *basileia* is used, by their subjects, of other powerful royal women, especially those without husbands present in their households, including Penelope as discussed by the suitors (*Od.* 4.770) and by the chorus of the Persian queen in Aesch. *Pers.* 623. But in democratic fifth-century Athens the term *basileus* was so strongly associated with the Great King of Persia (see Hdt. 7.174) that it could not fail to have slightly unsettling overtones in any Athenian context, even a theatrical enactment of events that happened several centuries ago. *basilea* is the standard term for eastern barbarian queens such as Candaules' wife in Herodotus (1.11.1). Agamemnon and Menelaus are called *basileis* at 113; the Herald address the palace of his *basileis* (518); Agamemnon is called *basileus* by the chorus as they formally greet him at 782, and lament him at 1489* and 1513*.

85–7   What's the news? What indication or persuasive report have you received that makes you send orders round to perform sacrifices? Lit., 'What [is] the matter? What [is] new? Perceiving what, or by persuasion of which report, do you make sacrifices by orders sent around?' The chorus intimate that they can see multiple sacrifices being performed round the city, an observation they go on to elaborate. In such references, the fictional world of the tragedy and the real environment of the theatre to an extent blend, since in the Athenian theatre of Dionysus both audience and chorus could see large portions of their city to the south and west of the Acropolis, and multiple sacrifices were performed at the Dionysia festival.

88–91   all the gods: Clytemnestra is apparently being careful to extend her gratitude to every possible divinity with an interest in Argos, or at least to be seen to do so. **we cultivate in our city:** The adjective *astunomos* implies 'officially' endorsed public cults (see Pind. *Nem.* 9.31). Pausanias reports that the most important Argive temple was that of Apollo Lykeios (2.19.6–7), but the sanctuary of Hera outside the city, her other temples under the titles 'Antheia', 'flowery' and 'Akraia' 'Of the Height' (2.22.1, 2.24.1) and her festival, held within the racecourse (2.24.2), were at least as important. It is strange that Hera plays so small a part in this Argive tragedy: see Introduction, p. 46. Pausanias' account of Argos (2.19.3–2.24.4) also mentions temples, sanctuaries, altars and cult images of Apollo 'God of Streets' (2.19.8), Athena, Zeus under several titles, Demeter, Persephone, Pluto, the childbirth goddess Eileithyia, the Seasons, Asclepius, Artemis, Leto, Poseidon, the Dioscuri, Dionysus, Helios and the River Inachus, as well as numerous heroes. **supreme:** The adjective *hupatos* is a regular epithet of Zeus (*Od.* 1.45, *Il.* 19.258; see 55–7*, 509*); in a Delphic oracle delivered to the Athenians in the fourth century BCE, the Athenians were recommended to sacrifice to several gods, the two under this title being Zeus and Athena, who will emerge as the chief agents in the theological conclusion of the *Oresteia*: see Introduction, p. 63. **of the Underworld:** Hecate had her own temple in Argos, at least by Pausanias' time (2.22.7), and a mysterious temple of burnt brick outside Argos housed images of the Maid and Pluto as well as the Olympian Demeter (Paus. 2.18.3). **the heavens:** The adjective *ouranios*, 'celestial', is used collectively of the gods, *theoi*, to distinguish them from mortals in the Homeric *Hymn to Demeter* 55. In Aristophanes' *Frogs* 1135 Euripides may imply that it was a word associated with Aeschylean pomposity and obscurity. **the marketplace:** The epithet *agoraios*, 'guardian of the agora', is used occasionally of Artemis and Athena (Paus. 5.15.4, 3.11.9), but is most commonly applied to Zeus as guardian of popular assemblies (Hdt. 5.46, Aesch. *Eum.* 973) or Hermes as patron of commerce (Ar. *Knights* 297). **ablaze with offerings:** The chorus do not specify the type, although what follows suggests the use of frankincense, myrrh, or an unction made of fragrant juniper or cedar wood and berries. Bloodless offerings typically included fruit, barley or wheat cakes which could be burnt and libations using wine, honey and milk. Animals usually sacrificed included cattle, goats, sheep and pigs.

92–3 Everywhere flames are rising all the way to heaven: Lit., 'One light [from here and another] from elsewhere rises heaven-high.' The verb *anischein* is used of the rising sun at Xen. *Cyn.* 6.13. Aristotle singles out the adjective *ouranomēkēs* as a compound and unfamiliar word 'appropriate to an emotional speaker'. Once again, the stress is on the vertical axis (4, 51–4*), drawing the audience's attention to the skies above what they can see in the theatre. On light and dark and fire symbolism see Introduction, pp. 63–5.

94–5 bewitched: For this sense of *pharmassein*, 'to medicate', see Ar. *Thesm.* 534 and Plato, *Symp.* 194a, 'bewitch by flattery'. Some of the animal and vegetable fats used in ancient lotions and potions were highly combustible. **pure balm:** In *Anabasis* 4.4.13 Xenophon's men anoint themselves with a *chrima* made of pork fat, sesame, bitter almonds and turpentine.

96 salve: The masculine noun *pelanos* designates any sticky, gum-like semi-liquid substance, especially a viscous mixture of meal and oil offered to the gods by being burnt on an altar. Electra pours one on her father's tomb in *Choeph.* 92; see also *Pers.* 204, Eur. *Ion* 707. **deep inside the palace:** The audience's uneasy awareness of the unseen activities, here relating to unguents, in the interior of the palace later becomes a preoccupation in the Cassandra scene (1310–14). On the importance of the dramatic setting just outside the house see Hall (2010b) 129–31.

97–9 You should tell us: Lit., 'Having told us'. Whether or not she is visibly and physically present (see 83–4*), Clytemnestra is addressed by the chorus again; they plead for reassurance about the reason for all the ritual activity. **right:** The feminine noun *themis* implies something sanctioned by deeply ingrained custom and religious sensibility, such as obeying Zeus' imperatives to honour guests, hosts, suppliants and oaths (see, e.g., *Od.* 14.56, *Il.* 11.779), but it is also used in the *Odyssey* to identify a particular form of behaviour as appropriate to women. Eumaeus says that it is *themis* 'for a woman to weep when her husband has died elsewhere' (14.129–30). See also 214–17*, 250–1*, 1431*. **and mend my troubled mind:** Lit., 'become the healer of my anxiety'. Although *Paiōn*, 'Healer', is the proper name of a doctor in the *Iliad* (5.401) and, like *Paian*, can serve as an epithet of Apollo (146*) or Asclepius (Ar. *Plut.* 636), it can also designate a hymn to a god, often a victorious one, usually Apollo or

Artemis (see 645*, Hom. *Il.* 1.473, Aesch. fr. 350.4). But it can also simply mean 'healer' (Soph. *Phil.* 168; cf. Hom. *Od.* 4.232). *merimna* literally means 'care', 'solicitude' or 'anxiety', but the concrete noun 'mind' is required in English to make sense of the following clauses. On the paianic strand in *Agamemnon* see Swift (2018).

100–3 one minute ... mind: Lit., 'which one minute is ill-minded; but at another minute, hope, appearing gentle from the sacrifices, wards off insatiable worry and grief that heart-eats the mind'. Aeschylus is the undisputed master of evoking tense and uneasy states of mind through his creative use of vocabulary. Here the chorus vacillate between despair and the optimism inspired by their observation of the city-wide burnt offerings. They badly need Clytemnestra to communicate with them. The adjective 'heart-eating', *thumoboros*, is applied to Strife (Eris) in the *Iliad* (19.58). **hope ... sacrifices:** By describing hope (*elpis*) in such visual terms, the chorus almost personify her as the sole spirit who remained in the jar opened by Pandora in Hesiod's *Works* 96–9. Her head seems to be depicted, protruding from the jar, on an Attic red-figured amphora dated to 450–430 BCE in the British Museum (1865,0103.28): see Neils (2005). Theognis 1136–46 recommends that men worship Hope, 'the one good god left amongst us', assiduously. The Watchman hopes for discharge from his duties (20–1*). On Hope see also 1059. **gently:** Hope is 'sweet' and the 'heart-fostering nurse of old age' at Pindar fr. 214.1–3 and 'golden' at Soph. *OT* 157–8.

104–256 Parodos
Disappointed that Clytemnestra has not responded to them, and probably returned indoors, the chorus cease their processional anapaests and embark on their sung and danced lyric *parodos*, one of the greatest pieces of poetry in ancient Greek and world literature. Martin West, a scholar not prone to expressions of enthusiasm, described it as a 'great cantata' which reveals 'the awesome workshop of Aeschylus' mind' (West (1979) 2, 5). It is divided into six corresponding strophic pairs, with a single, additional, different stanza or 'mesode' inserted solely after the first pair. The chorus fuse memories of the past with addresses to the gods. This is a summary of the subject matter they cover. On the impact of the transitions between dactylic, trochaic and iambic lyric metres see the Metrical Appendix.

Strophe 1   The chorus recall an omen outside the palace when the army was mustering for the Trojan expedition. Two eagles devoured a pregnant hare.

Antistrophe 1	The chorus report, in direct speech, the prophet Calchas' interpretation of the omen at the time. He divined that it meant that the expedition would take Troy, but also that Artemis was angry with the eagles. His direct speech, interrupted only by the repeated refrain at stanza end (121, 139, 160), continues until near the end of the mesode.
Mesode	The chorus continue to quote what Calchas uttered after the omen. He said that Artemis favours baby animals and the omen is marred; he then prayed to Apollo to intervene with his sister to prevent her from imposing adverse winds, thus 'precipitating another sacrifice' which would cause family conflict.
Strophe 2	The chorus interrupt their recollections of the past to sing a hymn to Zeus which extends over three stanzas. They sing that they can think of no other entity to invoke to ease their anxiety.
Antistrophe 2	Zeus has succeeded in vanquishing his father, who had vanquished his grandfather, and those who praise Zeus gain wisdom …
Strophe 3	… if they praise him as the one who taught humans the hard lesson that learning comes through suffering.
Antistrophe 3	The chorus return to their recollections, singing that the fleet was afflicted by adverse winds at Aulis.
Strophe 4	Delay cause by North winds caused hunger, mental problems and damage to the fleet. Calchas made a pronouncement that had something to do with Artemis and made the Atreidai weep.
Antistrophe 4	Agamemnon's response is recollected in direct speech. He said that he faced a terrible dilemma but decided to sacrifice his own daughter rather than fail his allies.
Strophe 5	The chorus condemn his decision as sacrilegious.
Antistrophe 5	Iphigenia's pleas were ignored. Agamemnon instructed the priests to gag her and hold her over the altar.
Strophe 6	Iphigenia tried to use eye contact to beg for her life. The chorus recall how she used to sing at her father's symposia.
Antistrophe 6	Calchas' prediction was fulfilled. Justice ensures that people who have suffered learn from it. But whatever will be will be.

104–7 I have the authority: The chorus base this claim on the argument that old people retain potency through their ability to use speech cogently even when they have lost the physical strength to fight. Nestor in the *Iliad*, despite his great age, is much valued for the advice he can give (10.17–20, 1.247–9, 4.291–311, 2.362–8; see Falkner (1995) 9–22); he says that it is the right of the elders to urge on the horsemen by words and counsels (4.322–4). In the *Odyssey*, the ancient Phaeacian Echeneus was excellent in speech and skilled in wisdom (9.52–9). Xenophon reports that, when Cerasus was attacked, it was three elderly citizens who sought an interview with the Greek assembly (*Anab.* 5.7.17); for further examples see Richardson (1933) 34–6. But the audience may have understood the chorus' authority as partly deriving from their age because it means that they were eyewitnesses of the events they are about to recall, as is implied by 248*. See further the impression Agamemnon made on them when he left (798–803). **to speak out loud:** The verb *throein* implies making an announcement or statement to a large or public audience (Soph. *Ajax* 67, *OC* 597). At 1137* Cassandra uses it of herself when she is about to inform the chorus about what she has suffered. **the leaders':** *andrōn ekteleōn* seems to mean 'perfect men' or 'perfected men', but Rodighiero (2018) may be correct in arguing that it means all the heroes of the Greek expedition against Troy. **For, in my old age, persuasion, the power of songs, is still breathed on me from the gods:** Lit., 'Life that has grown with me still breathes persuasion, power of songs, from the gods.'

108–15 I sing … tail: Lit., 'How the double-throned might of the Achaeans, the like-minded command of Hellenic youth, a furious bird-omen, sends with spear and avenging hand against the Teucrian land, the king of birds to the king of ships, [of which] one [was] black and the other white from behind.' In English, 'I sing' needs to be added, and the effect of the delayed nominative subject 'bird-omen' of the verb 'sends' needs to be reproduced by repeating 'how'. The title 'king of ships' consolidates from 45–7* and 51–4* the thread of accounts of sea voyages and also of maritime imagery (see van Nes (1963)), much of it related to monarchical or divine power, which weaves through the play (147–50*, 182–3*, 192–5*, 222–7*, 235–8,* 405*, 556–7*, 613–80 (the Herald's account of the storm and the shipwreck), 689–91*, 897–8*, 899–900*, 1005–13*, 1617–19*). A passage in Aristophanes' *Frogs* (997–1003) implies that naval metaphors were particularly associated with Aeschylus; *Agamemnon* lines 108–11 also provides the prototype for *Frogs* 1284–92. **double throne:** See above, 43–4*. **unified:** Lit., 'with mind together', 'thinking alike'; despite the double command, the chorus make it clear that the brothers were in full agreement. **furious:** *thourios* is a variant of *thouros*, 'rushing', an epithet of the impetuous war-god Ares (Hom. *Il.* 15.127), on whom see 374–6*; it is used by the chorus of *Persians* of Xerxes, rushing headlong into the invasion of Greece (73). **bird-omen:** *ornis* can mean not just 'bird' but 'bird portent' (Hom. *Il.* 13.821, *Od.* 20.242) or even just 'portent' (*Il.* 24.219). Divination by birds' movements and cries, ornithomancy, was deeply embedded in Greek culture by the archaic age. Hesiod was believed to have composed a poem entitled *Ornithomanteia*. On one side of an Athenian black-figured skyphos of the late sixth century BCE attributed to the Theseus Painter (Naples Archaeological Museum 16211), a huge bird devours a hare watched by two transfixed men in helmets; in a similar scene on the other side, the bird clutches a snake in its talons. For such bird omens in Homer see, e.g., *Il.* 12.201–9, 13.821–3; *Od.* 2.146–93, 15.160–218 and Collins (2002). In *PV* 484–8, Prometheus cites, amongst the modes of divination he has gifted to mortals, the one that reads 'the flight of large birds of prey (*oiōnōn*) with crooked talons'. In Aristophanes' *Birds* the avian chorus cites its role in divination as one of the advantages it bestows on humans, although the birds believe that humans are too credulous about bird signs (716–22). Several epigrams on bird omens are included in the collection by Poseidippus of Pella found on papyrus, edited by Bastianini and Gallazzi (2001) and translated by Gutzwiller (2005). On birds in *Agamemnon* see Introduction, p. 58. **avenging hand:** *praktōr*, 'executive', is a variant on Zeus' title *praktēr*; 'accomplisher' (Soph. *Trach.* 251) and in tragedy comes to mean 'punisher' or 'avenger' (in Aesch. *Eum.* 319 the Erinyes use it substantively of themselves). **Teucrian:** The Teucer alluded to here, the son of the River Scamander and Idaea, the nymph of Mount Ida, was the earliest king of the Troad. His daughter married Dardanus, who, on succeeding to the throne, changed the name of the people from Teucrians to Dardanians (ps.-Apollod. *Bibl.* 3.139; Diod. Sic. 4.75.1). **birds' king to the kings of ships:** The word order in the translation is designed to reproduce the chiasmus in the Greek, which emphasises the equivalent status amongst their respective realms of eagles and Atreidai. On the term *basileus* see 83–4*. The noun *oiōnoi* often specifically implies any large birds of prey (see Hom. *Od.* 16.216), but the word 'king' removes any doubt that that the eagle is meant here, rather than, e.g., a vulture (32*; see Pind. *Ol.* 13.21, Ar. *Birds* 515). **one black, one with a white tail:** Despite its name, the magnificent golden eagle (Aquila chrysaetos) has the darkest plumage of any eagle seen in Greece. The white-tailed eagle (Haliaeetus albicilla), still to be seen in the Peloponnesian mountains, is, as its name suggests, difficult to mistake visually for any other eagle. Both golden and white-tailed eagles prey extensively on hares. As Rose (1958) 13 points out, the 'appearance of two eagles of the same sex is of itself portentous, for the raptors are solitaries and hunt either alone or with their mate only'.

117–18 close to the palace … place: The portent occurred in or very near the precise space outside the palace where the play is set and the chorus are performing (Sommerstein (2010) 171–7 is clearly correct, despite the efforts of Heath (2001) to locate the omen at Aulis). **on the right:** Lit., 'from the spear-wielding hand's [side]'. This is a graphic way of saying 'from the right-hand side' appropriate to the warlike context. It was almost always better for a portent to appear on the right of its viewer's field of vision (see Hom. *Il.* 14.315–21, *Od.* 2.146–54), just as the right was considered auspicious in Greek culture and philosophy more generally, notably in Pythagoras' 'Table of Opposites'; it was associated there with the masculine, light, straight and good, while the left was associated with the feminine, dark, crooked and bad. See Lloyd (1962), Lovibond (1994) and Hall (2018b) 35–6. On an inscription from Ephesus, with instructions for divination, in the British Museum (museum no. 867,1122.441), which was created in the sixth century BCE, there is a detailed analysis of the meanings of birds flying from right to left and vice versa: 'In flying from right to left if the bird shall get out of sight it is lucky, but if it shall raise its left wing, and whether it raises it or hides, it is unlucky; and if, in flying from left to right, it should get out of sight in a straight line, it is unlucky; but if raising the right wing … .' **conspicuous place:** The more visible the site, the more authoritative the portent. But the chorus may have been understood as implying that it was sufficiently public for them to know so much about it.

119–120 eating baby hares, creatures still in the womb, deprived of a last escape: Lit., 'eating the hare-offspring [*laginan … gennan*], big-conceived [*erikumona*] womb-fruit [*phermata*]'. The word *laginan* is here adjectival. On very young creatures see 49–50*. The obscurity of the language, reflected across many centuries of frantic editorial activity which produced textual variants, is appropriate for the oracular description of a mysterious portent. The gruesome detail is reminiscent of the sacrifice of 'the foetuses of quivering goats' made by Vera, Priestess of Artemis on Patmos in the second or third century CE, a cult said to have been installed by Orestes on his return journey from Tauris after the events dramatised in the *Oresteia* and Euripides' *Iphigenia in Tauris*. See the inscription in Merkelbach and Stauber (1998) 169–70, discussed in Hall (2013) 142–3. A marble statuette of a girl holding a hare has been found in Artemis' sanctuary at Brauron (Bevan (1986) 415); so have several terracotta figurines depicting females holding hares around the archaic sanctuary of Artemis at Kanoni, Corfu (see Lechat (1891) 32, 38, 55–6, 66–8).

121 Sing the song of sorrow: Lit., 'Utter the Ailinos, Ailinos' or 'say, "alas for Linos, alas for Linos"'. The *linos*-song seems to have been a traditional refrain, performed by a young boy at harvest-time on the shield of Achilles (Hom. *Il.* 18.569–71), which came to be identified with or personified as a hero called Linos. He was somehow associated with Adonis (Sappho fr. 140b), the hero beloved of Aphrodite whose untimely death was mourned noisily by Greek women at their midsummer Adonia festivals. Their song was supposedly introduced from the Near East, and, according to Hesiod fr. 255, was performed by singers and citharists 'in feasts and choruses', when Linos was named at both the beginning and end of their songs. The despairing cry *ailinos* appears in dirge-like contexts elsewhere in Greek tragedy (Soph. *Ajax* 627; Eur. *Her.* 348, *Or.* 1395); see Stephens (2002–3). **but let good prevail:** This complete line, with its imperative *eipe* and indirect command *nikatō*, also rounds off the following antistrophe (139) and mesode (158–9*). The prayer that good may prevail is intended to avert the omen's bad implications; it may be compared with the apotropaic hymn to Apollo sung by the Achaeans at *Iliad* 1.73. On Aeschylean repeated refrains, the butt of jokes in Ar. *Frogs* 1264–97, see Moritz (1979) *passim*. The sentence condenses, into two gnomic clauses, the mood and import of the entire play and indeed *Oresteia*. The situation is terrible and must be lamented, but there remains hope that goodness will win out in the end: emotional pessimism, cerebral optimism. It is the epitaph to one of Oscar Wilde's bleakest poems: see Introduction, pp. 3–4 and Hall (2024) 174.

122–3 trusted army seer: Calchas is not named until 156*, after his speech interpreting the eagle omen is reported. The adjective *kednos* implies a relationship of reciprocal trust between people doing one another a service, such as kings and subjects, masters and slaves, messengers and their audiences, parents and children, or husbands and wives (Ar. *Thesm.* 62, Hom. *Il.* 17.28, *Od.* 13.170, 1.335, Pind. *Pyth.* 4.117, Hes. *Theog.* 169). See below, 261* and 622*. At least one professional diviner or soothsayer (*mantis*) accompanied ancient Greek armies (see Bearzot (1993)), the most famous examples being Xenophon's four named seers in the *Anabasis*: Silanus the Ambraciot, Arexion the Arcadian, Euclides of Phlius and Basias of Elis (5.6.18, 5.6.34, 6.4.13, 7.8.1, 7.8.10). The pious Xenophon claims (5.6.29) to have learned divination skills from being present at many sacrifices. On the precise meaning of *mantis* see 1202*. **noting … tempers:** Lit., 'having seen the warlike Atreidai [being] double in respect of their two spirits'. The point may be that the visual difference between the two eagles is reflected in the visible difference between the brothers' appearances, as well as indicating their divergent personalities, but since the chorus have reassured us that the Atreidai were unanimous about the expedition (108–15*), Calchas' observation strikes a note of unease. It is intriguing that Menelaus in the *Iliad*, deeply frustrated on the battlefield during the fight for Patroclus' corpse, and glancing from side to side warily, is likened to 'an eagle, which men says has the sharpest sight of all winged creatures under heaven; the swift-footed hare, crouching underneath a leafy bush, is not unseen by him, but the eagle swoops upon him and seizes him and takes away his life' (17.673–8).

124   leaders of the army: Lit., 'as the escorting authorities'; *pompous* needs to be taken adjectivally.

125   Aeschylus' decision to make the chorus report Calchas' own words, in direct speech, lends a hieratic intensity to the verse.

126–7   this expedition: The feminine noun *keleuthos* is a poetic word, appropriate to oracular language, meaning a pathway or road, but often in a cosmic rather than literal, everyday sense (of the winds, Hom. *Od.* 5.383; constellations, Soph. *Trach.* 131; the gods, Hom. *Il.* 3.406; or of abstractions like Persuasion, 28 Parmenides B 2.4). Here, as at Aesch. *Pers.* 758, it is an elevated term for a voyage or expedition. See Becker (1937) 7–13. **shall take:** Lit., 'takes'. The present tense may be used for vividness, or imply an action continuous with the expedition that is already, at the time Calchas is prophesying, in the process of being launched, but present tenses are also typical of oracular language that strictly speaking describes future events. **Priam's city:** On the recurrent and resonant use of Priam's proper name see 40*.

128–30   Fate: The Homeric divinity Moira (*Il.* 24.209) is usually negatively presented and often appears in formulaic phrases as the agent, bringer or harbinger of death (*Il.* 4.517, 18.119; see Alexiou (1974) 113). Homer usually refers to a single Moira, as Aeschylus does here; in the *Iliad* she is a personification of fate which spins out the thread of each person's life when they are born (24.29); she oversees the consequences of what they do in line with the wishes of the gods (5.613, 20.5). In Aeschylus' striking image she is virtually personified as the destroyer of the Trojans' livestock. See also 1535–7* and Schlögl (1991) 59–65. **abundant publicly owned livestock in its entirety:** Lit., 'all its abundant-publicly-owned flocks-and-herds'. The neuter noun *ktēnos* implies cultivated beasts, both sheep and cattle; it is sometimes used to mean 'animals' as opposed to 'humans' (68 Democritus B 57). Calchas speaks of animal deaths, but not of the human inhabitants of Troy. Moreover, his actual predictions of Greek victory are neither extensive nor laudatory and he swiftly moves on to admonition. This is the first of a series of references, most of which are menacing and figurative, to pastoral activities. The chorus say that the mind of a woman is easily convinced, like a field that is grazed by incoming livestock (485–7). The typhoon that assaulted the fleet is conceived as an incompetent shepherd who loses his flock (654–6). The allegorical lion-cub grew up to slaughter the family sheep (728–31); judging a character is compared with judging livestock (795; see also 796–8); in her mendacious speech of flattery, Clytemnestra compares Agamemnon to a dog that watches the cattle-pens (895–6), but later points out that he owned abundant fleecy flocks from which he could have selected a sacrificial animal instead of her daughter (1416).

132–4 Only … beforehand: Lit., 'Only let no grudge from the gods darken Troy's great bridle-bit, forged beforehand, mustered.' Metaphors from metalwork become important later in the play: 151–4*. This one makes the audience visualise the Greeks as imposing a bridle on the Trojans, with a touch of irony since one of the Trojans' own Homeric epithets had been 'horse-taming' (e.g. *Il.* 4.352). On other metaphors from the equipment used for constraining animals see 218–21*, 326–8*. **grudge:** The feminine noun *aga* is a certain correction for the manuscripts' *ata*, in which the long first alpha prevents correct scansion. In the context, too, what threatens the Greeks is not delusion sent by the gods (359–61*), but divine indignation. **darken:** Aeschylus is mixing metaphors with his customary panache. On the pervasive theme of light versus darkness see Introduction, pp. 63–5.

134–8 out of pity … the eagles' feast: Lit., 'For in pity pure Artemis, bearing-a-grudge against her father's winged hounds for sacrificing the wretched cowering-thing offspring-and-all before birth, hates the eagles' feast.' **pure:** The adjective *hagnos* is used more often of Artemis than any other divinity (e.g. Hom. *Od.* 5.123, 18.202), but after Homer it is also used in connection with virginal young people (Pind. *Pyth.* 4.103, Eur. *Hipp.* 102, Plato *Laws* 8.840d). The chorus later apply it to Iphigenia's voice (245). **Artemis:** She is the first named female divinity in the play. See further Introduction, p. 47. Unlike the chorus, who speculated that the god angered by an attack on the young of birds of prey might be Pan, Zeus or Apollo (55–7*), Calchas knows exactly which divine portfolio contains oversight of infant or embryonic fauna. **angry:** The adjective *epiphthonos* means either feeling *phthonos* (envy plus malice) towards another agent, or being the object of *phthonos* felt by another agent towards one (921–2*). **winged hounds:** This is a striking description of the eagles; *ptēnos* is usually applied to birds. But see Aesch. *PV* 1022 (also of Zeus' eagle), Eur. *IT* 193 (of horses). On wings and flying see 390–5*. **for sacrificing:** The middle voice of *thuein* suggests a sacrifice made to consult the gods' views on a proposed journey or military strategy (Hdt. 5.44, 9.10, Xen. *An.* 6.4.9, Thuc. 5.54). But it is a remarkably bold metaphor to use, not of humans sacrificing, but of birds devouring prey, reminding the audience that Calchas has identified the eagles with the Atreidai. The question of who the hare's unborn offspring 'represent' within the omen and Calchas' interpretation of it, as elliptically reported by the chorus, has produced a longstanding scholarly controversy: the candidates proposed include the murdered sons of Thyestes, the young Greek soldiers and/or the Trojans who are to die during the war, and Iphigenia herself, in a strange dialectic where the victim that Artemis demands is simultaneously the cause of her rage and the price of its appeasement. The goddess's concern for the unborn leverets themselves might, however, be sufficient to trigger her wrath. Aeschylus has carefully left the question unanswered to enhance the audience's metaphysical confusion. **distressed:** It is unusual to find the emotive term *mogeros* applied to anything other than a suffering human person or household, as at Aesch. *PV.* 565, *Sept.* 827, Eur. *Tro.* 783, 790, Soph. *El.* 93. **cowering creature:** Aeschylus' feminine noun *ptax* is equivalent to the masculine *ptōx* (which the Erinyes in *Eumenides* 326 use of the cowering Orestes) and elsewhere sometimes applies specifically to hares (Hom. *Il.* 17.676, 22.310). **along with her unborn brood:** *autotokos* seems to mean 'children and all', while *pro lochou* means 'before the birth'. In the *Iliad*, Agamemnon says to Menelaus that he wanted their men to destroy all the Trojans, even those still in their mothers' wombs (6.57–60) The verb *stugein* means 'to hate' more strongly even than *misein*. It implies that the emotion is expressed, not merely felt (see Eur. *El.* 1017), and is often used of divine detestation of a shocking human crime. At Aesch. *Sept.* 691 Eteocles says that the whole family of Laius is 'loathed' (*stugēthen*) by Apollo.

139 Sing the song of sorrow, but may good prevail: See 121*.

140 Beautiful One: The adjectives *kalē* as here and *kallistē* were cult titles of Artemis in Arcadia (Paus. 8.35.8) and on a sepulchral inscription found at Aleppo (CIG 4445); Paus. 1.29.2 says there were two wooden images of Artemis *Aristē* and *Kallistē* ('Best and Most Beautiful') at the Athenian precinct of Artemis outside the walls beyond the Academy. Some scholars think that this should be in the vocative as an apostrophe and amend the verb 'demands' accordingly. Views of this passage on Artemis are compiled by de Paoli (2018).

141　raging lions' tiny cubs: Lit., 'to the tiny dews of raging lions'. In Homer the epithet *maleros* always applies to fire (e.g. *Il.* 9.242, 20.316, 21.375), so may have associations that point up the contrast with the lions' damp, 'dewy' brood. There are several further lion images in the play and trilogy, which Knox (1952) regards as all enriching the 'parable' of the lion cub (717*): see also Saayman (2014). Artemis, as Mistress of Animals, is sometimes portrayed with lions and lionesses, for example on a relief on a terracotta pithos of the late seventh century BCE in the National Archaeological Museum of Athens (Museum no. 355). The adjective *leptos* is used by Herodotus to distinguish small livestock such as goats from large cattle (8.137). The feminine plural noun *drosoi* is a striking way of implying the moist, fresh quality of new-born mammals; in the *Odyssey* another word for dew, *hersē*, signifies young lambs and kids (9.222); Hesychius glosses *hersai* as 'kids born in winter and tender young cattle', adding that *drosoi* can mean the same. But dew is to have more disturbing associations later in the play (1390*).

142–3　delights ... countryside: It is unusual to find *terpnos* used subjectively of the agent experiencing pleasure rather than the object which gives pleasure: perhaps the translation should suggest that the suckling young find the goddess delightful. **suckling young:** The striking compound 'breastloving' recurs at 719* of a lion cub in a long allegory. It is not a big conceptual leap to make a goddess involved in childbirth under her title *lochia* (Eur. *IT* 1097) take delight in lactation. Artemis was honoured as protectress of the young in her epithets *paidotrophos* (Paus. 4.34.6) and *kourotrophos* (Diod. Sic. 5.73). Breastfeeding is repeatedly associated with violence in both this play (717–19*) and in Clytemnestra's dream and execution by Orestes in *Choephori* (530–4, 906–28). **roam the countryside:** It is a delicate touch to apply to wild animals the epithet *agronomos*, famously used of Artemis' other companions, the nymphs, in *Od.* 6.106. One of Artemis' ancient cult titles, *agrotera*, related her to the countryside (Hom. *Il.* 21.471, Xen. *Cyn.* 6.13). Xenophon built his temple of Artemis near Scillus in the Peloponnese in a rural valley which contained 'every type of creature that is hunted' (*Anab.* 5.3.8).

144–5　demands the fulfilment ... but the apparition was marred: Lit., 'demands to fulfil these joint tokens, [which are] on the one hand (*men*) auspicious, yet on the other (*de*) the visions of the birds [are] blameworthy'. The manuscript reading *strouthōn* ('of sparrows' or 'of ostriches' or, at a stretch, 'of birds') is an interpolation and corrupt. It does not fit the dactylic metre. It has also caused the ousting of the precise original reading. But it found its way into the text because someone copying the play out was clear that what Calchas meant here was the bird omen. The distinction here seems to be between the favourable outcome *predicted* by the signs (that the Greeks would capture Troy) and the disturbing nature of the omen itself. Calchas is moving on from interpretation of the signs to an attempt to influence the future behaviour of the angered divinity. The term translated 'joint signs', *xumbola*, suggests the splitting of an object such as a coin between two parties to an agreement (Hdt. 8.86), and this perhaps insinuates the idea that Artemis may feel her covenant with Zeus has been broken. He may be in charge of punishing crimes against *xenia*, but her portfolio includes taking care of mammalian young.

146 And I call on Paean with the cry *iē*: *Paian* (or *Paiēōn* or *Paiōn*), 'physician' or 'healer' (see above, 99*), is a cult title of Apollo, and *iē* is an exclamation especially associated with Apollo's worship. See Hom. *Hymn to Apollo* 517, Soph. *OT* 154. Calchas, sing the chorus, hoped that Apollo, as Artemis' brother, would be able to intercede with her.

147–50 to prevent her ... adverse winds of long duration: Lit., 'So she may not create for the Danaans any adverse-winded long-duration ship-detaining un-voyages.' While the accumulation of compound adjectives heightens the oracular obscurity, the feminine noun *aploia* was a standard term for detention in port (Thuc. 4.4, Hdt. 2.119). Calchas is going well beyond his interpretation of the bird-portent to predict (correctly) the way in which Artemis will wreak revenge. On ships and ship imagery see 108–15*.

151–4 and precipitating ... man: Lit., 'hastening another sacrifice, without law, that cannot be feasted on, innate craftsman of conflicts, unafraid of the male'. Calchas unmistakeably refers to the human sacrifice of Iphigenia as lawless and not providing sacrificial meat that can be eaten, although the oracular language still requires efforts from the chorus' audience to decode it. *sumphuton*, 'in-born', seems to be the first reference in *Agamemnon* to the notion that the family is cursed across generations: see Introduction, pp. 52–7. Metaphors drawn from the world of craft and metallurgy are used in reference to injustice and especially by and of Clytemnestra; they are drawn from the spheres of forging (151–4*), coin minting (390–5*, 440–4*), bronze smithery (611–12*), sword sharpening (1260–3, 1535–7) and welding (1566). See also the 'rightful craftsman' (1405–6). On the neuter noun *neikos* see 1377–8*. **disrespect of woman towards man:** The adjectival phrase *ou deisēnora* is in agreement with *tektona*, 'craftsman', but it is crucial in bringing Clytemnestra and the theme of a challenge to patriarchy into Calchas' word-picture. See also 1405–6*.

154–5 For there awaits … child: This remarkable sentence concludes the chorus' quotation of Calchas' divinatory utterance. It piles up adjectives, accumulates alliterative effects with '*m*' and '*p*' sounds, and combines two grim images suggestive of Clytemnestra as a fearsome housekeeper and as wrath personified. **terrible:** On the recurrence of terror see Introduction, p. 3. **resilient:** Literally 'rising again', i.e., impossible to suppress. **treacherous:** On Clytemnestra's guile see 1129*. Aegisthus is called *dolomētis* at *Od.* 3.308, and Clytemnestra is given the same epithet by the ghost of her husband at *Od.* 11.422. Taking this into account, as well as the remaining question mark over the importance of her relationship with Aegisthus in *Agamemnon*, it may be significant that *dolios* is an epithet of Aphrodite (Bacchylides 17.116, Eur. *Hel.* 238). **housekeeper:** In the masculine, *oikonomos* means 'estate manager' (Xen. *Oec.* 1.2), and it is used in the feminine of a wife running a household responsibly in Lysias 1.7. **remembering:** On the theme of memory see 34–9* and Introduction, p. 15. In *Eumenides*, the Erinyes urged on by Clytemnestra proudly say they 'remember evil deeds', *kakōn te mnēmones* (382–3). **wrath:** In imagining Clytemnestra as a personification of rage, the chorus use the strong noun *mēnis*, usually felt in archaic and classical poetry only by gods (Hom. *Il.* 5.34, Pind. *Pyth.* 4.159; see 649* and 701*) and semi-divine heroes such as Achilles (Hom. *Il.* 1.1; see Hdt. 7.134). **that avenges a child:** Lit., 'child-avenging'. The first child to come to mind may be Iphigenia, but the problem of abused children, the play will reveal, extends at least a generation further back in the family.

156–7 such fateful things: The unusually extended separation of pronoun and adjective in *toiade … morsim'* heightens the audience's concentration on the important words sandwiched between. **Calchas:** The famous seer is finally named. The Byzantine chronicler John Malalas may have been crystallising Calchas' image in the ancient world when he described him as 'short, white, totally grey including his beard, hirsute, and a very fine seer and reader of omens' (*Chron.* 5.105). The son of Thestor, Calchas was the augur of the Greeks during the Trojan War and played a major role in the Aulis incident as narrated in the epic *Cypria*. He 'knew what is, what will be, and what was' (Hom. *Il.* 1.70). After the war he was believed to have encountered another seer, Mopsus, in Colophon, further down the coast of Asia Minor from Troy. Mopsus defeated him in a prophecy competition and Calchas died (Hesiod fr. 214). See further Nünlist (2006) and Clarke

(2021). For what we know about the reality of such 'freelance' prophets in the ancient world see Johnston (2008) 109–43. **shout out:** The *klaz-* stem implies a loud, piercing noise; see 48*, 201. **inferring ... began:** Lit., 'from the bird-omens pertaining-to-the-road'. This could mean the precise route taken by the birds rather than the journey about to be undertaken by the humans.

158–9 in tune: The word *homophōnos* means either 'speaking the same language' (Hdt. 3.98) or 'sing in unison' ([Arist.] *Pr.* 921a7, Nicomachus, *Harm.* 11.5). Here the metaphor implies that the third and last time the refrain is sung (see 121* and 33*), its message of mixed sorrow and hope for an eventual resolution is 'in unison' emotionally with Calchas' interpretation of the omen. In effect, the chorus repeat Calchas' paean at 146–54; see Haldane (1965) 38.

161–3 Zeus ... address him: Some scholars have argued that the last iteration of the refrain and the entire 'Hymn to Zeus' from here to 180 report in direct speech an uninterrupted continuation of Calchas' utterance (Egan (2007), with further bibliography). This is plausible, but the *effect* of the chorus singing the hymn themselves would have been very little different even if the audience was somehow sure they were quoting Calchas. The hesitancy in choosing a cult title or epithet for Zeus is unusual, and has precipitated avalanches of discussion amongst scholars who believe that it indicates important developments in religious thought. But the chorus are in an unusual situation and their hesitation is characteristic of their theological bewilderment throughout this play. They are concerned to nurture a good relationship with the most important god, whose responsibilities included punishing the worst crimes against kin, but are reluctant to specify the particular capacity in which they need to ask for his help here. They have just narrated an incident in which an unlawful sacrifice was prophesied and they are about to describe it in shocking detail. The effect in context is 'to enhance the mood of grim foreboding, to foreshadow dire consequences from Agamemnon's terrible act' (Parker (2009) 137; see Rosenmeyer (1955) 255–6 and Schenker (1994)), especially stressed by the ancient liturgical formula 'whoever he may be'. No wonder they are apprehensive and careful with their language: see Carawan (2017) and Smith (1980) for an interesting if dogmatic commentary. **if this designation ... approval:** Lit., 'if being called this is dear to him'. **I have no point of comparison:** Lit., 'I have not [anything] to guess is similar'. This is an ancient idea: in the *Iliad*, Zeus himself is never compared with anything or anyone else, the supreme Greek deity inheriting from those of Ancient Near Eastern Literature a legacy of incomparability (see Ready (2012)). The chorus are certain that the correct divinity to invoke in the current circumstances, with anxiety running high, is Zeus rather than, say, Apollo or Pan (see above, 55–7*). **weigh everything up:** On Aeschylus' vocabulary for intellectual activity see Introduction, p. 62 and, on weighing imagery see 63–7*. **fruitless burden:** For the neuter noun *achthos* being used metaphorically see also 626. **from my anxious thoughts:** The feminine noun *phrontis* contains the ideas of both consciousness or feeling and worry.

168–9   The one … great: Ouranos, Zeus' grandfather. It is not possible to reproduce the double negative in the Greek without generating periphrasis or nonsense in English. Aeschylus takes just 12 words to tell the story of the rise and fall of the first cosmic patriarch, castrated by his disaffected son Kronos on behalf of his mother Earth and his siblings, as narrated in detail in Hesiod's *Theogony* 132–92. On the importance of Hesiod's account to the *Oresteia* see Hall (2018b) and (2021b); Introduction, pp. 55–7. Ancient sources do not address what happened to Ouranos after his mutilation, but Greeks continued to invoke him as a witness of oaths (Hom. *Il.* 15.36) and initiates into Orphism prayed to him as 'father of all, from whom the world arose' (Orphic Hymn 4.1–2, 'To Ouranos'). The idea that the original Olympian hereditary succession ran far from smoothly and involved intergenerational and intrafamilial violence is too disturbing for the chorus to dwell on. By not naming Ouranos or Kronos (171–2*), but curiously making them seem more important because the audience must work to identify the erased parties, Aeschylus is using a form of the rhetorical figure of *paralepsis* or *praeteritio*. **overconfidence in every battle:** Lit., 'over confidence (*thrasos*) that made him attempt any battle at all'.

171–2   the one who came next: This is the Titan Kronos, Zeus' father. The story of the second cosmic patriarch's vanquishment by a wily son, partly on behalf of the mother (Rhea) and his siblings, is here compressed from Hesiod, *Theog.* 453–506. **victor:** Zeus. The noun *triaktēr* summons up the striking image of Zeus defeating his father in wrestling; it is connected with the verbs *triazein* and *apotriazein*, to win a wrestling match by throwing the opponent in three bouts. See the comic poet Thougenides fr. 2 and schol. Aesch. *Choeph.* 339. There was a tradition that Zeus had wrestled with Kronos at Olympia, or that he had had founded the Olympic Games in honour of his victory over Kronos (Paus. 5.7.10, 8.2.2). On wrestling and the motif of the third fall in the trilogy see Poliakoff (1980). Both the number three (33*) and athletics metaphors are prominent in the play, including allusions to wrestling, relay racing, archery and probably the pankration

(63–7, 228–30*, 304*, 314*, 343–4*, 540*, 786*, 1206*, 1245*, 1377–8*, 1562*, 1648*: see Swift (2010) 166–7. In *Eumenides*, the moves and counter-moves by prosecutor and defendant in the trial of Orestes are likened to a series of throws and holds in a wrestling match (589). **is gone:** Where? What happened to Kronos after Zeus defeated him in the Titanomachy differs in ancient sources, but the usual view was that he was held in captivity with most of the other Titans in Tartarus (Aesch. *PV* 221–3). The play's audience may not have shared the chorus' view that there was no point in praying to Kronos: in Attica he had a significant festival called the Kronia as well as cults (Paus. 1.18.7), and a cult at Olympia (Pind. *Ol.* 1.111, Paus. 6.20.1); sacrifices were offered to him at the oracle of Trophonius in Lebadeia (Paus. 9.39.3–4).

173–5 peals forth: On the verb *klazein* see 48*. **victory praise-song:** Immediately after an image from wrestling, the adjective *epinikios* of a prayer, usually used adjectivally with a word for 'song' or 'hymn' (Pind. *Nem.* 4.78; Diod. Sic. 5.29), suggests a choral performance like those composed by Pindar and Bacchylides for victors in the great sporting festival competitions. **he'll acquire good sense about everything:** Lit., 'he shall achieve being sensible in respect of all'. This is a peculiar expression, since *phrenōn* is formed from a verb that normally means to make someone else see sense (e.g. Cassandra clarifying matters to the chorus at 1183), but it may be idiomatic and proverbial, like the English 'see sense' (see Eur. *Alc.* 327).

176–8 praising him ... suffering: The participles *hodōsanta* and *thenta* are in the accusative to agree with *Zēna* at 173: 'praising him as' is not in the Greek but needs to be inserted to make sense in the English translation. **who ordained the law ... suffering:** Lit., 'the one who established learning through suffering to be authoritative'. The principle that there is a direct causal relationship between suffering and learning—*pathei mathos*—jingles aurally like a proverbial expression, like so many phrases across the *Oresteia* (Ahrens (1937)). As Sommerstein (1993) points out, this does not mean that the person who learns is always identical with the person who suffers, nor that the person who suffers *must* learn as a result. There are plenty of individuals who suffer in the *Oresteia* but are dead before they have time to learn anything from the experience. The point the chorus makes is vaguer and intended to offer some comfort—there must be something positive, for any given community or for the human race as a whole, to emerge eventually from suffering. See the reading of Gagarin (1976) 139–50. Aeschylus seems to be implying that the principle did not apply before Zeus introduced it; this may have reminded the audience of the golden race of mortals under the blissful regime of Kronos (who was brought to mind in the preceding stanza at 171–2*) when they lived without any work or suffering whatsoever (Hes. *Theog.* 109–19). Sadly for the house of Atreus, the law of Zeus that is enacted in the course of the play is not that the sufferer learns, but that the doer of evil pays the penalty: see 1564*.

179–80 Anguish ... drips over the heart in sleep: Aeschylus brilliantly evokes the despair inflicted by dreams that recover unhappy memories in these famous lines (see Introduction, p. 94). Aristotle discussed how sense-impressions we have acquired while awake leave traces in our perceptual organs, such as the eyes and ears, and may be reproduced by the imaginative property inherent within them when we sleep (*On Dreams* 459a–460a). On *ponos* see 1*; on memory, 34–9*. The theme of sleep recurs, reaching its climax with the tableau of the sleeping Erinyes in *Eumenides*. In *Agamemnon*, the Watchman fears falling asleep (17); Clytemnestra speaks cryptically of information received by a sleeping mind (275*), of mountains that are unsleeping (290–1*), of the victorious Greeks getting a good night's sleep at last at Troy (335–7*), of her disturbed sleep during the nights while Agamemnon was away (891–4*, 1150*) and her intention of not being conquered by sleep when she has important matters to see to in the palace (912–13*). The chorus sing of Helen's image appearing to Menelaus and slipping away down the paths of sleep (424–6*) and long to fall into an everlasting sleep to escape the palace crisis (1448–54*). Dripping and drops—of dew, tears and blood—are also recurrent images in *Agamemnon* (60–2*, 887–90, 1121–3, 1310, 1350–1). **over the mind:** Lit., 'in front of the heart'.

181 wisdom comes: The Greek uses the 'gnomic' aorist common in proverbial generalisations. Aristotle says that maxims are particularly appropriate to characterising the speech of the elderly (*Rhet.* 2.1395a). Here, as at 1425*, [*to*] *sōphronein* is equivalent to *sōphrosunē*, one of the four cardinal Greek virtues, along with courage, intelligence and justice (Hall (1989) 121–30). It can mean simply 'moderation', 'self-control', 'respectfulness', 'right thinking' or even 'sanity' (Aesch. *PV* 982, *Pers.* 829, Thuc. 8.24), but it often, as seems likely here, suggests that this quality has had to be acquired (Hdt. 3.64, Aesch. *Eum.* 1000) or recovered after temporary delusion (Plat. *Phaedr.* 241b). See North (1966) and Rademaker (2005).

182–3 It seems ... severity: In the translation, 'it seems to me' corresponds to the particle *pou*, which slightly 'softens' the impact of what could be construed as a criticism of the gods. **favour:** The feminine noun *charis* is an important word in *Agamemnon*, where reciprocity is a prominent—and problematic—principle, usually implying something pleasant bestowed within the context of a reciprocal relationship (354*, 417*, 728*, 821*, 1043, 1058, 1544–7). But the idea of a severe or violent (*biaios*) favour is strikingly oxymoronic. **sitting augustly on the deck of the ship:** Lit., 'sitting on the august ship-bench'. The participle *hēmenos* is used of Zeus sitting on the peak of Mount Ida in the *Iliad* (14.158) and can be applied to magistrates (Eur. *Andr.* 699). It is here used (unusually; see 'sitting at the oars', but in the dative, at Eur. *Cycl.* 16) with the accusative of a noun, *selma*, a bench or deck of a ship; *semnon* implies that the chorus see the gods as sitting on the top deck from which the captain could look down upon the rows of oarsmen; this may be inspired by Zeus being described as *hupsizugos*, 'high-throned', at *Iliad* 4.166, a motif shared with or inherited from Ancient Near Eastern honorific titles; see West (1997) 114. It is one of the several metaphors using the image of an oared ship and its crew in the play: see 108–15*. Here the cosmic relationships between gods and men is envisaged in terms of a ship's personnel; at 1617–19 it is the political relationship between human rulers and their subjects. On the seats of the gods see also 519*.

184–91 And then ... rush: This is a syntactically troublesome sentence in which the initial nominative subject, 'the older commander' (i.e. Agamemnon), is given two participles, but no main verb, before being replaced by another nominative subject, 'the Achaean taskforce'. This may be intended to suggest psychological disturbance experienced long ago at Aulis or by the chorus as they recollect traumatic events, but it is jarring, even for Aeschylus. **without censuring:** On the basis of Agamemnon's famous first speech in the *Iliad*, where he harshly upbraids Calchas for always prophesying unpleasant events (1.105–8), Aeschylus' audience might have expected him to upbraid him on this earlier occasion, too. **breathed ... fortune:** Lit., 'blowing-in-unity with on-smashing fortunes'. The metaphor in *sumpneōn* is suitable for the context where winds are the issue: see 218–21*. Agamemnon's lack of resistance, indeed compliance, here is the first evidence that his priority is military victory regardless of the other damage it may entail; see Winnington-Ingram (1983) 78–100. **were oppressed ... running out:** Lit., 'were weighed down by food-container-emptying lack of voyage'. The chorus repeats the word *aploia* used by Calchas (147–50*). The adjective *kenangēs* is formed from *kenos*, 'empty', and the neuter noun *angos*, used of urns, buckets, jars, caskets and other containers, usually for food and drink (Hom. *Od.* 16.13, *Il.* 16.643; Hes. *Works* 613; Eur. *Ion* 32, 1337; Soph. *Trach.* 622). **Aulis region:** Lit., 'in places of Aulis'. The Greeks were stranded in the camp near their ships in the port, today housing a large cement-exporting operation, on the Boeotian coast opposite the city of Chalcis. **where the reverse tides rush:** *palirrothios*, 'refluent', used of sea-waves in the *Odyssey* (5.430, 9.485), is a perfect adjective for describing the straits of Euripus between the Aulis area and Chalcis. For 23 days each month, the flow changes violently every six hours from south to north and *vice versa*. The oceanographic reasons were first properly explained in Eginitis (1929); the puzzle was a familiar *topos* in ancient authors. In Plato's *Phaedo* (90c), Socrates compares the thought processes of people who think that nothing is certain or stable, but that everything goes up and down, to 'the tide in the Euripus'. Patristic authors claimed that Aristotle had committed suicide by jumping into the turbulent waters, frustrated that he could not explain them; see Hall (2016b) and (2017) 7–9.

192–5 Winds … cables: Lit., 'Bad-leisured hungry bad-anchoring blasts coming from Strymon—wanderings of mortals, unsparing of ships and cables'; *nēstides* is adjectival and *alai* is in apposition to *pnoai*. The militiamen at Aulis are not the only ones to fear hunger in the play: see 330–5*, 1014–15*, 1621–3*. Aeschylus paints a grim picture of the disintegration of both morale and equipment under the onslaught of adverse winds. This recalls one of the *Iliad*'s rare acknowledgements of the perishable nature of materials such as wood: Agamemnon uniquely observes that over the nine years that the Achaeans have been at Troy, the ships' beams have begun to rot and the ships' cables to unravel (2.134–5; see Hall (2025) ch. 4). On ships and ship imagery see 108–15* and on wandering 77–9*. **Strymon:** This is the great Thracian river, now called *Struma* by Bulgarians and *Strymonas* by Greeks, which flows from the mountains south of Sofia south-east and then south to disgorge into the Aegean near Amphipolis. The north wind, Boreas, is therefore implied.

196–8 Doubling the length of the delay: Lit., 'making the time as long again': **crushed:** *kataxainein*, literally 'comb' or 'card', is a strong word also used of stoning as a punishment (Soph. *Aj.* 728, Ar. *Ach.* 320) or grief that makes someone waste away (Eur. *Med.* 1030, *Tro.* 509). **flower of Argos:** Aeschylus had used this metaphor for the pick of the Persian forces at *Pers.* 59, 252, 925, but it was also used in prose, e.g. Thuc. 4.133.1 of the flower of the Thespian army that had fallen at Delium. It often has implications of youthful bloom (see Hom. *Il.* 13.484, Theogn. 994) or the freshness of something recently created. Flowers are repeatedly connected in the play's imagery with death and corpses: see 659*, 738–421*, 391–2*, 1459*.

198–204 the seer intoned: Calchas' words 'implicating Artemis' are not here quoted in direct speech, but the audience know that he recommended the sacrifice of Iphigenia. The effect of not yet mentioning it builds up the tension further. On the verb *klazein* see 48*. **another remedy:** The neuter noun *mēchar* implies an expedient or strategy to adopt in order to solve a problem (Aesch. *PV* 606); presumably Calchas' prayer to Apollo at 146–51 has constituted the first 'remedy'. **to the chieftains:** Aeschylus rings the changes on the terminology his characters use to denote the Atreidai; *promos* is suitable to the military context here, since in Homer it distinguishes the very foremost fighter even from others in the front rank (*Il.* 15.293, 7.75, 22.85). **bitter:** See 745*. **winter weather:** The neuter noun *cheima* is a regular term for the winter season (5*), but it can also mean wintry weather that arrives out of season—i.e., 'storm' (627*). **Artemis:** At this point some of the audience may have visualised the sanctuary of Artemis near the Euripus straits, visited by Pausanias in the second century CE (9,19.6–7; see also Strabo 9.2.8). He said the temple contained two marble images of Artemis, one carrying torches and one shooting an arrow, and the remains of the very plane-tree and fountain mentioned in the *Iliad*, where Odysseus describes them (2.307). Pausanias also saw nearby a bronze threshold said to have belonged to Agamemnon's tent. Remains from Mycenaean times attest continuous inhabitation of the region. In 1941, the site of the remains of a small temple of the fifth century BCE just south of Mikro Vathi (the exact address is Petrogianni 70) were speculatively identified as the Aulis Artemision by the archaeologist Ioannis Threpsiades, curator of Boeotian antiquities. The sanctuary was declared an official archaeological site in 1970. It may post-date Aeschylus' *Agamemnon*, but it is built over another edifice of Geometric date. **beating ... tears:** The vivid picture of the two brothers striking the ground and weeping sets the stage for the visualisation of the tragic events in the next four stanzas. There is no shame, for Homeric and tragic warriors, in weeping: see Monsacré (2018). The chorus-men may have struck the ground with their walking sticks as they sang this sentence.

205 saying: Agamemnon's is the second human voice to be quoted in direct speech by the chorus, as they bring to life their memories of the fateful day at Aulis. On embedded voices see Introduction, pp. 70–1.

206 dire calamity: Lit., 'a heavy doom'. In Homer a *Kēr* is a female personification of a warrior's death or doom. She may lead or carry a hero to the Underworld (*Il.* 11.332, *Od.* 14.207), overwhelm or envelop him (*Od.* 11.171, *Il.* 23.78–9). One appears on the shield of Achilles alongside Strife and Uproar (*Il.* 18.535). But, already in Homer, the feminine noun *kēr* can mean, as here, simply 'death' or 'doom' (*Il.* 1.228, 3.32, 2.352).

The repeated adjective 'heavy' may bring with it, however, the idea of the *kērostasia*, 'weighing of souls', the famous scene where Zeus puts the two *kēres* of Achilles and Hector into the scales, and Hector's is heavier (*Il.* 22.209–10). In the cyclic *Aethiopis*, Memnon's soul was probably weighed against Achilles', a scene depicted on several vases and apparently staged in Aeschylus' own *Psychostasia* (see Wiseman (2000) and 264–5*). The motif may have derived from Egyptian cultic imagery: see Dietrich (1964). On weighing imagery and oppressive heaviness see 63–7*.

207–8   smite … household: *daïzein*, 'cleave asunder', is an impactful verb associated in the *Iliad* (24.393) with violent and/or lethal injuries inflicted by bronze spears. **ornament:** This is the older meaning of the neuter noun *agalma*, which is not specifically associated with statues in archaic epic. See 738–42*. In *Eumenides*, Athena declares that the city of Athens is an ornament (*agalma*) to the gods worshipped on the altars of Hellas (919–20).

209–10   defiling: *miainein* can mean, without moral overtones, 'stain' or 'dye' (Hom. *Il.* 4.141, of colouring an ivory ornament), but where spilt blood is concerned, the resulting stain is almost always presented in a repellent light (*Il.* 4.146, 16.795). In Aeschylus it elsewhere has a suggestion of religious or moral pollution (*Supp.* 366; see below, 637*, 1669*), and the reference to 'paternal hands' makes the issue of kin-killing unmistakeable. On the Greek concept of religious–ethical *miasma* see Parker (1983). **with streams … blood:** Lit., 'with slaughtered-maiden streams'. Aeschylus' grotesque compound adjective, creating an image recurring at 214–17*, brings to sickening life the gender of the child he is to sacrifice. The neuter noun *haima*, blood, and its cognates, supplemented by the adjective *phoinios*, 'blood-coloured' or 'gory', occur with increasing insistence from mid-way through the play. Agamemnon is associated with the blood shed by both Trojan citizens and Trojan royalty (715, 828), and himself calls the gods' voting urns, in which he imagines them condemning the Trojans, 'bloody' (815). But it is his own blood that the chorus fear will be let (1020) in requital for blood previously shed (1338); it is his blood with which Clytemnestra's face is smeared (1428). Clytemnestra visualises Cassandra as a horse foaming with blood as it resists an imposed bit (1067); Cassandra, however, hopes that her blood will drain away gently in an easy death (1293). She says the Erinyes haunting the house, which reeks with freshly dripping blood (1309), drink human blood (1293). Clytemnestra declares it is the malign spirit afflicting the house that has lust for lapping blood (1478), while the chorus fear 'black Ares' advancing amidst streams of kindred blood (1509; cf. 643) and a deluge of blood raining on the palace (1534). Clytemnestra tries to change the discourse on blood in her proposal at the end of the play (1656) that a stop should be put to bloodshed.

212–13 How am I ... allies: On Agamemnon's articulation of his dilemma see Introduction, pp. 34–6. **deserter of the fleet:** This word is not otherwise attested, but the feminine abstract noun *lipostratia* means 'desertion of the army' in Herodotus (5.27) and Thucydides (6.76). **failing:** The verb *hamartanein* has a range of meanings illustrated in this play, from 'let someone down', as here, to 'forfeit' something (535) and 'err' (1194). On the cognate neuter noun *hamartion* see 537*. Agamemnon here uses the second of two successive rhetorical questions, a figure known as *hypophora*, reflecting his anguished deliberation. **allies:** The audience will have understood this as meaning the crews and their captains listed in the catalogue of Achaean ships in *Iliad* 2; this enacts a roll call, designed to suit the eighth century BCE, of the 28 contingents of Greeks, in more than 1000 vessels, who participated in the Trojan War centuries before the epic poem was written down. They come from mainland strongholds including Pylos, Lacedaemon, Mycenae, Argos, Athens and Boeotia (although no northern districts) and several islands, including Ithaca, Rhodes and Crete. See Visser (1997).

214–17 It's legitimate ... well: Lit., '[It is] right-in-religion (*themis*) angrily to desire in anger the wind-stopping sacrifice and virginal blood.' The pleonastic play on the *org-* stem and the alliteration of '*p*' and '*th*' sounds augment the effect of a jingling prophetic utterance. It is emphatically not stated, however, who is doing all this angry desiring, although many translators exculpate Agamemnon by saying that this must refer to the allies alone. The statement that it is *themis* to want an action involving both human sacrifice and kin murder could not sound more oxymoronic, since *themis* defines precisely the imperatives and basic taboos underlying ancestral Greek custom and morality (see 97–9*). This makes Agamemnon's ensuing wish that all be well sound shockingly inappropriate as well as deludedly optimistic.

218–21 put on the yoke-strap of necessity: This rightly famous image encapsulates the play's fundamental erosion of the distinction between freely chosen action (he put it on himself, the verb being the aorist indicative active of *duein*), but what he put on was a confining symbol of metaphysical compulsion: see Introduction, p. 35. A *lepadnon* is a wide leather strap which fastens an animal's neck to both the yoke and the girth: see Aesch. *Pers.* 191. It would not be inappropriate to capitalise 'Necessity', since the presocratic poets as well as others often personified metaphysical compulsion as a supernatural female (28 Parmenides B 8.30 and 10.6; 31 Empedocles B 116, where she is called 'unbearable), against whom even the gods do not fight (Soph. fr. 256, from his *Thyestes*, 'even Ares does not withstand Necessity'). As Otfried Müller lamented, it is often impossible in printing Greek of this date, whose authors did not distinguish between upper- and lowercase letters, to choose whether to capitalise and thus differentiate noun from proper name (Müller (1835) 166). Cosmic Anankē symbolises everything that neither humans nor gods have any power to change. The Aeschylean Prometheus, an immortal, laments that, against her, every skill, technology or stratagem is unavailing (*PV* 512); the elegiac poet Euenos produced a famous line, quoted by Aristotle, 'All that is done from necessity will bring pain' (*Rhet.* 1.1370a). But she has a transitive aspect. She can characterise the relationship between one agent and another. Anankē is often what the French call *force majeure*—it is what makes a superior power able, at will, to make an inferior one act or suffer without hope of resistance. To articulate the deified Anankē's unknowability as well as her ferocity, the Corinthians built a sanctuary for her, which she shared with Bia (Violence), but which (most unusually) custom prohibited people from entering at all (Pausanias 2.4.7). See further Hall (2014). **as if blowing … mind:** Lit., 'breathing a sacrilegious reverse wind of his mind, unholy, unhallowed'. The resolution producing the short syllables in *anieron* heightens the emotional effect. The metaphor in *pneōn* continues the wind imagery (692*). Aeschylus is fond of piling up adjectives beginning with privative alphas: see Introduction, p. 3. **he made a decision … unthinkable:** Lit., 'he changed his mind to think the all-daring'. The chorus vehemently reject Agamemnon's attempt to justify the decision to perform the sacrifice as in any way right in religious terms. The term *pantotolmon* of Agamemnon's decision is picked up at 1237*, where Cassandra calls the murderous Clytemnestra *hē pantotolmos*. Bremmer (2002) compares the version of the sacrifice of Iphigenia in *Agamemnon* with all the ancient variants on the story, a procedure which throws light on the unameliorated brutality of Agamemnon's decision in this Aeschylean version. On what little we know about Aeschylus' own lost tragedy *Iphigenia* see Deforge (1986) 102–3. This choral sequence has the effect of inserting a miniature tragic narrative within the frame tragedy in which the victim's killer finally becomes a victim himself: see Barbieri (2009).

222–7 For making … emboldens men: Lit., 'For shameful-planning, wretched, delusion, first cause of woe, emboldens mortals'. *aischromētis* is best read adjectivally. On *talaina* see 385–6*. The menacing adjectives describing delusion are lavishly accumulated, with a run of short syllables in *parakopa*, to emphasise the climactic decision Agamemnon is making and point out that the crime he is about to commit is premeditated, immoral, deluded *and* will have agonising repercussions. The Erinyes in *Eumenides* connect 'crazed, mind-destroying delusion (*parakopa*)' with the effect of their song on their victims (329); it means 'delirium' in medical writing (Hippocrates, *Aph.* 6.26). **The sacrificer of his daughter:** The agony entailed in the decision is emphasised by the double alliteration with *th*-, followed by the prominent *p* sounds. **putting her ... voyage:** Lit., '[as an] aid to woman-avenging wars and a [as a] prelude-ritual of ships'. On *proteleia* see 63–7* and on ships see 108–15*.

228–30   warlike: *philomachoi* includes resolved syllables to emphasise the bellicose temperament. **leaders:** The masculine noun *brabeus* originally means an adjudicator or umpire at the games (Soph. *El.* 690, 709, Plat. *Laws* 12.949a), perhaps lending this sentence the sinister implication that the sacrifice was callously treated almost like a sporting event (on athletics imagery see 171–2*). **disregarded:** Lit., 'put it in the accounts as of zero value'. **entreaties and her cries of 'father':** Lit., 'prayers and paternal invocations'. Although we emphatically do not hear Iphigenia herself in direct speech, the chorus have not forgotten the agonising moment before she was gagged when she did try to use her voice to save her life. It is touching to find Eduard Fraenkel, the father of two daughters, Edith and Barbara, as well as three sons, comment here that from this point 'onwards the theme of fatherhood becomes prominent' (see 231, 143, 244: Fraenkel (1950) vol. 2, 129–30).

231–5   to seize her confidently ... around her: Lit., 'with all confidence to take her [and hold her] high over the altar like a young she-goat [so that she would be] falling forward, and being flowed (*peripetē* opens with an emotive trio of short syllables) around by her robes'. The prescribed near-horizontal position of the young woman's body is best if most gruesomely illustrated on an Attic sixth-century BCE black-figured amphora in the British Museum depicting the sacrifice of Polyxena (1897,0727.2). **high:** *aerdēn* is adverbial. **like a young she-goat:** *dikan* (or *dikēn* in iambics, e.g. at line 3, 'like a dog') is an unusual preposition indicating similarity. It ultimately derives from the accusative of *dikē* and takes the genitive. I have sympathy with those critics who believe that Aeschylus is using this preposition to compound and complicate, at least on a subliminal level, what the *Oresteia* has to say about justice (*dikē*), or the natural rightness of the cosmic order; the double meaning of the term suggests 'the instability, the multiplicity and horrific entanglement of "orders"'; in this word, 'we see the way that Aeschylean language actively instantiates the very largest concerns of this vast trilogy at the smallest scale of poetic mechanics' (Wilson (2006) 188; see also Tralau (2016)). It seems strange to us that the word for the hybrid monster killed by Bellerophon is the same as the word for a young female goat, but in the *Iliad* the Chimaera herself is described as having the front of a lion, the rear of a snake or dragon and the middle of a she-goat (6.181). See also Sophocles fr. 502.2, from his *Shepherds*, 'offering green shoots to young she-goats' and Aristotle, *Hist. An.* 523a1. Although a great deal of scholarly ink has been expended on arguing about this simile (see, e.g., Tralau (2016) with bibliography), the simile would have been gruesomely appropriate to Aeschylus' audience. In his *Anabasis*, Xenophon reminds his troops that before the battle of Marathon the Athenians had vowed to Artemis to sacrifice to her a *chimaira* for every Persian they killed (3.2.12), and to his day sacrificed 500 every year in memory of the battle; in his *Hellenica* the Spartans sacrifice chimairas to Artemis Agrotera before battle during the Corinthian War, 'as is customary'. See also 142–3*. The foundation myth of the cult of Artemis at Brauron also involved a goat sacrifice; see Peradotto (1969a) 243–8 and Bowie (1993) 19–22. **falling around her:** Lit., 'wrapped around', 'wrapped up in', an unusual passive meaning of *peripetēs*, which more commonly has an active sense—'falling around', 'falling on' or 'falling in with' (Soph. *Ant.* 1223, *Aj.* 907). We learn more about Iphigenia's robes at 239*.

235–8   and with a gag … to stop: Lit., 'and to restrain, with her fair-prowed mouth's guard'. In the context of the frustration of the fleet, the choice of an adjective with a naval connection to indicate Iphigenia's beauty is probably not coincidental: on ship imagery see 108–15*. Jason uses *kalliprōros* to describe his ship the Argo at Eur. *Med.* 1335, although see Aesch, *Sept.* 533, where it describes the young and feminine-looking youth Parthenopaeus. **uttering a curse:** Lit., 'a cursing voice' (on the noun *phthongos* see 324–5*). That Agamemnon felt the need to take this precaution indicates that he was aware that the sacrifice was outrageous. In reality, even sacrificial animals had to give consent, and were induced to nod their heads. On curses see Introduction, pp. 67, 71. **with the violence … bit:** Iphigenia's gag is the third instance of a mechanism used for violent restraint of animals being applied to a human, but this is the first time it is not a metaphor (132–4*, 218–21*). **silencing:** The term *anaudos* usually means 'voiceless'; it is transferred from Iphigenia herself onto the force exerted by the bit; on silence see 34–9*. The enjambement extends the duration of the violent actions and emphasises the final words, which open the first line of the new strophe. The plural *chalinoi* is used of a horse's jointed bit in the *Iliad* (19.393).

239   yellow-dyed: Lit., 'things dyed with saffron'. The feminine noun *baphē* can mean an act of dyeing or dipping (612*), the object produced by such an action (Arist. *Pol.* 7.1334a8) or the dye itself (Theophr. *Hist. Plant.* 4.6.5). Saffron, collected from the stigmas of the *Crocus sativus* flower, was one of the most expensive products, in proportion to its weight and the work required to manufacture it, in antiquity. It was also associated with the clothing worn in relation to the cult of Artemis by adolescent girls, in their initiation rites, and in connection with childbirth, as well as young married women in erotic contexts (Ar. *Lys.* 44, 219). Saffron robes are included in the fourth-century catalogues of clothing dedicated by Athenian women to Brauronian Artemis (Cleland (2005) 9). It is unnecessary to assume that by the textiles the chorus specify here they mean a veil, as some, e.g. Armstrong and Ratchford (1985), have asserted.

240   kept on striking ... eye: Iphigenia may have been silenced, but she left her killers in no doubt about her emotional state; her emotive silent appeals are protracted by the use of the imperfect tense. On imposed silence see 34–9*. The verb *ballein* occurs in an equally gruesome context, of the murdered Agamemnon's blood hitting Clytemnestra, at 1390*; see also 947*. Eyes, to which the Watchman had introduced us at 15*, are later associated with several of the main themes of this drama (of course a visual medium), including sex: Menelaus misses Helen's erotic gaze (418–419*) and Helen's arrival at Troy results in erotic glances between lovers (738–42*); eyes express strong emotions: the chorus are advised by the Herald to greet Agamemnon with shining eyes (520–1); eyes produce tears of joy (541) and of misery (887–90); divine punishment is connected with eyes: Zeus smites malefactors on their eyes (466–70) and personified Uprightness abandons gold-encrusted mansions with averted eyes (776–7). But visual cognition is compromised. Although the chorus assert that the eyes of a fake friend give him away (796–8) and seeing things with one's own eyes offers reliable evidence (988–9), Aegisthus says that the chorus can't see what danger lies before them (1621–3). Bafflement at obscure riddling languages is like seeing things with clouded vision (1112–13) and oracular language is compared with a bride whose eyes can scarcely be made out from behind her veil (1178–9). For a detailed discussion see Fletcher (1999a).

242–3   standing out ... yearning to speak: The silence of painted figures became a standard *topos* in ancient literature, especially in full-scale ecphrasis. In Apollonius' *Argonautica*, the narrator says that Phrixus and his ram were so vividly portrayed on Jason's cloak that it was tempting to keep silent in the vain hope of hearing their words (1.763–7). In Catullus 64.132, the poet plays on this convention when he makes his wretched Ariadne launch into a first-person speech from the coverlet on which she is portrayed. But in this, the earliest surviving instance, the pathos of the moment is immeasurably heightened by the frustration of the gagged Iphigenia. The participle *prepousa*, 'standing out', further encourages the audience's internal eye to focus on the tragic girl's plight (see 6–7*): as Fraenkel (1950) vol. 2, 19 says, this passage is 'our earliest evidence for the clear definition of the individual figures being regarded as an essential quality in painting'. Aeschylus is partial to comparisons between characters and works of visual art (see further 418–19*, 799–801* and 1327–9*): when the character is female, the context is usually erotic or related to her death. Some such comparisons create an image of a character who is not present as an artwork in the audience's mind's eye (as here) and others construe as an artwork a character who is physically present. The audience may have been reminded her of a real painting or statue: the famous artist Timanthes painted this scene a few decades later (Pliny *NH* 35.10), and his version may be imitated in a Pompeii fresco (Naples National Archaeological Mueum inv. no. 9112). But such comparisons were no doubt also prompted by theatre's use of moulded and painted masks; moreover, they may have reminded audiences of a previous dramatic performance (on all these issues see Hall (2006) 99–141). If Aeschylus' *Iphigenia* antedated the *Oresteia*, the audience may here remember Iphigenia's costume and mask. The visual art analogy also operates in tragedy as a prompt to what Zeitlin (1994) 145 calls 'hyper-viewing', stimulating spectators to become conscious of their own contemplation of the masked characters before them.

243–5 she had sung ... banquet-table: Lit., 'she sang in her father's well-tabled men's rooms'. The pluperfect is required in English to translate the aorist *emelpsen*. The contrast between this remembered experience of the child Iphigenia's solo singing at a happy ritual and her enforced silence at her own sacrifice could not be more affecting. The implication that she was being killed by men she knew well from her father's banquets has a potent psychological force. Greeks contemporary with Aeschylus were accustomed to substantial households containing a separate room for the men of the family to entertain male guests in (Xen. *Symp.* 1.4). In Athens, respectable women, as opposed to prostitutes, dancers and musicians, did not usually participate in parties involving non-kin males and lavish consumption of wine (Cornelius Nepos *Praef.* 6–7; see Corner

(2012)). This *may* mean that there is something uneasy about the chorus' picture of the girlish Iphigenia, with no mentioned chaperone, singing for Agamemnon's men friends. There may be elsewhere in the play a slightly offbeat suggestion that Agamemnon and Iphigenia were very close indeed (1555–8*). But there is some evidence that respectable women family members served men, or at least prepared the food and tables, at small gatherings including close associates as well as kin (Menander, *Dyskolos* 555–69, 871–3). And Aeschylus is imagining life in a very different society from classical Athens—a Bronze Age monarchical palace in the Peloponnese. Polybius (4.20.8) reports that even in his day, amongst the Arcadians, the childen (his definite article is masculine but may be meant to include girls too) 'are by the laws trained from infancy to sing hymns and paeans, in which they celebrate in the traditional fashion the heroes and gods of their particular towns'. Menelaus may be imagined to have been present, since *Agamemnon* assumes that Menelaus resides in the same palace as Agamemnon at Argos, whereas later tragedies present him as having a separate household in Sparta (Hall (2018a)). This is the first of three banquets served on the table in the palace of the Atreidai recalled in the course of the play: the others are the occasions on which Paris visited it, leaving with Helen (399–402*), and the Thyestean feast (1595–602).

245–7 and with ... libation: Lit., 'and, a virgin, with her pure voice she used lovingly to honour her loved father's thrice-poured good-fortune hymn'. *ataurōtos*, 'un-bulled' is a graphic word meaning 'virginal' (see also Ar. *Lys.* 217), perhaps grimly appropriate in the context of a human being sacrificed like an animal. On bulls see 34–9*. Note the imperfect tense of *etima*, to imply repeated action, and the *figura etymologica* formed by *philou ... philōs*. On references to voices in the play see 324–5*. **chant:** See 97–9*. **third libation:** According to Pindar *Isthm.* 6.7–8, the third libation at a symposium was poured to Zeus *Sōtēr* (see also Ar. fr. 540 = schol. Plato, *Philebus* 66d, 512*, 897–8*, 897–8*, 1238*, 1384–7*), who was also thanked in sacrifices after safe voyages (Strabo 9.1.15). An Attic cup with an inscription dedicating it to Zeus Sōtēr has been found in the western Black Sea coastal colony of Callatis (Bîrzescu and Ionescu (2012) 386 with fig. 3). The third cup therefore came to symbolise good luck, and the third time to be held lucky (Aesch. *Choeph.* 1073, Plato *Rep.* 9.583b). Zeus himself is called 'the third one' at *Eumenides* 760. On the significance of the number three in *Agamemnon* and the *Oresteia* see 33*.

248 am not telling: The chorus' inhibition about speaking freely echoes that of the Watchman at 36–9. There was a version of the story of Iphigenia's sacrifice in which she was rescued by Artemis, who substituted a deer, taking the princess off to the land of the Taurians in the Black Sea; this version *may* already have been narrated in the lost cyclic *Cypria* (although see Hall (2013) 159), was retold in one version of Euripides' *Iphigenia in Aulis* (the spurious lines 1580–end) and is the premise of his *Iphigenia in Tauris*. But there is no indication elsewhere in the *Oresteia* that Aeschylus was aware of this tradition, let alone that he was suggesting that the audience be reminded of it here.

249 Calchas' arts … unfulfilled: The verb needs to be supplied in English. The litotes 'not unfulfilled' is perhaps intended euphemistically to soften the effect of this statement, given what the audience has been told about what 'Calchas' arts' had inferred from the omen of the eagles and pregnant hare. But the effect is sinister.

250–1 Justice … learn from it: Although the idea of law has been introduced earlier (41*), this is the first mention of the principle of justice, personified as a goddess, who, in collaboration with Zeus (she is often portrayed seated beside him as his ally or consort, e.g. Soph. *OC* 1377), is to dominate the theology of both play and trilogy. Clytemnestra is in no doubt that by killing Agamemnon she has Dikē on her side (1432*), and nor is Aegisthus (1607), but the chorus of *Choephori* are equally convinced that Orestes does (310–14). Aristotle discusses the use of arguments in court that assert that a killer may have done something strictly speaking illegal, but had acted justly because the victim deserved to die (*Rhet.* 2.1397b; see also 1505*). This sort of paradox creates the trilogy's nearly insoluble moral crisis, as Orestes understands it ('Ares will collide with Ares, Justice with Justice', *Choeph.* 461). Dikē was Zeus' daughter by Themis ('The Right Way of Doing Things'; see 97–9*; Hes. *Theog.* 901; Aesch. *Choeph.* 939) and one of the three Horae, along with Eunomia (Good Order) and Eirēnē (Peace). She watches how humans behaved; a beautiful fragment of Terpander says that she 'walks the wide streets and is a "helper in fine deeds"' (fr. 7.2). But whenever she is damaged by falsehood or corrupt legal proceedings, she reports it to Zeus so that the culprit can be punished (Hes. *Works* 256–64; Orphic Hymn 62.3–5). The epic poet of the third century BCE, Euphorion of Chalcis, asks Ares to set up in the marketplace images of Themis and Dikē, 'who leaps up like a tiger at once in anger at the deeds of men upon whom she looks—even them who provoke the gods and turn their commandments aside, and such as treat their feeble parents with arrogance, scorning the counsel of the living and the dead; or sin against the hospitable feast and the table of Zeus' (fr. 121, 2b.20–6 in Page

(1941) 496–7). On the archaic chest dedicated by Cypselus at Olympia, she was depicted as a beautiful woman defeating her opposite, Adikia, in a hand-to-hand struggle (Paus. 5.18.2). Unsurprisingly, she is the mother of the personification of 'peace of mind' (Pind. *Pyth.* 8.1, Hesychia), a psychological state which the chorus of this tragedy are incapable of obtaining. In *Seven against Thebes*, Polynices' golden shield is emblazoned with a picture of Dikē modestly leading a man in golden armour and saying that she is on the side of him and Thebes (644–9). In a lost play by Aeschylus, Dikē appeared as a speaking character, claiming that she helped Zeus overcome Kronos (fr. 281a.7–10*), who had begun their quarrel; she says that she rewards the just, writing the crimes of the unjust on the tablet of Zeus, thus at the proper time bringing fulfilment of what they deserve. In the *Oresteia*, she is equated with the anvil on which Aisa, the divine dispenser of each person's destiny, forges her sword (*Choeph.* 647–8); in the case of malefactors she is closely associated with the activities of the Erinyes (*Eum.* 510; Lycophron, *Alex.* 1035). But in this play, as in her claim in the 'Dikē play', she also bestows rewards on virtuous people; the chorus of *Agamemnon* know that 'she shines out' from the homes of the upright poor (733–5*), whereas riches cannot protect people who offend against her (382–4)*. **inclines her scales:** Dikē, like her father Zeus (206*), sometimes attracts the imagery of weighing: see Aesch. *Choeph.* 61–3 and Bacchylides, 4.11–12, 'If some god had been holding level the balance of Dikē'. **people who've suffered learn from it:** see 176–83*.

252–3   But you'll hear … prematurely: The chorus, who have spent most of their anapaests and parodos recalling the past, and generalising about the operations of Zeus and Justice, suddenly return the audience to the situation at hand and what will happen next. **let it be:** This is the third person imperative of *chairein* in the particular sense of 'let it depart' or 'let it be dismissed from the mind' (see 572*). **Worrying about it is:** These words need to be supplied to make sense in English.

254   It shall become … daylight: Lit., 'For it shall arrive clear dawning-simultaneously with beams'. On the motifs of dawn and light versus darkness see Introduction, pp. 63–5. **clear:** Connected with the verb *tetrainein*, 'pierce' or 'bore through', *toros* is to become a key term in *Agamemnon*, where the difficulty of achieving clarity about what language means is so fundamental. At 616* the chorus say that *toroi* interpreters can see through the superficial meaning of Clytemnestra's dissembling words; at 1062* they remark that the foreign Cassandra is in need of a *toros* interpreter; see also 616*, 1162*.

255   And so may ... well: Lit., 'And so may the things coming after these be success'.

256–7   which is the desire of this lone guardian of the Apian land: 'As wishes this single-guarding defensive-wall of the Apian Land'. In Aeschylus' *Suppliants*, performed five years before *Agamemnon* but set in a much earlier mythical time, the king of Argos is Pelasgus. He explains his genealogy and the name of his 'Apian land'. It took its name from Apis, a seer and healer son of Apollo, who arrived from Naupactus and relieved the area of a plague of monstrous serpents (260–70). **closest to the King:** *anchistos* can mean just 'near' or 'associated', but at Hdt. 5.79 it means close kin; the noun *anchisteia* denotes an intimate family relationship (Soph. *Ant.* 173; Plato, *Laws* 9.924d) and even the rights of relatives to inherit (Ar. *Birds* 1661). Some ancient scholiasts and modern scholars have taken the chorus here as referring to themselves as the sole remaining protector of the country, but it is surely a formal reference to Clytemnestra, even if the audience could hear a hostile undertow or ambiguity.

iii]   257–354   THE CHORUS AND CLYTEMNESTRA

Summary

The chorus and Clytemnestra engage in spoken dialogue. She tells them that Troy has been taken, but they are sceptical and require evidence. She delivers the first of her great orations, describing how serial beacon fires lit at intervals all the way from Troy have signalled the victory (281–316). The chorus ask her to repeat the account, but Clytemnestra makes a different, equally imposing speech (320–50), describing what must be taking place at Troy and expressing her hope that the Greek soldiers avoid committing sacrilege. The chorus say they now believe her and will thank the gods; she re-enters the palace.

258   Clytemnestra: The Queen must have (re)emerged from the palace by now (see 97–9* on whether this is her first appearance before the audience). She may be costumed to reflect her supervision of sacrificial ritual, or (if she had made a previous appearance), she may have changed her costume into something to underline her status as Queen Regent. Although many commentators, including Fraenkel (1950), vol. 2, 147, assume that when the chorus speaks iambics, the lines were delivered by the *koruphaios* or chorus leader alone, there is no evidence contemporary with the Athenian tragedians to support this assumption. Yet there is no doubt that the chorus leader bore considerable responsibility for the success of his ensemble's performance (Dem. 21.60, Aristot. *Pol.* 3.1277a). **to honour:** *sebizein* is a verb often used of honouring the gods, so it is perhaps a sign here that the chorus feel the need to emphasise the reverence they feel in her presence (see 943*), **sovereignty:** On the strong word *kratos*, again not a word usually used of the sort of power a woman would be expected to wield, see 10–11*.

259–60   For it's right ... throne: Lit., 'For it is right to pay respect to the wife of the leader man, his throne being bereft of a male' (the last three words form a genitive absolute). **out of respect:** In Homer, *tiein* is sometimes used of revering gods (*Od.* 13.129), but it is also the standard verb for men paying due respect to other men as kings, friends, allies or guest-friends (*Il.* 5.467, 9.63, 13.176, *Od.* 15.543). It is striking here because it is rarely found relating to the respect due to a woman; the chorus seem to feel the need to explain the formality of their own address. See also 315*.

261–3   whether ... nothing: Lit., 'if you are performing sacrifices having learned something trustworthy, or [having] not [learned something trustworthy but buoyed up] by hopes of good news'. The chorus have long been understandably curious about the reason for the citywide rituals that they noticed and described at 95–9, before they embarked on their lyric parodos. They repeat their request for an explanation now that Clytemnestra seems willing to respond to them, but immediately indicate that they fear she is acting on the basis of optimism rather than factual knowledge. On *kednos* see 122–3*. **But I hold no grudge if you say nothing:** Lit., '[There will be] no grudge against you-keeping silence' (*sigōsēi* is a femine active present participle of *sigan*). On *phthonos* see 921–2*. Again, the chorus seem anxious to please Clytemnestra.

264–5   There's a proverb ... night-time: Lit., 'On the one hand may dawn come, as [in] the proverb, with good news from her mother, the kindly time'. Clytemnestra does not greet or acknowledge by name the presence of the men of the chorus. Her cryptic tone, the ambiguous meaning of 'good tidings' to an audience who know there is a plan to murder Agamemnon, the appeal to proverbial wisdom and reference to a matrilineal relationship in combination make for one of the most sinister yet apt opening sentences anywhere for a character in drama. **dawn:** Although *Heōs* is not quite personified here, she is seen as emerging from her mother, who is what the Greeks euphemistically called 'the kindly time' (Hes. *Works* 560, Pind. *Nem.* 7.3). On night/Night see further also 337* and especially 357*. Dawn appeared as a character in Aeschylus' *Psychostasia*, of which only three fragments remain (279, 280, 280a), pleading for her son Memnon's life and possibly snatching away his corpse (Pollux 4.130; 4.130; see Wiseman (2000) 345–7). She was a second-generation Titan and, traditionally, her mother was not Night but either Theia (Hes. *Theog.* 371) or Euryphaessa (Hom. *Hymn to Helios* 31.2–3). If this proverb existed, it may have opened and closed with the two words beginning *eu*, to produce a chiming effect. Clytemnestra refers back to this assumed proverb at 279*. Compare Aristotle's metaphor for youth, 'the morning of life' (*Rhet.* 2.1389a).

266   You're about … hoped for: Lit., 'You shall learn a joy greater than hope to hear'. The neuter noun *charma* can mean either, as here, a concrete source of joy (Hom. *Il.* 17.636) or abstract joy itself (Hom. *Od.* 19.471).

267   Priam's city: See 40*.

268   It's difficult to grasp since it seems unbelievable: Lit., 'The utterance has fled on account of incredulity'. On the epistemological scepticism of the chorus see Introduction, p. 101.

269   Troy is under Achaean control … enough? Lit., '[I say that] Troy being [now of the] Achaeans'; or do I speak clearly'. She has condensed her message into three bald words, and emphasises this by sarcastically asking whether she has expressed herself with sufficient clarity. On *toros* see 254*.

270   I'm beginning to feel … tears: Lit., 'Joy creeps up on me eliciting a tear'. *hupherpein* implies stealth or secrecy (450*); the Herald will later feel like weeping with joy (541). But tears can be caused by misery, too. The chorus recall the Atreidai weeping as they struck the earth of Aulis (204*), and lament that Agamemnon will have no tears shed at his graveside (1490–1, 1548–50*). Clytemnestra claims to have suffered weeping fits while Agamemnon was away (887–90*). Cassandra envies Procne, who lived a life *free* from tears once transformed into a nightingale (1147–9*).

271   Yes … goodwill: Changes in emotion cannot of course be indicated by facial expression in masked theatre, but no doubt the chorus could have altered their posture or the angle at which they hold their heads in response to Clytemnestra's brusque statement of the news from Troy. This is a difficult line for an actor to deliver, and its interpretation depends on intonation and emphasis: Clytemnestra may be implying, with a hint of resentment, that they do not normally show such goodwill towards her, or simply be responding to them in the routine rhetorical formulae of palace bureaucracy.

272   proof … corroboration: The chorus' language is suggestive of legal proceedings, as if Clytemnestra was a litigant or witness in a trial. See 41*. She finally answers this question in her speech concluding at 315–16*.

273 unless some god has tricked me: This sounds more like a routine caveat than the expression of genuine doubt.

274 Is it the phantom-figures of dreams that have convinced you? Lit., 'Do you respect the persuasive phantoms of dreams?' On *phasmata* see 414–15*. Clytemnestra's reference to a divinity leads the chorus to consider the possibility that she is acting on information received in a dream, an allegation she is swift to repudiate (275). The chorus themselves later wonder whether they have been deceived by the evidence of the beacon-fires as if by things they have seen in dreams (491*; see also 980–3*). The Greeks believed that many dreams were sent by gods (Plato, *Apol.* 33c), and gods certainly featured in dreams catalogued in Artemidorus' *Interpretation of Dreams*, especially 2.33–40. But it was also assumed that such dreams could be deceptive. Penelope proposes that true dreams arrive through gates of horn, and false ones through gates of ivory, at *Odyssey* 19.560–7. The audience here will probably have been reminded of Agamemnon's famous false dream, sent by Zeus to trick him, in the *Iliad* (2.1–47). In tragedy dreams are always proved true, even though they may initially be misinterpreted (Hall (2013) 111–12). Amongst medics and philosophers there were sceptics who did not believe that dreams had any divine authority or predictive truth value (Hippocrates, *Reg.* 4.87; Aristotle, *On Dreams* 462b12–17; Epicurus, *Vatican Sayings* 24). Clytemnestra cryptically says that she has had dreams about Agamemnon suffering (891–4). On references to dreams in the *Oresteia* as a whole see Lennig (1969) 54–80.

275 I wouldn't accept … asleep: The feminine noun *doxa*, 'expectation', 'opinion' or 'belief', can denote, negatively, a 'mere' conjecture that is proved incorrect (Hdt. 8.132, Thuc. 5.105) or something that 'seems' to be so, or, as here, seems to *be*—i.e. the fantasies produced as dreams by our minds when they are asleep. It also refers to visions seen in dreams below at 421*, Eur. *Rhes.* 780 and Philostratus *Vita Apollonii* 1.23, and to hallucinations while one is awake at Aesch. *Choeph.* 1053 and in the late Greek medical writer Alexander of Tralles (1.17). The unusual verb *brizein* is used of Agamemnon when it is said that he was *not* asleep in the *Iliad* (4.223). Clytemnestra uses it of the baby Orestes at *Choeph.* 897; Orestes says the bloodshed that polluted him is 'sleeping', meaning that it is becoming less potent, at *Eum.* 280. On sleep in *Agamemnon* see 179–80*. It is interesting that in *Choephori* Clytemnestra is rather less sceptical about what a dream might portend (32–44), and she appears in a dream herself, witnessed by the Erinyes, in *Eumenides* (94–138).

276 some premature ... then: *apteros* means the opposite of 'winged' in the Homeric phrase 'winged words' (e.g. *Od.* 17.57), which is used of speech that meets its mark in the hearer. In *Agamemnon*, the feminine noun *phatis* is also elsewhere a rumour characterised in a negative light (8*, 456*, 611*), although its meaning is more neutral at 9 (a report expected from Troy), 1132 (of the message coming from oracles) and 1254 (of speech in the Greek language). *piainein* means 'to fatten', often in a rather derogatory sense (Pind. *Pyth.* 2.56, of being fattened on quarrels), and that is implied both here and at 1669*. The chorus assume that Clytemnestra has not verified the information. They here deride assumptions based merely on rumours, but are keen to hear any report at all about whether Menelaus' ship survived the storm (630–1) and acknowledge that the whole city has long talked about what actually happened at the Thyestean feast (1105). Clytemnestra complains that rumours about Agamemnon's death or injury at Troy were greatly exaggerated (866–8). Agamemnon likes to think that his fame as Troy's conqueror is indisputable (927), while Clytemnestra denies that any rumours circulated that she had been unfaithful to Agamemnon (611–12). The management of rumour and public opinion is also a political issue. The chorus, Clytemnestra and Agamemnon state that what 'the people' say cannot be disregarded by elites (457*, 881–4*, 938*); when it suits her purpose, however, Clytemnestra derides rumours as malicious (863, 874) or denies the importance of public opinion (939).

277 You really do ... girl: Clytemnestra's bitter expression of her frustration at the chorus' refusal to take her word seriously involves both the theme of childlike incompetence (see 74–5*) and gender. This child is grammatically and therefore definitely female, and would doubtless remind the audience of Iphigenia. Yet her wording is reminiscent of Diomedes' scornful response to receiving a wound in his foot from Paris in the *Iliad*, 'I am no more concerned than if I had been struck by a woman or a witless child' (11.389); see also Aeschylus, *PV* 986.

278 So at what time ... taken place? Lit., 'During what time has the city been sacked?' The genitive expresses duration of time. Perhaps the chorus are testing Clytemnestra by asking for such specific information, supplementary to the mere fact that the siege had finally been successful.

279 As I say, it was during last night, the one that gave birth to today: Lit., 'I say it is this light [emerging from] the kindly time now giving birth'. Clytemnestra, her time having been wasted by the chorus' derogatory suggestions of the unreliable means by which she had come by her information, wearily returns to the paedogonic dawn imagery with which she had begun the conversation in the first place (264–5*). Clytemnestra later uses the language of childbirth figuratively again (1391–2*); this invites a focus on her status as mother of Iphigenia, to which she draws climactic explicit attention at 1417–18*. On pregnancy see also the embryos of the hare at 134–8*.

280 And what kind of messenger could arrive so quickly: Lit., 'And who of messengers would arrive at such speed'. It would certainly take a single messenger travelling physically from Troy by land and sea much more than a couple of hours to arrive at Argos. But during Xerxes' invasion the Greeks had become fascinated with the Persians' different communication techniques, including the mounted courier system (*to angarēion*) in which relays of messengers mounted on swift horses passed the message from one to another in a relay; Xerxes used this system to send news home after Salamis. Herodotus describes it in detail at 8.98 and compares it with the torch relay races which the Greeks run in rituals for Hephaestus. A decree concerning arrangements at Athens for the festival of either Hephaestus or Prometheus, dating from the last quarter of the fifth century, includes instructions relating to torch races (IG I³ 82, lines 30–2). See also Sitlington Sterrett (1901).

281–316 The first of Clytemnestra's six great orations puts on display her powers of memory and rhetoric as she answers the chorus' question. She describes every stage of the beacon relay, which had brought the news by fire signals from Troy. The account draws a mental map of the northern Aegean Sea, a form of spatial description over which only Muses (in the catalogues of ships) and the god Hephaestus (who maps cosmic space on the shield of Achilles) have control in Homeric epic. The speech is resplendent with arresting visual details, especially colour terms and descriptions of the shapes made by features of landscapes (Sewell (1846) xxx). But Aeschylus' audience was learning to exert a different kind of spatial control across the Aegean, and the oarsmen in the audience will have known the regions she describes well: in Clytemnestra's words, they 'hear a dazzling confirmation of their own domination … in terms that foster imperial conquest. Aeschylus' evocation of these places and people … when viewed in the context of an aggressively expansionist state policy, is neither neutral nor innocent' (Rose (2009) 279). In mapping international space instantaneously, Clytemnestra shows herself in command of divine technologies of fire and cartography, just as she is in control of the action of the play: see Suksi (2017). According to the author of the pseudo-Aristotelian *de Mundo* 398a31–2, the Persian kings at Susa or Ecbatana could communicate with the most remote corners of their empire using fire signals. Aeschylus' audience will have been aware that the Persians used beacon relays; indeed, Mardonios probably used one to send word to Xerxes, then in Sardis, that he had sacked Athens for a second time (Hdt. 9.3.1). In his majestic Victorian translation of Herodotus, Rawlinson suggested that Mardonios' beacons were placed along the coast of Greece to Athos, then Lemnos and Asia: 'the line described in reverse order by Aeschylus (*Agam.* 272–290)— who may have taken his idea from the fact here noted, which would have come in part under his own observation' (Rawlinson (1880) 373 n.5). It is possible that the communication between Agamemnon and Clytemnestra is thus presented as something rather 'oriental', associating them with the hated Persian monarchy: see Introduction, p. 39 and Tracy (1986) 259–60. Clytemnestra's inclusion of divine names or allusions (Hephaestus, Hermes, Zeus) implicitly intimates that the gods themselves are somehow involved in bringing the news from Troy.

281   Hephaestus ... blaze: In answers to questions about the identity of an agent who did something, it is normal to supply the name but not repeat the main verb. Clytemnestra's language creates an image of the smith-god himself signalling with flames from Mount Ida, the peaks about 20 miles south-east of the ruins at Hissarlik, generally believed to be Troy. In the *Iliad*, Olympian gods take seats on this mountain to watch the Trojan War (e.g. 11.183). But Hephaestus here also personifies fire, or metonymically represents it, as at Hom. *Il.* 2.426. See also 280* and Hall (2018a) 383.

282–4   From one beacon-flame. ... fire: Lit., 'Beacon was sending beacon here from a courier of fire'. The imperfect tense indicates a repeated action. *angarou* is an emendation but a virtually certain one. **Hermaean crag of Lemnos:** The highest peak of Lemnos is now called Skopia or Vigla, standing at around 470 metres in the north-west of the island, which was of course Hephaestus' traditional residence (Hom. *Od.* 8.283–4, Hdt. 6.130.1) and home to one of his very few major local cults. Sophocles' Philoctetes, stranded on Lemnos, also mentions the Hermaean mount (*Phil.* 1459). Hermes, too, had an association with this island, along with nearby Samothrace; in these parts he and his phallic icons were connected with the ancient Pelasgian people and the mysteries of the Kabeiroi (Herodotus 2.51, Cic. *De Nat. Deor.* 3.2, Propertius 2.2.11, Servius on the *Aeneid* 8.619, 3.264). Aeschylus composed a play entitled *Kabeiroi* set on Lemnos (frr. 95–97a). The distance from Ida to Lemnos is about 50 nautical miles.

284–7   from that island: The distance here is about 44 nautical miles. **the peak of Zeus' Athos:** Athos, believed to have been formed from the body of one of the giants defeated in the Gigantomachy, is the easternmost of the three peninsulas of Chalkidiki. It was home to a temple of Zeus on the summit of its central mountain, which reaches the great height of 2033 metres. See Sophocles fr. 237, from his *Thamyras*, Capelle (1916) 39 and other references in Hübner (1985) 42 n.12. In the *Iliad* 14.229–30, Hera walks over the waves from Athos to Lemnos, a distance of about 44 nautical miles. Sophocles fr. 776 says that the shadow of the mountain of Athos reached all the way to Lemnos. **third:** some scholars have claimed that this brings to mind Zeus specifically in his capacity as Saviour (see 245–7*). **soaring high over the surface of the sea, the power of the torchlight travelled gleefully:** Lit., 'and aloft, so as to [skim] the back of the sea, the power of the traveller-lamp pleasurably'. The word *poreutou* is probably the genitive of the masculine noun *poreutēs*, 'traveller', since a feminine termination for the adjective *poreutos* was available. A line or lines have almost certainly dropped out of the manuscript tradition after this and there is no main verb. As so often, Aeschylus makes his audience think in terms of the great celestial spaces above them (4*). The evocation of the path of the light reflected gleefully on the 'back' or surface of the sea is a beautiful touch.

288–9   The pinewood torch ... message: Lit., 'the gold-beamed pine-torch, like a sun, having announced the light'. The participle *parangeilasa* needs to be translated as a main verb in English. Clytemnestra suggests that the light cast by the bonfires of Athos was intense enough to feel like sunlight. **Makistos:** Now named Kantili, this is a range of mountains in the north-western part of the island of Euboea, where the precipitous highest peak reaches 1246 metres. The distance between these two beacons, at well over 100 nautical miles, is far greater than the earlier two, and it is not feasible that the light of even an enormous bonfire could be seen across it. In reality, such a fire signal would have had to be passed from Athos to Euboea via a much larger number of stages: it is interesting, but may be mere coincidence, that the gap in the text occurs at this point.

290–1   The mountain ... messenger: Lit., 'He, neither delaying nor conquered witlessly by sleep, discharged the part of messenger'. Mount Makistos is virtually personified as a Watchman who needed to take care not to doze off, like the Argive Watchman at the beginning of the play (17); on sleep see 179–80*. The name *Mēkistis* was held by a Euboean tribe in the early fifth century and *Mēkistodoros*, 'gift of Mekistos', was the personal name of an Eretrian soldier later, which may mean there was a local hero called Makistos or Mekistos (also the name of one of the Seven against Thebes in some versions of that story (Apollodorus, 3.6.3; see Wallace (1936) 379–80)). **witlessly:** See 1401*.

**292–3	the flowing Euripus:** Lit., 'the streams of Euripus'. On the famous tides of the Euripus straits between Euboea and the mainland see 184–91*. This place name will, despite Clytemnestra's triumphant tone, certainly have reminded the audience of the stranded fleet and the sacrifice of Iphigenia a decade earlier. **Messapion:** This small mountain range, still called Messapio, lies in north-eastern Boeotia along the Euripus strait (Paus. 9.22.5). Its highest peak reaches 1021 metres. The distance 'as the crow flies' from the previous beacon is about 40 miles.

**295	bush heather:** *ereikē*, *Erica arborea* var. 'Alpina', is an evergreen bushy shrub common in mountainous areas of the southern Mediterranean. Theophrastus groups it with other bushy shrubs such as privet (*Hist. Plant.* 1.14.2).

**296	not losing any clarity:** *mauroō* is used of the gods blotting out or dimming the reputation of bad men in Hes. *Works* 325 and Theognis 192. It is a shortened form of the more common *amauroō*, which is found in connection with the light of the sun, moon and stars at Hdt. 9.10, *Anth. Pal.* 9.24, Xen. *Cyn.* 5.4.

**297	plain of Asopus:** The river Asopos, named after an early king of the area (Paus. 9.1.1, 298–9*), flows from its source on the northern slope of the Cithaeron mountain, south-west of Thebes, to the southerly part of the Euboean Gulf. The plain and heights south of the river near Plataea constituted a crucial site in the Athenians' memory, since they had participated in the protracted Battle of Plataea there in 479 BCE when Mardonios, despite the Persians' superior numerical force, was finally defeated. Perhaps the Athenians had experienced the light of a full moon across the valley at that anxious time.

**298	like a beaming moon:** On *dikēn* see 231–5*. The adjective *phaidros*, used of the sun in Aesch. *Eum.* 926, connotes joy as well as shining light and is often used of facial expressions: see 520*, 725–6*. **craggy Cithaeron:** Lit., 'rock of Cithaeron'. The mountain range which separated Boeotia from Attica was the backdrop scenery of many unhappy myths, especially those relating to Thebes (Antiope and her sons Amphion and Zethus; Pentheus, killed by his mother; the parricidal Oedipus; Actaeon). There was a tradition that Mount Helicon and a malevolent Mount Cithaeron were rivals, sometimes brothers, and had come into conflict. A poem by the Boeotian poet Corinna staged a singing contest between them in which Cithaeron was victorious (fr. 654); Hermesianax of Cyprus (*FGrH* 797 F 2) wrote that Cithaeron had killed their father and then tried to kill Helicon, whereupon they were both transformed into mountains; Cithaeron became the residence of the Erinyes (see Vergados (2012)), which might lend its name a sinister aspect in Clytemnestra's report.

299   and started up ... fire: Lit., 'aroused another handover of the escort of fire'. The feminine noun *ekdochē* is cognate with the verb *ekdechesthai* at 285.

300–1   The lookout team ... told to do: It is not clear why the Cithaeron watchmen were so assiduous, unless the association of the mountain with kin-murder and the Erinyes somehow explains it (298–9*). The use of the passive invites the question of who it was that had given the Cithaeron team its instructions: see 312*. **sent from far away:** *tēlepompon* picks up the *pompos* of fire in 299.

302   Lake Gorgopis: The proper name means 'staring-eyed'. 'Almost every lake and lake basin between Cithaeron and Corinth has been identified at one time or another as Lake Gorgopis', wrote Wiseman (1974) 539. His article argues persuasively that Aeschylus' Clytemnestra means what is now known as Black Lake (Mavro Limni), about five miles west of Pagae (now Kato Alepochorion) on the northern coast of Megara, near the border with Corinthian territory and the Isthmus. The lake is small but extremely deep, and its waters look dark because it is overshadowed by large cliffs to its south (see Wiseman (1974) plates 118–119). The *Etymologiconi Magnum* writes under the entry *Eschatiōtis* that this was an alternative for *Gorgōpis*, a name derived from Gorge, daughter of Megareus and wife of Corinthus; 'when she heard about the murder of her children, was overcome with pained grief and hurled herself into the lake'. If Aeschylus' audience were aware of Gorge's story, he is adding a reference to another mother who had experienced the death of her offspring, but sadly we know no more about Gorge. Some members of Aeschylus' audience may have recalled that the device on Agamemnon's Iliadic shield was a Gorgon 'of grim face' (*Gorgō blosurōpis*), 'staring terribly' (11.36–7).

303   Goat Mountain: Lit., 'mountain over which goats wander'. There has been controversy about this landmark's identity, too. Cartographically speaking, it must belong to the Gerania range (Thuc. 1.108.2), constituted by the only mountains between Cithaeron and the Saronic Gulf, of which the highest peak, at 1285 metres, is now called Loutraki. It towers over the Perachora peninsula, with its magnificent sanctuary of Hera Akraia, where Medea deposited the corpses of her sons on her flight from Corinth to

Athens. The component in the name *aigi-* and the idea of roaming may have brought to mind Clytemnestra's lover, once a wandering exile.

304   rite of fire: The masculine noun *thesmos* can mean a law or set of rules (Hdt. 3.31, Andocides 1.81), and is often found in the context of athletics competitions within epinician odes (Pind. *Ol.* 6.69, 7.88, 13.29); see 171–2*.

305–8   igniting: *andaiein* is a poetic compression *of anadaiein* 'to light up'. **beard:** A breathtaking image for the trail left by light cast (cf. Eur. fr. 836, from a tragedy about Phrixus) from a mountaintop bonfire. The firelight is here virtually visualised as a mature man. **these watchmen:** The abrupt change of subject from the light itself (302) needs the addition of a noun in English. **its blaze:** Lit., 'blazing', the feminine participle agreeing with *phlogos* in line 306. **the cape that faces:** Presumably this means the coastline above which Corinth is built, where there was no need for another bonfire, because the light penetrated from western Megara all the way to just outside Argos. **Saronic Gulf:** Pausanias 2.30.7 says that it was named after the hunter Saron, an early king of Troezen, who chased a doe into the sea, where he drowned. His body was buried in a sanctuary of Artemis. This brings the beacon relay into territory very familiar to the Athenians, whose western coastline formed one of the margins of the Saronic gulf, and who on a clear day could see its waters from the Theatre of Dionysus.

309   Arachnaion: This mountain, about 20 miles from Argos as the crow flies, with a clear view in daylight from its summit down to the Gulf of Argos, is 3737 feet high. Pausanias (2.25.10) says that there are altars of Zeus and Hera on its summit, and sacrifices were made to them there when rain was needed. Rupp (1976) has found sherds and the remains of burnt animals dating to the eighth–sixth centuries BCE on the western peak, Hagios Elias, where the last beacon fire in the relay would have been lit. The proper name means 'spidery' and was perhaps prompted by the mountain's numerous long, narrow spurs. See 1492*.

310–11   shot: After a good deal of variety in the verbs used of the torchlight and the various watchmen at the serial lookout points, Clytemnestra uses the same verb—*skēptein*—three times between 300 and 310, adding punchy rhetorical emphasis to the final climactic stages of the message's journey; on the significance of the number three see 33*. This line reminds the spectator of the Watchman's ecstatic response at 25* to his first glimpse of the light signal from what we now learn was the summit of nearby Mount Arachnaion. **this light:** The deictic *tode* implies that Clytemnestra, as she speaks, is gesturing to indicate the path taken by the light to the Watchman's lookout point on the roof, or to the palace as a whole (which the neuter noun *stegos* can also mean). **directly descended:** Lit., 'not ungrandfathered by'. This is a remarkable litotes and locution, imagining the serial bonfires as connected genealogically, which therefore interacts with the tragedy's theme of familial succession. **Ida:** See 281*.

312 These ... instructions: Lit., 'Such were the ordinances of torchbearers by/for me'. Clytemnestra makes it clear that she had organised the beacon relay herself. The image used to illustrate the light being relayed by serial bonfires is that of a relay race run by men carrying torches as at certain festivals (280*).

313 carried out ... other: Lit., '[the instructions] being fulfilled by handovers one from another'.

314 The winner ... the relay: Lit., 'The first and last to run wins'. Clytemnestra continues the analogy of the torchbearers' relay race from 312*. On athletics imagery see 171–2*.

315–16 That's the sort ... to me: Clytemnestra defiantly concludes with a direct answer to the chorus' sceptical request at 272* for proof and a *tekmar* (a clinching piece of evidence or pledge). **my husband has sent:** By implying that the message has come directly to her from Agamemnon, and that they must therefore have been in previous communication, Clytemnestra justifies her chorus' trust in her as acting for and in the best interests of her husband (259–60*). The emphatic 'to me' at the very end of her first great speech leaves us in no doubt of her confidence in her own status.

317 prayers to the gods: Clytemnestra, while ordering rituals across the city, and suggesting subtly that there was divine support for the success of the beacon relay and its message (281*, 282–4*, 284–7*), has since her arrival on stage rather conspicuously *not* included a conventional expression of gratitude to any gods for the good news. The chorus may be implying that this needs correction, as well as stating that a choral hymn will follow soon, as it does at 355*.

318–19 marvel: The chorus have been understandably impressed by the technological feat of the beacon relay, but the varied, colourful and potent language of Clytemnestra's oration has enhanced the pleasure. The chorus want her simply to repeat it in entirety. **so please tell it:** 'please' is inserted into the translation because the optative expression sounds rather more polite than an imperative would have done.

320–50 Clytemnestra asserts her authority by neither obeying the chorus' invitation to reiterate the beacon relay report nor even acknowledging the request. Instead, she delivers a second oration, equally dazzling rhetorically but increasingly ominous in tone. After a description of what she imagines has been taking place in Troy overnight, and the expression of a (from her) rather incredible wish that the Greeks refrain from committing any sacrileges, she ends on a note of sombre obscurity, implying that even if the Greeks' behaviour is impeccable, on their return they may find that the suffering of other dead people still needs to be addressed.

320   Today the Achaeans hold Troy: With lexical variations, Clytemnestra repeats a third time her lapidary central message (see 267 and 269*), as if concerned that the chorus may even now not have got her point or even have believed it.

321   In the city ... voices: Lit., 'I think an unmixed shout stands out in the city'. **loud:** This translates *prepein* (on which see 29–30*, 242–3*, 321*). **conflicting:** *ameiktos* implies that the voices are not homophonous and cannot blend into a single sound. **voices:** On *boē*, often the war-cry but here including cries of grief and suffering as well, see 48*. It is in keeping with the tragedy's fascination with the aural qualities of vocal expressions of emotion (Introduction, p. 70) that Clytemnestra's narrative of the fall of Troy begins with what it sounded like. Some voices can be heard more distinctly than others.

322–3   If you pour ... you could say: Lit., 'Having poured vinegar and oil into the same container, you would not label the two, standing antagonistically, as partners'. The optative *prosennepois an* has an indefinite singular generic 'you' as its subject: see Stanton (1997) 5. This is an unusual culinary metaphor, perhaps deliberately from a 'female' sphere of activity given Clytemnestra's concerns about her gendered self-presentation; she, however, uses the masculine participle *egcheas* in the image of the person hypothetically pouring oil and vinegar into a vessel, who is automatically gendered male since the subject is 'you'. But its application to the emotional difference between types of human vocalisation is remarkable, even in a speaker with such a striking and colourful idiolect. On the distinctive motif of mixing phenomena that 'should' be kept apart see 636–7*.

324–5   So you can hear ... fates: Lit., 'It is [possible] to hear voices of the captured and those who have conquered separately, their fate being twofold.' Clytemnestra is creating for her audience the horrible soundscape of post-siege Troy, so that through her we can imagine what both Greek and Trojan voices currently sound like. There is probably an echo of *Iliad* 4.449–51 here, where 'a great din arose; there were at the same time the groans of the slain and the triumphant shouts of the slayers, and the earth ran with blood'. On the verb *kratein* see 10–11*. In the Watchman's opening speech (37) he uses the same elevated, poetic noun denoting 'voice' (although it is masculine there) in talking about the power of speech that the palace walls do not have; the word implies a type of vocalisation that is distinctive (it is used of the Sirens at *Od.* 12.41 and 159) or the sound made by a musical instrument (Eur. *El.* 716; Plato, *Laws* 7.812d). The masculine noun *phthongos* was used by the chorus to characterise another voice that could not be heard, the gagged Iphigenia's at Aulis (235–8); see also 1630* on the voice of Orpheus.

326–8   For the defeated: *hoi* refers back to the conquered (*halontōn*) in 324. Despite the masculine definite article, at least some of these Trojans are of course women collapsed on the corpses of their husbands (*andrōn*), and presumably some of the siblings collapsed on the corpses of their brothers, and children on those of their fathers, are also female. Clytemnestra begins to move from her suggestive evocation of the Trojan soundscape to the horrific sights to be seen after the battle for Troy, although she stays with the acoustic theme of vocal lament with the main verb *apoimōzousi*, 'they bewail aloud'; like the more common *oimōzein*, this means to utter the 'meaningless' expression of pain or grief *oimoi*. **elderly fathers:** Lit., 'nurturing seniors'. The audience would no doubt have thought of Priam here. **captives now:** Lit., 'no more from a free neck'. This is a striking way of saying that these mourners, once free Trojans, are now slaves, the physicality bringing to mind the halters, yokes and bridles that have featured metaphorically earlier in the poetry (132–4*, 218–21*). It foreshadows others, especially the yoke of slavery imposed on Cassandra and the yoke of oppression Aegisthus wants to harness the chorus under: see 529*, 643, 842, 953, 1071, 1123–6*, 1640–2). On slavery see 1036–7*. **fate:** *moros* is a masculine noun related to *Moira* (see 128–30*), but in tragedy is never so personified (see Aesch. *Choeph.* 911). It is particularly associated with violent death, in Herodotus exclusively so (e.g. 1.117).

330–3   But for the victors … city: Lit., 'But night-wandering exertion out of the battle marshals hungers for breakfast [in] the others out of whatever the city contains'. There is something especially brutal about the image of ravenous Greek soldiers grabbing and devouring breakfasts at random while the defeated Trojans lament. Food and eating rarely feature in Greek tragedy, which is one of the central generic differences between it and comedy. On wandering see 77–9* and on hunger see 192–5*. **a busy night's work:** *nuktiplanktos*, like the whole sentence, implies the very opposite of collective military discipline. Clytemnestra's language when she is describing the activities of the ordinary Greek soldiers is also reminiscent of the language of the Watchman, who had used this adjective when describing his nocturnal ordeals (12–14*). Those who serve both Agamemnon and Clytemnestra are made to work night-long shifts. On *ponos* see 1* and on wandering, 77–9*. **has worked up:** *tassei* in a military context implies drawing up ranks and files, or marshalling, and so its use here ironically underlines that disciplined battle is not what these roaming individual soldiers had been engaging in at all. **huge appetite:** *nēsteis* is an alternative plural to *nēstides* (193). Hunger or fear of it is elsewhere associated with the lives of those subordinate to kings in *Agamemnon*: see also 192–5*, 1621*. **not according to rank: whatever straw ... happened to draw:** Lit., 'as each drew the lot of chance [out of the helmet]'. This metaphor simply means that each man ate what he happened to find on his own route around the town. The disorganised nature of the final conquest of Troy and the lack of coordinated action strike an offkey note before Clytemnestra even addresses possible sacrilege.

333–4 captured: The adjective *aichmalōtos* is frequently used of female war captives (see 1440*, Soph. *Trach.* 417), who are regularly referred to by the cognate feminine noun *aichmalōtis*; here the term may prompt the inclusion of Trojan women in the picture of the Greeks so speedily appropriating Trojan domestic housing, although Clytemnestra does not include rape explicitly amongst her list of potential war crimes. The audience in 458 BCE may well have remembered the way these captive women, including Cassandra, were depicted in Polygnotus' celebrated painting 'Iliupersis', recently installed in the Painted Stoa on the north side of the Athenian agora (Paus. 1.15.2). **released from the frost ... outdoors:** Lit., 'released from the open-air frosts and dews'. On dew see also 12–14* and 1390*.

335–7 like happy men: The image of someone enjoying an undisturbed night's sleep, and indeed the very word *eudaimones* (see 530*), stand out against the general picture of anxiety and sleepless nights evoked throughout this play (179–80* and Introduction, p. 6). But perhaps the wording '*like* happy men' suggests that there is something not quite right about the situation. **with no need for a guard:** Lit., 'unguarded'. On *euphronē* see 264–5*.

338–40 If they properly respect ... in their turn: The interlacing of the polyptoton *theous/theōn* with *halousēs* and *anthaloien*, which are formed from *haliskesthai* and *anthaliskesthai* respectively, gives this gnomic conditional sentence a jingling aural effect. In 458 BCE it would have been impossible for an Athenian audience not to be reminded of the Persians' looting of their Acropolis, and indeed the language here is not dissimilar to that in Aeschylus' *Persians* 807–12: see Hall (1996) 163–4.

341–2 I hope that no desire … shouldn't: Lit., 'May no lust fall before on the army to loot things they shouldn't, defeated by profits.' *empiptein* is used in a similarly destructive context, of the evil spirit at 1175* and 1468*. *emballein* occurs in a description of violent damage at 1468*. Metaphorical *erōs* here means a craving *like* sexual desire (see also 540*), but Ludwig (2002) 133 thinks that Clytemnetra 'may also be thought to have in mind the liaisons, rapes and enslavements attendant on sieges and the sacking of cities … . The violation of Trojan women and the violation of Trojan sacred space seem to link up … with a wider, theologico-political aim, the desire to violate.' But the audience must of course doubt the sincerity of Clytemnestra's purported hope here that the Greeks restrain themselves at Troy.

343–4 To get home safely … back again: Lit., 'For [they] must bend another leg of their race.' Clytemnestra imagines the Greek army as running such a race outward to Troy and then back again on the 'other leg of the *diaulos*'. On athletics metaphors see 171–2*.

345–7 Even if … that might befall: This is a chilling sentence with which to complete her account of what is happening at Troy. Even if two conditions are safely fulfilled—that the army does not commit sacrilege (which the audience knows well they did; visual representations of the cyclic *Ilioupersis* depict scenes of savage slaughter: Kennedy (2009) 58), and that no further calamities are imminent (the audience knows that a storm wrecked much of the returning fleet)—there is no guarantee that 'the misery of the dead' will not wake up again. By not identifying who these dead are (the troops killed at Troy? Iphigenia?), Clytemnestra cryptically augments the uneasy atmosphere she has already created. On the theme of avarice, which might motivate the Greeks to sacrilegious acts of plunder, see 378–80*.

348 That is what … words: Lit., 'Such things mark you (*toi*) you hear from a woman—me'. Clytemnestra may be understood both as pointing out that women can imagine and deliver war narratives and as referring back to the chorus' scepticism about the reliability of her account (272*). On the repeated discussions of what constitutes appropriate feminine speech see the Introduction, pp. 22–7.

349 But may what is good prevail: Clytemnestra joins Calchas before the fleet departed and the chorus in this wish, with slightly variant diction: see 121*. **unambiguously:** Lit., 'not indecisively when weighed in the scale'. *mē dichorropōs* implies that it will *not* be the situation that neither scale pan sinks. This particular litotes is used by both Agamemnon and Cassandra later in the play (815, 1272). The adverb is related to *rhopē* ('turn of the scale') and *rhepein* ('to incline or sink the scale'). On weighing imagery see 63–7*.

350   This benefit is the one I favour over multiple blessings: Lit., 'I chose this enjoyable advantage (*onēsin*) over many goods', which makes us wonder what exactly might be entailed by the unambiguous prevailing of the good. An alternative interpretation of Clytemnestra's cryptic line is the much blander, 'I chose this enjoyment of multiple good things'. A competent actor could bring out the double meaning by careful intonation.

351   good sense ... sensible man: This translation is an attempt to reproduce the aural effect of the two words containing the *phron-* element in the Greek. The chorus clearly think that this is a compliment to pay to a woman (see further 348*).

352–3   evidence: Lit., 'evidences'. The chorus use the more common noun, *tekmērion*, equivalent to the *tekmar* they requested earlier (272*); Aristotle traces the etymology of *tekmērion* from the older term *tekmar*, and defines it as a clinching piece of evidence regarded by all involved as irrefutable (*Rhet.* 1.1357b). **I'm getting ready:** As they speak, the chorus may be getting into formation ready for their imminent choral song: on the middle form of the verb *paraskeuazein* see also 1422. It is often found in military contexts, as in preparing for battle (Hdt. 1.71, 5.34, 9.96, Thuc. 2.80, 4.13, Xen. *Anab.* 7.3.35), and there are intimate connections in Greek thought between dance and military drill (MacNeill (1995); Hall (2010a) 155–6). It is conspicuous that Clytemnestra does not give them any encouragement, just as she has not thanked the gods herself.

354   A valuable reward ... achieved: On the litotes of *ouk atimos* see Introduction, p. 74; on *charis* see 182–3*, where the chorus complained that the favour of the gods was harsh and hard to win. Here they moderate that view, stating that their labours have *not* gone unrewarded by the gods, whom they are now to thank. **Labours:** On *ponoi* see 1*.

iv]   355–488   THE CHORUS

Summary

As Clytemnestra leaves the stage to enter (or re-enter: see 83–4*) the palace, the chorus begin a short anapaestic section, intoning the praises of Zeus and Night in thanks for the victory and getting into formation ready for the first choral ode, or *stasimon*, after the parodos. This consists of three strophic lyric pairs and an epode. What begins as a hymn in praise of the gods and the punishment of Troy for Paris' crime swiftly morphs into a wider meditation on human wrongdoing, especially committed by members of rich and powerful households, and its punishment. But here it is implied that the Atreidai are responsible for great suffering too. If the theme and memories of the parodos were centred on the sacrifice of Iphigenia just before the Greek fleet sailed for Troy, this ode's memories take us slightly further back into the past, and centre on the effect that the disappearance of Helen with Paris had on the Argive royal household, especially on Menelaus himself. But Menelaus' grief at his loss proves to be the pivot at the heart of the ode, because it reminds the chorus of the multiple bereavements suffered by ordinary Greek families like theirs, a pivot where the violent war-god Ares seems to oust providential Zeus as presiding deity. In highly allusive and subjective lyric passages such as these, an emotional continuum can provide the swivel between quite disparate subject matter. The war dead are here placed, in Aeschylean language, alongside Paris' crime and the suffering of Iphigenia, into the scales of justice constituted by the theodicy of the play.

355–366 Anapaests
During this introductory passage, as the chorus march and get into formation for their danced stasimon, they fulfil what would be expected of a public chorus in a Greek city consequent upon the news of a military victory. In elevated diction, they maintain their focus on thanking Zeus for castigating the enemy and describe the punishment.

355–6 Zeus my King: Hesiod calls Zeus the *basileus* of the gods (*Theog.* 886; cf. Pind. *Ol.* 7.34) but inscriptions show it was also a cult title of his (LSJ s.v. *basileus* I.2). This is the second hymn to Zeus performed by the chorus in the play, regardless of whether they were quoting a hymn first sung by Calchas on the day of the omen of the eagles (161–3*). **and kindly Night:** This is the divine personification of Night, whose lovers included Zeus (Hes. *Works* 17). Her epithet in Hesiod held the opposite force, 'deadly'. A primordial goddess, daughter of Chaos, she was mother of Aither and Day (see Hes. *Theog.* 123, 264–5*) but also of Death, Sleep, Dreams, Blame, Misery, the Hesperides, Moirai, Kēres and Nemesis (Hes. *Theog.* 211–24). No wonder the Greeks feared her and often euphemistically called her 'the kindly time' (264–5*, 335–7). Yet her son Sleep recalls in the *Iliad* (14.259–61) that she had been very kind to him when he was afraid of Zeus. **provider of great glory:** The punctuation of the English translation is designed to show that this phrase and the remainder of the sentence apply to Night, not to Zeus; this is clear from the feminine gender of *kteateira* in Greek. It is possible that the *kosmoi* ('ornaments', 'glories') were taken by the audience not to mean metaphorical signs of distinction obtained by victory, but the stars and heavenly bodies which are visible at night, as the Watchman observed (4*); the masculine noun *kosmos* was used in this way by Pythagorean philosophers (see the Orphic fragment 2 in Kern (1922) 93 and also the *Corpus Hermeticum* 11.7.3.15). Or perhaps listeners could hear both meanings at the same time.

357 you who threw: Night is compared to the netkeeper (*arktuōros*), who needed to be strong, skilled and agile and worked closely with the leader of a hunting expedition, since animals were netted before they were killed off with hunting weapons: see Xenophon *Cyn.* 2.3. The image of the hunting or fishing net of various types, designated by different words, occurs several times in the language of the play, both before and after the net which Clytemnestra uses to restrain Agamemnon's movements is brought physically into view with his corpse at 1372: see 358* (*steganos* and *diktuon*), 359–61* (*gangamon*), 1048* (*agreumata*), 1374–6* (*arkustata*), 1382 (*amphiblēstron*) and 1611 (*herkos*). Lloyd-Jones (1969) 98–9, citing parallels with Babrius' fable 4, 'The Fisherman and the Fish', makes a plausible case that it is fishing that Aeschylus evokes here. Agamemnon is caught in a physical net, prefigured by Clytemnestra's bizarre visualisation of his body with as many wounds as there are holes in a hunting net (868); Cassandra is compared with a wild animal trapped by hunting nets (1063*), although she imagines herself as a hunting hound on the scent (1184–5*). The Greeks attacking Troy are also imagined as hunters at 693*. Hunting and traps are singled out as the most distinctive images of *Agamemnon* by Dumortier (1935b) 71–87. **ramparts:** *purgoi* always refers to *defensive* walls, e.g. Hom. *Il.* 7.338. The Trojans are architecturally represented by the city's defensive walls rather than their royal palace: see also 827 and 1168–70. On the evolving image of Troy in the trilogy, and its ambivalent signification, see Fartzoff (2009).

358 impermeable mesh: The masculine noun *steganos* implies a leakproof covering, i.e., one so tightly woven that even 'not one of the young ones' could escape—a sinister metaphor for the effect of nightfall. A *diktuon* is a substantial (Xen. *Cyr.* 2.5) piece of netting, used for fishing (Hom. *Od.* 22.386, Aesch. *Choeph.* 506) or hunting on land (Hdt. 1.123, Ar. *Birds* 1083). In tragedy it is elsewhere used metaphorically, as in the 'net of delusion' (Aesch. *PV* 1078); Cassandra speaks of the 'net of Hades' at 1115*. The tragedy has already established the use of images from constraints used on domesticated and sacrificial animals (132–4*), and in this passage expands this repertoire to include metaphors from the world of hunting fauna in the wild: see 357*.

359–61 **nor any of the young ones:** *nearos* is a rather imprecise word meaning 'young', 'new' or 'fresh' (74–6*), but here, contrasted with *megas*, which implies large physical stature (Hom. *Il.* 16.776, *Od.* 18.4, Soph. *OT* 742), it must mean small children and therefore may well bring to the audience's mind the infamous execution of Astyanax, cast from the ramparts of Troy. Clytemnestra uses the term to mean either Iphigenia or Iphigenia plus the children of Thyestes (1504*). **escape:** Lit., 'overleap', 'achieve [going] beyond'. **great net:** A *gangamon* (neuter noun) is normally a small contraption consisting of a round net, suitable for catching oysters (Oppian, *Hal.* 3.81), perhaps to be used in conjunction with a special small piercing fork or trident (this appears to be the meaning of the feminine noun *gangamē* at Strabo 7.3.18). Aeschylus deploys a wide range of words for nets in the trilogy (357*), but the choice of this rare word here provides a strong guttural effect in conjunction with the polyptoton *megan ... mega ... megan* within five lines. **of slavery:** The theme of slavery is to become increasingly prominent in *Agamemnon* and will culminate in the miserable slave-chorus of *Choephori*: see 1036–7*. **all-embracing:** Lit., 'all-capturing'. **ruin:** This is *atē*, a force of destruction involving delusion, sometimes personified, and a daughter of Zeus by Strife, who was herself the daughter of Night (355–6*; see *Il.* 19.91, Hes. *Theog.* 230). Personified Atē seems to be compared with Clytemnestra by Cassandra at 1230* and is grouped by Clytemnestra with Justice and 'Erinys' as her collaborators at 1433*. But when not personified, *atē* can mean delusional and reckless crime (as, relevantly, in the original *atē* of Paris/Alexander at Hom. *Il.* 6.356) or, as here, the doom consequent upon it (Aesch. *Pers.* 822, Soph. *Aj.* 363; see also 386*, 1268, 1566). For a detailed discussion of Atē /atē in *Agamemnon* see Geisser (2002) 267–97.

362 **guardian of strangers:** On Zeus Xenios see 60–2*. There is probably a specific echo here of Menelaus' accusation of the Trojans in *Il.* 13.623–5: 'nor did you fear in your heart the harsh wrath of loud-thundering Zeus *xeinios*'.

364–5 **bending his bow:** Unlike his children Apollo, Artemis and Heracles, Zeus is not usually imagined or worshipped as an archer. The image, however, works well in conjunction with Night as Zeus-the-hunter's collaborator in the pursuit and destruction of Troy. **at length:** While Night only recently cast her net over Troy, Zeus has been perfecting his aim ready to discharge his arrow for much longer, perhaps ever since Paris took Helen to Troy. This is a grand image reminiscent of the powerful archer-potentates in Ancient Near Eastern art, for example Ashurnasirpal II and Crown Prince Shalmaneser III in the Neo-Assyrian wall relief panels from Nimrud in the British Museum (see Curtis and Reade (1995)). There are subsequent images of archers in the play: see 364–5, 535–6, 537, 628, 786, 1194. **prematurely:** *pro kairou* just might refer to space rather than time, 'short of the target/ mark', which would make a neater antithesis with 'beyond the stars'. On the stars and vertical axis in the play see 6–7*, 51–4*, 92–3*, 826* and Introduction, p. 58.

367–487　First Stasimon

The chorus perform a long choral ode in which they trace the crisis in Argos back further than the sacrifice of Iphigenia to Helen's departure for Troy. They continue to insist that Zeus must have authorised the Trojan expedition, but shift to painting an uncomfortably dark picture of the suffering caused by the war and the resentment it has caused amongst the general population. The metre is predominantly iambic and used with precision and ironically (see Metrical Appendix). The subject matter can be analysed as follows:

Strophe 1	Zeus must be behind the victory. Gods do concern themselves with human morality. Rich people wage war but wealth does not protect them from divine justice.
Antistrophe 1	The unjust man, compelled by Persuasion, is exposed and cannot escape after damaging his city. The gods destroy him. Look at Paris who offended against the laws of hospitality and stole a wife.
Strophe 2	She left her own people and caused an armada and a war and the destruction of Troy. Menelaus was inconsolable.
Antistrophe 2	He saw apparitions in dreams, but his sorrow is surpassed by the grief suffered by those many Greeks whom the war has bereaved.
Strophe 3	Ares sends men to Troy but only ashes return. Some of the bereaved feel aggrieved towards the Atreidai.
Antistrophe 3	It is bad when citizens speak resentfully.
Epode	Can we really believe the news brought by the beacon relay?

367　It's what they call 'the stroke of Zeus': Lit., 'They have [in their repertory of sayings the possibility] to say "the stroke of Zeus"'. It is not clear that the *plēgē* of Zeus was proverbial, but *plēgai* is used of Zeus' lightning strokes at Hes. *Theog.* 857. This feminine noun can designate a rather general godsent stroke of misfortune (Aesch. *Pers.* 251, *Eum.* 933, Soph. *Aj.* 137, 279). But the audience may recall this phrase when Agamemnon says he has been struck by a *plēgē* at 1343* and Clytemnestra uses the word of the third blow she struck him at 1386*.

368 track this down: *exichneuein* brings with it the association of tracing the path of a living creature through their footprints, as in Sophocles' *Trackers* (*Ichneutae*) fr. 314.166, of tracking cattle; it is used metaphorically of hunting down the Lydian 'stranger' in Euripides' *Bacchae* 352 and of tracking down the truth like a detective in the hypothesis to Menander's *Priestess* preserved in *POxy* 1235.49 (text and translation in Arnott (2000) 622–3).

369–72 They fared as he ordained: The aorist tenses might be gnomic; some translate this as 'People fare as he ordains'. **by whom:** The dative of the agent with the passive optative indefinite *patoit'*. **the favour of things which must not be touched:** On *charis* see 182–3*. *athiktos* is used in the neuter plural, as here, in a choral meditation on the divine punishment that awaits humans who break fundamental taboos at Soph. *OT* 891, and of land that must not be violated (the Delphic oracle, *OT* 897), but it can also imply female virginity or chastity (the tragedian Ion fr. 11, Eur. *Hel.* 795). Although the first three stanzas of this ode are ostensibly about Paris' violation of *xenia*, at this point it becomes likely that the audience would have been reminded of Agamemnon's sacrifice of Iphigenia as much as of Paris' relationship with Helen, especially since the ensuing discussion of the problems brought by extreme wealth applies quite as much to the Atreidai as to their Trojan foes. **is trampled underfoot:** *patein* is to become an important verb in *Agamemnon*, especially at 957* when Agamemnon walks on the priceless textiles, 1298* and 1357*. The idea of bad people trampling on what is sacred or just is also picked up later in the trilogy (Aesch. *Choeph.* 844, *Eum.* 110).

374–6 The penalty has been shown to be paid by the daring of those who breathe war in excess of what's right: Lit., 'Daring of those breathing Ares more greatly than justly has been demonstrated paying a penalty'. This is the best sense that can be made through necessary emendation of the text. For the metaphorical use of the war-god's name as meaning 'warlike spirit' see 48*. On his increasingly menacing but invisible presence in the play see also 74–6*, 108–15*, 438,* 439,* 472*, 642*, 643*, 645*, 1206*, 1509–12* and Introduction, pp. 46–7.

378–80 Let one's livelihood ... sense: Lit., 'Let [livelihood] be non-harming, so as to suffice for the one who has drawn the lot of good sense'. The noun 'livelihood' needs to be supplied in English from the general meaning of the previous sentence. *prapides* are equivalent to *phrenes*, originally meaning the physiological diaphragm (Hom. *Il.* 11.579), but coming to signify 'understanding' or 'mind' (Hom. *Il.* 24.514, Hes. *Theog.* 656). See Sullivan (1997) 137–51, 802* and, on Aeschylus' physiology of the emotions, Introduction, p. 62. The *prapides* are here in the genitive as being the reference of *eu*. The idea that excessive wealth leads to wrongdoing and/or unhappiness is of course a leitmotif of ancient Greek thought: see 381, 471, 776–7*, 1008–9*, 1638–9* and Desmond (2006) chapter 2.

381   For wealth provides no protection: Lit., 'For there is no defence of wealth'. The feminine noun *epalxis* refers to a physical edifice such as a defensive wall or line of battlements (Hom. *Il.* 12.381, Thuc. 2.13), continuing the play's metaphorical fusion of the concrete house or fortified palace with moral and metaphysical phenomena (see Introduction, pp. 69–70). **insatiably:** *pros koron* needs to be taken adverbially. **kicked:** *laktizein* used metaphorically, like 'trample underfoot' (369–72*), is consistently applied in *Agamemnon* to arrogant or stubborn behaviour (855*, 1624*). **altar of Justice:** See 250–1*. **into obscurity:** Pindar speaks in *Isthm.* 4.31 of the obscurity (*aphaneia*) of the fortune of people who attempt nothing.

385–6   Wretched Persuasion: The adjective *talas* in reference to people usually means that they are deserving of pity (Aesch. *Choeph.* 743, *Pers.* 445); in tragedy it is often found in reference to suffering or misery (Aesch. *Choeph.* 1069, *Sept.* 988) or the unpleasant phenomena that cause suffering, such as disease (Eur. *Tro.* 1084) or strife (Eur. *Hel.* 248). It was used of the delusion that made Agamemnon decide to kill Iphigenia at 222–3*. Karas (2022) 4–11 suggestively reads the references to Peithō in *Agamemnon* as allying her closely with the casting of destructive magical spells. But it is unusual to find *talas* oxymoronically (compare, however, 'the whip of Persuasion' at Pindar, *Pyth.* 4.219) describing a phenomenon often presented as a positive force in Greek life, such as persuasion (see, e.g., 104–7*)—a skill required in relationships to avoid sexual coercion, especially of males by females they intend to marry (see Cheiron's description of the 'hidden keys to sacred loves' of 'wise Peithō' at Pind. *Pyth.* 9.39), and in the city-state to bind citizens together and avoid conflict: see Buxton (1982). Athena expresses gratitude to Persuasion for helping her to control her way of expressing herself to the mutinous Erinyes at *Eumenides* 970 and this achieves a favourable outcome. It is thus directly *opposed* to the violence inherent in the verb *biatai* (Foley (2012)), of which it is the subject in this sentence. Some translators feel the need to translate it here with a more negative noun such as 'Temptation', but this is to weaken the paradoxical power of the Greek: Athena's deployment of persuasion 'reinforced' by *force majeure* in *Eumenides* continues this ambivalence (Hall (2015)). Peithō personified was the recipient of a cult at Sicyon and elsewhere (Hdt. 8.11, Paus, 2.7.7; Pirenne-Delforge (1991)); in religion she was closely associated with or subsumed to Aphrodite: at Athens her statue stood close to that of Aphrodite Pandemos, whose worship was said to have been instituted by Theseus at the time when he united the scattered townships into one great body of citizens (Paus. 1.22.3). Both goddesses were celebrated at the Athenian festival of the Aphrodisia (Pala (2010); see also Buxton (1982) 29–37). Peithō is often depicted in visual art alongside Aphrodite and/or Eros in erotic contexts, especially the abduction of Paris (Stafford (2000) 162–5; Rozenzweig (2004) 20), and such scenes may have been suggested to the mind's eye of the audience by this passage. **intolerable daughter:** The same adjective *aphertos*, which Aeschylus probably invented, is used later in this antistrophe of the damage that was inflicted on the community (395). It recurs in the Herald's description of the unbearable cold of Mount Ida (564) and in Cassandra's denunciation of the crime taking place indoors (1103). It is also used in *Choephori* and in *Eumenides*, e.g. at 146, when the Erinyes sing that, if they have lost track of their victim, it is an 'intolerable' (*apherton*) wrong. Peithō is an Oceanid in Hesiod (*Theog.* 346–9), and the daughter of Foresight (Promētheia) and sister of Fortune and Good Order in Alcman fr. 64. She is one of the Charites in later poetry (Nonnus 24.461), but in Sappho (fr. 90) and Aeschylus' *Suppliant Women* 1039 she had appeared as the daughter of Aphrodite. Aeschylus is here using paedogonic imagery (see Introduction, pp. 65–6) to explore the causal links between abstract ethical and metaphysical phenomena. **premeditated ruin:** On *atē* see 359–61*. Athenian laws did make a distinction in some types of case (especially a man killing his wife's lover, as in Lysias 1), between crimes committed on an impulse and those planned ahead; this distinction informed tragedy elsewhere: see Hall (2010c). **forces him on:** An accusative pronoun 'him' as the object of *biatai* needs to be supplied from the previous stanza. In the middle voice this verb can mean the powerful physical force of an army cornering an individual enemy on the battlefield (Hom. *Il.* 11.467) or of a vast sea wave hurling a swimmer onto dry land (Hom. *Od.* 7.278).

387–9 Every remedy: On medical imagery see 17*. **The wound can't be hidden:** Lit., 'the hurt part was not concealed'. The neuter noun *sinos* probably extends the medical metaphor implied in 'remedy', since its basic meaning in medical Greek is 'injury' (Hippocrates, *Fract.* 10). It is used metaphorically among the tragedians only by Aeschylus (561*, 734* of Helen), but see Herodotus 8.65. The aorist may be understood gnomically. **stands out like a light:** The effects of wretched Persuasion are like an injury to the body that can't be hidden; they are visually conspicuous like a light shining in a sinister manner. On *prepei* see 29–30*, 242–3*, 321*; on the recurring theme of light and darkness, Introduction, pp. 63–5.

390–5   Just like base metal … taint: Lit., 'In the manner of bad bronze, when tested by rubbing and applications [of the touchstone], he is black-clotted (since a child pursues a winged bird), having imposed an intolerable taint-mark on his city.' The accumulation of metaphors from different realms of experience—medicine, light and dark, metallurgy, proverbial wisdom about futile action—is dizzying. **tested:** The verb *dikaioō* from which this aorist participle is derived suggests a moral and quasi-legal rather than metallurgical judgement (see Thuc. 3.40 and 41*). **touchstone:** This noun needs to be supplied in English. The ancient Greeks called such a smooth stone, the size of a large board-game counter, and found in the Lydian river Tmolus, the 'Lydian' stone; it was used to test (*basanizein*) the quality of precious metals 'by comparison of marks made by the friction' (*tēi paratripsēi*, Theophrastus, *On Stones* 1.47, 4, 45; see also Plato, *Gorg.* 486d). The technology seems to have been introduced from Lydia to Greece during Aeschylus' boyhood. On metallurgy images see 151–4*. **child chasing a bird on the wing:** Even by Aeschylean standards this delicate image forms a jarring contrast with the context, which otherwise entails a sustained comparison of a man's moral mettle being tested with a lump of bronze's metal on the touchstone. But there is psychological continuity here: the generalised malefactor whom the chorus is discussing is deluded about the attainability of his goals and their moral probity, just like a child who thinks s/he can run fast or high enough to catch a bird in flight. On the figurative language of childlike incompetence see 74–5*. It was probably a well-known proverb: see Strömberg (1954) 15. Winged beings soar through the memories and images in this play in keeping with its early stress on the vertical axis. The eagles in the omen are 'winged hounds' of Zeus (136), and the Herald recalls that the cold at Troy in winter was so cold it killed the birds (563–9*); the Atreidai were like winged vultures flying against Troy (49–52), an empty rumour is 'wingless' (276), a dream is a 'winged vision' (426) and the gods gave Itys' mother the 'winged form' of a nightingale (1147). On birds in *Agamemnon* see Petrounias (1976) 129–40 and Introduction, p. 58. **intolerable:** See 385–6*. **taint:** Although it can designate the infliction of punishment (Aesch. *PV* 329), *prostrimma* in this context, after *tribōi* at 381, probably continues the metaphor of the touchstone being applied (see also 151–4*). The technology worked by rubbing a small amount of the metal to be tested onto a touchstone. The transferred metal forms a coloured stripe, which is compared with a stripe ground from an alloy of known high-quality composition. The man who has been shown to be 'black' internally is envisaged as leaving a dirty-looking stripe on his city rather than a bright golden one.

396–8   The gods ... things: Lit., 'On the one hand no god hears his prayers. But on the other hand [the god] destroys the unjust man conversant with these [things]'. *tōn* is demonstrative, as often in epic. **involved in:** For *epistrophos* meaning 'acquainted with' or 'conversant with', see Hom. *Od.* 1.177.

399–402   That was what ... wife: Lit., 'Such too [was] Paris, having arrived at the Atreidai's house, [when] he shamed the hospitality table by thefts of a wife.' Until this point in the choral ode, the chorus' generalisations might have applied equally to Agamemnon or Paris, but here the chorus pick up the reference made in the anapaests at 364–5* to Zeus aiming his arrow at Paris. **hospitality's table:** On *xenia* see 60–2*. On the Atreidai's dining table in *Agamemnon* see 243–5*. **by stealing:** This is typical of the ambivalence of the language used by all ancient authors about the degree of Helen's complicity in her departure from Sparta. Was it rape or elopement? See also 534*. This ode, by implicating Peithō (385–6*), with her connotations of erotic persuasion, and speaking of Helen walking through a gate apparently unconstrained (407–9), leaves the question only slightly open. Yet, ultimately, since Helen seemed willing to remain with Paris in Troy, no patriarchal ancient Greek audience, being largely indifferent to the issue of female sexual consent (unless a woman's *kurios* believed she had been raped and acted on that belief: see Sommerstein (2006)), would have been overly concerned with whether she went voluntarily in the first place.

403–4   tumult of shield-bearing warriors: Lit., 'the shield-bearing-men throng'. The language is purposely redolent of the battle-scenes of the *Iliad*; *aspistoras* is reminiscent of *aspistaōn* (always genitive plural, e.g. *Il.* 4.90) and *klonos* is a regular word for turmoil on the battlefield (*Il.* 16.331, 713), especially of thronging spears (5.167, 20.319); cf. also the 'throng of men' at Hesiod, *Aspis* 148 and of cavalry at Aesch. *Pers.* 106. **formation of companies** This rare word might, alternatively, mean 'settings of ambushes' (see Plutarch, *Life of Philopoemen* 13).

405 arming of ships' crews: Lit., 'sailor-armings'; see 108–15*. The chorus use a similar expression when later they describe, in an ominous passage, the departure of the Greek ships from the Aulis sands (987*).

406 bringing: This is the second of three semi-rhyming feminine participles alluding to Helen's actions in this sentence (*lipousa ... agousa tlasa*), the first and third being placed in syntactical first and last position, providing an aural frame for the striking visual contrast of the mustering at Aulis and Helen's allegedly blasé physical departure. **instead of a dowry:** A dowry of destruction is a powerful image. Aeschylus is updating poetic wedding protocols, however: greater stress is laid in Homer on the prices (*hedna*) paid *for* brides (e.g. *Il.* 16.178, 16.190, *Od.* 16.391) than on the dowry (*hē proix* or, as implicit in the compound adjective *antiphernos* here, *hē phernē*).

407–10 lightly: This is a brilliant choice of adverb combining the idea of swift motion and light-heartedness. When Paris leaves Helen's bed to return to the battlefield in the *Iliad*, he is compared with a stallion whose knees 'lightly' (*rhimpha*) bear him to where mares are pasturing (6.511). **through the gate:** In the context, where we are about to hear about the impact of Helen's departure on her own home, and since *bainein*, from which the main verb *bebaken* derives, of which Helen is the subject, more often connotes movement away from or departure than arrival (425*), this is more likely to refer to the gate of Menelaus' house or estate than to the gates of Troy. **daring what should not be dared:** The paradoxical *figura etymologica* of the two words sharing the same root verb, *tlaō*, adds to the aural impact of the closing participle (406*). **palace seers:** The precise meaning of the word *prophētai* has been much disputed; a few scholars have argued that the palace employed some kind of official spokesmen (see the discussion in Fletcher (1999b)). Since this play assumes that Menelaus and Agamemnon lived in the same palace at Argos, whoever these *prophētai* are, they are based in the joint residence. Perhaps they are simply the same as the domestic dream 'adjudicators' (*kritai*) who will be said to offer Clytemnestra interpretations of her snake-lactation dream at *Choephori* 37. It is interesting that the chorus do not here explicitly include Calchas. **began groaning:** This translates the imperfect tense of the verb *stenein*, on which see 18*. **saying:** The voice of the seers is the third to be quoted in direct speech by the chorus in *Agamemnon*, in the course of their articulation of their memories of the events leading up to departure of the Greek fleet— memories which form a kind of parallel tragedy within the audience's mind. The previous two speaking characters in this alternative embedded tragedy have been Calchas and Agamemnon, although at 228–30* we heard *about* Iphigenia's 'cries of father' before she was gagged. It is not, however, clear when the end point of the direct speech is meant to occur: suggestions have included the ends of every sentence up to and including line 431: see van Emde Boas (2022) 417–18.

411   Alas, alas: *iō* is an exclamation frequent in the anapaests and lyrics of tragedy, usually repeated twice and often in combination with other exclamations (see 1100*). It often signifies pain or lamentation, as here, but see 503*. The repetition of this and 'house' imbues the seers' quoted response with a formal and semi-ritualised flavour.

412   marriage-bed: The identification of the neuter noun *lechos* (which could mean just 'couch' or even 'bier') with the sexual relationship of married or quasi-married couples was so strong that it could metonymically replace the institution or the figure of the spouse (Hom. *Il.* 1.31, *Od.* 8.269, Soph. *Aj.* 491, *Trach.* 27, 360). At 50* the chorus had used it in the simile comparing the Atreidai with vultures to denote the content of the parent-birds' nest, now empty of their progeny. On other allusions to marriage beds see 27*. **traces of her lovemaking:** Lit., 'man-loving tracks'. The masculine noun *stibos* can mean specifically the imprint of a body part such as a hoof (Hom. *Hymn to Hermes* 353) or a foot (Aesch. *Choeph.* 205). Here it brilliantly evokes the actual dents made in the bedding by Helen's lovely body. The adjective *philanōr* implies the wife's desire for the husband especially; at Aesch. *Pers.* 136 the Persian wives whose men are far away in Greece are said to be smitten by a husband-loving desire, and Clytemnestra uses the same adjective, with devastating irony, below at 856*.

412–13   You can see … unreproachful: This translates the less implausible suggested emendations of an irredeemably corrupt line. Nevertheless, Aeschylus' intention to evoke Menelaus' misery, combined with the cuckold's unusual reluctance to blame Helen herself, remains apparent. On silence see 34–9*.

414–15   In his yearning for her across the sea: This is strongly reminiscent of Sappho fr. 16.7–11, in her poem about longing for Anactoria, who has left her 'as Helen left her most noble husband and went sailing off to Troy with no thought at all for her child or dear parents, but (love) led her astray … ' (trans. Campbell (1982)). **a wraith … household:** Although the primary reference of *phasma* ('apparition') in conjunction with the idea of ruling the household is probably Menelaus, whose grief makes him seem wraithlike, the audience might also imagine the spectral image of Helen somehow lingering, especially since they will have known of the

Stesichorean tradition that it was a fabricated image of her that was sent to Troy (frr. 192–3). At 274* the chorus had used the plural *phasmata* to refer to figures seen in dreams and the chorus here continue to discuss Menelaus' sad dreams about Helen at 421–6.

416–17   grace of beautiful statues: On *charis* see 182–3*, although here, as at 422 and 1206*, the favour granted is specifically erotic and so the word almost means 'sexual gratification' (cf. Hom. *Il.* 11.243, and, in the plural, fr. trag. adesp. 402). In Pindar fr. 123.14 personified Charis is twinned with Persuasion in an eroticised encomium where the authorial voice says he is under the influence of Aphrodite; cf. Plato, *Phaedrus* 254a. The statues have been thought by some scholars to be portraits of Helen at which Menelaus can no longer bear to look (Huddilston (1898) 5 and Lloyd-Jones's translation (1979) 39–40: 'And the charm of her beautiful statues / is hateful to her husband'). But this is overly specific, since, from classical times, statues of beautiful young women (and men) were believed to be erotically inflammatory (Osborne (1994); Hall (2006) 131–3). The text refers to unspecified beautiful statues, which might normally be expected to arouse Menelaus, but can have no effect on the depressive cuckold now. At the time of the *Oresteia* the term *kolossos* probably designated not 'colossal' size but a style in which the statue's legs were tightly held together or replaced by a pillar (Benveniste (1932)); Aeschylus may have meant statues of young women like those of the late sixth-century Attic *korai*. This is the second reference to visual artworks relating, in highly charged contexts, to significant figures in the play: see 242–3*.

418–419   In the absence of eye contact all ... departed: On Aphrodite as personifying sexual pleasure or desire see Hom. *Od.* 22.444; Eur. *IA* 1264. But this text has proved controversial: to whom do they eyes belong? The options are (i) that it is the statues (e.g. Steiner (1995) 179). Statues always lack 'real' eyes, and yet were universally thought in antiquity to stimulate the viewer, and indeed it was their eyes that were thought to be the most beautiful of all a statue's features (Plato *Rep.* 4.420c; see also *Hipp. Maj.* 290b). (ii) Menelaus. See the translation of Smyth (1957), 'In the hunger of his eyes all loveliness has departed.' In this view, Aphrodite (i.e. sexual passion) is missing because Menelaus 'has no eyes' for anyone any more. But *en achēniais* must mean a want or absence of something, and the missing eyes belong to (iii) Helen. See Lloyd-Jones' translation (1979), 39–40: 'and in the absence of *her* eyes, gone is all the power of love'. There is, however, a further possibility (iv), suggested by George Thomson (1966) 41, but routinely ignored: the nearest parallel to the form and thought expressed here is a proverb attributed to the Orphic thinkers: *cheirōn ollumenōn erren poluergos Athēnē* ('Without hands there is no Athena, goddess of handicrafts'; Orphic fr. 347 ed. Kern (1922), quoted in Orion of Thebes' etymological lexicon (163.23). This means 'No hands, no handicraft'. In the Aeschylus passage the thought could be equally proverbial: 'No eyes, no sex'. The ancients were clear that sexual attraction emanated from the desired person's eyes and passed into the smitten party through *their* eyes. In Hesiod, Eros flows from the Graces' eyes with their glance (*Theog.* 910–11); in Euripides' *Hippolytus* Eros distils desire upon the eyes (525–6). Menelaus and Helen can't see each other any more; the chorus' elliptical expression is gnomic and ambiguous. Without the eye contact between loved and beloved there can be no sexual desire. On the importance of eyes and the gaze in *Agamemnon* see 240*, and on visual artworks, 242–3*.

421–2 mournful … dreams: Lit., 'dream-appearing mournful apparitions are present'. On this meaning of *doxai* see 275*. On the recurring theme of dreams in the play and trilogy see 274*. **joy:** See 182–3* and 416–17*. Menelaus is assumed to have dreamt about his absent wife because he was visibly distraught about her in his waking state: Heraclitus said 'The waking have one world in common, whereas each sleeper turns away into a private world of his own' (89 B 15 DK).

423 someone: The chorus' ruminations shift from Menelaus' delusional dreams about Helen to a generalised comment on the futility of anyone dreaming about holding an unobtainable beloved in their arms. This shift is in preparation for the pivotal move from the individual experience of spousal abandonment to the communal experience of bereavement in the next sentence.

424–6 slipping through his arms: The basic meaning of *parallassein* is to change, deviate or change direction as winds do ([Aristot.] *Probl.* 945a36). But the reference to arms evokes the sense of a physical embrace. **is gone:** The perfect indicative of *bainein* often has the connotation of *going away*, i.e. disappearing (Soph. *Trach.* 134, Eur. *IT* 1289) and can even be a euphemism for dying (Aesch. *Pers.* 1002). The word here repeats the same form of the same verb used of Helen leaving Menelaus' palace at Sparta in the matching strophe at 406*. **momentarily:** The litotes of 'not hereafter' heightens the sense of loss after a fleeting moment of joy. No listener could fail to be reminded of the archetypal dream of the beloved in the *Iliad*, when Patroclus appears to Achilles and asks him to clasp his hand and promise to bury him (23.75). But when Achilles asks for an embrace and puts his arms out, 'he could not hold him, for his soul went like smoke, screeching beneath the earth' (23.100–1). **on wings:** Hecuba calls dreams 'black-winged' at Eur. *Hec.* 70–72 (see also the anonymous lyric fragment (no. 963 in Campbell (1993) quoted by Demetrius, *On Style* 143) and they are 'long-winged' in *Orphic Hymn* 86.1 ('To Dream'). On winged entities see 390–5*. **the paths of sleep:** The reported speech of Menelaus' palace seers concludes with Aeschylean poetry at its very finest; on sleep see 179–80*; this seems to me to be the most appropriate place to place the closing speech marks (see 407–10*).

427–8 Such are the sorrows … even these: These seemingly unremarkable two lines are of exceptional importance in the play's depiction of the tension between the Argive royal family's domestic problems and the widespread suffering that they have inflicted on the entire community. Returning from reported speech to their own subjective thoughts, the chorus of elderly Argives comment that, while Menelaus may have been cuckolded and miss his wife, countless households have lost a man at Troy and are suffering actual bereavement. This sentiment provides the pivot of the stasimon which henceforward focuses on the war dead. **of hearth and home:** The translation inverts the nouns in accordance with a familiar English idiom. The central hearth of the palace of the Atreidai is to become of increasing importance, while the unseen activity inside gains momentum after Agamemnon's return, as the place of domestic sacrifices (1311*, 1435*, 427–8*, 672*, 851–3*, 968–9*, 1036–7*, 1056–7*, 1311*, 1587–90*); it is notable that we are reminded here that every citizen family has its own domestic emotional and ritual centre constituted by the domestic hearth. **surpass:** The comparative form stresses that the public grief is of greater, rather than equivalent, magnitude.

429–31 Lit., 'Heart-unbearable grief in all cases for those who set out from Greece stands out in the homes of each'. **unbearable:** This compound adjective is inspired by the several Homeric formulae which combine the verb *tlaō* (I bear, withstand) with *kradiē* (heart), e.g. *Od.* 20.23. **heartbreak:** The feminine noun *pentheia* is not otherwise attested, but is a poetical form of the neuter noun *penthos*, perhaps suggesting a female personification of grief presiding in this house like a bereaved woman. **dominates:** On *prepei* see 29–30*, 242–3*, 321*, 387–9*.

432   heart: Lit., 'liver'. On the liver as the seat of emotions see Archilochus fr. 234, below 792*, where grief on the victim's behalf of false friends is said *not* to 'bite the liver', and Aesch. *Eum.* 135, where Clytemnestra is urging the Erinyes to feel pain on her behalf so as to act. This line constitutes a striking example of the chorus' ability to describe the physical sensations caused by mental pain (Introduction, p. 62).

433–6 This powerful evocation of the effect of multiple wartime fatalities on a community must have prompted many of Aeschylus' spectators to remember the family members whom each individual household had lost on military service. Shockingly high numbers of deaths are recorded on an inscription of 460 or 459 BCE, shortly before the first production of the *Oresteia*, commemorating the dead of one tribe, Erechtheis, alone (IG³ 1147); see Zaccarini (2020). **urns:** The neuter noun *teuchos* with the sense 'hollow vessel' and its visual instantiations serve diverse but unifying purposes in the play and trilogy (Introduction, p. 65). In a proleptic image of voting by casting ballots in urns, Agamemnon will later say that the gods cast their bloody ballots in the voting urn that would bring down Troy (813–16*); Cassandra speaks of the bath in which Agamemnon dies as a *teuchos* (1128*); Electra refers to the vase containing a libation with the same word (*Choeph.* 99), and it is used for actual voting in the Areopagus at *Eum.* 742. **ashes:** For the feminine noun *spodos* meaning ashes of cremated human cadavers see 443 below and *Choeph.* 687, where Orestes, reporting falsely his own death, speaks of his ashes in an urn far away. Eur. *Suppl.* 827 suggests that such ashes might be wiped on the head of mourners as a ritual sign.

438 **Ares … currency:** Lit., 'Ares gold-exchanger of bodies'. Gold has an equally negative resonance at 776–7*, where it is associated with the moral degeneracy of decadent wealthy families. On the increasing threat posed by Ares in the play see 374–6*. The image of the war-god trafficking bullion for men's vulnerable corpses reinforces the play's emphasis on the interconnection between wealth, callousness and human suffering. Bakewell (2007) 123 astutely points out that it is also related to the 'increased intersection of finances and war in fifth-century Athens'. There was increased conscription; payment for military service and the funding of financial support for war orphans were introduced. And as leader of the Delian League, Athens itself resembled the war-god, establishing equivalents between men and money, from its acceptance of tribute payments in a variety of currencies. Taken together, the metaphor's various dimensions probably had an unsettling effect on the Athenian audience at the time.

439 **who holds the scales:** Ares is not usually imagined as balancing the scales of warriors' fate in battle, as his father Zeus is (264–5*), but this striking picture of a merchant weighing bodies against golden ingots may have brought to mind the scene in Aeschylus' *Phrygians* (frr. 263–72) where Priam's ransom for Hector was visually weighed out, as reported by a scholion on *Iliad* 22.351.

440–4   weighty residue from the fires: Lit., 'heavy scrapings processed-by-fire'. The neuter noun *psēgma*, cognate with the verb *psēchein* ('rub down', 'wear away'), probably continues the metallurgical imagery (151–4*), since it can mean the dust rubbed off gold (Hdt 1.93, 3.94–5, 4.195). So may 'from the fires', since this participle in later Greek can denote ore that has been processed into bullion or coinage (Bakewell (2007) 124). On oppressively heavy weights see 63–7*. **easily stowed urns:** There may be a caustic undertone to the adjective *euthetous*, which in later Greek can mean 'convenient' (Diod. Sic. 2.57, 5.37, 21.21). The primary meaning of the masculine noun *lebēs* is 'cauldron' (*Il.* 21.362), but here it designates a container for cinerary ashes (as at *Choeph.* 686). Just as *teuchos* in the play refers both to the containers in which the ashes of the war dead are transported and Agamemnon's bathtub (433–6*), so does this noun (see 1129*).

445–51   They groan ... Atreidai: This is a beautifully crafted sentence, in which conventional eulogy of the war dead is undermined by the sting in the tail—'for the sake of another man's wife' (see 60–2*)—and moves into the first statement in the play that is overtly critical of the whole war project of the Atreidai. Although not quite in direct speech, the words of the Greek bereaved 'loved ones' (the subject of *stenousi*, on which see 18*) represent the first time the voices of the ordinary citizens have entered the soundscape of the play. **snarls:** *baüzein* is associated by a scholion here and by the grammarian Hesychius (B 357.1) with the sounds made by dogs. **under their breath:** Lit., 'silently'. A simple adverb suggests the recurrent theme of supressed speech in this tense nation (34–9*). **advocates:** A certain sarcasm underlies the choice, in the circumstances, of this legal term. Why would the general population need legal representation in a case regarding another man's marriage? On legal vocabulary see 41*.

452–5   beautiful men: The chorus' thoughts briefly shift back to Troy and their dead loved ones before developing the political thoughts instigated by the previous sentence. They use the same adjective, *eumorphos*, as they had used of the beautiful statues which Menelaus cannot bear to look at any more (416–17*). **enemy earth:** The noun needs to be supplied from the *gas* at 453. The three words beginning with *ech-* or *ek-* produce a powerful assonantal effect (on the significance of the number three see 33*), bolstered by the use of *(kat)echein* for the Greeks' possession of graves and conquest of enemy earth. This verb is sometimes associated with dead heroes' occupation of the area where they are buried, in a proprietorial manner that allows a cult to be established (Soph. *Ajax* 1165–7).

457 It is a grave matter ... angrily: Lit., 'Grave [is] the voice of citizens with ill-will'. As the stasimon reaches its darkly apprehensive conclusion, the chorus expand the idea of the grievances and resentment of the specific bereaved families to cover the entire citizen community.

458 It pays the debt: The metaphor of paying back a debt, as 'payback' in the form of reciprocal reprisal for an immoral act, is to become increasingly pervasive throughout the play and trilogy. The verb *tinein* is used of Troy paying the penalty at 537*, and Clytemnestra's future punishment by the chorus at 1430*. See also *Choeph.* 313. **curse:** The idea of a curse on members of an aristocratic family will have spoken loud to Aeschylus' audience (see Introduction, p. 56); for a brief account of how a public curse ritual was performed see Lysias 6.51. **ratified by the people:** Aeschylus probably invented this striking compound adjective, which will likewise have resonated with his spectators, the Athenian *dēmos*, just half a century after they had become the executive power in the state. The verb *krainein* was used of Zeus ordaining Troy's fate at 369; see also 1340. Although this line is not difficult to construe linguistically, its precise meaning in reference to the situation in Argos is rather obscure: there is no indication that any formal public curse on the Atreidai, incurred by the plethora of war dead, has been rubberstamped by any civic body at Argos. Sommerstein (2009) 53 with n.8 may well be right in translating 'it pays the debt of' as 'it is equivalent to'. He interprets this passage as meaning that furious public talk and official public curses 'are in effect the same thing', but measured in different units.

459–60 In my anxiety ... gloom: Lit., 'My anxiety awaits to hear something night-roofed'. On Aeschylus' mastery of the evocation of a mood of apprehension see 97–9*, 100–3* and, on architectural language, 1283*.

461–2 people with blood on their hands: Although the identity of the *poluktonoi* is not specified, the sacrifice of Iphigenia as well as the war dead must be suggested to the audience here. The same adjective is used in an enigmatic choral passage at 734*.

462–3 black Erinyes: See Aguirre (2010) and 58–9*.

465–6 by attrition ... obscurity: Lit., 'by fate-reversing rubbing-away of life they make obscure'. In archaic poetry, *amauros* often refers to dim or faintly perceived spectres (Hom. *Od.* 4.824, Sappho fr. 55.4), and later in this play describes a troubled or gloomy mind (546*; see also *Choeph.* 157). But the sense of *social* obscurity—becoming a 'nobody'—is already present in Hesiod *Works* 280–4, in a context which surely underlies Aeschylus' thought here: 'For whoever knows what is right and is prepared to speak it, to him far-seeing Zeus gives prosperity; but whoever deliberately bears false witness and perjures himself, and so damages Justice and commits a crime that cannot be repaired, that man's descendants are left obscure thereafter'.

466–70 amongst the unseen: Like the word *amauros* (465*), Aeschylus' language implies there is not much difference between being socially invisible and actually being dead. **excessive praise:** The typical early Greek concern about the consequences of receiving inappropriately high adulation is articulated later by Agamemnon himself (921–4*) and is fundamental to his entire scene. **The exalted … Zeus:** Lit., 'Heads are struck from Zeus upon the eyes'. The neuter noun *karēnon*, usually in the plural, can mean a single individual human, as in the Latin *per capita* or English 'per head' (Hom. *Il.* 11.500, *Od.* 10.521), or the heads of animals (*Il.* 23.260, 9.407), but it can also mean the summit of a mountain or a city (*Il.* 1.44, 2.117, 2.869, 9.24). The Greek leaves the precise meaning here ambiguous, but the general sentiment, that the gods like to bring down humans who become too eminent or arrogant, is commonplace (cf. Hdt. 7.10e.1, where Mardonius advises Xerxes: 'You see how the god smites with his thunderbolt creatures of greatness and does not suffer them to display their pride, while little ones do not move him to anger; and you see how it is always on the tallest buildings and trees that his bolts fall; for the god loves to bring low all things of surpassing greatness. Thus a large army is destroyed by a smaller, when the jealous god sends panic or the thunderbolt among them, and they perish unworthily; for the god suffers pride in none but himself').

471 I favour: For *krinein* meaning to choose between options see also Aesch. *Supp.* 396. **felicity:** The masculine noun *olbos* means human wellbeing, happiness or contentment of a kind sometimes explicitly distinguished from material wealth, *ploutos* (*Il.* 16.596, *Od.* 14.206; see 750–4*). **that attracts no envy:** On *phthonos* see 921–2* and on Aeschylus' penchant for the privative alpha see Introduction, p. 3.

472 sacker of cities: Aeschylus makes a noun cognate with the epithet *ptoliporthos*, which is elsewhere applied to the war-god Ares (Hom. *Il.* 20.152, Hes. *Theog.* 936, on whom see 374–6*), to the warriors Odysseus, Oïleus and Achilles (Hom. *Il.* 2.278, 2.728, 15.77) and later in this play to Agamemnon himself when the chorus greet him (783*). At that point Cassandra, who has been captured and witnesses her life having been taken under the control of others, will accompany him on his vehicle. See also his magniloquent conqueror-titles at 782–4 and 1227.

475–8 Announced ... by the gods: After exploring their fears of what is about to happen, the chorus reprise the scepticism with which they earlier greeted the news that Troy had been taken in the first place. Some editors, following Hermann (1852) and K.O. Müller (1835), divide this epode into three sections (475–8, 479–82 and 483–7), to be delivered by two semichoruses who disagree on the extent to which they should believe Clytemnestra's news. Sommerstein (2009) 57n. writes that such a division is 'unavoidable: the vacillating attitude which is sharply criticized in the second part of the epode (479–82)—that of those who first believe and then, for no particular reason, doubt the message of the beacons—is precisely that which is displayed in the first and third parts (475–8, 483–8), when we recall how unquestioningly the chorus had believed the news in 351–4 and at the beginning of the present ode'. This interpretation is plausible enough, especially in the light of the different opinions expressed by the chorus at 1346–71. Yet doubt, hesitation, mixed emotions and meandering trains of thought are wholly in keeping with the overall picture of bewilderment and apprehension painted in the play. A director today can of course legitimately choose how to distribute these lines. **deceit practised by the gods:** Lit., 'divine deceit'. On the sort of deception they mean see 274*. The neuter noun *psuthos* is a poetic variant for *pseudos*, which this chorus also uses in their epistemological confusion at 999 and 1089. The text has been emended and remains unsatisfactory, but the general sense of the overall contrast between truth and falsehood is clear.

479 childlike: On the figurative language of childlike incompetence see 74–5*. **mindless:** Lit., 'cut away in terms of his wits'.

480–2 when his heart has been inflamed ... beacon-fire: Lit., 'having been inflamed as to his heart by fresh message-transmissions of a beacon-fire'. The accusative 'inflamed' is probably consecutive after the *hōde*, with 'heart' in the accusative of respect. **to struggle when the story changes:** It is as if the chorus are preparing themselves emotionally for a retraction of the report that Troy has fallen. This ongoing uncertainty, as the next sentence demonstrates, is fundamentally related to Clytemnestra's gender.

483–4 A woman ... clarified: Lit., 'In a woman's warlike spirit, giving assent to favour before the thing is manifest, is a conspicuous [feature]'. The primary meaning of the feminine noun *aichmē* is a spear-point (Hom. *Il.* 6.320), but one of the metonymic meanings it acquired was 'fighting spirit' (Pind. *Nem.* 10.13).

485–7 A woman's mind ... infringed: Lit., 'Too gullible, the female pasture-boundary-marker is quickly handed over to be grazed by other livestock.' This sententious expression of sexism includes no few than five resolved long syllables, creating a pattering, scattergun aural effect that suits the chorus' estimation of the female intellect. The technical sense of *epinemein*, as 'turn one's livestock to graze on another's land', is demonstrated in e.g. Plato, *Laws* 8.843d and Aristot. *Pol.* 5.1305a26. This pastoral image is connected with others: see 128–30*. It is a striking way of expressing male fear that women are somehow psychologically porous and permeable (see Hall (1997) 115–18). **quickly meets its end:** The chorus' disdainful remark is given rhetorical edge by the rhyming and chiastic aural effect of *tachumoron* so soon after *tachoporos*.

v] 488–586   THE CHORUS AND THE HERALD

This scene is crucial for establishing important pieces of information, in particular that Agamemnon's arrival is imminent, and that he will not be accompanied by Menelaus. The Herald delivers two long speeches, the first of which sounds as though it is an official text, announcing the victory, that has been written or at least approved by high command (503–37); this is followed by 12 lines of stichomythia which show two different generations of Argive citizens in dialogue and reveal the chorus' discomfort with the current political situation. The Herald's second speech ruminates on the hardships suffered by the regular soldiers on board ship and in the Trojan camp, but concludes unconvincingly that all's well that ends well (551–82). The chorus' brief response shows that they now believe that the victory has been achieved and that the palace residents will want to know the Herald's news.

489   We'll soon know: Nearly 500 lines into the play, as far as the chorus is concerned, even the basic facts of the situation have yet to be clarified. Their speech, until 502 and the arrival of the Herald, is incorrectly attributed by the manuscripts to Clytemnestra, but she is not currently present on stage.

491   like dreams: This is another instance of the recurrent comparison of false perceptions to the phenomena experienced in the world of dreams (see 274*). **deceived our minds:** On the play's fascination with epistemology see Introduction, pp. 101–2.

493–5   I see there: At this moment the actor playing the Herald must come into view, from the assumed direction of the harbour, so that the chorus can point him out with the deictic *tonde*. In the Athenian theatre, since spectators could see the sea towards the right of their field of vision, he would probably have entered via the parodos taking the same direction. The port at which the remnants of the Argive taskforce disembarked is not specified in *Agamemnon*;

the Panhellenic fleet had mustered at Aulis, but the natural harbour for Argos was and is today Nauplion, which is less than seven miles away. It is, however, just possible that Aeschylus' audience thought of the harbour used in the fifth century by the landlocked Spartans, which was at Gythion on the Mani peninsula. **garlanded:** Lit., 'shaded'. **olive-twigs:** The olive was a symbol of victory (it was used for the victory crowns at the Olympic Games held in honour of Zeus; see Theophrastus, *Enquiry into Plants* 4.13.2), of peace (suppliant branches such as the one which Aristagoras of Miletus held in order to get access to the Spartan King Cleomenes at Hdt. 5.51 would have been of olive) and purity (they were sometimes held by pilgrims asking questions of the Delphic oracle—Hdt. 7.141). **He's encrusted with dusty dried mud, evidence:** Lit., 'Thirsty dust, sibling coextensive with mud, is witness to me'. An elaborate circumlocution offering an unusual detail to the costume-designer. On the use of legal language in the play see 41*.

496–7   that he's not about to use ... wood: Lit., 'that he will not make signs with smoke from a fire either voicelessly or kindling flame from forest wood'. A longwinded way of saying, perhaps with a jibe intended at Clytemnestra's elaborate system of beacon-fires, that the possibility of an orthodox verbal communication seems enhanced by the Herald's headgear and travel-worn appearance.

498–9   He'll speak out ... opposite kind: Lit., 'He'll speak out saying [what will make us] exult more [or]—but I decline an opposite report to these things'. The chorus interrupt themselves and the syntactical flow of the sentence in order to avoid saying something like 'or to make us despair'. They imply in this and the next sentence that they have already partially accepted the news of the victory and have been rejoicing, but the audience knows that this is far from the case.

500   May more good news be added to what we already know: Lit., 'May an addition of good happen to the good that [already] appeared'. This, like other compressed chiming lines using the term *eu* (121*), may well have been proverbial.

501–2   may he ... misjudgement: Lit., 'may he himself harvest-the-fruit of his error of mind'. The feminine noun *hamartia* can mean a criminal mistake of enormous gravity, as at 1197* and Plato, *Laws* 2.660c; Thucydides' Corcyreans, on the other hand, distinguish between actual wrongdoing (*kakia*) and an erroneous viewpoint (a *hamartia* of *doxa*, 1.32.5). Aristotle famously uses *hamartia* to denote the disastrous error of fact or judgement which causes the downfall of a tragic protagonist (*Poet.* 1453a). It is a strong word to use in this context, but then uttering an imprecation against one's fatherland would have been heard by Aeschylus' audience as a shockingly offkey, indeed immoral and possibly sacrilegious act.

503   Greetings: The emotion expressed by the exclamation *iō* needs to be inferred from the context. It can introduce a request for help from the gods (Aesch. *Sept.* 96), an articulation of grief (411*, 1305*) or a deprecation (1455). **earth ... fatherland:** Lit., 'paternal earth of the Argive land'. This phrase includes a variation on the *gē* or *gaia patrōiē* of Homer (*Od.* 13.88, resonantly of Odysseus' first sleep on the soil of Ithaca on *his* return from Troy).

504   I've reached you: The verb *aphikneomai* can take the accusative of the person arrived at (*Il.* 18.395, *Od.* 132) as well as the place (*Il.* 13.645, Aesch. *Pers.* 15). The Herald speaks to the earth of Argos as if to a human being. **on this bright day:** Lit., 'in this light'. The Queen in *Persians* uses the same phrase when she learns that Xerxes is safe (300–1) and a prosaic version of it became proverbial in the sense of a good day or day of delivery (Irwin (1974) 165–6). Compare Aegisthus' much more sinister first phrase, greeting the 'gracious *phengos* of the day that brings justice', when he finally emerges from the palace at 1577*. On light and darkness see Introduction, pp. 63–5.

505   Though ... one: Lit., 'Many hopes having been shattered, I [have] hit upon one.' On the recurrent theme of hope and the difficulty of sustaining it in hard times see 100–3*. **shattered:** The verb *rhēgnumi* often refers to ripping gowns in mourning (Aesch. *Pers.* 199, 468) or, in the passive, to walls or weapons being smashed or a ship being wrecked (Hom. *Il.* 12.198, 13.124, 21.165, 2.544; Dem. 56.21). All these associations are suitable for a Herald who has recently been through combat, bereavement and the wrecking of the Argive fleet.

506   expressed confidence: The imperfect tense emphasises the length of time he has been concerned about the whereabouts of his future burial. The verb *auchein* can mean 'declare' or 'boast' and several shades of meaning exist between these two (see also 871–2,* 1497*).

507   receive the burial I yearn for: Lit., 'to partake in a share of the funeral most dear to me'. The audience will have been reminded of all the men whose corpses were left behind in the enemy soil of Troy, as described in the foregoing ode (452–5*).

509–11   supreme god, Zeus: See 55–7* and 88–91*. The text implies that statues of Zeus, Apollo and Hermes were visible in front of the palace. **Pythian lord ... Scamander:** Where Zeus was neutral in the Trojan War, Apollo not only afflicted the Greeks with the plague in *Iliad* book 1 when Agamemnon offended his priest Chryses, but sided throughout with the Trojans. In books 15–16 he encourages Hector to lead an attack on the Achaeans, before helping him to demolish their fortifications and kill Patroclus. The use of the cult title *Puthios* (see, e.g., Pind. *Ol.* 14.11) is the first instance in the trilogy of Apollo being associated with his oracle at Delphi, where the opening of *Eumenides* is set (see also 1255*). **may your bows shoot no more arrows:** Lit., '[you] no more sending missiles from bows'.

512 be our saviour and healer: The epithet *Sōtēr* is more commonly applied to Zeus (245–7*), but Apollo was worshipped as Apollo Pythios Sōtēr in his surviving Doric sanctuary in the modern city of Arta, Ambracia; some Milesian soldiers made a dedication to 'Apollo Sōtēr of Didyma' on the island of Cos in the first century BCE (Packard Humanities Institute inscription no. 185850 lines 9–10). *paiōnios* means 'belonging to Paian' (see 146*) and therefore 'healing'. Agamemnon uses the same adjective referring to metaphorical pharmacological cures for potential political problems that lie ahead at 848*.

513 gods of the assembly: Although *agōnios* can mean 'of the athletic contests' (Pind. *Isthm.* 1.60, Soph. *Trach.* 26), it can also mean the gods of the assembly or in assembly, and *agōn* can just mean 'assembly debates' (see Aesch. *Suppl.* 189, 242, Plato *Laws* 6.783a, 845*). The gods indicated here are probably the same as those at 88–91*; a scholion on *Iliad* 24.1 explicitly says that Aeschylus uses the term *agōnioi* in place of *agoraioi*.

514–15 my own protector: The original meaning of *timaoros*, a contracted form of *timōros*, is 'avenger' (see 1280, 1324, 1578, Antiphon 1.2), but it could take the slightly less strong meaning of 'champion' or 'protector' (Hdt. 2.141). Hermes is addressed as the 'luck-bringing messenger of the immortals' in his Homeric *Hymn* 4.3 and is constantly engaged in delivering messages in the Homeric epics and other archaic literature, especially when the content might be irksome to the recipient (*Od.* 1.38, *Il.* 24.390, Hom. *Hymn to Demeter* 335). Offerings of animal tongues were made to him (Ar. *Peace* 1062). He is an important figure in the *Oresteia*, invoked by Orestes in the first line of *Choephori* in his chthonic capacity to assist the exile's communication with his dead father, and eventually appearing as a silent escort figure in *Eumenides* (see Apollo's command at 88–94). **much-loved Herald, by Heralds revered:** The chiastic structure adds a ritual dignity to this address and may have been a traditional formula in the worship of Hermes, possibly dating back to the Bronze Age: see Gulizio (2000).

516–17 heroes: This is an unusual form of the accusative plural of the masculine noun *hērōs*. These are the local and ancestral figures, including founders of cities and tribal patrons, to whom the Argives trace their descent. See Antiphon 1.27, Hdt. 1.168, Thuc. 4.87. The most famous Argive heroes included Inachus, Argos and Perseus. This is the only use of this word in Aeschylus' extant plays, although a libation is poured 'to the heroes' in his fragmentary *Epigonoi* (fr. 55.2). The term has changed meaning since the Homeric epics, where it seems connected with Panhellenic reputation, rather than the local aspects of cult in Aeschylus' day: see Shilo (2022) 114. **asking them to give ... combat:** Lit., 'to receive [being] kindly the force [coming] back, the remains of the spear'. The infinitive *dechesthai* is dependent upon *prosaudō* at 514. For the neuter noun *to doru* as metonymic for war or combat see, e.g., Hom. *Il.* 16.57, Thuc. 1.128, Aesch. *Eum.* 773.

518   I salute you: On *iō* see 411* and 503*. **palace:** The Herald addresses the physical house of Atreus almost as if it were a sentient being. See Introduction, pp. 69–70.

519   consecrated seats: Presumably these are honorific thrones of office for the kings (see Ar. *Frogs* 1515), unless the whole line means 'and divinities on sacred seats in the sun'. **gods:** The plural noun *daimones* here seems to be equivalent to *theoi*, as at Bacchylides 17.117–18, 'nothing that the gods' wish is beyond the belief of sane mortals'; see further François (1957). The adjective *antēlios* means 'opposite the sun', or 'looking east'. In *Prometheus Bound* the Titan claims that 'brick-built houses facing the sun' were one of the inventions he bestowed on humankind (450–1).

520–1   if ever ... manner: Lit., 'If [you did so] at some time long ago, receive the King with shining eyes duly after much time'. The three datives are of instrument, manner and time respectively. On the conventional Greek prayer form where the speaker bases their claim for a favour on a previous occasion when the god addressed had helped them see most famously Sappho fr. 1.5–7. **and with a shine:** Lit., 'shining'. See 298* and, on eyes, see 240*. The Herald talks to the statues as well as the house as if they were sentient; on the eyes of statues see 418–19*. His phrasing strikes a slightly troubled note by suggesting that these gods would not be as glad to see Agamemnon as they had been once upon a time.

522–3   bringing in the darkness a light: This high-flown ceremonial language works in synergy with the many manifestations of the light/darkness theme in the play and trilogy (see Introduction, pp. 63–5). On *euphronē* as a euphemism for night-time see 264–5*, where Clytemnestra uses similar language in *her* opening speech. The Herald perhaps implies that Agamemnon has been travelling overnight, thus making marginally less unrealistic his arrival so soon after the news of Troy's fall was delivered by the beacon relay. See Introduction, p. 98 and Hall (2010b) 44. **all these people here:** The Herald points out, for the statues' benefit, the members of the chorus and, by extension, the imagined collective inhabitants of Argos beyond the palace.

524–6 So greet him warmly: *alla* with an imperative often has no real adversative force, but is meant to heighten the persuasive impact. See, e.g., Hom. *Il.* 1.210, Pind. *Ol.* 6.22. **the one who has demolished ... foundations:** Lit., 'the one who has dug Troy down utterly'. **mattock:** The *makellē* of Zeus, which creates an agricultural image of him labouring to break up clods of earth, seems to have been proverbial (Soph. fr. 727, from his *Chryses*; Ar. *Birds* 1240). This is the first of a series of (mostly) violent images relating to arable farming. Paris 'mowed down' his city (535–6); Zeus' rain enables agriculture and the ploughing of furrows (1014–15); Clytemnestra talks of people who have acquired wealth as reaping a fine harvest (1044), but refers in a sinister way to the sowing of the earth in her speech over the corpses (1391–2). Later, she admits that the house of Atreus has reaped a great harvest of misery (1655). **Zeus the avenger:** *dikēphoros* is used by the chorus in Aegisthus' first line (1577), when he greets the light of the day that he perceives as having brought justice. See also *Choeph.* 120. 'Justice' is something that all murderers are unsatisfactorily associated with in the trilogy (see 250–1*). The Herald expresses the view that Agamemnon was acting as agent of Zeus' justice. **completely tamed:** The Herald continues his agricultural image; the very ground of what was the city of Troy has been brought under cultivation (for this passive sense of *katergazomai* see Theophrastus, *Causes of Plants* 3.1.3).

527 have been obliterated: Lit., '[are] not to be seen'. The language is almost identical to that of Aesch. *Persians* 811, where Darius is *censuring* Xerxes for his sacrilegious behaviour in Athens. Boasting about the destruction of enemy shrines is dangerous. The messenger is also confirming that what the rampaging Greeks did at Troy was precisely what Clytemnestra, insincerely, expressed the hope at 338–47 that they would *not* do.

528 population: Lit., 'seed'. No Trojans are alive at Troy any more. Since the neuter noun *sperma* can specifically mean semen (Pind. *Pyth.* 3.15, *Nem.* 10.17), the implication is probably that the entire *male* population has been wiped out, especially Astyanax. The female survivor Cassandra will be making an appearance shortly.

529 Such ... Troy: Lit., 'Having cast such a yoke round Troy'. **yoke:** See 132–4, 326–8*. Agamemnon has earlier been seen as putting a different metaphorical yoke-strap on *himself* when he decided to sacrifice Iphigenia (218–21*).

530 the King … blessed by fortune: The assonance of the three words beginning with alpha heightens the ceremonial ring to this line: on the significance of the number three see 33*. The adjective *eudaimōn* originally meant 'blessed with a good *daimōn*', and often refers to material wealth (Hdt. 1.133, Lys. 32.17), although in the philosophers it comes to mean a spiritual or psychological state produced by a virtuous way of life. Pindar pairs it with *humnētos*, 'lauded' (*Pyth.* 10.22). Here it probably combines the senses of great wealth and fame, both derived from sacking Troy. See also 335–7*.

531 men alive today: For the term *hoi nun*, with *brotoi* or *anthrōpoi* understood, see, e.g., Pind. *Ol.* 1.105, Hdt. 1.68.

532 affiliate: *suntelēs* probably has a technical meaning here, either an 'allied' community (Thuc. 2.15, 4.76) or 'sharing liability for paying a tax' (Dem. 14.20), as if the Greeks were collecting revenue from Paris and Troy simultaneously.

533 can boast: Lit., 'boasts aloud'. The verb *euchomai*, with or without the prefixes *ep-* or (as here) intensifying *ex-*, performs a significant function in the *Oresteia*. In Homeric epic this verb has two different meanings related to significant speech acts: the sacred sense 'to pray' (see Pulleyn (1997) 72–6) and the secular sense 'to boast' (as a warrior boasts about his genealogy and status or a killing on the battlefield): see Adkins (1969). Aeschylus plays these two senses off against one another. Boasting about inflicting suffering (as the chorus say Paris cannot any more) remains an important meaning of the verb in *Agamemnon*, whereas in the subsequent plays *euchomai* and the cognate noun *euchai* (prayers) always denote prayer (11 times in *Choephori*; see the first line of *Eumenides*). The word will be used of making vows to the gods at crucial moments in Agamemnon's scene (933, 962), but Clytemnestra will do the boasting, like a Homeric warrior, in relation to the killings, according to Cassandra (1262), Clytemnestra herself (1394) and the chorus (1474). **his feat … suffering:** Lit., 'the action [was] greater than the suffering'. This concise phrase sounds as if it could have been a proverbial saying. The implication here is that any distinction achieved by stealing a wife pales into insignificance beside the pain that has now been inflicted on Troy.

534 Convicted of: Lit., 'owing the penalty for' after being found guilty: see Ar. *Clouds* 34. On legal language in the play see 41*. **abduction:** The Greeks did not have a specific word for crime equivalent to 'rape' (see especially the first nine chapters in Deacy and Pierce (2002)), which allowed ancient authors considerable flexibility in the presentation of Helen's subjective contribution to her elopement/rape/kidnapping with/by Paris. On the problem of 'heroic' rape in ancient mythology see Lauriola (2022) and also 399–402*. When the noun *harpagē*, 'seizure', 'plunder' (see 'they steal *apharpagēi*', Solon 4.13) is used in the context of a marriageable young woman, in Greek eyes her husband or father, rather than she, was the wronged party. The word implies that the man who seized her had sexual intercourse with her, but it may not *necessarily* mean that she was unwilling (Hdt. 1.2.3). **theft:** The feminine noun *klopē* is usually used of the theft of money or valuables (Antiphon 2.1.6, Lys. 30.25). In Homer, Greeks and Trojans fight not just for Helen but for 'Helen and all her goods' (e.g., *Il.* 3.70), implying that Paris had stolen other booty from Sparta as well as its queen.

535–6   forfeited … . stolen: Lit., 'he missed the mark [by having to pay back] compensation money'. Aeschylus continues the legal and financial imagery, although *hamartanein* is ultimately related to archery (364–5*). **mowed down:** A striking verb, *therizein* means 'to do summer agricultural work', i.e. reap, harvest or cut down a crop. See 524–6*. **and its very land:** This is the meaning of *autochthonos* here. The central idea is the total amount of 'fine' paid by the Trojans—Helen was confiscated, their city was demolished *and* the surrounding land was destroyed. **in utter ruin:** The adjective *panōlethros* is etymologically formed from *ollumi* (I destroy), which, with other cognates, regularly appears in curse and oath formulae (see e.g. Aeschines 3.111).

537   Priam's sons: In sliding from Paris and his townspeople to his brothers, the chorus is developing the trilogy's underlying concern with the possibility of *escalation* and *collateral damage* in reciprocal revenge cycles, a concern already articulated in Hesiod's *Theogony*. See Hall (2018b). **have paid a double penalty:** Lit., 'have repaid their crimes double'—i.e., both Helen and the destruction of Troy plus its land. The neuter noun *hamartion* is a variant of *hamartēma*, a wrongdoing which, at least in Aristotle's opinion, lay on a scale somewhere between a misfortune and a serious intentional offence (*NE* 5.1135b18). Ethical words from this stem are ultimately metaphors from archery (364–5*), meaning a shot that doesn't even adhere to the target (1194*); they also include the verb *hamartanein* used just two lines previously and the feminine noun *hamartia* (1197*), which Aristotle was to make an important element in his definition of the tragic hero and his plot (*Poet.* 1153a).

539 I'm happy ... so will it: Lit., 'I shall no more gainsay (my) death to the gods'. The Herald has already told us that, while he was away, he never hoped to be buried in his fatherland (505–7).

540 craving: Clytemnestra has earlier used the masculine noun *erōs* in her stated hope that the Achaeans did not succumb to lust for booty at 341–2*. Eros was an important concept in early Greek political theory (Ludwig (2002)), and is what Pericles wanted Athenian citizens to feel for the values their city stood for, as its *erastai* (Thuc. 2.43.1); see Monoson (1994). It is less usual to find it designating a patriot's yearning for the very land of his fathers, but see *Eumenides* 852, where Athena warns the Erinyes that they will begin to yearn for her if they leave Athens. **oppress:** Lit., 'train you hard for athletics'. The sporting metaphor (see 171–2*) conveys the physical exhaustion that strong emotions can induce.

541 so that ... joy: Lit., 'so that [I produce tears] in my eyes because of joy': see 240*. **Yes:** The often elliptical style of stichomythia can result in the omission of words in the Greek which are however necessary to make an English translation sound natural. The sight of the earth of his homeland makes the Herald weep; previously the chorus painted a picture of the Atreidai weeping as they struck the earth of Aulis (204). See also 270*.

542 The affliction affecting you brings gratification: Lit., 'Sweet is this disease you were in possession of'. On the medical imagery see 17*.

543 If you explain: Lit., 'having been instructed'. **I'll master ... what you say:** Lit., I'll be tyrant over this speech'. Although this is an unusual metaphor for the process of understanding something, the Herald may be represented as unconsciously inferring from the chorus' enigmatic remark that they are not being entirely open with him, and thus expresses himself in language suggestive of political repression: the word occurs in a seemingly bland metaphor when Electra is *about* to criticise her mother's despotic behaviour at *Choeph.* 188. See also 828*.

544 you longed for: Lit., 'by desire for whom [you were] smitten'. **loved you in return:** On the use of erotic language in describing civic emotions see 540*.

546 we felt so dejected: Lit., 'from my dark mind'. On the adjective *amauros* see 465–6*.

547 What caused this hateful misery: Lit., 'Whence came this miserable hate on your spirit?' The neuter noun *stugos* can mean the object of hate ('hated', 558*), but here, as at 1308*, it means a state of mind that is abhorrent. The adjective *dusphrōn* can mean 'feeling bad' in the subjective sense, but also 'wishing ill [on another person]': see 607–8*, 832–3*.

548   I've long since ... policy: Lit., 'I maintain [since] long ago that being silent is an antidote to harm'. If the Herald hopes for any clarity about the tense political situation from the cryptic chorus, this line alone might be expected to foreclose any further enquiries. On the theme of silence see 34–9*.

549   Were you afraid of anyone? The imperfect tense expresses emotional duration. The Herald does not want to be fobbed off without identifying the precise source of the chorus' psychological tension. The audience will have supplied the answer 'Aegisthus and Clytemnestra' in their minds.

550   So much so ... as you said: Lit., 'So that now, the thing you [said]'. The Herald had said at 539 he was happy to die now that he had returned. It is a strong sentiment for a chorus to express, emphasising to the Herald the degree of their fear without naming the person(s) terrorising them. On terror see 12–14*.

551   Yes: See 541*. **There's been a good outcome:** Lit., 'It has been well accomplished'. The passive voice, without specifying what precise outcome is meant, seems a cautious, even evasive response to the strong emotion of the chorus' previous line. The Herald seems to misunderstand the chorus' point. They meant that they often longed for death because they lived in fear: he thinks they mean that they can now die happy since Agamemnon is returning. **But when ... long view:** Lit., 'But in respect of these things during a long time'.

552   fallen out well: On this type of dicing metaphor see 32*.

553–4   regrettable: Lit., 'to be blamed'. The Herald's evasive language would stimulate the audience into wondering what events he regards as blameworthy and how far back in time he is thinking. **But who ... lifetime:** This is a somewhat banal statement about the human condition, of the type that people who are struggling to find words in which to communicate painful information often use. The form of the rhetorical question has the ring of a familiar saying about it.

555   if I were to detail: No apodosis is supplied, although something like 'you would be appalled' is clearly implied; Aeschylus is using the break in construction to heighten the emotional effect.

556–7   the terrible bedding in narrow gangways: This is undoubtedly the general sense of a textually suspect phrase; the precise meaning of the word *parēxeis*, here translated 'gangways', has been much disputed. The Watchman had complained about his bedding, too, at 12–14*. **everything was lamentable, every hour of the day:** The reading of the manuscripts, 'not lamenting what, not being apportioned the share of a day?' is impossible and *ou lachontes* is certainly corrupt. A plural participle from a verb meaning 'suffer' or 'feel vexed at' (e.g. *aschallontes*) or similar is required to make sense of the transmitted Greek; the translation reflects the apparent general sentiment. A line meaning 'while we were at sea' or something equivalent may well have dropped out after line 555. This remains, however, a rare account of the discomfort suffered by regular troops on board ship in antiquity. On ships see 108–15*.

558   vile: On *stugos* see 547*.

560–2   Drops ... dribbling on us: Lit., 'Dews from the sky and meadowy ones from the earth were drizzling.' On the ambiguous connotations of dew in the tragedy see 12–14* and 1390*. The imperfect tense emphasises the continuity of the damp suffered by the soldiers. **constant threat:** For *empedos* meaning 'continuous' see Hom. *Il.* 8.521, *Od.* 8.453, Pind. *Pyth.* 12.14 (of slavery) and Soph. *OC* 1674 (of pain). On the neuter noun *sinos* see 387–8* and 738*. **wild:** Were the soldiers hirsute or lice-ridden or both? The meaning of *enthēros* at Soph. *Phil.* 698 and Ael. *NA* 6.63 is 'beastly' or 'like a beast'. But here it might well mean 'infested with beasts', i.e. lice or vermin, as at Eur. *Rhes.* 289 and Soph. fr. 314.222 (from his *Trackers*). Aeschylus may not have known that lice do not in fact flourish in damp environments or weather.

563–9   And if one were to describe ... grieving over this: Once again, the Herald, in his emotional state, changes construction midway, this time following a conditional protasis with a rhetorical question instead of with an apodosis. **that killed the birds:** The image of cold so bitter that birds froze to death heightens the picture of an ominous mountain snowscape. On birds in this play see Introduction, p. 58. **heat:** On the imagery of extreme cold and heat, which can indicate psychological as well as meteorological extremes, see also 968–9*, 1172, 1278. The Athenians suffered extreme cold on campaigns in Thrace, recalled in e.g. Plato, *Symp.* 220a and Ar. *Ach.* 138–9. **when the winds failed ... couch:** Lit., 'when the sea, having fallen, slept waveless on noon-beds because of the lack of winds'. This is a striking personification of Pontos taking a mid-day nap in the windless heat. On sleep see 179–80*. According to Hesiod, who emphasises his endless motion rather than his stillness, Pontos was the child of Gaia conceived parthenogenetically (*Theog.* 132–3). **while the dead ... again:** This is a rather strange way of saying that the dead are beyond all grief or further effort.

570   Why enumerate: Pebbles were used to assist arithmetical calculations, so *en psēphōi legein*, 'reckon in the pebble', means 'count precisely' (see Eur.

Rhes. 309, Dem. 18.229). **the lives expended:** The verb *analiskein* carries with it a sense of wastefulness (Soph. *Aj.* 1049, Thuc. 2.64) or disposability (Plato, *Politicus* 289c). We are not to be told the total number of fatalities, although the chorus have previously implied that every household had suffered a bereavement (435).

571 about bad luck: Lit., 'about malignant fortune'. *palinkotos*, a word Clytemnestra uses twice about malicious rumours (863, 874), here implies an element of resentment (cf. Eur. fr. 572.2), transferred from the person feeling it to the luck which has given him the feeling. Survivors of catastrophes where many have perished often feel guilty, having escaped alive, about recounting what they suffered personally.

572 The situation demands a celebration of these occurrences: 'I deem it worth being very glad at these happenings.'

574 the benefits ... scales: Lit., 'the profit prevails: the pain does not balance.' On weighing imagery see 206*; 264–5*. This sounds platitudinous and as if the Herald is in some emotional denial.

575–6 seemly ... to make this boast: The Herald is aware that boasting about the victory is potentially to provoke divine reprisals, and so reassures himself and the chorus that it is 'seemly' or appropriate to do so in the manner and degree he proposes. The audience are aware that he is carrying out orders of the high command and will have been primed. **on this bright day:** An alternative translation would read 'to the bright sunlight'. On the way even the imagery of sunlight is compromised see Introduction, pp. 63–5.

577–9 The Herald's boast turns him into a poet himself. It consists of an iambic version of an epigram he imagines being inscribed beneath items of Trojan armour which members of the Greek militia will dedicate in their temples. For an example of such an epigram see Leonidas of Tarentum's poem celebrating a victory over the Lucanians (*Greek Anthology* 6.131): 'These long shields taken from Lucanians, this row of bridles, and the polished spears hung either side, deprived of horse and man: for Pallas. Man and horse are both devoured by death.' The temple of Athena at Lindos, Rhodes, claimed to house several items taken at Troy and dedicated by Greek heroes, including weapons taken by Tlepolemus' men, Alexander's cap, taken by Menelaus, and quivers taken by Meriones and Philoctetes (see the 'Lindos Chronicle' ed. Higbie (2010) B 55–69, 78–87). Many such epigrams were to be read in public spaces in Athens in the wake of the Persian Wars: see Petrovic (2010). **for the gods:** The gods who received such spoils included Athena and Apollo. **across Greece:** The contribution to the Trojan campaign of all the non-Argives listed in the Homeric catalogue of ships in *Iliad* 2 is not foregrounded much in *Agamemnon* by its predominantly Argive cast. **a dazzling ornament:** The neuter noun *ganos* means 'brightness', 'sheen', or, in the context of liquids, 'gloss', or even the tang of a drink that brings refreshment (Eur. *Suppl.* 1150; see 1392*). **from the olden days:** Characters in Greek tragedy, except in detailed aetiologies, rarely seem aware that their actions will live in the imaginations and memories of subsequent generations. This is an important exception.

581–2 favour of Zeus: On *charis* see 182–3*, and on Zeus, Introduction, pp. 33–5. **made it possible:** This verb can mean 'make an end of' or even 'kill' (1275*), and that sinister overtone may be present here. **You've heard the whole story:** Lit., 'You have the whole speech.' This is a conventional conclusion to a messenger speech, but since the audience knew from the cyclic epic *Nostoi* that the Greek fleet had been battered by a storm after departing from Troy, they will have been aware that the Herald is hiding something momentous.

583 won the day: Lit., 'having been defeated'. Although *nikan* can mean 'to prevail' in reference to one person proving superior to another in debate rather than in war (e.g. Hom. *Il.* 18.252), as well as in reference to one opinion or judgement receiving more support or votes than another (*Od.* 10.46, Hdt. 5.36, Plato, *Laws* 7.801a), it is a strong metaphor for the chorus to use of themselves here; perhaps they have absorbed the military aura of the Herald's speech. But the implication may be that they had previously succeeded in maintaining their scepticism and remained 'undefeated' by Clytemnestra when she had imparted exactly the same information.

584 In old people ... stays young: Lit., 'For always in old people [the ability] to learn well is youthful.' This has the ring of a proverbial saying: Solon claimed (fr. 18), 'As I grow old I am always learning many things.' On the theme of old age see 72*.

586 besides being advantageous to me: Lit., 'besides enriching me'. The same word is later to be used with scathing sarcasm by Cassandra when she tells her priestly regalia to go and 'enrich' another woman (1268).

vi] 587–612 THE CHORUS, THE HERALD AND CLYTEMNESTRA

This extremely short triangular scene consists entirely of Clytemnestra's third extended speech. It fills out her character by showing her indirectly but publicly rebuking the chorus and treating the Herald with rudeness that borders on contempt. She concludes with another passage of elaborate oratory, heightened by rich imagery, in which she gives the Herald the wording of the response he is to relay to Agamemnon; it is a mendacious, cryptic and ominous assertion of her loyalty and sexual fidelity.

587 I raised a joyful shout much earlier: Lit., 'I shouted out for joy long before'. On the verb see 28*. Confusingly, the adverb *palai* can refer either to a long time ago, even to generations past (Ar. *Wasps*, Aristot. *Metaphys.* 12.1069a29), or to something said or done just a few moments previously (e.g. Soph. *Ant.* 181). Although her previous interactions with the chorus were earlier in the same day, Clytemnestra wants to emphasise her irritation that the chorus has had plenty of time to believe her rather than wait for external corroboration.

588 the first messenger at night in the form of fire: Lit., 'the first nocturnal messenger of fire'. Clytemnestra insists on the authenticity of the first 'messenger', i.e., the beacon relay. She neither addresses nor even acknowledges the presence of the Herald here, let alone welcomes him: see 264–5*.

589 desolation: The primary meaning of the feminine noun *anastasis* is a 'raising up' or 'resurrection' (Aesch. *Eum.* 648), so when applied to a city or to people it means 'making them get up and leave' (Aesch. *Pers.* 107, Hdt. 9.106, Thuc. 1.133). The survivors of the siege were all removed from Troy and taken away into slavery.

590 Someone said: Clytemnestra is not going to forget lightly that the chorus doubted the news when it came from her. She had explained their scepticism as partly resulting from her gender (271–7*); her suspicion was confirmed to the audience at 486–8*. Here she paraphrases what they said. The relationship between the chorus and Clytemnestra is portrayed as one of scarcely concealed hostility.

592 to get excited: Lit., 'to be lifted up in respect of her heart'.

593 I was being made out to be: Lit., 'I was appearing', the imperfect tense emphasising the persistence of the vilification. **deluded:** Lit., 'wandering' (see 77–9*). This word is used by some of the suitors in the *Odyssey* to insult Eumaeus the swineherd when he carries the bow into the hall for the contest (21.363).

594–5 the women … loud shout: Lit., 'and according to the female convention shrieked the *ololugmos* each in another place across the town'. The women of Argos, although never heard audibly, form a virtual second chorus in this part of the play. On the *ololugmos* see 28*. The verb *laskein* can mean the sound made when metal weapons are struck (*Il.* 14.25, 20.277) and the cries made by animals, especially birds (*Il.* 22.141, Hes. *Works* 207) and dogs (Homeric *Hymn to Hermes* 145; this is probably the canine sense to be understood of Scylla, *Od.* 12.85). When used of humans it means 'shriek aloud' (see 613–14*, 865*), especially, as here, and at 1426*, in a ritual or prophetic context. **applauding:** On the verb *euphēmein* see 28*.

597   the fragrant flame with sacrificial offerings: Lit., 'the sacrifice-devouring fragrant flame'. The chorus had described the women performing these rituals at 85–96. The description here, as there, appeals to the senses of hearing and smell as well as sight: see Introduction, pp. 59–60.

598   why should you report … now? Mid-speech, Clytemnestra finally acknowledges the presence of the Herald and directs an abrupt rhetorical question to him which sounds more like a dismissal.

600–1   revered: Although *aidoios* is used of kings in the *Iliad* (4.402), it more usually refers to a family member who has a legitimate claim to being treated with respect and compassion, especially a wife (*Il.* 21.460). In the context, with all that the chorus and audience already know, Clytemnestra's sarcasm and mendacity, further emphasised in the euphemism of 'the best way possible', take the breath away.

601–2   For what pleasure is greater in a woman's eyes? Lit., 'For what light for a wife is sweeter to see than this?' The neuter noun *phengos* can stand as a metaphor for joy or delight (Pind. *Pyth.* 8.97, *Nem.* 3.64). This rhetorical question begins Clytemnestra's public welcome of her husband, and introduces the type of hyperbolic rhetorical flattery which she will continue after he has physically entered (895–902). Here the effect on the audience is that of a sarcastic lie with a double meaning. No doubt the imminent return of Agamemnon offered pleasure to Clytemnestra, because the Greeks acknowledged that wreaking justified revenge could bring *hēdonē* (see 902*).

604   Deliver this message: Some scholars have complained that this terse command is inappropriately, even impossibly, abrupt. But it fits perfectly with Clytemnestra's peremptory style of address to all those she perceives as her inferiors.

605–10   These lines contain the content, in indirect speech, of the supposedly loving message which the Herald is to convey to Agamemnon, but 'translated' into the second person. It is remarkable for its flamboyant imagery, heavy irony and almost exclusive focus on the sender, Clytemnestra, rather than the recipient, Agamemnon.

605   he should come … for him: The first line of the message containing the actual imperative is almost telegraphically compressed and contains no word of greeting or affection from Clytemnestra. **his city yearns for him:** Lit., 'an object of desire to his city', or, more derisively, 'his city's darling'. See 540*.

606 faithful wife: The falsehood of this statement is underlined by its evocation of the view expressed by the ghost of Agamemnon to Odysseus in the Underworld, straight after he has related how he was murdered (*Od.* 11.456), 'there is no *pistis gunaixin* [faithfulness in women] any more'. On the effect of the expression here see Roisman (2018).

607–8 just exactly as: The *oun* in such phrases means something like 'in short', intensifying the effect of the previous line. Clytemnestra was left by Agamemnon, of course, in whatever psychological state the slaughter of Iphigenia had caused. This process is perhaps emphasised by the imperfect tense of the verb. **loyal dog:** It is a shame that the English word for a female dog has acquired such pejorative associations that it cannot be used here without distorting the meaning, since the metaphorical dog's femaleness is indicated in Greek by the ending of *esthlēn*. For this adjective meaning specifically 'loyal' see Soph. *OT* 611, *El.* 24. For the image of the faithful dog waiting for the return of the householder, and its hyperbolic connotations, see 895–902*. But see also Aristotle's observation that watch-dogs bark at a mere knock at the door, without waiting to see if it is a friend or a foe (*EE* 6.1149a). In this message Clytemnestra is foreshadowing the extravagant rhetorical style she will adopt with Agamemnon on his actual arrival. The Watchman had also compared himself to a watchdog: see 3*. **to those who bear him ill-will:** For *dusphrōn* in this sense, as opposed to 'miserable' (547*), see also 832–3* and Aesch. *Supp.* 511.

609–10 the same in every detail: Clytemnestra once again reiterates her perception that she has not changed since Agamemnon left, prompting the audience to think about exactly how things were left between her and Agamemnon when he departed. Although *she* may be thinking about Iphigenia, and thus saying in a veiled way that she has not forgiven him, she assumes he will be looking for reassurance that she has not been sexually unfaithful. **having broken no seal:** From presenting herself metaphorically as a guard-dog, Clytemnestra shifts to presenting herself as a document or vessel which would have a seal imprinted on it, an image with an unmistakable sexual overtone; but the neuter noun *sēmantērion* is an alternative form of *sēmantron*, meaning a seal on a written document (Hdt. 2.121, Eur. *IA* 325) and is thus, perhaps, an appropriate image with which to close a message, even one that is to be delivered orally. Herodotus also uses the similar word *sēmantris* of a clay seal stamped with a ritual signet ring (2.38).

611–12 gratification ... reputation: Knowledge of a scandalous reputation is rather oddly expressed syntactically as an *alternative* to experiencing sexual pleasure with another man, when a scandalous reputation would logically be the *result* of sexual activity. This constitutes another of the series of prompts to the audience to wonder about the extent of Aegisthus' involvement (27*). On the topic of rumours in the play see 276*. **dipping bronze:** Clytemnestra's final image in this speech, despite it being in a negative comparison, still prompts a picture of her engaged in the manufacture of bronze objects. Since the masculine noun *chalkos* frequently stands in poetry metonymically for arms or weapons (Hom. *Il.* 4.540, 3.292, 23.130 etc.), and the verb cognate with *baphas* here, *baptein*, is used in tragedy of swords plunged into murder victims' bodies, producing blood (Soph. *Aj.* 95, Eur. *Phoen.* 1578), Clytemnestra's sinister parting words imply that she knows no more about adultery than about slaughter—that is, the same amount about both. There has been an enormous amount of scholarship discussing what procedure she actually means, collected and discussed in Holm (2012). She may visualise the smith's task of tempering metal hot off the forge, especially the sharp edge of an axe, knife or weapon, by plunging it into cold water (see Soph. *Aj.* 651, Arist. *Pol.* 7.1334a8, Theophrastus, *Hist. Plant.* 5.3.3 and the gruesome simile at *Od.* 9.392). But bronze (unlike iron) is not so tempered. It is more likely that she means colouring a weapon with a dye by immersing it in a chemical bath, which was a familiar Bronze Age metallurgical technique. The audience may remember this bizarre image later, when she uses the same word of dyed textiles as Agamemnon treads the delicate floor-coverings (960) and when she appears soaked in blood over the corpses (1372). On craft imagery see 151–4*.

vii]   613–680 THE CHORUS AND THE HERALD

After Clytemnestra re-enters the palace there is a brief interchange in which the chorus tell the Herald not to believe Clytemnestra's self-presentation and then ask for news of Menelaus and, indirectly, the other returning Greeks (613–35). To this the Herald responds with his third oration (636–80), describing in vivid and painful detail last night's storm and shipwreck; he concludes that Menelaus may yet return, and then leaves abruptly.

613–14 is full of truth: Lit., 'brimming with truth'. The participle construction conveys a sense of mild conditionality: the Herald does not make it clear whether he believes Clytemnestra's boast about her fidelity, but seems to feel he should comment approvingly on this powerful individual's parting words. Some scholars think Clytemnestra should speak these lines before her exit, but that does blunt the effect of her sinister closing words, 'dipping bronze', as she turns on her heel to enter the palace. The Herald joins in the general discussion of the relationship between veracity and preconceptions about gender in *Agamemnon*, especially the assumption that women are unreliable custodians of the truth, issues well brought out in Park (2023) 170–90. **a high-minded wife:** For *gennaios* referring to nobility of soul or spirit rather than of birth see, e.g., Hdt. 3.140, Soph. *El*. 129. The topic of the correct deportment for women and wives recurs even in scenes where no female is present. **to utter:** The verb *laskein*, which often refers to animal noises of loud ritual utterances (594–5*), may seem harsh here, but Aristophanes suggests that it was associated with the delivery of high-flown tragic rhetorical pronouncements at *Frogs* 97.

615–16 **indoctrinate:** An English verb stronger than 'learn' is required to get the force of the participle *manthanonti* here. **astute interpreters:** On the recurring figure of the need to interpret obscure speech as if it were a foreign language see 616*, 1162*. **façade:** The basic meaning of the adverb *euprepōs* is 'with good appearance', so it acquired an alternative negative sense, 'speciously'. The chorus seem anxious to convince the Herald that Clytemnestra is not to be trusted.

617–19 **want to know ... alive:** Lit., 'I enquire about Menelaus, whether [he is] in a position to return again saved [and] has come with you.' For *nostimos* meaning 'able to return' see Hom. *Od*. 4.806 and 19.85. On Menelaus, so instrumental in the backstory to *Agamemnon*, see 842*. **sovereign:** On the significant term *kratos* see 10–11*.

620–1 **I cannot ... length of time:** Lit., 'There is no way that I could speak falsehoods [to sound] good for friends to reap the harvest of, over a long time'. Rather than supplying a direct answer, the Herald's rather circumlocutory response is intended to prepare the chorus for bad news. On *karpizesthai*, meaning 'harvest the fruit of' in a negative sense, see also 502*.

622 **If only ... pleasing:** Lit., 'Would indeed that you could be in a position to speak true things [that we would find] pleasing.' On the word *kednos* see 122–3*.

623 **The man disappeared:** Lit., 'The man [was] unseen.' The adjective *aphantos* is used repeatedly in this play in connection with seafaring; see 657 (the ships that were lost in the storm), 695* (the temporary marks left in the water by oars on the ship taking Helen to Troy) and 1007* (of an underwater reef).

625   Was he seen: Lit., 'having put out to sea visibly'. For this meaning of *anagein* in the passive voice see Hom. *Il.* 1.478, Hdt. 3.138.

626–7   storm: The terrible frequency of shipwrecks caused by bad weather in the ancient Greek world makes the chorus assume that this is a likely reason. **blight:** For *achthos* as a metaphorical burden of emotional difficulty see also 161–3*. **on everybody:** Lit., 'in common'. The chorus is subtly fishing for news of all the other seamen.

628   like a consummate archer: On archery images in the play see 364–5*.

629   You've described: Aeschylus is fond of using the verb *phēmizein*, which denotes socially or ritually significant speech, in the middle voice with a meaning like 'express in words': see also 1162, 1173.

630–1   Was he alive … seamen: Lit., 'Was the rumour among the other seamen telling of him being alive or dead?' Again, the chorus want to hear what has become of 'the other seamen' as well as Menelaus. On rumours and *phatis* see 276*.

632   so as to … information: Lit., 'so as to report back clearly'. On *toros* see 26*.

633   the Sun: On Helios as witness, often the sole witness, of events in Greek tragedy, which was played beneath the sun in broad daylight, see Hall (2010b) 2–3, 93–4. **the natural world:** Lit., 'nature on earth'.

635   rancour: The masculine noun *kotos* indicates inveterate ill-will, and in Aeschylus is usually borne by a god (Apollo at 1211, Zeus at *Suppl.* 347; also Aeschylus fr. 266.5, from his *Phrygians*), but later, at 1464, Clytemnestra accuses the chorus of *kotos* towards Helen. The chorus are notably swift to assume that the gods are angry with Agamemnon and his fleet.

636–7   to pollute: On the verb *miainein* see 209–10*. **auspicious:** *euphēmos* means that nothing should be said that might be ill-omened, and so sometimes indicates actual ritual silence. When Cassandra says that the chorus will soon see the death of Agamemnon, they order her to keep her mouth *euphēmos* at 1247*. The sense of fear surrounding the capacity of speech to affect events and to jeopardise safety is ever powerful in this play. **They should be kept … gods:** Lit., 'the honour of the gods [requires that they occur] separately'. One distinctive motif in the trilogy, closely related to the idea of pollution, is anxiety about keeping inimical or contrasting phenomena separate, so that one cannot taint the other. This reaches a climax with Athena's ambiguous warning to the Athenian citizens against 'polluting the laws with evil streams; if you stain clear water with filth, you will never find a drink' (*Eum.* 693–4). In *Agamemnon*, Cassandra imagines Clytemnestra's rage about Iphigenia as a drug to which she adds anger caused by the presence of Cassandra (1260–3), but the motif predominantly relates to mingling diverse vocalised phenomena: Clytemnestra bizarrely compares the contrasting shouts of triumph and despair to be heard in Troy with oil and vinegar that cannot blend (321–3). The Herald is unhappy that he must 'pollute an auspicious day' by voicing bad news, because they 'should be kept apart' for the sake of honouring the gods (636–7; see also 648); he compares his news with a victory-song of the Erinyes, a bleak contradiction in terms (645). The Chorus protest that Cassandra addresses Apollo in the idiom not of a paean but a dirge (1075).

639   a grim-faced messenger: Lit., 'a messenger with a hated/hateful face'. A very likely alternative adjective is *smoios*, which means something like 'scowling'. **dreaded:** Lit., 'that prayers had been made to avert'. **with news:** These words are inserted into the translation to make sense in English. **of an army's fall:** Lit., 'of a fallen army'.

640   communal wound … state: Aeschylus seems to be echoing Solon 4.17, where civic misconduct arising from greed is an 'ineluctable wound' that comes 'against the entire city'.

641   but on the other hand: The point of contrast is between the singularity of the event (the ruination of the army) and the multiplicity of individuals experiencing death or bereavement. **led out for sacrifice:** The verb *exagizein* is probably a compound of *hagizein*, 'make sacred with offerings' (Pind. *Ol.* 3.19). It is a remarkable locution, quite different from the characterisation of death as a glorious achievement in archaic Greek epic (although, at *Iliad* 17.516–24, a most unusual simile likens the way Aretus fell to the ground in death on the battlefield to a slaughtered sacrificial bull); it implicitly connects all the war dead with the sacrificed Iphigenia. See also 803–4*.

642   twofold whip which Ares loves: A *mastix* is most found in connection with horses (Hom. *Il.* 5.748, Hdt. 4.3), although it was the word used for the whip wielded by the Scythian archers who kept public order in Athens (Ar. *Thesm.* 933). Zeus (Hom. *Il.* 12.37) is sometimes imagined as wielding a whip, as are other gods (Aesch. *Sept.* 608). Although Ares was not usually associated with a whip in combat, he was strongly identified as a charioteer, ordering Terror and Rout to yoke his immortal horses (*Iliad* 15.119–20); one of his cult titles was *hippios* (Paus. 5.15.6). In the Homeric *Hymn to Ares* he is addressed as 'chariot-rider' with 'blazing steeds' (8.1–8). In the *Iliad* he lends the wounded Aphrodite his chariot and horses and Iris whips them on (5.352–66). He is depicted in *The Shield of Heracles* 57–65, standing in his chariot and driving on his galloping horses, whose hooves raise the dust. He holds a long whip as he stands in his horse-drawn chariot on an Attic black-figured early sixth-century vase by Sophilos in the British Museum (London 1971, 1101.1). On Ares in this play and trilogy see 374–6*.

643 double-edged destruction, a gory double blow: Lit., 'two-spear-pointed ruin, a gory yoked pair', i.e., the combination of a public catastrophe and private grief. The idea of Ares as a hoplite perhaps lies behind *dilonchon*, and as a charioteer behind *xunōrida*, which means a yoked pair of draught animals: see further 374–6*. On *atē* see 359–61*, on yoking 326–8* and on blood 209–10*.

644 laden: Lit., 'stuffed with'. **sorrows:** This is the same noun, in a different case, with which the Herald had begun this long and disturbing sentence.

645 this victory-song of the Erinyes: The Herald seems to be referring with the deictic *tonde* to the dark content of his own last few lines as constituting a 'victory-song of the Erinyes', a striking and possibly 'blasphemous paradox' (Fraenkel (1950) vol. 2, 321). The masculine noun *paian* can refer, amongst other things (146*), to a song of triumph after a military victory, usually sung in honour of Apollo (Hom. *Il.* 22.391–2). But it can also mean a battle-song (Aesch. *Pers.* 393), and can be addressed to Ares (Schol. Thuc. 1.50). Here it could imply either or both, especially as it is immediately undercut by being said oxymoronically to be sung by or for the Erinyes, on whom see 58–9*. The allusion to the Erinyes raises the question of whether the catastrophe he is about to describe was a punishment for some dire misdemeanour.

646 for a man ... deliverance: Lit., 'for one who comes well-messaged [with news] of delivery matters'. The sentence begins with what might be expected to be revealed subsequently as an objective accusative or accusative of respect, but, under the pressure of his emotions, the Herald suddenly changes construction and interrupts himself with a rhetorical question.

647 to a city rejoicing: This might be better translated 'to a city so as to make it rejoice', although the women of Argos had indeed been celebrating the fall of Troy with rituals for some time before the Herald arrived. **happiness:** The feminine noun *euestōs*, literally meaning 'wellbeing', is often found in the sense of a community and/or its ruler enjoying times of prosperity (Aesch. *Sept.* 187, Hdt. 1.185.1) and is used in this sense by Agamemnon at 929*. It was the title of a treatise by Democritus.

648   how shall I combine? The Herald abruptly changes construction, interrupting himself with a rhetorical question. On the imagery of comingling and separation see 636–7* and on *kedna* see 122–3*.

649   not unconnected with divine wrath: The litotes suggests the Herald is reluctant to state baldly that the cause of the storm was definitely the vengeful wrath of the gods, which is what the cognate feminine noun *mēnis* indicates at 701 (Zeus' wrath against Paris). See also 154–5* and Clytemnestra's ambiguous adverb *amēnitōs* at 1036*. Nevertheless, the phrase prompts the audience to ponder which god(s) should feel *mēnis* towards the Achaeans and why.

650–2   fire and sea, former bitterest of enemies: Following immediately after the mention of the wrath of the gods, it is tempting to see these nouns as standing for Hephaestus and Poseidon respectively. But both gods supported the Achaeans during the Trojan War. Aeschylus may be referring to the way Poseidon turned against the Achaeans and complied with Athena's proposal to destroy their fleet, as famously dramatised by Euripides in the prologue to his *Trojan Women*, although the fragmentary evidence for the cyclic epics which mention Athena's involvement, the *Iliou Persis* and the *Nostoi*, do not explicitly implicate Poseidon. Some scholars think that there are echoes of the elemental fight between the River Scamander and the fire which Hera makes winds drive across the plain of Troy in the *Iliad* (21.328–82), or that fire and sea here represent the elements as opposed in presocratic cosmology (see Introduction, p. 101). The role of fire in the destruction of the fleet is not developed by the Herald. Although ships with naked flames from lamps or braziers on board do burn even while sinking, this is odd. Perhaps he means that although fire had been on the 'side' of the Greeks at Troy when they set it ablaze, it now collaborated with the sea against them. **swore an alliance:** Although in a military context this verb can mean 'to ally with' in a morally neutral sense (Thuc. 5.48, 6.18), it can also possess darker overtones and mean 'conspire' or 'plot together' (Hdt. 7.235, Ar. *Knights* 236, Dem. 57.64). Torrance (2015) 285 suggests that it foreshadows the compact between Clytemnestra and Aegisthus and that, since this is the earliest example of this verb in Greek literature, 'the conspiratorial element seems to have been deliberately underlined'. **offered as pledge:** Lit., 'both showed proofs'. **the joint destruction:** Lit., 'both destroying'. The dual forms of the verb and participle stress the collusion between fire and sea, even though the Herald does not elaborate on the role played by fire.

653 **difficulties ... waves:** Lit., 'ill-waved evils had arisen'. Note the pluperfect.

654–6 **Winds from Thrace:** That is, winds coming from the same northerly direction as those that had caused the problems before the outward voyage at Aulis (192–5*), a sinister detail given that the Herald has suggested that the storm had something to do with divine wrath. In the *Iliad*, the north and west winds blow from Thrace (9.4–8) and all the winds seem to live there (23.230). **kept making:** The imperfect suggests that the storm lasted for an extended part of the night. **gouged forcefully by the horns:** The Herald imagines the force of the typhoon and rainstorm as an angry male horned animal, probably to be envisaged as a bull (on such imagery see 34–9*), headbutting the ships. **of the wintry typhoon ... rain:** Lit., 'by the wintry-weather of the typhoon and rain-drumming squall'. On adverse weather in the play see 5*. Cyclones do occur in the Mediterranean; 67 typhoons of tropical intensity are believed to have occurred between 1947 and 2014: see Nastos et al. (2015). **whirled ... malign herdsman:** Lit., 'by the whirling-movement of a malign herdsman'. The ships were previously said to be assaulted by the typhoon as if by a bull; the livestock imagery here continues as the typhoon is imagined, rather, as a bad shepherd whose flock disappears altogether. On pastoral imagery see 128–30*.

657 **disappeared:** See 623*.

658 **the bright sun's light arose:** Strictly speaking, in the compressed temporal context of this play's action, this is of course the same sunrise as the one just experienced in Argos, where daylight has dispersed the darkness at some point since the Watchman's prologue. On light and darkness see Introduction, pp. 63–5.

659 **abloom with corpses:** Since the verb *anthein* is usually associated with youthful beauty (Hom. *Od.* 11.320, Plat. *Rep.* 5.475a) or healthily flourishing plants and flowers (Hes. *Works* 582), it is an effectively dark image to see the surface of the sea like a meadow flowering with human bodies. See also 196–8*.

660–2 **we ourselves:** Strictly speaking this should be translated 'us' since it is one of the accusative objects of the verbs in the next line, but this makes for clumsy English through unnatural word order. **hull ungouged:** This is in the accusative of respect. The metaphor continues the image established in 654–6*. **a god:** Ancient Greek seamen dedicated offerings to several different gods in gratitude for safe return from a voyage, often under the titles *sōtēr* or *sōteira*. See 245–7*, 664*. **rescued us by stealthy action or verbal appeal:** Lit., 'stole us away or interceded/demanded'—covert interference and overt intercession are the two ways in which gods such as Thetis, Athena, Apollo and Hera operate in Homeric epic in order to further their own ends around the will of Zeus.

663   Fortune ... Saviour: Not being clear why his particular ship (which is also Agamemnon's) escaped being wrecked by the storm, the Herald attributes its survival to personified Chance or Fortune. The concept of *tuchē* is already seen as a non-human agent or intervening cause in human life in earlier poetry (although not in Homer): see Archilochus fr. 16, where it is paired with *Moira* as the chief determinant of a man's life; Pind. *Ol.* 14.15, Aesch. *Sept.* 426); see also 1647* and Aesch. *Eum.* 93. But Tuchē became an important Hellenistic goddess, and is already personified in Pindar's *Olympian* 12.1–4 (466 BCE), with the same title as here, Sōteira; there she is said to be a daughter of Zeus, whose first function Pindar says is the steering of swift ships at sea. The life-threatening hazards faced by ancient seamen mean she is frequently found in maritime contexts; Hesiod had made her the daughter of the sea divinities Tethys and Ocean (*Theog.* 360), and she was sometimes depicted with a rudder (Paus. 7.26.3); Pindar asks her to look after a port city (*Ol.* 12.2). For her evolution see Matheson (1994). On the title 'Saviour' see also 245–7* and 512*.

665   take in storm-waves: Lit., 'have storm of wave'. Although bilge-pumps became sophisticated in later antiquity, the threat posed by ships taking in water via the hull has been demonstrated by analysis of the wreckage of the Kyrenia, a merchant ship that was lost off northern Cyprus in the fourth century BCE; a contributory cause was extensive seepage (Steffy (1985) 95–6).

666   on rocky shores: Lit., 'on hard-stoned land'. The adjective *krataileōs* is a compound of *krataios* ('mighty') and *laas* ('stone').

667   a watery death: Lit., 'a marine Hades'. The name of the god of the Underworld (Hom. *Il.* 15.188) can already stand metonymically for the Underworld itself in Homer (*Il.* 23.244; see Pind. *Pyth.* 5.96). But given the emphasis that has been laid on the visual disappearance of Menelaus at 624–7, some of the original force of the proper name, which was probably compounded from privative alpha and *idein*, 'to see', may reverberate here. At 1115–18* and 1235–6* *Haidou* in the genitive is used adjectivally, meaning 'lethal', of the net in which Agamemnon is murdered and of Clytemnestra respectively.

668   what had befallen: If unqualified, *tuchē* can mean either good fortune (Theognis 130, Pind. *Nem.* 5.48) or bad (Aesch. *Suppl.* 380, Antiphon 6.1 and 1653*), although it has a neutral sense in the plural and very occasionally

(Soph. *Trach.* 724) the singular. Here it is not clear whether the Herald is thinking about his own shipmates' survival (good luck) or the afflictions of the fleet in general (bad luck). The sense would depend entirely on the actor's delivery, pauses and intonation.

669   we paid close attention to: Lit., 'we tended as herdsmen'. It is a shame that no obvious way seems apparent in English of continuing the Herald's run of pastoral imagery from 654–6*.

670   battered: The passive of the same violent verb is used of being pelted by a storm at Eur. *Andr.* 1129 and being dashed against rocks at Eur. *Hipp.* 1238.

671   are alive: Lit., 'is inhaling'. This turn of phrase has a particular resonance in the context of death by drowning. The audience will certainly have thought here of Odysseus (see 842*) as well as Menelaus.

672–3   the same to be the case with them: Lit., 'them to have the same situation'. There is great pathos in the idea of another messenger from the fleet, far away in another city, describing how the current speaker's ship had vanished during the storm.

674   May things work out for the best: The Herald joins the chorus and Clytemnestra in conventional expressions of guarded optimism (255–6, 349–50) which do nothing to allay the general mood of tense anxiety.

675   anticipate: The verb *prosdokan*, 'expect', can imply both hope and fear. The messenger has said nothing about whether Menelaus will be bringing Helen with him, although, as the chorus' imminent song demonstrates, she is much on everyone's mind.

676   any ray of the sun: See 633*. **discovers him:** The verb *historein* implies being in a position to report after making enquiries (Aesch., *PV* 632, Hdt. 2.113, Soph. *OT* 1150, Theophr. *Hist. Plant.* 4.13.1).

677   alive and well: Lit., 'living and seeing'.

678   if he does not yet … out: It is possible that this means the entire family line of the Atreidai: at 1603, we will learn that Thyestes cursed the whole *genos* of Pleisthenes. But in the context it is more likely to be a reference to the ancient tradition, as old or nearly as old as the *Iliad*, reported in Hesiod's *Catalogue of Women*, that Zeus decided to 'annihilate most of the race (*genos*, as here) of speech-endowed human beings' as a by-product of his conflict with some 'semi-gods' (Hesiod fr. 155 translated by Most (2018) 256–9; see Hall (2025) ch. 1). An ancient scholiast (D) commented on *Iliad* 1.5 ('Zeus' plan was being fulfilled') that in the epic *Cypria*, attributed to Stasinus, Earth begged Zeus to relieve her of the weight of the multitude of people, who were impious. So Zeus first brought about the Theban War, which destroyed very large numbers, and afterwards the Trojan one, 'with Momus as his adviser, this being what Homer calls the plan of Zeus, seeing that he was capable of destroying everyone with thunderbolts or floods'. (Momus, 'Blame', was the son of Night and brother of Misery according to Hesiod's *Theogony* 214). Momus advised against this, instead suggesting the Judgement of Paris and the birth 'of a beautiful daughter' (i.e. Helen). Thus the Trojan War came about, resulting in 'the lightening of the earth as many were killed'. The ancient scholar then quotes an invaluable fragment of the lost epic *Cypria* in which Earth begged Zeus to relieve her of the excessive and impious 'tribes of men' (*Cypria* fr. 1 in West (2003) 82–3). On the verb *exanalōsai* see also on *analōthentas* at 570*.

679   hope: On the theme of hope see 100–3* and Introduction, p. 3.

680   truth: The play's explicit problematisation of the establishment of truth is a recurring theme (Introduction, pp. 101–2). The Herald's last words are oddly abrupt, perhaps implying his desperation to get away from the tension between Clytemnestra and the citizen chorus as well as this sinister household and back to his own.

viii]   681–781   THE CHORUS: Second Stasimon

Summary
As the Herald leaves, the chorus are left alone in the theatre. They sing a choral ode with two fundamental functions: (i) to process the news he has delivered, both good and bad, and (ii) to set the mood for the arrival of Agamemnon, the next character to enter (with Cassandra), during the choral anapaests between 782 and 809. This choral sequence is structurally of great significance in providing the transition between the part of the play where Clytemnestra is in charge of both household and city-state, and her long-awaited confrontation with her husband, whom she has not seen since the sacrifice of Iphigenia.

This lyric, unlike the previous two, is not opened with a section of anapaests; the chorus explode into immediate song, accompanied by the music of the aulos-player, to express their emotions. These were increasingly stirred, but had to remain under control, while they heard from the Herald about the suffering of the Greek soldiers at Troy, the storm which attacked the fleet and the disappearance of Menelaus' ship. The lyric consists of four pairs of stanzas, the longest of which come first and the shortest last, in a mixture of lyric metres which eventually settle in the iambic (see Metrical Appendix). The subject matter breaks down as follows:

Strophe 1	Helen was rightly named since her name sounds like destruction. Her ship was followed by Greeks and the ensuing war was bloody.
Antistrophe 1	Zeus annihilated the Trojans for breaking the law of hospitality.
Strophe 2	A lion-cub was once reared in a human family who adored it.
Antistrophe 2	But when it grew up it devoured the household flock.
Strophe 3	When Helen arrived in Troy at first all was well. But then she brought suffering on Priam's family on account of Zeus Xeinios.
Antistrophe 3	People say that success engenders misery. But I think it is a wrong act that blights the family. Decency flourishes in poor households and leaves rich ones where a crime has been committed.
Strophe 4	Hubris generates more acts of Hubris, Recklessness and family curses.
Antistrophe 4	But Uprightness flourishes in the homes of the virtuous poor and avoids the households of the corrupt rich.

681–2 Who was it: The chorus open their song with a riddle, syntactically composed of a question containing another, embedded question. The frame question asks who named the woman responsible for so much suffering 'Helen', which the chorus suggest means 'Destroyer', but the direct question is never answered beyond posing another question in a parenthesis—was it an unseen entity, something more than a human being? Delaying the name 'Helen', however, until after the two adjectives which describe her as the spear-bride and the cause of the conflict not only lends rhetorical emphasis to the end of the question but suggests that, in a sense, the 'answer' to the really important riddle is not the invisible naming power after all, but the one named—the notorious woman, the force of destruction herself. **completely suitable name:** Lit., who was it who once gave 'the name in every respect truly ... ?' **to Helen, the bride of the spear, the cause of the conflict:** Lit., 'to Helen, with a spear as a bridegroom, contested on all sides'. These words need to be moved up from their position in the Greek three lines later to make sense in English of this long, complex sentence with its parenthetical internal question. Greek literature often makes judgements on whether names are properly assigned to their referents, a practice which reaches its culmination in Plato's *Cratylus*, where the names of figures in the *Iliad* are prominent amongst those discussed: Astyanax (392c–e), Hector (393a) Agamemnon (395a). One of the rarer criteria of appropriateness was that the name of an individual was predictive of their future actions and behaviour ('cledonomancy'; *'nomen omen'*), as the chorus is suggesting here. See Peradotto (1969b) and Eur. *Andr.* 105–6. On the significance of names see further above 160–2*, where the chorus are concerned to use the correct appellation for Zeus. *dorigambros* is one of several striking compound words used by Aeschylus to suggest the paradox of a wedding with miserable consequences: see, e.g., the spirit of vengeance in the form 'of a bride who brought woe' (749). On the theme of wedding rituals in *Agamemnon* generally see the Introduction, p. 52. Doyle (2009) hears reminiscences of Hesiod's Pandora in Aesychlus' presentation of Helen, the wife who brings destruction, here.

683–4   some invisible being: The chorus wonder if the name was thought up by some supernatural entity, one of the many unseen forces which they and other characters sense are at work in the universe; see 385 (the force of persuasion), 420–2 (figures in dreams), 462–3 (Erinyes), 635 (unspecified malign *daimones*) and 663 ('some god'). In *Eumenides*, of course, the cosmic 'unseen' is finally revealed when the Erinyes, Apollo, Hermes and Athena are all made visible to the audience. But no such supernatural/metaphysical certainty is available in the confusing world of *Agamemnon*. On the chorus' fascination with their own powers of visual perception, and their limits, see 248–9*, where they note that they did not actually see Iphigenia die.

685   with foresight of what was destined to happen: The possibility that the future can be divined is explored in the chorus' first description of the army seer's (Calchas') interpretation of the omen of the eagles and the hare (see 125*) and during Cassandra's discussion with the chorus of her own mantic gift (1199–213). The term for 'what was destined to happen' is a perfect passive participle, assumed to be formed from an attested verb *porein* (to 'furnish' or 'offer'), used as a neuter noun, which in Aeschylus several times indicates 'fate' or 'destiny'. See above, 68*.

686   whose tongue hit on the truth: Lit., 'directing his tongue with [accurate] fortune'. On the power of a tongue to frame or even affect history by naming an individual or an event see the Watchman's dark statement that a bull has stood upon his tongue, preventing him from telling more of what is going on behind closed doors (36–7), and the Herald's reluctance to 'pollute' an auspicious day 'with a tongue that reports bad news' (636–7).

689–91   true to her name: Lit., 'befittingly'. **Hell for ships, Hell for men, Hell for a city:** In the English language this is the most satisfactory equivalent of Aeschylus' grim pun on Helen's name, the first syllable of which, *Hel-*, is shared in ancient Greek by the aorist tense (infinitive *helein*) of a fundamental verb meaning to seize or destroy (present infinitive *hairein*): in all three compounds Aeschylus uses here, the first syllable therefore means 'destroying'. Helen brought hellish destruction upon the Greek navy, but the 'men' and the 'city' can both be heard as referring inclusively to Argos and Troy. On the significance of the number three see 33*. At 577, the reading of the inscription which the messenger suggested that the Argives erect was that, 'having taken' (*helontes*) Troy, they had nailed up the spoils of victory.

690–2 when she sailed out: This is another in the play's several images of the eastward journey by sea, which began, in the first sentence uttered by the chorus in their opening anapaests, with the image of the Atreidai assembling their fleet for the expedition to Troy (40–54*; see also 108–20). Specifically, this image of Helen sailing forth from Greece has been anticipated in the first stasimon, where she was described as 'slipping swiftly through the gates with unbelievable daring' (403–8), causing her own people to go to war, and inflicting on Troy a dowry of destruction. **her luxurious, expensive draperies:** The emphasis on the softness of Helen's draperies is one component in Aeschylus' sustained evocation of the richness of the lifestyle and luxurious possessions of the Atreidai and their wives (382*); this has already been a feature of the perfumed oils from inside the palace with which Clytemnestra tends the altar fires (95), and will shortly be materialised in the textiles which are to be strewn at the palace entrance (908–9*). Many editors here adopt the reading *habropēnōn*, 'softly woven', suggested by a French scholar in the early seventeenth century, since the adjective in the manuscripts, 'soft and expensive', is not attested elsewhere. But Aeschylus was quite capable of inventing interesting new compound words to suit his poetic purpose (see Ar. *Frogs* 928–32). Helen's draperies, probably suggesting the curtains round her bed (see 27*) rather than the awnings at the palace gates, are one of the series of significant fabrics in the play, including Iphigenia's yellow robes, falling around her when she was sacrificed (233, 239*), the great metaphorical 'net' of military violence which Zeus cast around Troy (358) and the inadequate bedding endured by the regular Greek soldiers (556). Helen's agency here is stressed by making her the subject of the verb, and by the omission of any mention of Paris/Alexander, who, the chorus have previously suggested, was the primary instigator of the elopement (363*, 532–3). They have even called it a 'theft' (399–402). The precise extent of Helen's own culpability, and the question of whether she was abducted or seduced, is much debated in Greek literature: see Hall (2010b) 177–8.

692   wafted by the breath of the strong west wind: Lit., '[wafted] by the breeze of giant Zephyros'. It is not clear why Aeschylus refers to the west wind as a giant here, unless it is simply that, as a member of the race of giants, Zephyros is a Titan, implying perhaps the elemental strength of the wind. Winds blow in and out of the poetry of the play, from the moments when the 'adverse winds' (147–9) and the winds 'from the Strymon' (192) were described as holding back the Argive fleet at Aulis, Agamemnon's yielding to the 'adverse winds of fate' (187) and the Messenger's description of the 'Thracian winds' which smashed the Greek ships against each other at Troy (654–5). Here Helen is blown with almost uncanny effortlessness to Troy by a breeze that blows from the correct direction for her intended voyage—the west; later the chorus will sing, in contrast, that at first Helen's erotic presence at Troy brought a sense of 'windless calm' (739). On winds and this wind imagery see Scott (1966) 462–6.

693   shielded huntsmen followed: The comparison of the Greek army with huntsmen, implicit in the correlation between Atreidai and the eagles ('the hounds of Zeus') who ate the hare (124–57*), and in the nets which Zeus cast around Troy (357*), now becomes explicit. The huntsmen are the subject of this clause, which is 'tacked on' through the connective *te* to the previous one, so that they effectively share with Helen the verb 'sailed' (691), even though it is in the singular.

694   the oars' traces: In English the plural 'traces' makes better sense. Words containing the stem *ichn-*, 'track', are also used in the play to signify the diagnosis or identification of divine activity (368*). **as they vanished:** The same term, here referring to the marks so briefly made in the seawater by the oars of Helen's ship before she landed at the river Simois, was used to refer to Menelaus' sudden disappearance from the Argive fleet, also in the eastern Aegean close to Troy (623*). **when they beached her ship:** These five words translate the participle *kelsantōn*, which is probably a possessive genitive attached to the 'traces' (*ichnos*); literally, 'the oars' traces as they vanished, [the traces] of those who had beached the ship'.

695   leafy: Literally, 'leaf-nourishing'. Rich foliage is here, as elsewhere in the play, a sign of vigour and health; the chorus complain that in human old age 'the foliage withers' (79–80). The sensuous ease with which Helen is perceived as travelling to Troy is pointedly in contrast with the physical ardours of the voyage of the common soldiers (555–7). **Simois:** Running down from Mount Ida, the Simois was a tributary of Troy's most important river, Scamander. It is one of the rivers which Tethys bore to Ocean in Hesiod's *Theogony* (342). In the *Iliad* Simois is the brother of Scamander, and like him supports the Trojans: Scamander calls on him for help when the battle-crazed Achilles attacks him (21.311–15).

696 sent by Strife to create carnage: Lit., 'on account of gory Strife'. I have printed *Eris* with a capital letter to indicate that the chorus is probably referring to the dread personification of conflict, the daughter of Night (Hesiod, *Theog.* 225), the goddess of bellicosity (*Iliad* 18.535, 2.48); see also Aeschylus' *Seven against Thebes* (726). On the difficulties caused by capitalisation conventions when editing ancient Greek, see 218–21*. In the epic *Cypria*, the Trojan War was ultimately caused by Eris, who appeared at the marriage of Peleus and Thetis, made the three goddesses quarrel and thus instigated the judgement of Paris (fr. 1). On Eris/eris see also 1459*.

699–701 divine wrath: On *mēnis* see 154–5*. **a marriage whose name meant misery:** Lit., 'a correctly named relationship by marriage', i.e. Helen's relationship with Paris, with all its fatal consequences. The Greek plays untranslatably on the four related meanings of the neuter noun *kēdos*, which can mean simply 'grief' (Hom. *Il.* 13.464) but also a relationship by marriage (Hdt. 7.189, Thuc. 2.29), or the funeral rites that relatives including those by marriage would be obliged to attend (Hdt. 6.58), or even just 'death in the family' (Hdt. 6.58). On the parallels between wedding rites and funeral rites see Introduction, p. 52, and Rehm (1994).

702 Divine wrath … hearth: The repeated 'Divine wrath' here has been supplied in the English translation to make it clear what it was that in due course (lit., 'in later time'), would be 'taking reprisals (*prassomena*) for the outrage (*atimōsin*) done to the law of hospitality (*trapezas*) and Zeus "partaker in the hearth"' by Paris. On the image of the hearth see 427–8*.

704–8 punishing: This has been supplied in English to make sense of the long Greek sentence: **those who baldly sang the song in honour of the bride:** A literal translation of this corrupt Greek sentence would read, 'those baldly honouring the bride-honouring song'. *ekphatōs* might mean 'impiously' rather than 'out loud'. On *tiein* see 259–60*. **marriage hymn:** The word *humenaion* may be a scribal interpolation and have ousted an adverbial phrase, but the context certainly requires a reference to the *humenaion* as sung in communities portrayed on shields in epic ekphrasis (Hom. *Il.* 18.493, Hes. *Shield of Heracles* 273). Hymen was the god of marriage, and is named *Humenaios* in wedding songs, the title which also produced the name of the genre (Sappho fr. 58.5; see also fr. 111.2, 4; Ar. *Peace* 1335). **which fell:** The Greek suggests the sinking of one pan in the scales; on weighing metaphors see 63–7*. **on the groom's family:** This is a striking picture of Paris' numerous relatives singing the marriage hymn, especially so soon after we have been invited to imagine the insulted dining table of Menelaus at Argos (399–402*).

709–12 **has learned to sing a different tune … dirges:** Lit., 'changing its learning to a hymn full of dirges, groans I suppose (*pou*) loudly'. At Hdt. 1.57 *metamanthanein* is used of unlearning one language (*glōssa*) and learning another instead. The adjective *poluthrēnos* is repeated with the same ending within the same sentence at 713, as if to emphasise the plurality of dirges it indicates. **bridegroom from Hell:** Lit., 'dreadfully mated'.

713–15 **Troy has endured … by her citizens:** The text is corrupt and has been emended. What is printed translates literally as 'Having endured [seeing] her whole life utterly besieged and full of dirges for the sake of her citizens' miserable blood'. On blood see 209–10*.

716–19 **thus:** *houtōs* suggests that this sentence will illustrate what was said in the previous one, so the expectation is that the comparison will involve Paris and Troy. The account of the young lion 'possesses several formal characteristics of fable', besides this use of *houtos*, including ring composition and 'its paradigmatic use as a cautionary tale' (Harris (2012) 547). Yet lion cubs feature in Herodotus' account of Cambyses' household recreations (3.32.1) and a pet who demanded huge quantities of meat in Juvenal's critique of the possessions of an absurdly wealthy man (*Sat.* 7.74–7). Fraenkel (1950) vol. 2, 342, who almost completely eschewed references to the recent history of Nazism in his commentary, added to the list of lion-owners here the name of Marshal Hermann Göring, who can be seen with his lion cubs at https://www.youtube.com/watch?v=gzDK4RVfARs. **reared:** The aorist may have a gnomic or 'habitual' force, in which case it and the all the other aorist verbs down to 736 would be better translated in English by the present tense. The question is whether the chorus is represented as thinking about a particular case or a general pattern of behaviour. Aeschylus fr. 452.1, 'One ought not to rear a lion cub in a city', is preserved because it is spoken by Aeschylus himself in Aristophanes' *Frogs* 1431; this might mean either that the image was ancient and proverbial or that this passage of *Agamemnon* was well known. **lion cub:** On lion imagery see 141*. **forcibly weaned while still craving breast milk:** Lit., 'milkless … breast-loving'. The detail is intended to emphasise that the cub was fostered very young. See 142–3*.

720 **Tame:** The masculine accusative *hameron* reveals the lion cub to be male, so at this point the audience would probably have associated it with Paris, although in the antistrophe Helen's 'adoption' by the Trojans comes to mind as well. Paris was exposed at birth because Hecuba had a dream in which she gave birth to a firebrand, but the baby was fostered by a herdsman. This story was already known to Pindar (fr. 52i(A).14–25); it may be much older and have featured in the *Cypria*. Both Sophocles and Euripides told it in tragedies entitled *Alexander*, in which the prince arrived at adulthood and was reunited with his parents. Sophocles' *Alexander* might have preceded the *Oresteia*, since he was competing at the Dionysia by 468 BCE. The fragments of Sophocles' play make references to a midwife (fr. 99), a nurse (fr. 98) and a herdsman (fr. 93). Much more of Euripides' *Alexander*, produced with *Trojan Women* in 415 BCE, has survived, and is superbly edited by Karamanou (2017). The most important testimony is the hypothesis (T iii = POxy. 3650 col. i, ed. Coles (1974)) which relates how Alexander was felt by the country people to be arrogant. He competed victoriously in games laid on at Troy. Hecuba did not realise that he was her son and conspired to have him killed. The foster-father herdsman appeared in the play to protect him by explaining who he was (see also 60–2*). This tradition, although not explicitly mentioned in *Agamemnon*, may well have illuminated the meaning of this strophic pair. **in his early life:** On *proteleia* see 63–7*.

721–2 He was good … elderly: On the imagery of childhood and old age respectively see 74–5* and 72*.

723–4 often he was held in the arms: The participle 'held' has been inserted to make good sense in English. The emendation *esk'* is a Homeric frequentative for *ēn*, 'he was', a form Aeschylus uses at *Pers.* 656. **like a newborn child:** In a complicated two-way comparison, this simile compares the metaphorical lion cub with a newborn human infant. See 49–50*.

725–6 with his beaming face … pangs: Lit., 'beaming-faced towards the hand and wheedling by compulsions of his stomach'. On *phaidrōpos* see 298*. **cajoling:** In Homer, *sainein* denotes a dog wagging his tail and fawning on a person (*Od.* 10.217, 16.6, 17.302; see also Soph. fr. 885), but it is also used metaphorically of humans (798*). The contrast between the feigned loving demeanour of the lion cub and its crude motivations ('compulsions of his stomach') strikes a sinister note.

727 in time: In the passive, *chronizein* means 'to be delayed' or 'to be extended' (Aesch. *Choeph.* 957; Andoc. 3.27), so here it implies that the cub has grown up physically.

728–31 true disposition: The neuter noun *ēthos* also means the natural character of animals at Eur. *Hipp.* 1329 (horses) and Plato, *Rep.* 2.375e (dogs). **inherited from his parents:** Lit., 'on his parents' side'. The preposition *pros* with the genitive has exactly this sense at e.g. Hdt. 7.99

and Plato *Theaet.* 173d. In the context, this will have made the audience think of Priam and especially of Hecuba, who had the dream that she was pregnant with a fire brand. They may even have known the tradition that she conspired to have Alexander killed in adulthood (720–3*). But the allegory might also suggest Helen, who comes to destroy Troy, like her father Zeus. **returning the favour:** In the context, this a savagely ironic use of the noun *charis* (on which see 182–3*). **he prepared ... flock:** Lit., 'he prepared a feast with sheep-slaughtering ruins'. This feast must put the audience in mind of the Thyestean feast (1242*). On pastoral imagery 128–30*, and on *atē*, which appears again at the end of the antistrophe, 359–61*.

733   its inhabitants suffered: Lit., 'for the inhabitants [there was]'.

734   at the damage ... butchery: Lit., 'a great injury with many fatalities', in apposition to the neuter noun *algos*, 'grief', in the previous line. On *sinos* see 389* and 561*. The chorus had used the word *poluktonoi* enigmatically in a passage about divine punishment of the murderous at 461–2*.

735–6   priest of ruin: This is a powerful image, as if Atē (359–61*) had sent whoever is now thought to be represented by the lion-cub (and the partnership of Paris and Helen may by now implied) on ahead of her to announce her imminent arrival. **to the household:** This is possibly better translated 'in the household'.

738–42   a disposition of unruffled calm: Lit., 'a mind of windless calm'. Aeschylus avoids naming Helen or Paris here; the chorus imagine instead the emotional impact that the couple's joint arrival made in Troy, followed by three phrases in apposition, of which the subjects are the neuter nouns 'ornament', 'glance' and 'flower' respectively. The imagery of a windless calm connects this ode with both the chorus' description of the fleet stranded at Aulis (190–1*) and the Herald's account of the storm and shipwreck (649–73). **ornament:** On this sense of *agalma* see 207–8*, where it had referred to Iphigenia as an ornament of her father's household. Wohl (1998) 85 shows how the term indicates that Helen is an object of incalculable worth within systems of aristocratic exchange. **soft glances passed between eyes:** Lit., 'soft shaft of eyes'—a beautiful phrase. On the involvement of sight and eyes in erotic relationships see 240*, 418–419* and Fletcher (1999a). **sexual attraction so sharp it hurts:** Lit., 'the heart-biting flower of sex'. An oxymoronic and sensual expression. On the metaphorical use of the noun *anthos* see 198–204*, 742*.

744–5   she changed tack: Lit., 'turning aside'. The abrupt transition to a feminine participle finally brings Helen before the eyes, although Aeschylus has another surprise in store, when the female subject is identified at the end of the sentence as an Erinys. **brought her marriage to a bitter end:** *epikrainein* means 'carry out', 'discharge' (see also 1340, 1546). The adjective *pikros* in this play connects the bitter weather which resulted in the death of Iphigenia (198), the fall of Troy (here) and Clytemnestra's triumphant reception of Agamemnon (970).

746   a curse on the people she lived with and talked to: Lit., 'hard as sharing residence, hard to be in conversation with'. The chorus conjure the strained intimacy of Helen's relationships with the Trojan royal household.

748   with Zeus god of guests escorting her: On this title of Zeus see 60–2*.

749   spirit of revenge whose marriage brought woe: I.e. 'an Erinys-bride who brought woe'; alternatively, it could mean 'an Erinys who brought woe on brides', meaning the widows of the Trojan men who were killed. On the references to Erinyes in the play see 58–9*, where the word appears in a similar context (Zeus sending a punishment against Troy) and in the same emphatic position at line and sentence end.

750–4   An ancient saying … long ago: Lit., 'An anciently uttered elderly saying has been created'; *gerōn* is here adjectival (for the image see 72*). The chorus introduce, cite and subsequently refute a piece of proverbial wisdom which asserted that success in itself automatically ends in disaster for the family which enjoys it. **a man's success grows to adulthood:** Lit., 'a man's prosperity having been brought big to maturity', an arresting personification. *olbos* usually refers to an all-round state of wellbeing and felicity rather than a subjective state of psychological happiness, but is often distinguished from wealth, *ploutos* (see Hom. *Il.* 16.596), which was seen as more dangerous to possess, especially in immoderation. **produces offspring:** The middle voice of this verb normally refers to the mother (Aristot. *HA* 585a34), or to both parents (Eur. *Suppl.* 1087) although there are occasional exceptions. Since the parental figure here is an abstract concept personified (albeit one grammatically gendered masculine), it is not clear whether it/ he is to be imagined fully anthropomorphically. Other concepts which in tragedy 'produce offspring' usually have a direct object: (masculine) time becomes a parent to nights and days (Soph. *OC* 618), the (feminine) earth produces children in the shape of dreams (Eur. *IT* 1262). **childless:** At Aesch. *Eum.* 1034, the Erinyes are addressed as 'childless children of Night'. On paedogonic imagery in the play see Introduction, pp. 65–7.

755–6   good fortune: On *tuchē* see 663*. **the family's insatiable despair:** Lit., 'the unsated misery of the family'. The adjective *akorestos* introduces the theme of excess, *koros*, which is in Greek thought closely related to hubris, the subject of the next stanza (763–7*). The feminine noun *oïzus* is in Hesiod (*Theog.* 214) personified as the goddess Misery, daughter of Night and sister of Blame (355–6*). Both wealth, the possession of which creates the desire to accumulate more, and intrafamilial violence are in Aeschylus consistently portrayed as 'insatiable': see Seaford (2012) 201–5.

757–8 I have a mind of my own and disagree: Lit., 'I am apart from others and of singular thinking.' It is interesting to find the chorus, rather than simply citing gnomic wisdom, actively wrestling with its moral implications. They do not accept that wealthy prosperity in itself ends in disaster: there needs to be culpability of some kind.

758–60 ungodly deed: Rather than the felicitous state denoted by *olbos*, sing the chorus, it is an active deed that goes against divine laws that puts a family at risk and is seen as a parent itself. In tragedy and lyric, *tiktein* in the present tense is elsewhere invariably used of the mother (e.g. Pind. *Ol.* 6.85, Aesch. *Eum.* 321), and in the next strophe of *Agamemnon* it will be used of the feminine Hubris (763–7*). **bearing a family likeness:** Lit., 'like its own descent'. The distinction between the impious acts which are 'born' out of a previous impious act, and the two generations of a family that commit the acts, is almost non-existent in this metaphorical scenario, as the chorus grapple with the idea of an intergenerational curse (see Introduction, pp. 55–7 and Helm (2004)). In Greek tragic theatre, masks may well have been sculpted and painted, and actors' voices deployed, to suggest family likeness (see Hall (2006) 103 and Cratinus fr. 275), and this might have been the case with the first cousins Agamemnon and Aegisthus, although parent–child resemblance would have to wait until *Choephori*.

761–2 For in upright households … turn out well: Lit., 'For the fate of right-thinking houses [is] always well-childed.'

763–7 Amongst wicked people: Lit., 'Amongst the wicked among/of men'. **old Outrage … new outrage:** *hubris* means either an attitude of insulting arrogance towards or violence against a being (human or god), usually possessing nearly equivalent or superior status (Hom. *Od.* 16.86), or a single insultingly arrogant or violent action against them (Hes. *Works* 146). See the exemplary study by Fisher (1992). Here the lack of definite articles makes it difficult to be clear whether the abstract concept or the single act is meant, although in such metaphorical poetry this may not matter. Hubris was closely associated with the idea of excess, especially excessive wealth and material consumption, a concept touched on in the previous stanza, when it is, however, the *misery* that bad behaviour causes which is 'insatiable' (755–6*). It was part of an age-old nexus of ethical beliefs prominent in Hesiod (Doyle

(1970)) that underlies Greek tragic story patterns, most succinctly expressed by Darius in *Persians* (820–2) when commenting on the Persians' impending defeat at Plataea: 'Mortals must not think thoughts above their station. For hubris flowered and produced a crop of calamity (Atē), and from it reaped a harvest of lamentation' (see Hall (1996) 164–5). See also Herodotus 8.77.1, where the Delphic oracle proclaims, 'Divine Dikē will extinguish mighty Koros, the son of Hybris, thinking to devour all', and Solon fr. 6.3–4, 'For excess breeds insolence, whenever great prosperity comes to men who are not sound of mind.' The nexus is often expressed metaphorically and, as here, paedogonically, i.e. in terms of animal reproduction (see Introduction, pp. 65–7). In Theognis 153, 'excess breeds hubris when prosperity (*olbos*) comes upon a bad man'; at Pind. *Ol.* 13.10, hubris is the mother of excess; at Aech. *Eum.* 533, hubris is the child of ungodliness; see also Soph., *OT* 873–6. **when the appointed day of birth arrives:** While neatly continuing the paedogonic imagery, and also the play's theme of childbirth (49–50*), the sense of inevitability experienced by pregnant women and their families approaching 'the appointed day' of delivery feeds into the sense of the inevitability of vengeful acts, however long delayed. The text is corrupt, but the general import of the chorus' ruminations is clear enough.

768–71   With it comes the spirit of Recklessness: Lit., 'and the *daimōn*, Recklessness'. This is the only time that the neuter noun *thrasos* seems to be personified in ancient Greek thought. At 168–9* the noun was used of Ouranos, in time ousted by Kronos. See also Aesch. *Pers.* 831 (in connection with Xerxes' arrogance). The thought seems to be that Hubris produces two children, another hubristic act and the spirit of Recklessness. The definite article *tan* is feminine because the *daimōn* [of] Recklessness is gendered feminine to make a pair with *hubrin*. **uncontrollable, unmanageable, unholy:** This is another string of adjectives in tricolon beginning with privative alpha (Introduction, p. 3), producing strong assonance for emphasis and the wide-open mouth that singers enjoy. **black blight:** On atē see 359–61*. **which take after:** See 758–60*.

773   Uprightness: The meaning of Dikē here is not quite 'justice'; it is a principle like 'the right way of doing things', or 'decency', contrasted with the hubris and recklessness denounced in the preceding strophe. See 250–1* and 524–6*. **shines brightly:** The intransitive *lampei* is used metaphorically of other moral virtues or benefits at e.g. Pind. *Ol.* 1.23 (fame), *Isthm.* 1.22 (excellence), Eur. *Ion* 476 (youthful bloom), Plat. *Phaedr.* 250d (beauty). But light has of course been one of the most prominent images in the play since the Watchman's prologue (see Introduction, pp. 63–5).

774–5 smoky, shabby homes: 'smoky' is not quite strong enough a translation of *duskapnos*, 'bad-smoked'. The point is the contrast between the moral blackness (see 769–70) of homes marked by hubris, however 'gold-encrusted' they may be (776*), and the actual darkness of the homes of the poor, nevertheless metaphorically illuminated by being morally upright. **right-thinking:** In the *Odyssey* (17.363), Athena inspires Odysseus to find out who were the right-thinking (*enaisimoi*) suitors, contrasted with the lawless ones (*athemistoi*).

776–7 averted eyes: On the importance of the eyes and the gaze in *Agamemnon* see 240*. **gold-encrusted mansions:** *chrusopastos*, 'shot through with gold', may have had an 'oriental' significance, since it is used of an honorific tiara which Xerxes bestowed on the Abderites (Hdt. 8.120). Gold had an equally sinister resonance at 438*. The noun *edethla* is an emendation, but a very likely one, providing variety with *melathra* in the strophe (770).

778 hands have been fouled: Lit., 'with filth of hands'. The masculine noun *pinos* is an interesting choice in the context of wealthy palaces, since it often refers to the greasy grime associated with poverty (Soph. *El.* 305, *OC* 1259).

779–80 the power that comes with wealth falsely praised: Lit., 'power marked counterfeit by the praise of wealth'. The metaphor in *parasēmon* is of counterfeit coinage (see 440–4* and Dem. 24.213). On wealth see 750–4*.

781 conclusion: On *terma* see 1177*.

ix] 782–974 CHORUS, AGAMEMNON, CLYTEMNESTRA [silent CASSANDRA]

Summary

The decisive episode in the play stages the homecoming of Agamemnon from Troy. As the chorus intone anapaests, perhaps moving into positions lining Agamemnon's route in a sort of guard of honour, Agamemnon and Cassandra enter the orchestra on a vehicle from the direction of the harbour (see 493–5*); the spectacle is suggestive of the iconography of weddings on Athenian black-figured vases portraying newly wedded couples as they arrive at the groom's family home standing together on a chariot accompanied by pedestrian attendants (Sutton 1997/1998). Cassandra and Agamemnon are probably accompanied by a military retinue. The elevation of the figure of the King continues the vertical axis of the visual field which will be dramatically overturned when he walks across the fabrics and when his corpse later appears sprawled in the bath. The vehicle may well have been steered by a silent driver and drawn by two real horses (see Arnott (1959) 178; in the production illustrated in Figure 4, however, it was drawn by men); in the *Iliad*, Agamemnon's elaborately decorated bronze chariot was driven by his squire Eurymedon (4.226–8), whose tomb was later in antiquity, at any rate, to be seen at Mycenae (Paus. 2.16.5). The carriage here, which may have been visibly loaded with war spoils (Seaford (2012) 198), is significant: Athena in *Eumenides* may, at least at the first production, have arrived from Troy in a chariot drawn by colts (403–6; see Arnott (1959) 177–9 and Himmelhoch (2005)); yet all the firm examples of a *human* vehicular entrance in fifth-century tragedy pertain either to barbarian characters such as the Queen and Xerxes in *Persians* or to a character portrayed as one way or another lapsing into the excessive luxury or despotism appropriate only to barbarians. Entrance on a vehicle may have been one of the tragedians' complex of dramatic 'danger signals', the significant vocabulary and symbolic acts by which the other tragedians also learned unmistakably to connote the 'otherness' of the barbarian or Greek despotic character (Hall (1989) 95–6, 205–6). Clytemnestra enters from the palace; perhaps she has altered her costume to reflect the high ceremony of the imminent royal reunion in a way that also hints at the splendour of the Persian court. The text does not indicate for certain when she appears; nobody refers to or addresses her before she speaks at 855. It is probably most plausible that she enters from the palace with her enslaved women to block Agamemnon's entry into the palace at the same time as Agamemnon arrives from the direction of the harbour.

The episode consists of the increasingly lengthy formal orations delivered on this solemn occasion by the chorus (782–809), the King (810–854) and his Queen respectively (855–913), followed by an edgy, largely stichomythic interchange between the psychologically estranged couple. It is the sole example of stichomythia between two individual characters, rather than with the chorus, in the entire tragedy, which lends it a particular tension and focus. She persuades him to tread on expensive textiles which are spread by her women slave attendants over the route leading from his vehicle to the palace doors (914–43) and he delivers his final speech of acquiescence before walking over the covered pathway into the house (944–57).

Cassandra has arrived with Agamemnon, but remains silent throughout. The vehicle and the textiles make for an awe-inspiring display of both military prowess and palatial wealth; Clytemnestra's victory in argument over her husband produces an atmosphere of dark apprehension. As

Agamemnon disappears, Clytemnestra delivers a triumphant speech in which she boasts about the family's wealth, expresses some more cryptic flattery of her husband and asks Zeus to consummate her prayer (958–74).

Anapaests

782–809 After concluding their third song and second stasimon, which has established that immorality, rather than prosperity, brings inevitable blight on a household, however rich, the chorus deliver a sequence of anapaests. Their words represent a speech of public welcome from Agamemnon's subjects, but it is a strange and uneasy one. This peculiar passage emphasises once again how inhibited public speech is in Argos, not least since the chorus spend more than half of what is supposed to be a speech of welcome self-consciously reflecting on what the proper tone and content of such a speech should be.

782–4 Greetings ... Atreus: The chorus begin grandiloquently enough, with Agamemnon's title, recent achievement and paternal inheritance. On the term *basileus* see 83–4*; on the possible connotations of 'sacker' see 472*. **Offspring:** The neuter noun *genethlon* is a rather elevated and formal word to use in an address; Agamemnon deploys it when addressing Clytemnestra at 914*.

786 either exceeding or falling short of: The mixed metaphors, coming from archery and racing respectively, are both from the sphere of athletics: see 171–2* and 364–5*.

787 the appropriate degree of politeness: Lit., 'the due measure of reciprocal favour'. On the word *charis* see 182–3*.

788–9 think that appearances are paramount: Lit., 'honour first seeming to be'. On the attention given in this play to the epistemological problem of distinguishing fact from appearance or opinion see Introduction, pp. 101–2. **what is right:** On *dikē* see 250–1*.

790–2 When someone's unsuccessful ... sigh: Aeschylus' dissection of hypocrisy in social interactions is psychologically acute. The chorus is describing hypocritical behaviour here in order to prepare Agamemnon for imminent criticism coming from people of inferior status. **no real pang ... core:** Lit., 'no bite of distress approaches the liver'. On the liver as seat of emotions see 432*, and on Aeschylus' physiology of the emotions, Introduction, p. 62.

793–4 feigning similar expressions: This seems to be the meaning of *homoioprepeis*. **force themselves to smile:** Lit., 'forcing [middle participle] their unsmiling faces'. The verb *biazesthai* feels strong in the context:

see 1509*. The audience may have been reminded of the description of a mutinous wife of a powerful male, Hera in the *Iliad*: angered by Zeus, and plotting to subvert his plan to support the Trojans for a time, she sat down among the gods, 'and she laughed with her lips, but her forehead above her dark brows was furrowed' (15.101–3).

795 judge of livestock: While the neuter plural noun *probata* is found in Homer denoting flocks of sheep and herds of cattle (*Il.* 14.124 and 23.550), this is probably an Aeschylean coinage. It may add a homely touch to the chorus' language, as do some of the other pastoral images (128–30*), but since they are really talking about Agamemnon's potential response to them it may also be suggestive of the Homeric phrase for a ruler, particularly Agamemnon, 'shepherd of the people' (e.g. *Il.* 2.243).

796–8 can't be taken in ... sham: Lit., 'it is not possible for eyes of a man to escape [his] notice, which although seeming [to come from] a kindly-minded attitude, fawn with watery fondness', a rather awkward change in construction after the indefinite clause in 795*. **fawning:** The faked blandishments of false friends are implicitly compared with a dog wagging its tail and cajoling its master: see 725–6* and 1228–30*. **is a sham:** The adjective *hudarēs* may continue the image of the judge of livestock, since it seems to have been used for the watery, pale grey colour of the eyes of sheep (Aristot. *GA* 779a322). But its more usual reference is to wine that has been excessively watered down (Pherecrates fr. 76.2, Xen. *Laconian Constitution* 1.3). It is also used metaphorically, of *philia*, to designate less intense forms of friendship, at Aristot. *Pol.* 2.1262b15. On eyes see 240*.

799–801 for Helen's sake: This is the first time that the chorus have named Helen except in the lyric song they have just completed: on the cliché see 60–2*. **you were portrayed most inartistically:** Lit., 'you were drawn/painted away from the Muses'. Agamemnon cut an unattractive or badly painted figure. The artwork analogy prompts the audience to visualise a scene at Aulis—perhaps the identical scene in which Iphigenia had been remembered, gagged in her yellow gown and looking like a figure in a painting (242–3*). This is a rare instance in tragedy of a character being likened to a figure in an artwork that is not beautiful: see Hall (2006) 134–6. It has sometimes been argued that *gegrammenos* here means not 'painted' but 'written', implying that Agamemnon is 'inscribed' upon the memory (Rose (1958) 58–9). It was once even suggested that the metaphor is an unusually transparent reference to the circumstances of the tragic competitions external to the world of the play, and that it alludes to the judges writing down their verdicts (as at Lysias 4.3): Agamemnon's conduct at Aulis was judged by his Argive chorus to have been the work of a 'bungler' at the tragic art (Petersen (1911) 22–3). Yet Triclinius was correct in seeing how antiquity understood the metaphor in his interlinear gloss on the passage, *ezōgraphēmenos*, which unequivocally means 'painted'.

802 exercising poor judgement: Lit., 'not steering the rudder of your understanding well', a difficult metaphor to translate into natural-sounding English, even though the context of the mustering of the fleet at Aulis makes the maritime metaphor relevant to the chorus' general point. On *prapides* see 378–80*.

803–4 in using sacrifices to stir up bravado: Lit. 'furnishing dying men with recklessness from sacrifices'. On *thrasos* see 168–9*, 768–71*. If the necessary emendation that inserts the word 'sacrifices' is correct, which is probable, the chorus took a very different view of the sacrifice of Iphigenia from that taken by the younger men who were stranded at Aulis waiting to sail. See also 'led out for sacrifice' (641*). **dying:** The present participle suggests that the chorus is thinking of the parlous conditions endured by the Greek seamen at Aulis which they had earlier described at 188–98, but there is a possibility that they also refer to all the subsequent deaths at Troy itself. As Odysseus says to the ghost of Agamemnon in *Odyssey* 11.438, without specifying when or where, 'For Helen's sake many of us died.'

805 with all my heart: Lit., 'not from the top surface of my heart'; it would be a challenge to translate the litotes here, a figure to which 'no hard feelings' corresponds in English.

806 I extend goodwill: Lit., '[I am] benevolent'. The chorus here present themselves as the formal spokesmen of the whole city-state.

807 discover by enquiry: This is the force of the verb *diapeuthesthai*, a poetical form of *diapunthanesthai* (see Plato, *Symp.* 172a). The chorus is tactfully suggesting that Agamemnon investigate, rather than wait to be told, whose conduct has been satisfactory.

808–9 guarding the state: Since the verb *oikourein* suggests keeping watch over or from within the domestic household (Soph. *Phil.* 1328, *OC* 343, Plato. *Rep.* 5.451d), despite the object 'state', and the mention of (male) citizens, the chorus are here nudging Agamemnon to think of Clytemnestra (and possibly Aegisthus—see below, 1123–6*) without of course being able to say so explicitly. **unsuitably:** On this ethical meaning of *akairōs* see Xen. *Cav.* 7.6. It is here a euphemism; the opposite of *dikaiōs* should be the much stronger adverb *adikōs*.

810 local gods: Agamemnon is punctilious about prioritising gods in his homecoming address, but it might be expected that he would take care to please them by listing them by name and function, or at least by detailed category, as Clytemnestra had at 88–91*. It is particularly noticeable that he does not mention any household gods (yet) or Zeus Xenios (60–2*), whom the chorus have so closely and repeatedly associated with the suffering inflicted on Troy. Nor does he thank any gods for his safe return after a dangerous storm. Agamemnon, indeed, turns what is supposed to be a prayer of gratitude into a violent account of Argive militarism.

811   who share the credit: It might be felt to be hubristic to claim that the credit is to be shared between him and the gods. It would be more theologically expedient simply to thank them.

812   the penalty I exacted: The relative pronoun (not translated into English) is genitive by attraction, since *prassesthai* takes double accusatives. It is striking that Agamemnon uses the egocentric first person singular rather than the plural that could encompass both his fellow soldiers and the gods.

813–17   For the gods did not hear any cases made: Lit., 'not hearing legal suits from a tongue'. Agamemnon 'bizarrely imagines the gods voting using the technical vocabulary of Athenian democratic procedures' (Shilo (2023) 36) in imagining the possibility of the gods holding a trial of some kind to hear the cases made by the Greeks and the Trojans respectively. But the account of the trial is cut short so that it consisted only of the jurors' votes, and all the votes going into the urn that led to conviction rather than the one that led to acquittal; on legal language see 41*. Cassandra echoes this image at 1287–90*. **Priam's:** The recurring proper name (40*) is here stressed by enjambement. **unanimously:** Lit., 'without oscillation'; see 349*. **urn:** The primary meaning of the neuter noun *teuchos* is a piece of gear or equipment, but it can also signify a kind of vessel or container. In the *Oresteia*, it links the gods' imaginary voting urn here with cinerary urns visualised in the imagination (435), Agamemnon's bathtub (1128), the visible vases used in ritual libations (*Choeph.* 99) and the visible urns used at Orestes' trial in Athens (*Eum.* 742). **in favour of the murderous destruction:** Lit., 'with respect to the man-killing destructions'. **The only thing ... was hope:** Lit., 'To the opposite urn hope was coming near, but it was not filled by the hand', or, alternatively, 'To the opposite urn, hope of the hand was coming near, but it was not filled'. On *elpis*, hope, see 100–3*.

818   smoke: Smoke featured in a different way, to indicate the chorus' distrust of smoke from beacon-signals, at 496–7.

819–20   winds of destruction ... blowing: Lit., 'the storms of destruction are *alive*'. On winds as a central image see 692*, and on *atē*, 359–61*. **dying embers:** At 435 and 443 *spodos* referred to the ashes not of the dead Trojans and their city but of the dead Argives returned in urns from Troy. The destruction has afflicted both sides. The Greek points a contrast between the winds of destruction that live and the embers that are dying at the same time. **the greasy vapours of erstwhile wealth:** Lit., 'the fatty winds of wealth'. An unusual image, implying that the smoke from a rich city in ruins will somehow be of a particularly greasy kind.

821–4 we owe the gods a permanent debt of gratitude: Lit., 'we should pay a much-remembered favour'. On the meaning of *charis* see 182–3*, and on memory, 34–9*. **we put up a fence of fury:** Lit., 'we fenced furious fixtures for ourselves'; the Argive fury has been transferred to their military fortifications and equipment. It is almost shocking that Agamemnon uses the first person, even if in the plural, when ostensibly thanking the gods. Clytemnestra uses the verb *phrassein* indirectly of herself luring Agamemnon into a position of vulnerability in her speech over his corpse at 1376*. **for a woman's sake:** On this wearisomely reiterated formula see 60–2*. **it has been pulverised by the beast of Argos:** Lit., 'the Argive beast pulverised the city'. The neuter noun *dakos* is used of the Theban Sphinx at Aesch. *Sept.* 558 and of ravening marine beasts that eat land mammals at *PV* 583. Here the line seems to conjure a picture of the Greek army as a noxious animal, in the subsequent line defined as the children of a horse, thus suggesting the wooden horse. **pulverised:** In a fragment of Aeschylus' *Toxotides*, the same verb is used of Actaeon's dogs tearing him limb from limb (fr. 244). Agamemnon's pleasure in the sheer extremes of the destruction inflicted on Troy goes far beyond what the context of thanks to the gods requires.

826 leapt and charged: Lit., 'launched its leap'. The image probably suggests the Greeks leaping out of the wooden horse. **at the waning of the Pleiades:** The star-nymphs, daughters of the Titan Atlas, were also known as the *Peleiades* (doves); Aeschylus fr. 312.3–4 says 'as wingless Peleiades they have the form of phantoms of the night', i.e. stars, on which see 4*. Some ancient etymologists believed their name was related to the verb *plein*, 'sail', because the constellation's visibility in Greece was commensurate with the sailing season (spring to the beginning of November): Hesiod, *Works* 618–20, 'But when the Pleiades and strong Orion begin to set, then remember to plough in season. But if desire for uncomfortable seafaring seize you; when the Pleiades plunge into the misty sea to escape Orion's rude strength, then truly gales of all kinds rage.' If the Greeks launched the final assault on Troy when the Pleiades were setting, then they undertook the return voyage at a hazardous time of year. Sommerstein (2009) 95 n.171 comments that this contradicts the usual tradition that Troy fell in the month of Thargelion (May/June), a tradition already found in fifth-century sources, and thus implies that the commanders made a rash and irresponsible decision to sail at that time.

827   Vaulting high over the ramparts: This is a bold and terrifying image. For the walls and towers of Troy see also 357 and 1168–70*. **ravenous lion:** When the Pleiades set, the constellation Leo reaches its zenith; Agamemnon is suggesting that the Argive army is the terrestrial counterpart of this cosmic entity, developing further the stellar theme first introduced by the Watchman (6–7*); see Pfundstein (2003). Lions have been associated previously in the play with both the wrath of Artemis and the destructive Helen–Paris partnership 141*, 735–6*. Although lions are symbols of power and royalty prominent in e.g. Babylonian and Hittite architectural decoration, and appear in *Gilgamesh*, they are phenomenally popular in Mycenaean art (Thomas (2004)) and regarded in Homer as one of the most mighty of beasts (*Il.* 17.20–1). The *Iliad* contains at least 28 similes in which heroic aggression is compared with a lion on the attack (see Hall (2025) ch. 5), and Alden (2005) argues that the Ionian Greeks, at least, were familiar with lions and lion hunting. The adjective *ōmēstēs* literally translates as 'eating raw flesh', and is used of fauna and monsters that predate on human flesh, including birds (*Il.* 11.454) dogs (*Il.* 22.67), fish (*Il.* 24.82), the Echidna and Cerberus (Hes. *Theog.* 300, 311), as well as rhetorically characterising humans as cannibalistic when they are extremely angry with another human (e.g. *Il.* 24.207; see Hall (1989) 27, 53 and n.175, 105 and n. 11, 126, 148).

828   slurped: This crude English word has been selected to suggest the onomatopoeic effect of the Greek *eleixan*, 'lapped' or 'licked up'. Clytemnestra uses the same verb of the way the Erinyes lap up her libations at *Eum.* 106. **royal blood:** Although the adjective *turannikos* certainly began in the fifth century BCE to acquire negative overtones associated with despotic behaviour, especially at Athens and in other democracies (Ar. *Wasps* 507, *Frogs* 108, Thuc. 6.60), in tragedy (including elsewhere in the *Oresteia*), since this genre was set in a distant, pre-democratic past, it can still simply 'kingly' or 'regal': see also *Choeph.* 479, Soph. *OC* 373, Eur. *Med.* 348, 740. But no doubt the audience could detect ambiguity here. There is certainly no ambiguity later when the chorus fear that there has been attempt to introduce a tyranny (1354–5*) and say that Aegisthus is a tyrant (1633*). See also 543*. On blood see 209–10*.

829   has been my extended preliminary address: Lit., 'I prolonged this preliminary address'. On *phroimion* see 31*. Agamemnon is prone to commenting on the length of speeches: see 916*. **to the gods:** For a purported address to the gods, the thanks to them were meagre in comparison with the part of the speech that was focused on his and the Greeks' own bloodthirsty achievements.

830–1   your sentiments ... view: Lit., 'In regard to your thinking, hearing it I remember it, I say the same things and you have me as an advocate.' This is a rather long-winded way of saying 'I reciprocate your sentiments'. Presumably Agamemnon is referring only to the last part of the chorus' speech at 805–9; he can scarcely share their view of the episode at Aulis, which it was courageous of them to mention, and so chooses to overlook that section of what they said. On legal language in the play see 41*. **am mindful of:** By intonation an actor could make this sound threatening. Is Agamemnon saying that he will not forget that they brought up the Aulis episode as soon as he arrived home? **advocate:** A *sunēgoros* in the strict legal sense was at Athens usually a public advocate selected by the state to conduct public prosecutions or defend laws against proposed changes (Ar. *Ach.* 715, *Wasps* 482), but the term occasionally just means 'in agreement with' in a solemn context (Soph. *Trach.* 1165); on legal language see 41*. Judging from what Agamemnon goes on to say, he means that he is in agreement with the need to discover who has behaved in his interests in his absence, and who, out of envy, has not; the latter attitude he has encountered all too often.

833   without envy: A significant emotion in this play (134–7* and 921–2*). Lines 832–8 were central to the psychoanalyst Melanie Klein's theory of envy as a primary infantile anxiety (Klein (1963) 280–1). In Pindar's epinician odes, negotiating the pitfalls of *phthonos* in others was a central concern of the victor at the games; his glorious homecoming was expected to arouse envious feelings in his fellow citizens: see Kirkwood (1984). For Plato, it is the opposite of *eunoia*, goodwill (*Laws* 1.635b); Aristotle says that true *philia* not only excludes any envy towards *philoi* but entails not even caring whether the *philos* knows that you have done something to assist them (*Eud. Eth.* 7.1239a). Agamemnon is ostensibly praising the chorus for expressing their goodwill towards him, but, as the speech continues, it emerges that he has bitter memories in mind of others' ill-will.

834–5   venom of malice: Lit., 'ill-willed venom'. At *Eum.* 478–9, Athena fears that if the Erinyes do not get their way they will infect the ground with the venom exuding from their thoughts. On *dusphrōn* see 547*. **borne ... malady:** Lit., 'the burden for the person who has acquired the disease'. It is not altogether clear whether the *nosos* refers to envy or the venom of ill-will, although the general sense that such negative emotions reduplicate themselves is clear. On medical imagery see 17*; on difficult emotions metaphorically seen as a burden see also 161–3.

836–7 his own pain ... others' success: Aeschylus brilliantly captures the combination of inwardly and outwardly directed negativity that is experienced by the individual convulsed by envy. The adjective *thuraios* means 'out of doors', so 'away from home', and by extension, as here, refers to someone in another household.

838–40 mirror of social interaction: This is a striking image for the process of learning an associate's true nature from prolonged exposure to them. Cf. Eur. *Hipp.* 429. **that the loyalty ... illusion:** Lit., 'the phantom of a shadow, men seeming to wish me well'. A metaphorical shadow is a frequent element in ancient Greek proverbial musings on the fragility of the human condition (see Cassandra's final speech at 1328*). Agamemnon knows well that people feign loyalty towards powerful figures, a point well brought out in the detailed discussion of this passage in Bollack (1983). In the *Iliad*, however, he requires displays of obedience without seeming to care whether they are sincere or not.

841 Only Odysseus: Although the audience have certainly been nudged to wonder what happened to Odysseus in the storm at 671*, this is the first (and only) time he is explicitly named in *Agamemnon*. **who didn't want to sail:** The story of Odysseus' attempt to avoid joining the expedition was mentioned in the *Odyssey* (24.117), where the ghost of Agamemnon remembers that it took a whole month to persuade him to join; it was related in the *Cypria*: when the party gathering the Greek leaders arrived on Ithaca, they detect 'Odysseus when he pretends to be mad, not wishing to join the expedition, by seizing his son Telemachus for punishment at the suggestion of Palamedes'. The story, to which reference was almost certainly made in Aeschylus' lost *Palamedes*, is told in further detail in Apollodorus' *Epitome* 3.7: the infant Telemachus was placed in the path of Odysseus' plough to expose that his madness was feigned.

842 once he was harnessed ... partnership: Lit., 'yoked he was my ready partner-horse'. On yoking see 326–8*. The adjective *seiraphoros* literally refers to the 'trace-horse', one that is harnessed at the side of the pair under the yoke, and assists them, so it can mean that it is a horse which, although cooperating, has relatively light work (see 1640*). But here, although it will have gained force from Agamemnon's arrival on a vehicle, it seems simply to be a metaphor for a cooperative partner. Odysseus is indeed Agamemnon's most trusted lieutenant in the *Iliad*, where his behaviour is cool and detached, quite unlike any of the other heroes: see Pache (2000). Agamemnon of course did fall out with most of the others, including Achilles and Ajax. The question here is what he is implying about Menelaus: the epic tradition did know of at least two occasions on which the Atreidai had quarrelled, and even a version in which the two had been consistent rivals for overall command. In the *Odyssey*, Nestor tells Telemachus that the brothers had quarrelled after the sack of Troy; Menelaus wanted an immediate departure, while Agamemnon wanted the Achaeans to remain. This was followed by another quarrel on Tenedos (3.136–64). Odysseus originally aligned in it with Menelaus but returned to Agamemnon's side. The quarrel tradition also featured in the cyclic *Nostoi*, and the brothers' disputes over the sacrifice of Iphigenia dramatised in Euripides' *Iphigenia in Aulis* may also have been prefigured by an epic source: see Sammons (2014). Agamemnon's singling out of Odysseus throws into sharp relief his failure to thank any of the other Greek chieftains or even common soldiers for their participation, or to mention his brother; it also may nudge the audience to remember that Agamemnon described, when his ghost met Odysseus in the Underworld, how he was murdered on return to Argos (*Od.* 11.385–465).

842–3 This statement applies: Lit., 'I speak about [him]'. Agamemnon thus rounds off his perfunctory compliment (or epitaph) to the sole Greek chieftain he feels has not let him down.

844–6 our collective gods: See 88–91*. **we shall set up an assembly to debate and deliberate:** Lit., 'having set up debates in assembly we shall deliberate'. On *agōnas* see 513*. A *panēguris* often refers to a gathering at a religious festival (Pind. *Ol.* 9.96), but it can denote any large meeting or assembly (Eur. *Heraclid.* 239, Thuc. 5.50). On deliberation see 10–11* and *bouleuteon* in the next sentence at 847. Agamemnon wants to emphasise publicly that his monarchy is at least one that has a formal procedure for consulting the wider populace.

848 healing: See 512* and, on medical imagery in the play, 17*.

849–50 This sentence uses the famous metaphor of the physical body to represent the state. The explicit expression *sōma politeias* does not seem to be used before the fourth century (Din. 1.110, Aristot., *Pol.* 5.1302b34–42, Renehan (1982) s.v. *sōma*), so this is a bold early instance in ancient Greek thought of the 'body politic' figure, on which see Brock (2000) 69–94. **by cauterisation or surgery:** For this technical sense of the verb *kaiein* see Hippocrates, *Art.* 11. The two verbs seem to have been regularly paired, but usually the other way round (Plat. *Gorg.* 480c, 521e; Xen. *An.* 5.5.18). **graciously:** The adverb jars in what could be taken as a rather threatening metaphor about burning away or excising an element of the citizen body. The several attempts which have been made to use these lines as evidence for Agamemnon's kind and responsible paternalism towards his people are wholly unconvincing.

851–3   household hearth: Lit., 'fireside home'. See 427–8* and 1310*. **gods:** The hearth was dedicated to the household gods dutifully tended together by the ideal husband and wife, wrote the Stoic Hierocles in his *On Marriage* (ed. Ramelli (2009) 76–7). **my attendant Victory remain constant:** Lit.: 'Victory, since she has followed me, remain firmly'. Agamemnon's closing words strike a strident note in comparison with the choral refrains earlier, where the wish is that the victory should go to what is 'good' (121*, 139, 158–9*). The wording implies that Victory (*Nikē*) has some agency, and so is semi-personified in Agamemnon's mind. Although often represented as an avatar of Athena, who was worshipped widely as Athena *Nikē*, *Nikē* in Hesiod is an independent goddess, the daughter of Styx and Pallas the giant; she helped Zeus rebel against Kronos and was granted permanent residence with Zeus in return (*Theog.* 373–401). In epinician odes she is goddess of victory in athletics and musical competitions (Pind. *Nem.* 5.42, *Isthm.* 2.26), but *Nikē* seems to have been adopted widely as the giver of military success around the time of the Persian Wars. She was mentioned as an arbitrator of the fortunes of war in an oracle of Bacis quoted by Herodotus (8.7).

854   Citizens: Clytemnestra might have been expected to address her husband first. She is concerned first and foremost with controlling the response of the Argives to the unfolding events. She does not seem concerned to reassure Agamemnon about her relationship with the citizens, nor about their wellbeing, either, despite their implication that she was acting officially as some kind of regent in his absence (259–60*): she matches her husband in the self-centredness of her opening speech in this encounter. **you respected elders of Argos:** Lit., 'this revered body of Argives'. A formal and high-flown title. In *Persians*, the chorus address the Queen as *presbos* to the Persians (623). See also 1393*. Lucas (1954) 60 was not unjustified in calling this oration 'perhaps the greatest speech in all Greek drama'.

856–7   on the subject of my love for my man: Lit., 'about my man-loving ways'. The adjective *philanōr* implies the woman's desire for the man especially (see 411*, where it is used in an erotic sense in relation to Helen); at Aesch. *Pers.* 136 the Persian wives whose men are far away in Greece are said to be smitten by a husband-loving desire. But for those cognisant of Clytemnestra's relationship with Aegisthus, the double meaning here is disturbing.

857–8 People get over their timidity eventually: Lit., 'In time, terror among humans wanes'. Clytemnestra's surface meaning is that she has somehow learned not to be so nervous about speaking publicly, but the idea that she now has more courage than at a previous time would sound threatening to those who anticipate that she might imminently seek revenge for much earlier outrages.

858–60 From my own experience and no one else's: Lit., 'not learning from others'. **intolerable:** Again, the reason why life was so difficult for her to bear is open to interpretation.

862 terrible: The adjective *ekpaglos* and the adverb *ekpaglōs* are often found in Homer charactering powerful emotions or states of mind (*Il.* 2.223 of anger, 3.57 of a yearning for home, 9.238 of madness, *Od.* 11.437 of hatred, 15.35 of grief).

863 malign rumours: On the adjective *palinkotos* see 571*. Clytemnestra, like her husband, is suspicious of the motives of all who interact with her. In this play, rumours are a powerful force, which both enrich its epistemological focus on the difficulty of obtaining certain knowledge and indicate its interest in the way that public opinions can affect political outcomes even in an undemocratic constitution (see 276*). Agamemnon uses the same feminine noun, *klēdōn*, in a more positive way of his own reputation at 927*.

864–5 for one messenger after another to arrive: Lit., 'and one to come, but another to bring in addition'. **reporting news:** These words have been inserted into the translation to make sense in English. **shrieking it out to the whole household:** Clytemnestra, who likes to be in control of the flow of information, implies that the messengers of doom should have passed their information to her privately. On the verb *laskein* see 594–5*.

866–8 When it comes to injuries … number: Lit., 'And if the man here had happened to receive so many injuries'. Agamemnon suffers one injury in battle in the *Iliad*, when the Trojan Coön stabs him below the elbow. He continues fighting and killing, with the blood welling up, until the wound dries, at which point the pain becomes unendurable and he retreats to the ships in his chariot (11.248–83). **rumours:** See 276* and, on *phatis*, 8*. **kept being conveyed:** The imperfect tense suggests repeated occurrence. **you'd say … net:** Lit., 'he would have been bored through more than a net to speak of'. This crude expression brings to mind the picture of Agamemnon's body pierced several times, which no doubt Clytemnestra has painted many times in her mind. *tetrainein* implies strong violence, but is found in medical contexts (Hipp. *De Aër.* 9). On the image of the net see 357*.

869 as frequently as reports were indicating: Lit., 'as reports were proliferating'.

870 like a second Geryon with three bodies: The Greek does not use any simile marker. Like most mythical allusions in *Agamemnon*, the comparison does not work except to prove a negative. Geryon was a monstrous cattle herdsman with three heads, son of Chrysaor and Callirhoe (Hesiod *Theog.* 287–94), who lived in the far west on a red island. One of Heracles' labours was to take Geryon's cattle and bring them to Eurystheus. The story was told most influentially in Stesichorus' lyric epic *Geryoneis* (Stesichorus frr. S7-S87) and is illustrated in archaic art (Brize (1980)). On the significance of the number three see 33*.

871–2 he'd boast ... I can't tell about the lower: Lit., 'he would claim that he had received triple cloaks of earth, much above and I don't speak of the one beneath'. The verb *exauchein* is a strengthened form of *auchein*, on which see 506*. The text has often thought to be corrupt. Many editors delete line 872 altogether. One reason is the similarity of the first two words to those of line 875, but near-repetition sound-linking two ostensibly different types of subject matter is not atypical of Aeschylean style. Moreover, the crudity of the image and the language are not as inappropriate as some have argued it is to the veiled insolence, violence and strangeness of Clytemnestra's rhetoric here (see also 1440–3*). Heracles' fight with Geryon was a popular theme in Athenian sixth-century vase-painting, for example in the black-figure amphora in the Cabinet des Médailles, Paris (no. 202). In this picture Geryon has three heads and upper torsos, but his lower torso and legs are those of a single individual. Clytemnestra invites speculation about the logistics of killing and burying such a three-headed creature. She implies that all three of Geryon's upper bodies needed to be killed but that far less soil was needed to bury his lower half—a flamboyantly gruesome train of thought in any context, let alone an ostensibly joyful speech of welcome to a loved one.

874 malign rumours: See 276* and 863*.

875–6 often cut me down ... neck: Lit., 'untied many nooses above from my neck violently tied'. A convoluted way of saying 'I often tried to hang myself, but others stopped me'; perhaps, while wanting to shock Agamemnon by telling him she had attempted suicide repeatedly, she is trying to create the impression that she is employing delicacy in her language. The effect after the previous bald images of Agamemnon's body pierced like a net or buried like Geryon's is bizarre. Women do take their own lives in tragedy, by both stabbing and hanging themselves: see Loraux

(1987) and Hall (2024) 107, 134. But proving wifely devotion by claiming to have attempted suicide is a rhetorical extravagance without parallel in the genre. The feminine noun *artanē* is used of the noose with which Jocasta hangs herself in Sophocles, *OT* 1266 and *Ant.* 54.

877–9   our child: The Greek does not make the gender of the child immediately clear, and the audience knew from the mythical tradition that Iphigenia and Orestes had at least one sister. The lengthy postponement of Orestes' name by hyperbaton heightens the suspense as to what Clytemnestra is about to say. **trustee of our mutual pledges:** Lit., 'authority over my pledges and yours'. These words sound oddly inappropriate in reference to a marriage where one parent has already killed another of the mutual children. **Orestes:** This is the first time the figure who gave his name to the whole tetralogy has been mentioned.

880–1   ally Strophius the Phocian … well-disposed to us: Strophius was king of Phocis, on the north coast of the Corinthian Gulf, a largely pastoral district in which Delphi was located. Mythographers made him Agamemnon's brother-in-law; he married Agamemnon's sister, who is variously named Anaxibia, Astyocheia or Cydragora (Paus. 2.29.4, Hyg. *Fab.* 117, schol. Eur. *Or.* 33), and Pylades was their son. Pindar says that Orestes 'went to the friend of the family, the old man Strophius, who dwelled at the foot of Parnassus. But at last, with the help of Ares, he [i.e. Orestes] killed his mother and laid Aegisthus low in blood' (*Isthm.* 11.34–7). The true reason why Orestes was sent to Phocis, which was presumably the desire of Clytemnestra and/or Aegisthus to obstruct his claim to the Argive throne if/when Agamemnon died, is not discussed in *Agamemnon*, but see 1645–7*.

881–4   twin disasters: It is not clear how far the two are causally related since the construction changes with the introduction of the conditional protasis to describe the second danger. **danger you were in:** The obvious meaning is that Agamemnon's life was in danger because he was fighting a war, and that if he died there would be an opportunity for revolution at Argos. But the audience knew he had come into conflict with several of his own leaders (see 842*) as well as facing a threatened mutiny from the common soldiers led by Thersites in *Iliad* book 2. Aeschylus, who had been born into the last years of the Peisistratid tyranny at Athens and watched it fall, had an ear finely attuned to the paranoia of those in power. **and the possibility that the populace might talk itself into anarchy:** Lit., 'and if people-uttered anarchy'. Again, this could refer to an attempt at revolution in Argos if news came of Agamemnon's death, or a revolution that had become more likely in his absence, or both. The adjective *dēmothrous* is used by Agamemnon subsequently (938*). The primary meaning of the feminine abstract noun *anarchia* is neutral, 'absence of a leader' (see Aesch. *Suppl.* 906, Hdt. 9.23), in which case Clytemnestra's fear may be of a revolution in favour of a democratic constitution rather than a monarchy, tyranny or oligarchy. But it can also mean 'lawlessness' or civic 'disorder' in a derogatory sense (Thuc. 6.72; Plato. *Rep.* 9.575a, Aristot. *Pol.* 5.1302b29). This instance may contain both senses at the same time. At *Eumenides* 696 Athena instructs the Athenians to avoid both anarchy and despotism.

overthrow the Council: The feminine noun *boulē* in this concrete sense was the word used of the councils of Greek chieftains in the *Iliad* (2.53), but also denoted the Athenian Council of 500 established by Cleisthenes (Hdt. 9.5, Ar. *Wasps* 590, Antiphon 6.40), although with qualification it could also refer to the council of the Areopagus (Aeschines 3.20, Thuc. 66). On deliberation see also 10–11*. On the implied workings of the political system at Argos in *Agamemnon* see Introduction, pp. 9–13. Herodotus says that at the time of Thermopylae, at any rate, Argos had both a monarch and an active and powerful *boulē* (7.149). It is interesting that Clytemnestra does not openly say that there was a danger of the people overthrowing the monarchy altogether.

884–5 it's human nature … down: Lit., '[It is] innate to humans to trample the fallen man more'. The verb *laktizein* is used of arrogant behaviour also at 381* and 1624*; on trampling see 369–72*. This sentence sounds as though it might be paraphrasing a well-known proverb (see Introduction, p. 74); compare Soph. *Ant.* 1029–30.

886 explanation: The feminine noun *skēpsis* can mean a plea in a court of law (LSJ s.v. *skēpsis* I.2), but in literary texts it usually has a negative overtone like the English 'excuse' or 'pretext' (Soph. *El.* 584, Hdt. 1.147, Dem. 19.100). It is therefore a strange and unusually honest word for Clytemnestra to choose here. **no deceit:** Clytemnestra associates herself, even if to deny it, with guile: see the adjective *dolios* at 154–5* and other references to trickery collected at 1129*.

887–90 streaming tears: Lit., 'onslaught-fountains of crying'. The adjective *epissutos* is used of the violent onslaught of pains during Cassandra's vatic seizure at 1150*. It is a surprisingly violent word to use of weeping episodes. Clytemnestra implies that she has stopped weeping now (*men*) only because the beacon relay finally gave her the message that Agamemnon's arrival was imminent, but (*de*) that her eyes remain sore. As ever, her language opens her motivations to more than one interpretation: as a bereaved mother, unable to avenge her child because the man responsible was away, whose absence had she been weeping for? On tears see 270*. **drop:** On the imagery and language of dripping see also 560–2*. **But my eyes:** Lit., 'I have damages in my late-sleeping eyes, weeping for the watchfires for you' (on eyes see 240*). She had implied to the chorus at 315–16* that she and her husband had been in communication about the beacon relay, and mentioning it in his presence here seems to confirm this.

891–4   I was repeatedly woken: The adverb is added to express the force of the imperfect tense. **low hum:** Lit., 'light flappings'. The feminine noun *rhipē* means a gust of wind, but is used of the sonic effect made by the flapping of wings (Aesch. *PV* 126) and even the quivering, vibrato effect of the notes sounded when a lyre's strings are struck (Pind. *Pyth*. 1.10). **a buzzing mosquito:** This is a vivid detail conveying sensorily the misery of hot summer nights spent in emotional pain, ironically recalling Penelope's complaint about her sleepless nights without Odysseus (*Od*. 19.515–17). On the fauna imagery in the play see Introduction, pp. 67–9. **you suffer more than was possible during the time I was asleep:** Lit., 'sufferings concerning you more than the time coincident with sleep'. Conacher (1987) 36 suggests that this reference suggests 'Clytemnestra's secret memory of another, adulterous, bed-fellow'. Clytemnestra may be telling the truth about her dreamlife here, but she does not say what emotions the visions of Agamemnon suffering aroused in her—despair or vengeful pleasure. Aeschylus' understanding of the different way that time works in the world of dreams—it can be accelerated or decelerated (see Hom. *Il*. 22.199–201) vastly in comparison with the 'real time' of waking experience—is noteworthy. On sleep see 179–80*.

895–6   Now, however: After no fewer than 40 lines on her own experience of the time covered by the Trojan expedition, she finally begins to talk about her husband, although still not addressing him directly in the second person (see 905*). **I'd salute my husband here:** Lit., 'I would call this husband here'. **the dog which watches the cattle-pens:** On canine, animal and pastoral imagery in the play see 3* and 128–30*. This is the first of seven honorific titular phrases she applies to Agamemnon in the course of this sentence. The hyperbolic adulation is so unlike the normal Hellenic mode of panegyric discourse that it prompted its wholesale excision by Dindorf (1870) xcii. She will return to this vein of rhetoric in the speech she delivers as Agamemnon enters the palace (968–72*). Ulrich von Wilamowitz Moellendorff (1927) 287–8 observed that several of these specific comparisons find astonishingly close parallels in an Egyptian hymn of the Middle Kingdom to Khakaure Sesostris III discovered on a hieratic papyrus (English translation in

Lichtheim (1973–80) vol. 1, 199–200), but Kranz (1933) 102 *may* have overstated the case in assuming that Aeschylus was acquainted with specific Egyptian literature. The important point is that he had a clear idea of the kind of anaphoric encomia rendered to barbarian monarchs by their subjects (see the Egyptian Danaids' heavily anaphoric panegyric at Aesch. *Suppliants* 370–5), and that his audience would have responded to the hubristic and un-Greek tone of Clytemnestra's language (Hall (1989) 206–7) as well as to its funereal overtones (Seaford (1984)).

897–8 forestay on which the ship's safety depends: Lit., 'forestay saviour of the ship'. The forestay is the most important part of the standing rigging on a sailed ship. Standing rigging means that it remains in the same position at the same tension and is not adjusted. It supports the weight of the sail and prevents it from falling backwards. See Hom. *Od.* 2.425, 12.409, *Il.* 1.434. On naval imagery, much of it defining kingly power, as here, see 108–15*. At *Choeph.* 264, the chorus address Orestes and Electra as 'saviours (*sōtēres*) of your fathers' hearth'; on the title *sōtēr* see also 245–7*, 512*. **pillar ... foundation:** Lit., 'footed pillar of the high roof'. Euripides seems to have had this passage in mind when Iphigenia, stranded among the Taurians, dreams that Orestes is a pillar of her family's ancestral palace and concludes that 'male children are pillars of the household' (Eur. *IT* 50–57). The adjective *podērēs*, which appears with a more literal reference to real feet in a macabre context at 1594*, often mean 'floor-length' in relation to robes (Eur. *Bacch.* 833, Xen. *Cyr.* 6.4.2), and may imply the long sweeping vertical line drawn by the pillar supporting the highest part of the ceiling. It might, however, refer to the separate base of an Ionic or Corinthian column. In either case, the pillar seems to be seen as performing the same function in a building as the forestay does on a ship. On architectural metaphors see 1283*. **only child:** Clytemnestra, interestingly, does not specify the child's gender: the adjective *monogenēs* is usually applied to sons to mean 'sole son' and not 'sole child'. Agamemnon, of course, had more than one daughter but only one son. Hesiod recommends having only a single son to avoid poverty and division of property (*Works* 376), but the value attached to a single son is clear from Herodotus 7.221, where the seer Megistias of Acarnania seizes an opportunity to send his 'only-born son', *mounogenēs pais*, away from Thermopylae before the battle.

899–900 land ... storm: These two comparisons resonate in the context of the terrible storm at sea from which Agamemnon was lucky enough to escape: see 654–70. On hope see 100–3* and on naval imagery see 108–15*.

There is a sinister echo here of *Odyssey* 23.233–40, where Penelope's relieved reaction of sincere joy as she embraces her husband is compared to that of shipwrecked sailors as they reach dry land.

901   spurting spring-water: Lit., 'stream from a spring'. Agamemnon is of course a traveller, but the streams of water Clytemnestra has in mind for him are not designed to quench his thirst. Aeschylus is partial to the imagery of springs and fountains (see Berman (2010)).

902   pleasurable ... pressing need: Lit., '[It's] pleasurable to escape every constraining necessity'. This apparent commonplace of homely wisdom, in Clytemnestra's mouth, acquires a menacing overtone given the proverbial pleasure which the ancient Greeks associated with wreaking revenge. As the Spartan general Gylippus was to say to the Syracusans 45 years later, before they joined battle with the hated Athenian invaders, 'nothing is more legitimate than to claim to sate the whole wrath of one's soul in punishing the aggressor, and nothing more pleasurable, as the proverb has it, than the vengeance upon an enemy' (Thuc. 7.68). Aristotle says that, when people dwell on the thought of revenge, 'the vision that rises before us produces the same pleasure as a vision seen in a dream' (*Rhet.* 2.1387b).

903   worthy of salutations of this kind: Clytemnestra acknowledges the obvious extravagance, to ancient Greek ears, of her adulatory comparisons.

904–5   let envy absent itself: Clytemnestra does not specify who might be made to feel envy by her salutations, but the implication here is that it is the gods. An expression of the desire that an encomium should not cause resentment is an intrinsic feature of ancient Greek panegyric: see e.g. Pind. *Ol.* 13.25, *Pyth.* 10.20. On *phthonos* see 921–2*. **we were previously enduring many hardships:** Clytemnestra's train of thought seems to be that extravagant praise should be exempt from the usual reprisals if the suffering of which the praise marks the end was sufficiently intolerable. Although much of what she has said about her own suffering has been mendacious, she was of course expected to put up with indescribable loss. **dear one:** Tragedy uses the neuter noun *kara* periphrastically meaning 'person' or 'individual', especially in affectionate personal addresses (Soph. *Ant.* 1, *OT* 40, *El.* 1164, *OC* 1631). Clytemnestra finally addresses her husband directly, even if the affectionate language is wholly insincere (and contrast how she addresses Aegisthus at 1654*).

905–7   get down: When Clytemnestra finally addresses her husband, it is in the imperative. She will repeat the command to Cassandra in identical language at 1039. **carriage:** The feminine noun *apēnē* may imply a four-wheeled chariot specially designed or fitted out for war: see Strabo

4.5.2. In epic it denotes a four-wheeled wagon drawn by mules, such as Priam's herald and Nausicaa drive (*Il.* 24.277–80, 322–7, *Od.* 6.56–82); in Pindar *Pyth.* 4.94–5 it is a regal carriage; Clytemnestra and her slaves ride one in Eur. *El.* 988 and Laius 'rolled out' of his in *OT* 812, where Finglass (2018a) 403–4 says that 'a substantial vehicle' is suggested, and also provides an interesting discussion of visual illustrations. This is the 'internal stage direction' indicating that Agamemnon does not arrive on foot but on some kind of wagon, on the connotations of which see 923–48*. **don't touch ... the foot that has conquered Ilium:** Lit., 'don't put on the ground, O King, this foot of yours, conqueror of Ilium'. This is another feature of Clytemnestra's attempt to portray Agamemnon as a barbarian monarch: a hymn to the Assyrian King Assunasirpal calls him 'the mighty hero, who has trampled on the neck of his foes, who has trodden down all enemies' (in Luckenbill (1926) 169; see Hall (1989) 207). See also the anaphoric Egyptian hymn in honour of Thutmose III translated in Lichtheim (1973–80) vol. 2, 36–7: 'I came to let you tread on Djahi's chiefs, I spread them under your feet throughout their lands. ... 1 came to let you tread on those in Asia.' The Greeks believed that the Persian monarchs did not put their feet in contact with the ground when they dismounted from vehicles, and even inside their palaces always walked on carpets (Heraclides of Cyme, 689 *FgrH* fr. 4; Athenaeus, 690 *FgrH* fr. 26; see Thompson (1956) 288 and Crane (1993) 122–3). On trampling see 369–72*. On feet and power in the *Oresteia* see the fine article by Levine (2015).

908–9 waiting for: Every detail of Clytemnestra's speech builds up the picture of her harsh personality. Surely her slaves would not have dared to start rolling out the carpets without an explicit order from her. **slave women:** The feminine noun *dmōiē* signifies a female slave taken in war (Hom. *Il.* 18.28); on slavery see 1036–7*. **of covering his path with material:** Lit., 'to spread the ground of his path with coverings'. The material used to cover the ground over which Agamemnon will walk is here unspecified. See the variety of terms, well discussed in Morrell (1996–7) 147–63 and Shea (2007), which are used in quick succession to describe the covering at 921–2*, 923–4*, 936*, 946*, 949*, 957*, 963*; they keep the audience focused on its precise quality as purple, woven, patterned, connected with the sea and priceless. **Hurry up! Let his path be swathed in purple:** Lit., 'Let there be immediately a purple-spread route'. This is an extraordinary theatrical coup. Purple textiles had an exceptional and electrifying tactile value in the eyes of Aeschylus' audience. The most detailed account of its production is in Pliny, *HN* 9.125–42. A substantial amount of dye was required to stain several yards of cloth. It has been estimated that to obtain just 1.4 grams of dye (the amount needed to infuse the trim of a single robe, let alone cover a pathway from the orchestra to the stage doors in the Theatre of Dionysus), as many as 12,000 shellfish had to be culled alive, and the vein containing their purplish mucus extracted and drained (if they died before processing, the liquid drained away and disappeared immediately). The procedure could only take place in late winter or early spring, before the egg-laying season, when the mucus became depleted. To make the renowned Tyrian purple, quantities of the mucus from the hypobronchial gland of two different types of murex were combined. The smaller species (*Hexaplex trunculus*) needed to be painstakingly crushed and steeped in industrial vats, and the ensuing pulp gradually distilled by heating and evaporation until the correct density was achieved. The larger species (*Bolinus brandaris*) was found only in deep water and had to be located by divers and dredged up in baskets from many fathoms below the surface. The vein of every larger murex needed to be delicately extracted by hand. No wonder that the Phoenicians' most famous export was, quite literally, worth more than its weight in gold, through the almost inconceivable amount of labour that has gone into creating its glowing, vibrant spectacle. See the excellent discussion and drawings in Marzano (2013) 142–60; see also Enegren and Meo (2017), especially Cooksey (2017) and Hall (2018d) 211. Irwin (1974) 18–19 with n.31 contains the best discussion of what precise shade of colour and/or degree of gloss and type of texture the adjective *porphureos* and its compounds suggested. Shea (2007) 44–5 offers an account of the amount of back-breaking work that was entailed by weaving large textiles, even after the women had acquired the necessary wool and dyes.

910–11   Justice: See 250–1*. Clytemnestra is in no doubt that *Dikē* is on her side (see 1432–3*) and is helping her bring Agamemnon into the house to receive his just deserts. But no doubt Agamemnon (if not the sceptical chorus) assumes that she is referring to his carrying out of the will of Zeus at Troy. **he did not expect:** Again, these words are laden with double meaning. The adjective *aelptos* can mean 'unhoped for', which is no doubt relevant to Agamemnon's fears of not surviving the war to return home, but for Clytemnestra it denotes her pleasure in his ignorance of what awaits him inside.

912–13   I will organise … mindfulness: Lit., 'My thinking, not conquered by sleep, will organise the other things.' Why would Clytemnestra feel the need to say she will not be overcome by sleep? What could be interpreted as a rhetorical flourish also has a more threatening implication in terms of her determination to stay conscious and alert and take full charge of everything. On sleep and wakefulness see 179–80*. **in the right way:** The meaning of *dikaiōs* here, despite its proximity to *dikē* at 910, is nearer to 'properly' or 'rightfully'. **In accordance with the gods and what is ordained:** Lit., 'with the gods ordained'. For a similar expression see Theognis 1033.

914–30 Clytemnestra, in her speech of welcome to her husband, has just reminded her slave women of her pre-existing order to swathe Agamemnon's pathway into the palace with cloths dyed with sea-purple. In his second speech Agamemnon, still mounted on his vehicle, responds to his wife's peculiar welcome address, with its exaggeratedly flattering tone. He is conversing with her directly for the first time since he went away. He does not answer her point by point; he ignores the first four parts of her speech which respectively consisted of (i) references to her misery and loneliness while he was away, (ii) evocations of her anxiety for his safety, which was exacerbated by rumours that he had been wounded or killed, (iii) the reasons for the absence of Orestes and (iv) extravagant praise of Agamemnon. He only responds (after a brusque opening apostrophe of her) to her fifth and final point—the suggestion that he walks a pathway strewn with cloths to the palace door. The kernel of his speech is the sentence at 618–22, with its triple negative imperatives, 'don't ... , don't ... and don't' (see 33*); some members of the audience will have remembered the Iliadic Agamemnon's fondness for speeches of prohibition, from his very first section of direct speech, which contains negative commands to Calchas beginning with the same conjunction as he uses to Clytemnestra, 'not' (*mē*, 1.26, 1.32).

914 Child of Leda: This neuter word for child, *genethlon*, lends Agamemnon's apostrophe to Clytemnestra an air of formality, parallel to the chorus' use of the same term when they welcomed Agamemnon as 'child of Atreus' at 784. He does not enquire about her wellbeing, nor express affection. He does not praise her for looking after the kingdom in his absence. Addressing his wife by referring to her mother's name, rather than her paternity, emphasises the play's interest in the mother–daughter relationship (see 265*) and the emotional implications of matrilineal descent; the chorus, more conventionally, first addressed Clytemnestra as a female child of her father ('daughter of Tyndareus', 83–4). The audience may well also be reminded here that Clytemnestra was the sister of Helen, the even more notorious daughter of Leda.

915 guardian of my household: The theme of 'guarding' has been prominent in the play since the prologue, delivered by the Watchman, who used the verb *phulassein* (8) from the same stem as the masculine noun *phulax* which Agamemnon deploys here. See also 337*. Clytemnestra earlier ordered the Herald to tell her husband that she had been a fine guard-dog to his home, and an enemy to those who did not have his best interests at heart (607–8). The masculine noun *oikos* here means the 'household' as a community rather than simply the architectural building; since the Watchman's first speech, however (18), we have known that this household has not been guarded in a way of which Agamemnon would have approved.

915–16 **your speech ... very long:** Lit., 'you stretched [your speech] out for a long [time]'. There is no noun here for 'speech' in Aeschylus' text. The feminine gender of the adjective reflects the common use of the feminine to denote indefinite abstracts. A hint of sarcasm inflects Agamemnon's comment, suggesting that it would have been preferable if Clytemnestra had spoken more briefly: at 59 lines long (his own oration had been 44 lines), it had certainly been substantially the longest of the play so far, even including those delivered by the Herald. Clytemnestra is a formidable and colourful orator, and it is interesting to contrast the chorus' response to her first substantial speech to them at 317–19: they want to hear her deliver it all over again. Agamemnon implies that he may indeed deserve panegyrics, but that she is not the most suitable person to deliver them. Critics who have responded to Agamemnon more favourably have suggested that this is a friendly, jocular remark (e.g. Fraenkel (1950) vol. 2, 414), but the tone of misogynistic rebuke is unmistakeable. **by other people than you:** As a fragment of Pindar has it, blame (*mōmos*) attaches to praise (*epainos*) spoken by a member of one's own household (quoted by schol. Pind. *Nem.* 7.89b = fr. 181 in Snell and Maehler (1975) 129). It is not clear who the appropriate panegyrists would be—perhaps poets or other military men. The chorus has of course already warned Agamemnon against susceptibility to flattery (785–98); see the discussion of Harriot (1982).

918–20 **stop cossetting me:** Lit., 'don't treat me delicately', with the verb from the same stem, *habr-*, as e.g. the adjective used to describe Helen's soft draperies at 690–2*. The concept of *habrosunē*, or 'delicacy', when applied to men and cities, by the end of the Persian Wars had become a key term in the semantic register of orientalism: see Aesch. *Pers.* 41, 133–9, 541–2, 543–5, 1073; Antiphanes fr. 91.2; Hall (1993a) 120–1. This is the first in Agamemnon's series of three baldly negative commands to his wife. **like a woman:** It is not clear whether this refers to Agamemnon or Clytemnestra, although the intonation of the actor playing Agamemnon could make it clear in performance which interpretation he favoured. Agamemnon may be suggesting that Clytemnestra's fawning behaviour is that of a woman;

on the other hand, he may mean that she is treating *him* as if he were a woman, or in a way that threatens his masculinity. There is considerable precedent earlier in the play both for explicit criticism of what was perceived as typically female behaviour (483–7*, 591–6, 613–14) and for comments that one sex is showing features to be expected in the other, for example Clytemnestra's manly brain (10–11*; see also 351*). Either way, since there was an elision in classical Greek thought of the barbaric and the feminine, if Clytemnestra is staging a welcome display suitable for an eastern barbarian monarch, then she is effectively effeminising the Greek monarch involved: see Hall (1989) 207–9. **like some barbarian man:** On *dikēn* see 231–5*. **prostrate yourself on the ground, gaping at me as you clamour:** Lit., 'don't gape at me with a fallen-to-the-ground acclamation'. The implication is that Clytemnestra (and perhaps her retinue of slave women) has performed prostration before Agamemnon—the honorific 'salaam', *proskunēsis*—in a potent piece of stage action by which she is attempting to liken the return of Agamemnon to the arrival of the supreme barbarian, the Persian King, at his court. In his *Persians* the chorus of Persian elders prostrate themselves before the Queen and probably before the ghost of Darius (152, 694–702; see Hall (1996) 6), and other barbarians in tragedy perform prostration before royalty: see Eur. *Phoen.* 293–4 (women of Phoenicia on their way to Delphi), *Or.* 1507 (a Phrygian male slave), and fr. adesp. 664.9 (Lydian slave women). Although the Greeks knelt and genuflected before the statues of gods, they were appalled when they witnessed Persian courtiers abase themselves thus before their king: two Spartan emissaries at Xerxes' court, according to Herodotus, flatly refused to do so (7.136); see Hall (1989) 96–7, 156 and 206–7. Aristotle identifies prostration as one of the distinguishing marks of honour an individual can receive in barbarian countries, equivalent to state privileges in Greek cities such as front-row seats and public burial and statues (*Rhet.* 1.1361a).

921–2 don't bring down envy in my path: Lit., 'don't make a pathway liable to envy'. The particular divine envy, with a grudge, which mortals incur if they arrogate to themselves divine privileges, is the *phthonos* of which Agamemnon is here afraid: the same term *epiphthonos*, in an active sense, was used of Artemis' grudge against him (133–4) and will be used in *Eumenides* of the Erinyes' malevolent danced assaults on the matricide Orestes (371). Purple-dyed trimmings were especially associated with robes made to offer to gods or to dress their statues (see Ferrara (2017) on a robe for Hera of Samos and Brøns (2017)), so gods might well begrudge their use in honouring a mortal. Agamemnon's concern to avoid inciting *phthonos* (on the political implications of which in classical Athens see Ellis (2023)) in either gods or his citizens is a typical feature of the epinician genre, celebrating the victorious return of celebrated figures to their home cities: see Kurke (1991); Sailor and Stroup (1999) 168–72; Steiner (2010); on epinician resonances in *Agamemnon* see also Swift (2018). **honoured:** The verb *timalphein* may have had a specifically ritual connotation (see Aristot. *Pol.* 7.1336b19). **fabrics:** The noun *heimata* here usually means items of outer clothing (*Od.* 6.214; Hdt. 1.55, 2.81): see 908–9*.

923–4 I don't believe a mortal can tread: Agamemnon is talking about literally treading on expensive textiles, but the image of trampling underfoot has earlier in the play been used metaphorically of sacrilegious disrespect for divine law (369–72*). On scholars' different explanations of the symbolic meaning of the textiles—aesthetic, ritual, moral and political—and Clytemnestra's determination to make Agamemnon walk up over them, see the discussion above at the beginning of Agamemnon's scene (801–965*). It is relevant to this line in particular that the Greeks seem to have been believed that the Persian kings were not supposed to touch the ground with their feet and used a carpet or a footstool to avoid it. **beautiful tapestries:** Lit. 'patterned fineries': see 908–9*. The fabrics are not only dyed with the purple pigment which required so much labour to produce (909*) but have also been woven or embroidered (*poikilos* can mean either) with complex different coloured threads, thus making them even more valuable, as Agamemnon is aware (948–9*). **without feeling afraid:** Named emotions play an extraordinarily important role in this tragedy (see above, 547*), and fear is amongst the most prominent among them (see 12–14*).

927 Rumours run rife: Lit., 'report shouts aloud'. Agamemnon is confident that his reputation is well enough established already. Another possible interpretation is that rumours (of a negative kind) spread even without the sort of ostentation Clytemnestra is proposing. On the importance of public opinion see the chorus' bleak warning that what the people say matters a great deal when they feel angry (457*), and Clytemnestra's chilling denial (611) that any rumours existed about her enjoying herself with any man in Agamemnon's absence. On rumours see 276*.

928–29 Only the man who dies content with his prosperity: Here 'content with' translates the adjective 'dear', in the Greek applied to the prosperity rather than the individual. The same term for 'prosperity' was used by the messenger in reference to Argos, revelling in its news of victory, at 647. Agamemnon is resorting to well-known proverbial wisdom in his attempt to round off his speech and get the difficult confrontation with Clytemnestra over. He is citing a slightly different version of the proverb previously quoted (although refuted) by the chorus, to the effect that happiness (*olbos*) that grows too great breeds dangerous excess (750–6). Even earlier, the chorus avowed that the best sort of happiness is that which does not attract envy, and that they would rather *not* be a sacker of cities (471–4). In Herodotus 1.32, Croesus, the stupendously rich king of Lydia, asked his Athenian guest Solon who was the happiest man he had ever seen. Croesus wrongly anticipated, given his own incomparable wealth, that the answer would be himself; but Solon said only that the happiest man would be the one who 'is free from deformity and disease, has no experience of evils, has fine children and good looks ... and besides all this he ends his life well'. See also the famous opening of Sophocles' *Trachiniae* 1–3, the (controversial) final lines of his *OT* (1527–30) and Ovid *Met.* 3.135. Proverbial and gnomic language is prominent everywhere in Aeschylean tragedy, but particularly so in *Agamemnon* (see 36–7*, 264–5*), where the ethical confusion makes all the characters and the chorus unusually concerned to identify any jointly held moral or religious certainties.

930 If I always act in accordance with these principles: The translation here slightly expands the rather elliptical text, which says, more literally, 'If in every circumstance I should act thus'. The potential optative with *an* in the conditional clause implies the probability that the condition will be fulfilled. Agamemnon makes the staggering claim that the principles on which he acts are likely to ensure that he will die with a claim on having been, life-long, a happy man. For a man whose child has died under any circumstances, let alone those in which Iphigenia was killed, the insensitive self-satisfaction of making this boast in front of her mother, while also parading his mistress in front of her, is breathtaking.

931 But next: The word *kai* in conjunction with the particle *mēn* is often used to introduce a new argument or counter-argument in philosophical dialogue or the orators (Ar. *Clouds* 1185, Plato, *Theaet.* 153b, *Gorg.* 452c, Dem. 21.56, 27.30). **tell me your true opinion on this question:** Lit., 'tell me this following not contrary to your true opinion'. Clytemnestra is prepared for Agamemnon's initial objection.

932 I won't compromise: This sentence, with its implication that Agamemnon always behaves consistently and in accordance with his conscience, rings especially hollow in the light of the chorus' earlier picture of Agamemnon wavering before he authorised the sacrifice of Iphigenia (205–14). Clytemnestra knows better.

933 **If you were afraid:** Agamemnon was afraid of displeasing his allies when he sacrificed Iphigenia (205–14*); there is menace in Clytemnestra's prompt to imagine that Agamemnon is frightened at this very moment. **would you make a vow to the gods:** The verb *euchomai* has a range of meanings from 'pray' and 'vow' to 'profess', 'declare', 'claim' and even 'boast' (see 533*). In this sense of a vow to the gods to do something see Hom. *Od.* 17.50, where Telemachus tells his mother to vow to the god that she will sacrifice hecatombs (with future infinitive, not present, as here). See 963*, where Clytemnestra uses the same verb with the accusative. Here it would have been impossible for the audience not to think of the sacrifice of Iphigenia, when Agamemnon brought himself to commit an outrage to please a god by an action which, far more even than walking on fabrics, might be thought *ought* to attract divine anger.

934 **someone with expertise:** Lit., 'someone knowing well'. The undertext here is obviously a reminder of Calchas' intervention after the omen of the eagles, reported by the chorus at 122–59. **perform it as a duty:** For *telos* in the sense of something done as an act of religious service see Pind. *Pyth.* 4.286, Aesch. *Eum.* 743, and 1202*. It would seem most peculiar to an ancient Greek if a god ordered someone to do something as obviously self-aggrandising as walk on an expensive set of textiles into one's own house, but perhaps that is part of Clytemnestra's point.

935 **Priam would have done it:** On the constant reminders in the play of the Trojan king, so recently deceased, see 40*. Clytemnestra is exploiting what she assumes is Agamemnon's innermost desire, whatever he says about respecting the gods and acting with restraint, to flaunt his status and success like a supreme barbarian monarch.

936 **tapestries:** Lit., 'patterned things'. See 908–8*, 923–4*.

937 This manipulative line is 'so constructed that we think at once of the suppressed antithesis, the censure of the gods' (Kitto (1956a) 25). But Agamemnon does not.

938 **voice of the people:** Lit., 'people-uttered rumour'. Agamemnon uses the same word, *dēmothrous*, which Clytemnestra had earlier used of a threat from the people that did need to be taken seriously (881–4*). On rumours see 276*.

939 **worth vying for:** The adjective *epizēlos* has a slightly different meaning from *aphthonētos*, implying emulation and striving as well as resentment. This sentence has the ring of a proverb.

940 **It's not womanly:** Lit., 'It is not a woman's [part]'. Just like the other male characters—the Watchman and the Herald as well as the chorus—Agamemnon directs commentary on appropriate gender roles at Clytemnestra (see Introduction, pp. 22–3).

941　conceding victory can be appropriate: This is a cryptic statement, but one in which Clytemnestra counters Agamemnon's prescriptive tone. Agamemnon had concluded his arrival speech with the wish that Victory could be his permanent attendant (851–3*): the concept matters a great deal in this marriage.

942　victory in this combat: The feminine noun *dēris* casts this struggle as an epic battle, for it is used of combat at climactic moments on the battlefield, such as the struggle between foemen over Patroclus' corpse (*Il.* 17.158).

943　Do it: Lit., 'obey!' **You're still in charge:** *krateis* is a robust word to use in the context, prefiguring Clytemnestra's assumption of sovereignty in the last line of the play (1673*). The text of this line has been emended slightly, since the manuscript reading 'hand over power to me willingly' does not sound as though Agamemnon would have found it persuasive. There is a good parallel to the emended text at Soph. *Aj.* 1353, where Odysseus reassures Agamemnon that he remains the commander even if he yields to friends.

944　undo: The verb is a poetic form of *hupoluein*, 'undo', 'loosen', where the prefix is separated from the verb it qualifies by tmesis. Agamemnon regards the textiles as sacred ground; Pythagoras told his followers to worship and sacrifice barefoot (Iamblichus 24.10) **shoes:** *harbulai* were ankle-boots, stoutly made and suitable for travelling over rough or muddy land (Hipp. *Art.* 62). Agamemnon's gesture is a half-hearted attempt at 'a gesture of modesty and of respect for the precious stuff, and also an attempt to minimise damage' (Jones (1988) 9). Fraenkel's determination to exonerate Agamemnon here produces an explanation for his surrender to Clytemnestra that few will find convincing today: 'one … reason why Agamemnon gives way is his reluctance to get the better of a woman … he proves a great gentleman' ((1950) 2:441). Phillippo (2018) persuasively argues that Orestes removes his footwear when approaching his father's tomb in *Choephori*, thus recapitulating his father's action here, but that when he enters the palace to murder his mother, he is shod.

945　which serve my footsteps like slaves: Lit., 'slave-like stepping of my foot'. A bizarre description of footwear which implies Agamemnon's arrogance. On slavery see 1036–7*.

946　purple products of the sea: The adjective *halourgēs* literally means 'sea-wrought', but in practice always means authentic sea-purple (as opposed to substitute made from plants), usually in reference to cloth (in the comic poets: a headband at Pherecrates fr. 106; bedspreads at Anaxandrides fr. 42.7). This is another new word for the cloth spread over his route: see 908–9*.

947 may no envy: On *phthonos* and Agamemnon's desire to avoid incurring it see 921–2*.

948 there's much at issue: Lit., 'much shame [it is]'. The term *aidōs* is ambiguous: besides 'shame' (1204*), it can mean respect for the opinion of others or of one's own conscience (Hom. *Il.* 15.657), or the respect in which someone is held (Aesch. *Pers.* 699, interestingly referring to the awe that the Persian chorus feel in the presence of the barbarian King Darius' spectre); in the Homeric *Hymn to Demeter* (214), Metaneira, queen of Eleusis, says that *aidōs* and grace shine from Demeter's eyes as it does from those 'of kings that mete out justice'. Agamemnon seems to mean that it is a mark of great honour and respect to his status with the *potential* for bringing shame upon him.

949 expensive textiles: Lit., 'woven things bought with silver'. Agamemnon may be so concerned to remove his outdoor footwear because he is entirely aware of how much the tapestries must have cost and that to risk damaging them was 'comparable to someone burning what are known to be real bank notes on stage' (Wyles (2020a) 92). This is yet another term for the floor-coverings: see 908–9*. A wife's ability to conserve the wealth of the household, as Clytemnestra is so signally failing to do, was much prized and praised in ancient Greek literature (see especially Xen. *Oec.* 7–9).

950 this foreign woman: This is the first mention of Cassandra, riding silently in Agamemnon's vehicle in priestly costume. All men who bring or have brought a second woman to their marital homes in a Greek tragedy die during it (the others are Neoptolemus in Euripides' *Andromache* and Heracles in Sophocles' *Trachiniae*). See further Introduction, p. 37, and 358*. Ordering Clytemnestra to welcome her husband's concubine graciously is emotionally brutal in the extreme.

951–2 a god looks approvingly: Agamemnon's repeated pious expressions of concern with divine opinion seem incongruous in the light of his actual conduct. **overlord:** Lit., 'the conqueror' or 'the one with power over'. A strong word for the master of a slave, especially in the context where Clytemnestra has spoken of her domination of Agamemnon (943*).

953 nobody assumes the yoke of slavery of their own free will: Later tragedies, especially those by Euripides, abound in such sententious generalisations about slaves and slavery: see Synodinou (1977) 77–109. On slavery see 1036–7*, and on yoking see 326–8*.

954–5   outstanding ornament: Lit., 'picked-out flower'. On *anthos* used metaphorically see 198–204*, where it has connotations of youthful vitality, and 742*, where it is associated with erotic desire. Here it contains both associations. **worth a great deal of money:** Agamemnon's insensitivity here is not only towards Cassandra. He implies that, unlike Clytemnestra and her expensive tastes in textiles, he is careful to accumulate valuable domestic goods. **a gift from the army:** Judging from Agamemnon's unilateral decision to expropriate Briseis from Achilles in *Iliad* 1, the audience may have heard this claim sceptically.

956   I've been compelled: The verb *katastrephein* means 'overturn' or 'turn upside down', and in the historians often denotes the subduing of a country or population and putting it under compulsion to pay tribute (Hdt. 7.51; see Thuc. 5.29). It is a potent military metaphor for yielding to his wife's strange request. See 941–3.

957   purple fabrics: Lit., 'sea-purples': see 908–9*. The feminine noun *porphura* is the name for the actual purple-fish (see Soph. fr. 504, from his *Shepherds*; Aristotle *HA* 528a10 and 909*), which is what it means in Clytemnestra's response two lines later at 959*, and it might do so here. Although it can stand metonymically for an item dyed purple (Aristotle *NE* 4.1123a23), it would not be out of the question, for a man who can describe his shoes as equivalents of slaves to his stepping feet (945*), to refer to himself as quasi-metaphorically treading on actual purple-fish.

958   sea: and who shall drain it dry? Clytemnestra, in her characteristically strange oratorical style, responds to Agamemnon's continuing stress on the high cost of purple dye by posing a rhetorical question which effectively denies that the sea itself is an unsustainable resource. She articulates two intersecting arguments: there is plenty of sea-purple in the sea and plenty of wealth in our house.

959–60   It produces ... silver: Lit., 'nurturing silver-worth ever-fresh juice of much purple-fish, dyes for clothes'. On the production of purple dye see 909*. Clytemnestra uses the same word, *baphē*, that she had earlier used in her sinister reference to dipping bronze (612). This adds plausibility to Verrall's psychological insight (Verrall (1889) n. on 949–53) that at this moment, 'it is to the eye of the queen ... as though already he walked in blood', although others have found this unconvincing (Whallon (1980) 66–7). **never fading:** One of the things most valued about authentic purple dye is that the colour of items treated with it became brighter with exposure to sunlight.

961–2   household is such ... how to be poor: Despite the perfunctory nod to gods, Clytemnestra's tone is alarmingly boastful.

963 **I'd have made a vow:** On *euchomai* see 533*. **many textiles trampled on:** Lit., 'a trampling of many garments': see 908–9*. **if the house had been allocated this task:** Lit., 'it having been pronounced to the house' (genitive absolute). A particular use of *prospherein* occurs when an oracle proposes a task to one consulting it (Hdt. 4.151, 5.63, both instances referring to the Pythia at Delphi).

964 **I was working out:** The participle *mēchanōmenē* is formed from a verb that in the middle voice so often contains negative connotations (devising or contriving an evil plot, Hom. *Od.* 3.207, 4.822, Hdt. 1.60) that Clytemnestra's imagined scenario, in which she needs to 'contrive' a ransom payment (*komistra*) for a life, sounds decidedly unnerving. **this person's life:** Lit., 'for this soul here'. Presumably Clytemnestra means Agamemnon; she is possibly pointing at him.

965–7 **the root remains:** Clytemnestra resumes the series of elaborate metaphors, some connected with extreme seasonal temperatures, with which she had first hailed Agamemnon at 895–902*. For the root as a metaphor for the stock from which a family springs see Pind. *Ol.* 2.46. On botanical imagery in the play see 79*. **against the searing Dog Star:** Lit., 'of the searing dog'. The adjective *seirios*, from which the proper name derives, means 'scorching'. Seirios was the brightest star in the constellation Canis Major, whose heliacal rising in high summer was said in a poem by Alcaeus (fr. 347.4–6) to make everyone thirsty and arouse women sexually, but enervate men, 'since it parches their heads and knees'. If this was familiar proverbial knowledge, it will have added paradoxical depth to Clytemnestra's supposed celebration of her husband.

968–9 **the domestic hearth:** On the symbolism of the hearth in *Agamemnon* see 427–8*. **warmth has come in wintertime:** The play seems to be set in the late autumn or early winter (826*); on weather imagery see 5*.

970–2 **when Zeus produces wine from the bitter unripe grape:** This is an exhaustingly elaborate periphrasis for the summer season (during which Zeus, as weather-god, provides the environment in which grapes ripen sufficiently to be harvested). On Zeus as weather-god see 1014–15*. **then coolness permeates the house:** Lit., 'then already coolness is in the house'. **if the man who is its consummate head is in residence:** This is a genitive absolute, lit. 'the consummate man frequenting the house'. The adjective *teleios* is a favourite of Clytemnestra's; she uses it with several shades of meaning. **Zeus, Zeus the fulfiller:** *teleios* was sometimes used of other gods, especially Zeus' consort Hera (Aesch. *Eum.* 214), but it was most commonly a title of Zeus (Pind. *Ol.* 13.115, *Pyth.* 1.67, Aesch. *Eum.* 28 and

Suppl. 526). Clytemnestra's unusual use of it in the previous line, apparently meaning 'consummate', in reference to her husband, seems dangerously arrogant so close to using it as a title of Zeus. But fulfilment and consummation are on her mind: she uses words with the *tel-* stem four times in the space of the last three lines of her speech as she follows her doomed husband into the palace. Elsewhere in the play she deploys the adjective in contexts to do with the death of Agamemnon, applying it to him when saying he was a 'fully grown' (i.e. adult) sacrificial victim (1504*) and to Justice, which she claims she has finally achieved for her daughter (1432*). The actor playing her is likely to have raised his hands in the ritual gesture of prayer as he delivered these lines.

x]   975–1068   THE CHORUS, CASSANDRA [SILENT], CLYTEMNESTRA

Summary

The chorus, who have earlier expressed their psychological tension and anxiety, are left in a state of terrified anticipation when Clytemnestra follows Agamemnon into the house. Cassandra remains in the vehicle while they sing their third stasimon (975–1034) in insistent, ringing lecythia (see Metrical Appendix). This is a much shorter song, consisting of two strophic pairs, which break down as follows:

Strophe 1	I don't know why I'm terrified. It's a long time since Aulis.
Antistrophe 1	I see that they have returned but fear the worst.
Strophe 2	A man's life is like a ship that can hit an unseen reef, but if excess wealth is offloaded in time things can work out.
Antistrophe 2	But a murdered man cannot be resuscitated. I am terrified and baffled.

Clytemnestra now re-enters from the palace, making everyone uncomfortable about what she has been doing during the stasimon. She barks a peremptory speech at Cassandra, telling her to submit to her lot as slave and enter the palace. This is followed by a short exchange with the chorus in which the Queen says that preparations have been made for an animal sacrifice at the central hearth and that they are to ensure Cassandra comes inside.

976–7   terror: Like the Watchman (12–14*), the chorus are gripped by feelings of fear; they previously told the Herald that they were afraid of someone in Argos (549*). **in front of my soothsaying soul:** Lit., 'standing in front of my soothsaying heart'. The adjective *prostatērios* is used as a title of Artemis (Aesch. *Sept.* 449) and also of Apollo, with the sense that his statue stood before the doors as a protective presence (Soph. *El.* 637). It may have been a term particularly associated with the language of oracles, since it is applied to Apollo in a prophecy quoted at Demosthenes 21.52, in which case the chorus seem to be imagining their heart/soul as some kind of oracular shrine with terror standing outside it.

979 unbidden and unwaged: The chorus imply that they are not fully in control of the direction in which this song is taking them, which is suggestive of a prophetic seizure. This single line is dactylic, appropriately given its prophetic subject matter.

980–3 Why doesn't a reassuring sense of courage … dream: Lit., 'nor persuasive courage sit on the dear chair of my mind to spit out [the terror] as if it were uninterpretable dreams'. The chorus would like to be persuaded into feeling confident that there was nothing wrong in the current situation. This opaque image perhaps continues the idea that the chorus' mind feels like an oracular shrine where a female or male priest might sit and interpret dreams, or alternatively reject the possibility of interpreting them. On dreams see 274*.

984–7 Time has grown old: Lit., 'time's youth passed'. In Aeschylus, time is presented as a great teacher: 'Time is a witness, and time is a sovereign power: when these two qualities combine, he becomes a judge and the most terrible of judges' (de Romilly (1968) 55; see also Beck (1975) 59–60). But here the effects of time are temporarily obscuring material evidence of all that happened at Aulis. Those events cannot so easily be erased from the memory. Sadly, the text of what seems to have been a powerful passage of poetry, reverberating with the chorus' earlier images of the fleet at and after Aulis (192–5, 693), has become irredeemably corrupt, especially the phrase about the sand, and the translation is therefore conjectural. **since the mooring-cables were cast from the sterns so the sand flew:** Lit., (translating a suggested restoration of the corrupt Greek text) 'since, from [or by] the throwings of the sterns, the sand flew up'. The text may, alternatively, hide an allusion to the plashing of the oars as the sailors began rowing (cf. Aesch. *Pers.* 396) rather than the idea of something being thrown. Regardless of the precise lexical details, the total image perhaps recalled the passage in the *Iliad* where the poet describes how the passing of time removed even the last vestiges of the Greek fortifications near Troy, which were obliterated after the war by Poseidon and Apollo; these gods inundated the shore for nine long days, before Poseidon smashed away every last beam and stone with his trident, made the coast of the Hellespont smooth again, and covered the beach with sand as if nothing had ever happened (12.15–33). The train of thought seems to be that the chorus attempt to calm their terror by reflecting that, since it is such a long time since what happened at Aulis, any repercussions would already have taken place. This of course contradicts their sentiments elsewhere that divine punishment, however delayed, is eventually inevitable 1525–7*.

988–9 I know they've returned: Lit., 'I know [the return]'. In fact, of course, the vast majority of the Argives have failed to return and even more bereavements have been inflicted on the offstage population whom the chorus represent. **from the evidence which I've seen with my own eyes:** Lit., 'from eyes … being witness myself'. On eyes see 240*. The unusual adjective *automartus* is picked up aurally at 991 by *autodidaktos*.

990–2 the lyreless lament of the Erinyes: Dirges were conventionally accompanied by the plangent *aulos* rather than the lyre: at *Eumenides* 331 the Erinyes say that their song is sung 'without the phorminx'. See also 1141–3*. On the Erinyes see 58–9*. **which it has taught itself:** Lit., 'self-taught', like Phemius the Ithacan bard in the *Odyssey* (22.347); the dactylic metre of this line enhances the epic resonance. The chorus' evocation of their sense of psychological struggle, between processing information they have received via their senses and a message of foreboding coming from within the interior of their body, is remarkable.

992–4 it can't fully feel: Lit., 'not altogether having'. **that hope brings:** Lit., 'of hope'. Hope (see 100–3*, 813–17*) is consistently presented as compromised in the play.

995–7 Not without reason do my innards speak to me: Lit., 'My innards are not in vain'. **my heart racing as it beats:** Lit., 'my heart being stirred in whirls'; *kear* is an apposition to *splagchna*. **in waves of fulfilment:** Lit., 'in fulfilling eddies'. **along with my sense of what's right:** Lit., 'in addition to my right-thinking mind'. This type of expression, relating to the physiology of the emotions (see Introduction, p. 62), is amongst the most difficult in Aeschylus to translate into English that sounds remotely natural. It is alien to the way we talk about fear and apprehension today. But, in poetic terms, the chorus brilliantly evoke their inner bodily and psychic sensations as memories of the past, tension in the present and fear for the future collide; they cannot reconcile their aversion to more violence with their conviction that wrongdoing should be—and is—always punished. The whirls and eddies also prompt recollections of the Herald's description of the storm and shipwreck.

998–1000 my expectations … unfulfilled: Lit., 'false [things] fall out from my expectation in the direction of unfulfilment'. The adjective *telesphoros* is repeated from the previous sentence for emphasis. On the metaphor from gaming with dice see 33*; the adjective *psuthos* is a favourite of the chorus in quasi-oracular contexts: see 475–8* and 1089*.

1001–4 Really excellent health knows no bounds: Lit., 'The boundary of very good health is insatiable.' This, the first of a series of metaphors in this strophe for exploring moral soundness and its opposite and its relationship with fate, is medical; on previous medical imagery in the play see 17*. **its neighbour, disease, shares a common wall with it:** Health and disease are now visualised as living side by side in a semi-detached dwelling (see *homotoichos oikia*, Is. 6.39), so that the one is constantly jeopardised by the other; *homotoichos* is found in psychological contexts elsewhere to express close affinity, e.g. between grief and madness at Antiphanes fr. 287, and anger and madness at Plutarch, *On Garrulity* 503e. **leans on it hard:** Lit., 'presses'. On architectural metaphors see 1283*.

1005–7 a man's destiny … reef: Although some words have dropped out of the text here, the sense is reasonably clear. What happens in a person's life is now seen as a ship, which may seem to be sailing along an unproblematic route, but can suddenly and unexpectedly strike (gnomic aorist of *paiein*) rocks that are hidden underwater. At 666* the Herald had said that the ship he was sailing in on return from Troy had been saved from running into rocks. On naval imagery see 108–15*.

1008–9 trepidation: Lit., 'act of shrinking from'. Personifying an emotion as a ship's captain taking the decision to jettison cargo is a daring literary choice, even for Aeschylus. **has previously jettisoned:** Lit., 'jettisoning'. The subject, the masculine noun *oknos*, is left dangling without a main verb. **wealth of possessions:** Lit. 'of possessed wealth'.

1010 by judicious use of the ship's crane: Lit., 'from a well-measured sling'. A *sphendonē* is a sling, whether medical (Hom. *Il.* 13.600, Hipp. *Art.* 16) or military (Thuc. 4.32), but it is found in a technical sense of a sling which formed part of a crane used for unloading ships (LSJ s.v. *sphendonē* I.2).

1011 the household is saved from sinking entire: Lit., 'The whole house does not plunge' (gnomic aorist). The household, in the nominative case, replaces trepidation as the subject of this sentence. It also replaces the hypothetical man's destiny as the comparand of the ship.

1012   overloaded with misery: Lit., 'brimming too much with misery'. Sad emotions, previously seen by the chorus as a metaphorical burden (63–7*, 161–3*), are here compared with a ship's cargo.

1013   doesn't submerge its hull: Since the hull was the part of a ship from which it was steered, this could be read as meaning that pre-emptive removal of some cargo could allow those in charge of the ship who represented the whole household or community (see 182–3*, 1617–19*) to remain in power.

1014–15   gift from Zeus: This is probably a periphrasis for rain. Pausanias says that there was in Argos an altar of Zeus Rain-God (Huetios, 2.19.8). The Athenians worshipped Zeus of Rain (*Ombrios*) on Mounts Hymettos and Parnes (1.32.2) and the Acropolis featured an image, perhaps created in response to a drought, of Earth beseeching Zeus to rain on her (1.24.3). Zeus once granted rain to end a drought after Aeacus' sacrifice to him (1.44.9, 2.29.8). See also Paus. 2.25.10 and, on Zeus as a weather god connected with viticulture, Clytemnestra's periphrasis at 970–2*. **annual ploughing of furrows:** Lit., 'from yearly furrows'. **oust the disease of famine:** This is a gnomic aorist. On agricultural imagery see 524–6*; on hunger and famine as themes see 192–5*. The chorus seem to conclude that a combination of paying attention to the gods and hard work will keep humans free from harm, but this heartening observation does little to dispel the fearful atmosphere created in the earlier lines of this strophe.

1019–20   a murdered man's dark blood has fallen before him: Lit., 'the fatal black blood has fallen in front of him'. The chorus believe that a murder cannot remain forever unavenged, although it is interesting that they gender the murder victim here specifically male, perhaps to avoid directly saying that Agamemnon will have to pay for Iphigenia's death sooner or later. On blood see 209–10*.

1021   call him back to life: The verb *anakaleisthai* (middle) is used specifically of calling someone up from the world of the dead at Aesch. *Pers.* 621. **by incantations:** The verb *epaeidein* is used of the song with magical powers by which the Sirens tried to bewitch Odysseus at Xen. *Mem.* 2.6.11. Aeschylus had written exactly such an incantation himself, replete with aural jingles and repetition, for delivery by the chorus of *Persians* (633–80) at Dareios' tomb, from which they successfully entreat him to appear: see Hall (1996) 153–4. But Dareios is now a god rather than a murdered mortal.

1022–4   Not even he: The reference is to the hero-doctor (and later divinity in his own right) Asclepius, the kindly healer, usually depicted with his trademark serpent and staff. He was the son of Apollo and Coronis (Apollod. 3.10.3). The story of his death is told in Pindar, *Pyth.* 5.55–8. He was tempted to bring back to life one whom the jaws of death had already seized, so Zeus killed both Asclepius and his patient with a thunderbolt. The man he brought back from the dead is identified diversely as Hippolytus, Tyndareus, Capaneus, Glaucus, Hymenairos and Lycurgus (see Stesichorus fr. 194, from his *Eriphyle*). The storyline was popular, being told not only by Stesichorus but in an epic *Naupactica*, a shorter poem devoted to Asclepius by the fifth-century BCE poet Telestes (fr. 807), and another poem by the fifth-century poet Cinesias (fr. 774). There was a tradition that the potion he used to revive the dead came from the blood that had coursed through the right side of the veins of the Gorgon (ps.-Apollod. *Bibl.* 3.121). **who properly knew:** The *ortho-* part of the compound suggests knowledge of divine affairs; see *orthomanteia* at 1215. **was allowed by Zeus to do so without being harmed:** The text as transmitted is unmetrical. The translation reflects the more sensible proposed emendations.

1025–9   one fate ... prevent another fate from gaining the upper hand: In one of the most egregiously obscure sentences in a play abounding in obscurity, the chorus reflect that sometimes the gods are conflicted; a human destiny preferred by one god can defeat or be defeated by a human destiny preferred by another. Here the rival fates could be identified with Clytemnestra/Iphigenia and Agamemnon respectively. Despite its difficulty, the sentiment undoubtedly expresses the fundamental dilemma faced in the *Oresteia*, that obtaining justice for one individual may require ignoring another victim's claim to justice. **my heart could take precedence over my tongue and become open to view:** Lit., 'my heart, having anticipated my tongue, could be conspicuous in respect of these things'. The chorus, as so often, imply that they feel inhibited about expressing their true feelings, which must remain invisible and in darkness (1030).

1030–2   drones: The aural effect of the verb *bremein* is difficult to specify because it indicates sounds from a wide range of sources: a sea-wave (*Il.* 4.425), a headland (Soph. *Ant.* 592), wind (*Il.* 14.399), armour (Eur. *Heraclid.* 832), men (Aesch. *PV* 424), a mob (Aesch. *Eum.* 978), a lyre and a song (Pind. *Nem.* 11.7). Perhaps it signifies a sense of soundwaves vibrating. **darkness ... light:** The repeated imagery that equates metaphysical confusion with darkness and true understanding with light is never far from this chorus' manner of speaking (see Introduction, pp. 63–5). **unravel:** Lit., 'wind off [from a ball of wool]'. A powerful textile-related metaphor for cognition, perhaps suggestive of the Moirai, spinners of mortal fates (Hom. *Il.* 24.209–10), with their golden distaffs (Bacchylides, fr. 24.7–12; see also Aesch. *Eum.* 334).

1035 Get yourself indoors too: Clytemnestra, re-entering from the palace, abruptly addresses a harsh imperative to Cassandra without apostrophising her. It is revealing that she knows Cassandra's name even though Agamemnon had not used it.

1036–7 benevolently: Lit., 'without malevolence', a peculiar and grating expression; on privative alphas see Introduction, p. 3 and also 649*. How could Zeus' enslavement of anyone possibly be described as an act of benevolence? Clytemnestra attributes Cassandra's plight to Zeus, as the god who others in the play have stated had been ultimately responsible for the destruction of Troy (Introduction, p. 33) and/or as the god of household possessions including slaves. **a joint partaker in the holy water:** Lit., 'partner of the water-basins'. Domestic slaves routinely participated in a household's religious rituals, including sacrifices and libations at the domestic hearth. **numerous slaves:** Clytemnestra has already had an opportunity to display her household's assets in terms of female slaves, at least, in the floor-covering scene (908–11). **the god who guards possessions:** This is Zeus. At Aesch. *Suppl.* 445 it refers emphatically to Zeus' protection of household possessions. There was a shrine of Zeus *Ktēsios* in Piraeus (Antiphon 1.16). Clytemnestra refers to this particular god amongst the several worshipped in the palace to underscore brutally that Cassandra is now a possession. The other Trojans who have been enslaved were highlighted earlier, and from this moment onwards the wretched treatment Cassandra can expect, as well as her fragile rights, are a pervasive theme in her scene (see 326–8*, 359–61*, 908–9*, 945, 953, 1040–1*, 1045*, 1056–7, 1071, 1084, 1123–6*, 1326*). Golden (1990) 151 explores how Aeschylus exploits the paradox that a woman, a foreigner *and* a slave has a more accurate understanding than anyone else in the play of what is really happening, on both the human and divine levels. McCoskey (1998) illuminates the discourse around Cassandra's enslavement from historical narratives written by women in the antebellum American South.

1039 Get down from this carriage: This is an unusually clear internal stage direction showing that Aeschylus intended the silent Cassandra to remain on the vehicle throughout Agamemnon's scene and the chorus' despondently anxious stasimon that followed it. Clytemnestra repeats, in identical language, her command to Agamemnon at 906, thus drawing attention to the intimacy and parallelism between her prospective victims.

1040–1 Alcmena's son: Clytemnestra, perhaps significantly, prefers not to name Heracles but to use his matronymic. Heracles was enslaved to the Lydian queen Omphale as a punishment for killing Iphitus. In Sophocles'

Trachiniae (8–53, 274–80) the Omphale episode serves both as part of the recent back-story and (as here, although the ever-cryptic Clytemnestra does not spell it out) as exemplar of a man in a woman's power. Ion of Chios wrote a satyr play called *Omphale* (on which see Hall (2006) 154–5), as did Achaeus. In Ion's, both Heracles and the satyr chorus seem to have donned women's clothing. On the story as represented in ancient visual arts see Schauenburg (1960). No doubt the theme of the powerful woman dominating a man famed for his vigorous masculinity appeals to Clytemnestra in the present circumstances. **eating the coarse bread of slavery:** Lit., 'to encounter slavery's barley-bread'. This reference to barley-bread (as opposed to the much more palatable wheaten bread, from which it is distinguished at Ar. *Eccl.* 606, Antiphanes fr. 225.1–2, and Xen. Cyr.1.2.11), sounds as if it may have been proverbial. Zenobius says that *maza* in a proverb implies something second-best (1.12). The inferiority of food allowed to slaves is a constant complaint in, for example, Aristophanic comedy, and a particular preoccupation of Cario in *Wealth* (Hall (2020a) 227–8, 232–5).

1042   if this fate bears down of necessity: Lit., 'if compulsion of this fate inclines in the balance'. On weighing metaphors see 63–7*.

1043   something to be grateful for: On *charis* see 182–3*. Clytemnestra's emotional brutality persists. **inherit ancient wealth:** It seems to have been customary to draw such distinctions between the behaviour of the wealthy by heredity and the nouveaux riches (Lys. 19.49; Ar. *Rhet.* 2.1387a24). Aristotle says that people who acquire a fortune for themselves are meaner with money than those who inherit it (*NE* 4.1120b).

1044   reaped a fine harvest: On agricultural metaphors see 524–5*.

1045   savage: The root meaning of *ōmos* is 'raw', 'uncooked' or 'unripe', of foodstuffs (Hom. *Il.* 22.347 and Theophrastus *de Vertigine 2*); of vegetables (Antiphanes fr. 186.2) and ears of barley (Lucian, *Ass* 17); this makes it particularly apt for a family which has not been accustomed to possessing slaves in any number and has not learned the most expedient way to handle them. Clytemnestra succeeds in combining class snobbery with insensitivity towards slaves in general and Cassandra in particular. Yet morality in terms of the ways in which slaves are treated is not often assessed in literature before the late fifth century BCE. **beyond the general rule:** A *stathmē* is a line drawn by a carpenter (Hom. *Od.* 5.245), but metaphorically it could mean a regulation or customary rule (Pind. *Pyth.* 1.62). Clytemnestra implies that there was a sense of the appropriate degree of cruelty that could be meted out to slaves, and to exceed it was to incur disapproval. On other references to enslavement in the play see 1036–7*.

1046   the treatment that's customary: Clytemnestra claims that she will treat Cassandra exactly as custom dictates. But Cassandra is no ordinary slave. Given that it was considered inappropriate for a man to bring his concubine to his marital home, there is no 'customary treatment' for Clytemnestra to mete out.

1047   It's you: The chorus are concerned that Cassandra does not realise that Clytemnestra has ordered her to get down from the vehicle and enter the house. This implies that she has made no response to Clytemnestra's remarks whatsoever.

1048   Since you're caught in destiny's hunting-nets: Lit., 'being in fateful hunting-nets'. Orestes uses the same neuter plural noun *agreumata* in both *Choeph.* 998 and *Eum.* 460 of the net in which Agamemnon was murdered and which Orestes redeployed. On nets and net imagery see 357*.

1049   you may obey, if you are compliant; but perhaps you'll disobey: This is a strange comment from the chorus, but indicative of their puzzlement at Cassandra's apparent unresponsiveness to her plight.

1050–1   unless she speaks: Lit., 'unless she is possessed of'. **some unknown barbarian language:** In the *Iliad*, the Trojans, including Cassandra, speak identical Greek to the Achaeans; only some of their allies are said to speak another tongue (2.804, 4.437–8; see Hall (1989) 19–20). But by the fifth century BCE the Trojans had become identified with the Phrygians (Hall (1988)), historical inhabitants of north-west Asia Minor, whose Indo-European tongue, although containing Greek words (Plato. *Crat.* 410a), and bearing strong similarities to Greek (Brixhe (2008)), was distinct from it. Nevertheless, the Athenian tragedians followed Homer in making their Trojans speak Greek, while describing them as *barbaroi*, non-Greek speakers. See also 1198–201*. **like a swallow:** The comparison of incomprehensible foreign speech with the twittering of birds, especially swallows, became a standard trope: see Ar. *Birds* 199–300, 1292–3, 1681–2 and *Frogs* 681–2 with Hall (2020b) 208.

1052   I'm inducing her with words she understands: Lit., 'I'm inducing her with speech inside her understanding'. Clytemnestra is (as it turns out, correctly) sceptical that Cassandra does not understand Greek.

1053   Under the circumstances: This is a much milder formulation to describe Cassandra's plight than the fateful hunting-nets to which the chorus had referred at 1048*. They seem increasingly sympathetic to her.

1054   leave your seat: Aeschylus has taken scrupulous care with the internal stage directions in the case of Cassandra, who has apparently not even stood up.

1055–6 I don't have leisure-time to waste: Lit., 'leisure [is] not at hand to wear down'. Clytemnestra is increasingly impatient, making the audience wonder what exactly she has been doing inside.

1056–7 The animals: In the plural, *mēla* denotes either sheep or goats or both. **the central hearth:** The word *mesomphalos* most commonly applies to the Delphic oracle, as at Aesch. *Sept.* 747 and *Choeph.* 1036. Cassandra is to be killed in a place that is here presented as a bizarre distortion of the temple of Apollo at Delphi, where *Eumenides* opens. Clytemnestra has previously spoken of participating with the other household slaves in the domestic cult of Zeus Ktesios (1036–7*), so a sacrifice to him seems likely to be her surface meaning here, although the audience will be fearing that she means another sacrificial victim altogether. As Zeitlin (1966) elegantly demonstrates, this reference to sacrificial rituals opens the Cassandra scene, which will be drawn to a close with Cassandra's own ironic characterisation of these very same rites (1309–12).

1058 gratification such as we never hoped to experience: Lit., 'for us never having hoped to have this joy'. On the flexible concept of *charis* see 182–3*, and, on the theme of hope, 100–3*.

1059 if you are to take any part in this: Perhaps newly acquired slaves were sometimes keen to incorporate themselves swiftly into the religious rites of a household out of real piety or practical expedience.

1060 if you don't understand and don't grasp my meaning: As soon as she has said this, Clytemnestra realises its absurdity and abruptly changes addressee to the chorus in the apodosis of the next line.

1061 you there: This abrupt address, at least to a group of free elders rather than a slave woman (1059), is decidedly peremptory. **with a barbarian hand:** The word *karbanos* is rare; it seems to have been equivalent to *barbaros* (Hall (1989) 118, 140); Aeschylus had previously used it in *Suppliants* both to denote Egyptian speech (129) and in the context of outrageous behaviour (914). Clytemnestra here gives the chorus permission to use violence against Cassandra (although some scholars have quaintly assumed that she is telling them to use sign language that a non-Greek speaker could understand).

1062 foreign woman: The chorus, like Agamemnon (951), use the feminine form of the much milder term *xenos* for a foreigner (a term which can include a Greek from another city-state), where Clytemnestra has used *barbaros* and *karbanos* (1051*, 1061*) in association with Cassandra's language. **clear interpreter:** See 26* and 616*.

1063 she's acting like a wild creature that's just been seized: Lit., '[Her] demeanour is of a newly caught beast.' On animal and hunting imagery see 357*. The actor playing Cassandra may have been cowering or moving wildly at this point.

1064   she's crazed: The chorus are later to speculate about the precise source of Cassandra's perceived madness (1140*). The verb *mainomai* covers a wide range of mental disturbances, including divine possession (*Il.* 6.132, where the god is Dionysus). Plato *Phaedr.* 244a–b uses it of the Delphic priestesses. See also 1140* and 1427*.

1065   that's just been seized: Clytemnestra picks up but transfers to Troy the adjective which the chorus had applied to Cassandra herself at 1063*.

1066   to tolerate the bit: This image and the masculine noun *chalinos* create a direct parallel between Cassandra, soon to be murdered, and the description of Iphigenia's sacrifice at 235–8*.

1067   discharged her temper in bloody spume: Lit., 'foamed out her bloody temper'. This savage picture is of a horse being violently broken in, with blood-flecked, foaming saliva pouring from her mouth, on which image see also an indirectly relevant comment at 1327–9*. Xenophon explains the different types of equestrian bit and how to control a horse's movements using them at *On Horsemanship* 10.6–12. On blood see 209–10*.

1068   No, I'll not throw more words away on being disrespected: Lit., 'I'll not be dishonoured having thrown [away] more [words]'. Clytemnestra re-enters the palace. She has no time to waste.

xi]   1069–1330   THE CHORUS AND CASSANDRA, NO LONGER SILENT

Summary

After the chorus speak three lines to Cassandra, the first part of this episode, the whole of which is beautifully analysed by Valakas (2002) 80–1 (see also Taplin (1978) 59–60, Bollack (1981) and Delattre (2017)), constitutes the earliest known lyric exchange (*amoibaion*) in which the individual actor takes the lead in interchanges with the chorus (1072–177) rather than *vice versa*. The first solo singing voice in the tragedy transforms the psychological atmosphere: the musicologist Aristoxenus said that speech begins to sound like song when we are emotional (*Elements of Harmony* 1.9–10). Cassandra sings 14 times in seven strophic pairs and the chorus respond to each utterance. At first, Cassandra opens each stanza with lyric verses, which become dominated by dochmiacs, to which the chorus respond in spoken iambic trimeters. But the psychological roles begin to change in the second part of the exchange (1114–77), when the chorus begin to respond in sung dochmiacs, as if coming under Cassandra's vatic and emotional influence. Cassandra seems intermittently unaware of their presence as she vocalises her disjointed thoughts on the bloodshed at Argos and Troy; she ignores some of their worried questions; they assert at the end of both halves of her song that they are at a complete loss (1113, 1177). But Cassandra at last shifts into the iambic metre, and the remainder of the scene consists of her four speeches, with three stichomythic exchanges with the chorus inserted between them. They do not like what they hear, especially her reference to the murder of Agamemnon (1246), but she pointedly responds that they are now the deluded ones (1247–55). She shockingly discards her priestly equipment, predicts that the current carnage will be avenged and walks into the palace to certain death. On the metre, especially the dochmiacs, see Introduction, p. 43 and the Metrical Appendix.

Over the last 24 hours Cassandra has suffered multiple bereavements, enslavement, probably rape and certainly a terrifying storm at sea. The impact of this traumatised young woman's sudden movement as she descends from the carriage and vocalisation at 1072 can scarcely be overstated. After more than 1000 lines in which no individual character has performed lyrics, the aulos-player strikes up and a previously static, silent figure bursts into movement and song. A precious piece of evidence suggests that tragic audiences found emotive the precise moments of change, the acoustic gearshifts from one type of metre and delivery to another. The pseudo-Aristotelian *Problem* 19.6 is discussing vocalisation in tragedy and says that it is contrast or 'unlikeness' that is effective: 'contrast is emotive in situations of great misfortune or grief; regularity is less conducive to lamentation'. See further Hall (2012) 12–13.

Amoibaion (1069–177)

The content of this lyric exchange can be broken down and summarised as follows:

Strophe 1	Cassandra: O Apollo!
	Chorus: Why call on him?
Antistrophe 1	Cassandra: O Apollo!
	Chorus: She keeps miserably addressing a god unconnected with misery.
Strophe 2	Cassandra: Apollo, this is the second time you have destroyed me.
	Chorus: She seems about to prophesy concerning herself.

Antistrophe 2	Cassandra: Where have you brought me?
	Chorus: To the house of the Atreidai.
Strophe 3	Cassandra: It's a god-hated slaughterhouse.
	Chorus: The foreign girl is a good murder detective.
Antistrophe 3	Cassandra: The proof is those dead babies.
	Chorus: You may be a prophet but we don't need one!
Strophe 4	Cassandra: What's this new trouble?
	Chorus: I don't know but I did understand your former reference.
Antistrophe 4	Cassandra: Woman, are you bathing your husband with outstretched hands?
	Chorus: I'm baffled by your riddles.
Strophe 5	Cassandra: What's that deathly net? Let the hostile company sing victory!
	Chorus: Why are you mentioning an Erinys? I'm miserable.
Antistrophe 5	Cassandra: The cow is holding the bull in cloths and stabbing him in the bath.
	Chorus: Oracles cause problems.
Strophe 6	Cassandra: Why have you brought me here except to die?
	Chorus: You're mad and mourn like the nightingale for her son.
Antistrophe 6	Cassandra: At least she got changed into a bird; I'm about to be killed.
	Chorus: How long are you going to continue raving?
Strophe 7	Cassandra: Alas for Paris' marriage, and the River Scamander. I'm going to die.
	Chorus: I do understand this and am heartbroken for you.
Antistrophe 7	Cassandra: My poor city and father.
	Chorus: I've no idea where this is leading.

1069 I, however, since I pity her: The chorus' attitude serves to throw Clytemnestra's brutality into sharp relief and also shows once again that they retain the ability to think and act independently of their overlords.

1070 wretched woman: This word recurs throughout the Cassandra scene: Cassandra addresses Clytemnestra as *talaina* at 1107 and describes herself as such at 1138, 1158, 1260 and 1274; the chorus call her *talaina* again at 1274; see also 1143 (the nightingale) and 1295 (the chorus labelling the many sad things Cassandra has spoken of). **Leave this carriage:** Pillinger (2019) 42–3 comments that here and in the next line the chorus themselves become 'interpreters', who echo but rephrase Clytemnestra's bridle imagery and harsh instructions into a gentler, more encouraging suggestion that Cassandra should try to make a new start in life, which of course is the furthest thing from her thoughts. Cassandra presumably gets down from the vehicle at this point. It may be removed out of view by those who pulled it in or by stage hands if it was drawn by horses (see 782–957*). Alternatively, it may have remained visible; in one university production I saw in my youth it was mounted by Clytemnestra and Aegisthus at the end of the play when they assert their tyrannical authority and reactivate the vertical visual field. The valuables Agamemnon amassed at Troy and which Aegisthus says he is appropriating (1638–9*) were stacked up behind them.

1071   Give in to necessity and try on this new yoke: The verb *kainizein* means 'inaugurate'. On *anankē* see 218–21*, where the chorus used similar language linking necessity to a yoke-strap when describing Agamemnon's decision to sacrifice Iphigenia, although here they probably refer to the proverbial 'yoke of slavery' (953*; on yoking see also 326–8*).

1072   *Otototoi popoi da*: When Cassandra finally breaks her silence after nearly 300 lines on stage, her first utterance still does not answer the question of whether she speaks Greek, since she utters an exclamation of grief that probably transcended linguistic boundaries in the eastern Mediterranean. *otototoi* (the *ot*-syllable repeated a varying number of times, between two and six), sometimes with double *t*, occurs in threnodic passages of all three tragedians, especially those sung by barbarians (Aesch. *Pers.* 268, 918, Eur. *Or.* 1389) and/or women (Soph. *El.* 1245, Eur. *Andr.* 1197, Eur. *Troj.* 1294, *Ion* 789); see further Heirman (1975). In Aristophanes' *Birds* (1043) there is a city where the people are called Ototyxians, with a play on Olophyxians, the inhabitants of Olophyxus or Olophyxia, a hybrid Greek-barbarian town in Chalcidice near Mount Athos (see Hdt. 7.22, Thuc. 4.121.4). ***popoi*:** This is another alliterative exclamation, which in Homer expresses pain, anger or surprise (*Od.* 17.248, *Il.* 21.420); the Erinyes utter it when they are pained that they have let Orestes escape (Aesch. *Eum.* 145). In later antiquity *popoi* was said to be a Dryopian (aboriginal Greek, from around Mount Oeta) word meaning 'gods' (Plutarch, *How a Young Man Should Listen to Poetry* 22c–d) or statues of gods (*Et. Magn.* 823.32). ***da*:** The scholiast here suggests that this is a Doric form of *gē*, or 'Earth': see also *Et. Magn.* 60.8.

1073   O Apollo O Apollo: Compared with Zeus, Apollo has not so far been prominent in the religion and theodicy of this play (although see 55–7*,

146*, 509–11*, 512*). But his influence is profound on Cassandra's psyche henceforward, as it is on Orestes' psyche in *Choephori*, and Apollo finally becomes a physical presence in *Eumenides* (from line 64, where he visits his own oracle at Delphi) as Orestes' protector and advocate.

1074 Why did you start wailing *ototoi*? The prefix *an-* on the verb implies breaking out into an utterance. At *Choeph.* 327 the verb *ototuzein* is used in connection with funeral rites, indirectly those of Agamemnon; see also Ar. *Peace* 1011, where it refers to the performance of a monody in Melanthius' *Medea* (Melanthius T 4a); it is clear that the verb was in Greek tragedy especially associated with lamenting females. See also Ar. *Thesm.* 327. **Loxias:** This cult title of Apollo was explained in later antiquity as referring to his oblique (*loxios*), i.e., obscure oracles (see Lucian, *Jup. Trag.* 28, Lycophron, *Alex.* 14, 1467), or (once Apollo had become firmly identified with Helios) because the ecliptic (the apparent path of the sun during the year) was called the *loxios kuklos* ('slanting cycle', see Aristot., *Metaphysics* 12.1071a16; Aratus, *Phaenomena* 527).

1075 It's not appropriate for him to be associated with mourning: Lit., 'He is not such as to meet a mourner'. The chorus' shock is palpable at the association of the gleaming, cerebral Olympian god of healing, the 'far-shooter' who keeps his distance from mortals, with the miserable sounds uttered during a dirge. Xenophanes, according to Aristotle *Rhet.* 2.1400b, said that laments were to be performed for mortals but sacrifices for gods. On unease about paradoxical blending of genres of song see also 636–7*, 645.

1076–7 See 1072*, 1073*.

1078–9 with ill-omened words: The chorus discuss Cassandra in the third person, rather than addressing her again, because she has not replied to them. The strong participle *dusphēmousa* emphasises just how disturbingly profane they find threnodic exclamations in connection with Apollo. **whose presence doesn't belong:** Lit., 'who should not arrive to stand by'.

1081–2 god of the streets: Here, *aguiat'* seems to be a vocative form of *Aguieus*, a cult title of Apollo derived from the feminine noun *aguia*, 'street'. At Ar. *Wasps* 875, Bdelycleon invokes a conventional statue or altar of Apollo at his household's front door as 'Lord, King, Neighbour, Aguieus of the front door and front gate'. Cassandra apparently recoils on seeing the image of Apollo at the entrance to the palace (509–11*), which implies that she has certainly by now at last descended from the carriage. **my destroyer. For you have destroyed me:** Cassandra derives Apollo's name etymologically from the verb *apollumi*, 'destroy', although the original (Doric) form of his name was probably *Apellōn*; some Doric states, including Delphi and Epidaurus, named a calendar month 'Apellaios'. **utterly:** Lit., 'not slightly'. **a second time:** Apollo had previously caused her great harm by making nobody believe her prophecies after she spurned his advances, as she explains to the chorus at 1209–13.

1083 she seems: Cassandra's posture indicates that she has entered some kind of mantic trance. **about to prophesy:** The verb *chraō* in this sense is normally used of a god making a proclamation via an oracle, especially Apollo via the Delphic oracle (Hom. *Od.* 8.79, Hom. *Hymn to Aphrodite* 132, 396, Hdt. 1.55). It would not normally be expected that an individual mortal would utter a prophecy about themselves.

1084 in a mind even though it's enslaved: Lit., 'even in an enslaved mind'. On Cassandra's new servile status see 1036–7*.

1085–6 See 1081–2*.

1087 To what kind of house? Cassandra's question could imply she is already sensing the revulsion that will soon overwhelm her (1090–2*). Although she has previously addressed Apollo, it is not entirely clear whether she is talking to Apollo or Agamemnon.

1088 that of the Atreidai: The chorus answer her as if she had asked 'whose house?' rather than 'what kind of house?' It is extremely unlikely that Cassandra would not by now be clear that the palace belonged to Agamemnon; perhaps the chorus' peculiar next sentence, about Cassandra's understanding and the truth of their statement, is an acknowledgement of this.

1090–2 No, it's a house: The combination of the particles *men* and *oun* can indicate a correction, or a greater focus on the detail of an argument, and have semi-adversative force: 'no, rather' (Ar. *Knights* 13; Plato, *Crat.* 44b). Cassandra responds directly to the chorus for the first time. **witness to:** On the idea that the very material fabric of the building contains consciousness see Introduction, pp. 69–70. **foul kin-murders, beheadings:** Lit., 'kin-murdering head-cut evils'. With some misgivings I translate Kayser's emendation of the manuscript reading. The transmitted text reads 'nooses' rather than 'head-cut', and problematically demands a metrical feature called epic correption that does not appear outside dactylic verse. The other possible problem is that death by hanging has not been a feature of the Atreidai's backstory, at least as far as we know; but at least two women in this household, Aerope and Pelopia, may have killed themselves in texts that we have lost (see 1569–70*). This sentence is a turning-point: it is the first time Cassandra has answered the chorus, or even acknowledged anyone else's presence (except, in a sense, Apollo's). **human abattoir, floors spattered:** Although the text needs slight emendation, the overwhelming power of this image and indeed of the whole sentence represents Aeschylean poetry at its most formidable.

1093–4   seems keen-scented, like a dog: The adjective *heuris* is also used of a dog tracking with its nose at Soph. *Aj.* 8; a good sense of smell is a requirement in a hunting dog (Xen. *Cyn.* 4.6). On canine imagery see 3* and, on the sense of smell, 597* and Introduction, p. 60. **is on a trail where she'll detect murder:** Lit., 'she's tracking [things] from which she will discover murder'. This is the first time the chorus have explicitly said that murder has been committed in the palace of the Atreidai.

1095   Yes, for: In tragic dialogue and Plato, *gar* often requires that 'yes' or 'no' is supplied from the context, where further evidence is to be produced (Soph. *Ant.* 450, Plato, *Symp.* 194a). Cassandra responds to the chorus for the second time.

1096–7   these babies howling: The deictic and the participle suggest that Cassandra, in her visionary state, can see *and hear* the murdered sons of Thyestes clearly and believes that the chorus can, too: these children's miserable voices are therefore added to the previous miserable vocalisations evoked in the soundscape of the play (see 276–9). **devoured by their father:** This is a reference to the Thyestean feast, the first time it has been explicitly mentioned. The dead boys, who are probably part of the household's cacophonous resident chorus Cassandra perceives at 1188–93, will be described by her in more detail at 1217–22. They are identified by the Argive chorus as Thyestes' children at 1242–4, and both Clytemnestra and they understand that the violence has its origins in the 'sacrifice of young ones' and 'congealed blood of children devoured' (1504, 1513); when Aegisthus eventually appears, he describes in disgusting detail the butchery of his older brothers when he was still a tiny baby (1592–9). Cassandra is not currently prophesying, but divining what has happened in the house a generation ago.

1098–9   Yes: *kai mēn* often indicates affirmation. **your famous mantic power:** Lit., 'your mantic fame'. The chorus, shocked at her evocation of Thyestes' act of unwitting cannibalism, imply that it is unnecessary for her actually to *demonstrate* her mantic gift to them. **we're not looking for any prophets:** The chorus' experience of prophets in the past has not been positive (156–7). The effect of this barb is reinforced by the same verb as they had just used of Cassandra's mantic activity, *mateuein* (1094), but with a slightly different sense, and by the play on *mat-* and *mant-* sounds.

1100 *Iō popoi!* On *popoi* see 1072*; it is here preceded by another exclamation of strong emotion, *Iō*, on which see 411* and 503*. **Whatever's the plan?** Lit., 'what is s/he planning?' Cassandra stops responding to the chorus and asks a question about what she can 'see'; it is either rhetorical or addressed to Apollo. This stanza does not identify the gender of the individual planning evil, and it spoils the tension and the ambiguity of Cassandra's statement to translate it as 'she'. Cassandra suddenly moves from voicing an intimation about past murders to wondering in rhetorically powerful question form what is about to happen in the imminent future.

1102 **planned:** Lit., 's/he is planning', changed in the translation to the passive for the same reason as in line 1100*.

1103–4 **incurable:** On medical imagery see 17*. **help is far away:** Lit., 'help stands absent at a distance'. The audience might conceivably understand this to mean Menelaus, whose whereabouts are unknown and who is feared dead (617–23*), but it is much more likely that they think of Orestes, who has been raised in Phocis (880–1*).

1105 **I have no idea:** The chorus are entirely bewildered by Cassandra's mysterious statement about an impending catastrophe. **the others; the whole city resounds with them:** This is the first time that we have been told that the memory of the Thyestean feast remains very publicly alive in Argos.

1107 **wretched woman:** Only now is there clarification of the gender of the person whose actions are so disturbing Cassandra.

1108–9 **bathing your husband, who shares your bed, to make him glisten?** Lit., 'brightening the bed-sharing husband with baths?' Cassandra starts to describe concretely exactly what she believes is happening inside simultaneously. A man's corpse would normally be washed by his widow and other close female relatives, but Clytemnestra is washing him *before* his death. In Greek epic, the bath of a hero after battle or journey, assisted by women and presented in a positive light, was far from unusual (Grethlein (2007)), but on one momentous occasion in the *Iliad* it is associated with a warrior's death. Immediately before she learns of her husband's expiry, Andromache is at home inside the walls of Troy, weaving, after ordering her slaves to prepare a hot bath for Hector to soothe him on his return (*Iliad* 22.442–4). The participle *phaidrounasa* here seems sinister, but in this particular stanza Cassandra says nothing explicit to suggest Clytemnestra is doing anything more elaborate than helping her husband take a bath. On Clytemnestra's bed and bedpartners see 27*. Bridegrooms as well as brides took ritual baths before wedding feasts (Oakley and Sinos (1993) 15, with figs 10–13), so this perverted scene of ablution has nuptial as well as funereal resonances, and reminds us that Agamemnon is being washed by one wife while his 'spear-bride' visualises the scene from the other side of his palace wall.

1110–11   she's stretching out first this hand and then the other: Lit., 'she holds forward stretchings hand from hand'. The action Cassandra ambiguously describes could simply be part of Clytemnestra's activities in helping her husband wash. These lines may be illustrated in a fragmentary Lucanian crater of about 400 BCE in the Herbert Cahn collection in Basel, discussed in Hall (2005a) 58–9 (see Figure 7 and the cover of this book), on which the faces, especially the eyes and the wrinkles, suggest the effect created by theatrical masks. Here a woman, not in the first flush of youth, appears to be holding in her left hand the greaves of the mature, bearded, seated man; her right hand seems to be on his head. The left hand of a mostly invisible third party is visibly pressing the seated man's head down. If this image represents Clytemnestra and Agamemnon, which seems likely, then she is, however, not attacking her husband single-handedly, as she claims in this play.

1112–13   I'm baffled: The chorus' bewilderment increases as events develop, and they repeat the same part of the same verb both at 1177 and 1530. **obscure prophecies emanating from riddles:** Lit., 'by dimly perceived prophecies out of riddles'. The adjective *epargemos* literally means 'with a white film over the eyes' (Aristot. *HA* 609b16, 620a1), so this a strikingly sensory metaphorical description of prophecies that defy interpretation: see 240*. When Cassandra later ceases singing and begins to speak in intelligible iambic trimeters, she says that she has stopped talking in riddles (1183*).

1114   *E, e, papai papai*: These are further incoherent exclamations, *papai* being associated with extreme agony, either psychological (Aesch. *Pers.* 1032) or, more often, physical (Soph. *Phil.* 746, 754, 792). **What's this that appears?** Cassandra is describing in concrete detail what her clairvoyance allows her to see going on or about to go on behind the palace walls; since oracular language often uses the present tense (126–7*), temporal precision is not to be expected.

1115–18   hunting-net of Hades: This is the first reference to the net with which Clytemnestra restrains Agamemnon in order to stab him and which Orestes will have spread out in front of the palace after he has murdered her and Aegisthus in *Choephori* (981–1000); he describes it there as a snare, a shroud and, once again, a hunting-net. On imagery of the hunt see 132–4* and 358*. Hades is a son of Kronos and Rhea; when the universe was divided between him and his brothers Zeus and Poseidon, he received the world of the shades of the dead (Apollod. 1.1.5, 2.1), the horrors of which he was determined to keep concealed from both mortals and other gods (Hom. *Il.* 20.61–5). He is sometimes called 'Underworld Zeus' (Zeus *katachthonios*, Hom. *Il.* 457). See also 667*. **a snare that sleeps with him:** Because *arkus* is a feminine noun, the article *hē* before *xuneunos* is also feminine, making the ensnaring net equivalent to Clytemnestra, Agamemnon's consort, herself. **the accomplice in murder:** Once again gendered feminine. But the *xun-* element clearly indicates that the net is not the only contributor to the murder (Plato. *Gorg.* 519b, *Tim.* 46d). Cassandra's words could be construed as meaning that the net is Clytemnestra's co-murderer, or alternatively that someone else altogether, in addition to Clytemnestra/the net, is involved. On Clytemnestra and Agamemnon as bedpartners see 27*. **faction:** This is one possible meaning of *stasis*, which is used by Theognis and Herodotus to refer to a party formed for seditious purposes (Theog. 51, Hdt. 1.59, 1.173). In *Choephori* it is used of the group of mourners praying for vengeance gathered at Agamemnon's grave (114, 458), but in *Eumenides* it is the Erinyes themselves who say that they form a *stasis*, 'company' or 'faction', that directs the affairs of men (311). Alternatively, *stasis* might here refer to a personification of factionalism or discord (see *stasin emphulon* at Solon 4.19; Thuc. 2.65), but the chorus' response at 1119* suggests that they have understood Cassandra to mean the Erinyes. Wilson and Taplin (1993) 172 regard Cassandra's image as 'a prime instance of submerged self-referentiality, since it is an enigmatic, subliminal prefiguring of what later becomes literal. This image of a choros—the product of Kassandra's prophetic/poetic vision—will of course take on a theatrical reality in the *Eumenides*, where it will be described again as a stasis (*Eum.* 311)' and its relation to political stasis will 'be explicitly thematised'. **that never gets enough of this family:** Lit., 'insatiate towards this family'. The adjective *akoretos* is equivalent to *akorestos*, which the chorus had used of a family's despair at 756. **raise the triumphal cry:** See 28*. **over a condemned victim:** Lit., 'over a sacrificial victim condemned to be stoned to death'. This mysterious phrase, with its jarring reference to stoning, in a context where the death is indoors and has so far only been connected with a bath and a net, could refer either to Agamemnon (currently being executed) or to Clytemnestra; the chorus later threaten Aegisthus with public curses and death by stoning for involvement with the murder of Agamemnon (1616*).

1119 Erinys: The chorus assume that by *stasis* at 1117* Cassandra had meant the Erinyes as a collective. This assumption may have been consolidated by her reference to Hades in the same stanza (1115*). In the *Iliad*, Althaea, angry with her son for killing her brother, kneels down and beats the earth with her hands and calls upon Hades and Persephone, and from Erebus she is heard 'by the Erinys who walks in darkness, she of the ungentle heart' (9.565–72). Hades and the Erinyes were closely connected in Greek cult, including at Athens (Paus. 1.28.6); in some accounts, the Erinyes were the daughters of Hades or his equivalent, Chthonian Zeus (see, e.g., Orphic Hymn 69.1–2, to the Eumenides). Cassandra calls Clytemnestra 'mother of Hades' at 1235–6*. On Hades see also 667*. The chorus are so disturbed by the direction Cassandra is taking that after these two iambic lines they begin to sing lyrics at 1121–3; the same iambic to lyric transition occurs in the corresponding 1130–5, after which the chorus sings for the remainder of the amoibaion.

1120   to raise a cry: See 28*. **don't cheer:** Lit., 'do not brighten me'.

1121–3   Yellow-stained drops … life's light: The chorus' first sung sentence in the amoibaion is corrupt and difficult. The text as printed would translate, more literally, as 'Onto my heart ran a yellow-dyed drop, as when, falling at the critical moment, it comes to an end along with beams of the setting life'. It is an image expressing the physiological corollary of painful emotion similar to that at 179–80*, where anguish had been said to drip over the heart or mind during sleep. Here, however, it merges into a picture of someone physically collapsing in death like a setting sun. The close echo of Iphigenia's yellow-dyed robes falling around her when she was sacrificed over the altar is not coincidental (239*), although there is perhaps a sense, also, of a complexion becoming sallow pale in death. Aristotle fr. 243 Rose states that in people who are terrified, blood runs towards the heart from other part of the body, resulting in pallor. For further discussion see Irwin (1974) 53–4. **falling:** The drop coursing over the heart now seems to drip in a manner suggestive of blood. **at the critical moment:** The term *kairia*, related to the noun *kairos* ('the opportune moment'), when applied to injuries can mean 'lethal' or 'mortal' in the sense of bringing death (see Hdt. 3.64, Xen. *Cyr.* 5.4.5 and 1353*) and so could here be translated 'fatal'.

1124   destruction: On *atē* see 359–61*.

1125–6   Ah! Ah! *a* is a cry which precedes a negative address, such as insult, or (as here) a compassionate exclamation (Hom. *Il.* 17.201, *Od.* 14.361, 20.351). **Look, look!** In her clairvoyant state, Cassandra seems to assume that others can see what she can. **Keep the bull away from the cow:** The shocking comparison emphasises that the couple once had a sexual relationship (see 245–7*); it will have reminded the audience of the words of Agamemnon's ghost to Odysseus in *Od.* 11.411—Aegisthus and Clytemnestra had killed him 'like a bull at the manger'. On bull images see also 34–9*. This may also continue the imagery of wedding rituals, since bulls were sometimes sacrificed for wedding feasts (Oakley and Sinos (1993) 12 and fig. 2). **in cloths:** The masculine noun *peplos* can refer to any piece of weaving, not just a garment, and often refers to textiles used to cover corpses at funerals (Hom. *Il.* 5.194, Eur. *Hec.* 432). On the textile in which Agamemnon was caught to be stabbed see also 1115–18*.

1127 a device that has a handle of black horn: Some translators have assumed that the Greek means, rather, 'a cunning movement of her black horn', as if Cassandra sees Clytemnestra's assault on Agamemnon as similar to a cow butting a bull. But Bronze Age, archaic and classical Greek swords often had handles made of antler wood, ebony, ivory, or other animal bone. Presumably Cassandra is not seeing in her mind's eye with precise simultaneity what is going on inside the house, since Agamemnon's death cries do not come until later (1343, 1345); she is here, at least, pre-empting events by just a few minutes. On the precise nature of Clytemnestra's weapon see 1260–3*.

1128 vessel of water: On *teuchos* see 433–6*.

1129 a fate in a treacherous, murderous bath: Lit., 'a fate of a treacherous and murderous basin'. The issue of the trickery involved in persuading Agamemnon to take a bath, thereby disarming him (see also 154–5* and 886*), is soon to become more complicated. The chorus agree that the murder was aggravated by the premeditated scheming involved (1495–6*). But Clytemnestra will counter that Agamemnon had himself used deceit to ruin the household (1521*). Aegisthus traces the use of malicious guile back to Atreus (1582*). But he also, confusingly, claims both that he was personally responsible for plotting Agamemnon's death (1609) and that the actual trickery was obviously Clytemnestra's idea (1636), since she is female. The upshot is that deceit is practised, or said to be so, by all the murderers in this blighted family's history.

1130 good at judging oracles: Lit., 'topmost in the judgements of oracles'.

1131 I think these mean something bad: Lit., 'I liken these to something bad'. There is possibly a grim humour here, given the utterly bizarre images which Cassandra has been communicating to them.

1132–5 What good pronouncement … prophecy: It is a commonplace in ancient Greek literature that a displeasing prophecy produces an expression of scepticism about the reliability of all forms of divination. See, e.g., Hom.

Il. 1.108, Soph. *OT* 390–8. **Through predicting bad things, their skill and wordiness:** Lit., 'Through bad things wordy skills'. **frightened:** See 12–14*.

1136 *Iō iō*: See 411* and 1100*. **the misery of my ill-fated destiny:** Lit., 'the ill-fated fortunes of miserable [me]'.

1137 **pouring it in on top:** These four words translate the single adverb *epenchudan*, an emendation of the unmetrical manuscript reading, which means something to do with pouring over or in addition. The adverb is otherwise unattested, but formed on analogy with the adverb *chudēn*, 'pouringly'—i.e., in substantial quantities. This implies that Cassandra sees her suffering as a supplement to Agamemnon's.

1138 **why did you bring me here?** This is most likely to be addressed to Agamemnon, but it might be Apollo.

1139 **to die, and not alone:** Lit., 'that I might die together'. If the previous line was addressed to Agamemnon, this could be translated 'to die with you', but the Greek leaves this ambiguous. Cassandra's mantic gift allows her to see that, despite Clytemnestra's claim that she would not be especially ill-treated (1043), if Agamemnon dies she has no chance of survival.

1140 **Your mind is crazed:** During much of this sequence, the chorus alternate personal reflection with direct address to Cassandra in the second person. **possessed by a god:** Lit., 'borne [off] by a god' (this means the same as *theophorous* at 1150). Despite Cassandra's addresses to Apollo, the chorus are not at all clear what is happening to her. At 1173–6 they speculate that she has been attacked by a malicious *daimōn*.

1141–3 **an unmelodic melody:** This is a resonant case of litotes to denote an inappropriate or unpleasant musical performance. Aristotle (*Rhet.* 3.1408a) discusses the poets' fondness for such negative phrases as 'stringless' or 'lyreless melody'. **about your own plight:** Lit., 'about yourself'. **like the chirruping nightingale … sorrows:** Lit., 'like some chirruping [female thing] insatiable of crying out—alas—groaning 'Itys, Itys' in her pitifulness-loving heart, the nightingale, throughout her life with sorrows flourishing on both sides'. The adjective *xouthos* is associated elsewhere with the nightingale's song and seems to mean 'quivering' or 'vibrating' (Ar. *Birds* 214, 676, 744). This is an excellent description of all the varied sequence of sounds made by the male nightingale (the female is in reality mute); for other ancient references see the estimable Thompson (1936) 16–22. On birds in *Agamemnon* see Introduction, p. 58, and on the relationship between this image and the musical dimension of the play in performance, Pillinger (2019) 50–4. **alas:** *pheu* is yet another exclamation expressing strong emotion, in tragedy usually grief (Aesch. *Eum.* 841).

It's not clear whether the chorus are paraphrasing what the nightingale or Cassandra is saying, or interjecting this exclamation in their own voice, as it were. **'Itys, Itys':** This was the name of the son of an Athenian princess usually named Procne, who was turned into a nightingale, and her Thracian husband Tereus, who was turned into a hawk or a hoopoe. Procne's story has points of contact with that of the house of Atreus, since she killed her child Itys and fed him to the unwitting Tereus in an act of revenge, similar to the Thyestean feast (1597*), to punish him for raping and mutilating her sister Philomela (who was turned into a swallow). The full story was enacted in a famous tragedy by Sophocles named *Tereus*, which was in turn parodied in Aristophanes' *Birds* (see Hall (2020b) 200–3) and became elaborated in later classical authors, especially Ovid in *Metamorphoses* (6.401–674). But Aeschylus had already explored the parallel between female tragic lament and the nightingale's story in his *Suppliants*, where she is named not Procne but Metis: the chorus says someone who knows about birdsong would think he heard 'the voice of Metis, the piteous wife of Tereus, the hawk-chased nightingale, who was forced to depart from her green leaves and laments pitifully her customary places; she composes the story of her the fate of her child, who was killed, slaughtered by the hand of his enraged unnatural mother' (60–7). **For a death so abundant in sorrows:** *amphithalēs*, 'blooming on both sides', can mean a person who has two living parents (Hom. *Il.* 22.496), and so this passage might conceivably mean that the fate of Itys involved evildoing by both parents (so Sommerstein (2009) 137 n.246). But at *Choeph.* 394 *amphithalēs* just means 'abounding'.

1146 *Iō iō*: See 1072*. **the clear-voiced nightingale:** *ligus* in description of a sound means sweet, penetrating and well-articulated; whether the lyre (Hom. *Il.* 9.186, *Od.* 8.67), the voice of the Muse (Hom. *Il.* 24.62), the authorial voice in an address to the Muse (Alcman fr. 28) or an orator (Hom. *Il.* 1.248). After Hesiod and always in Aeschylus it is used of sad sounds (Aesch. *Pers.* 332, 468).

1147–9 **the gods wrapped her in a winged body:** Lit., 'the gods cast on her a winged body'. Cassandra is thinking of Metis'/Procne's metamorphosis. On winged beings see 390–5*. **a sweet life free from tears:** The loss of other sources for this myth in Greek literature before and in the fifth century BCE means that we cannot be sure that any other author said that the Athenian aristocrat, once a nightingale, was no longer conscious of her previous suffering, which is the explanation offered by a scholion on this line. On tears see 270*. **being split open by a double-edged shaft:** This is a brutal description of a brutal act. Cassandra is quite clear that she is about to be killed. Unfortunately, the neuter noun *doru* does not clarify exactly what weapon she is envisaging, because its basic meaning is 'wood' or 'stick' of wood; it came to mean the shaft of a weapon and then, often in Homer, specifically a spear. On Clytemnestra's weapon see 1260–3*.

1150–1   these agonising onslaughts of divine possession: Lit., 'on-rushing divinely possessed agonies'. On *epissutos* see also 887* and 1140*.

1152–3   And why do you set these horrors to a tune with cacophonous shrieks and piercing refrains? These lines provide a precise description of the type of vocal performance Aeschylus wanted from the actor playing Cassandra. The point seems to be a jerky alternation, suggestive of serial onslaughts of sensation, between screams and passages with a clear melodic line. A *klangē* is often found coming from the mouths of fauna including birds (Hom. *Od.* 11.605), pigs (Hom. *Od.* 14.412), wolves and lions (Hom. *Hymn to the Mother of the Gods*, 14.4), serpents (Aesch. *Sept.* 381) and dogs (Xen. *Cyr.* 4.5); see also on the related verb *klazein* (48*). The adjective *orthios* in reference to a sound means 'shrill' (Aesch. *Pers.* 389, Soph. *Ant.* 1206, Eur. *Tro.* 1266), and indeed an *orthios nomos* was a technical term for a traditional melody performed at a very high pitch (cf. [Aristot.] *Probl.* 920b20, Hdt. 1.24, Ar. *Ach.* 16).

1154–5   How can you know what the limits are: Lit., 'From where do you have limits?' The chorus seem to be wondering whether there is any end in sight to Cassandra's frenzy, or any limit to its weirdness. The primary meaning of the masculine noun *horos* was a stone set up to mark the boundaries of a piece of land (*Il.* 21.405) or the direction of a roadway, as in the metaphor in Bacchylides fr. 11.1–2: 'There is one guide-mark (*horos*), one pathway (*hodos*) to happiness for mortals: the ability to keep an ungrieving spirit throughout life.'

1156   *Iō*: See 1072*. marriage of Paris: From thinking about the mythical example of the mourner turned into a nightingale, and her own imminent death, Cassandra now moves back in time to the fateful union of Paris and Helen previously replayed in the chorus' imagination; they had also meditated on the harm it brought to Paris' kinfolk (704–8*). Attempts to identify this as Paris' earlier marriage to the Mount Ida nymph Oenone are unconvincing: see Vandersmissen (2013).

1157–61   Cassandra unifies her past and her future through the beautiful imagery of rivers. the waters of the Scamander, drunk by my ancestors: Lit., 'the ancestral drink of the Scamander'. Scamander was also himself ancestor of the Trojan royal house (Diod. Sic. 4.75.1), its first king and the father of Teucer (on whom see 108–15*). He was the son of Tethys and Ocean (Hes. *Theog.* 337–45). He plays an important role in the *Iliad*, when he fights Achilles (21.211–383). The gods had their own name for him, Xanthus (Hom. *Il.* 20.74), and the importance of the river to the Trojan royal family is revealed when Homer tells us that Hector's private name for his son (and Cassandra's nephew) Astyanax was Scamandrius (*Il.* 6.402). In the chorus' evocation of Helen's arrival at Troy it had been Scamander's brother and tributary river, Simois, that they had named (695*). **I used then to be raised and nurtured:** Lit., 'I was growing to maturity with nurturings'. **Cocytus:** This is one of the rivers of the Underworld, the name of which derived from the verb *kōkuein*, 'utter a shrill lament' (see 1314*). In the *Odyssey*, Circe gives Odysseus directions for navigating his way in the Underworld. After he has crossed the stream of Ocean, he is to beach his ship beside a grove of Persephone and proceed into Hades at the point where the rivers Periphlegethon and Cocytus, which is a branch of the Styx, join the Acheron; the place is marked by a rock (10.508–15). **Acheron:** This is the major river (sometimes a lake or swamp, below at 1555–9 a ford) of the Underworld, identified with several rivers known to the ancient Greeks—including the one that still bears its name in Thesprotia, Epirus (Thuc. 1.46)—for example, one near Hermione in Argolis (Paus. 2.35.7) and another near Pontic Heraclea (Xen. Anab. 6.2.2). It name was sometimes thought to be derived from the neuter noun *achos*, 'sorrow'; Clytemnestra later imagines the dead Agamemnon being reunited with Iphigenia in the region of these Underworld rivers (1555–9*). For Ancient Near Eastern equivalents of the notion of the body of water that needs to be passed to the Underworld, see West (1997) 155.

1162   words whose meaning is all too clear: Lit., 'excessively clear word'. On *toros* see 254*. The chorus finally seem to comprehend that Cassandra is sure she is about to die.

1163   a newborn: See 49–50*, 723–4*.

1164   murderous pain: *phoinios* elsewhere in the play retains more of its primary sense of the redness of blood, on which see 209–10*. Here *dakos* denotes the bite of a noxious beast rather than the beast itself, which is what it means at 821–4* and 1232*.

1165   while you, because of your agonising fate, whimper horribly and shriek: Lit., 'you shrieking horrible whimpers on account of your painful fate'; *threomenas* is the feminine genitive present participle of *threomai*, a rare verb used only of women. This line offers another clue as to the sounds the actor playing Cassandra was emitting.

1166 heart-breaking: Lit., 'fragmenting'. The consistency of the chorus' ability to empathise with Cassandra's pain is striking.

1167 *Iō*: See 1072*. **ordeals:** On *ponoi* see 1*. The alliteration of '*p*' sounds in this stanza adds to its nostalgic pathos.

1168–70 the frequent sacrifices of grazing animals slaughtered by my father to save its walls: Lit., 'the many-slaughtered sacrifices of grazing animals on behalf of the ramparts by my father'. The piety and frequent sacrifices performed by the Trojans, especially Priam and Hector, on both Mount Ida and the Trojan citadel, are stressed in the *Iliad* (4.44–9, 22.171–3, 24.34–5). The walls of Troy have also symbolised its community at 357 and 827. **they effected no cure that prevented:** Lit., 'they furnished no cure'. On pictures of pastoralism see 128–30* and on medical imagery see 17*.

1172 my mind inflamed: Lit., 'hot-minded': on heat and cold in the play see 563–9*. **shall soon collapse to the ground:** Lit., 'shall soon throw [myself] to the ground'. If this emended text is correct, it has Cassandra comparing her own soon-to-be-dead body with the material walls of Troy in the past, as in her previous stanza she had used rivers to connect her past in Troy and her imminent death.

1173 This statement confirms your previous words: Lit., 'What you uttered [is] following the former'.

1175 spirit: On the term *daimōn* see 683–4*, and on the violent verb *empitnein*, 341–2. Cassandra has been in no doubt that Apollo lies behind her mantic seizure, which is now abating, but the chorus have angrily denied that this can be possible at 1078–9* and were speculating about which supernatural being could have possessed her at 1140*.

1176 about distress, suffering and death: Lit., 'lamentable death-bringing sufferings'. This line is metrically climactic, since it contains the first and only full resolved dochmiac in the entire amoibaion (see Metrical Appendix).

1177 I've no idea where it will end: Lit., 'I'm without resource as to the finishing line'. This is said, of course, at the precise moment when her song does end. On the chorus' bafflement see 55–7*, 1105* and 1112–13*.

1178–9 no longer glance out from behind her veils like a newly wed bride: The amoibaion closes and Cassandra utters her first iambic lines. The image links the moment with the references to the ill-omened wedding celebrations of Paris and Helen earlier made by both the chorus (704–8*) and Cassandra (1156*). As Cassandra begins to speak, now at last unaccompanied by instrumental music, she may finally stand still as she turns to address the chorus. She paradoxically produces one of her strangest metaphors, likening her oracular utterance itself to a veiled bride whose eyes can scarcely be seen: on wedding imagery see Introduction, p. 52, and on eyes see 240*. The importance of the bride's veil in wedding rituals is discussed and richly illustrated in Oakley and Sinos (1993) 16–33 with figs. It would be dramatically effective if the actor playing Cassandra had just removed a veil from his mask, or lifted it back to show more of the mask, thus marking the end of the frenzy. Plutarch (*On the Cessation of Oracles* 6 =*Mor.* 397a–b) implies that, at least in his day, the Pythia avoided expensive purple raiment and burned only bay leaves and barley meal, rather than incense, when she was divining. The only certain surviving representation of the Pythia at work is on an Attic red-figure kylix by the Kodros Painter from Vulci in central Italy, dated to about 440–430 BCE (Antikensammlung Berlin, Altes Museum, F 2538). She is wearing a diaphanous veil with a patterned edge over the top of her head, but has pushed it back from her face partially to reveal her hair. Her gown is relatively simple and she holds a bowl and a sprig of bay leaves. One ancient vase-painting probably related to a tragic performance shows Cassandra, still at Troy, holding a branch and in a swoon, collapsed on a seat by a tripod. She is being comforted by an older woman, presumably Hecuba. She wears a simple diaphanous dress and a headband, her hair flowing over her shoulders in four ringlets (Apulian volute-krater of c. 320 BCE attributed to the Underworld Painter in Berlin (1984.45); photo and discussion in Taplin (2007) 252–4).

1180–1   It will spring up on me like a fresh wind blowing against the rising sun: Lit., 'it seems a bright [wind] about to leap on [me] towards the risings of the sun'. This is another extraordinary metaphor, interconnected with all the sun and weather imagery in the play (5*), describing how it subjectively feels to be in a mantic trance, even if a calmer one now than heretofore. Cassandra is keeping the chorus and audience on tenterhooks: will she erupt into song again? Casandra's string of images is remarkable. As Lebeck (1971) 54 comments, there are three elements: 'the simile of a bride whose glances are concealed beneath her veil; the double image of brightness diffused by the rising sun and of the strong morning wind blowing towards its rays; the simile of waves which swell and break as the wind lifts them upwards in the direction of the sun. Before one word picture is complete the next encroaches upon it.'

1181–3   to surge against its rays like a wave: The fresh wind of new mantic illumination is now likened to a sea breaker rising high above the rising sun on the horizon: on sunrise and sea-waves during last night's storm in the Aegean, of which Cassandra is herself a survivor, see 650–70.

far greater than this calamity: This could be understood as her personal misery or as the prospective murder of both her and Agamemnon. **through riddles:** See the chorus' complaint at 1112–13*.

1184–5 be my witnesses: Cassandra at last fully acknowledges the chorus' presence and invites them to follow her thought processes. **as I track the odour:** Lit., 'as I sniff the track'. Cassandra configures herself as a hunting hound on the trail of quarry. See 3*, 357*, 607–8*, 891–4*, 1093–4*. On appeals to the sense of smell see Introduction, p. 60. **crimes committed long ago:** Cassandra's details will start with the conflict between Thyestes and Atreus (1193*), but see 1569–70* on allusions to episodes in the family's earlier history.

1186 a chorus: Cassandra envisages ghostly victims of crimes past as a chorus haunting the interior of the house. See Introduction, p. 71. **singing in cacophonous unison:** Lit., 'singing together but not euphonious'.

1188–90 A troupe of revelling kinsfolk of the Erinyes: Lit., 'A revelling procession of kin Erinyes'. The Erinyes here are seen as those of the actual family dead: see 58–9*. **have guzzled human blood:** Instead of the wine the participants in the ritual procession, *kōmos*, would normally drink, these Erinyes have acquired their 'Dutch courage' through drinking human blood. See 209–10*, Aesch, *Choeph*. 577–8 and *Eum*. 264–6.

1191 chant their chant: Lit., 'hymn their hymn'.

1192–3 about the original felony: The accusative is in apposition to *humnon*. Presumably this refers to Thyestes' sexual encounter with Atreus' wife Aerope; see also 1197, 1469 and 1569–70*. **each in turn:** This implies that each Erinys takes up her joint utterance in succession, rather as the chorus-men of the tragedy may do at 1346–71*; this is not quite what was indicated by *xumphthongos*, 'in unison', at 1187. **spurning:** Lit., 'they spat out'. **loathing its abuser:** Lit., 'hostile to its trampler', Thyestes. On the metaphor of trampling see 369–72*.

1194 Have I missed the target or made a hit like an archer? Cassandra, priestess of Apollo, the god of mantic vision and archery, fuses both aspects of the god in an account of her own prophetic utterance. See 364–5* on other archery imagery.

1195 Or am I a false prophet: The second of Cassandra's two questions indicating her insecurity about being believed perhaps reflects the kind of insulting language in which she later says she had always been derided at Troy (1273–4*).

1196 Bear witness on oath: Cassandra seems to need assurance that her diagnosis of the past crimes in the palace is correct, or at least reassurance that the chorus believe her. It may well be that Sommerstein (2012) 91–3 is right in thinking that the correct reading of the Greek is *mē eidenai*, in which case Cassandra is saying 'bear witness on oath that *you* do *not* know' the misdeeds of the household; he argues that she, 'in effect, is calling the members of the chorus as witnesses to the story of Thyestes' adultery, and challenging them, if they can, to deny on oath that they know the story to be true. This appears to be exactly what Athenian litigants did to witnesses who refused to give the testimony they desired', by a process called *exōmosia* 'swearing out', or in other jurisdictions *ekmarturia* ('testifying out'). On oaths see also 1284, 1432–3, 1569–70.

1197   spoken of since long ago: This presumably refers to Thyestes' affair with Aerope, which must have taken place at least three decades previously. See also 1192–3, 1469 and 1569–70*.

1198–1201   how could an oath: The chorus, insensitive to Cassandra's desperate fear of not being taken seriously or believed, do not see the point of swearing an oath (see Fletcher (2012) 49–50), although they are kind enough to affirm that her diagnosis is correct, leading her to confide further in them. **honourably:** According to Aristotle, *gennaios* referred to consistency of moral character, distinct from the nobility inherited by birth and designated by the adjective *eugenēs* (*Hist. Anim.* 1.488b 18). **provide a cure:** On *paiōnios* see 146* and 848*. **you speak the truth:** Lit., 'speaking you are correct'. **house that speaks another tongue:** On the Trojans' language see 1050–1*.

1202   The seer Apollo: The noun *mantis* is usually applied to a human diviner rather than a god (Hom *Il.* 1.62, 1.106, Thuc. 8.1, Pind. *Pyth.* 11.33, Aesch. *Sept.* 382), but in the *Oresteia* it is distinctively used of Apollo here, at *Choeph.* 559 and *Eum.* 169, and of the Pythian priestess at *Eum.* 29. See also 1275*. It is derived from a putative Proto-Indo-European root **men*, and suggests an altered mental state. A passage in Pindar has been used to distinguish it, in the Delphic context, as a term applied to the priestess herself, from the term used for the attendants; they were each called a *prophētēs* (a word referring to speech rather than mental state) and were involved in delivering the message to the questioner (Pindar fr. 150). But, in practice, both Apollo and the Pythia are referred to by both nouns: see Maurizio (1995) 70, with references in nn.11–14.

1203   lovestruck: Curiously, the same metaphor had been used by the chorus of their longing to see the Herald at 544*. It seems odd that the chorus are surprised at the idea of a male Olympian god desiring a female mortal, since this is wholly consonant with standard patterns of Greek mythology.

Apollo pursued at least 33 mortal women in extant Greek literature in addition to four men and 16 nymphs.

1204 I was ashamed: On *aidōs* see 948*.

1205 Delicacy is more of an option: Lit., 'treat themselves with delicacy'. A metaphorical use, referring to psychological delicacy, in the reflexive middle voice, of the verb which Agamemnon had used to deride Clytemnestra's indulgent physical cossetting of him at 919*.

1206 he wrestled with me: Lit., 'he was a wrestler'. On athletics metaphors see 171–2*. There was a tradition that Apollo had once excelled at the Olympic Games, outrunning Hermes and defeating Ares (on whom see 374–6*) at boxing (Paus. 5.7.10). Wrestling features in another story of Apollo's desire for a mortal woman at Pind. *Pyth.* 9.26–8; he falls in love with the nymph Cyrene when he sees her wrestling, bare-handed, with a lion. **desire:** On *charis* in an erotic context see 417*. This interchange probably reminds the audience that Cassandra has presumably been raped by Agamemnon very recently.

1207 Did you two join in the rite that might produce children? Lit., 'Did you two come by custom to the work of children?' This is as close to asking whether Cassandra had penetrative sex with Apollo as Greek tragic diction can come.

1208 I gave my consent but deceived Loxias: This mysterious line has triggered a great deal of wholly speculative and sometimes prurient scholarship concerning the precise physiological nature of Cassandra's sexual experience with Apollo (see Debnar (2010)). I think we should take her at her word. She gave her consent to join him 'in the rite that would produce children' but in the event did not.

1209 of the god-inspired art: Lit., 'by the divinely inspired arts'. The chorus want to know the exact order of the developments in her relationship with Apollo. She has previously told them that her ability at divination was bestowed upon her by him (1202*).

1210 I was already foretelling: Cassandra implies that, before Apollo approached her sexually, she was already engaged in public prophetic activity, which she has also said was a function bestowed upon her by Apollo. Their relationship is longstanding. This detail about the complicated relationship between them seems to matter to Aeschylus' presentation of this most enigmatic of characters.

1211 How did no damage come to you: Lit., 'How were you undamaged'. The adjective *anatos* is related to the concept of *atē* (359–61*). **anger:** The masculine noun *kotos* is one of Aeschylus' favourite words for wrath, tinged with a desire for revenge, in a god (635*, *Suppl.* 347 (Zeus), fr. 266.5, from his *Phrygians* (*Dikē*)), but see also Clytemnestra's rage at 1261* and her own words at 1464. The chorus' question stems from their correct assumption that mortal women who spurn gods' sexual advances have little hope of escaping unhurt.

1212   I became unable to convince: Lit., 'I was not persuading'. Cassandra's punishment meant that the Trojans would no longer believe any of her predictions.

1213   the truth: Lit., 'trustworthy things'. It further heightens Cassandra's tragedy that she has at last, too late, found a sympathetic if uncomprehending audience.

1213–14   *Iou iou*: This exclamation, usually repeated twice, as here, is most frequently associated with grief or other negative feeling (Dem. 19.20, Soph. *Trach.* 1143, *OT* 1071, Aesch. *Eum.* 1214), but see 25*. It here heralds the arrival of a new wave of mantic inspiration (albeit expressed in iambics) in Cassandra after her brief, rational dialogue with the chorus.

1215   true divination: See the similar compound *alēthomantis* at 1241, and also 1022, where Asclepius' knowledge of supernatural matters is indicated by a compound beginning with *ortho-*. Mason (1959) 85 comments that Cassandra is now determined 'to convince the chorus that this time, as always, she has spoken truly, as if the one thing she must do before her death is to break through the barrier of disbelief which has always been her fate'.

1216   makes me reel: Lit., 'whirls me around'. **its unwanted onset:** Lit., 'with its ill-preluding prelude'. On the neuter noun *phroimion* see 31* and 829*.

1217   those young ones: Another recurrence of the theme of the young of animals (142–3*, 716–19*), perhaps to be identified with the 'chorus' and 'revelling troupe of kinsfolk of the Erinyes' that Cassandra had seen at 1186* and 1188–90*. On the vision and the deictic 'those' see 1258–9*.

1218   figures in dreams: This evocation of phantom-like beings helps the audience imagine what it is that Cassandra can see in her clairvoyant mind's eye: on the importance of dreams and their visual quality see also 12–14*, 80*, 179–80*, 274*, 491*, 891–4*. Ghosts of the dead were most commonly seen in dreams, as the ghost of Clytemnestra appears in the dream experienced by the Erinyes at *Eum.* 94–139. Compare Aesch. *PV* 1218. For the neuter noun *morphōma* see also Clytemnestra's strange language about reported deaths of Agamemnon at 874.

1219–22 children killed by their kinfolk: Although Iphigenia was very young when she died, the obvious reference for this is the two little sons of Thyestes murdered by Atreus; their gruesome fate is to be described in more detail by their surviving brother, Aegisthus, at 1590–602. **they stand out conspicuously:** In the context of a visual description, *prepous'* suggests a painting in which shadow and perspective puts emphasis on these children's bodies (6–7*, 29–30*, 242–3* 321*, 387–9*). **their hands brimming:** This horrific image is made worse by the detailed vocabulary that follows it relating to meat and guts—words usually found in the specific context of animal sacrifice (e.g. Hdt. 2.40, Hom. *Il.* 1.464, *Od.* 3.9, 20.252, Ar. *Pax* 1105, *Knights* 410). **flesh:** On the coarse connotations of *bora* see 1597*. **their father tasted:** This is Thyestes (see commentary on 1584–602), not named here. The verb *geuesthai* adds a sensory touch more macabre than a more basic word for eating would have done.

1123–6 I can tell: Lit., 'I tell'. **a strengthless housekeeping lion:** This would obviously be interpreted as meaning Aegisthus, who has no doubt been on the audience's minds since the mention of Clytemnestra's bed by the Watchman (27*; see also 1108), but who has still not been named a single time; *analkis* means having no *alkē*, 'strength', 'martial valour' or 'power to defend', and is used precisely of Aegisthus (and the stay-at-home suitors of Penelope) in the *Odyssey* (3.375, 4.334); *oikouros* in reference to a male (as opposed to a wife, about whom it can be complimentary: see Dio Cassius 56.3) implies an effeminate shirking of the male duty to leave the household and fight, or even draft-dodging (see Dinarchus 1.82 and cf. 1626*). It also associates this Aegisthus-lion with the 'housekeeper' image used earlier of Clytemnestra's wrath (154–5*; see also 808–9*). On lion imagery see 141* and 827, where Agamemnon's army at Troy was likened to a very different kind of lion. **turns over in bed:** There may be more to the verb here, a frequentative form of *strephein*, 'turn', than this translation suggests. It can suggest a freedom to move around in a place or amongst people (e.g. Hom. *Il.* 9.463), occasionally with a sexual overtone (Eur. *Alc.* 1052), although the suggestion that it here means 'claiming a husband's rights' (LSJ) is rather too strong. The implication is simply that Aegisthus feels perfectly at home in the main palace marriage bed: see other references to it discussed at 27*. **plots:** On the *boul-* stem see 10–11*. **my master:** Cassandra has not previously referred to Agamemnon by any title, and this one expresses her awareness of her newly enslaved status (see 32*). But the strange comment following this implies she has not truly digested the implications of her enslavement. **yoke of slavery:** See 326–8*, 953 and 1071 and other references at 1036–7*.

1227 The admiral of the fleet and the destroyer of Ilium: Cassandra now gives him his full titles as commander of the Trojan expedition (see also 472, 782–4, 905–7), despite knowing him herself now just as 'master'. Aeschylus puts a much greater stress on Agamemnon's role as naval commander than the *Iliad* had done—a response to his contemporary Athenians' identity as a sea-power: see Rosenbloom (1995).

1228–30 what evil fate she will furnish him with: Lit., 'what she will make ready with evil fate'. The relative pronoun is at an unusual distance from the verb. **having licked him with the tongue of a hateful hound and cocked her gleaming ear towards him:** Lit., 'the tongue of a hateful hound having licked [him] and having stretched out her gleaming ear'. The Greek incongruously gives the tongue an ear, both participles grammatically agreeing with *glōssa*, but the audience will have understood a change of subject from the tongue to its possessor—i.e. the female hound representing Clytemnestra in Cassandra's vision. Clytemnestra had likened herself to the faithful dog awaiting her master's return at 607–8*. See also 725–6*. At Hesiod *Theog.* 771 Cerberus fawns (*sainei*, see 725–6) 'with his tail and both his ears' to trick those who arrive in the Underworld into entering the house of Hades and Persephone, but he also ensures that they can never leave. The shade of Agamemnon calls Clytemnestra 'dog-faced' at *Od.* 11.424, adding at 11.427 that there is nothing 'more doglike' (i.e. shameless) than a woman. **clandestine Ruin:** Cassandra as good as identifies Clytemnestra with a personification of covert *Atē*, on which see 359–61*.

1231–3 female murderer of a male: The term *thēlus* often suggests biological sex (it is related to *thaomai*, 'I suck', used of human lactation at e.g. Hom. *Il.* 24.58; see Plato, *Crat.* 414a and Ar. *Lys.* 881, where *athēlos* means 'not breastfed'), and is often applied to animals (Hom. *Od.* Od.4.636, 14.16, Pind. *Ol.* 3.29, Hdt. 3.102); it therefore helps to extend the comparison of Clytemnestra with a dog and forms a bridge to the series of mythical female monsters to which Cassandra will liken her. It is specifically the opposite of *arsēn*, 'male', or its equivalent *arrēn* here, as at e.g. Plato, *Rep.* 5.454d and Aristot., *Metaph.* 1.988a5. The term *phoneus* was used in legal contexts to signify a murderer (Antiphon 4.3.3). On legal language see 41*. **What kind of unlovely monster should I call her?** Lit., 'What unlovely monster could I alight upon naming her? On *dakos* see 821–4* and 1164*.

1233 amphisbaena: This is the earliest reference in classical literature to the species of mythological snake with two heads, one at each end, which was perceived as going in two different directions at once (thus the name). Dicephaly (two heads as a congenital deformity) does occur more often in snakes than in most other animals, but the heads are at the same end. Aristophanes in his *Storks* (fr. 457) mentioned an amphisbaena, which is also described in Aelian, *On Animals* 8.8, 9.23, and Pliny the Elder, *NH* 8.85, who points out that having two heads from which to dispense poison makes it twice as deadly. **Scylla:** This sea-monster, encountered by Odysseus, forms a pair with the whirlpool Charybdis; in the *Odyssey* she barks like a dog (and an etymological connection, probably false, is suggested between her name and the noun *skulax*, dog, at 12.86); she has 12 feet, six long necks and mouths, each of which contained three rows of sharp teeth (*Od.* 12.85–92, 12.245–59). In classical art her appearance is different: she is a beautiful trident-wielding sea-goddess with a single torso and fish tail, but with two or more upper bodies and heads of dogs attached to her waist; see, e.g., the Paestan red-figured calyx-krater signed by Asteas, c. 340 BCE, formerly in the J. Paul Getty Museum, Malibu (Malibu 81.AE.78) and now in the Archaeological Museum of Paestum. On the paradox of the twin conceptions of her appearance see the excellent Hopman (2012). Aeschylus is likely to have been interested in Scylla, since he composed at least two plays about Glaucus (frr. 25a to 42a; see Wright (2018) 23–6), a sea-god who in some narratives loved Scylla (Ovid, *Met.* 13.898–14.74). She was often known by her matrilineal descent, as daughter of Kratais (*Od.* 12.126) or Lamia the shark (Stesichorus in his *Scylla*, fr. 220). Because Odysseus' wanderings became identified in the ancient imagination with the western parts of Italy, a town there was named after her (Pliny the Elder, *NH* 3.73). Plato includes her, with the Chimaera and Cerberus, in a list of fabled monsters of hybrid form (*Rep.* 2.588c). These are the only mythical comparisons in the play which are not negative in import (see Introduction, p. 101): Clytemnestra is the equivalent, not the opposite, of the amphisbaena and Scylla; similarly, in *Choeph.* 612–22, the chorus invoke the crime of 'dog-minded' Scylla as offering a parallel to Clytemnestra's felony.

1234　to cause harm to sailors: Lit., 'damage of sailors'. In the *Odyssey*, Odysseus narrates in Phaeacia the awful incident when Scylla dragged six of his crewmen 'writhing up towards the rocks. There at her doors she gulped them down shouting and stretching their hands towards me in the dreadful death throes. That was the most pitiable thing I ever saw with my eyes while I was exploring the pathways of the sea' (12.255–9).

1235–6　seething: The verb *thuein* in Homer is usually used of elemental forces such as a wind (*Od.* 12.400), a swollen river (*Il.* 21.234), a stormy sea (*Il.* 23.230) or the earth seething with gore (*Od.* 11.420), but metaphorically it could be used of an individual raging around angrily (*Il.* 1.342) or with a weapon (*Il.* 11.180). **mother of Hades:** See 667* and 1119*. Of course, Clytemnestra was not technically Hades' mother, but the many scholars who have worried about this have rather missed the power of the image. **who breathes war:** The same metaphor had been used by the chorus of indefinite malefactors at 375–6*; metaphors involving the same verb are quite frequent in the play (219, 1206, 1309) and cf. *Choeph.* 34 and 951; they offer actors an opportunity for a distinct kind of vocal delivery pointed up by exhalation. **she raised the triumph shout:** See 28*, and especially *Choeph.* 942, where exactly the same verb with the same prefix is used by the triumphant chorus while Orestes is killing Clytemnestra.

1237 all-daring woman: At 221* the chorus had used the similar formulation *to pantotolmon* of Agamemnon's decision 'to dare to think the unthinkable' and sacrifice Iphigenia. **as in the battle rout:** Lit., 'as in the [moment] of battle when the rout [of the enemy begins]'. At 941–3 Agamemnon and Clytemnestra had characterised their dialogue as a battle (*machē*, 941) which one of them must win.

1238 feigning delight at his safe return: This is an excellent description of Clytemnestra's conduct throughout the play so far. But it raises the macabre question of whether Clytemnestra would rather he had died at Troy (an unfulfilled possibility she mulled over in some detail at 861–73) or return so that she could have the satisfaction of killing him herself. On Agamemnon's *nostimos sōtēria*, safe homecoming, which he would probably have attributed to Zeus, see 245–7*.

1239 It's all the same whether I convince anyone of any of this: See 1212*. Cassandra senses, correctly, that the chorus do not actually believe that Agamemnon is about to die: see Greenhalgh (1969) 257–8.

1241 pitying me: Cassandra has at least noticed that the chorus are sympathetic towards her. **a prophet who speaks all too truly:** The issue of her veracity now recurs obsessively in her speech: see 1215*.

1242–3 Thyestes': This is the first time he has been named in the play, despite several allusions to the horrible banquet and to his adulterous relationship with Aerope (1096–7, 1105, 1192–3, 1197, 1219–22). **feasting on his children's flesh:** Lit., 'feast of the children-meat'. **I understood and I shuddered and terror seizes me:** The tricolon with an expanded third element is 'a very old and certainly pre-rhetorical form of emphatic expression' (Fraenkel (1950) vol. 3, 574). On the somatic apprehension of emotions see Introduction, p. 62; the verb also suggests the sort of movements the chorus-men might have been executing during Cassandra's prophetic seizure and might be making now. Terror is the most frequently mentioned emotion in the play (12–14*).

1245   I completely lose track: Lit., 'I run having fallen off the course.' The chorus feel like runners who have strayed even from the designated racecourse. On athletics imagery see 171–2*. Although they are understandably reluctant to face the truth of the situation, they come over as somewhat obtuse in having no idea how to decode Cassandra's several images about females murdering males.

1246   Agamemnon dead: Lit., 'the fate of Agamemnon'. Cassandra has not previously used his proper name. The statement here could not be balder.

1247   Don't speak inauspicious words: Lit., 'Lull your mouth [to make it] auspicious of speech.' On *euphēmos* see 636–7*. A harsh, contentious tone enters the dialogue between the chorus and Cassandra for the first time.

1248   no healing god: Cassandra surely means Apollo, whom she is about to repudiate altogether; see 146*. Her point is that if there is no divinity in charge who can prevent Agamemnon being murdered, then there is no divinity to offend by using bald language. **this prediction:** Lit., 'this speech'.

1249   may it somehow not happen: The chorus' hope, alongside their apparent inability to act on Cassandra's information, might appear incongruous, but although they pity her, they have at no point said that they believe everything she says.

1250   You do your praying: their concern is killing: This is a wonderfully scornful antithesis. Cassandra lurches from opacity to lucidity that is even more terrifying and responds to the chorus' more combative tone towards her. The plural raises an interesting question about the degree of cooperation between Clytemnestra and Aegisthus and indeed any others involved.

1251   which man is organising this woeful deed? Lit., 'this woe is prepared by which man?' On *achos* see 1157–61*. As so often, the vocabulary creates links between the several murders in the family's history, since the verb *porsunein* is used later by Clytemnestra in oblique reference to Agamemnon's preparation of Iphigenia's sacrifice (1374*).

1252   You're surely deluded about the meaning of my prophecies: Lit., 'You were deluded about my prophecies'. The verb *parakoptein* here means to suffer from the delusion, *parakopē*, which the chorus had earlier said made Agamemnon decide to sacrifice Iphigenia (223*). Cassandra is turning the tables on the chorus. Who is deluded now?

1253   That's because: Here *gar* explains the reason why they have not yet grasped her meaning. **I don't understand:** The chorus repeat this verb from

1112. Even if the chorus are slow to decode allegorical language, Cassandra has in fact specifically named neither Clytemnestra nor Aegisthus.

1254   I know the Greek language: Cassandra is frustrated either by their assumption that the perpetrator is male, or because they have not understood the 'strategy' (bath, net, stabbing), or because she fears that, like the Trojans before them, they do not believe her. In her mind, she has made herself completely clear, and she has certainly been using excellent Greek, even if her content is somewhat opaque. On the Trojans' language see 1050–1*. Diller (1961) 48–9 points to the paradox that Cassandra, who at first seemed to be ignorant of Greek, comprehends the major metaphysical issues of play and the nature of life and death better than anyone else in the tragedy.

1255   Pythian oracles: This is the first time these have been mentioned in a trilogy during which they will become increasingly important (see 509*). The chorus' sentiment is quite aggressive, yet the obscure language of the Delphic pronouncements was notorious: see Introduction, pp. 41–2 and Lucian, *Zeus Tragoedus* 28: 'You spoke rightly, Apollo, when you praised those who speak clearly, even if you don't do exactly the same in your prophecies, being ambiguous and riddling and tossing virtually everything into no man's land, so that those listening to you need another oracle to explain them.'

1256   *Papai*: See 1114*. In Cassandra's third (see 33*) and final wave of delirium, she settles, perhaps contrary to expectation, into iambic trimeters rather than the lyrics which were previously the vehicle for her mantic possession. She now focuses primarily on her own fate and the prediction of a future avenger which is to be fulfilled in *Choephori*. **the fire:** This is the first time that Cassandra has expressed her mantic frenzy in terms of fire; it is not only appropriate to the fire imagery across the play, most notable in the account of the beacon relay, but is suggestive of sacrifice and funeral pyres, both of which suit her topic well. The famous unquenchable fire at Apollo's Delphic temple was tended on the altar of Hestia.

1257   *Ototoi*: See 1072*. **Lycian Apollo:** This is the second cult title Cassandra has used of the god (1081–2*). Alternatively spelled *Lukios*, it was derived in different ways in antiquity. Apollo was worshipped in Lycia (Pind. *Pyth.* 1.39), but also at Lycoreia on Mount Parnassus, at Argos and Athens (Paus. 2.9.7, 2.19.3, 1.19.4). In most places where this title appears, however, wolves (*lukoi*) were involved in the related myth or cult. At Argos, the worship of Apollo Lukeios was founded after a wolf attacked a herd of cattle (Plut. *Pyrrh.* 32); Apollo taught the Sicyonians how to rid their territory of wolves (Paus. 2.19.3). An iron wolf stood at Delphi (Paus. 10.14.4). Apollo is called *lukoktonos*, 'wolf-slayer', at Soph. *El.* 7. In his commentary on the *Aeneid* 4.377, Servius offers other explanations, relating the title to e.g. Apollo's later identification with the sun via the adjective 'white' (*leukos*; others suggested a connection with the rare feminine noun *lukē*, meaning dawn twilight); Servius also suggests that Apollo slept in the form of a wolf with Cyrene, the foundation nymph of the city-state that took her name in Libya. For Cassandra, the wolf connotation leads into her impending equation of Aegisthus with a wolf. *oi* **me, me:** This is yet another exclamation of grief.

1258–9 this two-footed: Cassandra begins this mantic speech with a vision marked by a deictic, 'this', just as her previous speech had begun with a vision and the deictic 'those young ones' at 1214–18. **lioness:** On lion imagery see 141*. Agamemnon' army had been likened to a ravening lion at 827*, and Aegisthus to a cowardly one at 1123–6*. Now it is Clytemnestra's turn. **mating with the wolf:** On the sexual relationship between Clytemnestra and Aegisthus see 1453*. It may be relevant that wolves appeared in a proverb about unnatural love between different species (Plato, *Phaedr.* 241d, wolves and sheep) and that 'to live the life of a wolf' was proverbial for living by rapine (Polyb. 16.24.4). **noble lion:** Cassandra's uncritical attitude to Agamemnon, given his instrumentality in her plight, is noteworthy.

1260–3 As if concocting a drug: This sentence begins with the image of Clytemnestra adding (*enthēsein*) an extra ingredient (retribution against Agamemnon for insulting her by bringing Cassandra to their marital home) to the potion constituted by her pre-existing rage (*kotos*, see 1211*) against him (see 636–7* on the motif of blending). But this pharmaceutical image is mixed with the financial metaphor of a wage or fee put on that insult (*misthos*). **she boasts:** On the shades of meaning attached to the verb *euchesthai* and its compounds in the play see 533*. **sharpening her sword:** On the craft of metallurgy see 151–4*. Cassandra, for the first time, uses a word for Clytemnestra's weapon that unambivalently means 'sword' (see the 'device' at 1127 and the 'shaft' at 1147–9*). The chorus will later refer to the murder weapon with another ambiguous term, *belemnon* (1495–6*), although Clytemnestra herself refers to Agamemnon's death by the sword (1529–30*). Nothing in *Agamemnon* suggests that she used the 'manslaying axe' she calls for at *Choephori* 889: see also Introduction, pp. 82, 84. There has been a perhaps disproportionate amount of scholarly fascination with this topic: see, e.g., Prag (1991), Davies (1987) and Sommerstein (1989b).

1265 things that make me ridiculous: Lit., 'these mockeries of myself'. Cassandra probably means not that the priestess's outfit was inherently ridiculous but that, because she was not believed, everyone scorned her.

1266 **staff:** The plural noun probably does not mean that she held more than one. Chryses, the Asiatic priest of Apollo, in the *Iliad*, comes to the Achaean ships 'holding the chaplets (*stemmata*) of far-shooting Apollo in his hands on a staff (*skēptron*) of gold' (1.15; see also 1.28). In a rare ancient Greek depiction of the Pythia (1178–9*), she holds a sprig of bay in one hand and a dish in the other. **garlands:** These *stephē* were probably equivalent to *stemmata*, which were made of combed-out wool wound around an olive branch (schol. on Soph. *OT* 3; cf. Eur. *Or.* 12). At *Plutus* 39 Cario asks Chremylus, who has been to consult the Delphic oracle, 'What then did Phoebus bark out of the *stemmata*?', which implies that the prophetic vestibule was festooned with them. On a Greco-Etruscan bronze *cista*, Apollo sits in his Delphic shrine with a substantial branch of a bay tree at least equivalent to his own height and a network of woollen fillets stretched out over the *omphalos* (navel-stone; see the drawing in Holland (1933) 210 fig. 7).

1266 **You I shall destroy:** Whatever these accoutrements looked like (and of course Cassandra is not a Pythian priestess exactly like the one who opens *Eumenides*), the Cassandra-actor here throws them onto the floor, and possibly breaks and/or tramples upon them (see 369–72*), obedient to a very graphic internal stage direction. This is an act of extreme and shocking sacrilege. Wyles (2011) 68 argues persuasively that as a semiotic dismantlement of her stage character this prefigures her impending death.

1267 **By throwing you down I repay you:** Lit., 'I repay you [by making you] fallen.' Even Cassandra's relationship with her priestly equipment is expressed in terms of reciprocity and payback.

1268 **enrich some other woman by ruining her:** Lit., 'enrich some other woman with ruin'. A scathingly ironic use of the verb *ploutizein*, used in a non-ironic sense meaning 'to benefit' at 586.

1269 **Look, Apollo himself is stripping me:** Cassandra has previously addressed Apollo and his statue (509–11*, 1081–2*), but here she seems to sense him visually; the idea of him stripping her has particularly unpleasant connotations given that he had wanted sexual intimacy with her (1203–8).

1270 **my prophetic outfit:** See 1178–9* and 1266*. Sommerstein (2009) 155n. suggests that what is meant here is the *agrēnon*, 'a reticulated woollen over-garment worn by "Teiresias or other prophets" on stage (Pollux 4.116, cf. Hesychius α776, 777)'. He also astutely observes, 'Agamemnon, before being helplessly slaughtered, will have a net-like robe thrown over him; Cassandra, before going open-eyed to her death, deliberately divests herself of the net-like robe she is wearing.' **having watched closely:** The verb *epopteuein* implies assertive scrutiny, inspection or overseeing

(Hom. *Od.* 16.140, cf. Hes. *Works* 767); Apollo wanted to observe every detail of Cassandra's suffering consequent upon the punishment he inflicted on her.

**1272	by friends turned enemies:** Lit., oxymoronically, 'by loved enemies'. On the polarisation of *philoi* and *echthroi* in Greek tragedy, the best study remains Blundell (1989). **in vain:** Presumably, Cassandra means that their scorn was futile both because it was not fair and because it did not stop her prophesying.

**1273–4	vagabond:** This is a feminine noun equivalent to *agurtēs*, which Plato pairs with *mantis* (on which noun see 1202*) to mean an itinerant figure offering oracular services door-to-door for pay (*Rep.* 2.364b). In *OT* Oedipus insults Teiresias by calling him a 'conniving *agurtēs*' (388). Cassandra may previously have quoted another word that had been used to insult her at 1195*. **a wretched beggar woman starving to death:** Lit., 'a beggar, she-wretch, starving to death'. The asyndeton and the four consecutive harshly derogatory terms, especially with skilled delivery, create an effect of shocking brutality. On hunger see 192–5*.

**1275	the prophet has undone me, the prophetess:** *mantis mantin* has a chiming aural effect. For *ekprassein*, meaning 'to undo' or 'ruin', see Eur. *Hec.* 515, Soph. *OC* 1659.

**1277	my father's altar:** Presumably she refers to the altar of Apollo in Troy; the audience might imagine her have spent her days tending it in the past. Alternatively, it is an oblique reference to the tradition that she sought refuge in Athena's temple only to be raped by Locrian Ajax (see Eur. *Tro.* 70). **chopping-block:** The same word is used by Dikaiopolis in Aristophanes' *Acharnians* of the execution block from which he delivers his great political oration (318, 355, 359, 365). *Agamamnon*, however, does not make clear exactly how Cassandra is killed: in a rare visual depiction of Clytemnestra's assault on her, a cup by the Marlay Painter (ARV 1280.64 = Ferrara T 264, c.430 BCE), Clytemnestra raises an axe over the suppliant Cassandra, against the background of an altar, a bay plant and a tipped-over tripod (see Introduction, p. 84 and Easterling (2005) 34–5 with fig. 2.1).

**1278	hot and gory sacrifice:** The temperature of the body and its constituent parts is a constant sensory interest in this play (563–9). The *pro-* prefix in *prosphagma* implies that she is being sacrificed for someone else (Eur. *Hec.* 41, *IT* 243).

**1279	we shall not die unavenged:** Cassandra's last concrete insight consists of her memorable prediction of the plot of the next play in the trilogy, *Choephori*. The plural suggests that she means herself and Agamemnon, although the context of her visions of the dead in the previous generation (1096–7*) may make her 'we' even more capacious than that.

1280–1 Another shall come: This is Orestes, but Cassandra speaks in the oblique language associated with the Delphic oracle (see Introduction, pp. 42–3). **to avenge:** Lit., 'avenger'. The oracular utterance interlaces two words with the root *tim-* across 1279–80. **A mother-killing offspring to get redress for his father:** The neuter noun *phituma* means the shoot of a plant. This line creates a striking chiasmus. In Aristotle's *Rhetoric* (3.2.14) it is noted that Orestes 'corrects' the term 'mother-slayer' to 'father-avenger' in his altercation with Menelaus (Eur. *Or.* 1587–8); Aeschylus, typically, here allows the paradox of the two ways of thinking about Orestes' act to stand unresolved.

1282 a wanderer, alienated from this land: Orestes repeats this phrase at the end of *Choephori* when, now a polluted murderer, he once again departs from Argos (1041–2); see also *Eum.* 884. On wandering see 77–9*.

1283 he's returning: For *kateimi* in the sense 'I return' or 'I return home from exile' see Hom. *Od.* 13.267, Hdt. 1.62, 3.45, 5.62. **to put the copingstone on his family's devastation:** Lit., 'to put the top stones on the wall of the ruinations of his loved ones'. A *thrinkos* is the top row of stones in a wall, or coping (Hom. *Od.* 17.267, Aristot. *Phys.* 7.246a18), or even a frieze (Hom. *Od.* 7.87); metaphorically it came to mean 'finishing touch' (Eur. *Tro.* 489, Plato *Rep.* 7.534e). Orestes is seen as a builder in an image equating his family's tragic history with the material edifice of their house. In a comedy by Pherecrates, Aeschylus claimed that he had 'built up' (*exoikodomēsas*) a great art to bequeath to future dramatists (schol. Ar. *Peace* 749 = Pherecrates fr. 100), which shows awareness of Aeschylus' own fondness for architectural metaphors. For others see 459–60, 897–8*, 1001–4* and 1459*.

1284 a great oath has been sworn by the gods: The tragedy has already implicated Artemis, Zeus and Apollo in its theodicy; by the conclusion of *Eumenides* almost all the Olympians have been invoked as approving of the way divine justice has been dispensed. But who is swearing this oath and what role do the gods play? It is possible that Cassandra is predicting the oath which, in *Choephori*, Pylades reminds Orestes that he swore to kill Clytemnestra (900–1); the context implies that the god was Apollo. Roberts (1984) 44 and 46 n.18 may be correct in suggesting that Orestes swore an oath to Pylades, who came from Crisa and thus had a strong association with Delphi. See Fletcher (2012) 40–1. On oaths see also 1432–3, 1569–70.

1285   his dead father's prostrate corpse will bring him back: Lit., 'the stretching out of his recumbent father will bring him'. The neuter noun *huptiasma* graphically asks the audience to think of Agamemnon's lifeless body being manhandled.

1286   lament so pitifully: Cassandra's decision not to sing any kind of dirge for herself, after her extreme displays of psychic disturbance, comes as a moving surprise. Several tragic characters sing their own dirges with motifs that suggest 'a basis in popular belief outside the confines of tragic drama' (Alexiou (1974) 113).

1287–90   Because I saw, first: Cassandra had two chances—life in Troy or life as Agamemnon's concubine. She sees correctly that she now has no possibility of survival. **by judgement of the gods:** Cassandra sees the fall of Troy as a punishment following a legal decision passed by a jury of gods, echoing Agamemnon's brutal image at 813–18*. **ending up like this:** On this sense of *apallassein* see Hdt. 5.63, Eur. *Med.* 786, Aeschines 2.38. The Watchman had yearned for an end to his labours using the cognate noun *apallagē* in the opening line of the play. **to meet my fate:** Lit., 'to experience [what I shall]'. **endure:** On this meaning of *tlaō* see the similar point about Agamemnon's death made by the chorus at 1453*.

1291   I address these doors as those of Hades: To pass through the 'gates of Hades' is a metaphor for death in the *Iliad* (5.646, 9.312; see also *Od.* 14.156). It is a terrifying way of thinking about the Argive palace doors that were presumably cut into and painted on the scenery representing the house (Introduction, pp. 69, and 223). On Hades see 67*, 115–18*, 1115*, 1119, 1235–6, 1384–7, 1528.

1292   I pray: On the many meanings of *euchesthai* and its compounds see 933*. **fatal:** On this meaning of *kairios* see 1123* and 1353.

1293–4   without a struggle: The adjective *asphadastos* is related to the verb *sphadaizein*, used of the rapid movements of unbroken horses (Aesch. *Pers.* 194), wounded horses (Xen. *Cyr.* 7.1.37), fish flailing on land (Polyb. 34.3.5) and human death throes (Plut. *Ant.* 76). **my blood flowing away:** Cassandra's picture of an optimally pain-free death succeeds in creating the opposite impact. On blood see 209–10*. The audience will have known from Agamemnon's account of her death in the *Odyssey* that it was difficult (11.421–6): he relates that all the floor swam with blood, 'but the most pitiful voice I heard belonged to Priam's daughter Cassandra, whom wily Clytemnestra slew over my body'. The same detail, Cassandra's piteous death cry, was also recalled by Philostratus the Elder in his description of a painting of the scene (*Imagines* 2.10): 'The most prominent place in the scene is occupied by Agamemnon ... but even more striking in its pathos is the figure of Cassandra—the way Clytemnestra, her eyes crazed, her hair flying, her arm savagely raised, stands over her with the axe, and the way Cassandra herself, tenderly and in a state of inspiration, has tried to throw herself upon Agamemnon as she hurls her fillets from her and as it were casts about him the protection of her prophetic art; and as the axe is now poised above her, she turns her eyes towards it and utters so pathetic a cry that even Agamemnon, with the remnant of life that is in him, pities her, hearing her cry; for he will recount it to Odysseus in Hades in the concourse of souls' (trans. Fairbanks (1931)).

1295–8 You've been talking at great length: See Agamemnon's almost identical comment on Clytemnestra's speech at 916*. The length at which men speak is not similarly regarded as worthy of comment. But the chorus' attitude, in acknowledging that much of what Cassandra has said has been wise, is far kinder than Agamemnon's had been towards his wife. **If you truly know:** On *etētumōs* used of true knowledge about a religious matter see also 681–2*. **how is it that you're walking:** This is an internal stage direction showing that Cassandra must have started moving in the direction of the palace doors she apostrophised at 1291*, as well as something about her gait and demeanour. **like an ox driven by a god:** This is a striking incidence of the prevalent bovine imagery (34–9*) as well as the motif of animal sacrifice (Introduction, p. 66). Cassandra may look as though she is being coerced into moving, but no equivalent of an ox-driver is visible to the human eye.

1299 There's no longer time for escape: Lit., 'there is no escape with a duration of more time'.

1300 the one who's last has time on his side: Lit., 'the last one is senior with respect to time'—a strange phrase that sounds like a proverb. The superlative *hustatos* recurs twice more in contexts of extreme pathos relating to Cassandra's death at 1324* and 1445*.

1301 This day has come: On the significance of the critical, last or fatal day in Greek epic and tragedy see Hall (2011) and Murnaghan (forthcoming).

1302 you bear misery courageously: Lit., 'you are miserable from a courageous mind'.

1304 happy people: See 530*. **are talked about like that:** The verb *akouein* can function in tragedy as the passive of *legein*, and mean 'to be called' (e.g. Soph. *OT* 903).

1305 is a good thing: On *charis* see 182–3*. The chorus are stretching the convention of a comforting platitude to its limits.

1306   *Iō*: See 1072*. **father, for you and your noble children:** Cassandra recalls her family, the last of whom have so recently been killed as Troy fell, one last time. She has not named and does not here name Priam: see 40*.

1307   terror: On the ever-present sense of fear in this play see 12–14*. This internal stage direction implies that Cassandra has used posture and gesture in an arresting way.

1308   Alas, alas: See 1143*.

1309   something hateful in your mind: The chorus, because they cannot see or hear anything to elicit such a violent response from Cassandra, assume that the horrifying thing she is reeling from exists only in her mind's eye.

1310   reeks of murder and dripping blood: Lit., 'breathes blood-dripping murder'. On the sense of smell see Introduction, p. 60, and on blood see 209–10*.

1311   from the victims sacrificed at the hearth: The chorus assume that Clytemnestra had carried out her proposed sacrifices for the whole household, including the slaves (1036–7*, 1056–7*), and that it is the blood of the animals that Cassandra can smell. The Cassandra scene closes with an ironic twist on the same sacrificial rituals that Clytemnestra had announced before she entered the palace.

1312   vapour: The masculine noun *atmos* implies moist air, often with an odour (Aesch. *Eum.* 138, [Aristot.] *Probl.* 862a4, 908a21).

1313   Syrian incense enhancing the halls: Lit., 'a Syrian ornament to the halls'. A bizarre response, but it suggests that scented products imported from Syria were really used in burial rites.

1314   to bewail: The verb *kōkuein* means to shriek at a high pitch as a sign of grief, usually in funereal contexts and in epic and most tragedy always used of women (Hom. *Il.* 18.37, 19.284, 19.541; see 1157–61*).

1314   Let that be enough of life: Lit., 'Let the life suffice'.

1315   strangers: Cassandra is about to make a formal appeal to them within the terms of the laws of hospitality (1320*); in Attic law, importance was attached to whether a prosecutor in a case of violence had explicitly called on passers-by who were later to be summoned as witnesses. **as a bird fears a bush:** This sounds like a proverb denoting unjustified fear, and continues the series of ornithological images used by and in connection with Cassandra since 1050–1*.

1316   bear witness to this for me: Cassandra asks them to remember what she said now at a later time, when another man and a woman die; she wants them to acknowledge then that what she predicted was true. Of course, the chorus of old Argive men is not present in *Choephori* to do so when Clytemnestra and Aegisthus are both killed, but Orestes calls upon 'all the men of Argos' to come in due course to bear witness to the manner in which he has carried out the executions (1039–40).

1320 As your guest, about to die, I claim this favour: The verb *epixenoō* in the active voice means 'be entertained as a guest' or 'visitor' (Isoc. *Ep.* 6.2, Aristot. *Pol.* 7.1327a13); in the middle voice it implies that Cassandra is claiming something on her own behalf as a visitor (cf. Soph. fr. 146, from his *Mustering of the Achaeans*). There is a bitter irony here given the reception she is in reality about to receive.

1321 I pity you: The chorus do not actually respond to her request to affirm or deny it. **death you foretell:** Lit., 'prophesied death'. Aristotle says that events that are imminent excite the most pity, and singles out pity for those we witness when they are about to die, especially when the doomed individual is noble, 'both because the sufferer does not seem to deserve their fate and because the suffering is before our eyes' (*Rhet.* 2.1386b).

1322–5 one more speech—or a lament, my own lament: Lit., 'Once more I want to speak a speech or lament, my own.' A *rhēsis* implies a formal oratorical statement, such as might be given by messengers (Pind. *Nem.* 1.59) or to an assembly (Aesch. *Suppl.* 273, 615) or army (Hdt. 8.83); in real life it would be in prose: see Reiner (1938) 21. A *thrēnos* was a rhythmical utterance, sung or at least intoned, often with inarticulate noises quite unsuited to a *rhēsis* (Weiss (2017)). Cassandra has already voiced noises and many lines, some in song, that could be construed as threnodic, in lamenting Priam and the Trojans. But here she grimly indicates that, as her last utterance, this polished proclamation is to be the equivalent of a lament. But it also contains a prayer for someone to avenge her death, which was one function of the ancient—and more modern—Greek lament in cases of murder, as demonstrated in the long *kommos* of *Choephori*: see Holst-Warhaft (1992). **to the sun, my last daylight:** On the importance of the sun in Greek tragedy as witness to the passage from life to death see Hall (2010b) 2–3, 93. On the pathos of the word *hustatos* in the context of Cassandra's death see 1300*. **that my enemies may pay to my master's avengers a penalty for my murder, too:** The text is corrupt, although the general sentiment is clear; the translation reflects the emended text.

1326 by putting to death a slave: This would have made sense to Aeschylus' audience; in Athenian law, domestic slaves had what can seem a surprising degree of legal protection, as members of free households, from outrage and violence (Dmitriev (2016)). It has been Cassandra's humiliation and lack of rights as an enslaved person that have previously been emphasised (1036–7*). Isocrates (18.53–4) provides information about a trial at the court of the Palladion where two men had hidden a female slave and prosecuted a mutual enemy in the court of the Palladion for killing her; their case was sensationally derailed when she was presented, alive, in court. **achievement:** The neuter noun *cheirōma* implies a deed done with the hand, but the English term 'handiwork' does not quite convey the scornful sense of the Greek. Cassandra has put her finger on what to many modern readers seems to be Clytemnestra's only indefensible crime.

1327–9 When successful: The neuter plural participle refers back to *pragmata*. **one could liken it:** According to Photius, Aeschylus used *prepsai* (s.v.) transitively in the sense 'to liken to'. **to a sketch:** The feminine noun *skia* means a shadow (see 838–40*); it was used to mean an outline or shadow in the arts of drawing and painting (Dionysius of Halicarnassus, *Isocrates* 4), so *skiagraphein* meant to paint with shadows (Plato, *Rep.* 7.523b, *Parm.* 165c), for example in theatre scenery. But the word *skia* is also common in proverbs about the human condition (Pind. *Pyth.* 8.95, Soph. *Aj.* 126 and Soph. frags. 659.6 (from his *Tyro*) and 945: 'O wretched race of mortal men, we are nothing, just shadows, an excessive weight inhabiting the earth'), for example at 839*. **a wet sponge wipes the picture out with its strokes:** Rose (1958) 95 is almost alone in interpreting Cassandra's words here as referring to the erasure of writing rather than painting and suggests that the metaphor suggests wiping out rough notes with lamp black and water, as in Suet. *Aug.* 85. But a picture seems more likely: her words were reformulated by a character in Euripides' *Peleus* (fr. 618), who remarked that prosperity (*olbos*) is something that god can erase (*exaleiphei*) even more easily than a painting (*graphē*). Cassandra, played by a man behind a painted mask, compares human life, as well as her own particular living self, to a painting about to be erased as shading in a picture dissolves when water is applied to it. To become impervious to water, painted figures needed to be applied using encaustic techniques (Plato, *Tim.* 26c). The process to which Cassandra refers may also be illuminated by Plutarch, *De Fortuna* 99a–b: an artist once painted a horse, and could not achieve the result he wanted in portraying the froth and foam-flecked breath coming from the animal's mouth. After many failed attempts, he flew into a rage and threw his sponge, full of wet paint, at the easel. The desired effect was achieved. Iphigenia, Agamemnon, Helen and possibly the ghosts haunting the palace have all been created as visual artworks in the audience's imagination previously (242–3*, 416–19*,

799–801*, 1219–22*); here the focus is metaphysical (Hall (2006) 140–1). It is moving to find Eduard Fraenkel, a Jewish refugee from National Socialism, observe ((1950) vol. 3, 623): 'In her own lot and that of her nearest and dearest she has experienced the vicissitudes of fate, the sudden change from fortune to misery, from misery to utter annihilation. But her thought pierces deeper: what is happening to her is no other than what is happening time after time to the generality of men, almost all of them lament only their fall from fortune to misfortune, unconscious of their ultimate nothingness.' On Aeschylus' use of the conditional in statements about fate see Matino (1998) 200–1.

1330 this fate I pity far more than the other one: The meaning is that the obliterated picture corresponding to ill fortune is more to be pitied than living the illusory, shadowlike life that is the lot of humans who are enjoying prosperity. Fraenkel (1950) vol. 3, 627, atypically allows himself an emotional response to Cassandra's final words: 'There are no eruptions of frenzy any longer. Unfathomable misery speaks in a low voice.'

xii]   1331–1371   THE CHORUS [AND AGAMEMNON offstage]

Summary

After Cassandra enters the palace, the chorus intone a few ominous anapaestic lines which implicitly equate the wealth Priam had possessed with that of Agamemnon, and express foreboding that Agamemnon may indeed be about to die in requital for blood he had shed (1331–42). They are interrupted by Agamemnon's two death cries (1343, 1345) and respond to each in the rapid-fire metre called the trochaic tetrameter, before an agitated debate in iambic trimeters on how to react (1346–70). At the end of this they agree that they need more information before taking a decision.

Anapaests

1331–3 It's human nature: Lit., 'It is natural for all mortals'. **not to get enough:** The adjective *akorestos* is a word favoured by the chorus (756*, 1002*). **nobody denies it entry:** Lit., 'nobody keeps it out, denying'. On this sense of *eirgein* see Hom. *Il.* 23.72, Thuc. 4.9. **notable:** Lit., 'that fingers point out'.

1334 'No further entry': Lit., 'Do not enter any more'.

1335–6 blessed ones: Originally an epithet of the gods (*theoi*, Hom. *Il.* 1.339), *makares* is already used on its own to designate them in Hom. *Od.* 10.299. It is frequent in inscriptions. **on him:** This means Agamemnon, to whom the thoughts of the chorus very swiftly revert after Cassandra's exit, to the extent that they do not even need to name whom they are thinking about. **the capture of:** Lit., 'to seize [the things] of Priam'. On the constant references to Agamemnon's achievement in comparison with Priam's see 40*.

1337   honoured by the gods: Tyrtaeus 4.3–5 speaks of the Spartan 'kings honoured by the gods' who are counselled by 'aged elders'.

1338   for earlier bloodshed: Lit., 'for blood of earlier ones'. The chorus do not want to specify either Iphigenia or the children of Thyestes, apparently. On blood see 209–10*.

1339–40   by dying on behalf of the dead bring to fulfilment punishment for other deaths: The triplet *figura etymologica* of words with the *than*-stem reinforces aurally the pendulum-like nature of the system of reciprocal murder; on the significance of the number three see 33*.

1341–2   could boast: See what Paris could no longer boast, *exeuchetai*, according to the Herald, at 533. **free from harm:** This is an adjective that occurs in similar expressions in both *Choephori* (1018) and *Eumenides* (315); see also 387–9*. The chorus' rhetorical question expresses an ancient theme of Greek thought, that the unexpected vicissitudes of life mean that nobody can be called happy until they have met their end (Hdt. 1.32).

1343   *Ōmoi*: The chorus' intoned thoughts are shockingly interrupted by a cry from backstage in the basic iambic metre of speech. This sound is closely related to the grief-struck exclamation *oimoi*: see 326–8* and the chorus' characterisation of Agamemnon's cries as *oimōgmata* at 1146. **Fatal blow:** On this meaning of *kairios* see Cassandra's wish at 1121–3*.

1344   Be silent: During this trochaic tetrameter, the third different metre within three lines—a dense series of acoustic gearshifts to emphasise the crisis—it is possible that the pipe music accompanying the chorus' anapaests at 1331–42 had not ended, to make Agamemnon's urgent interruption more dramatic, and that this command is addressed to the musician. The metre will return at 1649 for the agitated closing sequence of the play, when physical violence seems once again on the cards. Aristotle recommends that orators avoid rhythms that bear a resemblance to the trochaic, because it is associated with dancing in comedy as the metre of running or tripping (*Rhet.* 3.1408b–1409a). On the use of the excited trochaic tetrameter in Greek tragedy see Drew-Bear (1968). The command is the culmination of the play's accumulated references to the impositions of silence at critical moments or on difficult issues (34–9*). **that he's fatally wounded:** The word 'that' has been added to the translation to make it sound more natural in English.

1345 a second time: These iambic words constitute the last time Agamemnon's voice is heard. We learn later that it took three blows to finish him off (1384–7*; see also 1553*).

1346–7 groans: See 1143*. Two more panicked trochaic lines, probably spoken by the chorus leader. But each of the following 11 pairs of iambic trimeters were probably delivered individually by the other members of the chorus, possibly interrupting or even speaking over each other to create an effect of panic and confusion. On a purely dramaturgical level, something needs to happen on stage while the tableau of Clytemnestra and the corpses is hastily prepared behind the scenes, to be revealed so terrifyingly at 1372*. **let's pool advice:** Some have said that the instinct to talk rather than act makes the chorus look weak and ineffectual, and even that the contrast drawn 'between the decisiveness of the heroic personages and the imbecility of the council reveals a glimpse of the anti-democratic tendencies of the poet' (Sidgwick (1905) xii n.1). Mader (2021) sees it as a satirical comment on ineffective rhetorical deliberation as it was experienced in the Athenian Assembly. The episode is, rather, psychologically credible and dramatically effective, conveying the sense that the civic society of Argos is threatened with total fragmentation by the murderous crisis within the royal household. Moreover, although the chorus expressed a guarded welcome to Agamemnon (802–5), it was only after stating that they did not approve of what happened at Aulis (799–804). He is not a beloved king whom they would do anything to rescue, even though they seem to dislike the alternative rulers more. Moreover, it later transpires that Aegisthus has at his disposal a group of armed private bodyguards (1650*), who enter with him at 1577; the elderly chorus will presumably have been aware of this throughout. **pool advice ... safety:** Lit., 'communicate with one another any deliberations [that will lead to] security'. On the *boul*-stem see 10–11*.

1348–9 summon the townspeople here to the palace to help: Lit., 'proclaim the cry-for-help (*boēn*) to the people [to come] hither to the palace'. Agelaus uses similar language at Hom. *Od.* 22.133, when he senses that he and the other suitors are in grave danger, and suggests that someone climb on a rostrum and tell the people that help (*boēn*) is needed immediately. See also Aesch. *Suppl.* 730. The first chorus-man to speak reverts to iambic verse: on the effect of the metrical shift in this pivotal sequence see Scott (1984) 67–8.

1350–1 apprehend: Lit., 'fall upon', the same verb as the chorus use of the malevolent *daimōn* that attacks this family at 1468*. **lay charges:** Lit., 'put the matter to the test'. **while the sword still drips fresh blood:** Lit., 'with a newly flowing sword'. The obvious idiomatic English equivalent is 'to catch someone red-handed'.

1352–3 vote to do something: The middle form *psēphizesthai* means 'cast one's vote with a pebble' (see Hdt. 9.55), as the Athenian jurymen of the Areopagus do in *Eumenides* (709–10). Here the meaning is more like 'resolve' (Hdt. 7.207). **Hesitation is useless at a critical time:** Lit., '[It is a] critical time not to delay'. The feminine noun *akmē* literally means the sharp 'edge' of a weapon or razor (Pind. *Pyth.* 9.81), but in contexts of time is similar to *kairos* (on which see 1121–3*), with which it is paired at Ar. *Plut.* 256; it can mean 'the most opportune' or the 'critical' moment (Aesch. *Pers.* 407, Isoc. *Ep.* 1.1).

1354–5 It's plain to see: Lit., 'It is present to see'. **Their prefatory actions:** The verb *phroimiazesthai*, 'to perform the prelude', is related to the neuter noun *phroimion*, on which see 31*, 829, 1216. The use of the third-person plural leaves open the question of who exactly is involved in the activity inside. **signal that they are imposing a tyranny:** Lit., 'effecting signs of tyranny'. It has been objected that this 'is a curious anachronism. The Argive elders talk of "tyranny" as if they were members of a free Greek republic' (Sidgwick (1905) 67). But Aeschylus presents the archaic monarchy in Argos as including some representation of the opinion of the people, replaced (as many constitutional monarchies were in Greece historically) by a tyranny ushered in by a violent coup: see also 828* and 1633* and Introduction, p. 13.

1356–7 we're wasting time: The verb *chronizein* can imply undergoing a simple passage of time (727*), sustainability (847*), or a sensible caution and avoidance of precipitate or impulsive action (Aristot. *Rhet.* 2.1380b5), but the context here requires a negative sense. **they're trampling:** See 369–72*. **the very name of hesitation:** Lit., 'the repute of delay'; the chorus imply that taking one's time is often a commendable approach, but not when one's enemies are making swift progress. **their hands are not idle:** Lit., 'they are not slumbering with their hand'.

1358–9 what plan could occur to me to suggest: Lit., 'what plan I might happen upon to speak'. **The person carrying out a deed needs to do the planning too:** This speaker seems to think it is pointless urging action without having any idea what that action should be.

1360–1 to bring a dead man back to life by talking: This recalls the chorus' song at 1019–24*, when they reflected that, ever since the death of Asclepius, there had been no possibility of ever resurrecting a murder victim.

1362–3 we should prolong our lives just to surrender: Lit., 'prolonging life to yield thus'. This speaker is prepared to risk his life rather than be ruled by Agamemnon's killers. **to people who disgrace:** Lit., 'to disgracers', a striking noun derived from the common verb *kataischunein*, 'bring shame on'.

1364–5 It's better to die: Although *kratein* in this play is a key word denoting *force majeure* and political power (10–11*), here it has the much milder sense of one opinion about the best course of action prevailing over another (Thuc. 4.104, Eur. *Hipp.* 248). **less bitter:** Lit., 'riper', the comparative of *pepōn*, an adjective used of sun-ripened fruit (Hdt. 4.23, Ar. *Knights* 260); on the sense of taste in ancient literature see the overview of Rudolph (2018), and, on archaic and classical Greek poetry, Hitch (2018). At 550* the chorus had told the Herald that even death would be pleasurable given the fear in which they are living.

1366–7 divine from the evidence just of groans: Lit., 'divine from the evidences of groans'. The verb *manteuesthai* is here derogatory, implying that better evidence is needed.

1368–9 Our anger about this must be based on certain knowledge: Lit., 'We must, being angry, know clearly about these things'. On epistemological problems see Introduction, pp. 101–2.

1370–1 With the support of the majority on all sides I approve this policy: Lit., 'Being replete from all sides I praise this.' The last chorus-man to speak is confident that all agree with the need for certain information; perhaps they have used gesture and posture during the previous four lines to indicate this. **to acquire clear information:** Exactly how this might be achieved, given the chorus' fear of entering the house, is not clarified. But the problem of certainty is suddenly solved by the appearance of Clytemnestra, and the chorus speak as one from this point onwards.

xiii] 1372–1576 THE CHORUS AND CLYTEMNESTRA

Summary

The Queen stands over the corpses of Agamemnon in his bathtub and of Cassandra. Her magnificent robes (unless she changed her clothes to 'bath' her husband) and her mask are now spattered with blood. The tableau may have been rolled out from the doors of the palace on the theatrical mechanism known as the *ekkuklēma* (Pollux 4.128). It was in use in the later fifth century BCE, where it is signified by the verb *ekkuklein* (Ar. *Ach.* 408–9, of Euripides being 'rolled out' of his house; see also *Thesm.* 96, of the tragedian Agathon, the evidence assembled in von Möllendorff (2015) and Lucarini (2016)). But it is not certain that this device was in use as early as 458 BCE, and the tableau could equally well have been arranged and uncovered by stagehands (Taplin (1977) 442–9). Clytemnestra is apparently not holding the murder weapon, since there is no reference to its *visible* presence in the text (but see 1260–3* for the several references to it).

The episode stages the fundamental political conflict of the play, between Clytemnestra and the citizens of Argos, and its length and complexity show Aeschylus finding the amoibaion, where speech contrasts with song, 'a flexible instrument, capable of development and adaptation in accordance with the needs of the individual dramatic situation' (O'Daly (1985) 3). The amoibaion is, however, prefaced by an iambic section of 35 lines (1371–1406), consisting of Clytemnestra's extraordinary speech over the corpses (where we might have expected a messenger speech) and two lines of shocked protest at her effrontery from the chorus, followed by her six lines of snarled retort: she carried out the killing herself and Agamemnon is now a corpse.

In the amoibaion, the chorus are partly attempting to offer some kind of funeral lament for the dead monarch (see Alexiou (1974) 134), but as the dire nature of the situation sinks in, they become combative with Clytemnestra. She is defiant and repudiates most of their points, but gradually begins to join them in exploring the role of the past and of supernatural agents in the suffering of the house of Atreus; the episode ends with the antagonists reaching a bitter, uncomfortable, partial and temporary accommodation (Conacher (1987) 53). The formal, metrical structure of the amoibaion consists of eight statements sung by the chorus in lyrics. Clytemnestra responds to the first two in spoken iambics. She does not follow the chorus into full sung lyric, but her third to eighth responses are in the intoned anapaestic rhythm, suggesting a slight psychological shift in her: see further Marshall (2024) and the Metrical Appendix. The 'argument' of this crucial altercation can be summarised as follows:

Strophe 1   Chorus: You are disgusting. The people curse you and banish you.

Clytemnestra: You banish *me* when you brought no charge against Agamemnon although he killed our daughter? I'm happy to meet you on equal terms. Let the winner rule.

Antistrophe 1   Chorus: You are crazed, covered in blood and must be punished.

Clytemnestra: I acted justly to avenge my daughter. I am not afraid since I have Aegisthus. Killing Cassandra was a bonus.

Strophe 2   Chorus: I would like to die. I have lost my King to a woman's violence. Another woman—Helen—caused the war. The strife in the house has been longstanding.

Clytemnestra: Don't ask for death and don't blame Helen for the war fatalities.

Antistrophe 2   Chorus: A malign spirit rules through two women whose regime is bad.

Clytemnestra: You are right about the malign spirit. It has been fattened three times.

Strophe 3   Chorus: You are right that the spirit is wrathful and fate unsatisfied. But it is Zeus' work.

O my King how shall I lament you?

Clytemnestra: I'm not just Clytemnestra: I incarnate retaliation for the Thyestean feast.

Antistrophe 3   Chorus: Even if retaliation for that is a factor, you are still to blame for *this* murder.

O my King how shall I lament you?

Clytemnestra: He deserved to die because he killed Iphigenia and did it by trickery.

Strophe 4   Chorus: I'm at a loss and fear more violence. I wish I were dead. How is the King going to receive a proper funeral?

Clytemnestra: That's not your business but ours. Iphigenia will welcome him to Hades.

Antistrophe 4   Chorus: Zeus' rule is that the doer suffers, so how do we stop the family curse?

Clytemnestra: I want to swear an agreement with the evil spirit to stop the reciprocal murders.

1372   to suit the occasion: Lit., 'seasonably', 'when the time was right'. For this meaning of *kairiōs* see also Eur. *Rhes.* 339. Clytemnestra begins not with an address to the chorus or to the sun, but with a self-absorbed comment on her own previous mendacious rhetoric. It is also suggestive of the contrived oratory necessary to an adversary at law, and Clytemnestra sees the chorus as self-appointed judges of her actions (1412, 1421). On legal language see 41*.

1373 the opposite: I.e., the opposite of the speciously welcoming sentiments she has previously articulated about and to Agamemnon.

1374–6 wanting to hurt: Lit., 'preparing hostilities against'. Although this is a general statement about human behaviour, it is interesting that Clytemnestra uses a masculine participle; the chorus used the same verb in reference to the prospective murder of Agamemnon, of which they assumed the perpetrator would be male, at 1251*. **enemies:** The translation does not convey the forceful polyptoton of *echthra echthrois*. **fence the prey in with hunting-nets:** Lit., 'fence nets of calamity'. With *arkustata* compare 1115–18*, where Cassandra compared Clytemnestra herself with an *arkus* (hunting-net), and other references to nets discussed at 357*. **too high for it to jump out over them:** Lit., '[resulting in] a height bigger than a leap out'. The accusative is a type of cognate or internal accusative describing the result of the main action, i.e., putting up a fence of nets. This is an arresting metaphor for telling sufficient lies to avoid any risk of the failure of a murder plot.

1377–8 This struggle: The masculine noun *agōn* here may retain a connotation of an athletics contest: see 171–2*. It occurs at similarly crucial points in other Aeschylean plays (Durand (2005)). Clytemnestra's combat with Agamemnon may be over, but the word also seems programmatic as she enters into her great quasi-legal dispute with the adversarial chorus. **an old dispute:** The feminine noun *neikē* is like the neuter *neikos* (see also 151–4), which can mean a physical altercation (Hom. *Il.* 24.107), but is often found in the context of exchanges of insults or abuse (Hom. *Il.* 7.95) or legal proceedings (Hom. *Od.* 12.440). On legal language in the play see 41*. This old dispute may include the argument between Atreus and Thyestes, but is more likely to direct the audience's minds to the sacrifice of Iphigenia. **was of old given no little thought:** The wording of the *figura etymologica palai ... palaias* continues the aural effect. Clytemnestra's litotes ('no little thought') here is emphatic, creating a picture of sustained brooding on what had happened.

1379 I stand where I struck: If the *ekkuklēma* is used, and it pushes the bodies forward out of the house, rather than the scene simply being disclosed, this is not literally true, but Clytemnestra may mean that she stands in the same place in relation to Agamemnon's corpse as when she dealt the blows. It is not made clear when Cassandra was killed, and her voice is not heard from backstage. **the deed has been done:** This phrase often has a slightly more negative connotation, meaning 'after the crimes were committed' (Hdt. 4.164, 8.94, cf. Eur. *Bacch.* 1039).

1381–3 I threw all around him: This is the first of four verbs in the vivid present tense as Clytemnestra relives the killing, probably using gestures to enact it mimetically (lit., 'I throw … I strike him twice … I deal his fallen body yet a third blow ... he strikes me with dingy drizzles'). The verb *peristichizein* seems to be related to *peristoichizein*, to surround with lines (often in a military context; see Polybius 8.5.2), but Pollux does say that a *stoichismos* is specifically an act of surrounding with hunting nets (5.36). Clytemnestra is quite clear that the net was intended to help her kill him easily, just as if he were a large wild animal or shoal of fish. **an impenetrable net:** Although *apeiros* usually means 'boundless', 'innumerable' (e.g. Hdt. 1.204), it seems to have a special meaning in tragedy, when applied to textiles, of being inescapable (see Soph. fr. 526, from his *Polyxena*, of an ominous *chitōn*; Eur. *Or.* 25). An *amphiblēstron* is anything thrown around an object to engulf it; Aeschylus rings the changes on words for nets throughout the play (see 357*). **as if for fish:** See 358*. **a costly, evil textile:** Lit., 'an evil wealth of garment'—a typical Aeschylean oxymoron.

1384–7 his limbs went limp: Lit., 'he relaxed his limbs'. The physical and sensory detail of Clytemnestra's 'blow by blow' account of the killing is most disturbing: she is the only murderer in Greek tragedy who personally reports the minutiae of the violence she has inflicted. **I dealt his fallen body yet a third blow:** The word 'body' has been supplied to make sense in good English. The *ep-* in *ependidōmi* implies an additional blow, over and above the two already dealt, reinforcing the play's metronomic allusions to the ritual and rhetorical power of the number three (see 33*). Steiner (2016) 161–7 argues persuasively that in this speech Clytemnestra is grimly playing on a comparison between her three blows and the triple libation poured at the symposium, which the chorus have mentioned in another grisly context at 245–7*. Steiner also argues, slightly less plausibly, that in the image of Agamemnon's sharp jets of blood there is an allusion to the popular symposium game of *kottabos*, in which a drinker flicked drops of wine left at the bottom of the cup at a designated target. **as a prayer of gratitude:** Lit., 'as a votive favour'. The adjective *euktaios* occurs in a fragment of Aeschylus (55) denoting the third libation at dinner parties, poured to Zeus *Sōtēr* (see 245–7*), and there is certainly some play on the language of that ritual convention here. On *charis* see 182–3*. **infernal Hades:** On Hades see 667*, 115–18*, 1115*, 1528*, 1119, 1235–6*, 1291. The same phrase meaning 'under the ground', *kata chthonos*, is used of the place where a body is buried at Soph. *Ant.* 24 and of the Erinyes at Aesch. *Eum.* 115. Hades is called *chthonios* at Eur. *Alc.* 237. But he is addressed as Zeus *Katachthonios* at Hom. *Il.* 9.457 and as Zeus *Chthonios* at Hes. *Works* 465, so it is just possible that the correct reading is *Dios* here. On similar titles in Ancient Near Eastern literature, see West (1997) 373.

saviour of corpses: Clytemnestra is presenting the killing of Agamemnon as an animal sacrifice to Hades, the Underworld god who is grimly called *sōtēr*, because she is suggesting an analogy between the three-blow killing and the thrice-poured ritual libation to Zeus Sōtēr. The concept of Hades as a *saviour* of corpses borders on the bleakly humorous; one of his cult titles was 'Receiver of Corpses', *nekrodegmōn* (Aesch. *PV* 153).

1388   he lay and gasped out his life: Lit., 'having fallen he set his own spirit in motion'. This is an unusual use of the verb *hormainein* (which usually means 'ponder'), probably close to the sense of *horman*, 'urge on' (see also Pind. *Ol.* 3.25). The masculine noun *thumos* is used in the frequent Homeric sense of one's breath of life, which physically departs the body when one is killed (e.g. Hom. *Il.* 6.17, 5.852; see also Eur. *Bacch.* 620).

1389   as he breathed out sharp jets: Lit., 'breathing out sharp slaughter'. On breathing see Introduction, pp. 61–2.

1390   with dingy drizzles of gory dew: Lit., 'with murky drop of bloody dew'. The adjective *eremnos* is customarily applied to Earth (Hom. *Od.* 24.16), night (Hom. *Od.* 11.606) or a hurricane (Hom. *Il.* 12.375). The feminine noun *psakas* is used to distinguish rain that merely drops from a raging storm at 1534*, but in the plural it is also used of wine at Critias 88 B 1 DK; it may be reminiscent of the blood rain that is twice sent as a portent to the battlefield in the *Iliad*, once to signal that many deaths were about to occur (11.53–4); on another occasion Zeus sheds blood-rain in honour of his son Sarpedon, who is soon to die (16.459–61). Dew appears in Greek literature in association with fertility and regeneration; wheat ripens with dew on its ear (*Il.* 23.598–9); Ithacan wheat and grape crops are wonderful and rain and abundant dew never fail (*Od.* 13.244–5). In Pindar, reputations for glorious achievements grow like a tree under refreshing dews (*Nem.* 8.40). Clytemnestra, who fuses metaphorical wine with Agamemnon's actual blood here (Zeitlin (1965) 473), may feel regenerated by the bloody dew in which she rejoices, and the murder will certainly increase her fame. On dew see also 12–14*, and on blood see 209–10*.

1391–2   which I delighted in: Lit., 'rejoicing'. **than the sown earth is refreshed by Zeus' gift of rain:** Lit., 'than [what is] sown by the Zeus-given refreshment'. On *ganos* see 577–9*, on Zeus as god of rain, 970–2*, 1014–15*, and on arable farming, 524–6*. Menelaus' heart at Patroclus' funeral games in the *Iliad* 'was gladdened like the corn when it ripens with the dew on its ears when the fields are bristling' (23.598–9). **when the flower-buds are**

born: Lit., 'in the childbirths of the bud'. Clytemnestra's analogy recalls her hyperbolic comparison of the joy she claimed Agamemnon's return brought her with spurting spring-water's appeal to a thirsty traveller at 901*, except that here the spurts are of blood rather than water. On childbirth imagery see 49–50*. Moles (1979) sees an erotic metaphor here, in which Clytemnestra's pleasure suggests an orgasm as Agamemnon ejaculates his blood; although sexual undertones are not made explicit, audiences may intuitively come to the same conclusion.

1393 revered citizens of Argos: This is an ironically respectful form of address: see the chorus' more sincere address to the Persian Queen at Aesch. *Pers.* 623 as well as Clytemnestra's earlier, ceremonial apostrophe of the Argive chorus, in front of Agamemnon, at 855*.

1394 be joyful, if you feel joy: This expression really means 'I do not care whether this pleases you or not', but cf. 1049*. **exult:** On the various shades of meaning attached to the verb *euchomai* and its compounds see 533* and cf. 1262.

1395 If it were proper: Lit., 'if it were [one of] fitting things'. Clytemnestra's concern with propriety in this context is scathing and perhaps deliberately ludicrous. She also invites us to picture her sacrilegiously pouring libations over her husband's cadaver even as she says it would be improper.

1396 with more than justice: Pindar calls Nemesis *huperdikos* at *Pyth.* 10.44.

1397–8 He filled the mixing-bowl: Clytemnestra metaphorically imagines the tribulations inflicted on the household by Agamemnon as ingredients in the bowl in which wine was mixed with water at a symposium (see the other image of libations being poured at a drinking party, where Iphigenia had sung, at 245–7*). **has drunk the very last drop:** The *ek*-prefix in *ekpinein* means 'to drink until the cup is empty' (Soph. fr. 483.1, from his *Pandora* or *Hammerers*). Clytemnestra optimistically fantasises that Agamemnon will be the last household member to suffer a tribulation.

1399 your insolent mouth: On the *thrasu*- component in the compound see 768–71*.

1400 make such a boasting speech: Lit., 'boast [making such a] speech'. The chorus also accuse Aegisthus of boasting, using the same verb, at 1671*. It is curious that the chorus here express shock at Clytemnestra's language rather than at her crime. **a woman who delivers:** Lit., you who [gendered feminine] boast'. **over your husband:** The preposition *epi* with the dative can mean simply 'near' (Hom. *Od.* 13.408) or 'beside' (Hom. *Il.* 7.133), but is used specifically in the *Iliad* meaning 'over the body' of a dead hero (11.261). It can also have a connotation of hostility (Hdt. 1.61, Soph. *Phil.* 1138), so it might better be translated here 'against'.

1401   as if I were an inane woman: Clytemnestra revives her earlier annoyance with being appraised as if she conformed with the stereotypical view of the female intellect (177*).

1402   my heart does not tremble as I address people who are aware: Lit., 'with heart without tremor I speak to those who know'. The adjective *atrestos* is found in military contexts at Aesch. *PV* 416 (of Amazons or women, like Medea, of Colchis) and Soph. *Aj.* 365 (Ajax on his own prowess).

1403–4   it's all the same: Clytemnestra has previously expressed disregard for public opinion (937), unlike Agamemnon (938).

1405–6   this right hand of mine: The actor playing Clytemnestra is likely to have lifted his right arm menacingly at this point. **a rightful craftsman:** Strictly speaking, this seems to be grammatically in apposition to 'this right hand of mine', which explains why an adjective governed by the masculine noun *tektōn* (carpenter, craftworker) is feminine. But the audience might have heard it as referring to Clytemnestra herself—'a rightful she-craftsman': cf. the 'craftsman of conflicts' at 151–4* and 1604*, when it is Aegisthus' turn to claim responsibility for the murder, saying that he was 'its rightful stitcher' (*dikaios ... rhapheus*).

1407–9   have you fed upon: The outraged chorus assume that Clytemnestra must have ingested some mind-altering substance to make her commit such an egregious crime and incur the penalty attached to it. **eaten or drunk:** Lit., 'edible or potable'. **nourished by the earth:** This would cover both plants and land fauna. **rising from the churning sea:** On fishing see 1381–3*.

1410   this sacrifice: This is presumably a euphemism for 'murder'; a *thuos*, strictly speaking, is an offering of a burnt sacrifice in distinction to a libation (Hes. *Works* 338). **pronouncement of the people's curse:** Lit., 'curses uttered by the people'. The chorus deploy the same word as Agamemnon had used of rumours that endanger a leader (938), and Clytemnestra had used of a threat from the people that she claims did need to be taken seriously (881–4*). On rumours and politics see 276*.

1411   You cast him out, you cut him off, and an outcast you shall be yourself: The Greek here sounds as if it may reflect the traditional language used in formal public denunciations or imprecations, with its triple rhetorical structure (see 33*); the chorus is threatening Clytemnestra with imminent banishment. The object 'him' and the reflexive 'yourself' need to be added to make sense in English. The solemn ritual effect is heightened by the clattering anaphoric repetition of verbs with the *ap-* stem and *apopolis*, 'cityless' and the most unusual 11 successive short syllables produced by a completely resolved dochmiac. Clytemnestra is threatened with the exile that Thyestes, Aegisthus and Orestes have all suffered or are suffering now.

1412   mightily hated: Lit., 'a mighty hate-object'. The chorus had previously compared Clytemnestra with a 'hateful' (*misētos*) dog (1228–30*).

1412–13   you sentence *me* to banishment ... public curse: Clytemnestra slightly rewords the three-part 'sentence' the chorus passed on her at 1410–11*. For *phugē*, meaning a punishment of official banishment, see Soph. *OT* 659, Lys. 13.74, Plato, *Apol.* 21a, 37c, *Laws* 1.638a. On legal language see 41*. In the Greek, one long and ornate period stretches all the way to the end of line 1418: 'Clytemnestra pleads her case like an advocate in court' (Fraenkel (1950) vol. 3, 667). Clytemnestra not unfairly infers that, since the mechanism apparently exists for the people to banish her for murder, the citizen body represented by the chorus could have implemented it when Agamemnon murdered Iphigenia. This is a good question; the audience may have been unclear about the state of the legal system, if any, in Bronze-Age monarchical Argos, or have assumed that the difference may lie in Agamemnon's status of immunity as monarch, the different relationship between a father and a daughter compared with that of a wife to a husband, or simply Clytemnestra's gender.

1414   brought no charge against: Lit., 'brought nothing opposed to'. For *enantion* with the dative case meaning 'against' in a hostile sense see Hom. *Il.* 20.252, Eur. *Or.* 624.

1415   who paid no heed to the sacrifice: Lit., 'who sacrificed, paying no more heed'. See Clytemnestra's injunction to Aegisthus to 'pay no heed' to the chorus' protests at 1672*. **as if she were:** Lit., 'as if of'.

1416   abounded: Cf. the criticism of overly abundant households at 377*. **fleecy flocks:** On the visual images of sheep and shepherds see also 128–30*.

1417–18   The most beloved product of my labour pains: Lit., 'my dearest birth-pang'. For Clytemnestra and the language of childbirth see 49–50*. **was used to cast a spell on Thracian winds:** Lit., '[as] an enchantment-song of Thracian winds'. These are the 'winds from the Strymon' to which the chorus had referred at 192, but they are also reminiscent of the 'Thracian winds' that destroyed the fleet, according to the Herald, at 654–6*. Cf. the metaphorical verbalised charm (*epōidos*) against terrors at Plat. *Phaed.* 78a.

1419   shouldn't you have banished: For the verb *andrēlatein* as a punishment for murder decreed in a court of law see Plato, *Rep.* 8.565e. **polluting acts:** See 209–10*, also in the context of the death of Iphigenia.

1421–4   on the understanding that: This is a necessary English expansion of the simple Greek *hōs*. **I'm prepared:** To describe her preparedness for combat, Clytemnestra uses a participle of the same middle voice of the verb, *paraskeuazein*, by which the chorus had denoted their preparations for performing a pious choral ode at 353*. **defeat me by force:** Lit., 'win against me by hand'. Clytemnestra's challenge to an apparently physical trial of strength is astonishing: see Introduction, p. 23. **on equal terms:** cf. Plato, *Phaedr.* 243d. Clytemnestra is a woman; they are men. There is one of her but 12 of them; she does, however, know that Aegisthus and his bodyguard are near at hand, even if the audience has not yet been told this. **for you to rule over me:** Clytemnestra seems to acknowledge the possibility of a democratic revolution.

1425   though taught late in the day: Lit., 'taught late'. **how to control yourself:** See 181*, where the chorus sang that even the unwilling learn how to *sōphronein* eventually. Clytemnestra uses an explicit threat of coercion against these representatives of the Argive citizen body for the first time.

1426   have bellowed overbearingly: Lit., 'bellowed overbearing things'. On the verb *laskein* see 594–5*. This gives us a clue as to the type of vocal delivery of which the actor playing Clytemnestra was capable.

1427   your mind is crazed: The sole instance of *epimainesthai* in Homer suggests sexual madness—it is used of Anteia's lust for Bellerophon (*Il.* 6.160). **of bloodletting:** At Aesch. *Eum.* 164 the same adjective *phonolibēs* is used by the Erinyes of the blood-soaked throne of the younger gods.

1428   congealed blood is clear to see: Lit., 'A fatty glob (*lipos*) of blood is conspicuous.' It would be a dramatic sight if blood had been applied to the mask of the bellowing actor playing Clytemnestra. On blood see 209–10*.

1429   Dishonoured: It is possible that the correct reading here is *antiton*, 'paid back', a simplified form of *antititon*. The asyndeton here implies impulsive, abrupt and emotional self-expression.

1430   for each strike you must still be struck in requital: Lit., 'it is necessary yet to pay back blow for blow'. The translation attempts to reproduce the polyptoton but does not quite reproduce the alliteration in this powerful line, consisting of three words beginning with '*t*' and with the accent on the first syllable; this replicates aurally the three strikes to which the chorus refer.

1431   just ordinance: This is concrete instance of the abstract principle of *themis*, on which see 97–9* and 214–17*.

1432–3   The female divinities to whom Clytemnestra says she slaughtered Agamemnon make an impressive and terrifying troika: on the significance of the number three see 33*. For Justice see 250–1*. **Ruin:** On *Atē* see 359–61* and on the Erinys see 58–9*. Clytemnestra's oath creates a jarring effect: it is 'as if she has just recited a law at a trial, while simultaneously enacting an occult rite' (Fletcher (2012) 49). She seems to have made some kind of vow to offer a sacrifice if she kills Agamemnon, but the sacrifice, performed out of gratitude to the trinity of female supernatural entities to whom the vow was made, is simultaneously the fulfilment of what she asked of them. Moreover, the oath is also offered, as if in court, to affirm the truth of a piece of testimony to something quite other—that Clytemnestra is unafraid. On oaths see also 1569–70*.

1434   hope does not tread for me in the house of fear: A resonant way of saying that she is optimistic and unafraid, combining in one line four of the tragedy's central themes and images: hope, fear, treading and the house, on which see 103*, 12–14*, 369–72* and Introduction, pp. 3, 61, 69–70 respectively. The line also draws attention to the domestic life lived unseen behind the palace façade.

1435   as long as Aegisthus kindles the fire on my hearth: This is the first occasion on which anyone in the play actually names the man whose presence behind the scenes has long been hinted at. The image of kindling the fire may well have an erotic overtone, and the hearth is the conceptual centre of the household (427–8*). But the image of Aegisthus tending the fire inside while Clytemnestra deals with the palace's public relations also effeminises him.

1436   as formerly: The question of exactly when Clytemnestra and Aegisthus formed their relationship is never answered in the play. This line also stresses once again how little the chorus and audience know about the extent of Aegisthus' involvement in the murders.

1437   shield of confidence: The only shields mentioned so far in the play have been those of the Greek force invading Troy (404*, 693*). The metaphor may imply that Aegisthus provides Clytemnestra with confidence in the militia at their disposal (see 1650*).

1438   Here lies the man who inflicted outrages on me, his wife: Lit., 'He, outrageous to his woman/wife here, lies'. The adjective *lumantērios* is derived from *lumainesthai*, which means 'to maltreat' or 'to inflict indignities on' in the most reprehensible way (Hdt. 1.214, 9.79, Isoc. 20.9).

1439   but was the fondling: The neuter noun *meiligma* refers to something with soothing properties, such as the scraps of food which appease a dog's hunger (Hom. *Od.* 10.217), words which calm someone down (Aesch. *Eum.* 886) or propitiatory offerings to the dead (Aesch. *Choeph.* 15). In the context of Agamemnon's sexual relations with war captives at Troy it is chilling. **every Chryseis:** Besides Chryseis, Briseis and now Cassandra, Agamemnon was not linked with any other war captive at Troy, but Clytemnestra's rhetoric underlines her point that he had committed adultery without a second thought for her. She does not accept the sexual double standards of her era. Fraenkel (1950) vol. 3, 679, misses the psychological complexity of this point in remarking that 'Clytemnestra exaggerates here, for the purposes of self-justification, the insult done to her by Agamemnon's relations with Chryseis and Cassandra'.

1440–3   So does: The verb has been supplied to make sense in English. **his war captive and diviner and bed partner:** The repetition of *kai* intensifies the strangeness of the same person being his diviner and his bed partner. **paramour:** The word *xuneunos* means exactly the same as *koinolektros* in the previous line, adding further emphasis to the insult this had caused Clytemnestra. On this most contested of marriage beds see 27*. **pounded by the sailors' masts beside their benches:** Lit., 'mast-rubber of the sailors' benches'. This is more obscene than anything anywhere in Greek tragedy, and the shock factor is emphasised by the enjambement. It is not surprising that so many editors have accepted a nineteenth-century emendation to *isotribēs*, 'equally consorting with', but Clytemnestra's idiolect can accommodate very low registers (871–2*). The *trib-* element may imply frequent interaction or experience with something (Ar. *Birds* 636, Hdt. 3.134), but there is also a physical overtone of 'grinding' or 'pounding' (Ar. *Thesm.* 486, Plato, *Phaed.* 117b), certainly sexual. Sommerstein (2009) 175–7 with n.306 cites an anecdote about a Corinthian prostitute who spoke of her work as 'lowering masts' (Strabo 8.6.20).

1444–7   like a swan: The bird sacred to Apollo (Ar. *Birds* 870, Plato, *Phaed.* 85b). This is the earliest reference in ancient Greek and subsequent literature to the popular tradition that swans sing at the moment of death, in some versions for the first time or more beautifully than ever before. Socrates in Plato's *Phaedo*, facing his own imminent death, says that while swans do sing earlier in their lives, they do so most prolifically and beautifully as they expire (84e–85a). Many other ancient authors subsequently alluded to the song of the dying swan (e.g. Aelian, *N.A.* 2.32, 5.34, 10.36, Oppian, *Cyn.* 2.548, Cicero, *Tusc. Disp.* 1.30.73, Ovid, *Met.* 14.429–30, *Her.* 7.1–2, Seneca, *Phaedra* 302); Harris (2012) argues that Aeschylus' source here was an Aesopic fable. In his *History of Animals* Aristotle writes that swans fly over the open sea, and that sailors off the coast of Libya 'have come across many singing with a mournful voice, and they could see that several of them were dying' (10.615b2–5). A century later the proverb 'to sing one's swan song', still current today, was cited by Chrysippus (see Athenaeus 14.616b and cf. Polybius, 30.4.7 and 31.12.1). Although some ancient authors were sceptical (the ornithologist Alexander of Myndos, quoted at Athenaeus, 9.392c, and Pliny *NH* 10.32.63), Arnott (1977) 152 points out that the whooper swan and some other wild species of swan have a peculiarly shaped trachea inside the breastbone, 'and when it dies, the final expiration of air from its collapsing lungs' produces a wailing sound like that of the flute. On birds in *Agamemnon* see Introduction, p. 58. **has sung:** Lit., 'having sung'. **her last:** On the pathos of the word *hustatos* in relation to Cassandra's death see 1300*. **death-dirge:** The word *goos* was used of the lament of the bereaved vultures at 55–7*.

1447   to my bed she's brought a dainty extra morsel to relish: Lit., 'an additional dainty morsel of my luxury of the bed'. A noun cognate with *paropsōnēma* means metaphorically a lover who is 'a bit on the side' in Ar. fr. 191. Clytemnestra's distasteful characterisation of the death of Cassandra combines the idea of a luxury food with sexual pleasure; it is the first time the erotic aspect of her relationship with Aegisthus has been so openly acknowledged; this line alone refutes Aeschylus' claim at *Frogs* 1044 that he had never created a sexual female character. On Clytemnestra's bed see 27*.

1448–54   I wish that: Lit., 'would that'. **neither agonising nor protracted:** *periōdunos* is found denoting extreme pain in a medical treatise (Hipp. *Acut.* 34) and Plato's *Laws* (9.873c). On *demniotērēs* see 51–4*. **eternal, everlasting sleep:** The theme of sleep has been constant in the play (179–80*), and the chorus have earlier expressed a near-death wish on account of living under the regime which operated in Agamemnon's absence (Introduction, p. 3). **has been slain:** The verb *damazein* can mean 'make a woman subject to her husband' (Hom *Il.* 18.432) and is indeed related to the feminine noun *damar* meaning 'wife' (Hom. *Il.* 3.122). In the context where Agamemnon's suffering at the hands of women is highlighted (the word *gunaikos* in the identical genitive case is repeated chiastically for emphasis at 1453–4), this participle therefore probably implies a degree of effeminisation. **on account of a woman:** On the formulaic blaming of Helen see 60–2*. **at a woman's hand:** The pairing of these two women perhaps highlights, for the first time (although see 83–4*, 914*), that Helen and Clytemnestra were sisters. The chorus here combine the topics of Clytemnestra's killing of Agamemnon and the deaths caused by Helen in the same way as Odysseus does when responding to the dead Agamemnon's account of his own death in the *Odyssey* (11.436–9): Zeus visited terrible hatred on the Atreidai 'through the counsels of women from the outset. Many of us died for Helen's sake and Clytemnestra set a snare for you when you were far away'. Helen and Clytemnestra are paired in Hesiod fr. 247.6–8 as adulteresses.

1455 *Iō iō*: See 1072*. **demented Helen:** The adjective *paranous* probably indicates the same kind of delusional behaviour as the noun *parakopa* at 223*.

1456–7 **one woman who destroyed so many—so very many:** See 60–2*. The particular wording here recalls the opening of the *Iliad* (1.3–4), where it is the *mēnis* (wrath) of Achilles which 'destroyed so many lives (*pollas ... psuchas*) of heroes' at Troy.

1459 **you have festooned yourself with your final, unforgettable flowers:** Lit., 'you flower-bedecked yourself in final form, always to be remembered'. In this extraordinary image, Helen ornaments herself for eternity with flowers symbolising men's deaths. Flower imagery has been used in connection with death and corpses repeatedly in the play: see 196–8*, 659*, 738–421*, 391–2*. On the themes of memory and forgetting see 34–9*. **strife that brought the man misery:** Lit., 'strife, misery of the man'. On *eris* cf. 696* and on *oizus* see 755–6*. **inbuilt:** The adjective *eridmatos* is formed with the intensifying prefix *eri-* and the verb *demein*, 'build', which produces an effective aural combination with *eris*. The idea seems to be that rivalrous conflict was a structural part of the material edifice of the Argive palace. On architectural imagery see also 1283*. **of old:** Lit., 'then'. This could mean at almost any point in the previous traumas suffered by the family.

1462 **Don't pray for death as your fate:** Lit., 'Neither pray for the fate of death'. On the several meanings of *epeuchesthai* see 533*. Clytemnestra here relinquishes spoken iambic trimeters for anapaestic, musically accompanied verse, as if emotionally affected by the chorus' naming of Helen.

1463 **weighed down:** For the same verb *barunein* in the context of psychological oppression see 189 (the Achaeans marooned at Aulis) and 836 (people blighted by envy). **thoughts:** This noun needs to be supplied in English.

1464 **And don't divert:** Lit., 'Nor divert'. **your rage against Helen:** Clytemnestra makes the important point, only infrequently stated in ancient literature, that the people who did all the killing at Troy did not actually include Helen. On *kotos* see 1211*.

1465–6 **calling her:** These words are supplied in English to clarify the meaning of *hōs*. **man-killer:** The chorus of Aeschylus' *Seven against*

Thebes use the same striking word of the deadly Sphinx (777), and the early historian Hellanicus of Lesbos used it of the Amazon Melanippe (4 *FgrH* F 106.2). **by individually destroying many Danaan souls:** This is Clytemnestra's detailed response to the chorus' charge against Helen at 1456–7*.

1467   infinite pain: On *algos* see 733*, where the lion cub which comes to represent both Helen and Paris is said to grow up and inflict *algos*. The adjective *axustatos* is formed from the verb *sunistamai* and fundamentally means 'not solidified' or 'unformed', so without definite delineation or boundaries. It clearly sounded memorable to the fifth-century BCE audience: it is one of the adjectives used to deride Aeschylus' rugged and obscure style by the smart younger men in Aristophanes' day (*Clouds* 1367).

1468   Malign spirit: On the recurring assumption that the household is under the malevolent influence of a daimonic entity, a *daimōn*, see 635*, 768–71*. **swoop down:** Lit., 'fall upon'. See 341–2*.

1469   the two Tantalids: The obvious men referred to here are Agamemnon and Menelaus, husbands of Clytemnestra and Helen. But, by alluding to their great-grandfather, Aeschylus perhaps encompasses Atreus and Thyestes, whose conflicted relationship also involved a 'difficult' woman, Aerope: see also 1197, 1469 and 1569–70*.

1470–1   through women: In the context, this might be understood as Clytemnestra and Helen, who have both played roles in the Argive royal family's catastrophe. But it might also suggest Aegisthus, whom the chorus call a woman at 1625*. **heart-breaking:** Lit., 'heart-biting'. **reflects their temperament:** Lit., 'is equal to their soul'. There have been several suggestions that the regime at Argos in Agamemnon's absence has involved great cruelty (550).

1472–4   like a hateful crow: On *dikan* see 231–5. The distinction between corvids, including the crow (*korōnē*) and the raven (*korax*), was not made at all systematically at this time, and either bird may have been in Aeschylus' mind's eye. But the most accurate translation, 'corvid', would not have the required rhetorical force here. Aristotle noted that, where food was scarce, crows often made appearances singly or in pairs rather than in flocks (quoted by Aelian, *NA* 2.48). It is most unfortunate that the treatise on bird-signs 'and the voice of crows' by the Alexandrian grammarian Theon has not survived. The collection of ancient Greek proverbs relating to the crow in Foufopoulos and Litinas (2005) 27–8 shows how apt a comparand the crow is for Clytemnestra, at least in the chorus' eyes: the crow was conceptually paired with the vulture (see 49–50*) and placed in antithesis to the nightingale (1141–6), and its song was proverbially hard on the ears; it was regarded as polluting to altars (Aesch. *Suppl.* 730), and particularly to relish pecking out the eyes of dead creatures. A terrifying curse (although of a much later date) in which a father disowns his children, preserved on a papyrus from Antinoupolis, abhors and casts them out 'for ravens to devour their flesh and peck out their eyes' (Pap. Cairo Maspero 3.67353.19).

sings her vaunting song: Lit., 'vaunts that she hymns her hymn'. On the verb *epeuchomai* see 533*; Clytemnestra is boasting like an Iliadic warrior on the battlefield. *Humnoi* are, properly, expressions of gratitude to gods (Pulleyn (1997) 49), which would normally accompany animal sacrifice, so this is a barbed word to choose to describe Clytemnestra's recent utterances. A word with the metrical form v – has dropped out here, perhaps describing the song as unpleasant.

1475 you've put your stated opinion right: Lit., 'you corrected the opinion of your mouth'. Clytemnestra, while disapproving of the chorus' expressed death wish and their criticism of Helen at 1448–61, is undismayed either by their identification of the malign *daimōn* afflicting the whole family or by the insulting characterisation of her as a vaunting crow at 1468–74. She is keen for them to accept her view of the reality and validity of the theodicy in accordance with which she believes she is acting.

1476–7 thrice-fattened malign spirit: The *daimōn* (see 1468*) has now gorged three times: on the children of Thyestes, on Iphigenia and, most recently, on Agamemnon. On the significance of the number three see 33*.

1478–80 lust: On *erōs* see 540* and on the gendering and sexualisation of revenge, Introduction, p. 56. **for lapping blood:** The graphic compound adjective recalls the ravening lion (i.e. the Greek army) who, Agamemnon says, licked up (*eleixen*) the blood of the Trojan aristocracy at 828*. On blood see also 209–10*. **is nourished by him in the belly:** The word *neira* seems to be a contracted form of the feminine noun *neiaira*, 'lower abdomen'. The spirit may be imagined as nursing his desire for revenge in his physical guts, or as nursing such a desire in Clytemnestra and other murderous members of the family. **new blood is discharged:** The neuter noun *ichōr* means the special blood coursing in the gods' veins at e.g. Hom. *Il.* 5.340, but seems to have encompassed any organic fluid, including blood (Plato, *Tim.* 83c, Aristot. *HA* 521b2), gall (Hipp. *Acut.* 1), or 'sero-purulent discharge' (Hipp. *De capitis vulneribus* 19, Aristot. *HA* 630a6). For a full discussion of this monstrous spirit see Moreno (2010).

1481 that keeps house: The chorus had said at 154–6*, 'there awaits a terrible, resilient, treacherous housekeeper (*oikonomos*), a remembering wrath (*mēnis*) that avenges a child', and Cassandra had suggested that Aegisthus was a 'housekeeping (*oikouros*) lion' at 1123–6*. Here the sinister housekeeper is the more ancient malign spirit that keeps on attacking the family.

1482   heavy with wrath: On the recurring language of oppressive weight see 63–7*, and on *mēnis*, 154–5*; the epic associations of the latter are reinforced by the dactylic metre of this line.

1483–4   an evil tale: The masculine noun *ainos* is cognate with the verb *ainein* (1481), as in the English 'speak a speech' or 'tell a tale'; the assonance with the *ai* in *daimōn* aurally structures this sentence. **ruinous:** On *atē* see 359–61*. **never satisfied:** See 755–6*, 1115–18*, 1331–3*.

1485   it's the work of Zeus: Lit., 'through Zeus'. At the moment of their highest anxiety about the continuing cycle of murders, the chorus need to reassure themselves that there must be a cosmic order behind all this, ordained by Zeus. He dominated the theology of the earlier part of the play (43–4*), yet it is possibly to him, in his infernal avatar, that Clytemnestra has dedicated her murderous sacrifice (1384–7*).

1486   cause of all, implementer of all: These two epithets create an anaphoric aural effect and return to the theological idea of Zeus' omnipotence (160–83). Zeus did have one well-known cult-title beginning with *pan-*, *Panhellēnios*, 'of all the Greeks', under which he was worshipped at Dodona and which had associations with the Delphic oracle (Paus. 1.44.13, Pind. *Nem.* 5.19, Hdt. 9.7).

**1487–8   The two rhetorical questions beginning with *ti* continue the anaphoric effect, supported by the repetition of *Dios* from 1485. The chorus is trying to reconcile the idea that Zeus must be behind all they have witnessed with the sacrilege and savagery it has entailed. Alexiou (1974) 161, with examples in nn.3–4, comments on this passage that it was traditional in the ancient dirge 'for the speaker to begin by expressing anxiety' lest he or she should fail 'to find words adequate to the occasion. This initial hesitation is most frequently expressed by means of questions'. The chorus are aware that there is no adult male of the family available to organise the funeral, as would normally be the practice, and Clytemnestra weaponises this opportunity to take charge. See the discussion of this scene in relation to Athenian funeral rites in Aeschylus' day in Hame (2004) 515–23 and (2008) 5–6.

1489   my King, my King: This line provides more repetition; on *basileus* see 83–4*. Lines 1489–96 are repeated at 1513–20.

1490–1   how shall I weep for you? Whatever can I say: The chorus utter more rhetorical questions. The implication is that the strange and terrifying scene before them is not conducive to the correct performance of the expected behaviours—weeping (see 270*) and eulogies—at an orthodox *ekphora*, where the body was brought out from the family home into public view before the funeral (see Kavoulaki (2005)). **from the heart of a friend:** See 805* where the chorus put aside their disapproval of what had happened at Aulis to welcome Agamemnon home *oud' aphilōs*, 'in a not unfriendly way'.

1492 this spider's web: Lit., 'weaving of a female spider'; the usual word for spider is the masculine noun *arachnēs*. Perhaps the image here was suggested by the name of the Argives' local mountain, Arachnaion (309*), from which the light emitted by the last beacon-fire arrived at Clytemnestra's palace. The female task of weaving seems to be linked to spiders in Hesiod's *Works and Days* 775–9, where it is recommended that the best day of the month for shearing sheep and gathering fruit was the twelfth, 'for on it the air-flying spider spins its web all day long, and the knowing one [i.e. the ant] heaps up its pile, and a woman should set up her loom and get on with her work'. It may be that it is relevant in this context, where Clytemnestra is presenting herself as a victor, that there was a tradition that the Delphic oracle had ordered that the victors at Olympia be crowned with branches from the wild olive in the sanctuary that was wreathed in the web of the spider (30 *FgrH* III.6). In Xenophon's *Memorabilia*, Socrates says that the hetaera Theodote deploys an art like that of the spider who weaves a fine web to attract male victims from whom she can derive her livelihood (3.11.5–6). Aegisthus applies a weaving metaphor to himself at 1604*. On the skill of the spider see Aristot. *HA* 622b–3a. On breath and breathing see Introduction, pp. 61–2.

1494 dishonourable bed: The adjective *aneleutheros* implies that whatever Agamemnon is lying in/on does not befit his status as a free man. The feminine noun *koitē* can mean 'the act of going to bed' (Hdt. 1.10; cf. 566*), but it may indeed refer to some kind of rough bedstead or bier here (Hom. *Od.* 19.341, Eur. *Hipp.* 132). It often means specifically a marriage bed (Aesch. *Suppl.* 804, Soph. *Trach.* 17), and such a connotation would not be inappropriate in this context, where Agamemnon is seen with two of his bed-partners, one alive and one dead: see 27*.

1495–6 slain in a treacherous killing by your wife's hand: On the play on *dameis* and *damar* (*damartos* is a necessary supplement but also provides further alliteration on the *d* sound in *doliōi*) see 1448–54*. On the issue of Clytemnestra's cunning see 1129*. **a double-edged weapon:** On the vexed question of the precise nature of the lethal weapon see 1260–3*. The word *belemnon* is unhelpful; it seems to be a variant of another neuter noun, *belos*, which, while it can often mean a missile like a dart or javelin, can alternatively mean a glance struck by the eye (see 240* and 742*), a shaft, dart or other missile (Hom. *Il.* 4.465, *Od.* 9.495, 20.305), a sword (Ar. *Ach.* 345, cf. Soph. *Aj.* 658) or, apparently, an axe (Eur. *El.* 1159).

1497   are you proclaiming: On *auchein* see 506*.

1498–9   Do not suppose: This is an unusual use of *epilegesthai*, although see Hdt. 1.78 where it means 'think over', and Hdt. 7.49, 'anticipate'. **Agamemnon's woman:** She assumes that the chorus think of her disrespectfully as little more than a woman Agamemnon has had sex with. The adjective *Agamemnonian*, combined with the feminine noun *alochos*, which puts the emphasis on the sharing of a bed (see 27*) and can mean 'concubine' as well as 'wife' (Ho, *Il.* 9.336, *Od.* 4.623), produces diction reminiscent of Pindar's version of the myth enacted in the *Oresteia* in his *Pythian* 11, for the sprinter Thrasydaeus of Thebes, probably dated to 474 BCE: Clytemnestra 'with the grey bronze sent the Dardanian daughter of Priam, Cassandra, alongside the Agamemnonian soul (*agamemnoniai psuchai*) to the shady bank of Acheron, the pitiless woman'.

1500   Taking on the appearance: The same verb is used of the figure who frightened Xerxes by appearing to him in a repeated dream (Hdt. 7.15).

1501   bitter: The adjective *drimus* carries with it a sense of real sensory discomfort, since it is applied to acrid, foul-smelling smoke at Ar. *Wasps* 146, sharp-tasting radishes (Xen. *Mem.* 1.4.5) and pungent medicines (Hipp. *Fract.* 27). **spirit of retaliation:** Presumably this entity is not easily distinguishable from the malign *daimōn* of previous stanzas (1468*). An *alastōr* is a specifically vengeful spirit (Aesch *Pers.* 354, Soph. *OC* 788); the proverb 'alastōr of the Pelopids' apparently meant 'utter ruin' (Xenarchus 1.3). Zeus was entitled 'Alastōr' in *Orphic Hymn* 73.3 (to *Daimōn*).

1502   against Atreus and his foul feast: Lit., 'of Atreus the harsh banqueter'. Clytemnestra is making the remarkable claim that she incarnates the spirit of vengeance which, Aegisthus will later tell us, Thyestes set in motion by his curse at Atreus' 'foul feast' (1600–2).

1504   an adult sacrifice to supplement: Lit., 'having sacrificed an adult in addition'. On *teleios*, meaning 'adult' here, see 970–2*. The prefix *epi-* in *epithuein* means 'besides' or 'after'. **that of young ones:** Lit., 'to young ones'. The word *nearoi* had been used of the Trojan youths who perished at 359*.

1505   not to blame: The term *anaitios* leaves room for a distinction to be drawn between whether Clytemnestra is denying that she had carried out the deed, because a supernatural spirit had done so, or claiming that she *was* responsible for the act, but it was justified (see 250–1*): on *Agamemnon*'s depiction of fledgling legal concepts see Introduction, p. 65.

1506   Who will testify? A good question in a context where Athena has not yet founded the first lawcourt; on legal language see 41*.

1507–8   the spirit of retaliation: See 1501*. **accomplice:** For the noun *sullēptōr* in a legal context discussing who was the cause of a death see Antiphon 3.3.10. The chorus, who insist that Clytemnestra must take primary responsibility, concede that the vengeful spirit aroused by the Thyestean feast may have played some role in the murder. **coming from a father's side:** By using the adverb *patrothen* the chorus avoids specifying which father, although in context it must be Thyestes, unless the meaning is simply 'for generations', as at IG 22.237.8, 'friends of the people from the time of our fathers'.

1509–12   Black Ares: The chorus have previously called *Atē* 'black' at 769*. The violence of Ares has earlier in this play been associated with military combat (374–6*); this is the first time in the trilogy that it refers to domestic murder, but this use of the war-god's name will be recalled in *Choephori* 461 where Orestes defines the trilogy's nearly insoluble moral crisis: 'Ares will collide with Ares, Justice with Justice.' **comes on with force:** For this meaning of *biazesthai* see Aesch. *PV* 1010, Soph. *Aj.* 1160 and Thuc. 1.77, where it is opposed to *dikazesthai*, 'behave in the morally right way'. **streams of kindred blood:** Lit., 'kindred streams of blood'. *epirrhoē* is a powerful feminine noun, which reappears in an equally important image in Athena's speech at *Eum.* 694, of the evil streams with which the pure waters of civic integrity should not be polluted. **for the congealed blood of children devoured:** Lit., 'for the child-devouring clot'. On blood see 209–10*.

1513–20   These lines constitute a repetition, suitable in a threnodic ritual chant, of 1489–98*.

1521   unworthy death: See 1494*. Clytemnestra denies that Agamemnon's death was inappropriate to him on the ground that he had committed a criminal act involving an underhand tactic, by which she presumably means tricking her and Iphigenia into believing that Iphigenia was to be married to Achilles at Aulis. **ruin on the household by treachery:** Lit., 'treacherous ruin on the household'. On the theme of *dolos*, cunning or teachery, see 1129*.

1525–7   he snatched away my offspring by him … what he did: Lit.,

'Suffering fit things having done fit things to my hoisted-up offspring by him'. The neuter noun *ernos* means the sprout or shoot of a plant or tree (Hom. *Il.* 17.53, Eur. *Med.* 1213) or a 'sprig' used in the garlands worn by victors at the games (Pind. *Nem.* 11.29). Metaphorically it came to mean 'child' or 'offspring', as here (Pind. *Nem.* 6.37, Aesch. *Eum.* 661, 666). The participle *aerthen* may bring to mind the physical lifting up of Iphigenia over the altar described by the chorus at 231–5*; on the other hand, *aeirein* means 'lift and take away', so 'remove' in an aggressive manner at Aesch. *Eum.* 847 and Plato *Rep.* 9.578e. **much bewailed Iphigenia:** Finally, after more than three-quarters of the play has passed, Iphigenia's proper name resounds around the theatre. The tears Clytemnestra claimed to have shed in Agamemnon's absence (887–90) were perhaps not fictitious at all. **His fitting agony befits what he did:** Lit., 'Having done fit things, suffering fit things'. The phrase *axia drasas axia paschōn* sounds proverbial (not unlike the less acoustically striking English saying 'make the punishment fit the crime'. The two verbs are found as oppositional pairs—the doer and the sufferer—elsewhere in tragedy, for example at Aesch. *Pers.* 813, *Eum.* 868, and cf. in *Choeph.* 313, the 'ancient saying *drasanti pathein*, 'let the doer suffer'; cf. also 1564*.

1528   let him make no big boasts in Hades: The audience would have been reminded of all that passes between Odysseus and the shade of Agamemnon in *Odyssey* 11.385–464. The dead king's ghost claims, among other things, that he fought back hard against Clytemnestra and that she has shed shame on other women, even those in the future and those who may be virtuous. On Hades see also *Agamemnon* at 1291*.

1529   of execution by the sword: Lit., 'by sword-annihilating death'. The same compound adjective, *xiphodelētos*, is used of Orestes' imminent attempt to kill Clytemnestra at *Choeph.* 729. On the issue of the weapon Clytemnestra used to murder Agamemnon see 1260–3*. **for what he started:** Clytemnestra veers between tracing the cycle of bloodshed back to the Thyestean feast and claiming, as here, that it was inaugurated by Agamemnon.

1530–2   I'm deprived of any mental resource to deal with this: Lit., 'Deprived of a handy care of thought'. **I have no idea:** Lit., 'I am resourceless'.

1533–4   the loud rattle of a home-wrecking deluge of blood: Lit., 'the home-wrecking bloody rattle of rain'. On rain see 1014–15* and on fear see 12–14*. The diction is reminiscent of the Herald's description of the 'gusts of pelting rain' (*zalēi t'ombroktupōi*) that afflicted the fleet at 656. **it isn't just drizzling any more:** Lit., 'the fine-drop-rain (*psakas*) abates'. On both the word *psakas* and the omen of blood rain see 1390*. The chorus fear that a pattern of occasional murder may be replaced by a denser spate of atrocities. On weather imagery see 5* and on blood see 209–10*.

1535–7 Fate is sharpening justice's blade: Lit., 'Fate is sharpening justice'. On *moira* see 128–30*; on the imagery of metallurgy and weapon-making, 151–4*. **for another damaging deed:** Lit., 'another action of harm', presumably the revenge killing of Clytemnestra predicted by Cassandra at 1281–5. **sharpening blocks:** The traditional translation 'whetstone' is too archaic to be understood by most modern English speakers, and fails to provide the rhetorical emphasis of the polyptoton *thēganē/thēganaisi*.

1538 earth, earth: See 503*, 633*, 871–2*, 1072*. Perhaps these two words should be capitalised; see 218–21*. **I wish that:** Lit., 'would that'. **you'd taken me:** The chorus' third statement of a death wish (see 550*, 1364–5*).

1539–40 occupying: See 454*, where the same verb, *katechein*, is used of the Argive dead 'occupying' the earth at Troy. **silver-sided:** Lit., 'silver-walled'; see 949* and 959–60*, where silver had also been used to emphasise the wealth of Agamemnon's household through its lavish deployment of purple dye. **bathtub:** The same feminine noun, *droitē*, is used for Agamemnon's death-bath at both *Choeph.* 999 and *Eum.* 633. Vermeule (1979) 13 and n.22 discusses the association between bath and biers in the Greek imagination and funeral ritual.

1541 Two obvious but good questions. How can an orthodox funeral take place when the murder victim's murderer holds supreme power in both his household and the state?

1542 Are you going to: The chorus have no suggestion of an alternative member of the royal household to conduct the funeral. **bewail:** On the root of this verb see 1314*.

1544–7 complete this with: The word 'this' has been supplied to make sense in English. *epikrainein* usually means 'accomplish', 'bring to pass' (see 744, 1340), but at *Odyssey* 4.132 it refers, in the passive, to the golden ornaments which 'topped off' or provided the finishing touches to the silver wool-working basket belonging to Helen. **a favour that is no favour:** This is a typically Aeschylean litotes. On *charis* see 182–30*. **in return for momentous deeds:** This presumably refers to the sacking of Troy.

1548–50 tearfully delivering: Lit., 'sending forth with tears'. On tears see 270*. **a eulogy over the grave:** Lit., 'a tomb-side praise'. **shall feel sincere mental pain:** Lit., 'Shall feel pain with truth of mind'. On the chorus' dislike of hypocrisy see 790–4, and on Agamemnon's fear of false friends see 833–7.

1551–2   to concern yourself with this responsibility: Although the details of Agamemnon's interment remain unclear in *Choephori*, it does became clear that his body was mutilated, he was not lamented properly, the public was excluded and Electra was not involved (429–50). **At our hands:** Lit., 'by us'. Clytemnestra's plurals here and in the next line keep everyone guessing about the extent of Aegisthus' participation.

1553   down he was struck: Lit., 'down he was killed'. The triple anaphora of verbs beginning with the *kata-* stem, and the ritualistic effect it creates, combined with the run of four dactyls and the additional alliterative effect of *k* in *kai* and in the next line, produce a brutal aural soundscape to match the activities described: on triple effects in rhetoric see also 33*.

1554   There will be no mourners from outside the household allowed at his burial—a blunt and savage response to the chorus' string of questions in the previous stanza.

1555–8   but his daughter Iphigenia: It is Clytemnestra who, for a second time (see 1526), names the maiden the chorus could not bring themselves to when they abruptly truncated their description of her sacrifice at 248. **with an embrace:** Lit., 'embracingly'. **as she ought:** The effect of the picture painted in this sentence depends entirely on the intonation of the actor playing Clytemnestra. She could be sincerely indicating how things should always have been between Agamemnon and Iphigenia, even perhaps implying that their relationship had been inappropriately close, or she could be using lacerating irony. **fast-flowing ford of miseries:** This means the Acheron (see Cassandra's prediction of herself singing mantic songs by this river at 1157–61*).

1560   blaming arises in return for blame: The chorus' use of polyptoton, as so often, aesthetically and aurally enacts the issue of reciprocity.

1561   The battle outcome is hard to judge: Lit., 'hard fought things to judge'. The chorus for once seem to acknowledge that Agamemnon and Clytemnestra each had a valid case to make.

1562   The defeater is defeated: The verb *pherein*, here in 'dialectical' *figura etymologica* again, was sometimes associated with carrying off the booty in battle (Hom. *Il.* 6.480) or the prize in athletics competitions (Hom. *Il.* 23.663), and this sort of victory seems to be meant here. See 171–2*. This stanza, the last lines sung by the chorus in *Agamemnon*, crystallises the moral and juridical conundrum of the entire tragedy. If it is unavoidable that the doer of evil must pay the penalty, because that is Zeus' law, then how can a stop ever be put to the family curse?

1563   While Zeus remains on his throne, it remains true: The word 'true' needs to be inserted to make sense in English. *mimnein mimnontos* (on this verb see 74–5*) provides yet a fourth *figura etymologica* in this stanza. On the chorus' dogged insistence on Zeus' ability to apply this cosmic rule see Introduction, pp. 49–50.

1564   that the doer suffers: See 1525–7*. **that is the rule:** Cf. 304*. This now seems to be the ordinance of Zeus that has been enacted in *Agamemnon*, rather than the more constructive and edifying principle which the chorus earlier said he had taught humanity, that learning comes through suffering (176–83*).

1565   family curse: Lit., 'cursed family line'. On the curse see Introduction, pp. 52–7.

1566   is welded: Probably an image from metallurgy (see, e.g., Hom. *Il.* 15.389, Pind. *Nem.* 7.78 and 151–4*) rather than from medicine or ceramics, contexts in which the verb *kollaō* is also common in classical Greek. **destruction:** On *atē* see 359–61*.

1568   this oracular statement: Clytemnestra picks up on the idea that the family line is cursed and 'welded to destruction', agreeing with the chorus that this is the situation. The adversarial parties have found some tentative common ground.

1569–70   for my part I am willing: This slightly more conciliatory Clytemnestra now speaks in the singular. Is she not so sure that Aegisthus has completed his acts of vengeance? She seems naively optimistic that she can individually put an end to the cycle of retaliation. **to make a sworn agreement:** Lit., 'making oaths'. Clytemnestra imagines a transaction like those in archaic homicide law that allowed a murderer to pay a sum in compensation to the victim's family for their loss. But such an oath cannot be made with a supernatural entity, and Clytemnestra anyway fails to follow any such oath up with the ritual or invocation which would be required to validate it (Fletcher (2012) 50). **the malign spirit of the Pleisthenids:** Clytemnestra had earlier fused herself with the *alastōr* of the house (1501*), but now sees herself as separate from the malign *daimōn*, from which the *alastōr* is barely distinguishable; indeed, she is willing to swear to an agreement with him (for discussion see Geisser (2002) 304–31). On this single occasion, she refers to the family as the 'Pleisthenids'; Aegisthus will call them 'the *genos* of Pleisthenes' at 1603*. This creates a problem in terms of the audience's understanding of the evolution of the mythical curse on the descendants of Tantalus, who is only mentioned tangentially in this play. Pleisthenes is a mysterious figure about whose connexion with the family curse and 'malign spirit' we are not well informed. One ancient tradition put him in the same generation as Atreus and Thyestes, making him the illegitimate son of Pelops (scholia on Pindar, *Ol.* 1.144c–e). Another said he was one of the sons of Thyestes, borne illegitimately by Aerope, and eaten by Thyestes (Hyginus, *Fables* 246). Another claimed that Pleisthenes was the son of Atreus and the father of Agamemnon (Hesiod fr. 37a), but had died young, so Agamemnon and Menelaus were brought up by their grandfather Atreus (Hesiod fr. 37b). A scholiast on Tzetzes' commentary on Homer's *Iliad* adds to this version the intriguing detail that Pleisthenes was a hermaphrodite or lame and wore women's clothing (Hesiod fr. 37c). Yet another tradition puts him in the same generation as Orestes, claiming that he was a son of Helen whom she took with her to Troy (*Cypria* fr. 9). It is possible that the audience were aware of one, some or all these versions. Clytemnestra might be expected, rhetorically speaking, to want to push the curse back as far in time as possible, so the mysterious father or half-brother of Atreus and Thyestes might be the most likely guess. There were tragedies about the generation of Atreus and Thyestes, including a *Thyestes* by both Sophocles and Euripides; a spectacular Apulian amphora in the Boston Museum of Fine Arts (1991.437), attributed to the Darius painter, portrays the murder of Atreus by Thyestes, with Aegisthus, Pelopia (on whom see 1090–2*) and an Erinys named *Poinē* ('Punishment') present (see the photograph and fascinating discussion in Taplin (2007) 241–3), but there is no figure there to be identified as Pleisthenes.

1570   to acquiesce: For this sense of *stergein* see Hdt. 9.117. Aesch. *PV* 11. **in what has happened:** Lit., 'in these things'. It is not clear whether Clytemnestra is accepting solely that the death of Iphigenia has now been fully avenged, or whether she is accepting the entire tragic history of the 'Pleisthenids'.

1571   let him be willing: This needs to be supplied from 1569, to point up the parallelism between the two parties to the oath. **to go:** Lit., 'going'.

1572   with intrafamilial deaths: Lit., 'by deaths, perpetrators'.

1573–4   the possession of a small share of wealth is wholly sufficient: This is a surprising and interesting claim, although neither Clytemnestra's earlier behaviour nor her presentation in *Choephori* (see, e.g., lines 136–7) suggests that she had any serious intention of embracing a modest lifestyle. See also 1638–9*, where Aegisthus says he will use Agamemnon's money to support his own regime.

1575–6   if I can rid the palace of the madness of reciprocal murders: Lit., 'to me, ridding the palace of reciprocally murderous madnesses'. This is a breakthrough moment in terms of Clytemnestra's attitude to killing. Up to this point, her own murder of Agamemnon, at least, has been presented by her as a rational choice in the circumstances and she has shown no signs of losing control. But, once again, Clytemnestra's sense of the potential effect of her own intervention in the cycle of violence seems optimistically exaggerated. These lines follow '*m*' sound alliteration with an intricating interlacing of '*a*', '*l*', and '*ph*', creating a gentler closing soundscape than hitherto in this exchange. The feminine noun *mania* is particularly associated with divinely inspired frenzy (e.g. Eur. *Bacch.* 305; Plato, *Phaedr.* 405a), but also has a more secular, medical application (Hipp. *Aph.* 7.5; Hdt. 6.75). The plural of *mania* is used to mean something similar to what Clytemnestra is articulating here when Iris tells Lyssa, the divine personification of berserk violence on the battlefield, to afflict Heracles, about to kill his wife and three children, with 'madnesses (*manias*) and infanticidal mental disturbances' (Eur. *HF* 835–6). There was a sanctuary of the Maniai in Arcadia, and Pausanias says that some claim that it was there that madness first overtook Orestes after killing his mother; Pausanias believes that *Maniai* was a title of the Eumenides/Erinyes (8.34.1).

## XIV]	1577–1653	THE CHORUS AND AEGISTHUS

Summary
Shortly after the Queen and the populace appear to reach a tense truce at the end of their amoibaion, and she disappears back inside leaving the corpses visible, Aegisthus emerges from the palace with an armed personal bodyguard, perhaps consisting of 12 men to provide a match for the chorus. The audience are left to ask whether she has talked to him and asked (or instructed) him to meet the indignant citizens himself. A director could even choose to have Clytemnestra and Aegisthus encounter one another wordlessly as they moved in different directions across the threshold. It is something of a shock to imagine that such a body of militiamen had been accommodated within throughout the foregoing action; perhaps, retrospectively, it explains why Clytemnestra had felt so little fear. Aegisthus is himself armed, defiant, inflammatory and triumphant. If he was acted by the same actor who played Agamemnon, the similarity of voice and gait may have underlined that the characters are first cousins. In spoken iambics, after exulting over Agamemnon's corpse and offering the audience the final extended oration of the play, in which he traces today's events back to the curse his father had invoked upon Atreus and his descendants, he claims responsibility for Agamemnon's death. The sheer length of

time for which Aegisthus has been nursing his murderous resentment is greater even than Clytemnestra's ten-year-old grievance: Aristotle says that crimes appear worse to juries the more brutal they are and when they have been long premeditated (*Rhet.* 1.1375a). Beginning with the chorus' announcement that he can expect to be cursed and stoned to death, pure mutual hatred is then expressed by both him and the old men in a disjointed iambic interchange, where no set pattern of number of lines emerges: the chorus have five, followed by Aegisthus with eight, the chorus with three, Aegisthus with five, the chorus with three, Aegisthus with seven and the chorus with six, as if representing an ill-disciplined shouting match. But as soon as the chorus mention Orestes, the metre shifts to the excited trochaic tetrameter at 1649, indicating the possibility of violence breaking out, and Aegisthus sets his guards on the elderly citizens. Weapons are drawn and death threats uttered; combat seems inevitable.

1577   light: On *phengos* see 504*, 601–2*. This apostrophe to the light makes it difficult to agree with critics who have argued that Aegisthus enters via an outdoor route rather than from within the palace. **that brings justice:** The same adjective, *dikēphoros*, was used by the Herald to describe Zeus as he mowed down the Trojans at 525–6, and will be used by Electra of the saviour that is needed in Argos at *Choeph.* 120. All the parties in this saga believe that justice is on their side.

1578   I can say: Lit., 'I could say'. **who wreak revenge:** The word *timaoros* is equivalent to *timōros*, which has been used by the Herald of his divine champion, Hermes, at 514*, and in Cassandra's prophecies of an avenger (Orestes) who will come subsequently, at 1280* and 1324*.

1579   do oversee: For a more negative view of divine scrutiny of human affairs see what Cassandra says about Apollo, using the same verb, at 1270*. **miseries:** On the neuter noun *achos* see 1157–61*, 1555–8*. These apparently conventional sentiments express something rather shocking: for most of his life, Aegisthus has been unable to subscribe to the orthodox providential view that the gods punish human injustice.

1580–1   I welcome the sight: Lit., 'seeing dearly'. **clothes:** See 1125–6*, where Cassandra used the same word of the same object. **woven by the Erinyes:** See 645*, 58–9*, 462–3*, 749*, 990–2*, 1119* and especially 1188–90*, where Aegisthus' collaborator Clytemnestra had claimed that the Erinys was one of the three female divinities to whom she had sacrificed Agamemnon.

1582   fully expiating: The English adverb 'fully' translates the force of the *ek-* prefix. **schemes:** On cunning and trickery see 1129*. This introduces the theme of the guile involved in the Thyestean feast, as in the luring of Iphigenia to Aulis and in Clytemnestra's entrapment of Agamemnon; it will be repeated when the chorus of *Choephori* (726–7) ask for the assistance of Hermes, god of stealth and cunning (*dolios*), in the wreaking of revenge.

1583 his father Atreus, when ruling this land: Aegisthus carefully avoids calling Atreus 'king', since that would implicitly acknowledge that the throne had rightfully belonged to Atreus.

1584–6 when his sovereignty was disputed: Lit., 'being disputed in his power'. The elliptical nature of this reference to the conflict between Atreus and Thyestes is frustrating. Aegisthus has no vested interest, of course, in elaborating on the reasons for the struggle between his father Thyestes and uncle Atreus, because it would reflect badly on Thyestes, who in most versions of the story both contested his older brother Atreus' right to the throne and seduced Atreus' wife Aerope. Aeschylus may have known the version of the myth in which the movement of the sun and the stars from east to west only came about when Zeus reversed their motion from west to east in order to show his support for Atreus in the dispute over the succession and the golden lamb (Plato, *Statesman* 268e–269a; schol. Eur. *Or.* 988; see also 1584–6*). Later versions, notably the 'golden lamb' ode in Euripides' *Electra* (699–746), on which see Rosivach (1978), relate how the brothers had fought over which one of them owned a god-given golden lamb, the possession of which indicated the right to sovereignty (see also 6–7*). The most detailed synthesis is in a very late source, Tzetzes, *Chiliades* 1.18.423–51, according to whom Aegisthus did not share a mother with his unfortunate older brothers; he was the product of incest and brought up to take care of goats in the mountains, since Thyestes had slept with his own daughter and impregnated her. **banished:** cf. Aesch. *Eum.* 221, where the same verb is used by Apollo of Orestes' later banishment from Argos. **to make it clear:** Lit., 'to speak clearly'. On the *tor-* stem in this play see 26*.

1587–90 returned again, a suppliant at the hearth: Once again, it is unhelpful that we are not told why Thyestes returned from banishment and became a suppliant at the hearth; the nature of his misdemeanours against Atreus might imply that he was unlikely to receive a whole-hearted welcome. This is, of course, the hearth at which Clytemnestra says Aegisthus now kindles the flames (1435; see also 427–8*). **he met a safe fate personally:** Lit., 'he found a secure fate himself'. **since he did not die and spill his blood:** Lit., 'so as not dying to put blood on'. Later versions claim that Thyestes survived to become king of Mycenae, but that he was ousted by Agamemnon and Menelaus with the help of Tyndareus; he was then forced to take refuge on the island of Cythera off the southern coast of the Peloponnese, and died there. Pausanias says (2.18.1) that, in his day, the tomb of Thyestes was to be seen on the right-hand side of the road if you walked from Mycenae to Argos; a stone ram adorned it.

1590–3   This man here's father: The body of Agamemnon is clearly still visible on stage, presumably with that of Cassandra. Aegisthus does not ever call Atreus his own uncle. **offered my father hospitality:** The adjective *xenia* is positioned an unnaturally long way away from the noun, *daita*, it qualifies. **with more zeal than love:** Aegisthus seems to have a mordant sense of humour. **pretending to mark the day generously by serving meat:** Lit., 'seeming to conduct a carnivorous feasting day'. **of his children's flesh:** See Cassandra's words at 1242*.

1594–5   He broke off: Lit., 'he was crushing into small pieces'. The imperfect tense probably emphasised that this gruesome task would have taken time, but the lacuna in the text makes it impossible to be sure. **the toes:** Lit., 'the parts about the feet'. **and the fingers from the hands:** Lit., 'the topmost combs of the hands'. Aegisthus is using slightly circumlocutory language for the details of the butchering of his brothers' corpses. The masculine noun *kteis* ('comb') is used of several different objects where there are parallel lines adjacent to one another, such as in a loom-comb (*Anth. Pal.* 6.247), a rake (*Anth. Pal.* 6.297.5), cutting-teeth (Poll. 2.91) or bivalve shellfish (Anaxandrides fr. 42.62, cf. Aristot. *HA* 525a22). Kin-killing was one of the most serious offences Greek ethics could contemplate. But compounding it with the eating of human flesh outraged every religious sensibility. The two fathers of Agamemnon and Aegisthus had between them contrived to do both at the same time. Cannibalism (which in this instance, since Thyestes was unaware of what he was eating, would more correctly be termed 'anthropophagy'), was presented in even the earliest Greek literature as a sign of the utmost barbarism: Achilles imagines devouring part of Hector raw in the *Iliad* (22.346–8), but even in his wildest fits of anger, and despite the close connection between the alimentary and the retaliatory evidenced in the story of Cronos, the best of the Achaeans stops short of such an atrocity. Human flesh-eating in Greek thought is practised only by such cultural outlaws as the Cyclopes of the *Odyssey* and remote savages located by ethnographers beyond the margins of civilisation. The eating of humans by humans is explicitly proscribed in Hesiod (*Works and Days* 276–80), for consuming members of your own species is regarded as the way of beasts. If humans are to preserve that important boundary between themselves and animals, they must absolutely abjure the consumption of human flesh. This incident is one of the most repellent episodes in Greek myth, along with the story of Tereus' devouring of his son Itys' flesh (see 1144–5*); it is portrayed in the tragedy as an outrage which threatened to erase all distinctions between humanity and bestiality.

1595 **on his own:** At Hom. *Od.* 13.14, the adverb *andrakas* means 'each man individually'. Presumably it is only Thyestes who has been served with human flesh, perhaps at his own separate table, to spare the other diners the sacrilege. It is unfortunate that some precious text, probably describing the culinary preparation of the obscene meal, has gone missing before this.

1596 **in ignorance:** Besides the Aesopic fables, few of which it is possible to date securely, Aeschylean tragedies are the earliest extant texts to use the noun *agnoia*, which was subsequently to become inseparable from philosophical discussions of excusable misdemeanour committed in ignorance and crimes committed wittingly; *Agnoia* was even to be personified and appear as a goddess on stage in New Comedy. See Cinaglia (2013). **parts he did not recognise:** Lit., '[things] not distinctively marked'. He recognised them neither as human flesh nor as having any connection with his sons.

1597 **food:** Aegisthus' distaste for the event he is narrating is conveyed by his choice of the feminine noun *bora*, a coarse word. It is often used to describe what is eaten by carnivorous animals (Aesch. *PV* 583, Eur. *Phoen.* 1603), including dogs (Ar. *Knights* 416) and lions (Arist. *NE* 3.1118a23); it can mean human flesh when cannibalistically eaten by humans or hominids (1220*, Hdt. 1.119, Eur. *Cyc.* 127) as well as simple fare (Soph. *Phil.* 274) or food eaten gluttonously (Eur. *Suppl.* 865). **which could not salvage:** The adjective *asōtos* implies that there was already a problem in the family rather than that this feast was the first cause of the conflict: see 1569–7*. **as you see:** This is a prompt to the Aegisthus actor to point to the corpse of Agamemnon again.

1598 **ill-omened:** Lit., 'not auspicious', an understatement, and a litotes, at the same time. Cf. 104.

1599 **he screamed:** On *oimōzein* see 326–8*. **fell backwards:** The posture Aegisthus is visualising is suggested by the occurrence of *anapiptein* in reference to rowers leaning back at the oar (Xen. *Oec.* 8.8) or horse riders (Xen. *Eq. Mag.* 3.14). **the slaughtered flesh:** Lit., 'the slaughter'. **spewing it out:** This meaning is produced by reading *apo* with *erōn* together, like the compound *exeraō* 'spew out', 'purge by vomiting' in Hippocrates, *Diseases of Women* 2.121. This disgusting scene had clear comic potential: it was presumably the character Thyestes who in Aristophanes' lost comedy about preparations for a tragedy to be performed at a drama competition, *Proagon*, said, 'I'm a wretch who has tasted the guts of my children? How can I contemplate roast pig-snout now?'

1600 He invoked an intolerable doom on the Pelopids: Atreus and Thyestes' father has not so far been named, but the context makes him by far the most appropriate ancestor to name here: he was said to have been chopped up, cooked and partially eaten at a banquet of the gods (a narrative alluded to but roundly dismissed as false by Pindar in *Olympian* I, performed 18 years prior to *Agamemnon*), before being brought back to life and given a prosthetic shoulder.

1601 with a kick to the dining-table … curse: Lit., 'adding to the curse in corroboration (*xundikōs*) a kick of the dinner'. On legal language see 41*. On the Atreidai's ill-omened dining table see also 399–402.

1602 Pleisthenids: See 1569–7*. The direct speech stands out from the narrative, with Aegisthus repeating verbatim his own father's curse.

1603 why you see this man fallen here: Lit., 'it is available to you to see this man fallen'. The deictic gives Aegisthus yet another opportunity to gesture at the corpse.

1604 designer of this murder, and rightly so: Lit., 'righteous stitcher of this murder'. The verb *rhaptein* is a regular metaphor for contriving a plot: see Hom. *Od.* 3118, Hdt. 9.17, Eur. *IT* 681, *Andr.* 811. Aegisthus' co-conspirator Clytemnestra was imagined as a female spider weaving the net at 1492*. This is the first time in the play where the suggestion is raised that the *plan* for the murder was Aegisthus' work rather than Clytemnestra's. It is revealing that Aegisthus uses a metaphor from the female sphere of textile production, where Clytemnestra had compared herself or her murdering hand with a (male) craftsman (1405–6).

1605 me, the third son, he drove out: It seems unwise of Atreus, if he was prepared to commit child-murder, to have spared any son of Thyestes, however tiny. In some versions Aegisthus was only the two murdered boys' half-brother: he was the product of Thyestes' incestuous rape of his own daughter Pelopia (see 1569–70*). Aegisthus is yet another exile from his homeland in the trilogy (1283*, 1411*). On the significance of the number three see 33*.

1606 baby in swaddling clothes: Nearly identical diction is used by

Cilissa, the nurse in *Choephori* 755, as she remembers tending the infant Orestes. On babies and small children in *Agamemnon* see 49–50*.

1607   Justice: On *Dikē* see 250–1*.

1608   Outsider: On *thuraios* see 836–7*. **I took this man on:** On the precise meaning here of the middle voice of *haptein* rests our understanding of the role Aegisthus did or did not play in the actual killing of Agamemnon. The basic meaning is 'take hold of for oneself', but it can also mean 'engage' (Soph. *Ant.* 179), 'attack' (Pind. *Nem.* 8.22, Ar. *Lys.* 365), 'feed on' (Thuc. 2.50) and physically 'lay hands on' (Plato, *Laws* 11.913a, *Rep.* 2.360b). Aeschylus is preserving ambiguity on this point.

1609   pondering every kind of unpleasant scheme: Lit., 'putting together every scheme of ill deliberation'. But did he do this on his own? Clytemnestra, after all, is a woman who can deliberate like a man (10–11*).

1610   death would be fine: Aegisthus adds himself to the list of those who have stated past or present willingness to die in the play.

1611   nets: For the neuter noun *herkos*, usually in the plural, meaning a net for catching birds or animals, see Hom. *Od.* 22.469, Pind. *Nem.* 3.51, and the metaphor at Eur. *Bacch.* 958. At Herodotus 7.85, in the plural, it means the coils of a lasso, which would provide a striking image here. At 257* the word had been used in the singular in the different sense of a 'defensive wall' by the chorus in praise of Clytemnestra. On nets and hunting imagery see 357*. **of Justice:** See 250–1*. This is the fourth claim that justice was on his side that Aegisthus has made in the course of this single speech (see also 1577, 1604, 1607).

1612   Aegisthus: The chorus use only a bald vocative, and no epithet or respectful address, when they respond to Aegisthus' garish and gloating first oration over his rival's corpse.

1613   wilfully: *hekōn* has a range of meanings from 'being willing' or 'readily' to 'consciously', but in legal and quasi-legal contexts it might best be translated 'intentionally' or even 'with premeditation'.

1614   on your own: Aegisthus has not explicitly denied that anyone else was involved, but this is how the chorus have heard his statement at 1604. The trilogy never reveals what exactly happened behind the scenes during the murder of either Agamemnon or Cassandra.

1615–16   you, personally: Lit., 'your head'. **public curses and death by stoning:** Lit., 'people-thrown stoning curses'. See 1409* and 1413*; the chorus had threatened Clytemnestra with curses and exile rather than curses and capital punishment.

1617–19   at the lower oar: The oarsman at the lowest of the three levels on the trireme, the *thalamitēs*, provided crucial muscle energy, but had the least power to alter the direction of the ship. His oar was the shortest and he was paid least. See schol. Ar. *Frogs* 1106 and Hall (2022a) section 2. **those with power over the ship sit on the top deck:** An early instance of the image of the ship of state; Aeschylus had earlier used the image of a cosmic ship (182–3*). On the verb *kratein* and the noun *kratos* see 10–11* and 1673*; Aegisthus and Clytemnestra in these last scenes deploy such vocabulary repeatedly. The neuter noun *doru* can refer to anything made of timber, including a ship's plank (Hom. *Il.* 15.410), and thence came by synecdoche (*pars pro toto*) to mean simply 'ship' (Pind. *Pyth.* 4.27, Aesch. *Pers.* 411). Medda (2017) vol. 3, 429 reviews the evidence and argues that *zugon* here must mean the top deck, from which the helmsman steered the ship. For similar metaphorical expressions see Eur. *Ion* 595 and *Phoen.* 74.

1619–20 You're old: Lit., 'being an old man'. **oppressive:** Lit., 'heavy'. For the recurring language in psychological contexts of heavy weights see 63–7*. **to be taught at your age, when the lesson is self-control:** Lit., 'to be instructed at such an age to control yourself [being the] stated [topic]'. The threat sounds almost identical to Clytemnestra's at 1425* ('you will surely know, though taught late in the day, how to control yourself'); this implies to an attentive audience that the couple have pre-emptively discussed how to respond to a mutinous Argive citizenry. On old age see 72*.

1621–3 In terms of schooling the elderly, fetters and hunger pangs are: Lit., 'To teach even old age, a fetter and hunger pangs'; 'are' needs to be supplied in English. On old age see 72* and on the fear of hunger see 192–5*. **outstanding physicians of the mind:** The superlative of *exochos* creates a menacing effect, in the context, equivalent to a threat of torture, since it is usually found in positive contexts praising a man's excellence or eminence (Hom. *Il.* 2.188, Eur. *Supp.* 889). The noun *iatromantis* means 'physician and seer', and is a bizarre way of describing a means of torture, since its reference is normally to sons of Apollo skilled in benign medicine and healing (see, e.g., Aesch. *Supp.* 263) or of Apollo himself, as both seer and healer, by his Pythia, at *Eum.* 62. Fraenkel (1950) vol. 3, 767 comments that here the term 'has become an instrument of cruel sarcasm' and thus might have had 'the effect of blasphemy'. On medical imagery see 18*. **Do you have eyes and not see:** Lit., 'Not seeing do you see'. See 240*.

1624 kick against the pricks: This proverbial expression about the futility of resisting sharp goads, drawn from disciplining animals or equestrianism, is also used in reference to obedience to higher political authority in the mysterious ending of Pindar's *Pythian* 2.94–6; the poet there warns people discontented with the despotic regime of Hieron of Syracuse to accept it quietly. The image of kicking, *laktizein*, has featured metaphorically earlier in the play (381*).

1625   You woman! Lit., 'O woman'. For the suggestion that Aegisthus is somehow deficient in terms of the stereotypical male virtues see 1123–6*. **Lingering until men:** Lit., 'Awaiting men'. The chorus basically accuse Aegisthus of draft-dodging, a source of great resentment in classical Athens, especially when those accused of it were rich and privileged (see, e.g., Lys. 6.46, 30.26). Draft-dodgers were pilloried as effeminate (see Aristophanes on Amynias, *Clouds* 658–93). Diodorus reports that the law against draft-dodging and deserters in Thurii punished offenders quasi-theatrically by making them sit in the marketplace in women's clothes (12.16.1–2; cf. Plato, *Laws* 12.944d–e; Christ (2004) 33–4).

1626   keeping house: See 154–6* and 1481*, where the *oikouros* (housekeeper) has been Clytemnestra and the 'malign spirit' that assaults the household respectively, although here it certainly implies evasion of military duty (Christ (2004) 53). **a husband's bed:** On the bed Clytemnestra has shared with both Agamemnon and his cousin see 27*.

1627   a military commander: The chorus feel that the military status and accomplishments of Agamemnon somehow make his premeditated killing off the battlefield even more deplorable.

1628   shall give you reason to weep: Lit., '[are] the first cause of cryings'. The pretentious bombast of Aegisthus' language is a feeble echo of Clytemnestra's oratorical bravura, and, in this context, Fraenkel may be responding accurately when he states (vol. 3, 772) that the furious 'boor Aegisthus becomes more and more vulgar'.

1629   Your voice is the opposite: Lit., 'You have the opposite tongue to Orpheus's'. This *negative* mythical comparison (see Introduction, p. 101) is a strangely abrupt one to make while delivering a series of threats, and is seemingly unrelated to any previous imagery or allusion in the play. Perhaps it sounds hackneyed, as though Aegisthus is not as original a speaker as his lover is. The second play of Aeschylus' tetralogy *Lycurgeia*, entitled *Bassarids*, enacted the story of Orpheus' dismemberment by the maenads of Thrace, the Bassarids. Euripides may have been remembering Aegisthus' bizarre negative comparison when he made his Iphigenia begin her appeal to her father to save her life with the contrastingly beautiful lines (*IA* 1211–14) 'If I had Orpheus' eloquence, father, to move the rocks to follow me by sung spells, or to enchant with my words anyone I wanted, I would have resorted to it.'

1630 he led every being to him: Lit., 'he led everything'. **with his delightful voice:** 'Lit., by his utterance with delight'. On the noun *phthongos* see 324–5*.

1631–2 childish yelps: On the figurative language of childlike incompetence see 74–5*. The word *'hulagma'* is used of the noise made by dogs at Eur. *IT* 293. Clytemnestra also refers to the chorus' angry words as 'yelps' at 1672. This is the first of the serial comparisons with animals which characterise the final showdown of this tragedy. **shall be led away:** The contrast between the effect of Orpheus' vocal expression and that of the chorus is further pointed using the same verb as at 1630. Aegisthus is threatening arrest without even claiming that an actual crime, beyond 'provoking' him, has been committed. **overpowered:** On the *krat-* root see 10–11* and 1617–19*.

1633 am I really to think you: Lit, '[are] you really to me'. **tyrant:** The chorus are using the noun *turannos* in both its technical sense, as a ruler who has attained power by a coup rather than hereditary inheritance, and qualitatively as someone whose despotic power is maintained non-consensually by terror and physical force. See 828*.

1635 to carry out the killing yourself: Lit., 'to carry out this deed in a self-killing way'. If a tyrant is to be able to maintain power after a violent coup, the chorus feel, he at least needs to be capable of violence himself.

1636 a woman's task: Lit., 'for a woman [to do]'. This may be better translated 'the woman's task'. It depends on whether Aegisthus is invoking the common stereotype of female wiles (see 1129*) or simply introducing his point that he would have had difficulty inveigling Agamemnon into a vulnerable position. He should probably be understood as meaning both.

1637 as an enemy of his from long ago: In addition to the enmity inherited from his father Thyestes, the audience may have brought other ancient episodes in the relationship between Agamemnon and Aegisthus to bear on their interpretation of this statement: 1569–70*.

1638–9 using this man's money: Contrast Clytemnestra's claim at 1573–4* that she would be content with a modest amount of wealth if only the intra-familial conflict would cease. Aegisthus is leaving us in no doubt that he intends to run a tyranny; the killing of Agamemnon was not a simple case of violent revenge. Aegisthus is a fine exemplar of the tragic tyrant, in possessing 'all four of the characteristics exhibited by the historical *turannos*: preoccupation with money, abuse of ritual, kin-killing and endogamy' (Seaford (2012) 131).

1640–2 I'll impose a heavy yoke: Lit., 'I will yoke with heavy [yokes]'.

On the language of weight see 63–7* and on yoking animals see 326–8*. **well-fed:** lit, 'barley-fed'. **trace horse:** On *seiraphoros* see also 842*. Trace-horses needed to be particularly strong in chariot racing, because, as Fraenkel observes (Fraenkel (1950) vol. 3, 777–8), in wheeling round the turning post 'the outside horse on the right had to make the widest turn. Naturally they were particularly well fed.' On chariot-racing imagery in *Agamemnon* see Solez (2012), and, across the *Oresteia*, Himmelhoch (2005). Aegisthus does not conceive a relationship with anyone disobedient as collaborative. **combined with:** Lit., 'sharing a house with'. The picture evoked is of a prisoner in a dark cell being starved. **softened up:** Lit., 'soft', metaphorically meaning 'compliant'.

1644 didn't you slay: *enarizein*, which originally meant 'strip the armour from' an opponent after killing him in battle (Hom. *Il.* 17.187, 17.413), then came to mean 'slay in combat' (Hes. *Shield of Heracles* 194). The chorus are distinguishing a more honourable military killing from a domestic murder by guile. The imperfect tense may imply intention. **his wife:** It might be more effective to translate *gunē* here as 'a woman'.

1645–7 pollution: On *miasma* see 209–10*, 636–7*, 1251* and 1419*. **to this land and this land's gods:** Note the emphasis provided by the repetition of the *chōr-* stem. **is alive so that he can return:** Lit., 'sees the light so that having returned'. On previous references, explicit and inexplicit, to Orestes see 877–91*, 1103–4* and 1280–3*. This is the strongest indication in the play that Orestes could not return to Argos safely and is effectively an exile. In *Eumenides*, Orestes will himself use this phrase to denote the possibility of acquittal by the Athenian jury (746).

1648 victorious in the contest: *pankratēs*, 'all-powerful', is an epithet of Zeus (Aesch. *Sept.* 255, *Eum.* 918), Moira (Bacchylides 16.24), Hera (10.44), Apollo (Eur. *Rhes.* 231) and Athena (Ar. *Thesm.* 317). But in reference to a mortal combat it probably suggests a victor in the athletics event called the *pankration*, a fusion of boxing and wrestling (Pind. *Nem.* 5.52, Hdt. 9.105, Thuc. 5.49).

1649 you've a mind to: On this use of *dokein* see 16*. The metre here shifts to the rapid-fire trochaic tetrameter, which indicates psychological tension, until the end of the play. It has not been heard before, except in the chorus' two responses to Agamemnon's iambic death cries at 1344* and 1346–7 (see Wills (1963)).

1650 my loyal guards: Aegisthus addresses his personal bodyguard, who had entered with him at 1577. The noun *lochitēs* means a member of a *lochos*, an armed band or contingent, usually of infantry (*Od.* 20.49, Aesch.

Sept. 56, Xen. *Cyr.* 6.3.21, where it consists of 20 men). The possession of a bodyguard could be used as evidence that an individual is aiming at a tyranny according to Aristotle, *Rhetoric* 1.1357b; where the goal of democracy is freedom, the goal of tyranny is self-protection (*phulakē, Rhet.* 1.1366a; see also Solon fr. 11.3). **not far to seek:** Lit., 'is not far'. A strange litotes at a time of crisis. The actors playing the guards seem to have responded by unsheathing their swords, to judge from the chorus' response. Aegisthus was finally provoked into initiating a threat of immediate violence by the chorus' second comment on his non-involvement in the physical killing of Agamemnon.

1651   let everyone draw their sword and get ready: Lit., 'let each one make ready their hilt-grasped sword'. Sommerstein (2009) 201 n.342 assigns this line to a new speaking character, the captain of Aegisthus' bodyguard, combining suggestions by Verrall and Thomson. This is certainly possible, and could be dramatically effective, especially if the next two lines are distributed as Sommerstein suggests. There is, moreover, a character, a doorman, who speaks a single line in *Choephori* (657), and in that play the same word, *lochitai*, is used of Aegisthus' bodyguard. But Sommerstein also denies outright the possibility that the chorus members can be wearing swords. Aristotle's *Politics* 2.1268b states that the Greeks used universally to wear arms, just as they used to buy wives; the right to be armed is a constant feature of his discussion of the rights of free citizens of any age in some Greek city-states. Leaning on a walking-stick is not incompatible with wearing a sword. On an *Iliad*-related scene depicting Greek warriors at Troy and items of armour, painted on an Apulian vase, the elders Nestor and Peleus are depicted in the upper section; both are white-haired and leaning on staffs. But the seated figure (probably Nestor) also has his sword sheathed in its scabbard ready for action by his right hand. Agamemnon and Menelaus may have been imagined to be armed with swords when beating the ground with their staffs at 202–3. The tableau here in *Agamemnon* is almost unique in Greek tragedy: an incident of *stasis* or civil war is imminent. Euripides' *Orestes*, his most detailed response to the *Oresteia* produced exactly 50 years later, culminates in a not dissimilar scene, with a murderous Orestes, Pylades and Electra in possession of the Argive palace and a furious Menelaus calling on the citizens to arm themselves and revolt (Hall (1993b)).

1652   don't spurn death: Aegisthus also unsheathes his sword, perhaps goaded by the chorus' derision of his lack of experience of combat at

1625–6, and for a second time states his preparedness to die (see 1610–11). Sommerstein (2009) 201, however, gives this line to the chorus.

1653   to accepting ears: Lit., 'to those accepting'. **we embrace the opportunity:** Lit., 'we choose the chance'. Sommerstein (2009) 202–3 gives this line to Aegisthus, accepting a very slight emendation of this line (*g'* for *t'*), to read, 'We accept the omen of "to die", and we opt for that outcome!' Ultimately, especially in performance, this textual controversy is insignificant. Both sides are shouting threats at one another, and about to resort to physical violence.

xv]   1654–73   THE CHORUS, AEGISTHUS AND CLYTEMNESTRA

Summary

Clytemnestra enters from the palace for the last time to take charge. She may still be drenched in blood or have changed into a clean and magnificent new costume representing her newfound status as co-tyrant of Argos. This brief three-way altercation continues to the end of the tragedy in the tetrameters which 'represent the temporary triumph of the guilty' (Otis (1981) 63). Clytemnestra insists that enough blood has been shed and repeats her wish that the cycle of violence has at last come to an end. She attempts to pacify Aegisthus, despite his protests at the way the chorus speak to him, and sends the mutinous chorus home. The play ends on an even more fragile note of temporary armistice than had her long amoibaion earlier.

1654   O dearest of men: Clytemnestra addressed Agamemnon, insincerely, as 'dear one' at 905, but this superlative expression is the first sincerely affectionate address made by one royal character to another in the entire play. **not one more bad thing:** Although Clytemnestra has previously spoken of the madness of reciprocal murder and said that she wants it to stop (1575–6), she goes considerably further here in seeming to concede that what she and Aegisthus have done was not a simple matter of obtaining justice.

1655   these are a substantial and miserable harvest to reap: Lit., '[are] many to mow to completion, a miserable summer [harvest]'. By 'these' Clytemnestra means the entre situation at hand. On the imagery of arable farming, which Clytemnestra has used much less negatively before, see 524–6*.

1656   enough calamity: Clytemnestra repeats again her wishful thinking that the cycle of violence has been put to rest. **Let's shed no more blood:** She is directing Aegisthus to call off his guards before the actual blood of civil war is spilt in front of the palace. This is the last mention of blood, which has flowed so copiously in both the action and the imagery of the play: see 209–10*. If the actor playing Clytemnestra has changed costume and cleaned his mask since her previous appearance, this plea will be visually reinforced.

1657–8 respected elders: In order to lower the psychological temperature, Clytemnestra uses a polite form of address to the chorus with more apparent sincerity than at 854 and 1393. **before you suffer … must suffice:** The text is horribly corrupt and has been emended, but the general sense is apparent.

1659 if these troubles were to prove sufficient: Lit., 'if it became enough of these troubles'. This is Clytemnestra's third statement that she would like the conflicts to be over: see 1574–6 and 1656.

1660 kicked: Lit., 'struck'. On the imagery of kicking see Introduction, p. 61.

1661 what a woman says: Clytemnestra remains acutely aware of the protocols surrounding appropriate speech for a woman (see Introduction, pp. 22–3). Here she seems to imply that it is a female role to foster peaceful resolution of male conflict.

1662 but it's intolerable: These words need to be supplied to make sense in English. Aegisthus rather pathetically and with infinite pettiness appeals to Clytemnestra to allow him to take reprisals against the chorus for their responses to him in this episode. **should pluck flowers of rash speech:** This is a vivid expression of Aegisthus' indignation. Flower imagery in this play has often had peculiarly negative connotations: see 196–8*, 659*, 738–42*, 1391–2*, 1459*.

1663 jeopardising: Lit., 'to make trial of'. **destiny:** The noun *daimōn* here means simply 'fate'.

1664 to make such a mistake in judgement: Lit., 'to miss the mark of a self-controlled judgement'.

1665 grovel: The verb *prossainein* is usually used of fawning dogs (Soph. fr. 1082, Arr. *Cyn.* 7.2); cf. 725–6*. The chorus refuse to be intimidated, and it is they, rather than Clytemnestra, who respond to Aegisthus' appeal to her for support against them.

1666 I remain in your midst: Lit., 'I am with you'. An understated but sinister threat.

1667 if god directs Orestes' return home: Lit., 'if god guides Orestes aright to come here'. The chorus, with considerable courage, say Orestes' name, thus stressing that Aegisthus' hold on power is precarious.

1668 I have personal knowledge of how exiles feed on hope: Lit., 'I know, I, that exiled men feed on hopes.' Aegisthus is yet another exile from his homeland in the trilogy (1283*; 1411*, 1605).

1669 get fat: The chorus here may imply that Aegisthus' decadence may result in him becoming physically corpulent, although *piainein* also has a metaphorical sense connoting a psychological form of inflation: see 276*. **as you pollute:** On *miainein* see 209–10*, 636–7*.

1670 Aegisthus seems incapable of the dignity required to stop responding with further threats and small-minded insults to the chorus' goads.

1671 Boast away to build up your confidence: Lit., 'Boast being bold'. **like a cock beside his hen:** Lit., 'like a cock near the female'. The cock was the proverbial male creature derided as one that 'fights at home' rather than fighting or taking on competition further afield: see Pind. *Ol.* 12.14, *endomachas*. At Aesch. *Eum.* 866, Athena forbids further civil war within Athens conducted by any 'bird within the house', *enoikios ornis*. Aeschylus probably uses the term 'female' because the feminine *alektruaina* meaning 'hen' had not yet been coined: see Ar. *Clouds* 666.

1672–3 Pay no heed: For Clytemnestra's other, impassioned use of this verb see 1415*. **yelps:** See 1631–2*. **I and you:** Although 'I' is a supplement (necessitated by the metrical truncation of the line in the manuscripts), like *kalōs*, 'in good order', at the end of the next line, it is a likely one. If it is correct, it is interesting that Clytemnestra inserts herself before Aegisthus here. **put things in good order:** In a circle back to the opening speech of the play, this statement is reminiscent of the Watchman's complaint in the prologue that the household was not being managed properly (19*). **joint rulers of this house:** Clytemnestra ominously ends the play with the dual form of the key verb *kratein* (see 17*, 1617–19*, 1631–2*, 1672–3*), asserting the power in the household of the couple who have performed the coup. But, given the sensitivity of the situation with the angry Argives, she does not here claim to hold the *kratos* over the state. This is an ambivalent and edgy note on which to conclude what she has earlier presented as a moment of supreme triumph; there is no choral epilogue to provide closure or ease the tension. The cosmic and international sweep of the world inhabited by the citizens of Argos, conjured in the opening part of the play, has steadily become more constricted, until the single focus is on this troubled couple and their stifling, bloodstained household.

METRICAL APPENDIX

Greek tragedy originated in choral dancing, which combined melodic and rhythmic enunciation of words with movement. As the metrical expert Aristoxenus of Tarentum put it, time is articulated by the three things that are subject to being measured by it: speech, song and bodily movement.[1] It is a sad truth that we have lost all access to the music and choreography of Aeschylean lyric choruses, which extended over a significantly higher proportion of the time his plays took to perform than those of Euripides and Sophocles.

We know that they were played in specific musical modes ('scales', or tunings of notes at specific intervals), in early tragedy usually the 'manly' Dorian and the more sensuous Mixolydian. We know that they were accompanied by the plangent-sounding instrument known as the auloi, which consisted of two reeded pipes, similar to small oboes, played simultaneously by a single performer. We know, too, that the basic units of choral songs in Aeschylus are serial pairs of matching stanzas (strophe plus antistrophe) in which each pair is metrically different (AA BB CC rather than AA AA AA), although sometimes a pair or even a single stanza is followed by a single stanza in a variant metre called an epode or ephymnion.

The metres were marked not by stress but by the length or shortness— the 'quantity' of vowels; they were immensely varied and complicated. Different lyric metres were associated with specific types of subject-matter, the worship of particular gods, and the evocation of discrete genres and their related emotions. Aeschylus has in *Agamemnon* created an elaborate network of aural resonances as certain metrical patterns recur and are further developed, like his imagery, morphogenetically (see Introduction, pp. 73–4). The lyric iambic metre is particularly prominent, linking the crimes of Agamemnon and Paris across individual choral odes. Resolution of long syllables is rare in these iambics, but there are a few instances deployed on strongly emotional words (*anieron*, 'unhallowed', 220; *parakopa,* 'delusion', 223; *philomachoi*, 'warlike', 230; *peripetē*, 'flowing around her', 233; see also the 'twittering' effect of the five instances at 485–6 when the topic is female credulity). Repeated use of the same metre in several odes

---

1   In Westphal (1885) 74.

is most unusual; the only parallel in extant Greek tragedy is the recurrent Ionic a minore in Euripides' *Bacchae*. Such patterning continues across the whole *Oresteia*: the second strophe and antistrophe of the third stasimon of *Agamemnon*, for example, which expresses the chorus' abject terror (1001–2 = 1018–19), uses runs of three and short, light syllables in succession; these are later recalled in the terror-inducing 'binding song' of the Erinyes in *Eumenides* (328–30 = 334–6).[2]

Aristophanes' *Frogs* contains parodies of Aeschylean lyrics which reveal that they were thought to create such an idiosyncratic effect that the tragedian could be accused of 'trimming all his tunes into one' (1262); the comedy also indicates that his lyrics were associated with extensive repetition, use of dactylic metre, high-flown, bombastic poetic language and lamentation—all characteristics a modern reader does not find it difficult to identify in the choral odes of *Agamemnon*.

We know nothing for certain about the dance movements, although there are suggestive references to certain actions like striking the ground, and to breathing, eyes, hands and feet (see Introduction, pp. 58–62). A precious passage in Athenaeus implies that Aeschylus was also thought to have used striking choreography, indeed to have invented new dance-movements, which he insisted on teaching to the chorus-men himself (*Deipn.* 1.21e).[3]

The chorus also use runs of anapaests, a formal-sounding marching rhythm, accompanied by the auloi. It is suitable for their entrance (40–103), for getting into formation for the first stasimon (355–66), for ceremonially greeting Agamemnon on his return (782–809), for accompanying Cassandra's resolute walk into the palace (1331–42), and for attempting a formal ritual of obsequy (1505–12, 1513–20). Clytemnestra also shifts into this metre during her exchange with the chorus at 1462. Twice in the play, the dialogue shifts from the standard iambic metre to the faster trochaic, which may also have been accompanied by the auloi. The first instance is extremely brief, when the chorus respond to Agamemnon's death cries (1344, 1346–7); the second is when Aegisthus' bodyguards and the chorus seem about to come to blows; it extends to the end of the play (1649–73).

Tragic audiences found emotive the precise moments of change, the acoustic gearshifts from one type of metre and delivery to another. The

---

2   Edwards (2002) 96–8. Battezzato (2020) offers penetrating insights into the development of the identities assumed by the chorus members and the nature and function of the choral odes across the trilogy.

3   See Weiss (2023) 243.

pseudo-Aristotelian *Problem* 19.6 states that what makes vocalisation especially effective in tragedy is contrast or 'unlikeness': 'contrast is emotive in situations of great misfortune or grief; regularity is less conducive to lamentation'.[4]

The audience was exposed, in *Agamemnon* alone (itself only one in a group of four plays performed sequentially), to no fewer than twenty-two aural 'gearshifts', at a conservative count; this does not even include alterations in lyric metres (dactylic, iambic, dochmiac etc.) within songs, or the repeated contrast of speech, intoning and singing internal to the two *amoibaia* the chorus share with Cassandra and Clytemnestra respectively. I say 'aural' rather than 'metrical' because these gearshifts marked not only a shift from spoken verse unaccompanied by the music to accompanied verse, but a shift in the nature of the vocal delivery from speech to recitative or song.

A word should be said about colometry (line division on the printed page). Some Byzantine manuscripts suggest that a system of colometry was used at times in copying out the lyric sections, but the situation remains extremely vexed: 'In any given lyric section of a dramatic poet there may almost as many differing colometries as there are editors'.[5] This is especially the case with *Agamemnon*, because the most important manuscript, M, does not contain so much of the play's lyric content. Different editions of the text separate and join lines in multifarious ways on a quest for Aeschylus' original poetic and phrasing design; this was of course tightly bound up with his music, which is entirely lost. The colometry offered in this edition owes most to Denys Page's OCT of 1972; I have also learned from the analyses in Fleming (2007).

1–39:   Spoken iambic trimeters (the Watchman)

40–103:   Chorus: intoned anapaests

104–264:   Lyric parodos
When the chorus move from intoned anapaests to full sung lyrics, in a long strophic pair and epode describing an omen which occurred a decade ago and Calchas' interpretation of it, the overwhelmingly dominant metre is the dactyl with two short syllables (– vv) rather than two long ones (– –). Dactyls are inherited from heroic epic narrative, and also suggestive of the metre of

---

4   See further Hall (2012) 12–13.
5   Fleming (2007) iii.

the Delphic oracles. The second strophe (160–7) introduces a very different trochaic metre (basic unit – v), especially the hypnotic string of syllables known as the lecythion (– v – v – v –) with the new meditation on the supreme power of Zeus. This sounds imposing and solemn: weighty trochaic stanzas similar to this are one of the linking metrical features that appear across the entire *Oresteia*. But from the fourth strophe until the end of the song, with only the briefest of interruptions, the chorus settle into a lyric iambic metre while they recall the sacrifice of Iphigenia. This metre sounds slow, and is used by Aeschylus 'only when he wants a particularly smooth effect';[6] the sad story, told in this long rhythmical surge, feels acoustically self-contained as a mini-tragedy within the frame tragedy; a run like this of six stanzas rooted in a single metre is rare. Calchas' advice and Agamemnon's appalling response are recounted in the fourth strophic pair in iambic metre and its variant feet the cretic (– v –) and the bacchiac (v – –), with the addition of the swaying choriamb (– vv –), which also had associations with prophetic utterance.[7] Aeschylus does disrupt the flow briefly, resolving long syllables to produce runs of three short ones in the fifth strophic pair, at the precise points when the chorus condemn the sacrifice as sacrilegious and when Iphigenia is forcibly gagged.

Strophe 1 (104–21) = antistrophe 1 (122–39).

```
    – v v  – v v  – v v  – v v  – v v  – –
    – v v  – v v  – v v  – v v  – –
    – –  – –
    – –  – v v  – –
  v – v –  –  vv  – v v  – v v  – –
         – v v  – –
    – –  – v v  – v v  – v v
         – v v  – –  – v v  – v
    – –  – v v  – v v  – v v
         – v v  – v v  – v v  – –
  v – v –  – v v  – v v  – v v  – –
    – –  – v v  – v̲
  – v v  – v v  – v v  – v v  – v v  – –
  v – v –  v – v –
  – v v  – v v  – v v  – –  – –
```

---

6 Kitto (1956b) 3.
7 Edwards (2002) 77.

Epode (140–59)

       v − v − − − v −
       v − v − − v v − v − −
       − − − v v − v v − −
       − − − v v − v − −
       − − − − − v v − −
       − v v − v v − v v − v v < − −>
       v − v − v v v − v − v
       − v v − v v − v v − v v − v v − v v − −
       − − − v v − v v − v v − v v − v v − −
       − − − v v − v v − −
          − v v − − − v v − v v − v
       − v v − v v − − − − − v v − −
       − v v − − − v v − v v − v v − −
       − v v − − − v v − − − v v − −
       − v v − v
        − v v − v v − v v − − − −

Strophe 2 (160–7) = antistrophe 2 (168–75)

       − − − v − v − v −
          − v − v − v −
       − v − v − v −
       − v − v − v −
          − v − v − v −
       − v v − v v − v v − v v − −
       − v − v − v − v − −

Strophe 3 (176–83) = antistrophe 3 (184–91)

       − v − v − v −
          − v − v − v −
       − v − v − v −
       − − − v − v − v −
       − v − − v − − v −
          − v − v − v −
       − v − v − v − v − −
       − v − v − v −

Strophe 4 (192–204) = antistrophe 4 (205–17)

v – v –   – v –   v – –

v – v –   – v –   v – –

v – v –

<u>v</u> – v –   – v –   v – v̄

v – –   – v –   v – –

<u>v</u> – v –   – v –   v – –

      – v – v – v –

– v v –   v – –

– v v –   v – –

– v v –   – v v –

– v v –   – v v –

      – v v –   – v v –

      – v v –   v – –

Strophe 5 (218–27) = antistrophe 5 (228–37)

v – v –   – v –   v – –

v – v –   – v –   v – –

v – v vv   v – v –

v – v –   – v –   v – –

v – v –   – v –   v – –

v – v vv   v – –   v – –

v – –   v – v –

      – v v –   v – v –

      – v v –   v – –

vv –   v – –

Strophe 6 (238–46) = antistrophe 6 (247–57)

v – v –   – v –   – v –

v – v –   – v –   v – <u>v</u>

v – v –   – v –

      – v – v – v –   v – –

v – v –   – v – v – v –

v – v –   – v –

v – v –   – v –   v – –

v – v –   – v –   – v –   – v –

v – v –   – v –   v – –

      – v v –   v – –

258–354:   **Chorus and Clytemnestra: spoken iambic trimeters**

355–66:   **Chorus: intoned anapaests**

367–488:   First stasimon
Like the long final section of the parodos, which narrated the atrocity at Aulis, the dominant rhythm of this ode is lyric iambic. This enables Aeschylus to use sound across separate songs to make implicit connections between the crimes committed by the Greek Agamemnon, the Trojan Paris and Helen, who was both Greek and Trojan.[8] There is a notable acceleration at 407–8 with resolution of a long syllable producing four consecutive short syllables at the very moment that Helen slips out of the gates *en route* to Troy, echoed in the corresponding 423 as the phantom slips out of Menelaus' reach. The first six of the seven stanzas all conclude with a mellifluous four-line period, clearly marked off from the iambic substance of the strophe or antistrophe, in the catchy 'Aeolic' measures known as the pherecratean (v v – v v – –) and the closely related glyconic (v v – v v – v –). The penultimate three lines of the third strophe and antistrophe all begin plangently with three long syllables, when the chorus think about the beautiful men they have lost, who now lie buried around the remains of Troy (452–4), and wish fervently they may never become either sackers of cities or slaves themselves (471–3).

Strophe 1 (367–84) = antistrophe 1 (385–402)

$$
\begin{array}{lll}
v - - & - v - & v - - \\
v - - & - v - & v - - \\
v - v - & v - v - & v - - \\
v - v - & - v - & - v - \\
v - v - & - v - \\
v - v - & - v - \\
v - - & - v - \\
 & v - - & - v - \\
v - - & - v - & v - - \\
v - - & - v - & v - - \\
v - v - & - v - & - v - \\
 & - v - & v - - \\
\end{array}
$$

---

8   Kitto (1955) 36–7.

```
− v v −   v − −
       − v − v v − −
       − v − v v − v
       − v − v v − v −
       − v − v v − −
```

Strophe 2 (403–19) = antistrophe 2 (420–36)

```
       v − v −   − v −   − v −
       v − v −   − v −
       − v −   v − −
       v − v −   v − v −   v − v −
       v − −   − v vv
                v − v −   v − v −   v − v −
       v − v −   − v −   v − −
       v − v −   − v − v − v −
       v − v −   − v − v − v −
       v − v −   − v −   − v − v − v −
                − v − v − v −
       v − v −   − v −
       − v −   − v −   v − −
                − − − v v − v
                − v − v v − v
                − v − v v − v −
                − v − v v −
```

Strophe 3 (437–55) = antistrophe 3 (456–74)

```
       v − v −   − v −   − v −
       − v −   − v − v − v −
       v − v −   − v −
       v − v −   − v −
       − v − v − v −
                − v − v − v −
                − v − v − v −
       v − v −   v − v −
                v − v −   v − v −
       v − v −   v − v −
                − v v −   v − v −
                − v v −   v − v −
                − v v −   v − v −
```

$$- \text{v} \text{v} - \quad \text{v} - -$$
$$- - - \text{v} \text{v} - -$$
$$- - - \text{v} \text{v} - -$$
$$- - - \text{v} \text{v} - \text{v} -$$
$$- \text{v} - \text{v} \text{v} - -$$

Epode (475–88)

$$\text{v} - \text{v} - \quad - \text{v} -$$
$$\text{v} - \text{v} - \quad - \text{v} -$$
$$- \text{v} - \text{v} - \text{v} -$$
$$\text{v} - \text{v} - \quad \text{v} - \text{v} - \quad \text{v} - \text{v} -$$
$$\text{v} - \text{v} - \quad \text{v} - \text{v} - \quad \text{v} - \text{v} -$$
$$\text{v} - \text{v} - \quad - \text{v} -$$
$$\text{v} - \text{v} - \quad - \text{v} - \text{v} - \text{v} -$$
$$- \text{v} - \text{v} - \text{v} -$$
$$- \text{v} - \text{v} - \quad - \text{v} -$$
$$\text{v} - \text{v} - \quad - \text{v} - \text{v} - \text{v} -$$
$$\text{v} \text{vv} \ \text{v} - \quad \text{v} - \text{v} \ \text{vv} \quad \text{v} \ \text{vv} \ \text{v} -$$
$$\text{v} \ \text{vv} \ \text{v} - \quad \text{v} \ \text{vv} \ \text{v} -$$
$$\text{v} - \text{v} - \quad - \text{v} - \text{v} - \text{v} -$$

489–680:   Spoken iambic trimeters, chorus, Herald, Clytemnestra

681–781:   Second stasimon

These four strophic pairs introduce more rhythmical variety, since they are in contrasting metres, the first of which has not featured previously. As the chorus sing of Helen's arrival in Troy and how she brought it ruin, after a run mainly consisting of ringing lecythia, Aeschylus introduces both Ionics a minore and Anacreontics. Ionics a minore ($\text{v} \ \text{v} - -$) sound sensual and perhaps 'oriental' (they are prominent in Euripides' *Bacchae*) and therefore suitable for describing Helen's soft, expensive draperies (691–5). An Anacreontic (i.e., the eight-syllable unit $\text{v} \ \text{v} - \text{v} - \text{v} - -$) has a gay and lilting effect; it was used in monodies about love and partying. Choosing it to describe how Helen made the Trojans turn her wedding hymn into dirges is grimly ironic. The second strophic pair takes up the glyconics from the mellifluous endings of the stanzas in the previous ode to recount the interposed parable of the lion-cub. But the third strophe, as it returns to Helen's arrival at Troy, immediately reintroduces that iambic rhythm, which the previous songs have both established as the measure of crime and retribution. It is briefly ousted once again by Anacreontics, but it prevails to assert dominance in the final strophic pair, which explicitly lays out the ineluctable relationship between hubris and destruction. Is it only when the arrival of the (as yet) unpunished Agamemnon is imminent that 'this obstinate rhythm at last subsides'.[9]

Strophe 1 (681–98) = antistrophe 1 (699–716)

```
        − v − v − v −
                − v − v − v −
        − v − v − v −   − v −
                − v − v − v −
        − v − v − v −
        − v v −   v − v −
                − v v −   v − v −   v̲
        v v − v   − v v −
                v v − −   v v − −
        v v − v   − v − −
        v v − v   − v − −
        v v − −   v v − v   − v − −
                v v − v   − v − −
        − − − v v − v −
                − v v −   v − −
        vv v − v v −   −
```

Strophe 2 (717–26) = antistrophe 2 (727–36)

```
        v − − v v − v −
                − v − v v − v −
                − v − v v − v v̲
        − v v − v v − −
        − v v − v v − v
        − v v − v v − −
        vv v − v − v −
        vv v − v − v v̲
        − v̲ − v v − v −
                − v̲ − v v − −
```

Strophe 3 (737–49) = antistrophe 3 (750–62)

```
v – v –   – v – v – v –
v – –   v – v –
          – v –   v – –
v – –   – v –   v – –
– v v –   v – v –
– v – v v – v – –
v v – –   v v – –
              v v – v   – v – –
v v – –   v v – –
– – v   – v – –
          – v – v v – –
```

Strophe 4 (763–72) = antistrophe 4 (773–81)

```
v – v –   – v –
          – v –   – v –
          – v – v – v –
v – v –   v v v v –
          v – v –   v – v –
v v v v –   v v v v v v
          v v v v –   v – v –
– v v –   v – –
```

782–809:   **Intoned choral anapaests**

810–974:   **Spoken iambic trimeters: Agamemnon and Clytemnestra**

975–1034:   **Third Stasimon**
The chorus' abject terror is reflected in the choice of metre, the almost jingling lecythion, which is repeated insistently, even appearing in a hypnotic run of six in the antistrophe, and emphatically opening and closing the strophe. Standing out from this is the strongly dactylic fourth line of the first strophic pair, when the chorus are singing about prophecy and song—prophetic incantation and the lament of the Erinyes. This is the first and only ode in which the 'crime and punishment' iambic metre does not appear, thus reflecting the chorus' increasing metaphysical confusion.

Strophe 1 (975–87) = antistrophe 1 (988–1000)

```
            – v – v – v –
            – v – v – v –
            – v – v – v –   v – –
            – v v  – v v  – v v  – v v  – –
            – v – v – v –
            – v – v – v –
            – v –  – v –
                  – v – v – v –
        v – v –  – – v –   v – v v
            – v –  – v –
                  – v – v – v v
            – v – v – v –
```

Strophe 2 (1001–17) = antistrophe 2 (1018–34)

```
            v v v –  v v v –  v v v –
            v v – –  v v v v  v v –
            v v –  v v –  v v –  –
            – v v – v v –
            – v v – v v –
            – v v – v v –  v – v
            – v – v – v –
            – v – v – v –
            – v – v – v –
            – v – v – v –
            – v – v – v –
            – v – v – v –
            – –  – v v  – v v  – v v
                  – v v  – v v  – v v  – –
            – v – v – v –
```

1035–71:   Spoken iambic trimeters: Clytemnestra and chorus.

1072–1177:   Amoibaion: Cassandra and chorus

This extraordinary exchange uses metre to show how Cassandra and the chorus gradually exchange roles. At first, she is in a state of possession, expressed from 1081 in the interspersed dochmiacs (basic unit v – – v –, but the long syllables can all be resolved into two shorts, and the more shorts there are, the more agitated the effect). This is soon established as the dominant rhythm. The chorus at first respond to her in spoken iambic utterance, but at 1121 they become infected by Cassandra's psychic state, and launch into dochmiacs themselves. At this precise moment, she begins to 'come round' and slowly returns to a more normal state of consciousness, implied by the inclusion in all her remaining utterances of at least one iambic trimeter, which perhaps she speaks rather than sings. The chorus, meanwhile, exhibit increasing mental disturbance; in their penultimate line, at the emotional climax, they finally produce the sole fully resolved dochmiac in the entire amoibaion (v vv vv v vv, 1176), when they describe Cassandra's songs as full of distress and death (*goera thanatophora*).

Strophe 1 (1072–5) = antistrophe 1 (1076–9)

Cassandra:	vv v – v – –
	– – v – – –
Chorus:	2 spoken iambic trimeters

Strophe 2 (1080–4) = antistrophe 2 (1085–90)

Cassandra:	– – v – – –
	v – – v – – v –
	v̲ – v – v – v – v̲ – v –
Chorus:	2 spoken iambic trimeters

Strophe 3 (1090–4) = antistrophe 3 (1095–9)

Cassandra:	– v v – v – – v v – v v̲
–	vv v vv v – v –
	– – v – – – v – – – v –
Chorus:	2 spoken iambic trimeters

Strophe 4 (1100–6) = antistrophe 4 (1107–13)

Cassandra:	v – v – v vv – v –
	vv v v̲v̲ v – v v̲
	v̲ – v – v̲ – v – v – v –
	v – – v – – v – – v – –
	v vv v̄v̄ v –
Chorus:	2 spoken iambic trimeters

Strophe 5 (1114–24) = antistrophe 5 (1125–35)

Cassandra:	v – v – v vv – v –
	– – v – v – –

$$\overline{v} - v - \quad v - v - \quad v - v\,\overline{v}$$
$$\underline{v} - v - \quad v\;vv - \underline{v} -$$
$$v\;vv - v - \quad - v - \quad - v -$$

Chorus: 2 spoken iambic trimeters

$$v\;vv - v - \quad v\;vv\;\underline{vv}\;v -$$
$$v - - v - \quad v - - v -$$
$$v\;vv - v - \quad v - - v -$$
$$v - v - \quad - v -$$

Strophe 6 (1136–45) = antistrophe 6 (1146–55)

Cassandra: $vv\;v - \quad v - - \quad v\;vv - v -$

                $v\;vv - v - \quad v\;vv - v -$

                2 iambic trimeters

Chorus: $v\;vv - v - \quad v\;vv - v -$

                      $v - - v -$

                $vv\;v\;vv \quad - v - \quad - -$

                $v\;vv - v - \quad - v - \quad - v -$

                $v\;vv - v - \quad - vv - v -$

                $v - - v -$

Strophe 7 (1156–66) = antistrophe 7 (1167–77)

Cassandra: $v - v - \quad v - v\;vv \quad v\;vv - v -$

                $v - v - \quad - vv - v -$

                $v\;vv - v - \quad - vv - v -$

                      $- vv - v -$

                2 iambic trimeters

Chorus: $v\;vv\;vv\;v - \quad v\;vv - v -$

                $\underline{v} - v\;vv \quad v - v -$

                      $v - - v - \quad \overline{v}\;\underline{vv} - v -$

                $v - - v - \quad v\;vv\;vv\;v\;\overline{vv}$

                $- v\;v - v -$

1178–330:   **Spoken iambic trimeters, Cassandra and the chorus**

1331–42:   **Intoned choral anapaests**

1343:   **Spoken iambic trimeter: Agamemnon**

1344:   **Trochaic tetrameter: Chorus**

1345: **Spoken iambic trimeter: Agamemnon**

1346–7: **Trochaic tetrameters: Chorus**

1348–1406: **Iambic trimeters: chorus and Clytemnestra**

1407–1576: **Amoibaion: the chorus and Clytemnestra**
This metrical complexity of this sequence is expressive of the tense negotiation between the murderous Queen and her citizens, and the psychological shifts that mark each new stage in their confrontation. There is a sense of syncopation, with the Queen at first answering lyric stanzas with speeches of variable length, and the chorus sometime appending ephymnia to one or both stanzas in a strophic pair and sometimes not. The outraged chorus burst into furious song, their first strophe and antistrophe as headily dochmiac as their last response to Cassandra in the previous exchange; they include completely resolved dochmiacs and a total of eleven short syllables in succession in the emphatic line, 'You cast him out, you cut him off, and an outcast you [shall be yourself]', 1410). Clytemnestra is not in the same psychological state as the chorus. She does not relinquish the unperturbed medium of iambic speech until they infuriate her by blaming Helen for the war fatalities, whereupon she begins intoning anapaests (1062), and continues them until the end of the exchange. As she assumes this slightly more emotional mode of delivery, the chorus seem to calm down, relinquishing their dochmiacs for an interlacing of several metres, including iambics; note the dactylic line when they refer to the of a 'spirit that keeps house and is heavy with wrath' (1482, see 151–4). The chorus also deploy anapaests at 1489–96 = 1513–20 and 1537–50, when they are attempting to use the solemn language appropriate to a funeral procession.

Strophe 1 (1407–11) = antistrophe 1 (1426–30), followed respectively by 14 and 17 iambic trimeters (Clytemnestra):

Chorus: v v v – v –
         v vv v vv   v – v –
         v vv – v –   – vv v̲v̲ v –
         – v v – v – – v v – v –
         v̲ vv vv v v̲v̲ v vv – v –
         – v – v v – –

Strophe 2 (1448–54, followed by its own choral *ephymnion* 1455–61) =
antistrophe 2 (1468–74, no ephymnion). Clytemnestra now and for the
remainder of the amoibaion replies in intoned anapaests.

$$- \text{v v} - \text{v} - \quad - \text{v v} - \text{v} -$$
$$- \text{v} - \text{v v} - -$$
$$\text{v} - \text{v} - \quad - \text{v} - \quad \text{v} - -$$
$$- \text{v v} - \text{v v} - \text{v} - -$$
$$\text{vv v} - \text{v} - \text{v} -$$
$$\overline{\text{vv}} \ \text{v} - \quad - \text{v} - \quad - \text{v} -$$
$$- \text{v} - \quad - \text{v} - \text{v} - \text{v} -$$

Strophe 3 (1481–8, followed by anapaestic ephymnion at 1489–96) =
antistrophe 3 (1505–12, followed by the same ephymnion at 1513–20)

$$- \text{v v} - \text{v v} -$$
$$- \text{v v} - \text{v v} - \text{v} - -$$
$$- - \text{v v} - \text{v} - -$$
$$- \text{v} - \text{v v} - -$$
$$\text{v} - \text{v} - \quad \text{v} - \text{v} -$$
$$\text{v} - \text{v} - \quad \text{v} - \text{v} -$$
$$\text{v} - \text{v} - \quad \text{v} - \text{v} - \quad \text{v} - \text{v} -$$
$$\text{v} - \text{v} - \quad \text{v} - \text{v} - \quad \text{v} - -$$
$$\text{v} - - \text{v v} - \text{v} - -$$
$$- - \quad - - \quad \text{v v} - \quad \text{v v} -$$
$$- \text{v v} - -$$
$$\text{v v} - \quad \text{v v} - \quad \text{v v} - \quad -$$
$$- - \quad \text{v v} - \quad \text{v v} - \quad \text{v v} \quad -$$
$$\text{v v} - \quad \text{v v} - \quad \text{v v} - \quad -$$
$$- - - \quad - - - \text{v v} - \text{v} -$$

Strophe 4 (1513–18) = antistrophe 4 (1505–12)

$$\text{v} - \text{v} - \quad - \text{v} - \quad \text{v} - -$$
$$- \text{v v} - \quad \text{v} - \underline{\text{v}}$$
$$\text{v} - \text{v} - \quad - \text{v} - \quad \text{v} - -$$
$$\text{v} - \text{v} - \quad - \text{v} - \text{v} - \text{v} -$$
$$\text{v} - \text{v} - \quad - \text{v} - \quad \text{v} - -$$
$$\text{v} - \text{v} - \quad \text{v} - \text{v} - \quad \text{v} - \text{v} -$$
$$\text{v} - - \quad - \text{v} - \quad \text{v} - -$$

Strophe 5 (1530–6, followed by its own anapaestic *ephymnion* at 1537–50)
= antistrophe 5 (1560–6, no ephymnion).

```
v − v −   − v −   v − −
− v v −   v − v
v − v −   − v −   v − −
v − v −   − v − v − v −
v − v −   − v −   v − −
v − v −   v − v −   v − v −
v − −   − v −   v − −


− −   − −   v v −   v v −
− −   v v −   − v v   − −
− −   v v −   v v −   −
v v −   − −   v v −   − −
− v v   − −   − −   − −
− v v   − −   v v −   − −
− −   v v −   − v v   − −
v v −   v v −   v v −   −
− v v − v v − v v − v − −
  − v v −   v − −
v − −   v − −   − v −
```

1577–1648:   **Spoken iambic trimeters (Aegisthus and chorus)**

1649–73:   **Trochaic tetrameters (Aegisthus, Clytemnestra, chorus)**

EDITIONS

Unless otherwise indicated, these are the editions of fragmentary ancient Greek literature used throughout this book.

Greek comic authors:	Kassel, R. and C. Austin (eds) (1983–2001) *Poetae Comici Graeci*. Berlin: Walter de Gruyter & Co.
Greek elegiac poets:	Gerber, Douglas E. (ed. and trans.) (1999) *Greek Elegiac Poetry: From the Seventh to the Fifth Centuries BC*, Loeb Classical Library 258. Cambridge, MA: Harvard Univ. Press.
Greek epic cycle:	West, Martin L. (ed. and trans.) (2003) *Greek Epic Fragments: From the Seventh to the Fifth Centuries BC*, Loeb Classical Library 497. Cambridge, MA: Harvard Univ. Press.
Greek iambic poets:	Gerber, Douglas E. (ed. and trans.) (1999) *Greek Iambic Poetry: From the Seventh to the Fifth Centuries BC*, Loeb Classical Library 259. Cambridge, MA: Harvard Univ. Press.
Greek lyric poets (including Bacchylides):	Campbell, David A. (ed. and trans.) (1982–1993) *Greek Lyric*, 5 vols, Loeb Classical Library 143, 142, 476, 461, 144. Cambridge, MA: Harvard Univ. Press.
Greek tragic authors	Snell, Bruno and Richard Kannicht (eds) (1971–7) *Tragicorum Graecorum Fragmenta*, 4 vols. Göttingen: Vandenhoeck & Ruprecht.
Hesiod	Most, Glenn W. (ed. and trans.) (2018) *Hesiod. The Shield. Catalogue of Women. Other Fragments*, Loeb Classical Library 503. Cambridge, MA: Harvard Univ. Press.
Pindar	Race, William H. (ed. and trans.) (1997) Pindar. *Nemean Odes. Isthmian Odes. Fragments*, Loeb Classical Library 485. Cambridge, MA: Harvard Univ. Press.
Presocratic philosophers:	Diels, H. and W. Kranz, W. (eds) (1964–6) *Die Fragmente der Vorsokratiker*, 3 vols. Dublin and Zurich: Weidmann.

ABBREVIATIONS

ARV	Beazley, J.D. (1963) *Attic Red-Figure Vase-Painters*, 2nd edn. Oxford: Clarendon Press.
FgrH	Jacoby, Felix et al. (1923–) *Die Fragmente der griechischen Historiker*. Leiden: Brill.
LIMC	Lexicon Iconographicum Mythologiae Classicae, Zurich and Munich: Artemis & Winkler Verlag (1981–99). Zürich, München, Düsseldorf.
LSJ	Liddell, Henry George and Robert Scott (1996) *A Greek–English Lexicon*, 9th edn. Revised and augmented by Henry Stuart Jones, with a revised supplement ed. P.G.W. Glare. Oxford: OUP.
PGM	Preisendanz, Karl and Albert Henrichs (1973–4) *Papyri Graecae Magicae. Die griechischen Zauberpapyri*, 2 vols. Stuttgart: Teubner.

BIBLIOGRAPHICAL REFERENCES

Adkins, A.W.H. (1969) '*Euchomai* and *euchos* in Homer', *CQ* 19, 20–25.

Aguirre, Mercedes (2010) 'Erinyes as creatures of darkness', in Christopoulos et al., 133–41.

Ahrens, Ernst (1937) 'Gnomen in griechischer Dichtung (Homer, Hesiod, Aeschylus)', Dissertation, Halle. Würzburg: Konrad Triltsch.

Alden, Maureen (2005) 'Lions in paradise: lion similes in the *Iliad* and the lion cubs of *Il.* 18.318–22', *Classical Quarterly* 55, 335–42.

Alexiou, Margaret (1974) *The Ritual Lament in Greek Tradition*. Cambridge: CUP.

Andújar, R., T. Coward and T.A. Hadjimichael (eds) (2018) *Paths of Song: The Lyric Dimension of Greek Tragedy*. Berlin: de Gruyter.

Armstrong, David and Elizabeth A. Ratchford (1985) 'Iphigenia's veil', *Bulletin of the Institute of Classical Studies* 32, 1–12.

Arnold, Margaret (1984) 'Thomas Stanley's "Aeschylus": Renaissance practical criticism of Greek tragedy', *Illinois Classical Studies* 9, 229–49.

Arnott, W. Geoffrey (1959) 'Animals in the Greek theatre', *Greece & Rome* 6, 177–9.

— (1977) 'Swan songs', *Greece & Rome* 24, 149–53.

— (ed. and trans.) (2000) *Menander. Samia. Sikyonioi. Synaristosai. Phasma. Unidentified Fragments*. Cambridge, MA: Harvard UP.

Athanassakis, A.N. (ed. and trans.) (1977) *The Orphic Hymns: Text, Translation and Notes*. Atlanta, GA: Scholars Press.

Avezzù, Guido (2018) 'Reticence and *phobos* in Aeschylus's *Agamemnon*', *Comparative Drama* 52, 23–53.

Bailey, Philip James (1858) *The Age: A Colloquial Satire*. London: Chapman and Hall.

Bakewell, Geoffrey (2007) '*Agamemnon* 437: chrysamoibos Ares, Athens and empire', *The Journal of Hellenic Studies* 127, 123–32.

Barbieri, Michele (2009) *L'Ifigenia di Eschilo: Filologia e drammaturgia nell' Agamennone*. Florence: Società Editrice Fiorentina.

Barrett, James (2002) *Staged Narrative: Poetics and the Messenger in Greek Tragedy*. Berkeley, Los Angeles and London: Univ. Calif. Press.

Bastianini, G. and C. Gallazzi (eds) (2001) *Papiri dell'Università di Milano – Posidippo di Pella. Epigrammi*. Milan: LED Edizioni Universitarie.

Battezzato, Luigi (2020) 'I cori dell' *Orestea*', in *Il potere della parola: studi di letteratura greca per M. Cannatà Fera*, eds G.B. D'Alessio, L. Lomiento, C. Meliadò and G. Ucciardello, 7–22. Alessandria: dell' Orso.

Baudou, Estelle (2017) 'To tell the Trojan War today: contemporary performances of *Agamemnon*', *Atlantide – Cahiers de l'EA* 4276 (*L'Antique, le Moderne* 6), 61–71.

Bearzot, C. (1993) 'Mantica e condotta di guerra: strateghi, soldati e indovini di fronte all'interpretazione dell'evento "prodigioso"', in *La profezia nel mondo antico*, ed. M. Sordi, 97–12. Milan: Vita e Pensiero.

Beck, Robert Holmes (1975) *Aeschylus: Playwright Educator*. The Hague: Nijhoff.

Bednarowski, K. Paul (2015) 'Surprise and suspense in Aeschylus' *Agamemnon*', *American Journal of Philology* 136, 179–206.

Beer, Josh (2020) 'Ambiguity of word and place in *Agamemnon* 1–24', *Eranos* 111, 21–34.

Bennett, Florence Mary (1929) 'The character of Clytemnestra in the *Agamemnon* of Aeschylus', *Transactions and Proceedings of the American Philological Association* 60, 136–54.

Benveniste, E. (1932) 'Le sens du mot *kolossos* et les noms grecs de la statue', *Revue de Philologie* 6, 118–35.

Berman, Daniel W. (2010) 'A few words for springs in Aeschylus', in *Studies in Classical Linguistics in Honor of Philip Baldi*, eds B. Richard Page and Aaron D. Rubin, 1–5. Leiden and Boston: Brill.

Berti, M. (1930) 'Anacoluti eschilei', *Rendiconti della reale accademia dei Lincei* 6.6, 268–90.

Betz, Hans Dieter (ed. and trans.) (1986) *The Greek Magical Papyri in Translation*. Chicago and London: Univ. Chicago Press.

Bevan, Elinor (1986) *Representations of Animals in Sanctuaries of Artemis and Other Deities*, Part 2. Oxford: BAR International Series no. 35.

Bierl, Anton (2016) '*Melizein pathe* or the tonal dimension in Aeschylus' *Agamemnon*: voice, song, and *choreia* as leitmotifs and metatragic signals for expressing suffering', in *Voice and Voices in Antiquity*, ed. N.W. Slater, 166–207. Leiden: Brill.

Bîrzescu, I. and M. Ionescu (2016) 'Recherches sur la fondation de Callatis: L'apport de la documentation archéologique', in *Mégarika: Nouvelles recherches sur Mégare, les cités de la Propontide et du Pont-Euxin* in *Actes du colloque de Mangalia (8–12 juillet 2012)*, eds A. Robu and J. Bîrzescu, 381–92. Paris: Éditions de Boccard.

Blamire, Alec (1970) 'Pausanias and Persia', *Greek, Roman and Byzantine Studies* 11, 295–305.

Blasina, Andrea (2003) *Eschilo in Scena: Dramma e spettacolo nell'Orestea.* Stuttgart: J.B. Metzler.

Blundell, Mary Whitlock (1989) *Helping Friends and Harming Enemies: A Study in Sophocles and Greek Ethics.* Cambridge: CUP.

Bollack, J. (1981) 'Le thrène de Cassandre (*Agamemnon*, 1322–1330)', *Revue des Études Grecques* 94, 1–13.

— (1983) 'Le masque de l'amitié et le miroir du prince (*Agamemnon* 832–44)', *Hermes* 111, 180–90.

Bouquet, J. and É. Wolff (eds) (1995) *Dracontius: Œuvres*, vol. 3. Paris: Les Belles Lettres.

Bowden, H. (2005) *Classical Athens and the Delphic Oracle.* Cambridge: CUP.

Bowie, Ewen (2015) 'Stesichorus at Athens', in *Stesichorus in Context*, eds P.J. Finglass and Adrian Kelly, 111–24. Cambridge: CUP.

Boyer, Claude (1680) *Agamemnon. Tragédie.* Paris: T. Girard.

Brault, Pascale-Anne (2009) 'Playing the Cassandra: prophecies of the feminine in the polis and beyond', in *Bound by the City: Greek Tragedy, Sexual Difference, and the Formation of the Polis*, eds Denise Eileen McCoskey and Emily Zakin, 197–220. Albany, NY: Suny Press.

Bremmer, Jan N. (2002) 'Sacrificing a child in ancient Greece: the case of Iphigenia', in *The Sacrifice of Isaac*, eds Ed Noort and Eibert Tigchelaar, 21–43. Leiden, Boston and Cologne: Brill.

Brixhe, Claude (2008) 'Phrygian', in *The Ancient Languages of Asia Minor*, ed. Roger D. Woodard, 69–80. Cambridge: CUP.

Brize, Philip (1980) *Die Geryoneis des Stesichoros und die frühe griechische Kunst.* Wurzburg: Triltsch.

Brock, R. (2000) 'Sickness in the body politic: medical imagery in the Greek polis', in *Death and Disease in the Ancient City*, eds V.M. Hope and E. Marshall, 22–34. London: RTF.

Brøns, Cecilie (2017) 'Sacred colours: purple textiles in Greek sanctuaries in the second half of the 1st millennium BC', in Enegren and Meo, 109–17.

Brook, Adriana (2019) 'Reading Aeschylus through Seneca: scenes of capitulation in *Agamemnon* and *Thyestes*', *Illinois Classical Studies* 44, 1–24.

Buxton, R.G.A. (1982) *Persuasion in Greek Tragedy: A Study of Peitho.* Cambridge: CUP.

Cairns, Douglas and Vayos Liapis (eds) (2006) *Dionysalexandros: Essays on Aeschylus and His Fellow Tragedians in Honour of Alexander F. Garvie*. Swansea: Classical Press of Wales.

Cambitoglou, Alexander, Jacques Chamay and Brenno Bottini (1997) *Céramique de Grande Grèce: la collection de fragments Herbert A. Cahn*. Geneva: Akanthus.

Campbell, David A. (1982) (trans.) *Greek Lyric*, vol. 1. Cambridge, MA: Harvard Univ. Press.

— (ed. and trans.) (1993) *Greek Lyric, Volume V: The New School of Poetry and Anonymous Songs and Hymns*. Cambridge, MA: Harvard Univ. Press.

Capelle, W. (1916) *Berges- und Wolkenhöhen bei griechischen Physikern* (= *Stoicheia* 5). Leipzig and Berlin: Teubner.

Carawan, Edwin (2017) 'The "Hymn to Zeus" (*Agamemnon* 160–83) and reasoning from resemblances', in *Resemblance and Reality in Greek Thought: Essays in Honor of Peter M. Smith*, ed. Arum Park, 141–53. London and New York: Routledge.

Carr, Marina (2002) *Ariel*. Oldcastle, Co. Meath: Gallery Books.

Casazza, Joseph (2003) '"Taming the savageness of man": Robert Kennedy, Edith Hamilton, and their sources', *The Classical World* 96, 197–9.

Case, Sue-Ellen (1980) 'Peter Stein directs *The Oresteia*', *Theater* 11, 23–8.

Cerri, Giovanni (2012) 'Gli avvoltoi meteci in Aesch. *Ag.* 57', *Eikasmos* 23, 57–65.

Champlin, Edward (2003) 'Agamemnon at Rome: Roman dynasts and Greek heroes', in *Myth, History and Culture at Rome: Studies in Honour of T.P. Wiseman*, ed. D. Braund and C. Gill, 295–319. Exeter: Exeter Univ. Press.

Chesi, Giulia Maria (2014) *The Play of Words: Blood Ties and Power Relations in Aeschylus' Oresteia*. Berlin and Boston: de Gruyter.

Christ, Matthew R. (2004) 'Draft evasion onstage and offstage in classical Athens', *Classical Quarterly* 54, 33–57.

Christopoulos, M., E. Karakantza and O. Levaniouk (eds) (2010) *Light and Darkness in Ancient Greek Myth and Religion*. Lanham, MD: Rowman & Littlefield.

Citti, Vittorio (1994) *Eschilo e la lexis tragica*. Amsterdam: Hakkert.

— (2006) 'Some remarks on critics and editors of Aeschylus from the 17th to the 19th century', in Cairns and Liapis, 63–78.

Clarke, Anactoria (2021) '*Manti kakon*: the uncanny prophecies of Calchas in the *Iliad* and beyond', *Preternature: Critical and Historical Studies on the Preternatural* 10, 11–33.

Clay, D. (1969) 'Aeschylus' *Trigeron Mythos*', *Hermes* 97, 1–9.

Cleland, Liza (2005) *The Brauron Clothing Catalogues: Text, Analysis, Glossary and Translation*. Oxford: BAR Publishing.

Coates, D. Justin (2023) *In Praise of Ambivalence*. New York: Oxford Academic Books.

Cohen, David (1986) 'The theodicy of Aeschylus: justice and tyranny in the *Oresteia*', *Greece & Rome* 33, 129–41.

Coleridge, Samuel Taylor (1851) *Specimens of the Table-Talk of Samuel Taylor Coleridge*. 4th edition. London: John Murray.

Coles, P. (2011) *Unremembered Past: An Exploration of the Unconscious Transmission of Trauma across the Generations*, 1–10. London: Karnac Books.

Coles, R.A. (1968) 'A new fragment of post-classical tragedy from Oxyrhynchus', *Bulletin of the Institute of Classical Studies* 15, 110–18.

— (1974) *A New Oxyrhynchus Papyrus: The Hypothesis of Euripides' Alexandros*. London: ICS.

Collins, D. (2002) 'Reading the birds: *oiônomanteia* in early epic', *Colby Quarterly* 38, 5–36.

Collins, Mortimer (1871) *The Inn of Strange Meetings*. London: Henry S. King.

Conacher, D.J. (1987) *Aeschylus' Oresteia: A Literary Commentary*. Toronto: Toronto UP.

Conomis, N.C. (1964) 'The dochmiacs of Greek drama', *Hermes* 92, 23–50.

Conradi, Peter (2001) *The Saint and the Artist: A Study of the Fiction of Iris Murdoch*. London: HarperCollins.

Coo, Lyndsay (2013) 'A tale of two sisters: studies in Sophocles' *Tereus*', *Transactions and Proceedings of the American Philological Association* 143, 349–84.

Cooksey, Chris (2017) 'Recent advances in the understanding of the chemistry of Tyrian purple production from Mediterranean molluscs', in Enegren and Meo, 73–8.

Corner, Sean (2012) 'Did "respectable" women attend symposia?' *Greece & Rome* 59, 34–45.

Crane, Gregory (1993) 'Politics of consumption and generosity in the carpet scene of the *Agamemnon*', *Classical Philology* 88, 117–36.

Curtis, John and Julian Reade (1995) *Art and Empire: Treasures from Assyria in the British Museum*. London: British Museum Publications.

Dalzell, J.O. (1970) 'Pleisthenes in the "Agamemnon" of Aeschylus', *Hermathena* 110, 79–80.

Danek, Georg (2015) 'Nostoi', in Fantuzzi and Tsagalis, 355–79.

Daube, B. (1939) *Zu den Rechtsproblemen in Aischylos' Agamemnon*. Zurich and Leipzig: Max Niehans.

Daux, G. (1968) 'Chronique des fouilles et découvertes archéologiques en Grèce en 1967', *Bulletin de Correspondance Hellénique* 92, 711–14.

Davies, M. (1987) 'Aeschylus' Clytemnestra: sword or axe?' *Classical Quarterly* 37, 65–75.

Dawe, R.D. (1963) 'Inconsistency of plot and character in Aeschylus', *Proceedings of the Cambridge Philological Society* 9, 21–62.

— (1964) *The Collation and Investigation of Manuscripts of Aeschylus*. Cambridge: CUP.

de Beauvoir, Simone (1972) *The Second Sex*, trans. H.M. Parshley. Harmondsworth: Penguin.

de Jong, I.J.F. (1987) 'Paris/Alexandros in the *Iliad*', *Mnemosyne* 40, 124–8.

de Paoli (2018) 'Doce e selvagem: Ártemis (no "Agamêmnon" de Ésquilo)', *Anais de Filosofia Clássica de Rio de Janeiro* 12, 68–83.

de Romilly, J. (1968) *Time in Greek Tragedy*. Ithaca, NY: Cornell Univ. Press.

— (1970) 'Vengeance humaine et vengeance divine. Remarques sur l'*Orestie* d'Eschyle', in *Das Altertum und jedes neue Gute. Festschrift für W. Schadewalt*, ed. K. Gaiser, 65–77. Stuttgart: Kohlhammer.

Deacy, Susan and Karen F. Pierce (2002) *Rape in Antiquity: Sexual Violence in the Greek and Roman Worlds*. Swansea: Classical Press.

Debnar, P. (2010) 'The sexual status of Aeschylus' Cassandra', *Classical Philology* 105, 129–45.

Deforge, Bernard (1986) *Eschyle: poète cosmique*. Paris: Les belles lettres.

Delattre, Charles (2017) 'Le "complexe de Cassandre": interactions du chœur dans l'Agamemnon' d'Eschyle et au-delà', in *El teatro clásico en el marco de la cultura griega y su pervivencia en la cultura occidental, 20, El coro dramático, un personaje singular*, eds José Vicente Bañuls and Francesco De Martino, 291–324. Bari: Levante.

Denniston, J.D. and Denys Page (eds) (1957) *Aeschylus' Agamemnon*. Oxford: Clarendon.

Desmond, William D. (2006) *The Greek Praise of Poverty: Origins of Ancient Cynicism*. Notre Dame, IN: Univ. Notre Dame Press.

Devoldere, Luc (2019) 'The Making Of: Orestes in Ghent and Mosul', *The Low Countries* 18 June. Available at https://www.the-low-countries. com/article/the-making-of-orestes-in-ghent-and-mosul.

Di Martino, Giovanna (2019) 'Vittorio Alfieri's tormented relationship with Aeschylus: *Agamennone* between tradition and innovation', *Anabases* 29, 121–33.

Dietrich, B.C. (1964) 'The judgment of Zeus', *Rhein Mus.* 107, 97–125.

Diller, H. (1961) 'Die Hellenen-Barbaren Antithese im Zeitalter der Perserkriege', in *Grecs et Barbares*, eds H. Schwabl et al., 37–82. Vandoeuvres-Genève: Fondation Hardt.

Dindorf, G. (ed.) (1870) *Aeschyli tragoediae*. Leipzig: Teubner.

Dmitriev, Sviatoslav (2016) 'The protection of slaves in the Athenian law against hubris', *Phoenix* 70, 64–76.

Dodds, E.R. (1960) 'Morals and politics in the *Oresteia*', *Proceedings of the Cambridge Philological Society* 6, 19–31, reprinted in his *The Ancient Concept of Progress and Other Essays in Greek Literature and Belief*, Oxford: OUP. (1973) 45–63.

Dougherty, Carol (2017) '"These metoikoi": living with others, living as others in Aeschylus' *Oresteia*', *American Journal of Philology* 138, 577–604.

Dover, Kenneth J. (1977) 'I tessuti rossi dell' *Agamemnone*', *Dioniso* 48, 55–69.

Doyle, A. (2008) 'Cassandra—feminine corrective in Aeschylus' *Agamemnon*', *Acta Classica* 51, 57–75.

— (2009) 'Aeschylus' Pandora—Helen in the *Agamemnon*', *Akroterion* 54, 11–27.

Doyle, Richard E. (1970) 'Olbos, koros, *hubris* and *atē* from Hesiod to Aeschylus', *Traditio* 26, 293–303.

Drew-Bear, Thomas (1968) 'The trochaic tetrameter in Greek tragedy', *American Journal of Philology* 89, 385–405.

Dumortier, Jean (1935a) *Le Vocabulaire medical d'Eschyle et les écrits hippocratiques*. Paris: Les Belles Lettres.

— (1935b) *Les Images dan la poésie d'Eschyle*. Paris: Les Belles Lettres.

Durand, Marc (2005) *AGŌN dans les tragédies d'Eschyle*. Paris: L'Harmattan.

Durrell, Lawrence (1985) *Collected Poems: 1931–1974*. London: Faber & Faber.

Earp, F.R. (1948) *The Style of Aeschylus*. Cambridge: CUP.

Easterling, Pat (1973) 'Presentation of character in Aeschylus', *Greece and Rome* 20, 3–19.

— (1991) 'George Eliot and Greek tragedy', *Arion* 1, 60–74.

— (1993) 'Tragedy and ritual', in *Theater and Society in the Classical World*, ed. R. Scodel, 7–23. Ann Arbor: Univ. Michigan Press.

— (2005) '*Agamemnon* for the ancients', in Macintosh et al., 23–36.

Easterling, Pat and Edith Hall (eds) (2002) *Greek and Roman Actors: Aspects of an Ancient Profession*. Cambridge: CUP.

Edwards, Mark W. (1978) 'Agamemnon's decision: freedom and folly in Aeschylus', *California Studies in Classical Antiquity* 10, 17–38.

— (2002) *Sound, Sense, and Rhythm: Listening to Greek and Latin Poetry*. Princeton, NJ: Princeton Univ. Press.

Egan, Rory B. (2007) 'The prophecies of Calchas in the Aulis narrative of Aeschylus' *Agamemnon*', *Mouseion* 7, 179–212.

Eginitis, D. (1929) 'The problem of the tide of Euripus', *Astronomische Nachrichten* 236, cols 321–8.

Eliot, George (1887) *Romola*. Boston: Estes and Lauriat.

Else, Gerald F. (1977) 'Ritual and drama in Aischyleian tragedy', *Illinois Classical Studies* 2, 70–87.

Enegren, H.L. and F. Meo (eds) (2017) *Treasures from the Deep: Sea Silk and Shellfish Purple Dye in Antiquity*. Oxford: Oxbow.

Erasmo, Mario (2004) *Roman Tragedy: Theatre to Theatricality*. Austin: Univ. Texas Press.

Ewans, M. (2005) 'Agamemnon's influence in Germany: Goethe, Schiller, and Wagner', in Macintosh et al., 106–17.

Ewbank, Inga-Stina (2005) '"Striking too short at Greeks": the transmission of *Agamemnon* to the English Renaissance stage', in Macintosh et al. 37–52.

Fairbanks, Arthur (trans.) (1931) *Philostratus, Imagines. Callistratus, Descriptions*. London: William Heinemann; New York: G.P. Putnam's Sons.

Falkner, Thomas M. (1995) *The Poetics of Old Age in Greek Epic, Lyric, and Tragedy*. Norman and London: Univ. Oklahoma Press.

Fantuzzi, Marco and Christos Tsagalis (eds) (2015) *The Greek Epic Cycle and Its Ancient Reception*. Cambridge: CUP.

Fartzoff, Michel (2009) 'Troie dans l'*Orestie* d'Eschyle: l'adaptation dramatique d'une image ambivalente', in *Reconstruire Troie: Permanence et Renaissances d'une cité emblématique*, eds M. Fartzhoff, M. Faudot, E. Geny and M. Guelfucci, 167–85. Franche-Comté: Presses Universitaires de Franche-Comté.

Ferrara, Bianca (2017) '"A Lydian chiton with a purple fringe": the gift of the garment to the Hera of Samos and Hera of Sele', in Enegren and Meo, 118–30.

Finglass, Patrick J. (2005) 'Erinys or Hundred-Hander? Pindar, fr. 52i(a). 19–21 Snell-Maehler = B3.25–7 Rutherford', *Zeitschrift für Papyrologie und Epigraphik* 154, 40–2.

— (ed. and trans.) (2018a) *Sophocles: Oedipus the King.* Cambridge: CUP.

— (2018b) 'Stesichorus and Greek tragedy', in Andújar et al., 19–37.

Finley, John H. (1955) *Pindar and Aeschylus.* Martin Classical Lectures 14. Cambridge, MA: Harvard Univ. Press.

Fisher, N. (1992) *Hybris.* Warminster: Aris & Phillips.

Fittschen, Klaus (1969) *Untersuchungen zum Beginn der Sagendarstellungen bei den Griechen.* Berlin: Bruno Hessling.

Fleming, Thomas J. (2007) *The Colometry of Aeschylus.* Amsterdam: Hakkert.

Fletcher, J. (1999a) 'Exchanging glances: vision and representation in Aeschylus' *Agamemnon*', *Helios* 26, 11–34.

— (1999b) 'Choral voice and narrative in the first stasimon of Aeschylus' *Agamemnon*', *Phoenix* 53, 29–49.

— (2012) *Performing Oaths in Classical Greek Drama.* Cambridge: CUP.

Flower, M.A. (2008) *The Seer in Ancient Greece.* Berkeley: Univ. Calif. Press.

Foley, Helene (1985) *Ritual Irony: Poetry and Sacrifice in Euripides.* Ithaca, NY: Cornell Univ. Press.

— (2001) *Female Acts in Greek Tragedy.* Princeton, NJ: Princeton Univ. Press.

Foley, Megan (2012) 'Peitho and Bia', *Symplokē* 20, 173–81.

Föllinger, Sabine (2003) *Genosdependenzen.* Göttingen: Vandenhoeck & Ruprecht.

— (2009) *Aischylos: Meister der griechischen Tragödie.* Munich: C.H. Beck.

Fontenrose, Joseph Eddy (1971) 'Gods and men in the *Oresteia*', *Transactions and Proceedings of the American Philological Association* 102, 71–109.

— (1978) *The Delphic Oracle, Its Responses and Operations, with a Catalogue of Responses.* Berkeley: Univ. Calif. Press.

Foufopoulos, Johannes and Nikos Litinas (2005) 'Crows and ravens in the Mediterranean (the Nile Valley, Greece and Italy) as presented in ancient and modern proverbial literature', *Bulletin of the American Society of Papyrologists* 42, 7–39.

Fraenkel, E. (ed.) (1950) *Aeschylus' Agamemnon*. Oxford: OUP.

François, Gilbert (1957) *Le Polythéisme et l'emploi au singulier des mots ΘΕΟΣ ΔΑΙΜΩΝ dans la littérature grecque d'Homere a Platon*. Paris: Belles Lettres.

Fries, Almut (2016) 'The dochmiac in ancient metrical scholarship', *Graecolatina et Orientalia* 37–8, 21–36.

Furley, W.D. (1981) *Studies in the Use of Fire in Ancient Greek Religion*. Salem, NH: Arno Press.

Gagarin, M. (1976) *Aeschylean Drama*. Berkeley: Univ. Calif. Press.

Gagné, Renaud (2013) *Ancestral Fault in Ancient Greece*. Cambridge: CUP.

Gantz, T.N. (1977) 'The fires of the *Oresteia*', *Journal of Hellenic Studies* 97, 28–38.

— (1983) 'The chorus of Aeschylus' *Agamemnon*', *Harvard Studies in Classical Philology* 17, 65–86.

— (1993) *Early Greek Myth: A Guide to Literary and Artistic Sources*. Baltimore, MD: John Hopkins Univ. Press.

Garner, Richard (1990) *From Homer to Tragedy: The Art of Allusion in Greek Poetry*. London: Routledge.

Garvie, A.F. (ed.) (1986) *Aeschylus: Choephori*. Oxford: OUP.

— (2010) *The Plays of Aeschylus*. London: Bristol Classical Press.

— (2016) 'Editing Aeschylus for a modern readership: textual criticism and other concerns', in *The Reception of Aeschylus' Plays through Shifting Models and Frontiers*, ed. Stratos Constantinidis, 23–50. Leiden: Brill.

Geisser, Franziska (2002) *Götter, Geister und Dämonen: Unheilsmachte bei Aischylos – zwischen Aberglauben und Theatralik*. Munich & Leipzig: K.G. Saur.

Gemin, Marco (2020) 'Asseverazioni di verità nell' Orestea', *L'antiquité Classique* 89, 173–6.

Gladigow, B. (1962) 'Aischylos und Heraklit', *Archiv für Geschichte der Philosophie* 44, 225–42.

Goheen, R.F. (1955) 'Aspects of dramatic symbolism: three studies in the *Oresteia*', *American Journal of Philology* 76, 115–26.

Golden, L. (1958) 'Aeschylus and Ares: A Study in the Use of Military Imagery by Aeschylus'. PhD dissertation, Chicago.

Golden, Mark (1990) *Children and Childhood in Classical Athens*. Baltimore, MD and London: Johns Hopkins Univ. Press.

— (1994) 'Children's rights, children's speech, and *Agamemnon*', in *Ritual, Finance, Politics: Athenian Democratic Accounts Presented to David Lewis*, eds S. Hornblower and R. Osborne, 371–83. Oxford: Clarendon Press.

Goldhill, Simon (1984) *Language, Sexuality, Narrative: The Oresteia.* Cambridge: CUP.

— (1986) *Reading Greek Tragedy.* Cambridge: CUP.

— (1992) *Aeschylus: The Oresteia.* Cambridge: CUP.

Green, Richard (2002) 'Towards a reconstruction of performance style', in Easterling and Hall, 93–126.

Greenhalgh, P.A.L. (1969) 'Cassandra and the chorus in Aeschylus' *Agamemnon*', *Rivista di studi classici* 17, 253–8.

Gregory, Andrew D. (2016) 'Astronomy', in *A Companion to Science, Technology, and Medicine in Ancient Greece and Rome*, ed. Georgia L. Irby, vol. 1, 96–113. Oxford: Wiley Blackwell.

Griffith, Mark (1995) 'Brilliant dynasts: power and politics in the "Oresteia"', *Classical Antiquity* 14, 62–129.

Griffith, R. Drew (1998) 'Corporality in the ancient Greek theatre', *Phoenix* 52, 230–56.

Gruys, J.A. (1981) *The Early Printed Editions (1518–1664) of Aeschylus.* Leiden: B. de Graaf.

Gulizio, J. (2000) 'Hermes and e-ma-a2: the continuity of his cult from the Bronze Age to the historical period', *Živa antika* 50, 105–16.

Gutzwiller, Kathryn (ed.) (2005) *The New Posidippus: A Hellenistic Poetry Book.* Oxford: OUP.

Haldane, J.A. (1965) 'Musical themes and imagery in Aeschylus', *Journal of Hellenic Studies* 85, 38.

Hall, Edith (1988) 'When did the Trojans turn into Phrygians? Alcaeus 42.15', *Zeitschrift für Papyrologie und Epigraphik* 73, 15–18.

— (1989) *Inventing the Barbarian.* Oxford: OUP.

— (1993a) 'Asia unmanned: images of victory in classical Athens', in *War and Society in the Greek World*, eds J. Rich and G. Shipley, 108–33. London: Routledge.

— (1993b) 'Political and cosmic turbulence in Euripides' *Orestes*', in *Tragedy, Comedy and the Polis*, eds A. Sommerstein et al., 263–85. Bari: Levante.

— (ed. and trans.) (1996) *Aeschylus' Persians.* Warminster: Aris & Phillips.

— (1997) 'The sociology of Athenian tragedy', in *The Cambridge Companion to Greek Tragedy*, ed. P. Easterling, 93–126. Cambridge: CUP.

— (2002) 'The singing actors of antiquity', in Easterling and Hall, 3–38.

— (2005a) 'Aeschylus' Clytemnestra versus her Senecan tradition', in Macintosh et al., 53–76.

— (2005b) 'Iphigenia and her mother at Aulis: a study in the revival of a Euripidean classic', in *Rebel Women*, eds S. Wilmer and J. Dillon, 3–41. London: Methuen.

— (2006) *The Theatrical Cast of Athens*. Oxford: OUP.

— (2009) 'Deianeira deliberates: precipitate decisions in *Trachiniae*', in *Sophocles & the Greek Tragic Tradition* (for Pat Easterling, co-ed. with Simon Goldhill), 69–96. Cambridge: CUP.

— (2010a) 'Heroes of the dance floor: the missing exemplary male dancer in ancient sources', in *The Ancient Dancer in the Modern World*, ed. F. Macintosh, 145–68. Oxford: OUP.

— (2010b) *Greek Tragedy: Suffering under the Sun*. Oxford: OUP.

— (2010c) 'Medea and the mind of the murderer', in *Unbinding Medea: Interdisciplinary Approaches to a Classical Myth*, eds H. Bartel and A. Simon, 16–24. Oxford: Legenda.

— (2011) 'The social significance of the "Unity of Time"', *Atti Accademia Pontaniana*, suppl. 60, 145–54.

— (2012) 'The politics of metrical variety in classical Athenian drama', in *Music & Politics in Ancient Greek Societies*, ed. D. Yatromanolakis, 1–28. London and New York: Routledge.

— (2013) *Adventures with Iphigenia in Tauris: A Cultural History of Euripides' Black Sea Tragedy*. New York: OUP.

— (2014) 'To fall from high or low estate? Tragedy and social class in historical perspective', *PMLA* 129, 773–82.

— (2015) 'Peaceful conflict resolution and its discontents in Aeschylus's Eumenides', *Common Knowledge* 21, 253–69.

— (2016a) 'Citizens but second-class: women in Aristotle's *Politics*', in *Patriarchal Moments*, ed. Cesare Cuttica and Gaby Mahlberg, 35–42. London: Bloomsbury.

— (2016b) 'Atheism and atrocity at Aulis', online resource at https://edithorial.blogspot.com/2016/01/atheism-and-atrocity-at-aulis.html.

— (2017) 'Master of those who know: Aristotle as role model for the 21st-century Academician', *European Review* 25, 3–19.

— (2018a) 'Hephaestus the hobbling humorist: the club-footed god in the history of early Greek comedy', *Illinois Classical Studies* 43, 366–87.

— (2018b) 'Why are the Erinyes female: or, what is so feminine about revenge?' in *Revenge and Gender from Classical to Renaissance*

Literature, eds L. Dawson and F. McHardy, 33–57. Edinburgh: Edinburgh Univ. Press.

— (2018c) 'Euripides, Sparta & the self-definition of Athens', in *The Greek Superpower: Sparta in the Self-Definitions of Athenians*, eds A. Powell and Paul Cartledge, 29–52. Swansea: Classical Press of Wales.

— (2018d) 'Materialisms old & new', in *The Materialities of Greek Tragedy*, eds M. Mueller and M. Telò, 203–17. London: Bloomsbury.

— (2019) 'Black Sea back story: Euripides' *Medea*', in *Greek Theatre & Performance around the Ancient Black Sea*, ed. D. Braund, E. Hall and R. Wyles, 257–88. Cambridge: CUP.

— (2020a) 'In praise of Cario, the nonpareil comic slave of Aristophanes' *Wealth*', in *Ancient Greek Comedy* (essays in Honour of Angus M. Bowie), eds A. Fries and D. Kanellakis, 219–37. Berlin: de Gruyter.

— (2020b) 'Aristophanes' *Birds* as satire on Athenian opportunists in Thrace', in *Aristophanes and Politics*, eds Ralph M. Rosen and Helene P. Foley, 187–213. Leiden and Boston: Brill.

— (2021a) 'Eating children is bad for you: offspring of the past in Aeschylus' *Agamemnon*', in *Looking at Agamemnon*, ed. D. Stuttard, 13–27. London: Bloomsbury.

— (2021b) *Tony Harrison: Poet of Radical Classicism*. London: Bloomsbury.

— (2022a) 'Rowing and democratic memory: Salamis in Aristophanic comedy', in *Democracy and Salamis*, eds E.M.L. Economou, Nicholas C. Kyriazis and Athanasios Platias, 201–20. New York: Springer.

— (2022b) 'Our Greek tragic hope: young adults overcoming family trauma in new novels by Natalie Haynes and Colm Tóibín', in *Our Mythical Hope*, ed. K. Marciniak, 371–86. Warsaw: Warsaw Univ. Press.

— (2023) 'Sorrow but survival: the therapeutic moral example of the chorus of Aeschylus' *Agamemnon*', in *Η Έννοια του Ηθικού Χρέους στο Αρχαίο Ελληνικό Θέατρο*, ed. Andreas Markantonatos, 52–70. Athens: Hellenic Foundation for Culture.

— (2024) *Facing down the Furies: Suicide, the Ancient Greeks, and Me*. New Haven, CT: Yale Univ. Press.

— (2025) *Epic of the Earth: Reading the Iliad in the Era of Environmental Catastrophe*. New Haven, CT: Yale Univ. Press.

Hall, Edith and Fiona Macintosh (2005) *Greek Tragedy and the British Theatre, 1660–1914*. Oxford: OUP.

Hall, Edith and Rosie Wyles (eds) (2008) *New Directions in Ancient Pantomime*. Oxford: OUP.

Hallett, Judith (2016) 'Greek (and Roman) ways and thoroughfares: the routing of Edith Hamilton's classical antiquity', in Wyles and Hall, 216–42.

Hame, Kerri J. (2004) 'All in the family: funeral rites and the health of the oikos in Aischylos' *Oresteia*', *American Journal of Philology* 125, 513–38.

— (2008) 'Female control of funeral rites in Greek tragedy: Klytaimestra, Medea, and Antigone', *Classical Philology* 103, 1–15.

Hamilton, Edith (1957/1964) *The Ever-Present Past*. New York: W.W. Norton.

Hanson, Victor Davis (1991) 'Hoplite technology in phalanx battle', in his *Hoplites: The Classical Greek Battle Experience*, 63–84. London and New York: Routledge.

Hardy, Thomas (2002) *Jude the Obscure*, ed. Patricia Ingham. New York and Oxford: OUP.

Harriot, R. (1982) 'The Argive elders, the discerning shepherd and the fawning dog: misleading communication in the *Agamemnon*', *Classical Quarterly* 32, 9–17.

Harris, Ella Isabel (trans.) (1904) *The Tragedies of Seneca*. London: Henry Frowde.

Hazlitt, William (1825) *The Spirit of the Age*. London: Henry Colburn.

Heaney, Seamus (1996) *The Spirit Level*. New York: The Noonday Press.

Heath, John (1999) 'Disentangling the beast: humans and other animals in Aeschylus' *Oresteia*', *Journal of Hellenic Studies* 119, 117–47.

— (2005) *Talking Greeks: Speech, Animals and the Other in Homer, Aeschylus, and Plato*. Cambridge: CUP.

Heirman, L.J. (1975) 'Kassandra's glossolalia', *Mnemosyne* 28, 257–67.

Herrmann, G.F. (ed.) (1852) *Aeschyli Tragoediae*, 2 vols. Leipzig: Weidmann.

Higgins, W.E. (1978) 'Double-dealing Ares in the *Oresteia*', *Classical Philology* 73, 24–35.

Himmelhoch, Leah (2005) 'Athena's entrance at *Eumenides* 405 and Hippotrophic imagery in Aeschylus's *Oresteia*', *Arethusa* 38, 263–302.

Hitch, Sarah (2018) 'Tastes of Greek poetry: from Homer to Aristophanes', in *Taste and the Ancient Senses*, ed. Kelli C. Rudolph, 22–44. London: RTF.

Hoernle, E.S. (1921) *The Problem of the Agamemnon*. Oxford: Basil Blackwell.

Holland, Leicester B. (1933) 'The mantic mechanism at Delphi', *American Journal of Archaeology* 37, 201–14.

Holst-Warhaft, Gail (1992) *Dangerous Voices: Women's Laments and Greek Literature*. London: Routledge.

Hopman, Marianne Govers (2012) *Scylla: Myth, Metaphor, Paradox*. Cambridge and New York: CUP.

Hübner, Ulrich (1985) 'Die literarischen und archäologischen Zeugnisse über den vorchristlichen Athos', *Antike Welt* 16, 35–44.

Huddilston, John H. (1898) *The Attitude of the Greek Tragedians towards Art*. London: Macmillan.

Irigaray, Tiago (2018) 'The aidós of Clitemnestra: politics and power in Aeschylus' Agamemnon', *Rónai* 6, 4–14.

Irwin, Eleanor (1974) *Color Terms in Greek Poetry*. Toronto: Hakkert.

Johnston, Sarah Iles (1999) *Restless Dead: Encounters between the Living and the Dead in Ancient Greece*. Berkeley, Los Angeles and London: Univ. Calif. Press.

— (2008) *Ancient Greek Divination*, Malden, MA and Oxford: Wiley-Blackwell.

Jones, J. (1988) 'The House of Atreus', in *Aeschylus's The Oresteia*, ed. Harold Bloom, 5–29. New York, New Haven, CT and Philadelphia, PA: Chelsea House Publishers.

Judet de la Combe, Pierre (2001) *L'Agamemnon d'Eschyle: Commentaire des dialogues*, 2 vols. Paris: Septentrion.

Kaimio, Maarit (1970) *The Chorus of Greek Drama within the Light of the Person and Number Used*. Helsinki: Societas Scientiarum Fennica.

Kanellakis, Dimitrios (2020) 'Sacrifice, politics and animal imagery in the "Oresteia"', *Classica et Mediaevalia* 68, 37–69.

Karamanou, Ioanna (ed.) (2017) *Euripides, Alexandros: Introduction, Text and Commentary*. Berlin and Boston: De Gruyter.

Karas, Allannah (2022) 'Double-bind, baleful hope: Peithô's constraint in the *Oresteia*', *Illinois Classical Studies* 47, 1–23.

Kavoulaki, Athena (2005) 'Crossing communal space: the classical ekphora, "public" and "private"', in *Idia kai dēmosia: Les cadres "privés" et "publics" de la religion grecque antique*, eds Véronique Dasen and Marcel Piérart, 129–45. Liège: Presses universitaires de Liège.

Kennedy, Rebecca Futo (2009) *Athena's Justice: Athena, Arhens and the Concept of Justice in Greek Tragedy*. New York: Peter Lang.

Kern, Otto (ed.) (1922) *Orphicorum Fragmenta*. Berlin: Weidmann.

Kerrigan, John (1996) *Revenge Tragedy: Aeschylus to Armageddon*. Oxford: OUP.

Kirk, G.S., J.E. Raven and M. Schofield (1983) *The Presocratic Philosophers*. Cambridge: CUP.

Kirkwood, G.M. (1984) 'Blame and envy in the Pindaric epinician', in *Greek Poetry and Philosophy: Studies in Honour of Leonard Woodbury*, ed. D.E. Gerber, 169–83. Berkeley, Los Angeles and London: Univ. Calif. Press.

Kitto, H.D.F. (1955) 'The dance in Greek tragedy', *Journal of Hellenic Studies* 75, 36–41.

— (1956a) *Form and Meaning in Drama: A Study of Six Greek Plays and of Hamlet*. London: Methuen.

— (1956b) 'The Greek chorus', *Educational Theatre Journal* 8, 1–8.

Klein, Melanie (1963) 'Some reflections on the *Oresteia*', in her *Envy and Gratitude*, 275–99. New York: Delta Books.

Knoepfler, D. (1993) *Les Imagiers de l'Orestie. Milles ans d'art autour d'un mythe grec*. Zurich: Akanthus.

Knox, B.M.W. (1952) 'The lion in the house (*Agamemnon* 717–36 [Murray])', *Classical Philology* 47, 17–25, reprinted in his *Word and Action: Essays on the Ancient Theater*, 27–38. Baltimore, MD and London: Johns Hopkins Univ. Press, 1979.

Kock, T. (ed.) (1884) *Comicorum Atticorum Fragmenta*, vol. 2. Leipzig: Teubner.

Kokolakis, M. (1959) *Pantomime and the Treatise peri Orchēseōs*. Athens: Sideris & Co.

Kossatz-Deissmann, Anneliese (1978) *Dramen des Aischylos auf westgriechischen Vasen*. Mainz am Rhein: Philipp von Zabern.

Kranz, W. (1919) 'Zwei Lieder des *Agamemnon*', *Hermes* 54, 301–20.

— (1933) *Stasimon: Untersuchungen zu Form und Gehalt der griechischen Tragödie*. Berlin: Weidmann.

Kurke, Leslie (1999) 'Ancient Greek board games and how to play them', *Classical Philology* 94, 247–67.

Kwapisz, Jan, David Petrain and Mikolaj Szymanski (eds) (2013) *Riddles and Wordplay in Greek and Latin Poetry*. Berlin and Boston: De Gruyter.

Latham, Caroline (2016) 'Reanimating Greek Tragedy: How Contemporary Poets Translate for the Stage'. PhD dissertation, King's College, London. Available at https://kclpure.kcl.ac.uk/portal/en/studentTheses/reanimating-greek-tragedy.

Lather, Amy (2018) 'Olfactory theater: tracking scents in Aeschylus's *Oresteia*', *Arethusa* 51, 33–54.

Lauriola, Rosanna (2020) *Brill's Companion to Episodes of 'Heroic' Rape/ Abduction in Classical Antiquity and Their Reception*. Leiden: Brill.

Leahy, D.M. (1974) 'The representation of the Trojan War in Aeschylus' *Agamemnon*', *American Journal of Philology* 95, 1–23.

Lease, Emory B. (1919) 'The number three, mysterious, mystic, magic', *Classical Philology* 14, 56–73.

Lebeck, A. (1971) *The Oresteia: A Study in Language and Structure.* Washington, DC: Center for Hellenic Studies.

Lechat, H. (1891) 'Terrecuites de Corcyre', *Bulletin de Correspondance Hellénique* 15, 1–112.

Lennig, Robert (1969) 'Traum und Sinnestäuschung bei Aischylos, Sophokles, Euripides'. Dissertation, Tübingen.

Lesky, Albin (1966) 'Decision and responsibility in the tragedy of Aeschylus', *Journal of Hellenic Studies* 86, 78–85.

Levine, Daniel B. (2015) 'Acts, metaphors, and powers of feet in Aeschylus's "Oresteia"', *Transactions and Proceedings of the American Philological Association* 145, 253–80.

Lichtheim, M. (trans.) (1973–80) *Ancient Egyptian Literature.* Berkeley, Los Angeles and London: Univ. Calif. Press.

Lilja, Saara (1976) *Dogs in Ancient Greek Poetry.* Helsinki: Societas Scientiarum Fennica.

Lister, Henry (1923) *Clytemnestra.* San Francisco: La Bohème Club.

Llewellyn-Jones, Lloyd (2021) 'The use of set and costume design in modern productions of ancient Greek drama', online publication. Available at https://www.open.ac.uk/arts/research/greekplays/publications/essays/llewellyn-jones-set-and-costume-design.

Lloyd, G.E.R. (1962) 'Right and left in Greek philosophy', *Journal of Hellenic Studies* 82, 56–66.

Lloyd, Michael (1989) 'Paris/Alexandros in Homer and Euripides', *Mnemosyne* 42, 76–9.

Lloyd-Jones, Hugh (1970) *Agamemnon by Aeschylus: A Translation with a Commentary.* Englewood Cliffs, NJ: Prentice-Hall.

— (1971) *The Justice of Zeus.* Berkeley and Los Angeles: Univ. Calif. Press.

— (trans.) (1979) *Aeschylus: Oresteia. Agamemnon.* Englewood Cliffs, NJ: Prentice-Hall.

Loraux, Nicole (1987) *Tragic Ways of Killing a Woman.* English translation. Cambridge, MA: Harvard Univ. Press.

Lovibond, S. (1994) 'An ancient theory of gender: Plato and the Pythagorean Table', in *Women in Ancient Societies*, eds L.J. Archer, S. Fischler and M. Wyke, 88–101. London: Palgrave Macmillan.

Lucarini, Carlo M. (2016) 'The ἐκκύκλημα in the Greek theater of the classical age', *Hermes* 144, 138–56.

Lucas, F.L. (1954) *Greek Drama for Everyman.* London: J.M. Dent & Sons.

Luckenbill, D.D. (1926) *Ancient Records of Assyria and Babylonia*, vol. 1. Chicago, IL: Chicago Univ. Press.

Ludwig, P.W. (2002) *Eros and Polis: Desire and Community in Greek Political Theory*. New York and Cambridge: CUP.

Luz, Christine (2013) 'What has it got in its pocketses? Or, what makes a riddle a riddle?' in Kwapisz et al., 83–99.

McClure, Laura (1999) *Spoken like a Woman: Speech and Gender in Ancient Drama*. Princeton, NJ: Princeton Univ. Press.

McCoskey, D.E. (1998) '"I, whom she detested so bitterly", in *Women and Slaves in Greco-Roman Culture: Differential Equations*, eds Sandra R. Joshel and Sheila Murnaghan, 35–55. London and New York: Routledge.

Macintosh, F., P. Michelakis, E. Hall and O. Taplin (eds) (2005) *Agamemnon in Performance*. Oxford: OUP.

MacLeod, C.W. (1982) 'Politics and the *Oresteia*', *Journal of Hellenic Studies* 102, 124–44.

McNeil, L. (2005) 'Bridal cloths, cover-ups and kharis: the "carpet scene" in Aeschylus' *Agamemnon*', *Greece & Rome* 52, 1–17.

MacNeill, William (1995) *Keeping Together in Time: Dance and Drill in Human History*. Cambridge, MA: Harvard Univ. Press.

Mader, Gottfried (2021) 'The spectacle of inaction (*Ag.* 1343–71): Aeschylus satiricus?' *Hermes* 149, 501–10.

Marshall, Hallie (2023) '*Oresteia* on stage: Koun, Stein, Hall and Mnouchkine', in *A Companion to Aeschylus*, eds Peter Burian and Jacques Bromberg, 491–504. Oxford and New York: Wiley Blackwell.

Marzano, Annalisa (2013) *Harvesting the Sea: The Exploitation of Marine Resources in the Roman Mediterranean*. Oxford: OUP.

Mason, P.G. (1959) 'Kassandra', *Journal of Hellenic Studies* 79, 80–93.

Matheson, Susan B. (1994) 'The goddess Tyche', *Yale University Art Gallery Bulletin*, 18–33.

Matheson, William H. (1966) *Claudel and Aeschylus*. Ann Arbor: Michigan Univ. Press.

Matino, Giuseppina (1998) *La Sintassi di Eschilo*. Naples: M. d'Auria Editore.

Maurizio, L. (1995) 'Anthropology and spirit possession: a reconsideration of the Pythia's role at Delphi', *Journal of Hellenic Studies* 115, 69–86.

— (1997) 'Delphic Oracles as oral performances: authenticity and historical evidence', *Classical Antiquity* 16, 308–34.

— (2013) 'Technopaegnia in Heraclitus and the Delphic Oracles: shared compositional techniques', in Kwapisz et al., 100–20.

Mazzoldi, S. (2001) *Cassandra, la vergine e l'indovina. Identita di un personaggio da Omero all'Ellenismo.* Pisa: Istituti editoriali e poligrafici internazionali.

Medda, Enrico (2012) 'Aeschylus, *Agamemnon* 78: no room for Ares', *Classical Quarterly* 62, 39–44.

—— (ed.) (2017) *Eschilo. Agamennone, edizione critica con introduzione traduzione e commento*, 3 vols. [= *Supplemento n. 31 al "Bollettino dei Classici" dell'Accademia Nazionale dei Lincei*, Rome.

Mehrlein, R. (1959) 'Drei', *Reallexikon für Antike und Christentum* 4, 269–310.

Meiggs, Russell (1943) 'The growth of Athenian imperialism', *Journal of Hellenic Studies* 63, 21–34.

Meinel, F. (2015) *Pollution and Crisis in Greek Tragedy.* Cambridge: CUP.

Meridor, Ranana (1987) 'Aeschylus, *Agamemnon* 944–57: Why does Agamemnon give in?' *Classical Philology* 82, 38–43.

Merkelbach, Reinhold and Josef Stauber (eds) (1998) *Steinepigramme aus dem griechischen Osten.* Stuttgart and Leipzig.

Merkelbach, Reinhold and M.L. West (eds) (1967) *Fragmenta Hesiodea.* Oxford: Clarendon.

Merker, Raimund (2011) *Hinter der Maske des Feldherrn: Szenische und charakterorientierte Aspekte zur Agamemnonfigur bei Aischulos, Sophokles und Euripides.* Freiburg: Rombach.

Michelakis, Pantelis (2005) 'Introduction', in Macintosh et al., 1–20.

Miller, D.A. (1998) 'The Spartan kingship: some extended notes on complex duality', *Arethusa* 31, 1–17.

Millett, Kate (1971) *Sexual Politics.* New York: Avon Books.

Mitchell-Boyask, Robin (2006) 'The marriage of Cassandra and the "Oresteia": text, image, performance', *Transactions and Proceedings of the American Philological Association* 136, 269–97.

Moles, J.L. (1979) 'A neglected aspect of *Agamemnon* 1389–92', *Liverpool Classical Monthly* 4.9, 179–89.

Monoson, Sara (1994) 'Citizen as *erastes*: erotic imagery and the idea of reciprocity in the Periclean funeral oration', *Political Theory* 22, 253–76.

Monsacré, Hélène (2018) *The Tears of Achilles*, trans. Nicholas J. Snead, Introduction by Richard P. Martin. Hellenic Studies Series 75. Washington, DC: Center for Hellenic Studies.

Montiglio, S. (2000) *Silence in the Land of Logos.* Princeton, NJ: Princeton Univ. Press.

Moreno, Miryam Librán (2010) 'Aeschylus, *Agamemnon* 1478–1480', *Greek, Roman and Byzantine Studies* 49, 477–85.

Moritz, Helen E. (1979) 'Refrain in Aeschylus: literary adaptation of traditional form', *Classical Philology* 74, 187–213.

Morrell, Kenneth Scott (1996–7) 'The fabric of persuasion: Clytaemnestra, Agamemnon, and the sea of garments', *Classical Journal* 92, 141–65.

Most, Glenn W. (ed. and trans.) (2018) *Hesiod. The Shield. Catalogue of Women. Other Fragments*, Loeb Classical Library 503. Cambridge, MA: Harvard Univ. Press.

Müller, K.O. (1835) *Dissertations on the Eumenides of Aeschylus*. English translation. Cambridge: J. and J.J. Deighton.

Mund-Dopchie, Monique (1984) *La survie d'Eschyle à la Renaissance*. Leuven: Peeters.

Murdoch, I. (1977) 'Agamemnon Class, 1939', *Boston University Journal* 25, 57–8.

Murnaghan, Sheila (forthcoming) 'The singularity of the tragic day', in *Time, Tense & Genre in Ancient Greek Literature*, eds Connie Bloomfield-Gadêlha and Edith Hall. Oxford: OUP.

Murray, Gilbert (trans.) (1920) *The Agamemnon of Aeschylus*. Oxford: OUP.

— (ed.) (1937) *Aeschyli Septem quae Supersunt Tragoediae*. Oxford: Clarendon.

— (1940) *Aeschylus, the Creator of Tragedy*. Oxford: Clarendon Press.

Myres, John (1950) 'The structure of stichomythia in Attic tragedy', *Proceedings of the British Academy* 35, 3–35.

Nappa, Christopher (1994) '"Agamemnon" 717–36: the parable of the lion cub', *Mnemosyne* 47, 82–7.

Nastos, P.T., Karavana-Papadimou, K. and I.T. Matsangouras (2015) 'Tropical-like cyclones in the Mediterranean', *Proceedings of the 14th International Conference on Environmental Science and Technology, Rhodes, Greece, 3–5 September 2015*, online publication at https://cest2015.gnest.org/papers/cest2015_00407_oral_paper.pdf.

Neils, J. (2005) 'The girl in the pithos: Hesiod's Elpis', in *Periklean Athens and Its Legacy: Problems and Perspectives in Honor of J.J. Pollitt*, eds J.M. Barringer and J.M. Hurwit, 37–45. Austin: Univ. Texas Press.

Neuburg, Matt (1991) 'Clytemnestra and the Alastor (Aeschylus, Agamemnon 1497ff.)', *Quaderni Urbinati di Cultura Classica* 38, 37–68.

Nicholson, Eric (2018) 'Who watches the watchmen, especially when they're on edge? Liminal spectatorship in "Agamemnon" and "Macbeth"', *Comparative Drama* 52, 103–21.

Njoya, Wairimu (2020) 'The progress of law: Aeschylus's *Oresteia* in feminist and critical theory', *Political Theory* 48, 139–68.

Nooter, Sarah (2017) *The Mortal Voice in the Tragedies of Aeschylus.* Cambridge: CUP.

North, Helen F. (1966) *Sophrosyne: Self-Knowledge and Self-Restraint in Greek Literature.* Ithaca, NY: Cornell Univ. Press.

Nünlist, René (2006) 'Calchas', *Brill's New Pauly*, online resource at http://dx.doi.org.ezphost.dur.ac.uk/10.1163/1574-9347_bnp_e605610.

Nussbaum, Martha (2001) *The Fragility of Goodness: Luck and Ethics in Greek Tragedy and Philosophy.* Revised ed. Cambridge: CUP.

Oakley, John H. and Rebecca H. Sinos (1993) *The Wedding in Ancient Athens.* Madison: Univ. Wisconsin Press.

O'Daly, Gerard J.P. (1985) 'Clytemnestra and the elders: dramatic technique in Aeschylus, *Agamemnon* 1372–1576', *Museum Helveticum* 42, 1–19.

Osborne, Robin (1994) 'Looking on—Greek style. Does the sculpted girl speak to women too?' in *Classical Greece: Ancient Histories and Modern Archaeologies*, ed. I. Morris, 81–96. Cambridge: CUP.

Østerud, Svein (1976) 'The individuality of Hesiod', *Hermes* 104, 13–29.

Otis, Brooks (1981) *Cosmos and Tragedy: An Essay on the Meaning of Aeschylus*, ed. E. Christian Kopff. Chapel Hill: Univ. North Carolina Press.

Pache, Corinne (2000) 'War games: Odysseus at Troy', *Harvard Studies in Classical Philology* 100, 15–23.

Page, Denys L. (trans.) (1941) *Select Papyri, Volume III: Poetry.* Cambridge, MA: Harvard Univ. Press.

— (ed.) (1972) *Aeschyli septem quae supersunt tragoedias.* Oxford: Clarendon Press.

Pala, Elisabetta (2010) 'Aphrodite on the akropolis: evidence from Attic pottery', in *Brill's Companion to Aphrodite*, eds Amy C. Smith and Sadie Pickup, 195–216. Leiden: Brill.

Paleothodoros, D. (2010) 'Light and darkness in Dionysiac rituals', in Christopoulos et al., 237–60.

Paley, F.A. (ed.) (1845) *Aeschylus. Agamemnon.* Cambridge: J. & J.J. Deighton.

Parasinou, E. (2003) *The Light of the Gods: The Role of Light in Archaic and Classical Greek Cult.* London: Duckworth.

Park, Arum (2023) *Reciprocity, Truth, and Gender in Pindar and Aeschylus.* Ann Arbor: Univ. Michigan Press.

Parker, Robert (1983) *Miasma: Pollution and Purification in Early Greek Religion*. Oxford: Clarendon.

— (2009) 'Aeschylus' gods: drama, cult, theology', in *Eschyle*, ed. G.P.D. Mark, J. Jouanna, F. Montanari and A.-C. Hernández, 127–64. Vandoeuvres-Geneva: Fondation Hardt.

Patera, Ioanna (2010) 'Light and lighting equipment in the Eleusinian Mysteries', in Christopoulos et al., 261–75.

Pearson, A.C. (ed.) (1917) *The Fragments of Sophocles*, 3 vols. Cambridge: CUP.

Peradotto, John J. (1964) 'Some patterns of nature imagery in the *Oresteia*', *American Journal of Philology* 85, 378–93.

— (1969) 'Cledonomancy in the *Oresteia*', *American Journal of Philology* 90, 1–21.

Peretti, Aurelio (1939) *Epirrema e Tragedia*. Florence: Felice Le Monnier Editore.

Petersen, Eugen (1911) 'Zu Aischylos' *Agamemnon*', *Rheinisches Museum für Philologie* 66, 1–37.

Petrounias, Evangelos (1976) *Funktion und Thematik der Bilder bei Aischylos* [= *Zetemata* 48]. Göttingen: Vandenhoeck & Ruprecht.

Petrovic, A. (2010) 'True lies of Athenian public epigrams: rituals, half-truths and propaganda in the aftermath of the Persian Wars', in *Archaic and Classical Greek Epigram*, eds M. Baumbach, A. Petrovic and I. Petrovic, 202–15. Cambridge: CUP.

Phillippo, Susanna (2005) 'Clytemnestra's ghost: the Aeschylean legacy in Gluck's Iphigenia operas', in Macintosh et al., 77–103.

— (2018) 'Stepping onto the stage: Aeschylus' *Oresteia* and tragic footwear', in *Shoes, Slippers, and Sandals: Feet and Footwear in Classical Antiquity*, ed. Sadie Pickup and Sally Waite, 143–73. London: Routledge.

Pillinger, Emily (2019) *Cassandra and the Poetics of Prophecy in Greek and Latin Literature*. Cambridge: CUP.

Pirenne-Delforge, Vinciane (1991) 'Le culte de la persuasion: Peithō en Grèce ancienne', *Revue de l'histoire des religions* 208, 395–413.

Podlecki, Anthony J. (1999) *The Political Background of Aeschylean Tragedy*, 2nd edn. Bristol: Bristol Classical Paperbacks.

— (2006) '*Aischulos megalophōnotatos*', in Cairns and Liapis, 11–29.

Poliakoff, Michael (1980) 'The third fall in the *Oresteia*', *American Journal of Philology* 101, 251–9.

Pool, E.H. (1983) 'Clytemnestra's first entrance in Aeschylus' *Agamemnon*: analysis of a controversy', *Mnemosyne* 36, 71–116.

Pope, Maurice (1974) 'Merciful heavens: a question in Aeschylus' *Agamemnon*', *Journal of Hellenic Studies* 94, 100–13.

Popp, H. (1971) 'Das Amoibaion', in *Die Bauformen der griechischen Tragödie*, ed. W. Jens, 221–75. Munich: Wilhelm Fink.

Postgate, Raymond (ed. and trans.) (1969) *The Agamemnon of Aeschylus*. Cambridge: Rampant Lions Press.

Prag, A.J.N.W. (1985) *The Oresteia: Iconographic and Narrative Tradition*. Warminster: Aris & Phillips.

— (1991) 'Clytemnestra's weapon yet once more', *Classical Quarterly* 41, 242–6.

Pucci, Pietro (1996) *Enigma Segreto Oracolo*. Pisa and Rome: IEPI.

Pulleyn, Simon (1997) *Prayer in Greek Religion*. Oxford: Clarendon Press.

Purdy, Richard Little and Michael Millgate (eds) (1988) *The Collected Letters of Thomas Hardy*. Oxford: Clarendon Press.

Rademaker, A. (2005) *Sophrosyne and the Rhetoric of Self-Restraint*. [= *Mnemosyne*, supp. 259]. Leiden: Brill.

Raeburn, David and Oliver Thomas (2012) *The Agamemnon of Aeschylus: A Commentary for Students*. New York: OUP.

Ramelli, Ilaria (ed.) (2009) *Hierocles the Stoic: Elements of Ethics, Fragments, and Excerpts*, translated by David Konstan for the Society of Biblical Literature. Leiden: Brill.

Rawlinson, George (ed. and trans.) (1880) *History of Herodotos*, vol. 4. London: J. Murray.

Ready, Jonathan L. (2012) 'Zeus, Ancient Near Eastern notions of divine incomparability, and similes in the Homeric epics', *Classical Antiquity* 31, 56–91.

Rehm, R. (1994) *Marriage to Death: The Conflation of Wedding and Funeral Rituals in Greek Tragedy*. Princeton, NJ: Princeton Univ. Press.

Reiner, E. (1938) *Die rituelle Totenklage der Griechen*. Stuttgart and Berlin: Kohlhammer.

Renehan, Robert (1982) *Greek Lexicographical Notes: A Critical Supplement to the Greek–English Lexicon of Liddell–Scott–Jones* [= *Hypomnemata* 74]. Gottingen: Vandenhoeck & Ruprecht.

Reynolds, Margaret (2005) '*Agamemnon*: speaking the unspeakable', in Macintosh et al., 120–38.

Richardson, Bessie Ellen (1933) *Old Age among the Ancient Greeks*. Baltimore, MD: Johns Hopkins Univ. Press.

Robb, Kevin (1983) 'Preliterate ages and the linguistic art of Heraclitus', in his *Language and Thought in Early Greek Philosophy*, 153–206. LaSalle, IL: The Hegeler Institute, Monist Library of Philosophy.

Roberts, D.H. (1984) *Apollo and His Oracle in the Oresteia* [=*Hypomnemata* 78]. Göttingen: Vandenhoeck & Ruprecht.

Robertson, H. (1939) 'Legal expressions and ideas of justice in Aeschylus', *Classical Philology* 34, 209–19.

Robinson, E. (2011) *Democracy beyond Athens*. Cambridge: CUP.

Rodighiero, A. (2018) 'Aeschylus, *Agamemnon* 104–05, Homer and the epic tradition: a new survey', *Journal of Hellenic Studies* 138, 36–49.

Rodrigues, Marco Aurélio (2020) 'A "aemulatio" senequiana: o caso da tragédia "Agamêmnon"' *Classica* 33, 31–49.

Roisman, Hanna M. (2018) 'Loyal Clytemnestra γυναῖκα πιστήν (Aeschylus, *Agamemnon* 606)', *Giornale Italiano di Filologia* 70, 11–18.

Romagnoli, Ettore (1921) (trans.) *Tragedie di Eschilo*, vol. 2. Bologna: Zanichelli.

Rose, H.J. (1952) 'Review of Aeschylus, *Agamemnon* by Eduard Fraenkel', *Journal of Hellenic Studies* 72, 130–2.

— (1958) *A Commentary on the Surviving Plays of Aeschylus*, vol. 2. Amsterdam: N.V. Noord-Hollandsche Uitgevers Maatschappij.

Rosenmeyer, Thomas (1955) 'Gorgias, Aeschylus, and apate', *American Journal of Philology* 76, 225–60.

— (1982) *The Art of Aeschylus*. Berkeley, Los Angeles and London: Univ. Calif. Press.

Rosenzweig, Rachel (2004) *Worshipping Aphrodite: Art and Cult in Classical Athens*. Ann Arbor: Univ. Michigan Press.

Rosivach, Vincent J. (1978) 'The "Golden Lamb" ode in Euripides' *Electra*', *Classical Philology* 73, 189–99.

Röttger, Kati (2019) 'Translating tragedy: Molora and Yaël Farber's adaption of Aeschylus' *Oresteia* for the South African community', *South African Theatre Journal* 32, 35–47.

Rudolph, Kelli C. (2018) 'Introduction', in her *Taste and the Ancient Senses*, 1–21. London: RTF.

Rupp, David William (1976) 'The altars of Zeus and Hera on Mt. Arachnaion in the Argeia, Greece', *Journal of Field Archaeology* 3, 261–8.

Saayman, F. (2014) 'Dogs and lions in the *Oresteia*', *Akroterion* 38, 11–18.

Sailor, Dylan and Sarah Culpepper Stroup (1999) 'ΦΘΟΝΟΣ Δ᾽ ΑΠΕΣΤΩ: the translation of transgression in Aiskhylos' *Agamemnon*, *Classical Antiquity* 18, 153–82.

Salanitro, G. (1966) 'L'*Orestea* e la politica estera di Atene', *Siculorum Gymnasium* 19, 163–80.

Sammons, Benjamin (2014) 'The quarrel of Agamemnon & Menelaus', *Mnemosyne* 67, 1–27.

Sansone, David (2016) 'The size of the tragic chorus', *Phoenix* 70, 233–54.

Scapin, Nuria (2020) *The Flower of Suffering: Theology, Justice, and the Cosmos in Aeschylus'* Oresteia *and Presocratic Thought*. Berlin and Boston, MA: de Gruyter.

Scharffenberger, Elizabeth W. (2007) '"Deinon Eribremetas": the sound and sense of Aeschylus in Aristophanes' "Frogs"', *Classical World* 100, 229–49.

Schauenburg, Konrad (1960) 'Herakles und Omphale', *Rheinisches Museum für Philologie* 103, 57–76.

Schein, S.L. (1979) *The Iambic Trimeter in Aeschylus and Sophocles: A Study in Metrical Form*. Leiden: Brill.

Schlögl, Albert (1991) *Der Geschichtsbegriff der aischyleischen Tragödie*. Vienna: VWGO.

Schmidt, Wilhelm Schmidt (ed.) (1899) *Herons von Alexandria Druckwerke und Automatentheater*. Leipzig: Teubner.

Schnyder, Bernardette (1995) *Angst in Szene gesetzt: Zur Darstellung der Emotionen auf der Bühne des Aischylos*. Tübingen: Gunter Narr.

Scott, W.C. (1966) 'Wind imagery in the *Oresteia*', *Transactions and Proceedings of the American Philological Association* 97, 459–71.

— (1984) *Musical Design in Aeschylean Theater*. Hanover, NH and London: Univ. Press of New England.

Seaford, Richard (1984) 'The last bath of Agamemnon', *Classical Quarterly* 34, 247–59.

— (1987) 'The tragic wedding', *Journal of Hellenic Studies* 107, 10.

— (2012) *Cosmology and the Polis*. Cambridge: CUP.

Seidler, August (1811) *De versibus dochmiacis tragicorum graecorum*. Leipzig: Gerhard Fleischer.

Shea, Megan (2007) 'Clytemnestra's net: Aeschylus' *Oresteia* and the text of tapestries', *Journal of Dramatic Theory and Criticism* 22, 41–60.

Shelton, J. (1983) 'Revenge or resignation: Seneca's *Agamemnon*', *Ramus* 12, 159–83.

Shilo, Amit (2022) *Beyond Death in the Oresteia*. Cambridge: CUP.

Sideras, A. (1971) *Aeschylus Homericus: Untersuchungen zu den Homerismen der aischyleischen Sprache*. Göttingen: Vandenhoeck & Ruprecht.

Sidgwick, A. (ed.) (1905) *Aeschylus' Agamemnon, edited with Introduction and Notes*, 6th edn. Oxford: Clarendon Press.

Simpson, Michael (1971) 'Why does Agamemnon yield?' *La Parola del Passato* 26, 94–101.

Sitlington Sterrett, J.R. (1901) 'The torch-race: a commentary on the *Agamemnon* of Aischylos vv. 324–326', *American Journal of Philology* 22, 393–419.

Smith, Ole Langwitz (ed.) (1976) *Scholia Graeca in Aeschylum quae exstant omnia*, Part I. Leipzig: Teubner.

Smith, Peter M. (1980) *On the Hymn to Zeus in Aeschylus' Agamemnon*. Ann Arbor, MI: Scholars' Press.

Smyth, H.W. (trans.) (1957) *Aeschylus*, vol. 2, with an appendix by H. Lloyd-Jones. Cambridge, MA and London: Harvard Univ. Press.

Snell, Bruno and H. Maehler (eds) (1975) *Pindari Carmina cum Fragmentis*, vol. 2. Leipzig: Teubner.

Solmsen, Friedrich (1949) *Hesiod and Aeschylus*. Ithaca, NY: Cornell Univ. Press.

Sommerstein, Alan H. (ed.) (1989a) *Aeschylus' Eumenides*. Cambridge: CUP.

— (1989b) 'Again Klutaimestra's weapon', *Classical Quarterly* 39, 296–301.

— (1993) 'Pathos and mathos before Zeus', in *Tria Lustra: Essays and Notes Presented to John Pinsent, Founder and Editor of Liverpool Classical Monthly*, ed. H.D. Jocelyn, 109–44. Liverpool. Reprinted as ch. 11 of Sommerstein (2010).

— (1996) *Aeschylean Tragedy*. Levante: Bari.

— (2006) 'Rape and consent in Athenian tragedy', in Cairns and Liapis, 233–51.

— (ed. and trans.) (2009) *Aeschylus. Oresteia: Agamemnon. Libation-Bearers. Eumenides*. Cambridge, MA: Harvard Univ. Press.

— (2010) *The Tangled Ways of Zeus and Other Studies in and around Greek Tragedy*. Oxford: OUP.

— (2012) 'The judicial sphere', in *Oath and State in Ancient Greece*, Alan H. Sommerstein and Andrew J. Bayliss, with contributions by Lynn A. Kozak and Isabelle C. Torrance (= *Klio* 98.1), 57–119. Leipzig: de Gruyter.

Stafford, Emma (2000) *Worshipping Virtues: Personification and the Divine in Ancient Greece*. London: Duckworth.

Stanford, W.B. (1941) 'Gerard Manley Hopkins and Aeschylus', *Studies: An Irish Quarterly Review* 119, 359–68.

— (1942) *Aeschylus in His Style: A Study in Language and Personality.* Dublin: DUP.

Stanton, G.R. (1997) 'The generic second person in Aiskhylos' *Agamemnon*', *Mnemosyne* 50, 1–6.

Steffy, J. Richard (1985) 'The Kyrenia ship: an interim report on its hull construction', *American Journal of Archaeology* 89, 71–101.

Steiner, D. (1995) 'Eyeless in Argos: a reading of *Agamemnon* 416–19', *Journal of Hellenic Studies* 115, 175–82.

— (2010) 'The immeasures of praise: the epinician celebration of Agamemnon's return', *Hermes* 138, 22–37.

— (2016) 'Parting shots: Aeschylus, *Agamemnon* 1384 98 and symposia in the visual repertoire', in *The Cup of Song: Studies on Poetry and the Symposion*, eds Vanessa Cazzato, Dirk Obbink and Enrico Emanuele Prodi, 159–83. Oxford: OUP.

Stella, Luigia Achillea (1994) *Eschilo e la Cultura del suo Tempo.* Alessandria: Edizioni dell'Orso.

Stephanis, I.E. (1988) *Dionysiakoi Technitai.* Heraklion: Univ. of Crete.

Stephens, Susan A. (2002–3) 'Linus song', *Hermathena* 173/174, 13–28.

Stinton, T.C.W. (1965) *Euripides and the Judgement of Paris.* London: Society for the Promotion of Hellenic Studies.

Strömberg, R. (1954) *Greek Proverbs.* Göteborg: Wettergren and Kerbers.

Suksi, Aara (2017) 'Scandalous maps in Aeschylean tragedy', in *Myths on the Map: The Storied Landscapes of Ancient Greece*, ed. Greta Hawes. Oxford; online edn, Oxford Academic, 22 June 2017. Available at https:// doi.org/10.1093/oso/9780198744771.003.0012, accessed 21 July 2023.

Sullivan, Shirley Darcus (1997) *Aeschylus' Use of Psychological Terminology, Old and New.* Montreal and London: McGill-Queen's Univ. Press.

Swift, Jonathan (1937) *The Poems of Jonathan Swift.* Oxford: Clarendon Press.

Swift, L.A. (2010) *The Hidden Chorus: Echoes of Genre in Tragic Lyric.* Oxford: OUP.

— (2018) 'Competing generic narratives in Aeschylus' Oresteia', in Andújar et al., 119–36.

Synodinou, K. (1977) *On the Concept of Slavery in Euripides.* Ioannina: Ioannina Univ. Press.

Taplin, O. (1972) 'Aeschylean silences and silences in Aeschylus', *Harvard Studies in Classical Philology* 76, 57–97.

— (1977) *The Stagecraft of Aeschylus.* Oxford: Clarendon Press.

— (2005) 'The Harrison version: "so long ago that it became a song"?' in Macintosh et al., 235–51.

— (2007) *Pots and Plays: Interactions between Tragedy and Greek Vase-Painting of the Fourth Century B.C.* Los Angeles, CA: J. Paul Getty Museum.

Taplin, Oliver and Joshua Billings (2018) *The Oresteia: The Texts of the Plays, Ancient Backgrounds and Responses, Criticism.* New York and London: Norton.

Tarrant, R.J. (ed.) (1976) *Seneca's Agamemnon.* Cambridge: CUP.

Thalmann, W.G. (1986) 'Aeschylus' physiology of the emotions', *American Journal of Philology* 107, 489–511.

Thiel, Rainer (1993) *Chor und tragische Handlung im* Agamemnon *des Aischylos.* Stuttgart: Teubner.

Thomas, Nancy R. (2004) 'The early Mycenaean lion up to date', *Hesperia* suppl. 33, *XAPIΣ: Essays in Honor of Sara A. Immerwahr*, 161–206. Princeton, NJ: American School of Classical Studies at Athens.

Thompson, D'Arcy Wentworth (1936) *A Glossary of Greek Birds.* Oxford and London: OUP & Humphrey Milford.

Thompson, Dorothy Burr (1956) 'The Persian spoils in Athens', in *The Aegean and the Near East (Studs. H. Goldman)*, ed. Saul S. Weinberg, 281–91. New York: J.J. Augustin.

Thomsen, R. (1972) *The Origin of Ostracism* [= *Humanitas* 4] Copenhagen: Gyldendal.

Thomson, George (ed.) (1966) *The Oresteia of Aeschylus*, 2nd edn. Prague: Academia.

Thomson, James (1738) *Agamemnon. A Tragedy.* London: A. Millar.

— (1756) *Des Herrn Jacob Thomson sämtliche Trauerspiele aus dem Englischen übersetzt, mit einer Vorrede von Gotthold Ephraim Lessing.* Leipzig: Weidmann.

— (1780) *Agamemnon, tragédie en 5 actes et en vers, traduite de l'anglais de feu M. Thompson* [sic]. Paris: Duchesne.

Torrance, Isabelle (2015) 'Distorted oaths in Aeschylus', *Illinois Classical Studies* 40, 281–95.

Tracy, Stephen V. (1986) 'Darkness from light: the beacon fire in the *Agamemnon*', *Classical Quarterly* 36, 257–60.

Tralau, J. (2016) 'The justice of the chimaira: goat, snake, lion, and almost the entire *Oresteia* in a little monstrous image', *Arion* 24, 41–68.

Trendall, A.D. (1987) *The Red-Figured Vases of Paestum.* London: British School at Rome.

Trendall, A.D. and T.B.L. Webster (1971) *Illustrations of Greek Drama*. London: Phaidon.

Turyn, Alexander (1943) *The Manuscript Tradition of the Tragedies of Aeschylus*. New York: Polish Institute of Arts and Sciences.

Umachandran, M. (2019) '"The aftermath experienced before": Aeschylean untimeliness and Iris Murdoch's defence of art', *Ramus* 48, 223–47.

Usener, H. (1903) 'Dreiheit', *Rheinisches Museum für Philologie*, Neue Folge 58, 1–47.

Valakas, Kostas (2002) 'The use of the body by actors in tragedy and satyr play', in Easterling and Hall (eds), 71–94.

van Emde Boas, Evert (2017) 'Analyzing *Agamemnon*: conversation analysis and particles in Greek tragic dialogue', *Classical Philology* 112, 411–34.

— (2022) 'Aeschylus', in *Speech in Ancient Greek Literature*, eds Mathieu de Bakker and Irene J.F. de Jong, 407–27. Leiden and Boston: Brill.

van Nes, D. (1963) *Die maritime Bildersprache des Aischylos*. Groningen: Wolters.

Vandersmissen, Marc (2013) 'Hélène ou Œnone? Note sur les vers 1156–1161 de l'*Agamemnon* d'Eschyle', *L'Antiquité Classique* 82, 249–53.

Vaughn, John W. (1976) 'The watchman of the "Agamemnon"', *Classical Journal* 71, 335–8.

Vedelago, Angelica (2020) 'The interplay between Aeschylus and Seneca in James Thomson's *Agamemnon*', *International Journal of the Classical Tradition* 27, 40–61.

Vellacott, Philip (1984) *The Logic of Tragedy: Morals and Integrity in Aeschylus' Oresteia*. Durham, NC: Duke Univ. Press.

Vergados, A. (2012) 'Corinna's poetic mountains: *PMG* 654 col. i 1–34 and Hesiodic reception', *Classical Philology* 107, 101–18.

Vermaseren, M.J. (1982) *Corpus Cultus Cybelae Attidisque*, vol. 2. Leiden: Brill.

Vermeule, Emily (1966) 'The Boston *Oresteia* krater', *American Journal of Archaeology* 70, 1–22.

— (1979) *Aspects of Death in Early Greek Art and Poetry*. Berkeley, Los Angeles and London: Univ. Calif. Press.

Verrall, A.W. (ed.) (1889) *The 'Agamemnon' of Aeschylus*. London: Macmillan.

Visser, Edzard (1997) *Homers Katalog der Schiffe*. Stuttgart: Teubner.

von Blumenthal, A. (1939) *Ion von Chios, die Reste seiner Werke*. Stuttgart and Berlin: Kohlhammer.

von Humboldt, Wilhelm (1816) *Aeschylos' Agamemnon, metrisch übersetzt.* Leipzig: Ernst Fischer.

von Möllendorff, Peter (2015) 'Das Ekkyklema auf der tragischen Bühne', in *Translatio Humanitatis: Festschrift zum 60. Geburtstag von Peter Riemer*, ed. C. Kugelmeier, 31–55. St. Ingbert: Röhrig Universitätsverlag.

von Wilamowitz-Moellendorff, Ulrich (1914) *Aischylos-Interpretationen.* Berlin: Weidmann.

— (1927) 'Lesefrüchte', *Hermes* 62, 276–98.

Wallace, William (1936) 'An Eretrian proxeny decree of the early fifth century', *Hesperia* 5, 273–84.

Warmington, E.H. (trans.) (1935–40) *Remains of Old Latin.* 4 vols. Cambridge, MA: Harvard Univ. Press.

Wartelle, André (1971) *Histoire du texte d'Eschyle dans l'antiquité.* Paris: Les belles lettres.

— (1978) *Bibliographie historique et critique d'Eschyle.* Paris: Les Belles Lettres.

Waterfield, R. (trans.) (1988) *The Theology of Arithmetic: On the Mystical, Mathematical and Cosmological Symbolism of the First Ten Numbers.* Ann Arbor: Michigan Univ. Press.

Weiberg, Erika L. (2022) 'False reports and waiting wives on the home front in Aeschylus' *Agamemnon* and Sophocles' *Trachiniae*', *Classical Philology* 117, 282–302.

Weismann, W. (1972) *Kirche und Schauspiele.* Würzburg: Augustinus-Verlag.

Weiss, Naomi (2017) 'Noise, music, speech: the representation of lament in Greek tragedy', *American Journal of Philology* 138, 243–66.

— (2023) 'Music, dance and metre in Aeschylean tragedy', in *A Companion to Aeschylus*, eds Peter Burian and Jacques Bromberg, 242–53. Oxford and New York: Wiley Blackwell.

West, M.L. (1979) 'The Parodos of the *Agamemnon*', *Classical Quarterly* 29, 1–6.

— (ed.) (1990) *Aeschyli Tragoediae cum incerti poetae Prometheo.* Stuttgart: Teubner.

— (1992) *Ancient Greek Music.* Oxford: Clarendon Press.

— (1997) *The East Face of Helicon: West Asiatic Elements in Greek Poetry and Myth.* Oxford: Clarendon Press.

— (2000) '*Iliad* and *Aethiopis* on the stage: Aeschylus and son', *CQ* 50, 338–52.

— (ed. and trans.) (2003) *Greek Epic Fragments: From the Seventh to the Fifth Centuries BC*, Loeb Classical Library 497. Cambridge, MA: Harvard Univ. Press.

— (2015) 'The formation of the epic cycle', in Fantuzzi and Tsagalis, 96–107.

Westphal, Rudolf (1885) *Griechische Rhythmik*. Leipzig: Teubner.

Whallon, William (1980) *Problem and Spectacle: Studies in the Oresteia*. Heidelberg: Carl Winter.

Wians, William (2009) 'The *Agamemnon* and human knowledge', in his *Logos and Muthos: Philosophical Essays in Greek Literature*, 181–98. Albany, NY: SUNY Press.

Wilde, Oscar (2010) *Complete Works*. London: HarperCollins Publishers Inc.

Williams, Bernard (1993) *Shame and Necessity*. Berkeley, Los Angeles and Oxford: Univ. Calif. Press.

Wills, G. (1963) '*Agamemnon* 1346–71, 1649–53', *Harvard Studies in Classical Philology* 68, 255–62.

Wilson, Peter (2006) '*Dikēn* in the Oresteia of Aeschylus', in *Greek Drama III: Essays in Honour of Kevin Lee* [= *Bulletin of the Institute of Classical Studies*, suppl. 87], eds John Davidson, Frances Muecke and Peter Wilson, 187–201. London: ICS.

Wilson, Peter and Oliver Taplin (1993) 'The "aetiology" of tragedy in the *Oresteia*', *Proceedings of the Cambridge Philological Society* 39, 169–80.

Winnington-Ingram, R.P. (1954) 'Aeschylus, Agamemnon 1343–71', *Classical Quarterly* 4, 23–30.

— (1983) *Studies in Aeschylus*. Cambridge: CUP.

Wiseman, James R. (1974) 'The Road to Oenoe', *Hesperia* 43, 535–43.

— (2000) '*Iliad* and *Aethiopis* on stage: Aeschylus and son', *Classical Quarterly* 50, 338–52.

Wohl, Victoria (1998) *Intimate Commerce: Exchange, Gender, and Subjectivity in Greek Tragedy*. Austin: Univ. Texas Press.

Wright, Matthew (2018) *The Lost Plays of Greek Tragedy*, vol. 2. London: Bloomsbury.

Wüst, E. (1949) 'Pantomimus', *Realencyclopaedie* 18.3, 833–69.

Wyles, Rosie (2011) *Costume in Greek Tragedy*. London: Bristol Classical Press.

— (2020a) *Theatre Props and Civic Identity in Athens, 458–405 BCE*. London: Bloomsbury.

— (2020b) 'The Aeschylean sting in *Wasps*' tale: Aristophanes' engagement with the *Oresteia*', *Classical Quarterly* 70, 1–12.

Wyles, Rosie and Edith Hall (eds) (2016) *Women Classical Scholars*. Oxford: OUP.

Younger, John G. (1978) 'The Mycenae-Vapheio lion group', *American Journal of Archaeology* 82, 285–99.

Zeitlin, Froma I. (1965) 'The motif of the corrupted sacrifice in Aeschylus' *Oresteia*', *Transactions and Proceedings of the American Philological Association* 96, 463–508.

— (1966) 'Postscript to sacrificial imagery in the *Oresteia*' (*Ag.* 1235–37)', *Transactions and Proceedings of the American Philological Association* 97, 645–53.

— (1984) 'The dynamics of misogyny: myth and mythmaking in the *Oresteia*', in *Women in the Ancient World: The Arethusa Papers*, eds John Peradotto and J.P. Sullivan, 159–91. Albany, NY: SUNY Press.

— (1994) 'The artful eye: vision, ecphrasis and spectacle in Euripidean theatre', in *Art and Text in Ancient Greek Culture*, eds Simon Goldhill and Robin Osborne, 138–96. Cambridge: CUP.

Zhmud, Leonid (2016) *Forms and Transfers of Pythagorean Knowledge*. Berlin: de Gruyter.

Zimmermann, B. (1985) *Untersuchungen zur Form und dramatischen Technik der Aristophanischen Komödien* vol. 1, 2nd edn. Königstein: Hain.

ADDENDUM

Unfortunately, Leah Himmelhoch's Bloomsbury Academic edition of *Agamemnon* was published too late (2023) to be taken into detailed consideration in this book. She uses the Greek text by Herbert Weir Smyth which was published in the now superseded 1926 Loeb edition of Aeschylus (vol. 2) and is reproduced with Smyth's translation by the online Perseus project. The forthcoming proceedings of a 2024 international workshop at Groningen University devoted to the parodos of *Agamemnon* and organised by Saskia Peels and Felix Budelmann will do much to illuminate this extraordinary lyric ode.

INDEX

Printed and bound by CPI Group (UK) Ltd, Croydon, CR0 4YY

05/02/2025

14638971-0003